THE WORKS OF THOMAS TRAHERNE

Volume VII

Thomas Traherne (1637?–1674), a clergyman of the Church of England during the Restoration, was thought to be little known until the twentieth century, when his poetry and *Centuries of Meditations* were first printed. During the twentieth century, however, other significant works by Traherne were discovered; some were made available in print.

The Works of Thomas Traherne brings together for the first time Traherne's extant works, including his notebooks, in a printed edition. The two works in this volume were printed in the seventeenth century: *Roman Forgeries* (1673), which Traherne saw through the press, and *Christian Ethicks* (1675), published posthumously.

Roman Forgeries is a complex analysis of the 'False Decretals', forgeries produced by the Roman Catholic Church, making the Pope the supreme head of the Church, rejected by the Eastern Church, which fully accepted the Nicene Creed and the constitutions confirmed by the Ecumenical Church councils, which the forgeries attempted to alter.

Christian Ethicks is a book about the virtues every Christian ought to possess and practice as a witness to the world. It was published in a modernized version during the twentieth century; however, because of numerous errors, it was little help to Traherne scholars. Also parts of the text and poems were extracted and published separately without context. In 1968 the complete *Christian Ethicks* was published by Cornell University Press with a substantial introduction as well as notes and a bibliography; however, that too was not completely reliable. *Roman Forgeries* presented in this text is its first publication since the seventeenth century.

During the twentieth century it was assumed that Traherne was little known after his death in 1674. However, details in book descriptions and provenance indicate that through the centuries *Roman Forgeries* and *Christian Ethicks* had various owners. They were read, corrected, annotated and circulated.

THE WORKS OF THOMAS TRAHERNE

Volume VII

Christian Ethicks: or, Divine Morality.
Opening the Way to Blessedness,
By the Rules of
Vertue and Reason.

Roman Forgeries
Or a True Account of False Records
Discovering the Impostures and
Counterfeit Antiquities of the
Church of Rome.

Edited by
JAN ROSS

D. S. BREWER

Editorial matter © Jan Ross 2022

All rights reserved. Except as permitted under current legislation no part of this work may be photocopied, stored in a retrieval system, published, performed in public, adapted, broadcast, transmitted, recorded or reproduced in any form or by any means, without the prior permission of the copyright owner

First published 2022
D. S. Brewer, Cambridge

ISBN 978-1-84384-618-5

D. S. Brewer is an imprint of Boydell & Brewer Ltd
PO Box 9, Woodbridge, Suffolk IP12 3DF, UK
and of Boydell & Brewer Inc.
668 Mt Hope Avenue, Rochester, NY 14620-2731, USA
website: www.boydellandbrewer.com

A CIP catalogue record for this book is available
from the British Library

The publisher has no responsibility for the continued existence or accuracy of URLs for external or third-party internet websites referred to in this book, and does not guarantee that any content on such websites is, or will remain, accurate or appropriate

This publication is printed on acid-free paper

Printed and bound in Great Britain by
TJ Books Limited, Padstow, Cornwall

Contents

General Preface	ix
Acknowledgements	xi
Abbreviations	xiii
Introduction	xv
Christian Ethicks	xvii
General discussion of *Christian Ethicks*	xvii
Copies of 1675 *Christian Ethicks* held by various libraries	xix
Cambridge University Library, Cambridge	xix
British Library, London	xxi
Folger Shakespeare Library, Washington, DC	xxi
Brasenose College Library, Oxford	xxii
Worcester College Library, Oxford	xxiii
Weston Library (Bodleian), Oxford	xxiv
Roman Forgeries	xxiv
General discussion of *Roman Forgeries*	xxvi
Other anti-Roman Catholic works of the seventeenth century	xxix
Copies of 1675 *Roman Forgeries* held by various libraries	xxx
Folger Shakespeare Library, Washington, DC	xxx
Library of Congress, Washington, DC	xxxi
Hereford Library, Hereford	xxxi
Hereford Cathedral Library, Hereford	xxxii
Balliol College Library, Oxford	xxxii
Brasenose College Library, Oxford	xxxiii
Worcester College Library, Oxford	xxxiv
Weston Library (Bodleian), Oxford	xxxiv
Cambridge University Library, Cambridge	xxxv
Peterborough C.4.18	xxxv
Cambridge University Library 7.41.24	xxxvi
Union Theological Seminary Library, New York	xxxvii
British Library, London	xxxviii
Lambeth Palace Library, London	xxxix
Main Collection SR3, H1763.T7	xxxix
Sion Aarc Octavo	xxxix
General editorial principles	xl

Christian Ethicks — 1

To the Reader — 5
The Contents — 9
To the Reader (apology for errata due to author's death) — 15

Contents by chapter in abbreviated form:

Chap.	I.	Of the End of Virtue	17
Chap.	II.	Of the Nature of Felicity	23
Chap.	III.	Of Virtue in General	28
Chap.	IV.	Of the Powers … Soul	34
Chap.	V.	Of Knowledge	41
Chap.	VI.	Of Love and Hatred	49
Chap.	VII.	Of Eternal Love	55
Chap.	VIII.	Of the Excellency of Truth	63
Chap.	IX.	Of Wisdom	69
Chap.	X.	Of Righteousness	75
Chap.	XI.	Of Goodness	82
Chap.	XII.	Of Holiness	91
Chap.	XIII.	Of Justice	98
Chap.	XIV.	Of Mercy	103
Chap.	XV.	Of Faith	110
Chap.	XVI.	Of Hope	120
Chap.	XVII.	Of Repentance	128
Chap.	XVIII.	Of Charity to our GOD	136
Chap.	XIX.	Of Charity … Neighbour	147
Chap.	XX.	Of Prudence	155
Chap.	XXI.	Of Courage	164
Chap.	XXII.	Of Temperance … of Art	173
Chap.	XXIII.	Of Temperance in GOD	181
Chap.	XXIV.	Of Patience	188
Chap.	XXV.	Of Meekness	197
Chap.	XXVI.	Of Humility	208
Chap.	XXVII.	Of Contentment	217
Chap.	XXVIII.	Of Magnanimity	225
Chap.	XXIX.	Of Modesty	235
Chap.	XXX.	Of Liberality	238
Chap.	XXXI.	Of Magnificence	247
Chap.	XXXII.	Of Gratitude	258
Chap.	XXXIII.	The Beauty of Gratitude	269

An APPENDIX — 278
Textual Emendations and Notes — 287

Roman Forgeries   319

  A Premonition   325
  An Advertisement to the Reader   329
  An Abridgment of the Chapters   336
  Contents by chapter in abbreviated form:
    Cap. I.   *Of the Nature ... of Forgery*   339
    Cap. II.   *Of the Primitive ... Government*   342
    Cap. III.   *A multitude of Forgeries*   352
    Cap. IV.   James Merlins *Edition ... Councils*   360
    Cap. V.   *Divers Forgeries ... Isidore's Collection*   369
    Cap. VI.   *A further ...* Merlins *design*   378
    Cap. VII.   *Of* Francis Turrian *... Jesuite*   385
    Cap. VIII.   *Of* Peter Crabbe *... his Councils*   390
    Cap. IX.   *Of* Carranza *his* Epitome   395
    Cap. X.   *Of* Surius *his four Tomes*   396
    Cap. XI.   *Of* Nicolinus *his Tomes*   398
    Cap. XII.   Nicolinus *... Pope Sixtus V*   406
    Cap. XIII.   *The Epistle ... to Aurelius*   412
    Cap. XIV.   *Counterfeit* Canons *... Apostles names*   415
    Cap. XV.   *A Book called the Pontifical*   423
    Cap. XVI.   *Of the Decretal Epistles*   429
    Cap. XVII.   *Of* Higinus, *and* Pius   434
    Cap. XVIII.   *A Letter Fathered on* Cornelius   440
    Cap. XIX.   *The ridiculous Forgery ... of* Sinuessa   444
    Cap. XX.   *Divers things premised ...* Binius *opened*   453
    Cap. XXI.   *The counterfeit* Edict *...* Constantine   459
    Cap. XXII.   *The Donation of* Constantine *proved*   465
    Cap. XXIII.   Pope Melchiades *Epistle counterfeited*   473
    Cap. XXIV.   *Threescore Canons put into the* Nicene   476
    Appendix.   *Cardinal* Baronius *his Grave Censure*   483
  Textual Emendations and Notes   493

Appendix   515

  The Will of Thomas Traherne   517
  Wm. Brooke's ... discovery of Traherne's manuscripts   519
  Glossary   523

In Memory of
Anne Lamb

General Preface

Thomas Traherne (1637–1674) left a substantial body of work, primarily in manuscript form, when he died in 1674 before the age of forty. Only one of his works was published during his lifetime, *Roman Forgeries* (1673); and he was apparently preparing *Christian Ethicks* for the press, which appeared posthumously in 1675. The story of the discovery of Traherne's manuscripts is well known, beginning in 1896–7 when William Brooke chanced upon a group of manuscripts of Traherne's works in both prose and poetry. Included among them were the *Centuries* and what is now known as the Dobell Folio, which contains Traherne's autograph poems and the Commonplace Book.[1] In 1910 H. I. Bell found and published Philip Traherne's hand-written edition of Thomas's poems, *Poems of Felicity*.[2] In 1964 James Osborn unexpectedly discovered the manuscript containing the *Select Meditations*.[3] This was followed in 1981 by the identification of Traherne's *Commentaries of Heaven* by Elliot Rose.[4] It was not until 1996–7 that other Traherne manuscripts were discovered. 'The Ceremonial Law', an eighteen-hundred-line poem, was identified as Traherne's by Laetitia Yeandle.[5] Jeremy Maule found yet another Traherne manuscript in the spring of 1997,[6] which consists of four more works by Traherne, plus a fragment of a text. There are perhaps other missing notebooks and perhaps poems and treatises, as references in some of his works suggest.

---

[1] See Bertram Dobell, ed., *The Poetical Works of Thomas Traherne, B.D. 1636?–1674* (London, 1903; repr. 1906); *and Centuries of Meditations* (London, 1908).
[2] See H. I. Bell, ed., *Traherne's Poems of Felicity* (Oxford, 1910).
[3] 'A New Traherne Manuscript', *The Times Literary Supplement* (October 8, 1964): 928.
[4] 'A New Traherne Manuscript', *The Times Literary Supplement* (March 19, 1982): 324.
[5] 'Felicity disguisd in fiery Words: Genesis and Exodus in a newly discovered poem by Thomas Traherne', *The Times Literary Supplement* (November 7, 1997): 17.
[6] Denise Inge and Calum McFarlane, 'Seeds of Eternity: A New Traherne manuscript', *The Times Literary Supplement* (June 2, 2000): 14.

There has been no attempt to gather all Traherne's extant works into a uniform, printed edition, with the purpose of giving a sense of the manuscript or printed originals. The primary purpose of this edition, therefore, is to present a printed text of Traherne's extant works, both published and unpublished. In his 1903 introduction to Traherne's poems, Dobell wrote that 'there is a picturesqueness, a beauty, and a life about the manuscripts which is lost in the cold regularity of type',[7] to which Peter Beal has added that Traherne's texts 'should be edited according to manuscript, rather than according to individual "work" as defined by modern editors', since 'the MS is "the work"'.[8] This edition will present Traherne's texts by manuscript insofar as possible, giving due attention to the physical aspects and integrity of the manuscripts themselves, hoping to bring the reader as close as possible in a printed format to the manuscript originals and to the distinctive quality of Traherne's writings. His printed works will be edited with the same intention.

The text of Traherne's works will be printed in seven volumes, with the eighth containing his notebooks. Volume nine will include all annotations, notes and commentary germane to the previous volumes. Annotations in the separate volumes will be limited to textual notes, biblical references and immediately essential commentary. The arrangement of Traherne's works is not an attempt to represent them chronologically, since their dates are uncertain.

---

[7] *The Poetical Works of Thomas Traherne, B.D.*, pp. xxiii–xxiv.
[8] For a discussion of the manuscript discoveries through 1993, see the *Index of English Literary Manuscripts, Volume II: 1625–1700*, Part 2, compiled by Peter Beal (London and New York: Mansell Publishing Limited, 1993), pp. 477–506.

Acknowledgements

It is impossible to accomplish a work of this scope and complexity without the help of other scholars and especially librarians. Because of ill health, with limited ability to travel or walk long distances, as well as transportation interruptions caused by an international pandemic, it has been necessary to rely on the assistance of friends, librarians and other scholars to complete this volume. I am indebted to the staff of the Folger Shakespeare Library for allowing me to examine their copies of *Christian Ethicks* and *Roman Forgeries*, especially the late Betsy Walsh for helping with obscure readings in *Roman Forgeries* and for sending photographs of pages with inserted errata. I owe thanks also to Richard Willmott, who read through the copies of *Roman Forgeries* at the Hereford Library as well as the Hereford Cathedral Library taking detailed notes and helping with variants as well as printing errors in *Roman Forgeries*. Jane Cox was also a huge help, spending one winter afternoon at Hereford Cathedral Library, taking photographs and notes of the Library's copy of the book. Rosemary Firman, Librarian, Hereford Cathedral Library, very generously sent photos of various pages in the Library's copy of *Roman Forgeries*, as well as a written description of the book. I thank also Liz Kay, Librarian, Brasenose College, Oxford, and Stewart and Naomi Tilely, Librarians, Balliol College, Oxford, as well as Phoebe Bradley, graduate student at Brasenose College, who helped with book descriptions, obscure readings and notes as well as the insertions of errata into the text of *Roman Forgeries* held at the Bodleian Library, Oxford, Brasenose and Balliol College libraries, Oxford, sending photos of bindings and pages with questionable readings. Mark Bainbridge, Librarian, Worcester College, Oxford, has my sincere gratitude for sending photos of the copies of *Christian Ethicks* and *Roman Forgeries* as well as helping with book descriptions, notes, marginal glosses and insertions. I am indebted also to the staff of the Munby Rare Books Reading Room at Cambridge University Library for allowing me to examine their copies of *Christian Ethicks* and *Roman Forgeries*; thanks especially to Claire Welford-Elkin, Superintendent, a constant help in tracking down obscure materials. I am also indebted to the British Library, St Pancras, London, and the Weston Library

(Bodleian), Oxford, for allowing me to examine their copies of *Christian Ethicks* and *Roman Forgeries*. Lambeth Palace Library also has my sincere gratitude for giving me the opportunity to examine their two fragile copies of *Roman Forgeries*. I owe my greatest debt of gratitude to my husband, Allen, who has always been an encouragement and support to me and especially for his constant care and help.

Abbreviations

AV	Authorized Version of the Bible, 1611
BCL	Brasenose College Library, Oxford
BL	British Library, St. Pancras, London
Brook's Account	William Brook's Account of the discovery of Traherne's Manuscripts
CE	*Christian Ethicks*
Centuries / C	*Centuries of Meditations*
CH	*Commentaries of Heaven*
CPB	Commonplace Book
CUL	Cambridge University Library, Cambridge
CYB	*Church's Year-Book*
Dobell Folio	Bodleian MS. Eng. Poet. c. 42, Oxford
Edn.	Edition
EN	Early Notebook
Fol. / fols.	Folio(s)
HCL	Hereford Cathedral Library, Hereford
HL	Hereford Library, Hereford
Inducements	*Inducements to Retirednes*
Kingdom / KG	*The Kingdom of God*
LPL	Lambeth Palace Library, London
LC	Library of Congress, Washington, DC
MS. / MSS.	Manuscript(s)
ODNB	*Oxford Dictionary of National Biography*
OB	Balliol College Library, Oxford
Repr.	Reprint
RF	*Roman Forgeries*
SM	*Select Meditations*
SV / A Sober View	*A Sober View of Dr Twisses his Considerations, With a Compleat Disquisition of Dr Hammonds Letter to Dr Sanderson. And a Prospect of all their Opinions concerning GODS Decrees* (Vol. I, pp. 45–230)
NU / Union	Union Theological Seminary, New York, NY
WF/Folger	Folger Shakespeare Library, Washington, DC

WTN	Weston Library (Bodleian Libraries), Oxford
WCO	Worcester College, Oxford
Yale	Yale University Library, New Haven, CT

Introduction

Roman Forgeries and *Christian Ethicks* are two of three books by Thomas Traherne published during the seventeenth century. Traherne saw *Roman Forgeries* through the press but died before he was able to do so for *Christian Ethicks*, as the printer's apology 'To the Reader' indicates: 'The Author's much lamented Death hapning immediately after this Copy came to the Press, may reasonably move the Readers charity, to pardon those few Errata's [sic] which have escaped in the Printing by so sad an occasion.' *Roman Forgeries* was printed by S. and B. Griffin[1] and published by Jonathan Edwin.[2] No publisher is indicated on the title page of *Christian Ethicks*; it was however printed for Jonathan Edwin in 1675. The third book, *A Serious and Pathethical Contemplation of the Mercies of God*, was published by George Hicks and printed for Samuel Keeble in 1699.[3]

Contrary to the common understanding that Traherne's works were not widely read and fell into obscurity until the dramatic discovery

---

[1] S. and B. Griffin: Bennet Griffin, a London bookseller and printer in the Old Bailey, 1671–1700, and probably the son of Edward Griffin II (1638–52). His name is joined with that of his mother Sarah Griffin as a printer. Primarily a bookseller, Bennet published several notable works, including Bacon's *Sylva Sylvarum*, with an epitome of the *Novum Organum*, 1683 … and an *Epictetus* for Sam. Keeble, 1692 … His name appears first among booksellers selling Chauncy's *Hertfordshire*, 1700, after which nothing is heard of him (*A Dictionary of the Printers and Booksellers who were at work in England, Scotland and Ireland from 1668 to 1725*, by Henry R. Plomer, with the help of H. D. Aldis, E. R. McC. Dix, G. J. Gray, R. B. McKerrow, and Arundell Esdaile eds. [London: Printed for the Bibliographical Society, at the Oxford University Press, 1922], p. 134).

[2] Jonathan Edwin, London bookseller, at the three Roses, Ludgate Street, 1671–9, dealt in a variety of literature, from sixpenny pamphlets … to folio histories and classics. His first entry in *The Term Catalogues* was Michaelmas 1671 … his last was Easter 1679. A staunch Royalist and Churchman, Edwin issued several books against the Presbyterians and Dissenters (Henry R. Plomer, ed., *A Dictionary of the Printers … 1668 to 1725* [p. 111]).

[3] See Vol. IV, Introduction, pp. xl–xliv and pp. 312–434; references to various volumes of Traherne's works are to *The Works of Thomas Traherne*, ed. Jan Ross (Cambridge, 2005–).

of his manuscripts by Bertram Dobell in the late nineteenth century; the details in book descriptions and provenance indicate that through the centuries Traherne's *Roman Forgeries* and *Christian Ethicks* had various owners; they were read, corrected, annotated and circulated. The primary copy texts for this edition of both *Christian Ethicks* and *Roman Forgeries* are held at the Cambridge University Library; of necessity to confirm as correct a text as possible, especially for *Roman Forgeries*, both texts were collated against other copies, primarily those listed in this edition.[4]

There may have been more than one printed copy of *Roman Forgeries*: both have missing words and letters, irregular pagination and signatures; the irregularities, however, are not the same in all copies, for instance in some copies there are printed manicules as in those held at Brasenose College Library and Lambeth Palace Library, pages 152 and 291, whereas manicules are missing in other copies as in the two copies at the Cambridge University Library. Pagination is also erratic, for example Hereford Library prints page 82 upside down; Hereford Cathedral library prints '82' right side up; Hereford Library prints p. 223 as 226; Hereford Cathedral Library prints p. 223 as 203. This is a conjecture; there may have been also various compositors.

Both *Roman Forgeries* and *Christian Ethicks* were badly printed with crowded text, run-on lines,[5] various letters in superscript or subscript,[6] misplaced punctuation, irregular spacing,[7] the use of a capital italic letter instead of a roman as the initial letter of words,[8] missing as well

---

[4] *Christian Ethicks* has also been read against the mid-twentieth-century edition produced by Carol L. Marks and George Robert Guffey: *Christian Ethicks* (Ithaca, NY, 1968).

[5] Crowded text, run-on lines, see 'to our Perfection, both here and hereafter' printed as toourPerfection,both hereandhereafter, p. 15, sig. B8^r in 1675 Yale text.

[6] Various letters in superscript or subscript, see 'ornaments and trophies far' reads 'fa^r' in *CE*, p. 16, sig. B8^v in 1675 Yale text, which appears to have been corrected by hand in ink; WF, CUL, BL WTN read 'far'.

[7] Misplaced punctuation, irregular spacing; see *CE*, p. 19, sig. C2^r, 'an inferiour end, our Wisdom', printed as 'an inferiour end , our Wisdom' and 'all Worlds fit to be enjoyed' printed as 'all World$_s$ fit to be enjoyed' (the final 's' was inserted in Yale text). See also *CE*, p. 24, sig. C4^v, 'forasmuch as the Distinction' printed as 'forasmuch astheDistinctionbetween them' and *CE*, p. 33, sig. D1^r, 'worse than Sleep, because' printed as 'worse than Sleep, because without'; see also *CE*, p. 27, 'well order'd Habit of mind, which Facilitates' printed as 'well order'dHabit ofmind,whichFacilitates'; see also *RF*, p. 47, 'Greg. Cassander, Anton. Contius, the famous', printed as 'Greg.Cassander,Anton.Contius,the'.

[8] For instance, the word 'Bliss' is printed as '*B*liss'; see *Christian Ethicks*, p. 4, sig. B2^r in 1675 text.

Introduction xvii

as misplaced and misformed punctuation, such as the exclamation mark, printed at a slant,[9] two capital letters 'V' for the letter 'W',[10] a common practice in the seventeenth century. Italics have been maintained as they appear in the text.

Christian Ethicks

General discussion of Christian Ethicks

The full title of *Christian Ethicks* is printed as Christian ETHICKS: O R, Divine Morality. | Opening the WAY to BLESSEDNESS, | By the RULES of | VERTUE | AND | REASON. | By *THO. TRAHERNE*, B.D. | Author of the *Roman* Forgeries. | *LONDON,* | Printed for *Jonathan Edwin*, at the *Three* | *Roses in Ludgate-street,* | 1675.

It was registered with the *Stationers* 6 August 1674 and printed for Jonathan Edwin. The Entry reads as follows: 'Entred … under the hands of Master George Hooper and Master Warden Roycroft a book or copy entituled Christian Ethicks or, Divine morality opening the way to blessednesse by the rules of vertue and reason …'.[11] *The Term Catalogues* lists its publication for Michaelmas Term, 1674 as 'Christian Ethicks, or Divine Morality opening the way to blessedness by the Rules of Virtue and Reason. By Tho. Traherne, B.D., Author of the "Roman Forgeries". In Octavo. Price, bound, 5^s. Printed for Jon. Edwin at the Three Roses in *Ludgate street'*.[12]

Christian Ethicks is intimately connected to Traherne's other works. For instance the section in the 1675 text (pp. 503–4), 'Of Magnificence', 'THE best Principle whereby a man can stear his course in this World, is that which being well prosecuted will make his Life at once honourable and happy: Which is to love every man in the whole World as GOD doth. For this will make a man the Image of GOD, and fill him with the mind and spirit of Christ, it will make every man that is, the Representative of GOD and of all the World unto him. It will make a man to reverence GOD in all Mankind, and lift him up

---

[9] Such as the exclamation mark, printed at a slant, see *Christian Ethicks*, p. 544, sig. Mm 7^v, 'I am still with thee!'.

[10] See *Christian Ethicks*, p. 77 in 1675 text 'Which that we may'; 'Which' is printed with a double 'V' for the letter 'W'.

[11] See *A Transcript of the Registers of the Worshipful Company of Stationers: From 1640–1708 A.D.*, Volume II, *1655–75* (London, 1913), p. 487.

[12] See *The Term Catalogues*, ed. Edward Arber, Volume I, *1668–1682* (London, 1903), pp. 184–5.

above all Temptations, Discouragements and Fears. It will make him to meet the love of GOD, Angels, and Men, in every Person. It will make a man truly glorious, by making him pleasing to GOD, and universally good to every one; diffusive like the Sun, to give himself to all, and wise to enjoy their compleat Felicity', is reiterated with slight variations in Volume V in the section entitled 'Miscellaneous works from Osborn MS b. 308' under 'Untitled treatise: The best principle whereby a man can Steer his course':[13] 'The best principle whereby a man can Steer his course in this World is that of Love to God and man; which being well prosecuted will make his Life at once Honorable and Happy, Holy and Blessed, Divine and Glorious. The utmost Height of it is most easy and most Blessed. which is to love evry man in the whole world, as the Sovereign object of ones Desires, the Representative of God Angels and Men, the right object of all their Love, the freind of God and the End of all Things.' The short 'Untitled treatise' may have been written in preparation for *Christian Ethicks*, although it may have been intended to stand on its own as a separate work as well. It was Traherne's habit to self-borrow and shift sections from one work to another.

Christian Ethicks is connected to *Commentaries of Heaven*, as the numerous cross references in 'Textual Emendations and Notes' (pp. 287–318) indicate. For instance see 'Abundance', p. 11 in 1675 text and p. 21 in present text, with the cross reference to see *CH* under 'Abundance', Vol. II, p. 53–63. See also the reference to Traherne's use of nautical imagery on p. 12 in 1675 text and pp. 21, 22 in present text, 'RATHER then make Shipwrack of a good Conscience, we must do as Mariners in a storm'. 'Shipwrack' and mariners are common images in Traherne's works; see for instance *Inducements* (Vol. I, p. 13); *A Sober View*, Sect. 1, pp. 49, 51; *The Kingdom of God* (Vol. I, Cap. XL, p. 483); *Centuries of Meditations* 1.36; *Commentaries of Heaven*, 'Appetite' (Vol. III, p. 148); 'Assumption' (Vol. III, p. 288); 'Astrologie' (Vol. III, p. 313); 'Authoritie' (Vol. III, p. 430). See also, 'to Sail Smoothly, and attain the Haven', p. 12 in 1675 text and p. 21 in the present text. *Select Meditations* anticipates *Christian Ethicks* in *The Fourth Century*, 56–68 (Vol. V, pp. 380–8), where Traherne outlines the various virtues, a discussion similar in many points to that of *Christian Ethicks* but markedly different from it.[14] *Christian Ethicks* may be considered as an epitome of Traherne's fundamental principles clearly ordered and explained for the general reader.

---

[13] See Vol. V, pp. 438–61; see also Introduction, pp. xxx–xxxii.
[14] See Vol. V, 'Textual Emendations and Notes', pp. 428–31.

Introduction

The book is an octavo, badly printed. The pagination is erratic, with missing numbers, some upside down and others used twice. In some copies, signatures are also irregular and unclear. Because of the various bindings, the measurements of the books differ, ranging from approximately 168 mm long x 111 mm wide x 37 mm deep to 183 mm long x 122 mm wide x 43 mm deep and sewn on four to five cords. The paper ranges approximately from 165 mm long x 110 mm wide to 170 mm long x 120 mm wide, with three to four vertical chain-lines per leaf; the watermark appears at the bottom inner edge of the page, although there is not enough to identify it.

Copies of 1675 Christian Ethicks held by various libraries

Cambridge University Library, Cambridge

Cambridge University Library holds two copies of *Christian Ethicks*, one previously owned by John Venn, 1834–1923, logician and president of Gonville and Caius College, Cambridge, who collaborated with his son, John Archibald, on *Alumni Cantabrigienses* (see *ODNB*); the other by Geoffrey Keynes, 1887–1982, surgeon, writer, bibliographer and literary scholar, whose work on William Blake helped establish Blake as a central figure in the history of English art and literature (see *ODNB*).

1. *Christian Ethicks* (7.61.8): the book owned by John Venn was repaired in 1963 with a new spine, front and back board pastedowns and fly leaves. The boards and spine are dark brown mottled calf; 'Traherne / Christian Ethicks' is printed on the spine, which has three raised cords. Although this is not recorded in Venn's handwritten catalogue, the book was perhaps acquired later. The title page appears at A1^r, on A1^v written in graphite is 'From J. Venn, Sc. D. Caius College' plus a library stamp dated 9 June 1896; 'To the Reader' begins at A2^r and extends to a3^r; a3^v is blank; 'The Contents' begins at a4^r and ends at a8^r; the apology 'To the Reader' appears at a8^v; the text begins at B1^r.

2. *Christian Ethicks* (Keynes T.4.10): the book owned by Keynes is bound in dark brown calf; the spine, which has no title, is decorated with gold leaf. On the front board pastedown in the upper left corner is a former library stamp, 'Porkington[15] Library / Shelf 6 / No. 114'

---

[15] Porkington, an estate near Denbighshire, referred to as Brogyntyn / the National Library of Wales; from the library the arms by Gore family, Barons of Harlech or Brogyntyn, or referred to by the English as 'Porkington', Oswestry, Shropshire.

with '£45' plus the library class mark. Written in graphite on the recto side of the first free fly leaf in the upper right corner is 'Geoffrey Keynes'; at mid-page also in graphite and perhaps in Keynes's script, is 'Sir Orlando Bridgeman'; at mid-page is a list of 'Passages in verse' found in the 1675 *CE*:

pp. 326 (Aa2^v)
    344–5
    348–9
    383
    394–8
    425–6
    456.

'My Lady Myddelton her book' is written in ink across the top of the recto side of the second fly leaf; mid-page written in graphite (perhaps by Keynes) is 'of Chirk Castle / Denbighshire'. On the title page in ink at the upper left corner is written 'Ellen. Owen'.

'My Lady Myddelton' refers to Lady Charlotte Myddelton (born c. 1661), daughter of Sir Orlando Bridgeman, mentioned in Traherne's will. She was the second wife of Sir Thomas Myddelton IV (1586–1666) of Chirk Castle in Denbighsire. Charlotte Bridgeman Myddelton died in 1694; she had four sons who predeceased her and one daughter, Charlotte, who inherited £20,000; she married twice (1) the 6th Earl of Warwick (d. 1701) and (2) Joseph Addison (1672–1719), the essayist. There was no issue from either marriage. The Chirk estate and family title passed to Sir Thomas's younger brother, Richard.

It appears that Keynes, or perhaps someone else, read at least parts of the book, indicated by graphite lines drawn along the sides of selected passages at pp. 271–3 ('Of Charity towards God'), at pp. 275–7 ('Of Charity to our Neighbour'), and at p. 462 ('Of Magnanimity'). The title page appears at A1^r with A1^v blank; 'To the Reader' begins at A2^r and ends at a3^r; a3^v is blank; 'The Contents' begins at A4^r and ends at a8^r; the apology 'To the Reader' appears at a8^v.

Charlotte, Bridgeman's daughter, must have returned to her father's house in Teddington, where she was present at Traherne's death as mentioned in his nuncupative will:

> Thomas Traherne … dyed vpon or about the Seaven and Twentyth of September 1674 … then lying sick at the Lady Bridgmans house in Teddington … being then of perfect mind and memory by Word of Mouth with an intent to make his Will

Introduction xxi

and to settle and dispose of his Goods and Estate did vtter and speake these or the like words vizt. I desire my Lady Bridgman and her daughter the Lady Charlott haue each of them a Ring.[16]

British Library, London

Book description

The British Library holds one copy (1112.d.6) of *Christian Ethicks*, which is rebound in light brown cloth with a leather spine. The leather extends to both front and back boards; the corners at the fore-edge of both front and back boards are also covered in leather up to 30 mm. The book is sewn on five raised cords forming six blocks; printed on the second block in gold is 'TRAHERNE / CHRISTIAN / ETHICS [sic]' with 'London / 1675' at the bottom of the spine. The title page begins with A1^r, A1^v is blank; 'To the Reader' extends from A2^r to a3^r, a3^v is blank; 'The Contents' extends from a4^r to a8^r; the apology 'To the Reader' appears at a8^v. The text begins at B2^r.

Except for the name 'J. J. Ferris** [?]' on the first free end paper, there are no other marks of previous ownership. The book was acquired by the British Museum 6 September 1838 and rebound 1969.

Folger Shakespeare Library, Washington, DC

The Folger Shakespeare Library's single copy of *Christian Ethicks* is bound in speckled light tan calf similar to the first book near the fore edge in fig. 2.17, p. 41, of *Trade Bookbinding in the British Isles 1660–1800* by Stuart Bennett (London, 2004). It is sewn on six cords with 'CHRISTIAN / ETHICKS' printed in gold on the second red block. Both front and back boards are loose not however separated from the spine.

The Folger copy of *Christian Ethicks* (168–224q) is corrupt and unreliable in many ways. While examining the Folger copy, I discovered a major flaw: at some point the complete 'M' gathering (pp. 161–76) was replaced by the 'M' gathering of Joseph Briggs's *Sound considerations for tender consciencies*. The Folger Shakespeare Library has no holding for this work.[17] Gatherings after the 'M' signature are

---

[16] See Appendix, 'The will of Thomas Traherne, as registered in the prerogative court of Canterbury', pp. 445–6. See also Dobell, ed., *The Poetial Works of Thomas Traherne*, pp. 167–8.

[17] This flaw has now been recorded in the library's catalogue. The complete title of Briggs's work is *Sound considerations for tender consciencies: wherein is shewed their obligation to hold close union and communion with the Church of England*

also irregular. Readings from the Folger copy recorded in Volume VII of the Brewer edition of *The Works of Thomas Traherne* are from the few complete gatherings before the 'M' signature.

The full title appears at A1^r, followed by a blank leaf (A1^v); 'To the Reader' extends from A2^r to a3^r, followed by a blank leaf (a3^v); 'The Contents' begins at a4^r and ends at a8^r, the apology 'To the Reader' appears at a8^v; Chapter 1 of *Christian Ethicks* begins at B1^r. In the Folger copy, signatures A7^v (last leaf of 'A Premonition') and B1^r ('first leaf of 'An Advertisement') are continuous; there is no cancel, although there may be in other copies. This was possible to see because of the broken spine.

The front pastedown as well as the free end paper indicate four previous owners of the book: 'Mary Pitman her / Book ex dono / Mr. La: Smyth 1683' and 'Maria Brata Janiber / This Leaf not to be / taken out'. On the front board pastedown is the armorial bookplate of Montagu Egerton Loftus, with 'Loyal Amort' printed above the crest and 'Prends moi tel que je suis' under the crest. Above the bookplate is written in graphite '£20 /- /- / extremely rare'. The Folger purchased the book from Steven & Brown 9 July 1983.

In the margin of some pages are crosses (x) in graphite next to various lines, some of which do not appear in other copies of *Christian Ethicks*, indicating the book had been examined seriously at some point as well as the corrupt condition of the book.

Brasenose College Library, Oxford

The Brasenose College Library's single copy of the 1675 *Christian Ethicks* is bound in mottled brown calf; it appears to have been rebound with the old, perhaps the original, calf replaced over the new up to approximately 15 mm, with a new spine and sewn on 5 raised cords. On the first pastedown is written 'BRAS. TS. 10', perhaps a former class mark. There is also a book plate with a crest on the front pastedown. At the top of the crest is written 'Aula Regia et Coll', at the bottom, 'AENAE NASI'. At the corners of the crest are the following numbers: at the top left is '1'; at the top right '5', bottom left '0' and at the bottom right '9', forming perhaps the date '1509'. On the first free end paper written in ink is 'from Rodd, London / April 25, 1846'

and their fellow members in it, and not to forsake the publick assemblies thereof. In several sermons preached, upon 1 Cor. 1.10 and Heb. 10.25. By Joseph Briggs M.A. vic. of Kirkburton, in Yorkshire (London: Printed for Nathaniel Brooks and are to be sold at the Angel in Cornhil, 1675).

(perhaps a bookseller and date of purchase) as well as W. E. Buckley / Brasenose: Coll: Oxford'. At the bottom of the verso side of the first free end paper is written in ink: 'By Thomas Traherne.', under which is written in a lighter brown ink 'of Brasenose Coll. Oxford' as well as 'On the Title Page of his *Christian Ethics* [sic] / He calls himself the author of "The Roman Forgeries".' The title is at A1^r with A1^v blank; 'To the Reader' begins at A2^r and ends at a3^r; 'The Contents' begins at a4^r and ends at a8^r; apology 'To the Reader' is at a8^r; the text begins at B1^r. A portion of a watermark appears at the upper left corner of the leaf; it is however too small and incomplete to clearly identify it. There are also ink spots at various places throughout the text. There are no corrections to the text.

The provenance is indicated on the first free end paper where 'from Rodd, London / April 25, 1846' is written; to the right of the leaf written in ink is 'W. E. Buckley / Brasenose: Coll. Oxford'. This would be William Edward Buckley, who matriculated at Brasenose College in 1835. His collection of Brasenose authors was purchased in 1892. Written at the top of the title page is 'Fr. Wrangham' with what appears to be the letter 'w' followed by the numbers 11 / 5 (perhaps a date). This would probably be Francis Wrangham, 1769–1842, whose books were auctioned by Leigh Sotheby in 1843.

Worcester College Library, Oxford

Worcester College Library holds one book of *Christian Ethicks*. It is bound in brown mottled leather, which may be the original binding. It is very worn with scratches, which removed some of the leather revealing the board. The front board is detached; the back board is loose but attached. Both front and back boards are modestly tooled with two lines at the head, bottom, spine and fore edge of the book. The spine which has four cords also has marks of wear. Signature A1^r contains the title page; 'To the Reader' extends from A2^r to a3^r; 'The Contents' extends from a4^r to a8^r; the apology 'To the Reader' appears at a8^v; the text begins at B1^r.

There are a few corrections made to the 1675 text: Number '3' is written in ink at the bottom of the title page; at the penultimate line on page 9 is an addition in ink of 'Pe' to 'Per' (Perfection); p. 43, 'lov of the world that' has been inserted; p. 183, line 22 'the' has been deleted; p. 193, line 23 'of' has been added in the margin ('Holiness of God'); p. 199, second paragraph, line 12, 'Emazement' changed to 'Amazement', with 'A' written over the 'E' in ink; p. 205, second paragraph, line 4 'lower' changed to 'Lower' with 'L' written over 'l' in ink; p. 222, lines 6–8, to the first letter of each line has been added: 't' of 'the'; 'd' of deep and 'b' of 'ber', 'of number'; p. 260, last line 'h' added to 'im' in ink (him); p. 290, penultimate line, 'Decree' changed to 'Degree'; p. 295 (i.e. 294), second paragraph, line 4 'a' deleted ('the a Joy' to 'the Joy'); p. 337, line 2 ('that is') as well as penultimate line ('that is between'), the 's' of 'is' in both places has been provided in ink. On pages 324–5, 327–30, 332, 334–5, there are ticks and other marks in the margin indicating the text was at some point read. There is worming throughout the book. On the front pastedown are the current classmark (L.R.1.30) plus a previous classmark (XA.6.56) crossed through.

The stamp (H. A Pottinger / Worcester / Oxford) on the front pastedown indicates that it was owned by Henry Allison Pottinger (1824–1911), librarian of Worcester College from 1884 to 1911; it also suggests that it is likely the book as well as others was a gift to the Library. The *Worcester College Record* for 1910–11 describes Pottinger as 'gradually transferring to the shelves the whole of his huge and miscellaneous private collection', which must have been a prolonged process not a single bequest.

Weston Library (Bodleian), Oxford

Weston's single copy of *Christian Ethicks* is bound in brown mottled calf and sewn on four cords with five blocks. The book is in poor condition with both boards loose; the spine appears to have been replaced with a lighter calf, although this is uncertain. CHRISTIAN / ETHICKS is stamped in gold on the second block of the spine. There are no indications of ownership on the front board. Signature A1^r contains the title page with A1^v blank; 'To the Reader' extends from A2^r to a3^r with a3^v blank; 'The Contents' extends from a4^r to a8^r; the apology 'To the Reader' appears at a8^v; the text begins at B1^r.

Roman Forgeries

Although the least read and studied of his works, Traherne himself must have thought *Roman Forgeries* to be one of his most important works, since it is his first book to be published and perhaps the only one he saw through the press. The 1673 title page reads as follows: Roman Forgeries | Or a *TRUE* | ACCOUNT | OF | *FALSE RECORDS* |

Discovering the | IMPOSTURES | AND |Counterfeit Antiquities | OF THE | CHURCH | OF | ROME. | *By a Faithful Son of the Church of ENGLAND.* | *LONDON,* | Printed by *S.* and *B. Griffin*, for *Jonathan Edwin* at | the three Roses in *Ludgate-Street*, 1673. It is intimately connected to *Commentaries of Heaven*, which helps to date at least parts of that work, indicating that it may have been written either after *Roman Forgeries* (1673) or simultaneously with it. Under 'Antichrist' in *CH* Traherne alludes to the *Index Expurgatorious* (Vol. III, p. 109); also under 'Antichrist' he specifically refers to *Roman Forgeries* (Vol. III, p. 110)[18].

> With these forgeries he [the Pope] hath corrupted all the Stream of Antiquitie, and so muddled the Waters, that they must poyson them that drink it. But the Unspeakable Blessing of GOD is, that his ignorant rotten Counterfeit Records before a Wise and discerning Ey, are as easy to be distinguished, from the pure Bright and solid, Majestick Divine and Heavenly Truths, and Records indeed, as an Oyster shell is by a common Ey easy to be discerned from a piece of Gold. Concerning which we shall say nothing here, bec. we have prepared a whole Tract upon that theme, (an intire volume) fit to be published.[19]

Roman Forgeries however has been often regarded as a waste of Traherne's energy and time. Bertram Dobell thought the work to be a mistake and of little literary value: 'one can hardly help regretting that the book should have been written, for, well as it is done, it might have been done equally well by a writer of far inferior gifts, while it is impossible not to feel that Traherne was wasting his genius in its composition.... Within twelve months after the publication of "Roman Forgeries" its author was dead.'[20]

Roman Forgeries was entered with the *Stationers*' registers on 25 September 1673, under Jonathan Edwin: 'Entred for his copie under the hand of Master Warden Mearne a coppy or booke intituled *Roman forgeries, or a true account of false records detecting the counterfeit antiqui-*

---

[18] See also *CH*, 'Antiquitie' (Vol. III, pp. 114–23), and 'Apostasie' (Vol. III, pp. 124–7); for '*Atheism*', see 'Atheist' (Vol. III, pp. 324–32); see also *CH*, Vol. II, p. 524 where Traherne planned a topic under 'Idolatrie'.

[19] With these forgeries ... a whole Tract upon that theme, (an intire volume) fit to be published, see Vol. III, p. 110, lines 554–63.

[20] 'one can hardly ... its author was dead': see Dobell, ed., *The Poetical Works of Thomas Traherne*, pp. xlvi–xlvii. See also Appendix, Brooke's account, pp. 519–22.

xxvi   *The Works of Thomas Traherne*

ties of the Church of Roome, by Tho: Traherne, S.T.B.'[21] Without noting the author, *The Term Catalogues* for 1673 Michaelmas, 24 November, lists *Roman Forgeries* as 'Roman Forgeries, or A true Account of false Records, discovering the Impostures and counterfeit Antiquities of the Church of *Rome*. Price, bound, 3ˢ. Printed for J. Edwin at the Three Roses in *Ludgate street*'.[22]

General discussion of Roman Forgeries

Thomas Comber (1645–1699),[23] dissatisfied with Traherne's book, continued to expose the forgeries of the Roman Church in **Counterfeit Antiquities** | IN THE | COUNCILS | During the First Four CENTURIES. Together with An | APPENDIX | Concerning the |FORGERIES AND ERRORS | IN THE | ANNALS OF BARONIUS. | *By THOMAS COMBER, D. D.* | *Prebend of* YORK. | *LONDON* ,| Printed by *Samel Roycroft*, for *Robert Clavell* at the | *Peacock* at the West-End of S. *Pauls*, 1689:

> *When* Campian[24] *long ago undertook to defend the Roman Cause, he boasted, that* He was strengthned with the firm and powerful Guard of all the Councils, and that all the General Councils were on his side *(a) Which vain Brag the Writers from the Roman Church do frequently repeat to this very day. But he that with Judgment and Diligence shall peruse their own allowed Editions of the Councils, will easily discover the falshood of this Assertion: For there*

---

[21] *A Transcript of the Registers of the Worshipful Company of Stationers; from 1640–1708 A.D.* In Three Volumes, Volume II, *1655–1675* (London, 1913), p. 472.

[22] *The Term Catalogues*, ed. Edward Arber, Volume I, *1668–1682* (London, 1903), p. 154.

[23] Thomas Comber (1645–1699), dean of Durham, liturgist, controversialist and polemical writer, is best known for *A Companion to the Temple and the Closet; or a help to publick and private devotion, in an Essay upon the daily Offices of the Church*, 2 parts (London, 1672–6).

[24] Edmund Campian (c. 1540–1581), English Jesuit priest and martyr, ordained subdeacon at Douai in 1573. While on a pilgrimage to Rome in 1578, he was admitted into the Society of Jesus. When he returned to England to set up a Jesuit mission, he visited Catholic prisoners and hurriedly wrote his 'Challenge to the Privy Council', commonly referred to as 'Campion's Brag', wherein he proclaimed the purpose of his mission was 'to preach the Gospel, to minister the Sacraments, to instruct the simple, to reform sinners, to confute errors … to cry alarm spiritual against foul vice and proud ignorance, wherewith many [of] my dear country men are abused'. (*New Catholic Encyclopedia*, second edition, Volume 2 [Washington, D.C., 2003], pp. 921–2).

is such adding and expunging, such altering and disguising things in the Body of the Councils, such excusing, falsifying, and shuffling in the Notes, that a Judicious Reader will soon perceive these Venerable Records, truly set down and explained, do not favour them. But these Corruptions are carried on with such Confidence and Cunning, that an unexperienced and unwary Student, may be imposed on by this specious shew of Venerable Antiquity: For their sakes therefore, it's necessary to take a short view of that Fraud and Policy, which is so commonly made use of in those Editions of the Councils which pass through the Roman Mint, especially in those which are in most use among us, viz. This Edition of Severinus Binius *(b), and that of* Labbé *and* Cossartius *(c), wherein* Binius *his Notes are printed verbatim. Which useful design was begun by a Learned and Ingenious Gentleman, in a Tract entituled* Roman Forgeries, *printed at London, An.* 1673: *But that Author doth not follow the exact order of Time, nor doth he go much beyond the* Nicene Council, *and even in that Period he left out many plain Instances: And whereas he died before he had proceeded any further; I resolved to begin where he left off.*[25]

In several places however Traherne states the purpose and limits of the subject of his book *Roman Forgeries*:

> I shall not descend into the latter Ages, but keep within the compass of the first 420 years, and lay open so many of *frauds*, as disguize and cover the face of *Primitive Antiquities*, which ought to be preserved most sacred and pure. It is sufficient to prove, that all the *Streams* are infected by the *Poyson* that is thrown into the *Fountain-head*; and to expatiate downwards, would over-swell the Book, which is intended to be little, for the use and benefit of all. Neither shall I talk of the Fathers

---

[25] See The Introduction, sig. A². See also Dobell, ed., *The Poetical Works of Thomas Traherne*, pp. xlvi–xlvii. See Dobell's note, p. xlvii: '"Roman Forgeries" must have had some popularity in its time, for it is, unlike "Christian Ethicks," a tolerably common book. Fifteen years after its publication Dean Comber, a writer of some note in his day, published a work of similar character, and with the same title. As Traherne's book was published anonymously, Dean Comber has usually received credit for that as well as for his own work. The Dean was a man of considerable ability, and he would hardly have been pleased had he been told that he would only be remembered in future times as the writer who helped himself to a striking title at the expense of one who was much greater than himself.'

at large: I will not meddle with their *Amphilochius, Abdias, S. Denis, &c.* but keep close to *Records*, and *publick instruments of Antiquity*, which have the force of *Laws*: Such as *Apostles Canons, Decretal Epistles,* and *Ancient Councils*; which they have either depraved by altering the Text, or falsified, as it were, by Whole-sale, in the intire Lump: And I shall concern my self in the latter, more than the former (sigs. B6^r–B6^v in 1673 text and page 334 in present text).

As well as the following:

Did I follow them throughout all Ages, my work would be endless. We should find much foul Play in following Councils and Records of the Church: but for several weighty Reasons I have at present confined my self within the compass of the first 400 years next after the Death of our Lord, whose Name is not to be mentioned without praise and glory.

Note well: I go on thus, to observe particularly what Forgeries every collector of the Councils owneth, and what Emperours, Kings, and Popes, their books are dedicated to; and what priviledge, in all the principal parts of the Popes Jurisdiction, they come forth withal; and especially what a multitude of men have been encouraged to carry on this Design, that you might see the Conspiracy of the Members with the Head, and the general Guilt of that Church in so Enormous an Affair. To which we might add the innumerable *Armies* of Learned men that have cited them in that Church, and the Company of Captains that have defended them: But it had been better for them that they had never medled with the Protestant Objections, for they have made the matter worse than they found it, and bewraid themselves in all their Answers; nay, they have made the *Frauds* more eminent and notorious, by disturbing the Reader, while they give him Warning by their *Notes*, though the intent be to defend them. This I speak especially upon the last, from *Binius* downward (pp. 120–1 in original text and p. 397 in present text).

And see also *Roman Forgeries*, where Traherne writes the following:

How excessively the World was addicted to *Fables* about the time of *Isidore's* Appearance, we may see by the contents of the 2. *Nicene Council,* Dreams, Visions and Miracles being very rife in their best demonstrations; and among other Legends, a

> counterfeit *Basil*, a counterfeit *Athanasius*, a counterfeit *Emperour*, maintaining and promoting the Adoration of Images: As may perhaps in another Volume be more fully discovered, when we descend from these *first*, to succeeding Ages (pp. 34–5 in original text, p. 355 in present text).

'As may perhaps in another Volume be more fully discovered, when we descend from these *first*, to succeeding Ages' suggests Traherne may have planned to write another book about the forgeries of Church of Rome, to complement this one, a proposal, which perhaps inspired Thomas Comber's work on the same subject.[26]

Other anti-Roman Catholic works of the seventeenth century

Following the lead of John Jewel (1522–1571), Bishop of Salisbury, *An Apology of the Church of England* (1564) and William Perkins (1558–1600), *A Reformed Catholike, or, a declaration shewing how neere we may come to the present Church of Rome in sundrie points of religion and wherein we must for ever depart from them with an advertisement to all favourers of the Roman religion* (1597, 1598, 1611), anti-Roman Catholic literature continued to be written regularly throughout the seventeenth century: for instance, William Chillingworth, *The religion of Protestants a safe way to salvation* (London, 1638); Henry Hammond, D.D., Archdeacon of Chichester and Canon of Christ Church, *A defence of the Church of England against the exceptions of the Romanists, A discourse of heresy in defence of our Church against the Romanist, Alien alëtheuein, or A brief account of one suggestion of the Romanist against the dispatcher dispatched by Henry Hammond* (London, 1660) and *Of schisme a defence of the Church of England against the exception of the Romanists* (London, 1654). Edward Stillingfleet, *A Discourse concerning the idolatary practised in the Church of Rome and the danger of salvation in the communion of it in an answer to some papers of a revolted protestant* (London, 1671).

Besides *Roman Forgeries in the councils during the first four centuries*, Comber also wrote the following: *A Discourse concerning the second Council of Nice, which first introduced and established Image-worship*

---

[26] Thomas Comber, D.D. (1645–1699), *Roman Forgeries in the councils during the first four centuries. Together with an appendix concerning the forgeries and errors in and Annals of Baronius* (London, 1689). Comber's work is divided into two parts: Part I, *A brief account of the Roman Forgeries in the volumes of the councils, for the first three centuries*; Part II, *A brief account of the Roman Forgeries in the volumes of the councils, for the fourth century*.

in the Christian Church, anno Domini 787 (London, 1688), as well as *The Church History clear'd from the Roman Forgeries and Corruptions found in the Councils and Baronius. Being the third and fourth parts of the Roman Forgeries* (London, 1695).

Copies of 1673 Roman Forgeries held by various libraries

The book is an octavo, badly printed: pagination is erratic, with missing numbers, some upside down and others used twice. In some copies, signatures are also irregular and unclear. Like *Christian Ethicks*, because of the various bindings, the measurements of the books differ, ranging from approximately 165 mm long x 115 mm wide x 30 mm deep to 178 mm long x 118 mm wide to 43 mm deep and sewn on four to five cords. The paper ranges approximately from 163 mm long x 110 mm wide to 175 mm long x 115 mm wide, with three to four vertical chain-lines per leaf; the watermark appears at the bottom inner edge of the page, although there is not enough to identify it.

Folger Shakespeare Library, Washington, DC

The Folger copy of *Roman Forgeries* is bound in contemporary mottled calf with a gold-tooled decorated spine and sewn on four cords. On the front pastedown Traherne's name is written twice in graphite. The full title page appears at A1^r, the verses from the books of Timothy (1 Tim. 4:22, 2 Tim. 3:8) at A1^v; dedication to Bridgeman, A2^r; A2^v is blank; 'The Premonition' begins at A3^r and ends at A7^v; 'An advertisement to the reader' begins at B1^v and ends at B8^r; 'An abridgement of the chapters' begins at B8^v and ends at C2^v. The first chapter begins at C3^r. There are two blank leaves at the back of the book, plus a pastedown, perhaps taken from the last gathering with the following note in graphite: 'As probably blank / cut away / otherwise perfect from 16 / 6 / 24'.

According to the library records, there were three previous owners of the volume: George G(?) Clare, Sir Robert Leicester Harmsworth (1870–1937) and the William Andrews Clark Memorial Library. In February 1957, the Folger acquired the volume from a sale of duplicates from the William Andrews Clark Library. At this time it was listed as a duplicate, which they purchased from the library of Robert Harmsworth. There are no ownership marks on the volume of either of these two previous owners. Clare's signature however appears on the verso of the front fly leaf; the recto is blank.

Library of Congress, Washington, DC

Book Description

The Library of Congress copy of *Roman Fogeries* has been rebound in red cloth with paste downs on both boards, as well as end leaves replaced; there is no indication of previous ownership. The recto of the first free end paper is blank; on the verso of the first free end paper 'Thomas Traherne' is written in graphite at the top of the leaf. The full title page is at A1^r; verses from the books of Timothy appear at A1^v; at A2^r is the dedication to Bridgeman with A2^v blank. 'A Premonition' begins at A3^r and ends at A7^v; 'An Advertisement to the Reader' begins at B1^r and ends at B8^r; 'An Abridgement of the Chapters' begins at B8^v and ends at C2^v; 'A True Account … Church of Rome' begins at C3^r. Except for 'see the premon / tion' on page nine, no other changes have been made to the text nor is there any indication of provenance. 'See the premonition' in the margin of page 9 refers to signatures A3^v–A4^r, 'that the last Appeal should be made to Councils, and that the Person condemned in any Province should not be received, if he fled to others'.

Hereford Library, Hereford

Book Description

The Hereford Library's copy of *Roman Forgeries* has been tightly rebound in dark brown leather with six raised cords on the spine. At the top of the pages is a solid blue color with a sprinkling of colors on the outside and bottom edges. On the second block stamped in gold is 'Treherne [sic] / Roman Forgeries'. On the fifth block is the class mark in gold, 'L282', with '1673' at the bottom. On the title page Traherne's name does not appear nor has it been inscripted. On back of the title page is the number '20467' as well as the classmark. On A1^v (the page with verses from the books of Timothy) are what appears to be former classmarks as well as a Hereford Library stamp; at the bottom of the leaf written in graphite is the number '771714' and at the bottom inner edge, 'Collated / FM JM / 8.10.41.' On the first blank leaf in graphite is 'written by Thomas Traherne / £3 / 31–' with 'HERE' at the bottom.

The bookplates indicate at least two previous owners: Walter Charles James, whose crest appears on the first free end leaf and reads 'J'AIME A JAMAIS'; above the crest written in graphite is 'by Thomas Traherne /£3/3'; at the bottom of the leaf printed in graphite is 'HERE'. It was then in possession of the Hereford Public Library, Reference

Department with a note: 'This book was a gift of the Friends of the Art Gallery 1940'. 'Public Library Hereford' is stamped on the title page along with stamps reading 'Herefordshire Collection' and 'for reference only'. There are also Hereford Public Library stamps on various pages throughout the book.

Hereford Cathedral Library, Hereford
Book Description

The binding of the Hereford Cathedral Library's single copy is probably seventeenth-century in dark mottling. It has fine gold tooling on the front and back boards and is paneled in gilt with gold decorative lines forming a rectangle. At each corner of the inner section is a decorative fillet. The spine has five raised cords with 'ROMAN FORGE– / RIES' stamped in gold on a red background on the second block. The paper is marbled on the front board as well as the following leaf; it is also marbled on the last leaf and back board. Decorative gilt is rolled around the edges of boards. The binding is similar to the book as well as the spine pictured at the inner edge at the top of page 41 figure 2.17 of *Trade Bookbinding in the British Isles 1600–1800*, by Stuart Bennett (Oak Knoll Press / The British Library, 2001). On the title page under '*By a Faithful Son of the Church / of ENGLAND*' is written in brown ink 'By Tho. Traherne'. The full title page appears at A1^r, the verses from the books of Timothy at A1^v; dedication to Bridgeman A2^r; A2^v is blank; 'The Premonition' begins at A3^r and ends at A7^v. 'An Advertisement to the Reader' begins at B1^v and ends at B8^r; 'An Abridgement of the Chapters' begins at B8^v and ends at C2^v; The first chapter begins at C3^r.

Inside the front board is a bookplate with 'Hereford Cathedral Library / Purchased 1952'. It was bought from Bowes & Bowes, Cambridge, England, with no indication of further provenance.

Balliol College Library, Oxford
Book Description

The book is bound in English calf and modestly blind-tooled on a red spine. Sewn on four raised cords forming five blocks, 'ROMAN / FORGERIES' is printed in gold lettering on the second block, with straight gold lines at the sides of the block and double gold lines at top and bottom with a previous classmark, 'L. 24. / 12'(?). The Balliol crest is on the front pastedown. The full title page is at

A1^r, the verses from the books of Timothy appear on A1^v; at A2^r is the dedication to Bridgeman with A2^v blank; the Premonition begins at A3^r and ends at A7^v; 'An Advertisement to the reader' begins at B1^r and ends at B8^r; 'An Abridgement to the Reader' begins at B3^v and ends at C2^v; the first chapter of 'A True Account ... Church of Rome' begins at C3^r recto.

The book was a gift to the library. It was previously owned by George Coningesby (1692–1766), whose signature appears on the first front free leaf. There are also previous shelfmarks on the front leaves.

Brasenose College Library, Oxford

Book Description

The single copy of *Roman Forgeries* held by Brasenose College Library is bound in either late seventeenth- or early eighteenth-century calf over pasteboard. It is blind-tooled with a single fillet towards the outer edges of the boards. On the spine the text block edges are sprinkled red. It was rebacked and repaired in 1975. 'COMBER'S / ROMAN / FORGERIES' appears on the first block in gold lettering on the spine with 'B.N.C. / LIBRARY' in gold lettering at the bottom of the spine. The full title page is at A1^r, the verses from the books of Timothy appear on A1^v; at A2^r is the dedication to Bridgeman with A2^v blank; the Premonition begins at A3^r and ends at A7^v; 'An Advertisement to the reader' begins at B1^r and ends at B8^r; 'An Abridgement to the Reader' begins at B3^v and ends at C2^v; the first chapter of 'A True Account ... Church of Rome' begins at C3^r.

The book was owned by William Edward Buckley (1818–1892); with a note on the first free end paper: 'W. E. Buckley Bras: Coll: Oxford. From Straker, London. March 26. 1845.' The inscription at the top of the title page indicates it was also in possession of Fr. Wrangham, perhaps Francis Wrangham (1769–1842) whose books were auctioned by Leigh Sotheby in 1843.

Also on the first free end paper is written 'By Thomas Traherne. / of Brasenose College. / On the Title Page of his Christian Ethics [sic] / he calls himself the author of "The Roman Forgeries."' At the top of the title page is written 'Fr. Wrangham' with what appears as the letter 'w' and numbers 11 / 5'; on the title page under 'By a Faithful Son of the Church / of ENGLAND' in ink is 'written by Dr. Comber', heavily crossed through. In graphite is 'to wit', and written in bold 'see the list of Books at the end of the Traherne's [?]'".

Worcester College Library, Oxford

Book Description

The Worcester College Library's single copy of *Roman Forgeries* appears to have been rebound in cloth probably in the nineteenth century and sewn on four raised cords. There is no lettering on the spine. 'See the premonition' appears on p. 9; the only insertion from the errata is on p. 43, 'love of the World that'. No other changes to the text have been made. The full title page is at A1^r, the verses from the books of Timothy appear on A1^v; at A2^r is the dedication to Bridgeman with A2^v blank; the Premonition begins at A3^r and ends at A7^v; 'An Advertisement to the reader' begins at B1 recto and ends at B8 recto; 'An Abridgement to the Reader' begins at B8^v and ends at C2^v; the first chapter of 'A True Account ... Church of Rome' begins at C3^r.

The two signatures on the first free end paper indicate that it had at least two previous owners: one 'James Jones', who apparently bought the book in 1844 and that of Henry Allison Pottinger (1824–1911), Librarian of Worcester College from 1884 to 1911. The book was probably a gift to the Library by Pottinger. The *Worcester Record* for 1910–11 (p. 2) describes Pottinger as 'gradually transferring to the shelves the whole of his huge and miscellaneous private collection', which suggests a prolonged process not a single bequest.

Weston Library (Bodleian), Oxford

Book Description

The Weston Library's single copy of the 1673 book is perhaps bound in brown calf, with details tooled on the front and back boards. There is no lettering on the spine. 'See the / Premonition' appears in the margin on p. 9; and 'love of the world that' has been inserted on p. 43. The binding is in poor condition: the front and back boards are completely detached, with no lettering on the spine. It has been bound with *A Discourse on the Vanity of the Creature*, by a Person of Honour, 1673, Printed by J. Macock for Richard Royston, Book-seller to the Kings Most Excellent Majesty, 1673. On the first leaf before the title page is written, 'By Thomas Treherne [sic] on the Title page of his *Christian Ethics* [sic] of Brasenose Oxford. He calls himself "author of Roman Forgeries"'. There is no indication of provenance. The full title page is at A1^r, the verses from the books of Timothy appear on A1^v; at A2^r is the dedication to Bridgeman with A2^v blank; the Premonition begins at A3^r; 'An Advertisement to the reader' begins at B1^r and ends at B8^r;

'An Abridgement to the Reader' begins at B3^v and ends at C2^v; the first chapter of 'A True Account … Church of Rome' begins at C3^r.

Within the F signature (F6^r to F8^v), pages 65 to 80, pages 75, 76, 77, 78 are damaged; a clear line approximately 3 mm from the fore edge runs through the text hindering a complete reading. Except for 'see the Premonition' (p. 9) and 'the Lov of the World that' (p. 43), both inserted in ink, there appear to be no other changes to the text.

Cambridge University Library, Cambridge

Cambridge University Library holds two copies of *Roman Forgeries* as follows: Peterborough C.4.18 and 7.41.24.

Peterborough (C.4.18)

Book Description

1. The Peterborough copy held at Cambridge University Library is bound in dark mottled calf, with six raised cords on the spine. On both boards there are double lines on the spine, top, bottom and the fore edges of both the front and back boards with a set of double lines 30 mm from the verso (spine) side of the front board and 35.5 mm on the back board. The front and back boards have been modestly decorated with speckled gold at the fore edge of both front and back boards. There are no signs of ownership, such as names, dates or signatures, etc. throughout the book. The full title page is at A1^r, the verses from the books of Timothy appear on A1^v; at A2^r is the dedication to Bridgeman with A2^v blank; the Premonition extends from at A3^r to A7^v; 'An Advertisement to the reader' begins at B1^r recto and ends at B8^r recto; 'An Abridgement of the Chapters' begins at B8^v and ends at C2^v; the first chapter of 'A True Account … Church of Rome' begins at C3^r. On the verso side of the title page under the verses from the books of Timothy the number 2553:09 has been written in graphite; there is also a stamp reading 'Cambridge University Library / On deposit from / Peterborough Cathedral'.

On p. 9 at recto fore edge is written 'see the Premoni / tion'; p. 35 'now' is not deleted; p. 43 'Lov of ye World y^t' written in ink with 'obstinate perverseness' deleted; p. 55 reads 'Privy Councils' no change made; p. 66 (line 16) no '&' or 'and' inserted; p. 83 reads '1635' change from errata not made; p. 104 reads 'there is a fit', change from errata not made; p. 107 reads 'in the year 1618', change not made; marginal gloss Vid. Cap. no 'II' has been inserted; p. 137 reads '*Treatise of the*

xxxvi   *The Works of Thomas Traherne*

Right of the Fathers' change not made from errata; p. 157 reads 'Transceant', change not made from errata; p. 172 reads '*Pontifical Falsity*' change not made from errata; p. 222 (201) after 'that of these *Hermes*', 'one' has been inserted in ink after '*Hermes*'.

The Peterborough collection was acquired by Cambridge University Library in the 1970s. The collection is largely from the library of White Kennett (1660–1728), historian, antiquarian and bishop of Peterborough (1718–28), although there are books at one time owned by John and Simon Patrick, acquired by the Cathedral library in 1699. On the front pastedown is original classmark, A–2–9, now crossed out. This indicates that this copy of *Roman Forgeries* was a part of the ordinary Cathedral library not Kenentt's private library. Although the date 'Sept 25 1726' on p. 316 in the margin at the end of last paragraph may be in Kennett's script and indicates the time he finished either reading or examining the book. It was Kennett's habit to do this in his books. Books with these dates were acquired towards the end of his life (see Hall, pp. v–vi). There is a brief history of the collection in *Peterborough Cathedral Library: A catalogue of books printed before 1800 and now on deposit in Cambridge University Library*, ed. J. J. Hall (Cambridge, 1986).

Cambridge University Library 7.41.24

Book Description

2. *Roman Forgeries* (7.41.24): The second book of *Roman Forgeries* held at Cambridge University Library was repaired in 1946 with a new spine over which the original front and back binding has been replaced. It is modestly decorated with triple lines at the center of each board forming a rectangle with a floral decoration at each corner. There are new front and back pastedowns plus new front and back fly leaves, which are clean. It was catalogued several times without information about ownership or provenance.

On the title page above the title *Roman Forgeries* is an old classmark 7.41.26, with '26' changed to '24'. Under the title are previous classmarks written on either side of the second line of the title, '*Or a True*'.[27] Under the verses from the books of Timothy, the Cambridge University Library armorial crest has been pasted and reads '*Academiæ Cantabrigionsis / Liber*'[28] with the number 2553–09 written at the side. The full

---

[27] 'Ff.8.89' *Or a TRUE* '8.c.22'.
[28] Cambridge University library armorial crest ... '*Academiæ Cantabrigionsis / Liber*', see J. C. T. Oates, F.B.A., *Cambridge University Library / A History /*

Introduction xxxvii

title page is at sig. A1ʳ, the verses from the books of Timothy appear on sig. A1ᵛ; at sig. A2ʳ is the dedication to Bridgeman with sig. A2ᵛ blank; 'A Premonition' extends from at sigs. A3ʳ to A7ᵛ; 'An Advertisement to the reader' begins at sig. B1ʳ and ends at sig. B8ʳ; 'An Abridgement of the Chapters' extends from sig. B8ᵛ to sig. C2ᵛ; the first chapter of 'A True ... Church of Rome' begins at sig. C3ʳ.

'A True Account / of / *FALSE RECORDS;* / Discovering / The Forgeries / or / Counterfeit-Antiquities / of the / Church of Rome' begins at page 1 (sig. C3ʳ); at p. 9 (sig. C7ʳ) 'x see the / Premonition' is written at the outer margin in ink; p. 35 reads 'now', not deleted as directed by errata; p. 43, 'Lov of yᵉ World yᵗ' has been inserted in ink with 'Obstinate Perverseness' crossed through; p. 55 reads 'Privy Councils' with no change made from errata; p. 66 'and' has been inserted in ink following 'Magdenburge'; p. 83 reads 1635, with no change from errata; p. 104 reads 'fit' with no change from errata; p. 107 reads '1618' with no change from errata; p. 109, marginal gloss, 'Vid. Cap'., is missing 'II'; p. 137 reads '*Treatise of the Right of the Fathers*' with no change from errata; p. 157 (sig. N1ʳ) reads 'Transceant' with no change from errata; p. 172 (sig. N8ʳ) title reads 'Falsity' with no change from errata; page 201 (line 2) there is a caret with 'one' inserted in ink after 'that of these *Hermes*' to read 'that of these *Hermes* one at least was a Forgerie'.

Union Theological Seminary Library, New York

Book Description

On the title page of the Union Theological Seminar Library's 1673 copy, under '*By a Faithful Son of the Church*' was written at some point 'Dean Comber 1704'. After '*LONDON,* / Printed by *S.* and *B. Griffin*, for *Jonathan Edwin* at / the three Roses in *Ludgate-Street*', '1673' is replaced by '1704' in dark ink, again referring to Comber. The title appears at sig. A1ʳ with verses from the books of Timothy at sig. A1ᵛ; at sig. A2ʳ is the dedication to Orlando Bridgeman with sig. A2ᵛ blank; 'A Premonition' extends from sigs. A3ʳ to A7ᵛ; 'An Advertisement to the Reader' extends from B1ʳ to B8ʳ; 'An Abridgment of Chapters' extends from sigs. B8ᵛ to C2ᵛ; 'A True Account ... Church of Rome' begins at sig. C3ʳ. Written along the inner margin of the dedication to Bridgeman is 'Am. Art Auction Feb. 16, 1916' with no further indication of provenance. The Union copy was a reprint of the original so that no description of the original can be given.

From the Beginning to the Copyright Act of Queen Anne (Cambridge, 1986), p. 471.

British Library, London

The British Library holds two copies of *Roman Forgeries* as follows: 1019.c.19 and 861.D.10.

British Library (1019.c.19)

Book Description

The British Library's copy 1019.c.19 of *Roman Forgeries* has been rebound in blue cloth with a leather spine and corners on both front and back boards. ROMAN / FORGERIES is printed at the top of the spine and at the bottom in small print 'London / 1673'. The pastedown as well as the first leaf are clean, giving no indication of provenance. On the title page just under the title is written in ink '[Bish?] Dr Comber'. On the last free end paper is written in ink 'Collated and perfect. 4th Nov. 1727 OA'.

The signatures are also irregular. Full title is at A1^r with the verses from the books of Timothy at A1^v; A2^r contains the dedication to Bridgeman with A2^v blank; 'The Premonition' extends from A3^r to A7^v; 'An Advertisement … Reader' extends from B1^r to B8^r; 'An Abridgement of Chapers' extends from B8^v to C2^v; Chapter 1 begins at C3^r.

British Library (861.D.10)

Book Description

Both front and back boards of the British Library's copy 861.D.10 are bound in blue leather and decorated with double gold lines at the edge of the board and double gold lines at the center, forming a rectangle with a gold fillet at the end of each corner of the rectangle. Within the rectangle is a gold circle with an armorial crest, at the center of which is a rampant lion holding a flag. The back board is similarly decorated, within the circle is a griffin and the letters ID. The spine may perhaps be original with gold leaf speckled over brown leather. It appears to be sewn on five raised cords with gold leaf decoration between at least four blocks; the final block is missing.

The title page appears at A1^r with the verses from the books of Timothy at A1^v; the dedication to Bridgeman at A2^r with A2^v blank; 'The Premonition' begins at A3^v and ends at A7^v. 'An Advertisement' begins with B1^r and ends with B8^r. 'An Abridgement' begins at sig. C1^v and ends with C2^v; A True Account … Church of Rome' begins at C3^r.

Introduction

Lambeth Palace Library, London

Lambeth Palace Library holds two copies of *Roman Forgeries* as follows: Main Collection SR3, H1763.T7 and Sion Aarc Octavo, A69.3 / T67.

Lambeth Palace Main Collection SR3, H1763.T7

Book description

The book is bound in tan calf[29] and decorated with single lines at the four edges of both front and back boards and double lines at the middle, forming a rectangle with a decorative flower at each corner of the rectangle. The book measures approximately 117 mm long x 115 mm wide x 30 mm deep. On the title page under '*By a faithful son of the Church of ENGLAND*' is written in graphite 'Thomas Traherne'. There are four raised cords with the class number pasted over the last cord. On the pastedown of the last page is a previous classmark 'Ref. 7–4–60 f EM'. The page after the dedication to Bridgeman is blank. On page 259 'Our Lord Flavius Constantine' is underscored in ink as well as 'our Lord' after 'A NOTE'. On page 291 is a printed manicule at 'Face of the World. But such Councils'; on p. 152 there is also a printed manicule pointing to 'Devil is … deceive many'.

The title page appears at A1^r with the verses from the books of Timothy at A1^v; A2^r Dedication to Bridgeman; A2^v Blank; 'The Premonition' begins at A3^v and ends at A7^v. 'An Advertisement' begins with B1 and ends with B8^r. 'An Abridgement' begins at sig. C1^v and ends with C2^v; A True Account … Church of Rome' begins at C3^r.

Lambeth Palace Sion Aarc Octavo, A69.3 / T67

Book description

The book is bound in dark brown calf with barely discernible flowers attached at the top of each corner on both boards. The spine has been replaced as well as the top corner on both front and back boards. On the spine there are four raised cords, with ROMAN / FORGERIES stamped in gilt on the second block, 'TRAHERNE' is stamped on the third block and on the fourth, '1673'. There is some water damage at various places throughout the book.

---

[29] The book is bound in tan calf, not goatskin as listed in the library catalogue. I have this information from the Lambeth Palace Library senior librarian, Hugh Cahill.

The title page appears at A1^r with the verses from the books of Timothy at A1^v; the dedication to Bridgemen appears at A2^r with A2^v blank; 'The Premonition' begins at A3^v and ends at A7^v. 'An Advertisement to the Reader' begins with B1^v and ends with B8^r. 'An Abridgement' begins at sig. B8^v and ends with C2^v; '*A True Account of False Records ... Church of Rome*' begins at C3^r.

General editorial principles

In this edition I have attempted to represent faithfully Traherne's manuscripts and printed works in order to produce a clear, readable text. Because this volume contains two seventeenth-century printed works, I have followed the text insofar as possible, for instance Traherne's spelling, punctuation and capitalization have been maintained; the ampersand, S. for St. or 'saint', bec. for 'because', ch. for 'church' when used in 'Church of England' and H. for 'holy','y^t' and 'y^e', misplaced superscripts and subscripts, missing words, have been maintained as in the seventeenth-century printed text.

Also I have maintained the italics as they appear in the seventeenth-century printed text; many sections printed in italics are direct quotations from Traherne's sources. Scripture references or words, phrases, sentences and paragraphs may be italicized for emphasis.

Illegible words and phrases are indicated by an ellipsis within square brackets [...]. The rendering of uncertain words is indicated by square brackets plus a question mark [hid?]. Editorial additions such as commas, full stops, etc. for clarity, have been recorded with all textual emendations. Traherne's spelling is idiosyncratic and inconsistent, sometimes in harmony with general seventeenth-century conventions, for instance he often reverses the 'i' and 'e'; these have been noted with all textual emendations.

Because of the complexity of the text of *Roman Forgeries*, I have identifed many names mentioned in the text in Textual Emendations and Notes. These will be more fully discussed in Volume 9, Commentary. Any eccentric conventions of the texts within this edition are due to the peculiarities of the printed texts and have not always been noted.

Christian Ethicks

Christian
ETHICKS:
OR,

Divine Morality.

Opening the WAY to

BLESSEDNESS,

By the RULES of

VERTUE

AND

REASON.

By *THO. TRAHERNE*, B. D.
Author of the Roman Forgeries.

LONDON,
Printed for *Jonathan Edwin*, at the Three
Roses in *Ludgate-street*, 1675

TO THE
READER.

THE *design of this Treatise is, not to stroak and tickle the Fancy, but to elevate the Soul, and refine its Apprehensions, to inform the Judgment, and polish it for Conversation, to purifie and enflame the Heart, to enrich the Mind, and guide Men (that stand in need of help) in the way of Vertue; to excite their Desire, to encourage them to Travel, to comfort them in the Journey, and so at last to lead them to true Felicity, both here and hereafter.*

I need not treat of Vertues in the ordinary way, as they are Duties enjoyned by the Law of GOD; that *the Author of* The whole Duty of Man *hath excellently done: nor as they are* Prudential Expedients *and* Means *for a mans Peace and Honour on Earth*; that *is in some measure done by the French* Charron *of Wisdom. My purpose is to satisfie the Curious and Unbelieving Soul, concerning the reality, force, and efficacy of* Vertue; *and having some advantages from the knowledge I gained in the nature of* Felicity *(by many years earnest and diligent study) my business is to make as* visible, *as it is possible for me, the lustre of its* Beauty, Dignity, *and* Glory: *By shewing what a necessary Means* Vertue *is, how sweet, how full of Reason, how desirable in it self, how just and amiable, how delightful, and how powerfully conducive also to Glory: how naturally Vertue carries us to the* Temple *of* Bliss, *and how immeasurably transcendent it is in all kinds of* Excellency.

And (if I may speak freely) my Office is, to carry and enhance Vertue *to its utmost height, to open the Beauty of all the Prospect, and to make the Glory of* GOD *appear, in the Blessedness of Man, by setting forth its infinite Excellency: Taking out of the* Treasuries *of* Humanity *those Arguments that will discover the great perfection of the End of Man, which he may atchieve by the capacity of his* Nature: *As also by opening the Nature of* Vertue *it self, thereby to display the marvellous Beauty of Religion, and light the Soul to the sight of its Perfection.*

I do not speak much of Vice, *which is far the more easie Theme, because I am intirely taken up with the abundance of Worth and Beauty in* Vertue, *and have so much to say of the positive and intrinsick Goodness of its Nature. But besides, since a strait Line is the measure both of it self, and of a crooked one, I conclude, That the very Glory of* Vertue *well understood, will make all* Vice *appear like* dirt *before a* Jewel, *when they are compared together. Nay,* Vice *as soon as it is named in the presence of these Vertues, will look like* Poyson *and a* Contagion, *or if you will, as black as* Malice *and* Ingratitude: *so that there will need no other* Exposition *of its* Nature, to dehort Men from the love of it, than the Illustration of its Contrary.

Vertues *are listed in the rank of* Invisible things; *of which kind, some are so blind as to deny there are any existent in* Nature: *But yet it may, and will be made easily apparent, that all the* Peace and Beauty *in the* World *proceedeth from* them, *all* Honour *and* Security *is founded in* them, *all* Glory *and* Esteem *is acquired by them. For the* Prosperity *of all* Kingdoms *is* laid *in the* Goodness *of* GOD *and of* Men. *Were there nothing in the* World *but the* Works *of* Amity, *which proceed from the highest* Vertue, *they alone would testifie of its* Excellency. *For there can be no* Safety *where there is any* Treachery: *But were all* Truth *and* Courtesie *exercis'd with* Fidelity *and* Love, *there could be no* Injustice *or* Complaint *in the World;* no Strife, *nor* Violence: *but all* Bounty, Joy *and* Complacency. *Were there no* Blindness, *every* Soul *would be full of* Light, *and the face of* Felicity *be seen, and the* Earth *be turned into* Heaven.

The things we treat of are great and mighty; they touch the Essence *of every* Soul, *and are of infinite* Concernment, *because the* Felicity *is eternal that is acquired by them: I do not mean* Immortal *only but worthy to be* Eternal: *and it is impossible to be happy without them. We treat of* Mans *great and* soveraign End, *of the* Nature *of* Blessedness, *of the* Means *to attain it:* Of Knowledge *and* Love, *of* Wisdom *and* Goodness, *of* Righteousness *and* Holiness, *of* Justice *and* Mercy, *of* Prudence *and* Courage, *of* Temperance *and* Patience, *of* Meekness *and* Humility, *of* Contentment, *of* Magnanimity *and* Modesty, *of* Liberality *and* Magnificence, *of the* waies *by which* Love *is* begotten *in the* Soul, *of* Gratitude, *of* Faith, Hope, *and* Charity, *of* Repentance, Devotion, Fidelity, *and* Godliness. *In all which we shew what* sublime *and* mysterious Creatures *they are, which depend upon the* Operations *of* Mans Soul; *their great* extent, *their* use *and* value, *their* Original *and their* End, *their* Objects *and their* Times: *What* Vertues *belong to the* Estate *of* Innocency, *what to the* Estate *of* Misery *and* Grace, *and what to the* Estate *of* Glory. *Which are the* food *of the* Soul, *and the* works *of* Nature; *which were occasioned by* Sin, *as* Medicines *and* Expedients *only: which are* Essential *to* Felicity, *and which* Accidental; *which* Temporal, *and which* Eternal: *with the true* Reason *of their* Imposition; *why they all are* commanded, *and how wise and gracious* GOD *is in* enjoyning *them. By which means all* Atheism *is put to flight, and all*

Infidelity: *The Soul is reconciled to the* Lawgiver *of the World, and taught to delight in his* Commandments: *All* Enmity *and* Discontentment *must vanish as Clouds and Darkness before the Sun, when the* Beauty *of* Vertue *appeareth in its brightness and glory. It is impossible that the* splendour *of its* Nature *should be seen, but all* Religion *and* Felicity *will be manifest.*

Perhaps you will meet some New Notions: *but yet when they are examined, he hopes it will appear to the Reader, that it was the actual knowledge of true* Felicity *that taught him to speak of* Vertue; *and moreover, that there is not the least* title Signature A1ʳ contains the title page; 'To the Reader' extends from A2ʳ to a3ʳ; 'The Contents' extends from a4ʳ to a8ʳ; the apology 'To the Reader' appears at a8ᵛ; the text begins at B1ʳ. *pertaining to the* Catholick Faith *contradicted or altered in his Papers. For he firmly retains all that was established in the Ancient Councels, nay and sees Cause to do so, even* in the highest and most transcendent Mysteries: *only he enriches all, by farther opening the* grandeur *and glory of Religion, with the interiour depths and Beauties of* Faith. *Yet indeed it is not he, but* GOD *that hath enriched the Nature of it: he only brings the Wealth of* Vertue *to light, which the infinite Wisdom, and Goodness, and Power of* GOD *have seated there. Which though Learned Men know perhaps far better than he, yet he humbly craves pardon for casting in his* Mite *to the vulgar* Exchequer. *He hath nothing more to say, but that the Glory of* GOD, *and the sublime Perfection of* Humane Nature *are united in Vertue. By Vertue the Creation is made* useful, *and the Universe delightful. All the Works of GOD are crowned with their End, by the Glory of Vertue. For whatsoever is good and profitable for Men is made Sacred; because it is delightful and well-pleasing to GOD: Who being LOVE by Nature, delighteth in his Creatures welfare.*

There are two sorts of concurrent Actions necessary to Bliss: Actions in GOD, and Actions in Men; nay and Actions too in all the Creatures. The Sun *must warm, but it must not burn; the* Earth *must bring forth, but not swallow up; the* Air *must cool without starving, and the* Sea *moisten without drowning:* Meats *must feed but not poyson:* Rain *must fall, but not oppress: Thus in the inferiour Creatures you see Actions are of several kinds. But these may be reduced to the Actions of GOD, from whom they spring; for he prepares all these Creatures for us. And it is necessary to the felicity of his Sons, that he should make all things healing and amiable, not odious and destructive: that he should Love, and not Hate: And the Actions of Men must concur aright with these of GOD, and his Creatures. They must not* despise Blessings *because they are given, but* esteem *them; not* trample them under feet, *because they have the benefit of them, but* magnifie *and extol them: They too must* Love, *and not* Hate: *They must not* kill *and* murther, *but* serve *and pleasure one another: they must not scorn great and inestimable Gifts, because they are* common, *for so the Angels would lose all the happiness of Heaven. If GOD should do the most great and* glorious *things that infinite* Wisdom *could devise; if Men will resolve to be* blind, *and* perverse, *and* sensless, *all will be in* vain: *the most High and Sacred things will* increase *their Misery. This may give you some little* glimpse *of the excellency of* Vertue.

You may easily discern that my Design is to reconcile Men to GOD, and make them fit to delight in him: and that my last End is to celebrate his

Praises, in communion with the Angels. Wherein I beg the Concurrence of the Reader, for we can never praise him enough; nor be fit enough to praise him: No other man (at least) can make us so, without our own willingness, and endeavour to do it.

Above all, pray to be sensible of the Excellency of the Creation. for upon the due sense of its Excellency the life of Felicity *wholly dependeth. Pray to be sensible of the Excellency of* Divine Laws, *and of all the Goodness which your Soul comprehendeth. Covet a* lively *sense of all you know, of the Excellency of GOD, and of Eternal Love; of your own Excellency, and of the worth and value of all Objects whatsoever. For to* feel *is as necessary, as to* see *their* Glory.

The Contents.

CHAP. I.
OF the End, for the sake of which, Vertue is desired.

Chap. II.
Of the Nature of Felicity; excellency and perfection.

Chap. III.
Of Vertue in general. The distribution of it into its several kinds. Its definition.

Chap. IV.
Of the Powers and Affections of the Soul: What Vertues pertain to the estate of Innocency; what to the estate of Grace; what to the estate of Glory.

Chap. V.
Of the necessity, excellency and use, of Knowledge: Its depths and extents; its Objects, and its End.

Chap. VI.
Of Love and Hatred. The necessity and sweetness of Love. Its general use and efficacy. The several kinds of Love. Of the power, inclination and act of Love; its extent and capacity.

Chap. VII.
What benefit GOD himself does receive by his eternal Love: That when our Love is made compleat and perfect, it will be like his, and the benefit of it will be eternal.

Chap. VIII.
Of the excellency of Truth, as it is the object and cause of Vertue. The matter and form of Vertuous Actions. That their form is infinitely more excellent than their matter, and the Heathen *Morality infinitely defective and short of the Christian.*

Chap. IX.
Wisdom is seated in the Will; it attaineth the best of all possible Ends by the best of all possible Means.

Chap. X.
Of Righteousness, how Wisdom, Justice, and right Reason are shut up in its Nature. What God doth, and what we acquire, by the exercise of this Vertue.

Chap. XI.
Of Goodness natural, moral, and divine; its Nature described. The benefitsand Works of Goodness.

Chap. XII.
Of Holiness: Its nature, violence and pleasure. Its beauty consisteth in the infinite love of Righteousness and Perfection.

Chap. XIII.
Of Justice in general, and particular. The great good it doth in Empires and Kingdoms; a token of the more retired good it doth in the Soul. Its several kinds. That Gods punitive Justice springs from his Goodness.

Chap. XIV.
Of Mercy. The indelible stain and guilt of Sin. Of the Kingdom which God recovered by Mercy. The transcendent nature of that duty; with its effects and benefits.

Chap. XV.
Of Faith. The faculty of Believing implanted in the Soul. Of what Nature its objects are. The necessity of Faith: Its end; its use and excellency. It is the Mother and fountain of all the Vertues.

Chap. XVI.
Of Hope. Its foundation: its distinction from Faith; its extents and dimensions; its life and vigour; its several kinds; its sweetness and excellency.

Chap. XVII.
Of Repentance. Its original; its nature; it is a purgative Vertue; its necessity; its excellencies. The measure of that sorrow which is due to Sin is intollerable to Sence; confessed by Reason, and dispensed with by Mercy.

Chap. XVIII.
Of Charity towards God. It sanctifieth Repentance, makes it a Vertue, and turns it to a part of our true Felicity. Our Love to all other objects is

to begin and end in God. Our Love of God hath an excellency in it, that makes it worthy to be desired by his eternal Majesty. He is the only supream and perfect Friend; by Loving we enjoy him.

Chap. XIX.

Charity to our Neighbour most natural and easie in the estate of Innocency: Adams *Love to* Eve, *and his Children, a great exemplar of our Love to all the World. The sweetness of Loving. The benefits of being Beloved. To love all the World, and to be beloved by all the World, is perfect security and felicity. Were the Law fulfilled, all the World would be turned into Heaven.*

Chap. XX.

Of Prudence. Its foundation is Charity, its end tranquility and prosperity on Earth; its office to reconcile Duty and Convenience, and to make Vertue subservient to Temporal welfare. Of Prudence in Religion; Friendship, and Empire. The end of Prudence is perfect Charity.

Chap. XXI.

Encouragements to Courage. Its Nature, cause, and end. Its greatness and renown. Its ornaments and Companions. Its objects, circumstances, effects, and disadvantages: how Difficulties increase its vertue. Its Victories and Triumphs. How subservient it is to Blessedness and Glory.

Chap. XXII.

Of Temperance in matters of Art, as Musick, Dancing, Painting, Cookery, Physick, &c. In the works of Nature; Eating, drinking, sports and recreations: In occasions of passion, in our lives and Conversations. Its exercise in Self-denial, measure, mixture and proportion. Its effects and atchievments.

Chap. XXIII.

Of Temperance in God. How the Moderation of Almighty Power, guided in his Works by Wisdom, perfecteth the Creation. How it hath raised its own Glory and our Felicity beyond all that simple Power could effect by its Infiniteness.

Chap. XXIV.

Of Patience. Its original. How God was the first patient Person in the World. The nature, and the glory, and the blessed effects of his eternal Patience. The Reason and design of all Calamities. Of Patience in Martyrdom. The extraordinary reward of ordinary Patience in its meanest obscurity.

Chap. XXV.

The cause of Meekness is Love. It respects the future beauty and perfection of its object. It is the most supernatural of all the Vertues. The reasons and grounds of this Vertue in the estate of Grace and Misery. Its manifold effects and excellencies. Of the Meekness of Moses and Joseph.

Chap. XXVI.

Humility is the basis of all Vertue and Felicity, in all estates, and for ever to be exercised. As Pride does alienate the Soul from God, Humility unites it to him in adoration and amity. It maketh infinite Blessedness infinitely greater, is agreeable to the truth of our condition, and leads us through a dark and mysterious way to Glory.

Chap. XXVII.

That Contentment is a Vertue. Its causes, and its ends: Its Impediments, Effects, and Advantages. The way to attain and secure Contentment.

Chap. XXVIII.

Of Magnanimity, or greatness of Soul. Its nature. Its foundation in the vast vast Capacity of the Understanding. Its desire. Its objects are infinite and eternal. Its enquiries are most profound and earnest. It disdaineth all feeble Honours, Pleasures and Treasures. A Magnanimous Man is the only Great and undaunted Creature.

Chap. XXIX.

Of Modesty. Its nature. Its original. Its effects and consequences.

Chap. XXX.

The excellent nature of Liberality. Rules to be observed in the practice of it. Regard to our Servants, Relations, Friends and Neighbours must be had in our Liberality, as well as to the Poor and Needy. How our external acts of Charity ought to be improved for the benefit of mens Souls. Liberality maketh Religion real and substantial.

Chap. XXXI.

Of Magnificence in God. Its resemblance in Man. The chief Magnificence of the Soul is Spiritual. It is perfectly expressed in the outward life, when the whole is made perfect, and presented to God. God gives all his Life to us: and we should give ours all to him. How fair and glorious it may be.

Chap. XXXII.

Of Gratitude. It feeds upon Benefits, and is in height and fervour answerable to their Greatness. The Question stated, Whether we are able

Christian Ethicks

to love GOD more than ourselves. It is impossible to be grateful to GOD without it. A hint of the glorious Consequences of do doing.

Chap. XXXIII.

The Beauty of Gratitude. Its principal Caus. Amity and Communion are F the great effect of its Nature. The true Character of a grateful Person. Gods incommunicable Attributes enjoyed by Gratitude. All Angels and Men are a grateful Persons Treasures, as they assist him in Praises. He sacrifices all Worlds to the Deity, and supreamly delighteth to see him sitting in the Throne of Glory.

An APPENDIX.

Of Enmity and Triumph: Of Schism and Heresie, Fidelity, Devotion, Godliness. Wherein is declared, how Gratitude and Felicity inspire and perfect all the Vertues.

To the Reader.

The Author's much lamented Death hapning immediately after this Copy came to the Press, may reasonably move the Readers charity, to pardon those few Errata's which have escaped in the Printing by so sad an occasion.

CHRISTIAN ETHICKS

OR
DIVINE MORALITIE.

Opening

The Way to Blessedness

By

The rules of Virtue and Reason.

CHAP. I.

Of the End, for the sake of which, Virtue is desired.

'TIS the Prerogative of Humane Nature to understand it self, and guide its Operations to a Known End: which he doth wholly forfeit, that lives at random, without considering what is worthy of his Endeavors, or fit for his Desires.

THE End is that which crowns the Work; that which inspires the Soul with Desire, and Desire with a quick and vigorous Industry. It is last attained, but first intended in every Operation. All Means which can be used in the Acquisition of it, derive their value from its Excellency, and we are encouraged to use them only on the Account of that End, which is attained by them.

IT is the Office of *Morality* to teach Men the *Nature of Virtue*, and to encourage them in the Practice of it, by explaining its use and Efficacy.

THE Excellence of Virtue, is the Necessity and Efficacy thereof in the Way to Felicity. It consisteth in this, Virtue is the only Means by which Happiness can be obtained.

SINCE the Consideration of the End is that alone, which does animate a Man, to the use of the Means, they that treat of Virtue do worthily propose the End in the beginning, and first shew the Excellency of Bliss before they open Nature of Virtue. For it is a vain thing to discover the Means, unless the End be desired by those to whom the Nature and use of them, in their tendency to that End, is taught and commended; for if the End be despised, all endeavors are but fruitless, which instruct us in the Means; and the Knowledge of them vain, if they never be used or improved.

THAT Reason, whereby Man is able to Contemplate his End, is a singular Advantage, wherein he is priviledged above a Beast. It enables him not only to examine the Nature and perfection of his End, but the Equity and fitness of the Means in Order thereunto; and the singular Excellency of his first Cause, as its Glory and Goodness appeareth in the Design and Contrivance: Especially in making mans Happiness so compleat and perfect.

THE Heathens, who invented the name of *Ethicks*, were very short in the Knowledge of Mans End: But they are worse then Heathens, that never consider it.

THE more Excellent the End is, the more prone by nature we are to pursue it, and all the Means conducive thereunto are the more Desirable.

REASON, which is the formal Essence of the Soul of Man, guides Him to desire those Things, which are absolutely supreme. For it is an Eternal Property in Reason to prefer the Better, above the Worse: He that prefers the worse above the Better acts against Nature, and Swervs from the Rule of Right Reason.

WHATEVER Varieties of Opinion there are concerning Happiness, all conclude and agree in this, that Mans last End is his perfect Happiness: And the more Excellent his Happiness is, the more ought his Soul to be enflamed with the Desire of it, and inspired with the greater Industry.

THE more perfect his Bliss is, the greater is the Crime of despising it. To pursue an infinite and Eternal Happiness is Divine and *Angelical*; to pursue a Terrene and Sensual Felicity, is *Brutish*; but to place Felicity in Anger and Envy is *Diabolical:* the pleasures of Malice being Bitter and Destructive.

TO live by Accident, and never to pursue any Felicity at all, is neither Angelical, nor Brutish, nor Diabolical: but *Worse* then any Thing in some respect in the World: It is to act against our *own* Principles, and to wage war with our very *Selves*. They that place their Ease in such a Carelessness, are of all others, the greatest

Enemies and Disturbers of themselves.

IT is Madness and folly to pursue the first object that presents it self, under the Notion of felicity: And it is base to content ones self in the Enjoyment of a mean estate, upon a suspicion there is no true happiness, because the nature thereof is so much doubted in the World. The Disputations concerning its nature argue its existance. And we must cease to be Men, before we can extinguish the desire of being Happy. He only is truely Generous, that aspires to the most perfect Blessedness of which God and Nature have made him Capable.

BY how much Greater the Uncertainty is, by so much the more Heedful ought we to be, lest we should be seduced and deceived; in the Choice of Happiness: For the Danger is the Greater. And by how much the more Eager Men are in their Disputations, concerning it, by so much the more weighty is the Nature of the Theme to be presumed.

HASTINESS in catching at an unexamined Felicity, is the great Occasion of all the Error about it, among the Vulgar: who are led, like Beasts, by their *Sense* and Appetite, without discerning or improving any other faculty. The lip of the Cup is annointed with Hony, which, as soon as they taste, they drink it up, tho the liquor be nothing but Gall and Poyson. Being deluded with a shew, instead of *Pleasure*, they rush hand over head on their own *Destruction*.

IT is as natural to Man to desire happiness, as to live and breath: Sence and Instinct carry him to Happyness, as well as Reason: onely *Reason* should rectifie and direct his *Instinct*, inform his *Sence*, and compleat his *Essence*, by inducing those perfections of which it is capable.

THINGS Good in themselves, when they stand in Competition with those that are better, have the notion of Evil: Better Things are Evil, if compared with the Best; especially where the Choice of the one hinders the Acquisition of the other. For where Good, Better, and Best, are subservient to each other, the one is the better for the others sake; but where they interfere, and oppose each other, the Good are bad in comparison of the Better, and the Better worse than the Best of all. This is the Cause why Reason cannot acquiesce in any Felicity less than the Supreme: which must needs be infinite, because Almighty Power, which made Reason active, is illimited in its Operations; and never rests, but in the production of a Glorious Act, that is infinite in Perfection.

IF Felicity be infinite, the Loss is as great, that attends our Miscarriage, and the misery intolerable, that follows our Loss. For (our eyes being open) a Loss that is incomprehensible must needs produce a Greif unmeasurable, an Anguish as infinite as our Damage.

ALL inferiour felicities are but Miseries compared with the Highest. A farthing is *good* and pleaseth a Beggar in time of distress: but a piece of Gold is *Better*. An Estate of a thousand pounds a year is better than a Piece of Gold; but our Ambition carries us to Principalities and Empires. An Empire is more desirable than a Province; and the Wider, the Richer, the Better it is, the more Desirable. But the Empire of all the Earth is a Bubble compared to the Heavens: And the Heavens themselves less than nothing to an infinite Dominion.

PERFECT Felicity is not Dominion, nor Pleasure, nor Riches alone, nor Learning, nor Virtue, nor Honour; but all in Perfection. It requires that every Soul should be capable of infinite Dominion, Pleasure, Learning, and Honor for the full and perfect attainment of it.

IF all these be infinite and Eternal in that Felicity which is prepared for Man, those Actions are of inestimable Value, by Virtue of which his Felicity is gained; and it becomes his Wisdom and Courage to suffer many Things for so noble an End: Especially if in this Life it may in any measure be thereby acquired and enjoyed.

THE Great Reason why GOD has concealed Felicity from the Knowledge of man, is the enhancement of its nature and value: but that which most conceals it, is the Corruption of Nature. For as we have corrupted, so have we blinded our selves. Yet are we led by Instinct eagerly to thirst after things unknown, remote and forbidden. The truth is, our Palates are vitiated, and our Digestion so Corrupted, that till our Nature be purified by a little Industry, to make felicity Known, is but to Expose it to Contempt and Censure. It is too Great and Pure for perverted Nature.

THE Concealment of an object whets our Appetite, and puts an Edge upon our endeavours, and this carries some thing of Mystery in it; For whereas the Maxime is *Ignoti nulla Cupido, All Love comes in at the Eye*, we affect an Object to which we are Blind, and the more Blind we are, the more restless. We are touched with an unknown Beauty which we never saw, and in the midst of our Ignorance are actuated with a Tendency, which does not abate the value of our Virtues, but puts Life and Energy into our Actions.

THO Felicity cannot perfectly be understood, because it is incomprehensible to Men on Earth, yet so much of it may be discerned, as will serve to meet our Instinct, and feed our Capacity, animate our Endeavour, encourage our Expectation (to hope for more then we enjoy) enable us to subdue our Lusts, support us in temptations, and assist us in overcoming all obstacles whatsoever.

INFINITE Honors and Pleasures, were there no more in Felicity, are enough to allure us: but the fruition of all in the Best of Manners, in Communion with God, being full of Life, and Beauty, and Perfection in himself, and having the certain Assurance that all shall be included in his Bliss, that can be thought on; it is a Thing so Divine, that the very Hope of it fills us with Comfort here, and the Attainment with perfect Satisfaction hereafter.

HE that can enjoy all Things in the Image of GOD, needs not covet their fruition in a Baser Manner: Man was made in GODS Image, that he might live in his Similitude.

I am not so Stoical, as to make all Felicity consist in a meer Apathy, or freedom from Passion, nor yet so Dissolute, as to give the Passions all their Liberty. Neither do I perswade you to renounce the Advantages of Wealth and Honor, any more then those of Beauty and Wit: for as a Man may be Happy without all these, so may he make a Happy use of them when he has them. He may be happy with Difficulty without them, but Easily with them. If not in Heaven, yet certainly on Earth, the Goods of fortune concur to the Compleating of *Temporal Felicity*, and therefore where they are freely given, are not to be despised.

THAT which I desire to teach a man is, How to make a Good use of all the Advantages his Birth and Breeding; How in the Increase of Riches and Honors, to be Happy in their Enjoyment: How to secure himself in the temptations of Affluence, and to make a man glorious in himself, and delightful to others in Abundance: Or else if Affliction should arise, and the State of Affairs change, how to triumph over *adverse* Fortune, and to be Happy notwithstanding his Calamities. How to govern himself in all Estates so as to turn them to his own advantage.

FOR tho felicitie be not absolutely perfect in this World, nor so compleat in Poverty, as in a great and plentiful Estate; you are not to believe that wealth is absolutely necessary; because sometimes it is requisite to forfeit all for the sake of Felicity. Nothing is absolutely necessary to Bliss, but Grace and vertue, tho to *perfect* Bliss, Ease and Honour be absolutely necessary.

THERE are many degrees of Blessedness beneath the most Supream, that are transcendently Sweet and delightful: And it sometimes happens, that what is most bitter to *Sence*, is pleasant to *Reason*.

RATHER then make Shipwrack of a good Conscience, we must do as Mariners in a storm, cast our riches over board for our *own* Preservation. It is better losing *them*, then *our selves*.

VERTUE is Desirable and Glorious, because it teacheth us through many Difficulties in this Tempestuous World to Sail Smoothly, and attain the Haven.

CHAP. II.

Of the Nature of Felicity, its Excellence and Perfection.

THE *Peripateticks*, so far forth as they contemplated the Nature and Estate of man *in this World*, were Wise, in defining the Goods of the Body, Soul and Fortune to concur to Mans perfect Happiness. For Difficulties and Conflicts are not Essential to the Nature of Bliss, nor consistent with the fruition of its fulness and Perfection.

THERE is the Way, and the journeyes end.

IN the Way to Felicity many things are to be *endured*, that are not to be *desired*. And therefore is it necessary, to make a Distinction between the way to Felicity, and the Rest which we attain in the end of our Journey.

THE Goods of the Soul, are absolutely necessary in the Way to Happiness; the Goods of the Body are very convenient, and those of Fortune Commodious enough. But the lattter of these are not with too much eagerness to be pursued.

THE Goods of the soul are wisdom, Knowledg, Courage, all the Virtues, all the Passions, Affections, Powers and faculties. And these you know are absolutely necessary.

THE Goods of the Body are Health, Agility, Beauty, Vivacity, Strength and Libertie: and these shall in Heaven it self, together with those of the Soul, be enjoyed. By which you may discern that the Goods of the Body are real Parts and Ingredients of Happiness.

THE Goods of Fortune are food and Rayment, Houses and Lands, Riches, Honours, Relations and Friends, with all those convenient Circumstances without the Body, that are subject to chance. By which vertue is assisted, and of which a noble use may be made, in Works of Justice, Hospitality, Courtesie and Charity, which may redound to our greater Felicity here and in heaven.

THE more Honor and pleasure we enjoy, the Greater and more Perfect is our present Happiness: Tho many times in the Way to Felicity, we are forced to quit all these, for the Preservation of our Innocence.

GALLANT Behaviour in slighting all Transitory things for the Preservation of our Virtue, is more conducive to our future Perfection, then the greatest ease imaginable in our present condition.

IT is incumbent upon us, as a special part of our Care, to take heed, that we be not ensnared by the easiness of Prosperity, and that we do not set up our Rest in the *Way* to Happiness, nor deceive our selves in thinking the Goods of Fortune Essential: nor discourage our selves, by thinking it impossible to be Happy without them. Our Thoughts and Affections must be always disentangled, that we may run, with Alacritie the Race set before us, and close with the Sublimest Perfection of Bliss, as our only portion and Desire.

FELICITY is rightly defined, to be *the Perfect fruition of a Perfect Soul, acting in perfect Life by Perfect Virtue.* For the Attainment of which Perfection, we must, in the Way to Felicity, endure all Afflictions that can befall us. For tho they are not Parts of Felicity themselves, yet we may acknowledge them great Advantages for the Exercise of Virtue, and reckon our Calamities among our *Joys,* when we bear and overcome them in a virtuous Manner, because they add to our *Honour,* and contribute much to our Perfection, both here, and hereafter.

FOR this purpose we are to remember, that our present Estate is not that of Reward, but Labour: It is an Estate of Trial, not of Fruition: A Condition wherein we are to Toyl, and Sweat, and travail hard, for the promised Wages; an Appointed Seed Time, for a future Harvest; a real Warfare, in order to a Glorious Victory: In which we must expect some Blows, and delight in the Hazzards and Encounters we meet with, because they will be crowned with a Glorious and joyful Triumph; and attended with ornaments and trophies far surpassing the bare Tranquillity of idle peace.

WHEN we can cheerfully look on an Army of Misfortunes, without Amazement we may then freely and Delightfully contemplate the Nature of the Highest Felicity.

ARISTOTLE never heard of our Ascension into Heaven, nor of sitting down in the Throne of GOD, yet by a lucky Hit (if I may so say) fell in point blanck upon the Nature of Blessedness. For a perfect fruition by perfect virtue, is all that can be thought of: It implies our *Objective,* and our *formal* Happiness.

OBJECTIVE Happiness is all the Goodness that is fit to be enjoyed either in GOD or in his Creatures: while *Formal Happiness* is an active Enjoyment of all Objects by Contemplation and Love, attended with full complacency in all their Perfections.

PERFECT Fruition implies the Perfection of all its Objects. Among which GOD himself is one, Angels and Saints are next, the World also with all the variety of Creatures in it, the Laws of GOD, and his wayes in all Ages, his Eternal Counsels and Divine Attributes are other Objects of our Content and Pleasure. Unless all these be perfect in their Nature, Variety, Number, Extent, Relation, Use and Value, our fruition cannot be simply perfect, because a Greater and more perfect fruition might, upon the production of better Objects, be contrived, and no fruition can be truly perfect, that is not conversant about the highest things. The more Beautiful the Object is, the more pleasant is the enjoyment. But where Delight may be increased, the Fruition is imperfect.

A *Perfect Soul* is a Transcendent Mystery. As GOD could not be Perfect, were it possible there could be any Better Essence then he; so neither would the Soul be perfect, could any more Perfect Soul be created.

IT is a Soul in which no Defect, or Blemish can be discerned; perfect in the variety and Number of its Powers, in the fitness and Measure of every power, in the use and value of every Endowment. A perfect Soul is that whereunto nothing can be added to please our Desire. As all its Objects are perfect, so is it self. It is able to see all that is to be seen, to love all that is Lovely, to hate all that is Hateful, to desire all that is Desirable, to honour all that is Honorable, to esteem all that can be valued, to delight in all that is Delightful, and to enjoy all that is Good and fit to be enjoyed. If its Power did fall short of any one Object, or of any one Perfection in any Object, or of any Degree in any Perfection, it would be imperfect, it would not be the Master piece of Eternal Power.

PERFECT life is the full exertion of perfect power. It implies two things, Perfection of Vigour, and perfection of intelligence, an activity of life, reaching through all Immensity, to all Objects whatsoever; and a freedome from all Dulness in apprehending: An exquisite Tenderness of perception in feeling the least Object, and a *Sphere of activity* that runs parallel with the Omnipresence of the Godhead. For if any Soul lives so imperfectly, as to see and know but some Objects, or to love them remisly, and less then they deserve, its Life is imperfect, because either it is remisse, or, if never so fervent, confined.

PERFECT Fruition, (as it implies the Perfection of all objects) more nearly imports the intrinsick Perfection of its own Operations. For if its Objects be never so many, and perfect in themselves, a Blemish lies upon the Enjoyment, if if does not reach unto all their Excellence. If the Enjoyment of one Object be lost, or one Degree of the enjoyment abated, it is imperfect.

PERFECT *Vertue* may best be understood by a consideration of its Particulars. Perfect *Knowledg* is a thorow compleat understanding of all that may be Known. Perfect *Righteousness* is a full and adequate Esteem of all the value that is in Things. It is a Kind of Spiritual Justice, whereby we do Right to our selves, and to all other Beings. If we render to any Object less than it deserves, we are not *Just* thereunto. Perfect *Wisdome* is that whereby we chuse a most perfect end, actualy pursue it by most perfect Means, acquire and enjoy it in most perfect manner: If we pitch upon an inferiour end, our Wisdom is imperfect; and so it is, if we pursue it by feeble and inferior Means, or neglect any one of those Advantages, whereby we may attain it. And the same may be said of all the Vertues.

NOW if all Objects be infinitely Glorious, and all Worlds fit to be enjoyed, if GOD has filled Heaven and earth, and all the Spaces above the Heavens with innumerable pleasures, if his infinite Wisdome, Goodness, and Power be fully Glorified in every Being, and the Soul be created to enjoy all these in most perfect Manner; we may well conclude with the Holy Apostle, that we are *the children of GOD, and if Children, then Heirs, Heirs of GOD, and joynt heirs with Christ, if so be that we suffer with him, that we may also he glorified together. That our light Affliction, that is but for a Moment, worketh out for us, a far more exceeding and eternal Weight of Glory: That beholding as in a Glass the Glory of the Lord, we shall at last be transformed into the same Image from Glory to Glory, even as by the Spirit of the Lord.* For all his Works, of which the Psalmist saith, *They are worthy to be had in remembrance, and are sought out of all them that have pleasure therein*, are like a Mirror, wherein his Glory appeareth, as the face of the Sun doth in a clear fountain. We may conclude further that Vertue, by force of which we attain so great a Kingdome, is infinitely better then Rubies, all the Things thou canst desire, are not to be compared to her: So that with unspeakable comfort we may take Courage to go on, not only in the study, but the Practice of all Kind of Vertues, concerning which we are to treat in the ensuing Pages. For as the Apostle *Peter* telleth us, *He hath given to us all things that pertain to Life and Godliness, through the Knowledge of him that hath called us to Glory and virtue: whereby are given unto us exceeding great and precious Promises; that by these you might be Partakers of the Divine Nature, having escaped the Corruption that is in the World through lust. And besides this*, saith he, *giving all diligence, adde to your Faith vertue: and to vertue, knowledge; and to knowledge, temperance; and to temperance, patience; and to patience, godliness; and to godliness, brotherly kindness; and to brotherly kindness, Charity. For so an Entrance shall be Ministred to you abundantly into the everlasting Kingdome of our Lord and Saviour Jesus Christ.* Which Kingdom being so Divine and Glorious as it is, we have need to bow our Knees, *to the GOD and father of our Lord Jesus Christ, of whom the whole Family in Heaven and Earth is named, that he would grant us according to the Riches of his Glory, to be strengthened with might, by his Spirit in the inward Man, that Christ may dwell in our Hearts by Faith, that we being rooted and grounded in Love, may be able to comprehend with all Saints, what is the Breadth, and Length, and Depth, and Height, and to know the love of Christ which passeth Knowledg, that we may be filled with all the fulness of GOD.*

TO be Partaker of the Divine nature, to be filled with all the Fulness of GOD, to enter into his Kingdom and Glory, to be transformed into his Image, and made an Heir of GOD, and a joynt Heir with Christ, to live in Union and Communion with GOD, and to be made a Temple of the Holy Ghost; these are Divine and transcendent things that accompany our Souls in the Perfection of their Bliss and Happiness: the Hope and Belief of all which is justified, and made apparent by the explanation of the very nature of the Soul, its Inclinations and Capacities, the reality, and greatness of those Vertues of which we are capable, and all those objects which the Univers affordeth to our Contemplation.

CHAP. III.

Of Vertue in General. The Distribution of it into its several Kinds, its Definition.

BEFORE we come to treat of particular *Vertues*, it is very fit that we speak something of *VERTUE* in General.

VERTUE is a comprehensive Word, by explaining which we shall make the way more easy to the right Understanding of all those particular Vertues, into which it is divided. Forasmuch as the Nature of Vertue enters into knowledge, Faith, Hope, Charity, Prudence, Courage, Meekness, Humility, Temperance, Justice, Liberality, &c. Every one of these hath its *essence* opened in part, by the explication of that which entreth its Nature, which is *VERTUE* in General.

THE Predicament of *Quality* contains within it either Natural *Dispositions* or *Habits*: Habits may be either *Vertuous* or *Vicious*; Virtuous Habits are either *Theological, Intellectual, Moral,* or *Divine*. And these are branched into so many Kinds of Vertue, as followeth.

THE *Theological Vertues* are generally divided into Three, *Faith, Hope,* and *Charity*: which are called *Theological*, because they have GOD for their Principal Object, and are, in a peculiar manner, taught by his Word among the Mysteries of Religion. To which we may add *Repentance*; forasmuch as this Virtue, tho it be occasioned by sin, is chiefly taught by the Word of GOD, and respects GOD as its Principal Object. For which reason we shall account the Theological Virtues to be four, Faith, Hope, Charity and Repentance, to which, if we make them more, we may add *Obedience*, Devotion, Godliness.

THE *Intellectual Vertues* are generally reckoned to be five, *Intelligence, Wisdome, Science, Prudence, Art*. Which, forasmuch as the Distinction between them is over-nice and curious (at least too obscure for vulgar Apprehensions) we shall reduce them perhaps to a fewer number.

INTELLIGENCE is the Knowledg of Principles; *Science* the Knowledg of Conclusions. *Wisdom*, that knowledg, which results from the Union of both *Prudence* and *Art*, has been more darkly explained. The Objects of Wisdom are alwayes *Stable*; *Prudence* is that knowledge, by which we guide our selves in Thorny and *uncertain* Affairs; *Art* is that Habit, by which we are assisted in composing Tracts and Systems, rather then in regulating our Lives, and more frequently appears in

Fiddling and Dancing, then in noble Deeds: were it not useful in Teachers for the Instruction of others, we should scarce reckon it in the number of Vertues.

ALL these are called *Intellectual* Vertues, because they are Seated in the Understanding, and chiefly exercised in Contemplation. The Vertues that are brought down into action, are called *Practical*, and at other times *Moral*,¹ Because they help us in perfecting our Manners, as they relate to our Conversation with Men.

THE *Moral Vertues* are either Principal, or less Principal. The *Principal* are four: *Prudence, Justice, Temperance,* and *Fortitude.* Which, because they are the Hinges upon which our whole Lives do turn, are called *Cardinal,² and are commonly known by the name of *The four Cardinal Vertues.* They are called *Principal*, not onely because they are the *chief* of all Moral Vertues, but because they enter into every *Vertue,* as the four *Elements* of which it is compounded.

THE *less Principal* Vertues are *Magnificence* and *Liberality, Modesty* and *Magnanimity, Gentleness of behaviour, Affability, Courtesie, Trut*h and *Urbanitie,* all these are called *less Principal,* not because they are indifferent, or may be accounted useless, for then they would not be Vertues: but because, tho their Practice be of extraordinary Importance in their places, they are more remote, and less Avail in the Way to Felicity, and are more confined in their Operations.

DIVINE Vertues (which we put instead of the Heathenish *Heroical,*) are such as have not only GOD for their Object and End, but their Pattern and Example. They are Vertues which are seen in his eternal Life, by Practicing which we also are changed into the same Image, and are made partakers of the Divine Nature. *Wisdome, Knowledge* and *Truth,* in the Sublimest Height we confess to be Three: but we shall Chiefly insist upon *Goodness,* and *Righteousness,* and *Holiness.* All which will appear in *Divine Love,* in more peculiar manner to be handled.

BESIDES all these, there are some Vertues, which may more properly be called *Christian*: because they are no where Else taught but in the Christian Religion, are founded on the Love of Christ, and the only Vertues distinguishing a *Christian* from the rest of the World, of which sort are *Love to Enemies, Meekness* and *Humility.*

ALL these Vertues are shut up under one common Head, because they meet in one common Nature; which bears the name of *Vertue.*

---

¹ Marginal gloss: Manners *in Latine are called* Mores *whence the English word* Moral *is derived*.

² Marginal gloss: *Cardo* is a hinge.

The Essence of which being well understood will conduce much to the clear Knowledge of every one in particular.

VERTUE (in General) *is that habit of Soul by force of which we attain our Happiness.* Or if you please, *it is a Right and well order'd Habit of mind, which Facilitates the Soul in all its operations, in order to its Blessedness.* These Terms are to be unfolded.

1. *VERTUE is a Habit*: All Habits are either Acquired, or Infused. By calling it a Habit, we distinguish it from *a Natural Disposition*, or *Power* of the Soul. For a *Natural disposition* is an inbred Inclination, which attended our Birth, and began with our beings: not chosen by our Wills, nor acquired by Industrie. These Dispostions, because they do not flow from our Choise and industry, cannot be accounted Virtues. Tis true indeed that vertuous Habits are sometimes *infused* in a Miraculous Manner, but then they are rather called *Graces* then *Vertues*: and are *ours*, only as they are Consented to by our Wills, not ours by choise and acquisition, but only by Improvement and exercise. Tho they agree with Virtues in their Matter and their end, yet they differ in their Original and form. For as all Humane Actions flow from the Will and the Understanding, so do all Vertues, when they are rightly understood; whereas we are Passive in the reception of these, and they flow immediately from Heaven.

AND it is far more conducive to our Felicity, that we should conquer Difficulties in the attainment of Vertue, study, chuse, desire, pursue, and labour after it, acquire it finally by our own Care and Industry, with Gods Blessing upon it; then that we should be Dead and Idle, while virtue is given us in our Sleep. For which cause GOD ordered our state and Condition so, that by our own Labour we should seek after it; that we might be as well pleasing in his Eys, and as Honorable and Admirable in the *Acquisition* of vertue, as in the *Exercise* and Practice of it. And for these reasons GOD does not so often infuse it, and is more desirous that we should by many repeated Actions of our own attain it.

GOD does sometimes upon the General Sloth of mankind inspire it, raising up some persons thereby to be like salt among corrupted men, least all should putrifie and perish: Yet is there little reason why he should delight in that way, without some such uncouth and Ungrateful necessity to compell him thereunto.

FOR any man to expect that GOD should break the General Order and Course of Nature, to make him Vertuous without his own Endeavours, is to Tempt GOD by a presumptuous Carelessness, and by a Slothful abuse of his Faculties to fulfil the parable of the unprofitable Servant.

THE Powers of the Soul, are not vertues themselves, but when they are clothed with vertuous Operations, they are transformed into Vertues. For Powers are in the Soul, just as Limbs and Members in the Body, which may indifferently be applied to Vertues and Vices, alike be busied and exercised in either.

AS the Members are capable of Various Motions, either comely, or Deformed, and are one thing when they are naked, another when attired, and capable of being modified with several Habits: so are the Powers and Faculties of the Soul. As they are in the Nature of Man without Exercise, they are void and Naked: But by many acts of Vice or Vertue, they put on a Habit, which seems chiefly to consist in an Inclination and Tendency to such Actions, a Facility of Working, an Acquaintance with them, a Love to them, and a Delight in them; For by long Custome it turns to a second Nature, and becomes at last as Necessary as Life it self; a confirmed Habit being taken in and incorporated with the Powers of the Soul by frequent exercise.

2. IN the second Definition we add, that *Vertue is a right and well ordered Habit*. A *Habit* is something added to that which wears it, and every Power of the Soul is naked, without the Quality wherewith long Custom cloaths it. Much of the *Formal Reason* of Vertue is shut up in those Words, *Right and well ordered*. For confused, irregular, and careless Habits will be always erroneous and Deformed, and must consequently end in Dishonor and Miseries. He must aim at the Mark, that hits it, for only those actions that are well guided, produce right and well order'd Habits, which right and well orderd Habits alone can carry us to our Sovereign end.

A Mind in Frame is a Soul clothed with Right Apprehensions: Thoughts and affections well ordered, Principles and Contrivances well proposed, Means and Ends rationaly consulted, all considered, and the Best chosen. [Long Custom inuring us to the Benefit and Excellence of these, disposes the Soul into *a right and well ordered Habit, or Frame of Spirit*, which regards that Glorious End for which we were created.]

BY *force of which we attain our Happiness*. Idleness and vertue are as Destructive to each other, as fire and water. In all vertue there is some force, and in all Force much action. A vertuous Habit ceaseth to be virtuous unless it actually incline us to virtuous Operations. As the Powers of the Soul when they are well exerted turn into Vertues, so is it by that *Exertion* that we attain our Happiness. *Vertue is that right and well ordered Habit by force of which we attain our Happiness.*

ITS force is never expressed but in exercise and operation. Yet even when we are asleep, it may tacitely incline us and make us ready, when we awake, to be Vertuous. Perhaps the *Habit* Sleeps and awakes with the Body: but if the Habit and its Energie be the same thing; it still sleepeth when its Energie ceaseth: if they be Divers, the Habit may continue for some time without the force of its Operations.

BUT not to Divert into Blind and Obscure Corners: Whether the Soul of a man asleep may be stiled Vertuous or no; Whether the Habits continue in him at that time without their Acts, is nothing to our purpose. It is Sufficient, that when he is awake, he, that hath a Vertuous Habit, is in all his Actions inclined and Carried to his own Felicity, unless he falls into an oblivion worse than Sleep, because without some such Damnable and vicious Lethargy, he is always mindful of his Last End, and tends towards it in a Direct Line.

ALL his Actions derive a Tincture from the first Principle, *that Habit of Soul by which he is carried toward his own Felicity.* All those Actions, that Spring from that Habit tend to bliss, and by force of that Habit are made Vertuous, and with facility performed.

ALL the Difficulty is in the Beginning. Vertues in the beginning are like green fruits, sour and imperfect, but their Maturity is accompanied with sweetness and delight. It is hard to acquire a vertuous Habit at first, but when it is once gotten; it makes all Virtue exceeding Easie, nor Easie alone, but Happy and Delightful. For a virtuous Habit as certainly acts according to its own nature, as the Sun shines, which is light by Constitution. It acts freely, yet when it does Act, it must needs act Vertuous, and can do nothing else. For it is no vertuous Habit; but some other Principle that exerteth vicious and bad Operations.

HAPPINESSE is with so much Necessity the end of Vertue, that we cannot take a Due Estimate of the Excellence of Vertue without considering the tendency which it has to Felicity. For as the Means are extravagant (and indeed no means) that have no Relation nor Proportion to their End: so would all the Vertues be inept and Worthless (no Vertues) if they did not in some Sort conduce to our Happiness. For Happiness is the adequate End, which by nature we seek: Whether it be Glory, or pleasure, or Honor that we design, or wealth, or Learning; all that is Delightful, and Grateful to our reason, is comprehended in our Happiness. If we desire to glorifie GOD, or to please the Angels, or be grateful to men, it is because we love our selves and delight in our own Happiness, and conceit all those actions whereby we so do, either a Means, or a part of it. So that in the Partition and Distribution of Vertues we must take another Course to display their Glory, by exhibiting them in such a prospect, as that is, wherein their Place and office will appear in their Tendency towards mans last End, his Blessedness and Glory.

CHAP. IV.

Of the Powers and Affections of the Soul; What virtues pertain to the Estate of Innocency; what to the Estate of Grace; what to the estate of Glory.

TWO things in Felicity are apparent to the Eye, Glory and Treasure; and the Faculties of the soul do in a several manner affect both. The *Understanding* was made to see the value of our Treasure; and the freedome of *Will*, to atcheive Glory to our actions; *Anger*, to stir us up against all Difficulty, and opposition, that might stand in our ways; *Appetite*, to pursue the Pleasure in either; *Fear*, to heighten our concernment, that we might more dread the danger of losing that Happiness, wherein no less then Glory and Treasure are infinitely united: *Reason* it self, to compare Felicities and weigh which is the most perfect. *Desire*, to covet it; *Hope*, to encourage us in the pursuit of it; *Aversion*, for the avoiding of all Temptations and Impediments; *Love*, to the goodness of it; *Joy*, for its fruition; *Hatred*, to keep us from the Misery which is contrary thereunto; *Boldness*, to attempt it; *Sorrow* and *Despair*, to punish and torment us, if we fail to attain it. For these two, being unpleasant affections, serve to engage us in the pursuit of Happiness, because we are loath to experience the Sence of such Troublesome passions.

AMBITION and *Covetousness* are Inclinations of the Soul, by the one of which we are carried to *Glory*, by the other to *Treasure*. And as all the rest, so may these be made either Vertues, or Vices: *Vertues* when they are Means conducive to the Highest end; *Vices* when they distract and entangle us with inferior Objects.

THE Inclinations and affections of the Soul may be Defective or excessive in their exercise towards Objects. In relation to the Highest Object there is no danger of excess. We can never too violently either *love* or *desire* our Supream Happiness; our *Hope* can never exceed its greatness, we can never too much *rejoyce* in the fruition of it; Nor can we exceed in *Anger* or *Hatred* against those Things, that would bereave us of it; or too much *fear* the Misery of that Life, which will be ever without it; or be affected with too much *Sorrow* and *Despair* at the Losse of it. But if we look upon inferior Things, which are meerly Accidental to the nature of Felicity, such as the Favour of men, Injuries, Crosses,

Temporal successes, the Beauty of the Body, the goods of Fortune, and such like; our affections and passions may be too excessive, because the good or evil of these is but finite; whereas the Good of Sovereign Bliss is altogether infinite, and so is the evil of Eternal Misery.

WHEN our own Actions are Regular, there is nothing in the World but may be made conducive to our highest Happiness: Nor is there any value in any Object, or Creature in the World, but as it is Subservient to our Bliss. No member of the Body, no sence or endowment of any Member, no Inclination or Faculty of the Soul, no passion or affection, no Vertue, no Grace, no Spiritual Gift, no Assistance, no Means of Grace, nothing (how great or Precious soever) can be of any Value, but in order to Felicity. In real truth, nothing without this can be Great or Estimable. Every Vertue therefore must have this, in common with all the Laws and Ordinances, and Works of GOD, they must all directly or Obliquely tend to our supreme Happiness; upon this dependeth all their Excellency.

SOME Vertues are necessary in the Estate of Innocency, some in the Estate of Grace, some in the Estate of Glory.

WITHOUT *seeing*, it is impossible to enjoy our Happiness, or find out the Way unto it; therefore is *Knowledge* necessary in all estates: without *Loving* it is impossible to Delight in its Goodness. The Office of *Righteousness* is to render to every Thing a Due esteem; And without this it is apparent that no Treasure can be to us, (tho in it self never so great) of any value. *Holiness* is the conscience that we make of discharging our duty, and the Zeal wherewith we avoid the Prophaness of its Contrary. *Goodness* is necessary, because we our selves cannot without that be Amiable, nor unless we be Delightful to others, enjoy our selves, or acquire Glory. The office of *Wisdom* is to chuse, and pursue the Highest end, by the Best of all means that can be chosen.

THESE are Transcendent Vertues, whereby even GOD himself doth enjoy his Felicity. They are incumbent on us by the Law of nature, and so essentially united to our Formal Happiness, that no Blessedness or Glory can be enjoyed without them. Therefore are we to look upon them as the Life and Soul of Religion, as *Eternal* Duties in all Estates for ever to be exercised. They are all Exercised in the very fruition it selfe, as will more apparently be seen, when we come to every one of these Vertues in particular. They were enjoyed in the Estate of Innocency, without any need of a positive Law, by the very nature of GOD and the Soul, and of things themselves, and must be exercised in the state of Grace and will abide for ever in the state of Glory.

THAT Vertues might be *ours*, in being wrought by *our selves*; and be Vertues *indeed*, in being wrought with *Difficulty*; that we might be so much the more Laudable and Glorious in our eternal Condition, GOD gave us Liberty, in the beginning, that we might chuse what we would, and placed us in such an Estate; that, having in us only the Seeds and Principles of all Vertue, we might exercise our natural Powers of our own Accord, for the Attainment of that actual Knowledge, Wisdom and Righteousness, wherein the Perfection of our soul consisteth, and by which the Perfection of our Bliss is to be enjoyed. That being Naked by Nature, tho Pure and clean, we might cloath our selves with our own *Habits*, attain the Glory of those Ornaments, in our own Acts, for which we were created; And work our *own* Righteousness, in such a Way as GOD had appointed.

FOR the Glory which we were to attain, is that Goodness which we are to shew in our own voluntary Care and obedience; and that Goodness is chiefly expressed in the kind and Genuine Exercise of our own Liberty, while we are tender of Displeasing him, to whom we are Obliged, and so Good as to gratifie his Desires, tho we had no restraint upon us.

TO make our selves amiable and beautiful, by the Exercise of our own Power, produces another kind of Beauty and Glory, than if we were compelled to be good by all his preventing Power. All Goodness is spoiled by Compulsion. Our own Actions, springing from an interiour Fountain, deep within the Soul, when voluntarily and freely exerted, are more acceptable; and the Will, whence they spring, is more excellent and perfect. This I would have you to note well, for the intrinsick Goodness and Glory of the Soul consists in the Perfection of an excellent Will, and without this it might be a piece of Dirt surrounded with Gold; but no imputed or annexed value could make it a Jewel.

THE Actions of GOD, or of the Angels, or of other men towards it, add no value to the Soul, if it will do nothing of it self. If it be Idle or unactive, the more excellent the Actions of GOD, and of all other Creatures are towards it, so much the more deformed and perverse is the Soul: nor will all the Glory of its Powers and Inclinations excuse it, but the more Great and Divine they are, the more abominable will it make it self by abusing them, in frustrating their Inclinations.

FOR the removing of all Constraint, and the infusing of greater Excellency and Beauty into these holy Actions; which he required from them, it pleased GOD to make *Men* obnoxious to Temptations, that having obstacles to overcome, and disadvantages to strugle with,

Mans Righteousness might be more full of Vertue, and himself made capable of Victory and Triumph. For this End he seated him in a low Estate; even in an Estate of Trial: wherein was the Occasion of Exercising Faith and Hope, because his Felicity was distant from him: Faith in believing the Promises of God, and Hope in waiting for the Accomplishment of his Bliss: He had Occasions for Fear also, in relation to Gods Power and Justice, who was able to remove his Happiness, upon the least offence, and to bring upon him that Misery that was denounced for his Transgression. In this Estate of Trial, Prudence, which is conversant in nice Affairs, was to watch, and consider, and direct his Behaviour, in the midst of those Dangers and Temptations, that might possibly be expected: His *Temperance* was to be exercised in the Government of his Appetite; so that all inferiour satisfactions, and sensual Pleasures might be limited and ordered, as it most consists with his highest Happiness: *Humility*, in the acknowledgement of his own Unworthyness, who was taken out of Nothing; and Gratitude in a kind of just Retribution to his Benefactor, for all the Glory to which he was advanced.

ALL these Vertues are in themselves Delightful, and Easie in their Exercise; they immediately respect Felicity, and are by nature necessary to Mans enjoyment of it, they are consonant to Reason, and agreeable to the Circumstances of his Happy Condition: His Fear and Humility, which were in Paradise the severest, were aided and comforted, with a Transcendent Hope and Assurance, that upon his Diligent Care, he might be Eternally Blessed; and with the Sweet Sence of his Happy Change, and a Glorious Admiration resulting from the Comparison between his present Estate, and the Estate to which by his Creator he was to be exalted.

I will not say but there were more Vertues than these to be Exercised in *Eden*: But by these you may discern of what nature they all are, and conjecture they must be such as obedience to God, and Charity to one another.

ALL *Harsh* and *Sour* Vertues came in by Sin: and we are to look upon them, not as Vertues intended by God and Nature, but occasioned afterwards, because their Use and Existence is accidental.

WHEN we fell into Sin, we let Death and Misery into the World, contracted shame and guilt upon our selves, defiled our Nature with Deformities and Diseases, and made many Things upon that Occasion, necessary to our Happiness, that before were not so: And whereas they have a Mixture of *Bitterness* and *Advantage* in them, we may thank our selves for the *Bitterness*, and GOD for the *Advantage*: For as we by Sin forfeited our *Happiness*, for a new Obedience, consisting in the practice of proper Vertues, was necessary to recover it. Vertues, whose Names and Natures were of another kind, and never heard of before: All which we must look upon, not as Food, but Physick, and considering them under the notion of Remedies, not admire that there should be something in them Distasteful to Sence, tho they are now, when their Occasions are known, infinitely agreeable to Reason.

THEY are but an *Æquivocal* Offspring of the Fall: Sin could never beget such beautiful Children, as Meekness, Repentance, Patience, Alms-Deeds, Self Denyal, Submission and Resignation to the Divine Will, Fortitude, Contentment in all Estates, &c.

WHILE there was no Sin, there was no need of *Penitence;* while there was no *Pain* or Misery, no *Patience*; Without wrongs and Injuries there is no use of *Meekness*; nor place for *Alms-Deeds*, where there is no *Poverty*: no Courage, where are no Enemies. In *Eden* there was no ignorance, nor any Supernatural Verities to be confirmed by Miracles; Apostles therefore and Prophets, Ministers and Doctors were superfluous there, and so were Tythes and Temples, Schools of Learning, Masters and Tutors, together with the unsavoury Duty incumbent on Parents to chastise their Children. For as all would have been instructed by the Light of Nature, so had all been Innocent, and Just, and Regular: Whereupon no Magistrate had been needful to put any to Shame, no Courts of Judicature, nor Lawyers in the World. No Buying and Selling, and thereupon no commutative Justice, because the Blessed Earth had naturally been fertile, and abounded with rich and Glorious Provisions: Nakedness had been the Splendor and Ornament of Men, as it will be in Heaven: the Glorious Universe had been their common House and Temple, their Bodies fited for all Seasons, no Alien or Stranger, no Want, Distress, or War, but all Peace, and Plenty, and Prosperity; all Pleasure, and all Fellow Citizens throughout the World. Masters and Servants had been unknown, had we continued in that Estate, all had enjoyed the Liberty of Kings, and there had been no Dominion, but that of Husbands and Fathers, a Dominion as full of sweetness, as so gentle and free a Relation importeth. I can see no Use that there had been of *Trades* and Occupations, onely the pleasant Diversion that *Adam* had in dressing the Garden, and the consequents of that: I am sure there had been no Funeral *Pomps*, no *Sickness*, *Physick*, or *Physician*. There had been no *Faith* in the *Incarnation* of the Son of God, because no occasion for that Incarnation, no Ceremonial

Law of Moses, no *Baptism,* nor *Lords Supper*, because there were no supernatural Mysteries to be Typified, but the clear Light of a Diviner Reason, and a free Communion with God in the Right discharge of those Vertues, Divine and Moral, which naturally belong to the Estate of Innocency. All which Original and Primitive Vertues ought now to continue, as it were the Face of Religion beneath that *Mask* or *Vizor* of Ordinances and new Duties, which Sin and Corruption hath put upon it; Tho we have forgotten the Vertues of our first Estate, and are apt now to terrifie our selves with that *Disguise*, wherewith we have concealed their Beauty, by regarding only the Vertues, that were occasioned by Sin and Misery.

IT is a great Error to mistake the *Vizor* for the *Face*, and no less to stick in the outward *Kind* and Appearance of things; mistaking the Alterations and Additions that are made upon the Fall of Man, for the whole Business of Religion. And yet this new Constellation of Vertues, that appeareth aboveboard, is almost the only thing talked of and understood in the World. Whence it is that the other Duties, which are the *Soul* of Piety, being unknown, and the *Reason* of these together with their Original and Occasion, unseen; Religion appears like a sour and ungratefull Thing to the World, impertinent to bliss, and void of Reason; Whereupon GOD is suspected and hated, Enmity against GOD and *Atheism*, being brought into, and entertained in the World.

FOR it is an *Idea* connatural to the Notion of GOD, to conceive him *Wise* and *Good*: And, if we cannot see some *Reason* in his Ways, we are apt to suspect there is no *Deity*, or if there be, that he is Malevolent and *Tyrannical*, which is worse then none. For all Wisdom and Goodness are contained in Love: And if it be true that GOD is Love, he will shew it in our Beings, by making us Great and Excellent Creatures; in his Gifts and Bounties, by surrounding us with real and serviceable Treasures, in all his Laws, as well as in all his Works, by consulting our Welfare in the one and in the other. And as he makes the World Glorious and Beautiful for us to dwell in, so will he make such Actions and Vertues only needful to be exercised by us as are excellent and Divine: he will impose no Duties but such as are full of reason, and lead us more Advantageously to Bliss and Glory.

We are apt to charge our own Faults on God, by confounding all things: and because we see not how *Penitence*, and *Meekness*, and *Acts of Charity*, in relieving the Poor, directly and immediately bring us unto Bliss, are apt to repine at their Imposition. But when we see all these Virtues in their several Places and Offices, their Objects and their Uses, the Ends for which, and the occasions on which they were introduced, all are Delightful to the Reason of mans Soul, and highly Eligible, while GOD is adored and admired for the depth of his Wisdom and Goodness, and beloved for the Equity and Excellency of his Proceedings. For all these Occasional Vertues are but Temporary, when our Life, and this present World are past and gone as a Dream, Love, and Joy, and Gratitude will be all that will continue for ever, in which Estate, Wisdom and Knowledge, Goodness and Righteousness, and True Holiness shall abide, as the Life and Glory into which the Souls of all that are Blessed will be transformed. Repentance shall be gone, and Patience cease, Faith and Hope be swallowed up in fruition, Right Reason be extended to all Objects in all Worlds, and Eternity in all its Beauties and Treasures, seen, desired, esteemed, enjoyed.

Let it be your Care to dive to the Bottom of true Religion, and not suffer your Eyes to be Dazled with its Superficial Appearance. Rest not in the *Helps* and *Remedies* that it bringeth, but search for the Hidden Manna, the substantial Food underneath, the Satisfaction of all Wishes and Desires, the true and Cœlestial Pleasures, the Causes of Love, and Praise, and Thanksgiving founded in the Manifestations of Gods Eternal favour, especially in the Ends, for the sake of which all Helps and Remedies are prepared. For it is exceeding true, that *his Laws are Sweeter then the Hony and the Hony Comb, and far more precious then thousands of Gold and Silver.*

CHAP. V.

Of the Necessity, Excellency, and Use of Knowledge; its Depths and Extents, its Objects and its End.

KNOWLEDGE and Love are so necessary to Felicity, that there can be no Enjoyment or Delight without them. Heaven and Earth would be Dark and obscure, Angels and Men vain and unprofitable, all the Creatures base and unserviceable, Felicity impossible, were there no Knowledge. Nay GOD himself, without Knowledge and Love, could not well exist; for his very Essence is seated in infinite Knowledge.

GOD is Light, and in him is no Darkness at all; He is Love by nature and there is no hatred in his Essence. His very Godhead is all Perfection, by the infinite Knowledge and Love in his Nature.

THE Original of our Knowledge is his Godhead, His Essence and his will are the Fountain of it; and the stream so excellent, that in all Estates it is for ever to be continued, as the Light and Glory of the whole Creation.

THE understanding Power, which is seated in the Soul, is the Matter of that Act wherein the Essence of Knowledge consisteth: Its form is the Act it self, whereby that Power of knowing apprehendeth its Object.

ITS nature is invisible, like that of all other Spirits, so simple and uncompounded, that its form and matter are the same. For all Powers, when transformed into Act, are Acts themselves. And the faculty of understanding, in a Compleat and Perfect Act of Knowledge attains its Perfection, and is Power exerted, or an Act in its Exercise. For every Act is Power exerted.

THE Power of Knowing is vain if not reduced into Act; and the Soul a melancholly and Dreadful Cave, or Dungeon of Darkness, if void of Knowledge. Had GOD himself a Power of Knowing Distinct from its Operation, if he never exercised that Power, it would be useless to him. His Glory and Blessedness are seated in the Light of that Knowledge, which to us upon Earth appeareth *Inaccessible*.

IF we would *be perfect, as our Father which is in Heaven is perfect*, our Power of Knowing must be transformed (into *Act,*) and all Objects appear in the interior Light of our *own* understanding. For tho all

Eternity were full of Treasures, and the Whole World, and all the Creatures in it transformed into Joys and our Interest to all never so perfect; yet if we are Ignorant of them, we shall continue as poor and Empty, as if there were nothing but Vacuity and Space. For not to *be*, and not to *appear*, are the same thing to the understanding.

WERE a Man a Seraphim by his Essence, or something by nature more Glorious and Divine then the Highest Order of the most Blessed Angels, nay the greatest Creature that Almighty Power was able to produce, his Soul and Body would signifie nothing, if he were unknown to himself and were not aware of his Excellence.

IF you would have a solid Prospect of any Vertue, you must understand, that Vertues are Powers transformed into right, wise, and regular Acts, avoiding all extremes of *remissness* on the one hand, and *excess* on the other. The Extreams of Knowledge are Ignorance and Error.

FOR ought you know Heaven and Earth are as full of Treasures, as Almighty Power was able to create them, and you by Nature, the best and highest of all possible Creatures, made like GOD, for the highest and best of all possible Ends, and called to live in Communion with him, in all his fruitions: but being vilely corrupted, you have lost the sence of all these Realities, and are ignorant of the Excellences of your own Estate and Nature.

I am sure that GOD is infinite in Wisedom, Goodness and Power, and nothing is wanting on his Part, to perfect your Desires: But yet you may be blind, and idle, and ignorant, and dead in a manner, while you are wanting to your self, and have need of nothing, but clear and perfect apprehensions, but because they are Sottish and Erroneous at present, they may make you miserable, and Poor, and Blind, and Naked.

IF Sin had been like *Circe*'s Cup, and changed the shape of Mans Body, to that of a *Swine* or *Dragon*, the Depravation of his Nature had been plain and visible; yet without knowing what kind of Form he had before, it would not appear, because we should be unsensible of his first Form, and unable to compare the one with the other: But Sin is a *Moral Obliquity*, and the change it produceth in the Soul is *Spiritual*. It makes a man to differ far more from himself, than any alteration of Body can do; but withal so blinds his Understanding, that he does not remember what he was in his first Parent; Tho the first Man (who had experience of both Estates) was able to compare them, because in his Corruption, he might possibly retain a Sence of that Nature, and Life which he enjoyed in his integrity: Yet all his Posterity, that are born Sinners, never were sensible of the Light and Glory of an Innocent Estate, and for that cause may be wholy ignorant both of GOD and themselves, utterly unable to conceive the Glory of the World, or of that Relation, wherein they should by Nature have stood towards all Creatures.

IT is impossible to conceive, how great a change a slight Action may produce. It is but pressing the Wick a little with ones Finger, and a Lamp is extinguished, and Darkness immediately made to overspread the Room. The Glory and Splendor of the whole World would vanish upon the Extinction of the Sun: And one Instants Cessation from the Emission of its Beams would be its Extinction. A Soul is a more Glorious Thing than the Sun: the Sphear of its Activity is far Greater, and its *Light* more *Precious*. All the World may be filled with the splendor of its Beams; Eternity it self was prepared for it! Were there but one Soul, to see and enjoy all the Creatures, upon the suspension of its Light all the Creation would be rendred vain. Light it self is but *Darkness* without the Understanding.

THE Existence of many Souls is so far from abating the value of one, that it is by reason of their multitude more useful and Excellent. For the value of the Objects, imputes a Lustre and *Higher* value to the Light wherein they are enjoyed. And if Souls themselves are more excellent than all other Creatures, and are with, and above all other, to be enjoyed, that Power, whereby this Soul is able to enjoy them, is more to be esteemed, upon the account of those Souls, than for all the other Creatures, which are made for the same: GOD himself and his holy Angels are Objects of the Understanding. Those Felicities and Glories, which the Sun cannot extend to, the Soul can comprehend. All which, since their Fruition depends upon that Act of the Understanding by which they are *Considered*, reflect a Lustre, and add a value to that Knowledge by which the Soul does attain them. Whereupon it follows that the infinite value of all these is seated in the intellect; and as the Power, so the Act of Knowledg, on which their Fruition dependeth, is of infinite use and Excellency. As the loss is infinite, when the Soul is bereaved of them, so is the Dammage, which it suffers by failing of its Light, whether that Defect be voluntary, or imposed by some outward Impediment.

AS for the *Use* of Knowledge, it is apparent enough. For the Relation between the Use and Excellency of things is so near and intimate, that as nothing Useless can be at all excellent, so is every Excellence in every Being founded in its usefulness. The use of Souls is as great as their Excellency: The use of Knowledge as endless in Variety, as in Extent, and Value.

KNOWLEDGE is that which does illuminate the Soul, enkindle Love, excite our Care, inspire the mind with Joy, inform the Will, enlarge the Heart, regulate the Passions, unite all the Powers of the Soul to their Objects, see their Beauty, understand their Goodness, discern our Interest in them, form our Apprehensions of them, Consider and enjoy their Excellences. All Contentments, Raptures, and Extasies are conceived in the Soul, and begotten by Knowledge, all Laws, Obligations and Rewards are understood by Knowledg: All Vertues and Graces of the Mind are framed by Knowledge, all Advantages are by it improved, all Temptations discerned, all Dangers avoided, all Affairs ordered, all Endowments acquired; all the Ornaments of Life, all the Beauties of the inward Man, all the Works of Piety are affected by Knowledge. In the Light of knowledge all Pleasures arise, and as Fruits and Flowers are begotten in the Earth by the Beams of the Sun, so do all kinds of Joy spring from the Creatures, and are made ours, by the help of that Knowledge, that shineth on them; its last Off-spring are Eternal Thanksgivings and Praises. The Divine Image and the Perfection of Bliss are founded in Knowledge, GOD himself dwelleth in the Soul, with all his Attributes and Perfections, by Knowledge: By it we are made Temples of the Holy Ghost, and Partakers of the Divine Nature, And for this cause it is that St. *Paul* prayeth,[1] *That we might be filled with the Knowledge of his Will, in all Wisedome and Spiritual Understanding, that we might walk worthy of the Lord unto all pleasing, being fruitful in every Good Work, and increasing in the Knowledge of GOD, strengthened with all Might according to his glorious Power, unto all Patience and long-suffering, with Joyfulness giving Thanks to the Father, who hath made us meet to be Partakers of the Inheritance of the Saints in Light: who hath delivered us from the Power of Darkness, and translated us into the Kingdom of his Dear Son.*

THE Sun is a glorious Creature, and its Beams extend to the utmost Stars, by shining on them it cloaths them with light, and by its Rayes exciteth all their influences. It enlightens the Eyes of all the Creatures: It shineth on forty Kingdomes at the same time, on Seas and Continents in a general manner; yet so particularly regardeth all, that every Mote in the Air, every Grain of Dust, every Sand, every Spire of Grass is wholly illuminated thereby, as if it did entirely shine upon that alone. Nor does it onely illuminate all these Objects in an idle manner, its Beams are Operative, enter in, fill the Pores of Things with Spirits, and impregnate them with Powers, cause all

---

[1] Marginal gloss: Col. 1:9,10,11,12.

their Emanations, Odors, Vertues and Operations; Springs, Rivers, Minerals and Vegetables are all perfected by the Sun, all the Motion, Life and sense of Birds, Beasts and Fishes dependeth on the same. Yet the Sun is but a little spark, among all the Creatures, that are made for the Soul; the Soul, being the most High and Noble of all, is capable of far higher Perfections, far more full of Life and Vigour in its uses. The Sphere of its Activity is illimited, its Energy is endless upon all its Objects. It can exceed the Heavens in its Operations, and run out into infinite spaces. Such is the extent of Knowledge, that it seemeth to be the Light of all Eternity. All Objects are equally near to the splendor of its Beams: As innumerable millions may be conceived in its Light, with a ready capacity for millions more; so can it penetrate all Abysses, reach to the Centre of all Nature, converse with all Beings, visible and invisible, Corporeal and Spiritual, Temporal and Eternal, Created and Increated, Finite and Infinite, Substantial and Accidental, Actual and Possible, Imaginary and Real; All the Mysteries of Bliss and Misery, all the Secrets of Heaven and Hell are Objects of the Souls Capacity here, and shall be actually seen and known hereafter.

WERE Almighty Power Magnified by filling Eternity with created objects, and were all the Omnipresence of God full of Joys, it is able, when assisted by his Divine Knowledge, to look upon all: and tho every one of them should have an infinite Depth within, an Endless variety of Uses, a Relation to all the rest of the World, the Soul, as if it were able to contract all its strengths from all the expansions of Eternity and space, and fix them upon this Moment, or on this Centre, intirely beholding this alone, in all its fulness, can see its Original, its End, its Operations, Effects and Properties, as if it had nothing to consider but this alone, in a most exquisite and perfect manner.

IT is not to be denied, that every Being in all Worlds is an Object of the Understanding: nor can that of the Psalmist be doubted, *In his Presence there is fulness of Joy, and at his right hand there are Pleasures for evermore*: that is, his Omnipresence is full of Joys, and his Eternity of Riches and Pleasures: nor is it to be denied, that the Soul is by its Creation intended for *the Throne of GOD*. For it is made capable of his Omnipresence and Eternity, and, as the Apostle speaketh, *may be filled with all the fulness of GOD*, which fulness is adequate to the Immensity of his Eternal Power (of which you will see more in the Vertues of Love, Wisdom, Righteousness and Holiness:) This only is here to be noted, that Nature never made any Power in vain, but ever intendeth the Perfection of what it produceth; and prepareth objects for the understanding, the Perfection of which Power is the actual attainment of that Knowledge of which it is capable.

THE principal objects of our Knowledge are GOD, and a Mans self: The Kingdom of GOD, his Laws and Works, his Ways in all Ages, his Counsels and his Attributes, Mans Interest and Duty, Transactions of the World, the Thoughts and Actions of Angels and Men are considerable; which tho they may be stiled less material Objects of the understanding, yet in relation to GOD and a Mans self, are of great Importance.

GOD as he is the Life and fountain of all Felicity, the End of all Perfection, and the Creator of our Being, Almighty in Power, infinite in Wisdom and Goodness, Author of the universe, and Lord of all the Creatures, is most fit to be Known. *Plato* makes him the very *Light* of the understanding, and affirms, that as three Things are necessary to *Vision*, the Eye rightly prepared, the object conveniently seated, and Light to convey the *Idea* to the Eye; so there are three things required to compleat and perfect Intelligence, an understanding Eye, an Intelligible Object, and a Light intelligible in which to conceive it: Which last is GOD. Nor is the Royal Psalmist and Divine Philosopher *David* far from the Notion, while he saith, *In thy Light we shall see Light*. For GOD is the Light of the understanding. His Nature is the Light of all the Creation. Therefore it is said by Christ himself that the *Knowledge of GOD is Life Eternal*. For his Light is the Life of men, and without him we can do nothing. Till we Know his Nature, we cannot apprehend the Excellency of his Works: For all their Goodness is derived from him, and ends in him. His Love, moved him to create the World, and the principal End for which it was made, is the Glory of the Creator in the Felicity of his Creatures. The Glory of the Creatures is seen in his. By his Wisdom and Goodness we are guided to the Hope, and Investigation of their Excellence. His infinite bounty made them all our *Treasures*, that for the Perfection of their Beauty and Worth we might celebrate his Praises.

HE that would not be a stranger to the Universe, an Alien to Felicity, and a foreigner to himself, must Know GOD to be an infinite Benefactor, all Eternity, full of Treasures, the World it self, the Beginning of Gifts, and his own Soul the Possessor of all, in Communion with the Deity. That the Business of Religion is Complacency in GOD, and that GOD never laid aside his Wisdom in any Operation of his Power, never forgot to make the least of his Works agreeable to his Goodness. Nay rather he is so perfect, that his infinite Goodness, Wisdom, and Power, are exerted wholy and wholy Conspicuous in every Operation. It is the Beauty of Truth that maketh Knowledge of such infinite Value. For if all the Treasures of Wisdom and Knowing be ordained for a Wise and Knowing Man, if all Objects in the clear Light of Heaven and Eternity be laudable and Glorious, if Divine Wisdome hath so far obtained, that the number and Value of GODS Gifts is accurate, and exactly answerable to the nature of its causes; if every Soul, that will live in his Image, may be the friend of GOD, and acquire the Empire of the World, and be Beloved of Angels, and admired of Men; if fruition be the End of Knowledge, and all Things made that they may be enjoyed: Knowledge is the only Thing that enriches the Soul, and *the Knowing Man is the friend of GOD*. The Exercise and Pleasure of this Divine Amity is the End of the Creation, and the Perfection of the Soul.

The Knowledge of a Mans self is highly conducive to his Happiness, not only as it gives him Power to rejoyce in his Excellencies, but as it shews him his End, for which he was created. For by Knowing what Inclinations and Powers are in his Soul, he discerns what is agreeable with, and fit for his Essence; what objects and what Operations are conduciveto his Welfare, what means he is to use for the Attainment of his End, and what that is, wherein his Perfection consisteth. If the Powers of his Soul are illimited, his Desire infinite, and his Reach Eternal, if he be able to see and enjoy all Worlds, and all that is above all Worlds in the Image of GOD: If his Ambition carry him to be Pleasing to all Angels and Men, and to be Glorious in the Eyes of all Kingdoms and Ages; if his Abilities are indeficient for the fruition of all that is Excellent in eternity it self, it is a token that he is ordained for GOD, and the enjoyment of his Kingdom: and a wicked folly to restrain himself to the miserable Contentment of a Cell, or Cottage, and to delight in nothing but some fragments of the Creation, that in Comparison of the whole are infinitely Defective.

OF all other things I would have this most deeply engraven in the mind, that GOD hath exceeded all Imagination in the Works of his Hands, that he that overcometh shall be the Son of GOD and inherit all Things, that there is an infinite end why the secrets of all hearts shall at last be revealed, that in Heaven all Thoughts and Things shall be Known,that the Kingdome of Heaven is so Glorious, that all the blessed are Perfect Sovereigns, every one the Possessor and End of it all: that all Things proceeding immediately from GOD, are the Best that are possible: that the best and the worst things as ordered by him, are perfectly amiable, and subservient to Felicity, that he himself alone hath a Proper Right to all that is excellent, and that GOD is in every Thing to be enjoyed, that he is enjoyed only when his essence and his Works satisfie the Desires of perfect reason, and exceed all Wishes in filling and delighting the soul: That having filled the soul with infinite Wisdome, he has laid infinite Obligations upon us, and set infinite Rewards before us, made Laws infinitely amiable, and given us Duties infinitely Desirable: for which he deserves eternal Adorations and Thanksgivings.

CHAP. VI.

Of Love and Hatred. The necessity and sweetness of Love. Its General use and efficacy. The several kinds of love. Of the Power, Inclination and act of Love. Its extent and capacity.

BECAUSE Love is the most Desirable Employment of the Soul, the Power of Loving is to be accounted the most High and Noble of the Faculties. It is not seated by it self in the mind, but attended with a mighty Proneness and Inclination.

THERE is no Creature so unsociable and furious but it is capable of loving something or other. Wolves and Tygres live at peace among themselves, Lions have an Inclination to their Grim Mistresses, and Deformed Bears a natural Affection to their Whelps, expressed in their Rage, when they are bereaved of them. Things must either be absolutely Dead, or live in misery, that are void of love. Whatsoever is endued with Life and sence delights in easie and grateful Operations. Love is a necessary Affection of their Souls, because it is impossible to apprehend any thing Delightful, but it must be pleasing; and what is Pleasing must be Lovely. For to be Pleased, and to love are the same thing. If there be any difference, the pleasure we take in any Object is the root of that Desire, which we call Love; and the affection, whereby we pursue the pleasure that is apprehended in it, is part of the Love that we bear unto it; the end of which is the Completion of that pleasure which it first perceives: All is Love variously modified, according to the Circumstances wherein the Object is represented.

AS Love is the only Easie and Delightful Operation, so is Hatred of all other the most troublesom and tormenting. Displeasure and Enmity are the Ingredients of its nature; and the fruits of it (allyed to their Root) as Bitter as Gall, and Wormwood. Murder, and Vexation, and Grief are the off-spring of the one, with Separation, Contention, and Horror; Peace and Embraces are the Fruit of the other, with Praises and Complacencies, Honors, Services, Benefits and Pleasures. These are the little *Cupids* that flie about this cœlestial *Venus*, when it is, what it ought to be, the Mother of Felicity, and the Daughter of GOD.

ALL Creatures that are sensible of Pain or pleasure, must of necessity be addicted to Love and Hatred; to the Love of what is pleasing, to the Hatred of what is Painful. And if any Question be made, which of these Twins is the First born? the answer is; that they may seem Twins in respect of Time, but in nature Love is the first born, and the Mother of Hatred. For where nothing to be hated does at all appear, pleasant Things are Beloved for their own sake: whereas if there were no pleasant thing to be beloved, nothing could be hated, because nothing could be Hurtful, which appeareth by this, because where there is no Love, there is no Interest, and where there is no concernment, there can be no Affection, no Fear, or Hope, or Joy, or sorrow.

AS Fire begets Water by melting Ice, so does Love beget contrary passions in the soul of a living creature, Anger, Malice, Envy, Grief and Jealousie: not by its own nature, but by the accidental Interposure of some Obstacle, that hinders or endangers the fruition of its Object. Were there no Love of Ease and Pleasure, there could be no Anger or Quarrel between Competitors; no Emulation or Desire, no Aversion or Endeavour. All Enmity and Hostility Springs from a Contention, who shall enjoy what is Desirable; or from some other Principle of Envy or Revenge, in relation to what is Good: as is Obvious to Daily Experience.

LIFE and Love are so individualy united, that to live without Loving something is impossible. Even in Hell, where their whole Life seemeth to be spent in Detestation and Hatred, and actual Love is, like fire under those Embers, covered and continued, Could they put off self Love, all Love of Felicity, and Interest, their Torments would be gone: Punishments and Rewards are things impossible, where there is not self-Love: for without Love to something, Pains and Joys are equally Grateful.

AS *Love* is the Root of Endeavor, so is it the Spring of all the Passions: They all depend upon Love alone. We are *Angry* at that which stands in our Way, between our Love and its object: We *Desire* an absent Good, because we Love it: We *Hope* for it, when we conceive its Attainment feasible: We *rejoyce* in it, when we have it: We *fear* to lose it: we *grieve* when it is gone: we despair, if we cannot get, or recover it: We *hate* all that is opposite to it. And for this Cause is our Love, when well regulated, the greatest Vertue, because upon the right Choise of its Object, and true Goverment of it self, all the Powers and Affections of the Soul are well employed; and when we Love all that we ought as we ought to do, we fulfil all Laws, Hope and Fear, and Hate, and Grieve, and Desire, and Rejoyce, and do every thing in a regular Manner.

THERE is a Sensual and Brutish Love, there is a Humane and Divine: Brutish Love is of two sorts, the one Springs from a Harmony of Complexions and a Sympathy of Bodies, the other from the Consideration of Pleasure abstracted. The First of these is occasioned by a secret and unexpressible Agreement of Tempers, by which upon the presence of each other, the Senses are delighted, we know not why; it being a mystery in nature; and perhaps founded in a grateful Transpiration of Spirits from one to the other.

THE Consideration of Beauty seemeth peculiar to the Love of Men; because no Beast is observed to make any Distinction between Lineaments and Features, nor upon any account of shape and Colours to be delighted with each other. Wherein Man exceeds the Capacity of Beasts, in being able to note and admire the Workmanship of GOD in the decent Order of Symmetry and Proportion.

HUMANE Affection and Divine Love are near allyed, yet of several Kinds. If you take the Love of Reason in its utmost Height, it is always Divine. For it is conformable to the Love of GOD in its measures and Degrees, in its Effects and Causes. For the Love of GOD is it self the Love of perfect Reason. And as the Reason of his Love is Infinite and Eternal, so is its Operation. But in a lower Acceptation Humane Love differs from Divine; it being founded upon Temporal Causes, Vivacity, Wit, Learning, Beauty, Behaviour, Moral Honesty, Fidelity, Kindness, Goodness, Power, Majesty, Wealth, Nobility, Worth, Vertue, and the like. But all these may be exalted, when they are Sanctified, and made Divine by the superadded concurrence of Cœlestial Causes. For when a Man loves another, because he is made in the Image of GOD, and by the Beauty of his Soul is something more than Humane, this Love is made Sacred, and receives a Grace from the Influences of Religion.

DIVINE Love strictly so called, is founded on Eternal Causes, agreeable to the Life of Heaven, Delightful to GOD, and Pleasing to the Angels.

IF Divine Love be taken in the *highest* Sense, there is none but in GOD. For it is his Peculiar Prerogative to Love without Obligation or Reward, to be the Sole Author of all Felicity, and to over-flow with Goodness of himself freely, without any Motive, to prevent the Beauty and Existence of his Object, and to Love from all Eternity in an immutable manner: And this is the nature of Divine Love. Howbeit even here, are infinite Ends and Causes of his Love, tho they are all in Himself: For he Loves, that he may Love, and begets that Love which is his Essence. His Love is the foundation of all his Treasures, the Cause and End of the whole Creation, and that alone by which he proceeds from himself (to all his Creatures, and by those) to himself again for ever. All his Kingdome and Greatness and Pleasure, all his Wisdome and Goodness, all his Life and Perfection is seated in Love, which is his Beauty and his Holiness, his Bounty and his Godhead. He Loves therefore that he may be all Beauty and Goodness, and Holiness, and that he may enjoy himself and the Eternal Pleasure of his Essence in Glory and Blessedness for ever.

IT is GOD alone that Loves by his Essence, Angels and Men may Love by Inclination, but their Affection is Accidental to their nature, begins in time, may alter and cease. It is subject to Chance, Obligation and Reward, and ought to be guided according to the Pleasure of an Higher Agent. In this it differs from the Love of God, but in many things there is a great Agreement and proportion between them. For GOD has made the love of Angels and men so like his own, by extending their Knowledge to all objects, that infinite Perfections are contained in their love. It is as GODLIKE as any Thing created is capable of being; for Almighty Power and infinite Wisdome are employed in the production of it.

FOR the better understanding of this Love, we will consider it in the power of Loving, in the inclination to Love, in its act and Perfection. It may seem a surprizing verity; but the Power of Loving is as necessary to Blessedness and Glory as life it selfe; an inclination to love as necessary as the Power; and the act of Love as necessary as the Inclination. The world is useless without Life, and Life without Love, the Body without the Soul, the Soul without the Power of Loving, the Power of Loving without the Inclination, the Inclination without the Act.

IN the Power of Loving I shall note nothing at present, but its Extent and Capacity. In Beasts it is confined, but in Men it is Endless. As a Beast is unable to examine what spaces are above the Heavens, so is it unable to extend its Affections beyond the memory of things perceived, for a Beast cannot represent to it self the Idea's of its Progenitors; nor see into Ages that are before its birth, nor contemplate Objects that will be after it is Dead. But man can see, and know, and love any object, in any Age or Kingdom in the World. He can look into any Region, tho it be never so far removed and be as familiarly conversant with any Person or Transaction there, when represented once in a clear Light, as with any Object in his own country. He can look into *Eden*, consider *Adams* Dust in its first Creation, survey the Procedure of God in his Six Dayes Works, pass out of Time into Eternity it self, run up to the Original and fountain Head of all existence, ponder the nature of GOD, search in his Bosom for his Eternal Counsels, pierce into the Centre of the Earth, and survey the Circumference of all Immensity. His Love can follow his Knowledg in all its flights, while in spirit he can be present with all the Angels. He is able to Love not only his Family and Relations, but all the City and Country where he liveth, all the Kingdom, all the Cities and Kingdoms in the world, all the Generations in all Kingdoms, all the Spirits of Just men made perfect, all the Cherubims and Seraphins, and GOD blessed for ever. This is the extent: The capacity of Love is so alsufficient, that his Affection is not diminished, but the more he loves one, the more he is able, and the more inclined to love all that are united to him As in ordinary friendship, the more we love the Father, the more we love his Wife and all his children. For the more we love any Person, the more we love all that love him, or are beloved by him. As the reasons of our Love increase, so may our Love it selfe; the capacity of Love being so indeficient, that it never can be exceeded, or surmounted by its Object.

THE Capacity of Love being so exceeding vast, multiplies and heightens in the Soul of man, that is apt to overflow of its own Accord. For nothing is so prone to communicate it self as that Active Principle of Love; that Soul which is Generous and Divine, being disposed to the exercise of Love, because therein it findeth its Proper Element. The very Sun is not more inclined to communicate its Beams, then the Soul to love. For the Soul being made in the Image of GOD, who is Love by his Essence, must needs be like him in Power and Inclination, and is made for nothing else but the Attainment of its perfection, so that it can never rest, till it actually love after his similitude. Some Operation it must of Necessity have. For as all Life, so all pleasure is founded in Action.

IF Love in its Perfection be considered, all that is lovely is Beloved by the soul; all the Capacity of Love is filled with its objects, and all the Goodness of the Creator and his Creatures, at once enjoyed. It is the Life and pleasure and enlargment of the Soul, it is the Wisdom, and Goodness, and Glory of the Soul. I confess there be many Errors and Diseases in Love; and that Love is alwayes miserable, in its Effects, that is *vicious*: yet it so bewitches the Sences, that the Soul being captivated by the Force of present Delight is violently carried in an irresistible appetite to those Things which Reason condemnes, and advises to shun as Evil. *Medea's* faction most prevails in the World.

——— *Video meliora proboque,*
Deteriora Sequor.

LOVE is *then* a vice, when it is irrational and illegal, rebellious and Sensual, Blind, Defective, Unjust, Absurd. When Evil things are beloved, when Good things are preferred above the Better, and the Best neglected.

VERTUOUS Love is that which proceedeth from a well governed understanding, and is seated in a Will that is guided by Reason. It renders to all things their just Due, and is the Powerful Parent of all Kind of Vertues. This Love may be considered either in its Properties, or Effects, the last of which relate to the Soul it self, to the Conversation of the whole man, to all its Objects; when it is well understood, it will be found the proper and immediate Means by which we attain our Perfection and Felicity.

CHAP. VII.

What Benefit GOD himself does receive by his Eternal Love. That when our Love is made compleat and Perfect, it will be like his, and the Benefit of it will be Eternal.

BEFORE we can fully discern the Benefit of Love, or see the Glory of it in all its high and admirable Effects, we must consider what Love is and doth in GOD. For as we have said, *The Life of GOD is Love*; nay the Apostle saith, *GOD is Love*: By Loving he begot his Love. And if his Love be his Godhead, his Essence is an infinite and Eternal Act of Love, by extending which through all infinity, and by Loving Eternally, he begot his infinite and Eternal Essence: which is the Love that filleth all Worlds with Beauty and Glory. When you consider it well, An Act of Love is begotten by *Loving:* And if his Wisdome, and Goodness, and Blessedness, and Glory be seated in Love, his Love is his Wisdome which is the Son of GOD, and his Goodness, and his Glory, and his Blessedness. For all these, tho we conceive them diversly, are the same Thing: and of the Son of GOD it is said, that *he is the Wisdom of the Father, and the Brightness of his Fathers Glory*. He is the Life of the Father, *by whom also he made the Worlds*, and the Love of the Father *for whom all Things were created, that are in Heaven, and that are in Earth, visible and invisible, whether they be Thrones, or Dominions, or Principalities, or Powers: all Things were created by him, and for him.*[1] For GOD enjoyeth all Things by his Love, which is his Eternal Son; and made them as perfect and delightful as it was possible for things created to be, that he might take Pleasure in them. As he himself is made Glorious and Delightful in the Eyes of all Angels and Men *by* Love, so doth his whole Kingdom arise and Spring *from* Love; the Beauty and felicity of all his Creatures, their Joys and Praises, their Uses and Perfections are founded in his Love, by his Love he begetteth all his pleasures in himself, by his Love he made his Treasures infinite, and by that alone doth he take infinite Pleasure and Delight in himself and his Kingdome. Thus useful is the Love of GOD.

Had not GOD from all Eternity Loved, had he never desired, nor delighted in any thing; he had never exerted his Almighty Power, never communicated his Goodness, or begot his Wisdom, never enjoyed

---

[1] Marginal gloss: Col. 1.16.

Himself, never applyed himself to the Production of his Works, never appeared in his Glory to any eie whatsoever. Removing his Love we remove all the Properties and Effects of his Essence, and are utterly unable to conceive any Idea of his Godhead. For his Power, tho it be Almighty, yet if it be Dead and idle, is fruitless and Deformed. Idle Power is not the Essence of the Deity, but a meer Privation and Vacuity; or at least a positive Being as ignoble as it is unactive. The Reason of his Works is founded in Love, so are all the Obligations, that are laid upon his Creatures to adore him. All their Rewards are founded in Love, and by Love prepared: All his Laws are the Laws of Love, all his Attributes and Counsels are Love, in several formes, acting upon several occasions. When his Love communicates it self in Joys to innocent Creatures, it is *Goodness*; when it attains the most perfect End by the most perfect means, it is *Wisdome*; when it rescues guilty Creatures from Hell, it is *Mercy*; when it punishes the Rebellious it is *Justice*; when it inspires Obedience into any obstinate Person, it is *Grace*; when it delights in the Beauty of all its Works, it is *Blessedness*; when it appears in the perfection of its works, it is glory. For Glory is the perfection of Beauty, that ariseth from, and is seated in the lustre of excellent Actions, discovering the internal Properties of an excellent Agent, which is by those his Properties and Actions made Delightful to all *Judicious* Spectators.

NOR is it onely in GOD, but in us also that the fruits and Benefits of *Love* are ineffable. For by loving, as it ought to do, the Soul acquires its own Perfection, and is united to all its Objects. By loving as it ought to do, it is made Holy, and Wise, and Good, and Amiable. Onely by Loving does it embrace the Delights of which it is capable. Love is the root and Soul of those Actions for which a Creature is desired, and praised by others.

IT is an infinite Advantage, that we are able to live in GODS Image, if we please: For if GOD alone be infinitely Glorious and Blessed, there is no way for us to become Glorious and Blessed, but by being made, either by our selves, or some other, like unto him.

BY nature he hath implanted the Similitude of his power: which we are to improve by Grace, turning it into Act after his Similitude. To be able to Love is neither Grace nor vertue, but a meer Gift of GOD, a natural Endowment, which may be Blasted, or compleated. Actually to love is the Work of vertue; for by that Act we enjoy our Felicity.

HAD GOD limited and confined our understanding, our power of Loving had been shut up in Bounds. Had he made it infinite, but not prepared objects for the same, our Love had been deluded, and had lost its force. Had he made some Objects, but not so many as it was capable of Loving, it had been Superfluous and dissatisfied; Had he prepared Objects innumerable and Endless, but made them evil, our Love had been irrational, had he commanded us to Love them; Had he made more Objects then we were able to love, we had been discontented: But having made all Objects infinitely Amiable and Glorious, and filled his Immensity and Eternity with himselfe, and with the Lustre of his Actions, Love is an infinite Vertue, because nothing is wanting, but an Act of Love to enjoy them.

IF they are all Amiable in all Respects, they are all according to our Hearts desire, in their Natures, Places, Durations, Ends, Occasions, Causes, Uses, Service[s], Relations, Properties, Operations, &c. All things, as they immediatly proceed from him, are in all respects most perfectly pleasing. And if we have an Eye to see and discern this, and a Soul able to resent the Benefit; if our nature be so vast and perfect, as to see and take pleasure in all their Circumstances; it is the most unreasonable and *bruitish* thing in the world to withdraw our Affection from them, nay it is worse then *Diabolical*. For we Kill our selves, we blast our Felicity, we offend GOD, we slight the Beauty of all his Creatures, we break his Laws, we act against nature, we darken the Light and Splendor of our Souls, we deface his Image, we grieve his Love, we do the most vicious and abominable thing that is imaginable. But if we excite and awaken our Power, we take in the Glory of all objects, we live unto them, we are sensible of them, we delight in them, we transform our souls into Acts of Love and Knowledge, we proceed out of our selves into all Immensities and Eternities, we render all Things their Due, we reap the Benefit of all, we are Just, and Wise, and Holy, we are Grateful to GOD, and Amiable in being so: We are not divided from, but united to him, in all his Appearances, Thoughts, Counsels, Operations; we adorn our souls with the Beauty of all objects whatsoever, are transformed into the Image of GOD, live in communion with him, nay live in him, and he in us, are made Kings and Priests unto GOD, and his sons forever; There is an exact and pleasant Harmony between us and all the Creatures: We are in a Divine and spiritual Manner made as it were Omnipresent with all Objects (for the Soul is present only by an Act of the understanding) and the Temple of all Eternity does it then becom, when the Kingdom of GOD is seated within it, as the world is in the Eye; while it lives, and feels, and sees, and enjoyes, in every object to which it is extended, its own & its objects Perfection.

IF by our voluntary Remissness, or Mistake, or Disorder, we dote upon one Object, or suffer some few things to engage our Souls so intirely, as to forget and neglect all the rest, we rob all those we desert, of their due Esteem, and abridge our selves of that Liberty and Extent, wherein the greatness of our soul consisteth. As if the Sun, that is made to shine upon all the World, should withdraw its Beams from the Stars and the Heavens, and chuse to shine upon nothing else but a Spire of Grasse, a grain of Dust, or a little sand. We lose innumerable Objects, and confine our selves to the Love of one, by sacrificing all our Affection to that, become guilty of *Idolatry* in one respect, of *Atheism* in another. For we elevate that Creature which we love alone, into the place of GOD, and we rob the Creator of that supream affection which is due unto him: And in so doing bereave our selves of the Sovereign Object, in the fruition of which all the rest are happily enjoyed. Thus when a man so Loveth his Wife, or Children, as to despise all mankind, he forfeits his Interest in all Kingdoms, and the Beauty of all Ages is taken from his Eys, his Treasures are contracted, and his Felicity is maimed, and made Defective. When a Covetous man doteth on his Bags of Gold, the Ambitious on Titles of Honor, the Drunkard on his Wine, the Lustful Goat on his Women, the foolish Hector on his Dice and Duels, they banish all other Objects, and live as absurdly, as if a King should relinquish his Crown, and confine his Thoughts and Care to a Country Mannor.

I will not deny, but that there are many Disorders and Evils in the World, many Deformities, Sins, and Miseries: but I say two things; first that in the Estate of innocency, wherein all things proceeded purely from GOD, there was no Sin, nor sickness, nor Death, nor Occasion of Complaint or Calamity. Secondly, that all the Evils that are now in the world, men brought on themselves by the Fall: And there is great need of distinguishing between the works of GOD, and the works of men. For all that GOD did is Lovely and Divine: nothing is bitter and distasteful, but what we have done: himself surveyed the whole Creation, and pronounced concerning every Thing, that it *was exceeding Good.* So that *he* was in all his Works an Object of Complacency. To these we add two Considerations more; That of all the Evils and Mischeifs which men have introduced, there is not one left *uncorrected* in his Kingdome. Secondly, that GOD bringeth Order out of Confusion, Light out of Darkness, Good out of Evil, and by a Providence irresistable, and a Power infinite, so limiteth and divideth all, that even *Evils* themselves become the Matter of his Victory, the

Ground of his Triumph: They are all improved; and he makes the Greatest Evils Objects of Joy and Glory.

NOW if all Things before GOD are fit to be enjoyed, all Good Things perfect, all Evil overcome; if without any Change of Place or Scituation, all Things are naked and open before his Eyes, and there be no Walls to exclude, or Skreens to hide, no Gulph to pass, nor Distance to over come, but all things equally neer and fair; there is some Hope, that the same Felicity is prepared for the soul which is made in his Image, and that every thing, being fit for GOD, is full of infinite Depth and Beauty. For which Cause St. *John* being in the Spirit saw all the Kingdomes of the World, become the Kingdomes of the Lord and of his Christ, and heard *every Creature which is in Heaven, and on the Earth, and under the Earth, and such as are in the Sea, and all that is in them, saying Blessing, and Honor, and Glory, and Power, be unto him that Sitteth upon the Throne, and to the Lamb for evermore.* This we are the rather induced to believe, because *the Faithful Servant* is commanded to *enter into the Joy of his Lord*, and our *Masters Joys* are the Rewards of Believers. Our Saviour telleth us his *Lord will make his Wise Servant Ruler over all his Goods*, in one place, *and over all that he hath*, in another.

TO see beyond all Seas, and through all interposing Skreens and Darknesses, is the Gift of the Understanding, and to be able to Love any Object beyond the Skies, any Thing that is good from the Centre of the Earth to the Highest Heavens, is the Property of the Soul; which it exerciseth here by Parts, and Degrees, but shall at once exert at the Day of Consummation. The Infinity of the Father in the Son, & the Godhead of the Son in the Holy Ghost will entirely be enjoyed.

IT is the Glory of man, that his *Avarice* is insatiable, and his *Ambition* infinite, that his *Appetite* carries him to innumerable Pleasures, and that his Curiosity is so Endless, that were he Monarch of the World, it could not satisfie his Soul, but he would be curiously inquisitive into the original and End of Things, and be concerned in the Nature of those that are beyond the Heavens. For having met with an infinite Benefactor, he would not be fit for his Bounty, could any finite Object satisfie his Desire: and for this Cause is his Reason so inquisitive, to see whether every thing be Delightful to his Essence; which, when he findeth agreable to his Wish, and to exceed his Imagination, it is impossible to declare how his Avarice and Ambition will both rejoyce, how much his Appetite will be satisfied, and his Curiosity delighted. To sit in the Throne of GOD and to enjoy Communion with him, in those Things which neither Eye hath seen, nor Ear heard, nor hath it entered into the Heart of Man to conceive, is no mean thing: the Advancement is infinitely Greater, then we are able to understand. No young man can gaze upon a Beauteous face with greater Pleasure, no Epicures Sence be ravished with more Delight, than that which he apprehends in so Glorious a fruition.

THE very sight of other mens Souls, shining in the Acts of their Understanding throughout all Eternity, and extending themselves in the Beams of Love through all Immensity, and thereby transformed (every one of them) into a Sphear of Light comprehending the Heavens, every Angel and every Spirit being a Temple of GODS Omnipresence and Perfection; this alone will be a ravishing Spectacle to that Goodness, which delights to see innumerable Possessors of the Same Kingdome: Much more will the Perfection of the Kingdome it self, which by infinite Wisdom is so constituted, that every one is the Sovereign Object, the First born, and Sole heir, and End of the Kingdome; Every one the Bride of GOD, every one there a King, yet without Confusion, or Diminution, every one distinctly, enjoying all, and adding to each others fruition.

TO understand all this, and not to delight in it, is more miserable then not to understand it. To see it, without being able to enjoy it, is to pine away in a prison, from whence we see the Glory of a Palace, and repine in our misery at the Pleasures of those that are about it: To delight in these Things, without being affected with them; is impossible. Nor is there any Affection but that of Love, whereby we can enjoy them.

THE Angels see the Glory of GODS Kingdom and delight in it; the Damned see the Joys of the Blessed, and are tortured by them; the Wicked upon Earth neither see, nor are affected with them; the Saints on Earth apprehend them in part, and believe them, desire and endeavour after them; they wait with Expectation for the whole, and by certain degrees, as it were in a Glass, enjoy the Image and Reflection of them: As many as they comprehend, they actually delight in: for their love is awakened, and extended to the goodness of all they understand, which it feeds upon by meditation, and turnes into Nourishment, for the Benefit of their Souls, which are made more Great, and Strong, and Vigorous by their Fruitions. But without Love, it is easie to see, that no Goodness can be at all enjoyed.

GOD does desire Love from us, because his *Wisdom* very well knows, that without Love the World would be in vain, and the End of the Creation frustrated: his *Goodness* is diffusive and infinitly desires to communicate it self, which it cannot do, unless it be Beloved. To receive it, is the highest service we can do unto it, nothing being more agreeable to the Nature of his *Goodness*, then that it should be enjoyed. His *Blessedness* consisteth in the pleasure he taketh in the Felicity of others, and brancheth it self out into two Parts, the Pleasure of Communicating all to others, and the pleasure of receiving all from others, in the satisfaction which he taketh to see others Blessed, in the Returns of those joys and Praises, which are offered up to his Goodness and Glory. His *Glory* desires to be seen, and delighted in: To be esteemed and beloved: to be honored and admired, is natural to *Glory*, the Brightness of whose splendor is more Sensibly Pleasant in the Reflection of its face, and in the Joy that it makes in anothers Soul. His *Holiness* takes Pleasure in pure and upright Actions, of all which Love is the fountain. There is an *Objective fitness* and Excellency in Love, for which it is infinitely valued by him. It is one of the first and immediate Properties of Love to desire to be beloved, to make its object most Amiable and Beautiful, as well as Blessed; to be united to it, to have its own Goodness acknowledged, its Essence approved, its excellency desired, admired and delighted in; to see all its Actions, Appearances, Gifts and Tokens esteemed; and to feel its own Efficacy in the Grateful Acceptance it finds in the Raptures it occasions, in the flames it enkindles in anothers Soul. Now Love is the fountain of all Honour, Gratitude, Praise and Esteem: By Love the Soul is transformed into the Similitude of GOD, by love made Bright and Beautiful, all its Blessedness and Glory are founded in its Love, it is by Love it self made Communicative and Diffusive, and Great, and Rich, and as the Scripture speaketh, *fit for Delights*. All Obedience and service are founded in Love; And if a Creature, that is Beloved, must freely give up it self to anothers Pleasure, before it can shew its Love, or intirely be enjoyed; Love is of all other things in the World most fit to answer Love, because the very heart and Soul is given thereby to the Person that desires it.

LOVE is the Fountain of all Benefits and Pleasures. House, Estate, and Lands, Authority, Wealth, and Power, Life it self is consecrated and Devoted by a Lover to his Object. So that on our side all is given to GOD by Love, as well as by Love it is received from him. The Heavens and the Earth and all the Creatures are Gifts and Tokens of his Love, Men and Angels are a Present of his Love, which he hath infinitely adorned, and made endlessly serviceable to every Soul that is Beloved. All these his Love would have us to receive with a due Esteem, and therefore is it that of his Love he will have us to exercise our reason aright, and Love them as much as their Goodness deserveth. When we see and understand their Excellence, and Esteem them according to the transcendent value that appeareth in them, we adorn our selves with their fair Ideas, we enlarge and beautifie our Souls with Bright and clear Apprehensions, and which is much more, with regular and well ordered Affections, we enrich our selves, and increase our Greatness (in the fruition of his Gifts), we are lively, and pleasant, and vigorous Creatures, full of Knowledge, and Wisdome, and Goodness, and fit to offer up all these things unto him *again*, while we empty them as Helps and Advantages in that Service which we pay unto him: For our Love to himself is enkindled by these Incentives, and while we sacrifice our selves and them unto him, we delight in nothing more then to see him, that is so Great in Love and Bounty, the Author and Possessor of all His Glories.

CHAP. VIII.

Of the Excellency of Truth, as it is the Object and Cause of Vertue. The Matter and form of Vertuous Actions. That their form is infinitely more Excellent then their Matter, and the Heathen Morality infinitely defective and short of the Christian.

I do not see that *Aristotle* made the End of Vertue any other then a finite and temporal Felicity, which is infinitely short of that felicity which is here begun, and enjoyed for ever. He did not make GOD the Object and End of the Soul, and if all Acts are distinguished into their Kinds by their Objects and their Ends, those Vertues must be infinitely base, that have no other Objects or Ends, but Creatures; and those only Divine and Noble, that flow from an infinite and Eternal Original, respect an infinite and Eternal Object, rest in an Infinite and Eternal End. His Difinition of Felicity importeth all this, but his Behavior makes me to fear he did not understand it: As *Seneca* luckily hit upon that saying, *Deus me solum dedit toti mundo, totum Mundum mihi soli,* GOD gave me alone to all the World, and all the World to me alone; yet could not understand it. For had he Known what it was he said, he would have made a better use of it, and been more copious and explicite in the Illustration. An actual Respect had to infinite Obligations and Rewards, a Desire in every action to please an infinite and eternal Lover, to Glorifie a Divine and Endless Benefactor, to bring forth the fruits of infinite Benefits, and to be truely Grateful for all the Advantages of a mans Creation, that is made to have Dominion over all the World; these are higher and better Qualifications of those Vertuous Actions which Christians perform, than Heathens understood: And yet if nature were divested of its Corruption, the Natural Man, that is, no Christian, might, by the Light of Nature, be fitted to understand them. And the Truth is, I wonder much, (the World being so Beautiful and Glorious in every Eye, so really deep and valuable in Worth, so peculiarly applied to the use and service of every person;) that the Heathens did miss the fruition of it, and fail to measure them selves and their Felicity, by the Greatness of its Beauty, and the Joy which all the Creatures ought to produce in the mind of Man by their real Services. For the Earth is really better than if all its Globe were of beaten Gold, the Seas are better than if all their Abysses were full of

Diamonds, the Air is better, than if all the space between us and the Skys were full of Scepters, and the Sun alone a greater Treasure then all the wealthy Mines in the Indies: every man is surrounded with all the Light of their Advantages, and so much served by them, as if no man but himself were alive in the World. So that it is a natural and easie Investigation, even for Heathens themselves, to discern the mystery of Bliss, and to discover the misery of Humane Nature to be founded in some Disease of the Will, or Understanding: And to return from Inadvertency and Sloth, to Truth and Right Reason, which was the ready Way to true Felicity. For they Knew not the *Arcanum* or Hidden mystery of Divine Laws, nor the Excellency and Perfection of immortal Souls, which make every one a Soverain and Transcendent Creature; yet they might easily observe the miserable Effects of Eternal Solitude, and in external Services, how useful and comfortable men were ordained by Nature to be to one another.

EVERY man Loves to have many Eys fixt on his Beauty, and to have many Delightful Objects and Transactions for his own. Be the Theatre never so Magnificent, the Actions and the Actors are more Delightful to the Spectators than the Gildings, and Dead Engravings. Were all other men removed out of the World to make room for one, the empty Theatre would remain, but the Spectacle be lost, all the Cities, and Kingdoms, and Ages would be removed, with all that was lively, and rare, and Miraculous in all their Occurrences. Palaces, and Temples had been prevented, Houses and Villages, Fields and Vineyards! The World had been a Wilderness overgrown with Thorns, and Wild Beasts, and Serpents: Which now by the Labor of many hands, is reduced to the Beauty and Order of *Eden*. It is by Trades and Occupations that a man gets him Corn, and Wine, and Oyl, &c. all which he would have been without had he never seen any Company but himself; condemned to Idleness and melancholly. Vertues and Praises had been things unknown, Admiration and Honor, Love and Knowledge, the mysteries of Religion and Piety, all the speculations of Wisdom, for want of Education had been lost, at least the Sence and Exercise of these Bright and Glorious Things, for want of Conversation: Corrupted Nature being prone to afford no other fruits but Barbarism and Ignorance in that Solitary Condition. For the Powers of the Soul are improved by Tradition: and it is by the Information of others that our minds are awakened to perceive the Dignity of our own Nature, the Value of all the Creatures, and our Interest unto them.

But Religion teaches us far more, the Beginning and the End and of World, how highly we are honored, and beloved of GOD, the Manner wherein we are to converse with him, the transcendent Excellency of Souls, and the Divine Perfections of the Deity, What his Omnipresence and Eternity is, how we are to be enlarged in our Apprehensions and Desires, and prepared for infinite and Eternal fruitions; in what Quality, and Capacity, we are to live in the world, and Exercise Vertue, how we are to spend our Time, and employ our Powers on all Objects, every one as Lord of the Creation and the friend of GOD! How all Angels and Men are commanded to Love us as themselves, and by that Love to serve and delight us more, than by all other Actions and Offices whatsoever: That every Soul is a more excellent Being than the visible World, more nearly allyed to God, and more precious in it self than any Treasure whatsoever: That it is endued with Powers, Inclinations and Principles so fitly subservient and conducive to Blessedness, that any one of these is more Delightful then all inanimate Things; in the Contemplation and Enjoyment of which we may justly be lost in Wonder and Extasie. All this by the Light of Nature is asserted, but covered with so Gross a vail, that we discern it not, till it is newly revealed by the Ministery of Men. And upon all these Accounts are Men themselves, (which are generally mistaken to be Impediments) Means & Assistances of our Happy living.

BUT however familiar, and near, and easie these Great and evident Truths appear, it so happened, that the Heathen Philosophers were Blind unto them, and in the midst of their Searches after Felicity, failed of the Discovery; they became vain in their Imaginations, placing felicity in a meer Apathy, or conceited 'Auta,rkeia, a self-sufficiency, or in a brave Contempt of all misfortunes, in a forced Contentment Dark and empty, or in Sensual Pleasures, or in the Goods of fortune, either alone, or conjoyned with those of the Soul and Body, which they lamely enumerated, and knew not how to imploy; as if the Discovery of the highest and best Truths in nature, had been reserved for him that redeemed Nature, and the Plainest Truths had been appointed to honor and attend that Religion which brought supernatural Mysteries to Light, by the Preaching of the Gospel.

BY this last the Qualifications of an humble and pious Soul, a Penitent and Grateful Person, sensible (at once) of his infinite Guilt and Grandure, were introduced: Another foundation laid upon the Meritorious Death and Passion of GOD, the Son of GOD, a Second Love continued in the Deity to the miserable after an infinite forfeiture;

all the Oracles, and Visions, and Miracles, by which the Nature of Man is magnified, and Ages enlightned, the Ministry of Angels, and the Dispensations of Providence, by which the Care and Tenderness of GOD is shewn, the infinite measures and Violences of his Love, the infinite Variety and Number of Obligations, the present Advantages and Benefits, the Eternal Rewards, the Relation of GOD to Man as a Father and a friend, a Bridegroom and a King, a Light and Example, the sweetness of our Union and Communion with him, and the Gift of the Holy Ghost sent down from Heaven; all these Things which the Angels desire to look into, were by the Christian Religion (with the rest before mentioned) plainly revealed, with our victory over Death, the Resurrection of our Bodies, and Life Eternal.

IN the Light of these Circumstances the Interior form of Vertuous Acts more evidently appears. For to exercise Vertue in the Quality and Capacity of a Son of GOD, is another sort of Business, than to exercise Vertue as an ordinary Mechanick: and to do all things being clothed with a Sence of our Cœlestial Grandeur, as we are Heirs of the World, infinitely Beloved of GOD, ordained for his Throne, Delightful in the Eyes of all, Angels and Men, Beloved and honored by all the Creatures, made Partakers of the Divine Nature, intending and designing to Please all Spectators in Heaven and Earth (by the excellency of our Actions). This makes every little Deed as it were infinite within; while the *Matter* of the Action seemeth nothing; it renders the *Form* Divine and Blessed.

THE best Actions of the prophaner Heathen fell under the notion of *Dead Works*: By which name the Apostle calleth all wicked Deeds, to intimate the Privation of all that excellency that ought to be in Humane Actions. Every Deed and Thought of ours ought to be *Inspired* with Life from Heaven. The Light of the Understanding, and the vigor of the Will is the *Soul* that informes it. When it is void of Knowledge, and springs not from that series of GODS infinite Love, that ought to animate it, nor regardeth those Eternal Joys that are set before us, nor at all considers those Obligations that are laid upon us, it is bereaved of its *Vital* and *Essential* form, it is like a fair Carcase without a Soul, *unsensible* of those Interests and Concerns, that ought chiefly to be valued and promoted. And by this you may see clearly, that the Matter of a Good act falles infinitely short of that Perfection wherewith it ought to be inspired, if this *Soul,* or *Form* be wanting; which tho less visible to the Eye of flesh, is of as much greater Excellence and Importance, as the Soul in nature is above Body.

THUS when a Heathen giveth to the Poor, the matter of the Act is the very self same which a Christian man does: So is an Act of Courage, or Patience, in encountring Death; the subduing of the Appetite, and the Denial of a Lust, a piece of Justice against Interest and friendship, an Act of Prudence, Temperance, or Fidelity: In all these, if we respect the Matter of them, Heathens have acted (in a manner) as high as any Christian, and consequently appear to vulgar Apprehensions as Heroick and Stupendious. But consider the *inside*, the Heathen did it that he might satisfie his Conscience and please the GODS, that he might acquire honor and immortal fame, or please the generous Inclination of his own Soul, which delighted in Honor and Worth, or assert his own Principles, or save his friends, or preserve his Country. And doubtless these are Great and brave considerations, but they are *limited* and *finite*: and Sick of two Defects, (for the most part) that are incurable. They were Sacrifices of Obedience to false Gods, plain Idolatry, and attended with an ignorant Loftiness and Height of Mind, that confided in them: and besides this, they aspired to little more then a Glorious name in following Ages.

WHEREAS the Christian makes all Kind of Graces to meet and concentre in every Action, Wisdom, Goodness, Justice, Courage, Temperance, Prudence, Humility, Penitence, Patience, Meekness, Liberality, Cheerfulness, Gratitude, Joy in the Holy Ghost, Devotion, Piety, Faith, Hope, Charity, all Kind of Holiness; And his Action extends to all the Objects of these Graces, and includes their Causes. He remembers the infinite Obligations that are laid upon him by that Deity, which infinitely Loves him; the Benefit of the Creation, and the Glory of the Divine Image, the Guilt of the fall, and that blot and misery that lyes upon him, the Wonder of his Redemption, and the Love of Christ, his Death and Passion, the Miraculous Pains and Endeavors of GOD in all Ages, to reclaim him, the Giving of the Holy Ghost, and his holy Baptism, the New Covenant which he is in with GOD, the Height and Glory of his Place and station, the Beauty of the World, and his Dominion over all the Living Creatures, the Joy and Amity of all the Angels, the Benefit and Welfare of all his Neighbours, the Joy and Prosperity of future Ages; the Glory of GOD, the Honour of his Church, and the Propagation of Religion, the Salvation of others Souls, and the Eternal State and condition of his own, the Acquisition of a Cœlestial and Eternal Kingdom, and the Delight he taketh in an infinite Sphere of Eternal Joys, the fervent Desire he has to be Grateful to the Almighty; all these by the Light of his Divine and

Cœlestial Knowledge enter into the Act, for want of which the other work, that is wrought by an Ignorant Heathen, is in a Manner rightly called *a Work of Darkness*.

I do not speak this, as if I would discourage a Heathen from doing the Best that he is able; or condemn those reasons upon which he proceedeth in his Vertuous Deeds; No, nor as if all this were necessary to the Acceptance of an Action. But to shew how highly Christianity does ennoble the Soul of Man, how far more sublime its Principles are, and how far more perfect it makes his Actions: When they are what they may be: And withal to provoke Christians to a more Intelligent and lofty Practice of Christian Vertues, lest they differ not in their Morals from the better sort of Heathens. All these things are necessary to the perfection of an Action, tho not to its Acceptance; And GODS Omnipresence, and Power, and Wisdom, and Love ought to be considered in all places, among all Persons, upon all occasions; And the Blood of Christ, and the infinite Glory of Eternal Bliss. But that which above all I chiefly intend, is to shew what influence the great Perfection of Felicity hath upon all our Vertues: not only to stir us up to do them, but by entering their Constitution, to inspire them with their Beauty and form for their fuller Lustre, Glory and Perfection: That we may see also, how Great and Transcendent that Life must be, wherein every Act is capable of so much Majesty and Magnificence, if I may so speak, by reason of the variety of its Ends and Causes. And how abominable and absurd they are all that exclude GOD out of their Thoughts and Considerations; Who is alone the Fountain of all the Beauty in every Vertuous Deed, and the proper fulness, Cause and End of all its Perfection!

HOW Ambitious we ought to be of Knowledge, which is the Light wherein we are to adorn and compleat our selves, we may learn and collect from all that is said. It is rightly called *the Key of Knowledge*; it admits us into the spacious Recesses of every Vertue, openeth the Gate by which we enter into the Paths of Righteousness, that lead to the Temple and Palace of Bliss. Where all the Treasuries of Wisdome are exposed to the Eye of the Soul, tho hidden from the World. How Great and Amiable every Vertue is, how Great and Perfect it may be made, is only discerned by *the Eye if Knowledge*; It is by this alone that men come to discern how full of Reason Religion is, and with what Joy and Security and Sweetness it may be practised.

CHAP. IX.

Wisdom is seated in the Will, it attaineth the best of all possible Ends by the best of all possible Means.

KNOWLEDGE, how excellent soever it may be conceived, is without Wisdome like skill without Practice; which whether it be in Musick, or Painting, or in any other Art, as Government, Navigation, Preaching, Judicature, is altogether vain and fruitless, if it be not reduced into Act and Exercise. For Wisdome is that Excellent Habit of the Soul by which we chuse the most Excellent End of all those which may be Known, and actually prosecute it, by the best Means that are conducive thereunto.

TO Know the best of all possible Ends and not to embrace it, is the greatest folly in the World. To chuse and embrace it, without Endeavouring after it, is a folly contending with the other for Eminence. To chuse any means less then the best in Order thereunto, is a new piece of folly, even then when we pursue what Wisdom requires. For no less than the best of all possible Means is requisite to the Acquisition of the best of all possible Ends. And by all this we discern, that Wisdome is not a meer Speculation of Excellent Things, but a Practical Habit, by Vertue of which we actually atchieve and compleat our Happiness. For it is impossible for the best of Means (when they are well used) to fail; we may grow remiss, and suspend our Endeavor, which is another Kind of folly, and so be diverted from the best of all possible Means by some strong Temptation, or cease from using them through our own Inconstancy, or yield to some Light and easie Allurement, or be discouraged by some terrible Danger, and thus may abandon the Best of all Ends, but without some such folly it can never be lost.

POSSIBILITIES are innumerable, so that nothing less than infinite Wisdome can find out that which is absolutely the Best. But when the best of all possible Ends is by infinite Wisdome found out, it is an Easie thing for Wisdome, to discover that End to the Knowledge of others, to whom it is able to communicate it self by way of Gift and Participation.

WHAT the best of all possible Ends is, only GOD fully comprehendeth. But in General it is such, that it includeth all Kind of Goods in the highest Perfection, infinite varieties and Degrees of Possibility *turned into Act*, all Sweetness and Beauty, Empire, Dominion, and Power, all Riches, Pleasures, and Honors, Victories, and Triumphs, and Possessions, will be in it, and nothing possible or Desirable be wanting to it. GOD alone is the Best of all possible Ends, who includeth all things in himself as their Cause, and End: the Perfection of his Will is his Blessedness and Glory, and his Essence the only Means by which he can attain unto it. By himself it is that we come unto him in a manner afterward more fully to be explained. His Essence is the Best of all possible Means, by which he attains himself, and by which he is enjoyed. Our Conformity to his Essence is our Way, by a Wise Application of our Souls to that Eternal Act which is his End.

THAT Sweetness and Beauty are Attributes of the best of all possible Ends, is evident and clear: As it is also that these must be infinite in their Degree and Measure, because nothing but what is infinitely convenient, is absolutely Eligible. Now what is infinitely convenient is infinitely Sweet and Beautiful. What is infinitely Desirable is infinitely Good, because it is Agreeable to that Love wherewith every Existence intends it self, and pursues its own sublime Happiness.

IT is easie to conceive how GOD should be the End of his Creatures, but how he should really be his own End is difficult to understand: Because his Creatures are Defective, and have something besides themselves to aspire after: but GOD from all Eternity is infinitely perfect, and being all that he can be, needeth nothing that he can endeavor to attain. But if we consider the nature of Wisdome, which is a voluntary Act, we may be freed from the Despair of understanding the Mystery. For Wisdome must of necessity intend it self in its Operations, because it becometh Wisdome by doing the Best of all Excellent Things, and doth them all that it may be Wisdome, or Wise in doing them. It implies Deliberation and Freedome; being a Vertue seated in the Will and Understanding, It implies a Power of Knowing, and Chusing, and Doing all Things, it consisteth not in the Power of Knowing only, nor in [the] Power of Chusing, nor in the Power of Doing. Nothing else is Wisdome, but to chuse and do what we Know is absolutely most Excellent. Wisdome then is founded in the Act of Doing, nay it is the Act of Doing all that is Excellent. And if it be a free and voluntary Act, as it must needs be, because nothing is Wisdome, but that which guideth it self by Counsel freely, to a Known End, which it discerneth to be most Excellent, it implies an Ability to forbear, in him that is wise, by chusing to do what he might forbear. Had it forborn to

Christian Ethicks

do what is most Excellent, it had turned into folly, because it had by that means lost the most Excellent End: but by chusing to do all that was best, it became an act of Wisdome; which being most Lovely, it chiefly desired to be. And so by Chusing and Doing the most Excellent of Things, begot it self; and by it self proceeded to all its Operations, which must needs be infinite, if Wisdome be so, because any thing less would (if rested in) be infinitely Defective.

THAT Riches and Pleasures may be infinite, is evident from the Nature and extent of space, which is illimited and Endless, from the Omnipresence and Eternity of GOD, in which there is infinite Room for innumerable varieties, especially from his Wisdom and Goodness which are *Infinite Treasures*. It appears also from his Almighty Power, which is able in all Parts of his Omnipresence and Eternity, to work without any Bound or Period, without cessation at once to work in all Places of his Dominion, and throughout all his Immensity to act, and do what he will. So that in one Instant he can fill both Eternity and Time with enjoyments, Every Part and Particle of which shall be infinitely Delightful, because of the vigor of his Eternal Power in every Operation. Thus is he intirely Acting in Heaven, and Earth, and Hell, at the same time, and at all conceivable Distances beyond all Heavens ever Acting, because he is Willing, Decreeing, seeing and ruling there, and every where accomplishing his Counsel and Pleasure. His Essence and his Will are both the same, his Essence is his Act, and his Act his Pleasure.

BY exerting his Almighty Power he begot that Act, which is the Means and End of all his Endeavors. An Act of Wisdome infinite and Eternal is his Blessedness and Glory. We must take heed of conceiving GOD to be one Thing, and his Act another, for all his Wisdom and Goodness, all his Blessedness, and Life, and Glory are in the Act, by which he became the Fountain and the End of all Things. He became so freely, and yet was so by his Essence from everlasting, for Eternity is an infinite Length of Duration, altogether present in all its parts in a Stable manner. To fill one part of space with Treasures, and leave another Empty, was not Wise. Common Reason will instruct us, that it is better to have all spaces full of Delights, than some few or none And by his infinite Wisdome it is that he Knows how to enjoy, what he never needed, and to improve his Enjoyments by giving them away.

INFINITE and Eternal Wisdom does not onely imply the Possibility, but the certain Reality and Existence of Eternal Treasures. Where least you should wonder how such should be infinite, you must needs be informed that God is his own best and most perfect

Treasure. For if Treasures are by nature those precious Things, which are Means whereby we acquire our Ends, or those Things which we most Esteem, as the Sovereign Objects of our Joy; GOD is in both those respects his own *Wealth*, because his Essence is the *Means* by which he atchieveth all his ends, and the Sovereign End of all those Means which he by his Wisdom useth for his Ends. *For of him, and by him, and to him are all things*: As the Scripture witnesseth. Matter is the Dreg of Nature, and Dead without Power; Power is the Abyss of Nature, but void without act: Act is the Top and Perfection of Nature, it is the fulness of Power, the fountain and the means of all that is; for Power by transforming it self into Act, becometh an act, and by that Act produceth and perfecteth all its Works both outward and inward; so is it the Means of all its Productions: being so infinitely Simple and various together, that nothing but Power exerting it self is in the Nature of the Act by which it is exerted. All the Essence of that Act is the compleat Exertion of Eternal Power, and yet to it alone we ascribe the Original and Means of all: it is the Cause, and Means and End of it self, as well as of other Things, which for its own sake, are produced by it. For idle Power can do nothing: Meer Power is neither the Cause, nor the Means, nor the End of any thing. Power not Idle, but exerted, and throughly employed, is all Act: And this is the Cause of all its Productions, because of this Power exerting it self they spring: and the Means of all, because by this Power exerting it self, they are; and the End of all, because it did all, that it might be not *Idle*, but Power *Exerting* it self, or a Glorious Act in its full Perfection.

IT was an effect of infinite Wisdom, wherein GOD by one Act acquired himself, and all his Dominion, prepared his own, and his Creatures blessedness, made himself and all his Kingdome Glorious. But this is scarcely intelligible, because the manner of his Life is incomprehensible: we cannot tell how to conceive, what the Learned constantly affirm, that all Eternity is at one Time. All I shall observe in Order to the explaining of this Mystery, is onely this, that tho the World begins and Ends with Time, yet Eternity does immutably include Time, and the Operations of Divine Wisdom are various, and exactly fitted to their several Seasons, yet all the parts of Eternity are filled with Operations, which, tho they are one in GOD, like that of shining in the Sun, are manifold in Effects, as the Beams of the Sun in their different Works among all the Creatures.

IT is a natural Effect of infinite Wisdom to make every of its Treasures suitable to its own excellence. And that the Wisdom of

GOD has done, by making every the smallest Thing in his Kingdome infinitely serviceable in its Place, and station, for the manifesting of his Wisdom, Goodness, and Glory to the Eye of a clear Beholder. And this he hath done by making all his Kingdome one Intire Object, and every Thing in it a Part of that Whole, Relating to all the innumerable Parts, receiving a Beauty from all, & communicating a Beauty to all, even to all objects throughout all Eternity. While every one among Millions of Spectators, is endued with an Endless Understanding to see all, and enjoy all in its Relations, Beauties, and Services.

I cannot stand to enlarge on this, otherwise I might illlustrate it by a familiar Example. No single Part of a stately Monument is so Beautiful out of its Place, as it is in its Place: because if it be seen alone, it is not understood; for the Beauty that results from all, consists in Order and Symmetry, which by any division is broken to pieces. He Knoweth nothing as he ought to Know, who thinks he Knoweth any thing, without seeing its Place, and the Manner how it relateth to GOD, Angels and Men, and to all the Creatures in Earth, Heaven, and Hell, Time, and Eternity.

IT is an Act of Wisdome to prize and enjoy, what is by Wisdome prepared, and Because infinite Wisdome includeth all Wisdome, infinite Wisdome at once Knoweth, Chuseth, Doth, Esteemeth, and Enjoyeth, all that is Excellent. It is an Act of Wisdome to make ones self Good and Delightful to others, because Honor, and Peace, and Amity, are founded therein. It is infinite Wisdom to become infinitely Good and Delightful to others, and for that cause to be infinite in Bounty. For what is infinitely Good is infinitely *Glorious*. And therefore is it, that GOD needing Nothing in himself, gives all Things to others, Gives them in enjoying them, enjoys in Giving them, while his Goodness delights in the Felicity of others, and in being the Felicity of others. For by making them Great and Blessed he magnifieth himself; and by replenishing them increaseth his Treasures.

HOW little soever of this you are able to conceive, you may understand, that to be like GOD is the way to be Happy: And that if GOD hath put it in your Power to be like him, it is the extremest Madness in the World to abuse your Power, and to neglect his Treasures, but it is infinite Wisdome by the best of all possible Means to embrace and enjoy them, Because an infinite End is thereby attained, even GOD himself, who is thereby made the portion of the Soul, and its Reward forever.

THE best of all possible Means whereby we can acquire his Eternal Treasures, is to imitate GOD in our Thoughts and Actions; to exert our Powers after his Similitude, and to attain his Image, which is after GOD in *Knowledg, Righteousness,* and *true Holiness*. For by Knowing all Things, as GOD Knoweth them, we transform our Souls into an Act of Knowledge, most Bright and Glorious: By Loving all Things as GOD Loveth them, we transform our Wills into an Act of Love, which is most Sweet and Blessed. We enrich and Beautifie our selves with the Image of his Goodness, while we communicate our Souls (in our Powers) to all Objects in his whole Eternity. We magnifie our selves by magnifying Him in all his Works: We do right to our selves by doing right to GOD, and all other Things. Which for as much as we must here on Earth learn by Degrees, and can never perfectly accomplish the Work, till it is given us in Heaven, it is Wisdome to walk in the Paths of Righteousness as far as we are able, and to do those Things here, tho small and defective, which he will recompence with a Reward so perfect hereafter.

IF ever we be so happy as to come to Heaven, his Wisdome shall be our Wisdom, his Greatness our Greatness, his Blessedness our Blessedness, his Glory our Glory, All his Joys and Treasures shall be ours, his Life and Love ours, and Himself ours for evermore.

HIS Wisdome is made ours because it is the Light in which we shall see Light, and learn thereby to inherit all Things: the Exemplar and Original of our Wisdome; the Fountain and Patern of all our Joys, the Author and Inventor of all our Delights, the End and Sum of all our Desires, the Means of all our Felicity, our very Blessedness and Glory.

CHAP. X.

Of Righteousness. How Wisdome, Justice, and Right Reason are shut up in its Nature. What GOD doth, and what we acquire, by the Exercise of this Vertue.

RIGHTEOUSNESS and Wisdom are neer allyed. For to be Just towards all Objects is to render them their spiritual Due, their *Due Esteem*. It is Wisdom, because thereby we attain our End, and enjoy their Excellency. It is Right Reason, because to value all Things just as they are, rendering to them neither more nor less then they deserve, is to do Right to our selves and them, it is a Vertue, because by force thereof we attain our Happiness.

For the better understanding of this Vertue we must Know that there is a Righteousness of Apprehension, a Righteousness of Esteem, a Righteousness of Choise, and a Righteousness of Action. Righteousness of Thought is that Habit by Vertue of which we think aright; forming and framing within our selves aright Apprehensions of all Objects whatsoever. This, tho it be the First and smallest Part of Righteousness, is of Great importance; because no man can use that aright, the Nature of which he does not apprehend. He that mistakes his Hand for his Meat, will rise hungry from Table. He that mistakes a Fiddle for an Axe, will neither cut Wood well, nor make good Musick. The Misapprehension of Great and Transcendent Objects, whether visible or Spiritual, is not perhaps so Gross, but more pernicious and Destructive. He that apprehends GOD to be a Tyrant, can neither honour GOD, nor Love him, nor enjoy him. He that takes Vertues to be vices, and apprehends all the Actions of Religion unpleasant will loath and avoid them. He, that conceits Nothing in the World to be his own but this low Cottage and course diet, will think it needless to praise his Maker, and will deny himself to be happy in those narrow and Mean enjoyments. He that thinks all the Wealth is shut up in a Trunk of Gold, will little regard the Magnificence of the Heavens, the Light of the Sun, or the Beauty of the Universe.

RIGHTEOUSNESS in esteem is that Habit, by Vertue of which we value all things according as their Worth and Merit requires. It presupposes a right Apprehension of their Goodness, a clear Knowledge of all their excellencies. It is a Virtue by which we give to every thing that place in our Soul which they hold in Nature. It is wonderful both for its extent, and Value. For there is Room enough for all Objects in the esteem of the Soul, and it is by esteem that they are honored, perfected and enjoyed.

A wise man will actually Extend his Thoughts to all Objects in Heaven and Earth, for fear of losing the Pleasure they afford him, which must necessarily spring from his esteem of their excellency.

HONOUR and Esteem are neer akin. How the Creatures are honoured by esteem, needeth not to be unfolded: but how they are perfected by it, is a little Misterious. A thing is then perfected when it attains its End. Now the End for which all things were made is that they may be seen and enjoyed. They are seen that they may be esteemed, and by an intelligent and right esteem are all enjoyed. In our esteem therefore they find and attain their end, and by attaining that are consequently perfected. The Application of *Actives* to *Passives* is a mystery in Nature of very great and General Importance; In all Pleasures, Cures, and Productions. All satisfactions, Joys, and Praises are the happy off-spring of Powers and Objects well united. Both the one and the other would lie void and barren if they never met together: and when they meet their Union must be regular, wise and holy.

GOD is an Object of Mans Esteem: Which unless it were able to render him his Due and Quadrat with his Excellencies, a man could never be *Righteous* towards GOD. For that Esteem is void of Righteousness, that either exceeds, or falles short of its Object. If it becometh us *to fulfil all Righteousness*, it becometh GOD, to endue us with the Power of Esteeming all, that is Good and Excellent, according to the Worth and Value thereof. For which cause he enables us to Esteem all that we can see in Heaven and Earth, and in the Heaven of Heavens. For this Esteem is the Foundation of that choise which is the Original Spring of all excellent Actions. Even GOD himself meeteth his Honour in the esteem of our Souls. He is injured by the Sacrilegious Impiety that robs him of his Esteem; being infinitely Quick and Tender in apprehending, he is more jealous of his Honour, and more grieved when he loseth it then any other. His Wisdom and his Love are infinitly offended, when they are slighted and profaned; but pleased extreamly when they are sanctified and honored: and that they are by a just Esteem. And for this cause he hath made us able to attend him in all his Works, and in all his ways, and to have Communion with him in all his Counsels and Perfections that as our Saviour saith, *The*

Father loveth the Son, and hath given all things into his hand,[1] And again, *The Father loveth the Son, and sheweth him all things that himself doth:*[2] so we might become the Sons of GOD and see his Love and to delight in all that he hath done for us. For which cause he afterwards saith,[3] *Henceforth I call you not Servants, for the Servant Knoweth not what his Lord doth. But I have called you friends, for all Things that I have heard of my Father, I have made known unto you.*

THE Omnipresence and Eternity of GOD are so far from filling the Soul, that they fit it only to be filled with infinite Objects. For by the Indwelling of GOD all Objects are infused, and contained within. The Spiritual Room of the Mind is Transcendent to Time and Place, because all Time and Place are contained therein: There is a Room in the Knowledge for all Intelligible Objects: A Room in our Esteem for all that is worthy of our Care and Desire. I confess this Room is strange and Mysterious. It is the Greatest Miracle perhaps in Nature. For it is an infinite Sphere in a Point, an Immensity in a Centre, an Eternity in a Moment. We feel it, tho we cannot understand it.

WHATEVER we close our Eye against, we exclude out of our Knowledge. Whatsoever we Hate, we reject, tho we Know it. We give a Place in our Heart only to that, which we receive and embrace with a Kind Affection.

ETERNITY it self is an Object of Esteem, and so it is the infinity of Almighty GOD: there are infinite Causes for which they ought to be Esteemed. Our Esteem of these cannot be abridged, for upon the least substraction of the smallest Part, Infinity is lost, and so is Eternity. We must be able to esteem the utmost Extent of every Perfection of GOD, or our *Righteousness* in relation to that will be infinitely Defective. The Proportion, between our Esteem and its Object, is that wherein Righteousness is seated, if our Esteem be finite, it is utterly destroyed: for where the Object is infinite, instead of Proportion, there is infinite Disproportion.

FROM Righteousness in Esteem we proceed to Righteousness in Choice. We weigh and consider what is fittest to be valued, and what we find of greatest Esteem, we most desire. To prefer the Better above the worse is a righteous Choise; but to prefer the Worse, is abominable Impiety. The Election of GOD may be more strictly, or Generally conceived. His Election of perticular persons from the Rebellious

---

[1] Marginal gloss: Joh.3.25.
[2] Marginal gloss: Joh.5.20.
[3] Marginal gloss: Joh.15.15.

Mass of Mankind to be employed, as Ministers, in restoring the residue, is a matter of Grace; which is Arbitrary and free, is occasioned by the Accident of their General Rebellion, and his Mercy thereupon. Howbeit it is Righteous: for he does Right to himself, and to all his Creatures, and Perfections therein. For thereby notwithstanding the universal Apostasie of the World, he upholdeth and continueth his Righteous Kingdome. But the *Primitive Election* (by which, when he had considered the nature of all Possible Things, he chose the fittest and the Best) was wholy Natural. For according to the Merit of all Objects he chose them, which Merit nevertheless was to be infused by himself, in their first Creation. Whether a star were a Thing fit to be made, whether the Sun should be limited, whether his Image should be infinite, whether naked Spirits, or Bodies should be created, or Bodies and Spirits personally united: Whether Men should at first Instant be placed in Glory, or in an Estate of Trial, whether when they fell into Sin they should be redeemed or no, what Laws were most fitting under the Covenant of Works, what conditions were most proper for the Covenant of Grace; What Helps and Assistances Men should have, what Impediments and Obstacles; all these and many Millions of Objects more passed his Examination, in order to the Perfection of his Kingdome: as it did also whether he should *Create* a Kingdome or no? and look what surpassed in Esteem, as best and most Eligible, that he chose to create, and Perform. To fail in a Tittle had been an infinite fault, because had he in any one perticular preferred the Worse above the better he had contracted a Blot upon his own Wisdome and Goodness, and made the whole Creation deformed. For there is such a Love to Righteousness implanted in our Natures, that should GOD be unjust to a poor Indian beyond the Seas, we should be grieved at the Blemish, and any Blemish in him would blast our Felicity. For the Justice of the Soul is an impartial Thing, and its Severity Greatest, where its Expectation is the Highest. It is more easie with GOD to be infinitely Wise then with Man to be any thing; He may be Exact and perfect in every action with Greater Ease, then any other of his Creatures can, because he is Almighty, Omniscient, and Omnipresent: all the Advantages of his Wisdom, and Knowledge, and Goodness, and Power, would be Aggravations of his fault should he Sin against himself. The least offence would be an infinite Blot in him because committed against all Wisdome, Goodness, and Power, and a misery to us, because it would tend to the Ruine of his Creatures: The Accurate Perfection which he acquires in all his Ways, (having

to do with so many millions of Objects) becomes our infinite Joy, our
Amazement and Wonder, a Transcendent Cause of Complacency and
Adoration, it fills Eternity with Delights and Praises. The possibility
of doing otherwise, in him that is Subject to no Laws awakens our
Concernment: But the prevention of our fear, by the establishment
of our Security, supplies our contentment, he is an Absolute and free
Agent, and therefore we may fear a miscarriage in his Choise: but as
from all Eternity he hath determined himself, and is by his Essence
an Eternal Act of Wisdom and Righteousness, he secures our Felicity
and makes it more Great, because he is not imposed on by another, but
freely of himself, delights in the most Excellent things.

THIS relateth to the Righteousness of action, whereby GOD did
execute all his Decrees, and *does* Eternally. For Nothing is past, but all
things in him are immediately neer and present for ever. If you desire
further Information, concerning the Nature of Righteous Actions,
Those Actions are properly called Righteous, that are adequately fitted
to their ends and Causes. And in this respect there is in every being
under several Circumstances a several Righteousness.

THE Effect of Righteousness with men is Peace and Assurance
for ever: because Righteous men are Agreable to GOD and all his
Creatures: rightly answer all their Natures, and assist in the Harmony
of the whole Creation. It is Fruition and Blessedness, because all the
perfection and Goodness of GOD is, with his Kingdome, received into
the Soul, by the Righteous esteem of all Objects. It is the Beauty and
Glory of the Inward Man, because a voluntary Agent, that does incline
himself to such excellent Actions, is highly Amiable and Delightful to
be seen; Not only because his soul is transformed into an *Intelligible
World*, transcendent to all that is created, by the *Ideas* of GOD, and his
Works erected in the mind, but his *Affections* are framed in a living and
incomparable Order, according as every Cause and Object requires.
There is something in the Soul of a Righteous man, that fitly answers
all Obligations and Rewards, It is transformed into the Image of GOD
in such a sort, that in the *Righteous Act*, which it becomes, GOD for
ever dwelleth and appeareth.

THE Effect of Righteousness in GOD is so Great, that whereas
all Impossibles are stark naught, all things which it is possible for
GOD to do, are fair and excellent, all the Best are made actual, by the
execution of his Righteous Decree. By this the Son of GOD is in the
bosom of the Father, and the Spirit of GOD proceedeth throughout
all Eternities to his own perfection. For the Righteousness of GOD

is not like the Righteousness of Men, that may be permitted to sleep, and intermit their Operations, an Accidental Habit, distinct from their Essence, which may sometimes exist, when it doth not work; but it is Quick and Powerful, and ever in action and is indeed the Act it self which is his eternal Essence and his Son begotten of it self for ever. *For Wisdom[1] is more moving then any motion, she passeth and goeth through all things by reason of her Pureness, It is the Breath of the Power of GOD, and a pure Influence flowing from the Glory of the Almighty, the Brightness of the Everlasting Light, the unspotted Mirror of the Power of GOD, and the Image of his Goodness. Being One it can do all things, and remaining in it self, maketh all things new, and in all Ages entering into holy Souls, she maketh them Friends of GOD, and Prophets.* GODS Righteousness is the end and effect of it self. His Essence is an infinite and Eternal Act of Righteousness and Wisdome, which filleth his Kingdom with the Majesty of its Glory, and by coming into Being in a voluntary Manner giveth to all Things their Essence, and Perfection. Because it cometh into Being in a voluntary manner it is mysterious and incomprehensible.

THE Glory of this Act is derived from himself, and springeth purely from the Perfection of its pleasure. Of its Pleasure it is what it is, and as the Son of GOD is LIGHT of LIGHT, so he is Wisdome of Wisdome, Righteousness of Righteousness, Life of Life, and Goodness of Goodness. For it is infinite Wisdom that found out the Perfection of this Act, and Eternal Righteousness that first atcheived it. The Righteousness atcheived could not spring from any but Eternal Righteousness in it self atcheiving it, which is unbegotten in the Person of the Father, Begotten in the Person of the Son, and Proceeding in the Person of the Holy Ghost to all its Creatures and Operations, in its Actions, existing and abiding Perfect for ever.

IN GOD, to *Act* and to *Be*, are the same Thing. Upon the suspension of his act, his Essence would be gone; whereas our Essence may without its Act, or Operation, remain. And if his Act existeth, by Acting, his Righteousness is, and existeth of it self, and by it self compleateth its Essence forever. It is not the Power of being Righteous, but the Exertion of that Power, which is the Parent of Eternal Righteousness.

GOD, having such an infinite Delight in the Righteous Act, which *himself*, is, designed to make *us* such Righteous Acts as *himself* is. And when we perfectly do what we ought, we shall in Operation and Extent be like unto him, being *perfect, as our Father which is in Heaven is*

---

[1] Marginal gloss: *Wis.* 7.

perfect, for *we shall see as we are seen, and Know as we are Known*. In the mean time GOD hath taken care to endue us with Power, to make our perticular Actions compleatly Righteous. Every little Act we perform is a fruit & Off-spring of the whole Creation, infinite Love is delighted by it, infinite Glory and Blessedness acquired. A Creature of infinite Value is preserved, the Crown is put upon all GODS Works, and all the Spectators, Angels and Men, are Eternally pleased. For being done it is admitted into Eternity, and shall remain in its Place, and be visible for ever. *For[1] the Lord will Come, who both will bring to Light the hidden Things of Darkness, and will make manifest the Counsels of the Hearts: And then shall every man have Praise of GOD.* All that was done shall be remembred forever, and be praised and admired by the Holy Angels, Esteemed by all Saints, and Crowned with Acceptance by GOD Almighty. Which will turn to the Joy of the Righteous, because of the innate Goodness of their Souls, which moveth them to delight in nothing more then in becoming (in all their Righteous Actions) Objects of Complacency to GOD and his Creatures.

---

[1] Marginal gloss: 1.Cor.4.5.

CHAP. XI

Of Goodness Natural, Moral and Divine; its Nature described, The Benefits and Works of Goodness.

GOODNESS is a vertue of the first Estate, a Divine Perfection in GOD by which he is, and enjoys his Blessedness. In Men it is an Habit or an Act of the Soul, by force of which they Love, and delight in all that is Blessed. Tis that by which all Creatures Communicate themselves to others Benefit, all Living Creatures affect others, and delight in doing Good unto them. In GOD it is that infinite and Eternal Act from which all other Goodnesses spring, and on which they depend. The Nature of Goodness is founded in a *Convenience*, between that which is Good, and that to which it is profitable. If we consult its several Kinds, there is a *Natural* Goodness, a *Moral*, and a *Divine*.

NATURAL Goodness is the Aptitude of Corporeal Beings, to produce such profitable and healing Effects as the enjoyer desires. The Nutritive Power in Aliment, the Medicinal Vertue in Herbs, the Pleasing Quality in Perfumes, the Grateful Lustre in Precious Stones, the Comfortable Heat in fire, the Beautiful splendor in the Sun, the Refreshing Moisture in the Sea, the Reviving Nature of the Air, the solid Convenience and fertility of the Ground, all these are *Physically* Good. But this is Goodness in the meanest Degree, being no more then the natural fitness of Dead Agents that are made to act by a *Fatal* Necessity, without sence or Desire; tho their Action be answerable to the several Exigencies of other Creatures.

MORAL Goodness includeth all the Perfections of the former, and something more. For *Life* and *Liberty* enter its Existence; and it is *Wisely* exercised in *Love* and *Vertue*. A clear Understanding and a free will are the principles of those Actions that are *Morally* Good: they must flow from *Ingenuity* and *Desire*; tho the Person doing them be subject to anothers Empire, and made to give Account of his Actions. The Nature of its Excellence is very deep and retired, because it consists more in the *Principal* and *Manner* of its Operation, than the *Thing* that is *Done*; and is measured more by the *Intention*, then the *Benefit*. A mad man, or a fool, may by accident save a mans Life, or preserve an Empire, yet be far from that Goodness which is seated in the Will and Understanding. Which plainly shews, that the *Goodness* chiefly regarded is in the *Soul* of him that does any thing convenient, not in the *Benefit* received, but in the *Mind* of the Benefactor. And the Truth is that the *External Benefit*, tho it saves the Lives, and Souls, and Estates, and Liberties, and Riches, and Pleasures, and Honors, of all mankind, acts but *Physically* by a Dead or passive Application, the root of its influence and value is seated in another place, in the Soul of him whose Goodness was so Great as to sacrifice his Honor, and Felicity for the Preservation and Welfare of those whom he *intended* to save. It is seated in the *Counsel* and *Design* of the Actor. It is a hard matter to define it, but it is something like *a willing Conformity to the Interests and Affections of his fellow Creatures*, attended with a voluntary Convenience in a person Obliged and subject to Laws, to all those Obligations that are laid upon him, & to all the Rewards that are set before him, but especially to the Desires and Commands of his Superior, to whom he Naturally owes himself and desires to be pleasing. To Act upon Great and Mighty Principles, in a vigorous free and Generous Manner, for the sake of those that obliged him, and for the sake of those to whom his Kindness is shewn, increases the *Measure* of Moral Goodness: but its Perfection is seated in a Loyal Respect, and Perfect Gratitude to GOD Almighty. Who, by being infinitely Good to us, has infused and created such a Goodness in the Soul, that its principal Joy and Delight is to please him. For tho all Creatures consult themselves & their own Preservation, yet the force of Gratitude upon an Ingenuous Soul is very powerful. Moral Goodness is an Alacrity and Readiness of the Will, to sacrifice it self, upon consideration of the Benefits a Man hath received, to anothers Benefit, Enjoyment, Comfort, Satisfaction.

DIVINE Goodness is an Active and Eternal Principle, stirring up it self without Obligation or reward, to do the best and most excellent Things in an Eternal manner. It is proper only to GOD; Its Excellency is Supreme, its Beauty infinite, its Measure endless, its Nature ineffable, its Perfection unconceiveable. It hath no Cause, but it is the Cause of all other Things whatsoever. It is a *Living* and *Eternal Act* of free and undeserved Love, an indeficient Ocean of Bounty, which can never be fathomed, or (by finite Degrees be) wholy received. It is *Invisible* in its Essence, but *Apparent* in its effects; Incomprehensible, but manifest enough, to be *believed* and *adored*. It is an infinite and Eternal Essence, which is Good to it self, by being Good to all, infinitely Good to it self, by being without Bound or Measure Good to all its Objects. It is an infinite and Eternal Act, which continually ponders, and intirely intends the Welfare of others, and establishes its own (in a voluntary manner) by that intention: An Act whose Essence is seated in the Preparation of all Delights and the Communication of all its Glories. Its Felicity is Eternal and Infinite, yet seated intirely in the Felicity of others. It doth infinite Good, to all its Recipients Meerly for the sake of the Excellency of the Act of *Doing Good*. It delighteth in the Excellency of that Act, and useth all its power in doing Good, that the Act in which it delighteth might be infinitely perfect. And the perfect Act in which it finally resteth is the Goodness which all adore and desire. Its Sovereign Joy and Pleasure, is to be delightful to others. All its Creatures are Delightful to it self, only as they imitate, and receive its Goodness. Should we run into its Properties, they are innumerable and Endless; but as infinite in Beauty, as variety and greatness. It is the utmost Height of all Goodness as well as the Original, and end of all. It exceedeth Moral Goodness, as much as that exceedeth Natural, and infinitely more. In Physical Goodness there is a Mechanical fitness, and Dead convenience: but all it can pretend to, is the Benefit and Pleasure of Moral Agents. For the Sun and Moon, and Stars, and Trees, and Seas, and Minerals are made for Men. Whereas Moral Goodness is made to enjoy all Physical Goodness, that in a higher sphere it might be pleasing to GOD and is immediately subservient to his Divine & Essential Goodness.

THIS *Divine* Goodness is the first Perfection of the efficient Cause of the Worlds Creation, which of necessity derives an immediate Excellency into all the Creatures, because it is the most Communicative and active Principle that is. But the Necessity is attended with a Liberty no less then infinite. For it freely pleaseth it self in all its operations, and its Pleasure is to delight it self in the Acquisition of Felicity for others. Its freedom is a necessary Circumstance of its operation. For the Glory of its inclination and Kindness could not be, much less be seen, did it act by Necessity of Nature, Imposition, Chance or Accident. When the Act is in Being it worketh Physically, and it is no Wonder that such an Act should produce such Effects, and be so Beneficial. For when it is done it cannot be otherwise, but that such and such Effects must follow its Existence; They are as Natural as if they were Essential to it: All the Wonder is, what should determine the Liberty of the Agent at first to do such Great and Mighty Things for Others sake, and all that can be said, is his own Goodness and the Excellency of the Action. For it is not with GOD as it is with Men: few men will be at the expence of Doing, what all admire: all that receive the Benefit, applaud and delight in the Action; and so much the more by how much the more *Hazzardous*, and great, and Painful it was; but scarcely one will endure the Difficulty of an Heroick Deed for the sake of others. GOD on the contrary takes infinite Delight in the Action which all admire, and because it is infinity great and Heroick, and perfectly Divine, finds his Liberty and Ease in that Act, and is so taken with the Beauty of the Work, that his infinite Pleasure exceeds all the necessity and fate in Nature.

THAT Pleasure, which he taketh in promoting the Happiness of all Existences created and increated, is his Goodness. It is the infinite use of Perfect Liberty freely Delighted in: as Pleasant to himself as to all Intelligent Spectators and all Enjoyers. It is easie to discern that this goodness is the Foundation and Essence of his Happiness and glory.

BY it he becomes Delightful to himself, by it he becomes Delightful to others. By it he communicates all his Powers and Perfections with pleasure, and receives the Services of all the Creatures with high Satisfaction. By it he is concerned in the Joy of others, and enjoys their Blessedness. By it he is capable of all their Affections, and of the Services which his Laws require. By it all Angels and Cherubims are moved to admire and adore his Glory. By it all Creatures visible and invisible are made his Treasures. By it he is multiplied and magnified in every Soul, as the same Object is in several Mirrors, being intirely represented in every living Temple of his Eternal essence. By it he becometh his own end, and the Glorious Author, and the King of Heaven. By it he liveth a Divine and a Blessed Life, and by it he is what he is for ever. By it all the Graces, Exaltations, and Vertues of all his Creatures are made his Joys and their Persons and Praisers are Delightful to him. Of all his Laws and Decrees, and Counsels his Goodness is the fountain. It is the Original and final Cause of all our Thanksgivings. Our ease, and repose, and Satisfaction, our Bliss and enjoyment are founded in it, and caused by it. For its own Pleasure all our Delights are made exquisite in their place, and the most of them Eternal. For its own Glory it maketh all its Creatures Glorious, and prizeth its own Glory, because it is the Sovereign Delight of all its Creatures. It is every way compleat and perfect, as infinitely Convenient, as it is Great in Bounty, as Good to it self as to all others. There is no End of all its Perfection, and for that Cause it is *Incomprehensible*.

TO be made Partaker of the Divine Nature, without having the Goodness of Almighty GOD is impossible. Nor can we enjoy his Goodness, or bear the similitude of his Glory, unless we are good in like Manner. We enjoy the Goodness of GOD, and may be said to have it, either when we have its *Similitude* in our selves, or the *Pleasure* of it in others. Since the Goodness of GOD is the great Object of our Joy, its Enlargment is our Interest; and the more there are to whom he is Good, and the more he communicates his Felicity to every one the Greater Pleasures he prepares for us, and the more is our goodness therein delighted. To see innumerable Millions in Communion with him, and all of them made Glorious and Blessed, and every one seated in his throne, is the greatest Elevation of our Souls, and the highest Satisfaction in the World. When our Goodness meeteth his in all Places, and congratulates the Felicity of every person, we may then use the Words of our Saviour, because we are endued with the same *Mind* and Affection: And as he accepts all the Good that is done to his Members as done to himself, saying *Inasmuch as ye have done it to the least of these my Brethren, ye have done it to me*: Our Souls will reply, *Inasmuch as thou hast done all this to the least of these my Brethren, thou hast done it to me*, for loving our Neighbours as our selves, all Angels and Men will be our fellow Members, our Brethren, our other selves! As we delight in all Acts of Goodness for their own sakes, that are done to us, so shall we delight in all the Bounties of GOD for theirs, who are the partakers of them, and in GOD for this very reason, *Because he is good to all*. We shall be as Happy in others, as in our selves; and Esteem the Goodness of GOD our Felicity, because it hath prevented our Goodness, and done all for them, which were it undone, we should desire to do our selves. because our Goodness is a principle that carries us to delight in their perfect Felicity. Which that we may do the more Sweetly, and with more full Satisfaction and perfect Reason, his Goodness to all others is but the Perfection of Goodness to us, for they are all made Blessed for our fuller and greater Felicity.

HAD GOD withheld, or withdrawn his Goodness from all others, it had not been Greater to us, but less. The Stars are no hindrance to our Enjoyment of the Skie, but the Light and Beauty of the place which we contemplate. Were they all annihilated, the Heavens would be obscure. They do us many Services, of which we should be bereaved, by their Absence and Destruction. GOD by giving Beams and influences to them, made our Treasures more rich and fair, which are increased and multiplied by their Beauty and Number. Did the Sun shine upon us, and upon Nothing else, it would be less beneficial to us, than now it is. Its Beams that are scattered, seem to be lost; yet were they contracted upon one, his Body would be consumed, and all the rest of the World be dark about him; those Rays which fly from the Sun to the utmost parts of the World, illuminate all Objects, and from them more conveniently return to the Eye with their Beauty and Glory, which by those Rayes that are dispersed become visible and Profitable. They fall not all upon every single man, but work for him in other places, begetting Herbs, and Fruits, and Flowers, and Minerals, and Springs, and Trees, and Jewels, with all that is rich and delectable in the World for his fruition. It serves Beasts, and Fowles, and Fishes, for my sake, and for my sake does it serve even Men and Angels: That they, being more Divine and Glorious Creatures, might adorn Heaven and Earth with their Persons, which without them would be void and Empty. For we all desire to be seen, and Known, and Beloved, and for that Cause, without Living Agents, should be very Desolate and discontented.

THUS you see, if GOD had given all Eternity and Immensity to a man, if he had made no other Creatures but him alone, his Bounty had been defective: Whereas by the Creation of these he hath filled Eternity and Immensity with Treasures. All which he hath made ours by commanding them to Love us as themselves; fit to be enjoyed, and beloved by us, by filling them with his Goodness, and making them in his Image. For every one of them is to Love all his Creatures as he does, and to delight in the Beauty and Felicity of all, and to be the joy and Delight of all, as he is: And the Greater, and the Richer, and the fairer they are, the more Great and Happy are we, because they are made our Lovers and Friends, our Brides and Brethren, our Sons and Daughters, our Fathers, and our Servants, which the more Honourable and Excellent they are, the more Delightful: the more Glorious and Blessed these are, their Love is the more precious and Acceptable. True Goodness removes all Envy and Contention out of the World, and introduces nothing but Peace, and Bounty, and Joy, unspeakeable and full of Glory.

WE Love nothing more then to be Delightful to others, and to have our Glory seen is a natural Desire, which our Saviour has countenanced by his own Petition. It is our Interests, that the Eys should be innumerable, that see and admire the Glory which we had with the Father in some Sense before the World was; that they should see (I mean) how much we are Beloved of GOD from all Eternity; that there should be Millions of Blessed Persons to whom we may communicate our selves, concerns our Glory, as it doth also that, that they should be Great and Perfect, that are made to Admire and Delight in us. If we enter *Into his Eternal Glory*, as the Scripture saith, and our Bliss be individually one with his, or so perfectly like his, as is promised, it is no fault to desire Glory, for it is *Goodness* it self that desires Glory and Esteemeth all those its Best and Sovereign Treasures, that are capable of Loving and Delighting in it.

THERE is in the Goodness of GOD, and Men, and Angels, a Living Power, that is exquisitely tender in Sence and feeling, which as it feels and apprehends it self, doth also feel its Object, and apprehend both its own, and its Objects Excellences. By Vertue of which *Living Power*, it is able to delight in its own Goodness, and its Objects Glory. The Apple of its Eye is not more tenderly regarded, than the Person which it Loveth. It is afflicted in all our Afflictions, and crowned and delighted in all our Prosperities. It tendeth by its nature to the Benefit of others, and cannot endure the least Damage or Detriment to any. It infinitely hates the least Defect in it self, or in its Creatures. Nothing can be Evil to it, but what is Evil to another. Its Interests, and its Objects are so united, that it intirely lives, and sees, and feels, and enjoys, in others. All its inclination is to be doing Good, and it has no other Element than the Felicity of its Creatures. In friendship it appeareth, and from Love it proceedeth, it endeth in felicity. It hath many Great and Glorious Designes, all contending with each other for Supremacy. It cloths it self with Glory, and adornes its Essence with all Kind of Beauties. It endures all Afflictions and Hazzards, It undertakes all Labors, It builds a Palace, and provides a Kingdome for its Beloved. And yet when all is done nothing can exceed the Delight which it taketh in the Person of its Beloved. All the Honour, and Esteem, and Glory it desires, it findeth there, the Use and Value of all its Treasures consists in the Benefit they do to its Beloved. Infinite Goodness can be seated no where but in Love alone, for that onely is capable of infinite Benevolence and Complacency.

THE Liberal Soul deviseth Liberal Things, and by Liberal Things shall he stand. The more Good it doth, the more Good it is, and the more Good, the more Great and Honourable, the more Perfect and Happy. There can be no Excess in Goodness; because the more Delightful it is to its Object, and the more Divine and Glorious its Object is, the more abundant Pleasure it taketh in communicating all Felicities to its Object, & the more Great and manifold its Treasures are, the more Sweet and Precious the Things are which it giveth away, and the more its Beloved delighteth in them; by so much the more Admirable and Divine it is, its Goodness and its Blessedness are both the Greater. There is no Inconvenience which it can possibly meet, but a stop or Impediment. It cannot be hurt by it self, because its Essence is always overflowing, and the only Evil it can fear from others is the unkindness of its Object, or the Wrong that it may receive from free Agents. For Angels and Men being made free, that they may Love, and Honour, and Praise in a voluntary manner, and be, and become Good of their own Accord, (because they cannot be made *Morally* or *Divinely* Good, without the Liberty of their Concurrence, and their own Consent.) there is some fear, that they may abuse their Power, because for the more Illustrious use of it, they are left in the Hand of their own Counsel. Howbeit he has endeavoured as much as is possible, without prejudicing their Excellence, to secure their Duty; he hath infused into them the greatest Inclinations to goodness imaginable, and the Greatest principles of Honour, he hath shewn them the Glory and felicity of Goodness by his one Example, he hath commanded them by the Severest Laws that are possible to be Good, he hath founded their Peace and Pleasure in Goodness, he hath made the suspension of Goodness uncouth and unnatural, all evil Actions Dark and disagreeable, he has laid infinite Obligations upon them to exercise Goodness, and set Eternal Rewards before them. He hath made the Object unto which they must shew it extremly amiable, he hath given them all Advantages, Helps and Assistances. He hath prepared the Severest Penalties and Torments to punish the Omission of it. And for a Complement of all, will extremely be grieved, if they fail to shew it. This in the Estate of Innocency. Since the fall indeed we must be kind and Good to injurious Persons: but this is founded in his own Goodness toward us Sinners, and tho it be a difficult Work in the first Appearance, Carries us to higher and more Perfect Glory.

THAT such a Goodness as this should be, cannot be incredible to them that are acquainted with the Nature of the Universe: tho it seemeth hard at least, if not impossible to them that converse with peevish men. Being corrupt in their Understandings, they are narrow and base and servile in their Affections. They start at a shadow, and boggle at a feather. Sin hath transformed them into slaves and Cowards. They misapprehend the Nature of their Duty like *Fools*; that were made to be great and Mighty as *Kings*. They think they shall be undone, if they become too Great and Good: they fear they shall grow weak and Contemptible by Goodness: whereas nothing makes them so Amiable and Glorious as Excess of Goodness.

TO shew that there is such a Goodness as that, which infinitely delights in powring out its Glory upon all Creatures, the Sun was made: Which continues Night and Day powring out its Streams of Light and Heat upon all Ages, yet is as Glorious this day as it was the first Moment of its Creation. To shew this the Stars were made, that shine in their Watches and Glitter in their Motions only to serve us. The Moon was made to shew this Goodness, which runs her race for ever to serve us. The Earth was made to support us, Springs and Rivers expend their Streams to revive us. Fruits, and Flowers, and Herbs, and Trees delight us. All corruptible Things wast and consume away, that they may sacrifice their Essence to our Benefit. For if they were made Stiffe and unalterable they could not feed us, nor communicate their Essence and Perfection to us. The Emanations and Effusions of Minerals are unknown, but that of Spices and Odours is well understood. And if these by Disbursing their proper sweetness, become more sweet and enlarge themselves, if they are made Bright and fair for our sake, if they enjoy any Light and Pleasure in their Service, as the Sun and Stars do, as Herbs and Flowers do, as Beasts, and Birds, and Fishes do; the Goodness of the Creator is abundantly more clear and apparent herein, for in all those Creatures that perfect themselves by the Service which they do, the Service it self is a sufficient Recompence: while those upon which we feed, being more Corruptible, are exalted in their Beings, by being turned into ours. And the Trade of Bees, in the Hony they make for us, and the Warmth of sheep, in the fleeces they bear for us, the Comfort of Birds in the feathers they wear, and the Nests they build for us, and the pleasures of Beasts in the off-spring they beget and bring up for us, these things shew that *GOD is Good to all, and that his mercy is over all his Works.* And if any perish in our Service, the Bloody Characters of his Love and Goodness are the more Stupendious. All Nature is sacrificed to our Welfare, and all that we have *By pure Nature* to do (till Sin marres all) is to admire and enjoy that Goodness,[1] to the Delight of which we sacrifice our selves in our own Complacency. And in real truth, if it be a great Wonder that any Goodness should be thus infinite, the Goodness of all other Things without that Goodness, is a far Greater. If it be Wonderful, admire and adore it.

---

[1] Marginal gloss: *Note, All this is spoken for Encouragement and Imitation.*

CHAP. XII

Of Holiness: Its Nature, Violence, and Pleasure. Its Beauty consisteth in the infinite Love of Righteousness and Perfection.

THE infinite Love of his own Goodness is the Holiness of GOD. There are infinite Pleasures and perfections in its Nature, that Merit an infinite Esteem and Desire. His Goodness is all Beauty, and his Holiness all Fire and flame in pursuing it. His Holiness is all Beauty, and his Goodness all Fire and flame to enkindle it. The infinite Excess of his Eternal Goodness is its own Holiness, and the Beauty of Holiness is Excess of Goodness. For if Righteousness and Holiness be well distinguished, Righteousness is that Vertue by which GOD doth apprehend, affect and Esteem all Excellent Things according to their value, and chuse and do always the Best and most Excellent: Holiness is the Love which he beareth to his own Righteousness: Which being infinite, makes him infinitely enflamed with the Love of the most perfect Actions; and carries him with an infinite Ardor to the performance of them. For tho it be a Righteous Thing to esteem the Righteousness of GOD in an infinite manner, yet there is as much difference between Righteousness and the Love of Righteousness, as between an Object and the Affection embracing it. Tho here also the Affection & the Object are the same Thing: For this Holy Esteem and Love of Righteousness is Righteousness it self: for it does but render Righteousness its due, tho the Affection be infinite which it bears unto it.

HOLINESS (if it be strictly defined) is that Vertue in GOD, by which he Loveth the most Perfect Things, and infinitely delighteth in them. For by Vertue of this Affection he shunneth and hateth all that is profane, pursuing and delighting in all that is Holy. For the Object of Holiness may be Holy, as well as the Affection, Whereupon it followeth, that Holiness is of two kinds, either the Holiness of the Affection, or the Holiness of the Object. They bear a Relation to each other, yet are absolute Perfections in themselves. For the Hatred of all Defects, Imperfections, Blemishes and Errors is a Glorious thing in it self, yet relates to the Perfection of those Objects from which it would remove those odious Imperfections. The Perfection of all Objects when they are free from all Blemishes is a Glorious Thing in it self too, yet is Acceptable to that Affection, that desires to see a Compleatness and

Perfection in every Object. And all is resolved into the same Goodness of which we have been speaking.

FOR infinite Goodness must needs desire with an infinite violence, that all Goodness should be compleat and Perfect: and that Desire, which makes to the Perfection of all Goodness, must infinitely avoid every slur and Miscarriage as unclean: and infinitely aim at every Grace and Beauty, that tends to make the Object infinitely perfect, which it would enjoy. It cannot desire less then infinite Perfection, nor less then hate all Imperfection, in an infinite Manner. All Objects are made, and Sanctified by the Holiness of GOD. It is the measure and strength and Perfection of Goodness.

THE Holiness of GOD is sometimes, called in his Oracle, *The Beauty of Holiness*. As if all the Beauty of GOD were in this. It extends to all Objects in Heaven and Earth, from the Highest to the Lowest, from the Greatest to the Meanest, from the most Pure to the most profane, with a Goodness and Wisdom so infinitely perfect disposing all, that some way or other every Thing might answer its infinite Affection. It infinitely hates all that is Bad, and as infinitely desires to Correct the same. The Influence of that Affection, by which GOD abhorreth the least Spot in his Kingdome, reaches to the Perfection of every Object, and is [the] real & proper fountain of all the Perfection of Life & Glory. And for this Cause in all Probability, do the Angels so continually cry, *Holy, Holy, Holy, Lord GOD of Hosts*; because the Brightness of his Infinite Glory and Perfection appeareth in his *Holiness*, the violence of his Eternal Love, and the Excess of Goodness. It may be, also because all the Heights of Created Perfection owe themselves to this Holiness, all the Raptures and Extasies of Heaven depending on the Zeal wherewith GOD is carried to perfect Blessedness. All which are occasioned by those pure and Quintessential Joys, those most sublime and Perfect Beauties, which they see and feel every where effected by the irresistible Strength of that Eternal *Ardor*.

SINS of Omission have an unknown Guilt and Demerit in them. They unsensibly bereave us of infinite Beauty. To let alone that Perfection which might have been infinite, to pass by, or neglect it, to exert Almighty Power in a remiss and lazy manner, is infinitely Base and Dishonourable, and therefore unclean because so Odious and Distastful. *Lukewarmness* is Profane, as well as *Malice*. And it hath pleased GOD to brand it with a worse and more fatal Censure. No folly or iniquity can dwell with him; Omission is both. To be hated is to be rejected; but to be beloved Lukewarmly is to be embraced with polluted and filthy Armes. And for this Cause, the fire of his Jealousie burns most *devouringly* about the Altar. He will be sanctified in all them that draw nigh unto him, and but to touch his Ark irregularly, is to be consumed. Nor is this any other then a concomitant of his Holiness, and an evident Testimony of his Love to perfection, For it First shews, that on his own Part, he maketh our Powers Perfect, that we may be able to see and adore him worthily; and next that he delights in no Adoration but the most Worthy. It moreover shews that he infinitely delights in the Perfection of his own Actions, for otherwise he would not be so severe against the Imperfection of ours.

NOR is the reason of his Love to the utmost Perfection less then infinite: You Know that all impure Things upon Earth are dull and Obscure; as Vile in Esteem, as Base and faint in their Operations. Neither will a Lump of Dirt shine like the Sun, nor a Mudwall be Resplendent like polisht Marble. All Glorious Things have a Height of *Intenseness* in them; and owe most of their Beauty to the Motion of their Strength and Activity. But GOD is a more High and Necessary Thing than these. Perfection is his Essence, and he could not be himself upon any Abatement. It is a great Wonder! But the smallest Thing in the world may spare somewhat of it self rather than that which is infinite. Upon the least substraction, that which is infinite is made finite, and the Loss is infinite. We cannot be at all Beloved by Almighty GOD unless we are infinitely Beloved. For to Love and neglect us at the same time is impossible, and to be able to do infinite Things for us, and yet to do but some of them, is to Love and neglect us at the same time. Tis Love in what it does, & neglect in what it leaveth undone. The Reason why it is our duty to Love him infinitely, is because he infinitely Loved us. Did he not exert all his Power himself, he would never command us to exert ours. The Love of all Perfection is his Essence and must be infinite for its own Perfection. The least flaw in a Diamond abates its Price: one Tooth awry, or wanting in a Clock, doth make it useless. *Dead flies corrupt the Apothecaries Oyntment, so doth a little folly him that is in Reputation for Wisdome and Honour.* The Greater his Reputation and Wisdome is, the more Grievous a Disparagement is any Stain. Nor is GOD above these Rules, for his Essence it self is the [Rule] of ours: and the Higher his Divinity is the more Exquisite is its *Care* of its own Perfection. There is no Danger of being Severe in our Expectations, for GOD does infinitely hate any Defect in himself, more then we, tho we infinitely hate it; and enjoys himself only as he is an Object Worthy of his own infinite Love and Honour.

FROM GODS Love of Righteous Action it proceedeth, that he made ours so compleatly capable of becoming Righteous, and that he adventured a Power into our Hands of offending. It is a strange thing, that the Excess of the Hatred of all Sin should make Sin possible, and that the most perfect Righteousness should be the Accidental Cause of Unrighteousness. But yet it is so, an infinite Love to the Best of all Possible Things made the worst of all things that could be possible, excepting those that are impossible, which yet we need not except.

TO read these Riddles aright, you must understand, that even *Impossibles* themselves are conceiveable Things, and may be compared with *Possible*, and *Actual*. That the Highest and Best of all that are Possible, are the most Easie with GOD, and most near to his Nature; that inferior Possibles are more remote, and only thought on in the second place; that Things Impossible are the worst of *Evils*, and Things Actual the *Best* of GOODS. For nothing is impossible but that GOD should lye, or Dishonour, or displease, or deny himself, or abuse his Power, or suspend his Goodness, or injure his Creatures, or do some such thing, which is contrary to his Nature, yet very conceiveable, because he is a free Agent; and has a kind of Power, were it not prevented by his Eternal Act, whereby he is able to do these Impossible things. Nothing is Eternally Actual, but the Goodness, and Wisdome, and Holiness of GOD, or some such Thing; as his Righteousness, and Blessedness, and Perfection. All which spring from his Will, and are Eternally his pleasure, as well as his Essence. In the idle Power of being, and doing all Excellent Things, there is much Hazzard and danger; but he freely and voluntarily became all these from all Eternity. He wrought all Righteousness, and Wisdom, and Goodness from everlasting, and by so doing became the fountain of all that is Glorious from all Eternity. The Worst of all *Possible* Evils are the Sins of Men: Which have an infinite Demerit and Vileness in them, yet are truely possible. And the reason of their Possibility is thus accounted. Impossible, which are worst of all, are Sins in GOD.

TO make Creatures infinitely free and leave them to their Liberty is one of the Best of all Possible Things; and so necessary that no Kingdome of Righteousness could be without it. For in every Kingdome there are subjects capable of Laws, and Rewards, and Punishments. And these must be free Agents. There is no Kingdome of Stones nor of Trees, nor of Stars; only a Kingdome of Men and Angels. Who were they divested of their Liberty would be reduced to .the Estate of Stones and Trees; neither capable of Righteous Actions, nor able to Honor, or to Love, or praise; without which Operations all inferior Creatures and meer Natural Agents would be totally Useless. So that all the Glory of the World depends on the Liberty of Men and Angels: and therefore GOD gave it to them, because he delighted in the Perfection of his Creatures: tho he very well knew there would be the Hazzard of their abusing it, (and of Sin in that abuse) when they had received it. The abuse of it he infinitely hated yet could not prevent it, without being Guilty of a Greater Evil. He infinitely hated it, because those Actions of Love and Honor which should spring from the right use of it, were the onely fair off-spring, for the sake of which the whole World was made, and without the right use of their Liberty all Creatures, Angels and Souls would be in vain: he could not Prevent it without being himself Guilty of what in them he abhorred.

FOR himself to be Guilty, was the worst of Evils, and absolutely impossible. Twas better let them make their Power vain themselves, then do so himself. For the Author of that vanity, be it who it will, is the Author of the Sin. If *they* would make it vain, *He* could not help it, for him to divest them of the use of Liberty after he had given it, was as inconsistent with himself, as it was with their Beauty to abuse it: the Act of giving it by taking it away being made vain. He infinitely hated that the Liberty should be frustrated, which he gave unto men, for their more perfect Glory: he laid all Obligations upon them to use it well, and deterred them (as much as was possible) from abusing it, but would not transfer their fault upon himself, because he fore saw they were about to do it; which he certainly had done, had he made their Power vain *himself*, after he had given it. Either to refuse to give the Power, or Having given it, to interpose and determine it without their Consent, was alike detrimental to the whole Creation. For indeed it is impossible, that he by determining their Wills, should make them the Authors of Righteous Actions, which of all things in the World he most desired. There is as much Difference between a Willing Act of the Soul it self, and an Action forced on the Will, determined by another, as there is between a man that is dragged to the Altar, whether he will or no, and the man that comes with all his Heart with musick and Dancing to offer sacrifice. There is Joy, and Honour, and Love in the one, fear and constraint, and shame in the other. That GOD should not be able to deserve our Love, unless he himself made us to Love him by violence, is the Greatest Dishonour to him in the World: Nor is it any Glory or Reputation for us, who are such sorry Stewards, that we cannot be entrusted with a little Liberty, but we must needs abuse it.

GOD adventured the possibility of sinning into our hands, which he infinitely hated, that he might have the Possibility of Righteous Actions, which he infinitely Loved. Being a voluntary and free Agent, he did without any Constraint Love and desire all that was most high and Supreamly Excellent of all Objects that are possible to be thought on, his own Essence which is a *Righteous Act* is the Best: and the Righteous Acts of Saints and Angels are the Highest and Best next that which Creatures could perform: The very utmost Excellence of the most noble Created Beings, consisted in Actions of piety freely wrought: which GOD so Loved, that for their sake alone, he made Angels and Souls, and all Worlds. These Righteous Actions he so Loved, that for their sake he prepared infinite Rewards and Punishments. All the Business of his Laws and Obligations are these *Righteous Actions*. That we might do these in a Righteous Manner he placed us in a mean Estate of Liberty and Tryal, not like that of Liberty in *Heaven* where the Object will determine our Wills by its Amiableness, but in the Liberty of *Eden*, where we had absolute Power to do as we pleased, and might determine our Wills our selves infinitely, desiring and Delighting in the Righteous use of it, hating and avoiding by infinite Cautions and Provisions all the unjust Actions that could spring from it. If we Love Righteous Actions as he does, and are holy as he is holy, in all manner of Wisdome and Righteousness; then shall we delight in all Righteous Actions as he doth, shall Love Vertue and Wisdome as he doth, and prefer the Works of Piety and Holiness above all the Miracles, Crowns and Scepters in the World, every Righteous and Holy Deed will be as pleasing to us, as it is to him: all Angels and Men will be as so many Trees of Righteousness bearing the fruit of Good Works, on which we shall feast in Communion with GOD; Or if our Righteous Souls be vexed, as *Lots* Soul in *Sodom* was, in seeing and hearing the unlawful Deeds of the wicked, they shall be recreated and revived with the sight of GODS most Righteous Judgments, and with the Beauty of his holy Ways, by which he rectifies the Malignity of the Wicked, overcomes the evil of their Deeds, and turnes all the vices of men into his own Glory, and ours, in the Kingdome of Heaven. The Delights of Wisdome, and Righteousness, and Holiness are suitable to their Nature as those of Goodness are to the nature of Goodness: Which no man can enjoy, but he that is qualified for them, by the Principles of Goodness and Holiness implanted in his Nature. For as he that has no Eys, wanteth all the Pleasures of sight, so he that has no Knowledge wanteth all the pleasures of Knowledge, he that is void of Holiness, is void of the Sence which Holiness inspires, and he that is without Goodness must needs be without the Pleasures of Goodness, for he cannot delight in the Goodness of GOD towards other Creatures. To be Good, to be Holy, to be Righteous is freely to delight in Excellent Actions, which unless we do of our own Accord no External Power whatsoever can make us, Good, or Holy, or Righteous: because no force of External Power can make us free; whatever it is that invades our Liberty, destroys it. GOD therefore may be infinitely Holy, and infinitely desire our Righteous Actions, tho he doth not intermeddle with our Liberty, but leaves us to our selves; having no Reserve but his Justice to punish our offences.

CHAP. XIII.

Of Justice in General, and Particular. The Great Good it doth in Empires and Kingdoms, a Token of the more retired Good it doth in the Soul. Its several Kinds. That GODS Punitive Justice Springs from his Goodness.

THO following the common Course of Moralists, in our Distribution of Vertues, we have seated *Justice* among the Cardinal *Moral*; yet upon second Thoughts we find reason to reduce it to the number of *Divine* Vertues, because upon a more neer and particular Inspection, we find it to be one of the Perfections of GOD, and under that notion shall discover its Excellence far more compleatly, then if we did contemplate its Nature, as it is limited and bounded among the Actions of Men.

THE Universal Justice of Angels and Men regards all Moral Actions and Vertues whatever: It is that Vertue by which we yield Obedience to all righteous and Holy Laws, upon the Account of the Obligations that lye upon us, for the Publick Welfare of the whole World. Because we Love to do that which is Right, and desire the fruition of Eternal Rewards. There is much Wisdom and Goodness, as well as Courage and Prudence necessary to the Exercise of this Vertue, and as much need of Temperance in it, as any. For he that will be thus just must of necessity be Heroical, in despising all Pleasure and Allurements that may soften his Spirit, all fears and dangers that may discourage and divert him, all inferior Obligations and Concernes that may intangle and ensnare him, he must trample under foot all his Relations and friends and particular Affections so far as they incline him to partiality and sloth; he must be endued with Great Wisdom to discern his End, great Constancy to pursue it, great Prudence to see into Temptations and Impediments, and to lay hold on all Advantages and Means that may be improved, he must have a Great Activity and Vigor in using them, a Lively sense of his Obligations, a transcendent Love to GOD and felicity, a mighty Patience and Long-suffering, because his Enemies are many, his Condition low, his Mark afar off, his Business manifold, his Life tho short in it self, yet long to him, his undertaking Weighty, and his nature corrupted.

THEY otherwise define Justice to be that Vertue by which we render unto all their Due. Which is of large Extent if the Apostles

Commentary comes in for Explication, *For this Cause pay you Tribute also, for they are GODS Ministers attending continually on this very thing: Render therefore to all their Dues, Tribute to whom Tribute is Due, .Custom to whom Custom, Fear to whom Fear, Honour to whom Honour: Owe no man any thing, but to Love one another for he that Loveth another hath fulfilled the Law*. Kings, and Magistrates, and Ministers, and Parents, and Children, must have all their *Due*, and so must GOD, Blessed for ever: Adoration, to whom Adoration is due, and Obedience, to whom Obedience. In strict Justice we must render Hatred to whom Hatred is Due, and Love to whom Love. Hope is due to certain Grounds of Encouragement, and Sorrow to certain sorrowful Objects. But all our Passions must still be guided by the Rule of the Law, and all our Actions as Honour and Equity require.

PARTICULAR Justice is conversant in the Distribution of Rewards and Punishments, or else it observes the Rules of Equity and Reason in Buying and Selling. It is called particular, because the Exercise of it is not allotted to all, the Power of rendring Rewards and Punishments being committed to a few, namely to the Magistrates: and among Private persons many not at all accustomed to Buying and Selling. This Vertue, being to be exercised by some particular men, is particular Justice. However it has occasioned a Distinction in the Thing, whereby *Justice* is divided into *Distributive* and *Commutative*: the one being used in Courts of Judicature, the other in the Market.

IT was a notable Observation of *Plato*, that by reason of our Dim Eyes we are not able to see immediately what Vertue does in Secret in the Soul. And therefore he says, that as an Old man that is blear-ey'd if he hath something given him to read in little Characters, finds it necessary first to see the same in Capital Letters; so to observe first what Vertue doth in a Commonwealth, is expedient to him, that would understand what it doth in his own Soul. The Throne is upholden by Justice, the Majesty of Kings, and the Glory of Kingdomes is preserved by Justice. When Vertue is rewarded, and Vice supprest, the City flourisheth, as the Laws are the Rampart of Mens Estates, Justice is the Rampart of the Law, the Guardian Angels of every family, State and Kingdome. Kings and Counsellors, and Priests, and Soldiers, and Tradesmen, have all their several Office, and proper Duty in a Kingdome: and that Nation is blessed (with order and Beauty) where every one contains himself in his proper Duty. But where Tradesmen invade the Priests office and defile the Altar, the Soldiers turn Counsellors, and every Consellor deposes the King, nothing but Confusion can follow in such a State. The Senses and Members of the Body are like Tradesmen, they traffick with sensible Objects, the Irascible passions of the Soul are Soldiers, and very apt to rebel and Mutiny; the Conscience is the Priest in the Temple of the Mind; Right Reason is the King, and the Concupiscible Affections or smoother Passions, especially *Avarice* and *Ambition* may pass for Counsellors. They may do well to put a man in mind of his Interest, but when they depose Right Reason, and usurp the Throne, Ruine must follow in the Soul, the Passions will turn Counsellors, the Tradesmen invade the Temple, and all Rights (Sacred and Profane) be blended together. To sell offices of Trust and Places of Judicature, is for a King to do that himself which Rebels attempt in violence; to put unworthy men in places of Trust promiscuously, that will sell Justice by Retail, as they bought it by Whole Sale. Justice is a Severe Vertue, and will keep up all the Faculties of the Soul upon hard Duty. For otherwise it would not pay to Felicity its Due: But where its Care is remiss in taking an Account, and solid Goods are barterd away to counterfeit false Commodities, the Soul will grow loose and poor in a moment: All its Powers subordinate and Superior will forget their Duty, and the Healthy Estate of the Mind fall into Anarchy and Confusion. All its Hopes and Felicities will be lost, for want of that Justice which Distributes to every Power its proper office.

THERE are two passages that I mightily desire to be imprinted in the Memory of all the World: and they are both of our Saviour. The one is, *He that is faithful in a little, shall be Ruler over much:* The other is this, *Who then is that faithful and Wise Servant, whom his Lord hath made Ruler over his Houshold, to give them meat in due season: Blessed is that Servant, whom his Lord when he cometh shall find so doing. He that is faithful in a little, is faithful also in much.* To be Just in a little Silver and Gold, and accurate in deciding Causes between a Man and his Neighbour, are Actions that in their own Nature seem to have little tendency to Bliss and Glory. But when we consider that we are Servants for a time, entrusted by a Lord, that will come and examine what we have done, we are not to measure our Hopes by those little Acts, as they determine in a Moment, but in relation to the Recompences which our Lord will give when he cometh. For our Saviour hath added, *Blessed is that Seruant &c. Verily I say unto you that he shall make him Ruler over all his Goods. But and if that evil Servant shall say in his Heart my Lord delayeth his Coming; and shall begin to smite his fellow Servants, and to eat and drink with the Drunken, the Lord of that Servant shall come in a day when he looketh not for him, and in an hour that he is not ware of, and shall cut him asunder, and appoint him his portion with Hypocrites, there shall be Weeping and gnashing of Teeth.*

IF GOD should be loose and careless in his Kingdome, as it is infinitely Greater then all other Dominions, so would it quickly be more full of confusions: Especially Since the King would then himself be so loose and Careless. For Licence and profaness are of a spreading Nature, and such as the King is, such is the people. The vices of Kings do always punish themselves in the Imitation of their subjects, especially where the Distinction between Profane and Holy is lost, and there is no Hope and Fear of Punishments or Rewards. If GOD should declare it by any Act of his, to be a Thing indifferent whether men did well or ill; it would mightily abate the Rectitude of his nature, and Eclipse his Majesty. His Sovereignty would be slighted, and his Will despised, which ought infinitely to be dreaded. While Justice is infinite and there is an infinite difference put between Good and Evil, his Creatures we see are apt to abuse their Liberty, and Rebel, and become Apostates; tho they have an infinite pleasure to aspire after, and an infinite destruction, or Wrath to fear. What would they do, if the Divine Will were feeble and remiss, and exacted no reverence to its Law and Pleasure? It is the Height and Glory of GOD, that he sets an infinite Rate upon Excellent Deeds, and infinitely detests and abhors the Wicked. Their last ends are not more distant then their first Beginnings; in his Esteem, and Displeasure. Because he is infinitely Offended and displeased at Evil Deeds, he guards and fortifies his Law, deterres men from displeasing him by the fear of infinite Punishments; Encourages men to please him by proposing infinite Rewards, and the Truth is the infinite Approbation and Esteem which he hath for Wise and Holy Deeds, produceth a Delight and Complacency in them, which is the principal Part of the Reward. Nothing is more honourable then to be Praised and honoured by the King of Kings; The infinite Hatred of Evil Deeds is the very Torment it self, that afflicts the Wicked. Tis but to see how much we are hated of GOD, and how base the Action is, no other fire is needful to Hell: The Devils chiefest Hell is in the Conscience. They are obdurate and feared that cannot discern and feel the Wound which they inflict on themselves, who grieve and offend their Creator. It is easie to see, the Necessity of that Justice which springs from Holiness, and that GOD could not be infinitely Holy, were he not infinitely Just in like manner.

THAT his *Punitive Justice* springs from his Goodness, is next to be observed. He punishes them that are hurtfull to others. He is most severe in pleading the Cause of the Fatherless and the Widow. Himself is persecuted when his Saints are molested: and the faults for which the untoward servant was punished, are particularly those of *beating his fellow Servants*. A good man by how much the more tender and compassionate he is, by so much the more is he provoked at any gross Affront or abuse of the Innocent. Every soul is the Bride of GOD: and his own infinite Goodness, which deserves infinite Love, is infinitely Beloved by him. He infinitely tenders it and avoids its least Displeasure: but its Displeasure is infinite at every Sin, and consequently his Anger, when such a Sovereign Beauty as his infinite Goodness, is offended by it.

THE foundation of his Righteous Kingdome, and of the Room prepared for his Eternal Justice to Act in, is infinitely deeper, and must in other Discourses more full and copious (on that Theme) be shewn. And to those we refer you. All we shall observe here is, that this Punitive Justice being GODS infinite Zeal whereby he vindicates his abused Goodness: His goodness must of necessity proceed it, and be abused, before he can be Angry, and before his Anger can be accounted Justice. His Dominion is infinite, but cannot be Arbitrary (in a loose Construction) because it is infinitely *Divine* and Glorious.

CHAP. XIV.

Of Mercy, The indelible Stain and Guilt of Sin. Of the Kingdom which GOD recovered by Mercy, The transcendent Nature of that Duty, with its Effects and Benefits.

SUCH is the infinite Justice of God, and the Severity of his Displeasure at Sin, his Holiness so Pure, and his Nature so irreconcilable, his Hatred so real and infinite against it, that when a Sin is committed, his Soul is alienated from the Author of the Crime, and his infinite Displeasure will ever see the Obliquity, and ever loath the Deformity therein.

THE Person of a man is concerned, in (and always represented in the Glass of) his Action. Union between him and his Deeds is Marvellous. Tis so close, that his Soul it self is hated or Beloved in his Actions. As long as it appeareth in that deed which is Odious and Deformed, he can never be Beloved.

HOW slight soever our Thoughts of Sin are, the least Sin is of infinite Demerit, because it breaketh the Union between God and the Soul, bereaveth him of his Desire, blasteth his Image, corrupteth the Nature of the Soul, is committed against infinite Goodness and Majesty, being as the Scripture speaketh *Exceeding sinful*, because it is committed against infinite Obligations and Rewards, displeasing to all the Glorious Angels, abominable to all the Wise and Holy, utterly against all the Rules of Reason, and infinitely Opposite to the Holiness [of] God, who is of purer Eys then to behold the least Iniquity. So that unless there be some way found out to deliver the Soul from the Guilt of Sin, to blot out the Act and to purifie it from the Stain, there can be no Reconciliation between GOD and a Sinner. That an offence so infinite should be Eternally punished, is the most reasonable thing in the World.

NOTHING but infinite power and Wisdome is able to wash away Leprosie of guilt, and to restore the Soul to its former Beauty and Perfection. Without which all Pardon is vain, and the Soul dishonourable, and sick unto Death, as long as the shame and Confusion of its Guilt does lie upon it. Which cannot be removed by feeble Tears, nor by Acts of Indignation against our selves, nor by any Penitence or Sorrow of ours. For if these could prevail, the Divels might repent, and be cleared of their Trespasses; long agoe.

THAT no Law of Works can justifie Sinners is evident enough from that of the Apostle, *For if there had been a Law given which could have given Life, verily Righteousness should have been by the Law.*[1] GOD was not so prodigal, as without an infinite Cause to expend the Blood of his Son. And the principal Cause for which he came, was that he might *be made a Curse* and *Sin* for us, that we might be delivered from the Curse of the Law, and be made *the Righteousness of GOD in him.*[2]

THE reason why the Devils cannot be saved, is because the Son of GOD *took not upon him the Nature of Angels, but the seed of Abraham.* And there is no other name given under Heaven among men whereby we may be saved, but only the name of Jesus, who offered up himself a sacrifice for us, that he might purifie to himself a peculiar People Zealous of Good Work. He pacified the Wrath of God by his Death, and satisfied his Justice in our nature, and washed us in his Blood, and made us Kings and Priests unto GOD. To him be Glory and Dominion forever. Amen.

IT was the Design of Christ, and it became the Mercy of GOD in our redemption, to take away all the filth and Deformity of Guilt, in which the Perfection of his Love and Power appeareth. *Even as Christ also Loved his Church, and gave himself for it, that he might Sanctifie and cleanse it with the washing of Water, by the Word, That he might present it to himself a Glorious Church, not having Spot, or Wrinkle, or any such thing, but that it might be holy and without Blemish.*[3] For the Church of GOD being his *Bride*, and we *Members of his Body, and of his Flesh, and of his Bones*;[4] it was meet that we should be restored to the Perfection of Beauty, and if not recover the same, enjoy a Better Righteousness than we had before.

THE Light of Nature could discover nothing of all this, and therefore it was taught by Revelations, and Miracles, and Oracles from Heaven.

AS all things before his fall were subservient to mans Glory and blessedness, so all things after his fall became opposite to him; all creatures up braided him with his Guilt, every thing aggravated his Sin and increased his Damnation. The glory and Blessedness which he lost was his Torment, the Honour which he had before, was turned into shame; the Love of GOD which he had offended, increased his

---

[1] Marginal gloss: *Gal.* 3.21.
[2] Marginal gloss: 2 Cor. 5.21.
[3] Marginal gloss: Eph. 5.25, 26,27.
[4] Marginal gloss: Eph. 5.30.

Guilt, Eternity was a Horror to him, his Conscience a Tormentor, and his Life a Burden; Nothing but shame and Despair could follow his Sin, the Light of nature it selfe condemned him, and all that he could see was, that he was deformed, and hated of God. For that of the Psalmist is an Eternal verity, *Thou[1] art not a GOD that hath pleasure in Wickedness, neither shall Evil dwell with thee: The Foolish shall not stand in thy sight, thou hatest all Workers of iniquity: Thou shalt destroy them that speak leasing: The Lord will abhor the Bloody and Deceitful man.*

THE Express Declaration of GOD assured *Adam*, that his Recovery was impossible, *In the Day that thou eatest thereof thou shalt die the Death.* For not being able to dive into the Secret Reservation, which depended absolutely upon Gods holy Will and pleasure, as an Act of Sovereignty above the Tenor of the Law, all that he could see was, that he must *die the Death*, because the Veracity of GOD (as well as his nature) obliged him to fulfil the Denunciation of the Sentence: at least as *Adam* conceived.

IN the midst of this Black and Horrid Condition, the Mercy of GOD appeared like a Morning Star, and the Redeeming Love of GOD was that alone which was able by its Discovery to dispell the Mystes of Darkness that were round about him.

AS all things were before turned into Evil, by the force of Sin, and conspired to sink him lower into the Bottomless Pit; so all the Evils of his present condition were, by this infinite Mercy, turned to his Advantage, and his Condition in many Respects far better than before.

IT is fit to see how Sin enfeebled his Soul, and made him unable to serve GOD; that we might the better understand the Manner of his Recovery, and how his Spiritual Life and Power is restored, in the new strength which he received in his Saviour.

THE Account of it is this: By his *self Love* he was prone to desire all that was Profitable and Delightful to him: While therefore GOD infinitely Loved him, being apparently the fountain of all his Happiness, he could not chuse, (as long as he considered it) but Love GOD and Delight in him, it was natural and Easie to celebrate his Praises. But when he was hated of GOD, tho he could not chuse but acknowledge that hatred *Just*; yet his Self Love made him to look upon GOD in a Malevolent manner, as his Greatest Enemy and his Eternal Tormentor. All that was in GOD was a Terror to him. His power, his Eternity, his Justice, his Holiness, his Goodness, his Wisdome, his Unalterable Blessedness, all was a grief and Terror to his Soul, as long

---

[1] Marginal gloss: Psal. 5.4, 5,6.

as the Hatred of GOD continued against him, it made him desperate to think it would continue forever, and reduced him to the miserable slavery of hating GOD even to all Eternity.

BUT when the Love of GOD towards Man appeared, the Joy wherewith he was surprized, was, in all Likelyhood, so far beyond his Expectation, and his Redemption so far above the Powers of Nature, that his very Guilt and Despair enflamed him with Love. GOD appeared now so Welcome to him, and so Lovely above all that was before, that it was impossible for him to look upon GOD, and not to Love him with Greater Emazement and Ardor then ever. Self Love, that Before compelled him to hate GOD, carried him now most violently to the Love of GOD; and the Truth is, the Love of GOD in the Eye of the Understanding, is the influence of the Holy Ghost proceeding from the Father by the Son into the Soul of the Spectator.[1] For GOD is Love, and we therefore Love him, because he first Loved us. A faln man is Still a reasonable Creature, and having more reason to Love GOD then he had before, is by the pure Nature of his Essence infinitely more prone to Love GOD and delight in him, and praise him for ever, because he is so mercifully and so Strangely restored. Thus are we in Christ restored to the Exercise of that Power which we lost by Sin: But without him we can do Nothing.

WHEN all the Kingdom of GOD was at an End by the fall of man, and all the Labor of the Creation lost, by the Perversness of him for whom the whole World was made; GOD by his Mercy recovered it, and raised it out of the Rubbish of its Ruines, more Glorious than before. Which is the chief reason for the sake for which we introduce the Mercy of GOD, as our best pattern. For when a man has injured us, by Nature there is an End of all the Lovely Exercises of Peace and Amity. If natural Justice should be strictly observed; but then the Season of Grace arrives, and the Excellencie of Mercy shews it self in the Lustre of its Wisdome, and so our Empire is continued, our loss retrived: For by shewing Mercy we often recover the Love of an Enemy, and restore a Criminal to the Joy of our friendship. We lengthen out our Goodness, and Heighten its measure; we make it victorious, and cloath it with a Glory above the course of Nature. And all this we are enabled to do by [the] Coming of *Jesus Christ*, who hath restored us to the Hope of Salvation, and taught us a Way to increase our own Goodness by other mens Evils, to turn the vices of others into our own Vertues, and to Live a Miraculous Life of Worth and

---

[1] Marginal gloss: Psal. 5.4, 5,6.

Excellency in the midst of Enemies, Dealing with men better than they deserve, adorning our selves with Trophies by the Advantages of their vileness, making our selves more Honourable by the Ignominy they cast upon us, more Lovely and Desirable by the Hatred which they bear towards us.

 THE foundations upon which we Exercise this Vertue, are wholy Supernatural. To be kind to the innocent is but Justice and Goodness, but to be Kind to the Malevolent is Grace and Mercy. And this we must do, *because our Father which is in Heaven Causeth his Sun to rise on the Just and the unjust and his Rain to descend on the Righteous and the Wicked*. Because Mercy is the Head Spring of all our Felicities, therefore should we shew Mercy, as we have obtained Mercy. As the Blood was sprinkled upon the Tabernacle and all its Utensils; so is the Blood of Christ upon the Heathens, and the Earth, and all our Enjoyments. They are Daily Monitors of Mercy to us, because they are purchased by the Blood of Christ. For of him it is, that the Heavens declare the Glory of GOD, and the firmament sheweth his Handy work to us sinners at this day. The Salvation of Sinners being the only End for the sake of which we can be permitted now to enjoy them.

 THE Incarnation of our Lord Jesus Christ is an incredible mystery to them, that do not consider the Love of GOD towards Men, in the Creation of the World. But they that measure it by his Laws and Works, and see it in the value of their own Souls, would think it very Strange, if that Love which appeareth so Infinite in all other things, should be defective only in its Ways of Providence. They easily believe, it may express it self in the Incarnation. Especially Since all Ages are Beautified with the Effects and Demonstrations of this verity, that *GOD so Loved the World, that he gave his only begotten Son, that whosoever believeth in him should not perish but have Everlasting Life*. For Love is apt to transform it self into all shapes, that the necessity of its Object requires; and as prone to suffer as rejoyce with it, as apt to suffer for it, as with it. Many fathers have died for their Children, many for their Country, but the Love of GOD exceedeth them all. To be beloved in our Guilt is exceeding Wonderful: but this also is in the Nature of Love, it may be provoked with the Guilt, or moved with Compassion at the misery of a Sinner.

 WHERE the Love is extreamly violent, and the weak Estate of the Object fit for Compassion, it is more inclined to Pity than Revenge: Tho where the Object is strong, and endued with all advantages, it is more offended at the Outrage of its Rebellion.

WHETHER we consider the Nature of Man, or his Estate before the Fall, we have some reason to believe that he was more Beloved then the Holy Angels for there was more exquisite Care and Art Manifested in the Creation of his *Person*, and his *Condition* was fitted for a more curious Tenderness and Compassion, if he offended.

IF you look into the *Nature* of Angels and Men you will find this mighty Difference between them, Angels are more Simple Spirits, Men are Images of GOD carefully put into a Beautiful Case. Their Souls would seem equal to the Angels were they not to live in Humane Bodies, and those Bodies are Superadded, certainly for unspeakable and most Glorious Ends; the visible World was made for the sake of these Bodies, and without such persons as men are, it would be utterly useless. The Hypostatical Union of two Natures so unspeakable different as the Soul and Body are, is of all things in the World most mysterious and Miraculous. Man seems to be the Head of all Things visible, and invisible, and the Golden clasp whereby Things Material and Spiritual are United. He alone is able to beget the Divine Image, and to multiply himself into Millions. His Body may be the Temple of GOD, and when it pleased GOD to become a Creature, he assumed the Nature of Man. Angels are made Ministring Spirits for the sake of Man, and by him alone GOD and his works are United.

IF you respect his *Condition* he was made a little lower than the Angels, that he might be crowned with Glory and Honour; *Lower* for *a* Time, that he might be *Higher* for ever. The Angels were placed in such an Estate, that if they fell, it would be with more shame; yet if they stood, it would be with less Glory: For having the Advantages of Greater Light and strength, to Sin against them was more Odious, and to stand in them less Wonderful. While man, being more remote from GOD, was more Obnoxious to Dangers, and more Weak to resist them; His Want of Clear Light if he fell, would lessen his offence; And the Difficulties wherewith he was surrounded, if he stood, would increase his Vertue, which by consequence would make his Obedience more pleasing, and much augment his Eternal Glory. All which put together, when Angels and Men both fell, fitted Man rather to be chosen and redeemed; he being the Greater Object of Compassion and Mercy.

THE Degrees and measures of that Mercy which was shewn to Man in his Redemption, are very considerable. When he was Weak and unable to help himself, when he was Guilty, when he was an Enemy, when he was Leprous and deformed, when he was Miserable and Dead, before he desired, or Thought of such a Thing, God freely gave his Son to die for his Salvation, and condescended to propose a reconciliation. Which should teach us, tho higher then the Cherubims, and more pure then the Light, tho our Enemies are never so base, and injurious, and ingrateful, nay Obstinate and Rebellious, to seek a reconciliation by the most Laborious and Expensive Endeavors, to manifest all our Care and kindness toward them, pursuing their Amendment and Recovery. For the same Mind ought to be in us that was in Christ Jesus: who being in the form of GOD thought it no Robbery to be Equal with GOD, yet took upon him the Form of a Servant, and being found in fashion as a man, humbled himself to the Death, of the Cross: Wherefore GOD also hath highly exalted him, and given him a Name above every Name that at the Name of Jesus every Knee might bow. The very reason why we so infinitely adore him, being the incomparable Height and Perfection of his Mercy, expressed in his Humiliation and Abasement for us. If we would enter into his Glory, we must walk in the Way which he hath trod before us, for that only will lead us into it.

THO GOD hath in his infinite Mercy redeemed us from the unavoidable Necessity of being Damned, yet hath he with infinite Prudence ordered the Way and Manner of our Redemption: in such sort that we are not immediately translated into Heaven, but restored to a *new Estate of Trial*, and endued with Power to do new Duties, as pleasing to him, as those which he required from us in *Eden*. For he Loved a Righteous Kingdome from the Beginning, wherein his Laws were to be obeyed, Rewards and Punishments expected, and administred in a Righteous manner.

THE Great and necessary Duties in this second Kingdome are Faith and Repentance introduced by his Wisdom, and occasioned by Sin, necessary for our Justification, and Sanctification, and Superadded to the former.

THIS Kingdome of Evangelical Righteousness, being founded on the Blood of Christ, is by Death and Sin, and by the Supernatural Secrets of Love and Mercy, made infinitely more Deep and mysterious than the former.

CHAP. XV.

Of Faith. The Faculty of Believing implanted in the Soul. Of what Nature its Objects are. The Necessity of Faith; Its End, Its Use and Excellency. It is the Mother and Fountain of all the Vertues.

FAITH and Repentance are the Principal Vertues, which we ought to exercise in the Kingdome of *Evangelical Righteousness*: because by them alone a Sinner is restored to the Capacity and Power of living in the Similitude of GOD, in the Practice of his Divine and Eternal Vertues. For *without Faith it is impossible to please GOD*, because we can never believe that he is the Rewarder of all those that diligently seek him, without that Credit which is necessary to be given to the Discovery of his Love to them that are defiled by the Guilt of Sin. For as long as we think GOD to be an infinite and Eternal Enemy to all Offenders, we cannot use any Endeavor to please him, because we Know there is no Hope of Reconciliation, and the vanity of the Attempt appears like a Ghost that always haunts us, and stands in our Way to oppose and discourage us, in the Atchievment we would undertake. For to Fight with *Impossibility* is so Foolish a thing that Nature it self keeps us back from doing it. Till therefore we believe our Reconciliation possible, we have no Strength at all to endeavour our Salvation. Our Despair oppresseth and frustrates our Desires, with the inevitable Necessity of our Eternal shame, and Guilt, and misery.

TO believe that GOD will be so Gracious, as to pardon our horrible Apostacy and Rebellion, is a Work so Great, that GOD accepteth it instead of all other Works of Innocence and Piety: to believe that he hath given his Eternal Son to dy for us, and that he so Loved us as to come down from Heaven to suffer the wrath of GOD in our stead, is so much against the Dictates of Nature and reason, that GOD *imputeth this Faith alone for Righteousness*, not as if there were no Good Works necessary beside, but by this alone we are justified in his Sight, and our Justification cannot be ascribed to any other Work of ours whatsoever. Howbeit that which maketh Faith it self so Great a Vertue, is that we thereby receive a Power and an Inclination with all, to do those Works of Love and Piety, the Performance and the Reward of which was the very End of our Saviours Coming.

THAT there is implanted in Man a Faculty of *believing*, is as certain as that his Eys are endued with the Faculty of *seeing,* or his Soul with *Knowledge*, or any other Faculty. And that this Power implanted is of some *Use* in Nature, is as sure, as any Thing in the World. For nature never gave to any thing a Power in vain, this therefore being one of the Powers of the Soul, must have a certain *End* ordained for it: And its use is the Exercise of *Faith*, in order to that End.

OBJECTS of Faith are those Things which cannot be discovered but by the Testimony of others. For some things are known by Sence, some by Reason, and some by Testimony. Things that are Known by Sence, are present, some time or other, to the Senses themselves. Those Things which Reason discovers, are Known, as Effects are by Causes, or as Causes by Effects; a Good and rational Demonstration being made by the Concatenation of Causes and Effects depending upon each other, whereby Things remote from Sence are evident to Reason, because the one is necessarily implied by the existence of the other. But some Things there are, which have no such necessary Dependance at all: such are the fortuitous Occurences that have been in the World, with all those Actions of free Agents that flow meerly from their Will and pleasure. For of these, there can be no certaine Knowledge when they are past, but by History and Tradition. That the World was made so many years ago, that Man was created in an estate of Innocency that he fell into Sin, that GOD appeared, and promised the seed of the Woman to break the Serpents Head; that there was a Flood, that *Sodom* and *Gomorrah* was burnt by fire, that all the World spake one Language till the Confusion at *Babel*, that there were such men as *Julius Cæsar*, or *Alexander the Great*, or such as *Abraham*, and *Moses*, and *David*, that the children of *Israel* were in *Egypt*, and were delivered from thence by Miracles; that they received the *Law* in the *Wilderness*, and were afterwards setled in the Land of *Canaan*, that they had such and such *Prophets*, and *Priests*, and *Kings*: that *Jesus Christ* was born of the Virgin *Mary*, that he was GOD and Man, that he died and rose again, that he ascended into Heaven, and sent the *Holy Ghost* down upon his *Apostles*. Nay that there is such a City as *Jerusalem*; all these things can no other Way be understood but only by Faith, for no Light of Nature nor principle of Reason can declare such verities as these, among which we may reckon these, that all the Nations in the World, except that of the Jews, were *Pagans* and Idolatrous, till the *Gospel* began to come forth from *Jury*; that by the Miracles, and Perswasions, and Faith, and Patience, and Persecutions, and Deaths of the *Martyrs*, they were converted, and forsook their Dumb Idols, and erected Temples to the GOD of Heaven; that his Eternal Son was crucified in *Judea*; that such *Emperors* made such Laws, that such *Councils* were held in such Ages, that such and such *Fathers* sprung up in the Church; that there is such a Place as *Rome*, and *Constantinople*: these and many Millions of the like Objects, to them that live in this Age, and never stirred any further then the English Coast, are revealed only by the Light of History, and received upon Trust from the Testimony of others. Nevertheless there is as great a Certainly of these Things, as if they had been made out, by Mathematical Demonstration, or had been seen with our Eys.

FOR tho there are some *false* and some *Doubtful* Testimonies, yet there are also some that are *True* and *Certain*. And least all Faith should be utterly blind, and vain, and uncertain, there are External Circumstances and inward Properties, by which those Testimonies which are true and infallible are distinguished from others.

ALL those Things that are absolutely necessary to the Welfare of Mankind, the Knowledge of which is of general Importance, that are unanimously attested by all that mention them, and universally believed throughout all the World, being as firm and certain, as the Earth, or the Sun, or the Skye it self. We are not more Sure that we have Eys in our Heads, then that there are Stars in the Heavens: tho the Distance of those Stars are many Millions of Leagues from our Bodily Organs.

THE Objects and Transactions which in former Ages occur to our Eys, (I mean the Spiritual Eys of the intelligible Soul, that are seated within) are by Faith received, and brought to the understanding. When they are transmitted to our Knowledge, their Nature is apprehended immediately by the Soul, and their existence examined by Reason. There being certain clear and infallible Rules, by which their Truth or falshood may be discerned. And for this Cause is it that we are commanded, to *Try all Things, and hold fast that which is Good*; It is our Duty, to be *ready always to give a reason of the Hope that is in us.*[1] For Reason is a transcendent faculty, which extendeth to all Objects, and penetrates into all misteries, so far as to enquire what probability may be in them; what Agreement or repugnance there is in the Nature of the Things revealed; what Harmony or Contradiction there is in the Things themselves, what Correspondence in all the Circumstances, what consistence between those Things which we certainly *Know*, and

---

[1] Marginal gloss: 1 Pet. 3.15.

those which we are perswaded to *believe*, what Authority the Relation is of, what is the Design and integrity of the Relators, what is the Use and End of the things revealed, whether they are important or frivolous, absolutely necessary, meerly convenient, or wholy Superfluous, things to be abhorred, or things to be desired, Absurd or Amiable, what Preparations went before, what Causes preceded their Existence, what Effects followed, what Concomitants they had, what Monuments of them are now left in the world, How the Wise and Learned judge of them, what Consent and Unity there is in all the Relations, and Histories, and Traditions, of the Things reported.

WHERE there is no Repugnance between the Objects offered to our Faith and the Things we already know, no Inconsistance in the Things themselvs, no difference, no Contention between the Relators, no fraud in promoting, nor folly (discernable) in the first Embracing of the Things that are published, no Want of Care in Sifting and examining their Reality, nor any want (in the Hearers) of Industry, Skill and Power to detect the Imposture, there is a fair Way laid open to the Credible of such Objects attested and revealed with such Circumstances. But if the Things attested were openly transacted in the face of the World and had Millions of Spectators at the first, if they were so publick as to be taken notice of in all Kind of Histories of those times and places, if they were founded on great and weighty causes, if they were pursued by a constant Series, and succession of affairs, for many Ages, if they produced great and publick alterations in the World, if they overcame all suspicious oppositions, obstacles, and impediments, if they changed the state of Kingdoms and Empires, if old Records, and Monuments and Magnificent Buildings are left behind, which those Occurrences occasioned; our Reason it self assists our Belief, and our Faith is founded upon *Grounds*, that cannot be removed: Much more if the Things be agreeable to the Nature of GOD, and tend to the Perfection of Created Nature, if many Prophesies and long Expectations have preceded their Accomplishment, if the misteries revealed are attested by Miracles, and painted out many Ages before, by Types and Ceremonies, that can bear no other Explication in Nature, nor have any Rational use besides; if all the Beauty of former Ages is founded in, and compounded by their Harmony, if they fitly answer the Exigencies of Humane Nature, and unfold the True Originals of all the Disorder and Corruption in the world, if the Greatest and Best Part of Learning it self consists in the Knowledge of such affairs; if the Doctrines on which they attend, be the most pure, and Holy, and

Divine, and Heavenly; if the most of them are rooted in Nature it self, when they are examined and considered, but were not discerned nor Known before; if they supply the Defects of our Understanding and lead us directly to felicity, if they take off our Guilt, and are proper Remedies to heal the Distempers and Maladies of our Corruption; if they direct and quiet the passions of Men and purifie their Hearts, and make men Blessings to one another; if they exterminate their vices, and Naturally tend to the Perfection of their Manners, if they lead them to Communion with GOD, and raise up their Souls to the fruition of Eternity, enlarge their Minds with a Delightful Contemplation of his Omnipresence, enrich them with infinite varieties of Glorious Objects fit to be enjoyed, if they perfect all the Powers of the Soul, and Crown it with the End for which it was prepared: Where all these Things meet together, they make a Foundation like that of the Great Mountains which can never be moved. But if there be any flaw, or Defect, in these Things, if any of them be wanting, our Faith will be so far forth lame and uncertain, as our Reason shall discern its Cause to be failing.

NOW of all the Things that the World doth afford, the Christian Religion is that alone wherein all these Causes of Faith perfectly concur. Insomuch that no Object of Faith in all the World is for *Certainty* Comparable to that of Religion. Never had any Truth so many Witnesses, never any Faith so many Evidences, they that first taught and published it, despised all the Grandeurs and Pleasures in the World, designed nothing but their Eternal Felicity, and the Benefit of men, trampled all Honours and Riches under feet, attested the Truths they taught and revealed, by Miracles wrought, not in obscure Corners, but in the Eye of the Sun, many Nations far distant from each other were in a Moment reduced, and changed at a time. Millions of Martyrs were so certain of the Truth of these Things, that they laught at Persecutions, and Flames, and Torments. The Jews that are the great enemies of Christianity, confess those Histories, and Prophesies, and Miracles, and Types, and Figures upon which it is founded. They reverence the Book wherein they are recorded above all the Writings in the World, confess that they had it before our Saviour was born, and glory that it was theirs, before it was ours. Their whole Faith and Religion is made up of Such Materials, which being granted, it is impossible the Christian Religion should be false, Turks acknowledge the Historical Part. The Artifices of Corruptors have been all detected, and must of necessity so be as long as there are inquisitive Men in the World: All Schismaticks and Hereticks have cavilled and disputed about the true Interpretation of certain Texts, but never so much as Doubted, much less shaken the foundation. Nay when you look into Matters well, the very Certainty of the one was the occasion of the other. The great Moment of what they took for granted made the strife the more Eager.

THIS Advantage our Faith has above all, it is suspected only by Lazy and Profane, half witted men that are as Empty as self conceited, as rash as Wanton, and as much Enemies to Felicity and Vertue, as to Truth and Godliness. But the more you search into it, the more Light and Beauty you shall discern in the *Christian Religion*, the Evidences of it will appear still more deep and abundant, as endless in Number, force, and Value, as they are unexpected.

AMONG other Objects of Felicity to be enjoyed, *the Ways of GOD* in all Ages are not the least considerable and Illustrious. Eternity is as much Beautified with them, as his Omnipresence is with the Works of the Creation. For Time is in Eternity, as the World is in Immensity: Reason expects that the one should be Beautiful, as well as the other. For Since all *Time* may be Objected to the Eye of Knowledge altogether, and Faith is prepared in the Soul on purpose, that all the Things in Time may be admitted into the Eye of the Soul, it is very Displeasing to Humane Reason, that *Time* should be horrid, and Dark, and empty, or that he that has expressed so much Love in the *Creation* of the World, should be Unmindful of our Concerns in the Dispensations of his *Providence*. Especially Since the World, how Glorious soever it is, is but the Theatre of more Glorious Actions, and the Capacity of *Time* as Great and Large as that of the *Universe*, Ages are as long and as Wide as Kingdoms. Now if GOD have altogether neglected the Government of the World, all Time will be Dark and vain, and innumerable Bright and Delightful Objects, which were possible to be desired, denied to the Soul, and the better half of GODS Love be removed. But if GODS Will and Pleasure be Uniform in his Operations, and Time it self Beautified by this Wisdome, Goodness, and Power, as well as the World, our *Faith* will have a peculiar Excellency because, it is that by which all the Beauties in *Time* and *Providence* are enjoyed: Especially if it be able to see and feel them in clear Light, and in as lively a manner as the *Reason* of the Soul can do, when most fully informed. It is evident that without this *Faith*, the Greater half of our Felicity can never be enjoyed.

TO Know that we are Men, encompassed with the Skies, and that the Sun and Moon, and Stars are about us, with all the Elements and

Terrestrial Creatures, is matter of Sence and *Reason* as it is also, that we have the Dominion and use of them; and that such Excellencies and Degrees of Goodness are Connatural to them: But their utmost Perfection is discovered only by the Truth of Religion; that alone discloses their first Cause, and their last End, without which all their Intermediate uses are *Extremely* Defective: It is far more Pleasant to see the Infinite and Eternal GODHEAD from the incomprehensible Height of his Glory, stooping down to the abyss of Nothing, and actually making all these Transcendent Things out of Nothing for our sakes, then to see our selves at present surrounded with them. This is the first Act of all the Ornaments of *Time* and *Nature.* Which tho it be founded on clear Reason, yet is it an Object of our Highest Faith, as it is revealed by the Word of GOD: and therefore it is said, *Through faith we understand that the Worlds were made.* For Faith and Reason are not so divided, but that (tho formally Distinct) they may enter into each others Nature, and Materially be the same. The very same Object (I mean) that is Known to Reason, may by Faith be believed: *Reason* not destroying but confirming *Faith,* while it is *Known* upon one account, and *believed* on another. For there is a Mutual Convenience between these two, *Faith* is by *Reason* confirmed, and *Reason* is by *Faith* Perfected.

TO see GOD stooping down to Create the World, and Nothing follow, is not so Beautiful, as to see him afterward in the Act of making Man, and Giving him Dominion over all the Creatures. It is more pleasant to see Man made in GODS Image, then to see the World made for the use of Man. For the End of the Creation is that, upon which all the Perfection of its Glory does depend, and the more Noble *Man* is, for whose use the *World* was made, the more sublime and Glorious its *End* is. To see him placed in the Estate of Innocency, Light, and Glory, wherein he was secure from Death, and Sin, and Sickness, and Infelicity, if himself pleased, is very Delightful; so it is to see, that Nature never intended any of those Abortive Errors, that now so confound us: But to see the *End* why man was placed in such an Estate, to be his *Trial,* and the End of that his *freindship with GOD,* whose Exercise consisteth in voluntary Acts of *Gratitude* and *Amity*; and the End of those the Beauty of his Life, and his fuller Exaltation to Bliss and Glory; this is far more Pleasant then the other. To see him fall is infinitely Displeasing, but the fault is intirely charged on himself: And had GOD Eternally destroyed him, tho we perhaps had never lived to see it, yet we confess it would have been just in it self, and the Justice Adorable. But to see GOD exalting his mercy in pardoning the offence, and for all our sakes redeeming Man by the Death of his Son is sweeter still: as it is also to see his infinite Justice and Holiness in the *Manner* of our Redemption. To see him lay the foundation of our Hope on a certain Promise, seconded with his Long-suffering, yet defer the Accomplishment of it for our greater Benefit, wisely forbearing to send his Son till *the fulness of Time*, is very transporting, but the Reason of it is very Difficult to understand. His foresight of our Obstinate *Blindness* and *Incredulity* was the Cause of his Delay. That he might gain Time, before our *Saviour* came, to speak of him, to paint him forth, to make him the expectation of the World, and the Hope of all Nations; To see him for that End reveal himself to *Abraham*, *Isaac*, and *Jacob*, and bringing down their Posterity into the Land of *Egypt*, that he might make that Nation, out of which our Saviour was to spring, *Famous* by *Miracles*, and by his Conduct and Government of them, more *Glorious* then all Nations, to appear himself among them, and give his Oracles unto them, and to make them conspicuous to the Eye of all the World, by mighty Signes, and Wonders, and Judgments, punishing them for their offences, yet Graciously continuing a Seed among them, that *Christ* might be raised up according to the *Prophesies*, that went before concerning him. To see all the Mysteries of the Gospel painted out in so *Lively* a Manner, in all the Types and Figures of the *Ceremonial Law*, and that Service with so much splendor and Glory continued, before he came by the Space of two thousand years, wherein all the mysteries of his Kingdome are exhibited; to see *the Volumne of the Book in which it was written of him*, so highly magnified and exalted, by them that crucified him after it was written, and that now continue so much to oppose him as the *Jews* do; To see the *Prophets* at various Times, and in Divers manners, so clearly to describe all the particulars of his Life and Doctrine, his Eternity, his Godhead, the Hypostatical Union, his Incarnation in the Virgins Womb, his Poverty, his Meekness, his Miraculous Life, his Death and Passion, his Resurrection and Ascension into Heaven, the Sudden and Miraculous Conversion of the Gentiles, compared to a *Nation's being born at once*, the very *Town* where he should be born, and the *City* from whence the Law should go forth into all the World, and the *Temple* in which the Gospel should begin to be preached. To see the Accomplishment of all these Things attended with so many Glorious and Transcendent Wonders, and the utter subversion of that Nation, for their Incredulity when they had slain him; To see Kings and Queens become the *Nursing Fathers* and *Mothers* of the Church, and so many Glorious Empires receive his Law that was *hanged* on a Tree; To see Temples erected over all the World to a Crucified GOD, and Nations upon Earth adoring his Glory in the Highest Heavens; Especially to see the manner of his satisfaction, by way of *Sacrifice* in our stead, the laying of our Sins upon his Head, & the sprinkling of his Blood upon all Nations so lively represented, the Necessity of such a Saviour exhibited by the Rigor and Severity of the Law, his Person and his Office being pointed out in so particular a Manner; all this as it is sweet & Heavenly, so does it enrich the Contemplation of the Soul, & make it meet to walk in Communion with GOD in all *Ages*, adoring his Wisdome, and Goodness, and Power, admiring & delighting in the *fulness* of his Love, And all these most Great & Transporting Things we receive into our Souls by *Faith* alone.

BUT that which above all other Things is most satisfactory is to see Jesus Christ *the end of the Law*, and the Centre of time, the main Business of all the Dispensations of GODS Providence, and the only Hinge upon which all mysteries both of the Law and Gospel Principally turn.

HAD he come in the Beginning of the World, there had been no *Room* nor *Place* for all these Prophesies, and Figures, and Expectations, and Miracles, Preceding his Birth, we had had nothing but a *bare* and *naked* Tradition, that he had been in the world, which by the carelessness of men had passed away like a Dream, and died unprofitably; As we may plainly see by their Backwardness to believe these Things, notwithstanding their strength and Beauty, and the reiterated Appearances of GOD to excite and awaken Man-kind, notwithstanding his care to erect a Ministery among us, for this very end, *that Jesus Christ might be Known.*

HAD he not been GOD and MAN in one Person, had no satisfaction been necessary for our sins, had he not made satisfaction for us; there had been no Necessity of believing on his name. The light of nature had been sufficient to guid us to sorrow and Obedience; all this trouble and care might have been spared, all this Oeconomy might have been changed into a Government of less expence, and the most of these proceedings had been impertinent and superfluous. For they all receive their Attainment and Perfection in *Jesus Christ*, who is the fulness, and substance, and Glory of them.

NOR is it, the excellency of Faith alone, that it looks back upon Ages past: it takes in the Influences of all these, that it may bring forth fruit, in our Lives for the time to come. For what is it but the Faith of these things, attended with the Glory which is intimated by them, that made so many Divine and Heavenly persons, so many Wise and Holy Heroes, so many Saints and Martyrs! What can enflame us with the love of GOD, inspire us with Courage, or fill us with Joy, but the Sence of them! A true and lively Faith is among Sinners the only Root of Grace and Virtue, the only Foundation of Hope, the only Fountain of excellent Actions. And therefore it is observed by the Apostle *Paul*,[1] that *by Faith* Abel *offered a more Excellent sacrifice than* Cain, *by Faith Enoch* walked with GOD, *by Faith Noah* prepared an Ark, in which being warned of GOD, he saved himself from the general Deluge; *by Faith Abraham* did such Things, as made his Seed to multiply above the Stars of Heaven; *by Faith Moses* despised the Honours and Treasures of Egypt, and endured, as seeing him that was invisible; *What should I say more* (saith the Apostle) *For the time would fail me to tell of* Gideon, *and of* Barak, *and of* Sampson, *and of* Jeptha, *of* David *also, and of* Samuel, *and of the Prophets: who through Faith subdued Kingdoms, wrought Righteousness, obtained Promises, Stopped the mouths of Lions, Quenched the violence of fire, escaped the Edge of the Sword, out of Weakness were made strong, waxed valiant in fight, turned to flight the Armies of the Aliens. Women received their Dead raised to Life again; and others were tortured, not accepting Deliverance, that they might obtain a better Resurrection. and others had tryal of cruel Mocking and Scourges, yea moreover of Bonds and Imprisonments. They were stoned, they were sawn asunder, were tempted, were slain with the sword, they wandred about in Sheep-skins and Goat-skins, being destitute, afflicted, tormented; of whom the World was not worthy, they wandered in Deserts and Mountains, and in Dens and Caves of the earth.* All these things were done through *Faith*, while yet there were but a few Things seen to encourage them. But the whole Accomplishment of mysteries and myracles is far more fair, and vigorous, and enflaming; the Beauty of the whole Body of GODS Dispensations fitly united in all its Parts, being an eternal *Monument* of his Wisdom and Power, declaring the Glory of his Love, and Kingdom in a more Eminent manner, and making us *more then conquerors in and thorrow Jesus Christ, who loved us, and gave himself for us.*

---

[1] Marginal gloss: Heb. 11; see Heb. 11.7–17, 24–29, and 32–38.

CHAP. XVI.

Of Hope. Its foundation, its Distinction from Faith, its Extents and Dimensions, its Life Sand Vigor, its Several Kinds, its Sweetness and Excellency.

JANUS with his two Faces, looking backward and forward, seems to be a fit Emblem of the Soul, which is able to look on all Objects in the Eternity past, and in all Objects before, in Eternity to come. Faith and Hope are the two Faces of this Soul. By its Faith it beholdeth Things that are past, and by its Hope regardeth Things that are to come. Or if you please to take Faith in a more large and Comprehensive Sence, Faith hath both these Faces, being that Vertue by which we give Credit to all Testimonies which we believe to be true concerning Things past, present and to come: Hope is a Vertue mixt of Belief and Desire, by which we conceive the Possibility of attaining the Ends we would enjoy, and are stirred up to endeavour after them. Faith respects the *Credibility* of Things believed to be *True*; Hope, the *Possibility* and *Goodness* of their *Enjoyment*. The Simple Reality of Things believed is the Object of the one, the facility of their attainment, and our Interest united are the Object of the other.

HOPE presupposes a Belief of the Certainty of what we desire. It is an Affection of the Soul of very general Importance. Which forasmuch as it is founded on Faith, and derives its strength from the Sure Belief of what we hope to attain, and there can be no fruition of that which is not really *existent*, to lay the foundation of our Hope more firmly, we will again consider the Objects of Faith in the best Light wherein their apparent certainty may be discerned.

THE Objects of Divine Faith revealed in the holy Scripture may fitly be ranked into three Orders. For the *Matter* of the Bible being partly *Historical*, and partly *Prophetical*, and partly *Doctrinal*, the Objects of *Divine Faith* fall under these three Heads, of *Doctrine, History,* and *Prophesie*.

THE *Doctrine* of the Scripture is of two sorts: for some Doctrines are *Natural*, some are *Supernatural*. The Natural are again divided into two. For some of them are *Laws* that teach us our Duty, some of them *Propositions* only, or bare and Simple *Affirmations*, which we call Articles guiding our Apprehensions in the Truth of those Things which are meet to be Known. *Speculation* is intended in the one, and Practice in the other.

NATURAL Doctrines are Objects of Divine Faith, only as they are revealed by the Word of GOD. For the Authority of the Witness is that which maketh our Faith *Divine*. They are called *Natural*, because how ever Blind any man is, in his present condition; upon a diligent Search, those Things may be clearly discerned by the Light of Nature. Those Doctrines which are Objects of Divine *Faith*, and yet may be found out by the Investigation of *Reason*, are such as these. That there is a GOD, that the World was made, that man was created in GODS Image, that he hath Dominion over the works of his Hands, that he is or ought to be tenderly Beloved of all mankind, that he is to be good, and full of Love to others: that he is to render all Objects their Due Esteem, and to be Grateful for the Benefits he hath received of his great Creator: that the first Estate of the Worlds Creation was pure and perfect, that Sin came in by the Accidental abuse of the Creatures Liberty, that Nature is Corrupted, that Death was introduced as the Punishment of Sin, that the Soul is Immortal, that GOD is infinitely Just, and Wise, and Holy; that he will distribute Rewards, and Punishments according to Right; that there is such a Thing as Eternity and Immensity; that the Body is frail and subject to Diseases; that we receive all Things from GOD, and depend in the fruition of all upon his Power and Providence; that it is Wise to please him, and foolish to displease him; that Punishment is due to Sin, and that GOD hateth it; that Reward is due to Vertue, and GOD delighteth in it; that there is a Conscience in the Soul, by which it feels and discovers the Difference between Guilt and Innocence. That man is a Sinner, that he is prone to Evil, and Obnoxious to GODS Wrath, that nevertheless he is spared by the Long-suffering of GOD, and that GOD Loveth him, and desireth his Salvation. That there is a felicity and a Supream Felicity appointed for man: that he is a free Agent, and may lose it, if he pleases: that misery is the Consequent of the Loss of Felicity: that GOD delighteth in all those that Love and practice Vertue: that he hateth all those that drown their Excellencies in any Vice: that Sorrow and Repentance are necessary for all those that have offended GOD: that there is Hope to escape the Punishment of Sin, if we endeavour to live as piously as we ought. All these things are evident in themselves by the Light of Nature, because they may either be clearly deduced from the principles of Reason, or certainly discerned by plain Experience: And are therefore taught by the Word of GOD, either because they had need to be revived and raised up to light from under the Rubbish or our Fall, or because GOD would sanctifie Nature by his express Consent, or make its Dictates more remarkable and Valid by his Approbation, and confirm all by the Seal of his Authority: or because a fair Way is laid open by these to more retired and Cœlestial Mysteries.

FOR when we know these Things we are prone to enquire what GOD hath done, what Way there is to recover our ancient Happiness, what Remedies are prepared for the corruption of Nature, how the Guilt of Sin may be removed, how we may be aided and assisted in the works of Virtue, by what Means our Reconciliation with GOD is wrought, and in what manner we ought to demean our selves that we may be accepted of him? for the knowledge of our former health is necessary for the clear apprehension of our present Sickness, and the sense of our Infirmitie fits us for the Physician. When we know all that *Nature* can teach, and see something needful, that Nature cannot unfold; when we are condemned by our Conscience yet feel our selves beloved, find that we have forfeited all, yet see the Glory of the creation continued (for our use and service,) stand in need of an Atonement, yet Know not where to get it; our Exigency meeting with the grace of GOD, the sence of our Misery and Hope united, our own Guilt and GODS Mercy (of both which we have the feeling and experience,) adapts us for the Reception of the Holy Gospel, wherein those things are revealed that come in *most fitly* to answer our Expectations. Satisfaction for Sin by the Death of Christ, and the Incarnation of his GODHEAD above the course of Nature, for that End; His active and passive Obedience in our Stead, our Justification thereby, the application of his Merits to our souls by faith, the Glory which we owe him for so great an undertaking, the coming down of the Holy Ghost to Sanctifie our Nature, and the dignity of Both these Persons by reason of their Unity in the eternal Essence; for the manifestation of which the Mysterie of the Trinitie is largely revealed, these supernatural Points come in so suitably and are so agreeable to Nature, so perfectly fit in their places, so marvellously conducive to the perfection of the Residue, that the very Harmony and sweetness of altogether is enough to perswade us of their *Credibility*; and then the *Matter of fact* comes in with the Testimony and Authority of GODS Word, assuring us that these Things are so, by History and Prophesie. The Miracles at our Saviours Birth alone one would think enough to clear the business: much more if we take in all the Miracles of his life; wherein his Glory appeared, as of the only begotten of the Father;

more fully yet, if we take in the Miracles of his Death; and abundantly more, if the Glory of his Resurrection and Ascension be added. But especially the *Coming down of the Holy Ghost,* and the Power the Apostles received from heaven, all the Prophesies that went before, and all the successes that followed after, all the Faith and Learning of the Fathers, all the Canons and Decrees of Councils, all the Transactions of the World drawn down to our own Age in a continued series, illustrate and confirm all that is revealed.

BUT you will say, How shall we know such Histories to be true, and that such Prophesies and Prophets were in their several Ages; Since we never saw the same with our eyes, and there are many sleights and Fables in the World: How dost thou know there are any Antipodes? Thou didst never see them! Or that there is any Sea, which thou didst never behold! Or that the next River has a Fountain Head? Is not the Universal Tradition of all the world (wherein the Church of *Rome,* nay the Catholick Church, is but a little Part) a clear Light for a *matter of Antiquitie,* attended with a *Stream* of Effects and clear *Monuments* concurring together, without any Dissonancy in the Things themselves, or Contention of Parties? How dost thou know that there was such a man, as King *James,* or *William* the Conquerer. Is he not a mad man that will doubt, or Dispute it? All that thou hast to confirm thee in the certainty of these, and infinitely more, conspires together, to confirm thee in the certainty of the other. The History of the Bible is confest by Turks, and Jews, and Infidels, and which is far more, by the Testimony of the Church, which deserves to be believed above them all. And if the History be true, there were such Persons as *Adam, Enoch, Noah, Abraham, Joseph, Moses, Samuel, David, Solomon, Elias, Elisha, Josiah, Isaiah, Jeremiah, Ezekiel, Daniel,* and the rest of the Prophets; such persons as Jesus Christ, and his Apostles in such Ages; such Prophesies, and such Accomplishments at vast Distances; such Acts, and such Miracles, and such Doctrines upon such occasions: And if all this *Matter of fact* be true, tis impossible but these Doctrines must be Divine, which the Devil and wicked men so much Oppose and Blaspheme in the World. And if these Doctrines are true, then all the Promises of GOD are true, and there is a large foundation of Eternal *Hope* prepared for the Soul: because if all these Preparations be not Eternally disgraced by the feebleness of their End, the Glory and Felicity which is designed by them, is infinite and Eternal.

THAT all these Things are intended for thy Benefit, thou mayst clearly see, by thy very Power to see them, and by the Natural Influence which they have upon thy Estate and condition. For tho it may happen by some succeeding Accident, that thy Power to see and enjoy all may be bereaved of its Objects, when thine *Interest* is Eclipsed and forfeited by thy Rebellion, and the *Influence* of all may at last through thine own Default be *ineffectual* and *Malevolent* to Thee; yet thou art assured by the Nature of GOD, and of thy own Soul, that it could not be intended Evil from the Beginning; nay the very Order and disposition of the Things themselves importeth the Design to be Felicity and Glory. For all these Things were written for our Admonition, upon whom the Ends of the world are come: And the Apostle expresly saith, that[1] *whatsoever Things were written aforetime, were written for our Learning, that we through Patience and Comfort of the Scriptures might have Hope.* This Hope maketh not ashamed, because the Love of GOD is shed abroad in our Hearts, We Delight in Beauty, and by that very Inclination that we have unto it, are apt to Delight in any Thing that is Amiable. We delight to see the Order and Perfection of GODS Ways, and GOD himself taketh Pleasure in manifesting his Wisdome and Goodness, for the Behoof of our Souls, because he is Great in Bounty, and infinite in Love by his every Essence: Nay further we are every one Capable of all the Benefit that accrueth thereby, and by Nature fitted to celebrate his Praises for all the Advantages that by any of his Dispensations are imparted to us, and have Liberty to improve them all for the Acquisition of that Glorious End to which we are ordained. The Nature of GOD, which is hereby manifested to be Love to his Creatures, is that which enableth thee by this very means to honour and adore him, and by so doing to enter into his Kingdome, where he, that did all these Things for a farther End, will appear in Glory, and shew thee a Perfection of Life and Bliss, that is worthy of all this Care and Providence, being as great as thy Heart can Wish or desire.

HOPE is for its Extent and Dimensions vast and wonderful. All the Honour, Advancement, Exaltation, Glory, Treasure, and Delight, that is concievable in Time or Eternity, may be hoped for: all that the Length, and Breadth, and Depth, and Height, of the Love of GOD, which passeth Knowledge, is able to perform; All that Ambition or Avarice can desire, all that Appetite and Self-Love can pursue, all that Fancy can imagine Possible and Delightful; Nay *more then we are able to ask or think*; we are able to desire, and aspire after (if it be promised to us) the very throne of GOD, and all the Joys of his Eternal Kingdom. And the more Sublime its Objects are, the more Eagerly & violently

---

[1] Marginal gloss: Rom. 15.4.

does our Hope pursue them, because there is more Goodness in them to ravish our Desire.

TO fall from the Height of ones Hopes, where the Kingdome and Glory was infinite, to which we aspire, is to fall from the Height of Heaven into the Depth of Hell, it produceth a misery and Anxiety in the Soul, an Indignation and Sorrow, answerable to all the Greatness of our Objects, and the expectancies of our Hopes: Especially where the Hope is *Lively* and *Tender*, and *Strong*, and *Sensible* of all it conceiveth.

FOR it is the property of a true and lively Hope to Elevate the Soul, to the Height of its Object: tho dull and drowzy Hopes make no Impression or Alteration in the Mind. The Soul extends it self with a kind of Pleasure in its Wishes and in touching the Possibility of such Goodnesses, as it proposes to its self in its own Imagination. Love and Beauty even in *Romances* are Delightful: the very Dreams and *Ideas* of the Perfections of Bliss, have a Pleasure as well as their Reallity. The Desires of it are something more Rich and Sacred then the fancy or Imagination: but to Hope for such a Thing with a clear and joyful expectation, is to grasp at its fruition, with a faint Kind of Promise, that it shall at last be ours. Had our Hopes in *Spiritual* Things, as much *Sence* as they have in *Temporal*, those Beams of Assurance that enlighten our Hope and fill it with Glory, would infuse a solid Strength into our Desire and our pleasures would be so Great that we should not exchange them for all the Empires in the World. Especially if it ascended so high as to be founded on infinite and Eternal Causes, and the only fears that did chequer our Hope, sprung from Nothing but the Danger of being Wanting to our selves. For who would think, That when our Lives and Liberties are at stake, we should be false to our selves, that infinite Love and Power should be tendered to us, infinite Beauty and Goodness be before us, infinite Honour and Pleasure be offered us, Eternal Delights, inestimable Riches, Ever flourishing Joys, an infinite Empire be without fraud attainable, and we be so Treacherous and false to our selves, as to sleight it all! It is an Absurdity so incredible, that we should lose all these Enjoyments by our own Default, and bare Remissness that we shall hate our selves Eternally if we lose so fair an Advantage. Yet this is our Case, we daily do that which in point of Reason is impossible to be done, and for doing which we judge our selves Guilty of Eternal Tortures. All the Misery that is lodged in infinite Despair has comfort and refreshment answerable to it in infinite Hope. Tis the present food and Support of our Lives, 'tis the

Anchor of our Souls in the midst of all the Storms and Tempests in the World, 'tis the foretaste of Bliss and Cœlestial Glory, a Glympse and Appearance of the Beatifick Vision, without which to Live is to Dye, and to Dye is to perish for evermore.

THE Great Reason for which a right Hope is accounted so Great a Vertue, is because its Objects do really surpass all Imagination. The fulness of the GODHEAD in the Soul of Man, the Perfection of the Divine Image, a Transformation for Glory, to Glory, even as by the Spirit of the Lord, Communion with the Father, Son and Holy Ghost, infinite Love and Bounty, the Estate of a Bride in Communion with GOD, the Possession of his Throne, with another Kind of sweetness then the Bridegroom himself enjoys, the Resurrection of the Body, and Life Eternal, in a Kingdome where all Occasions of Tears and Fears shall ever be removed, Where all Regions, and Ages, and Spaces, and Times, and Eternities, shall be before our Eys, and all Objects in all Worlds at once Visible, and infinitely Rich, and Beautiful, and *Ours*! Our very Appetites also being ravished with Sensible Pleasures in all our Members, not inconsistent with, but springing from these high and Superior Delights, not distracting or confounding our Spiritual Joys, but purely Superadded, and increasing the same; while our Bodies *are made like to his most Glorious Body, by that Almighty Power whereby he is able to subdue All Things to himself*, all these infuse their Value; and the Hope that is exercised about these Things is a Vertue so great, that all inferior Hopes, which this doth Sanctifie, are made Vertues by it, but without this all other Hopes are Debasements and Abuses of the Soul, meer Distractions and delusions, and therefore *Vices*.

I Know very well that Presumption and Despair are generally accounted the Extreams of Hope, and the only vices that are Opposite thereunto. But I Know as well, that there may be many Kinds and Degrees of Hope, of which some may be *vicious*, and some *Vertuous*: and that some sorts of Hope themselves are Vices. When ever we make an inferior Desire the Sovereign Object of our Hope, our Hope is abominable, Idolatrous and Atheistical. We forget GOD, and magnifie an inferior Object above all that is Divine. To Sacrifice all our *Hopes* to Things unworthy of them, or to be Remiss and sluggish in *Hoping* for Things of infinite Importance, is apparently *Vicious*: But to be just to all our Encouragements; and to lift up our Eys to the Eternal GOD, with an humble Expectation; to wait upon him, and to hope for all that from his Bounty, which his Goodness has promised, to desire the most high and perfect *Proofs* of his Love, is the Property of a most Great and Noble Soul, by which it is carried above all the World, and fitted for the Life of the most high and perfect Vertue.

CHAP. XVII.

Of Repentance. Its Original, its Nature, it is a Purgative Vertue. Its necessity, its Excellencies. The measure of that sorrow which is due to Sin is intollerable to Sense confessed by Reason, and dispensed with by mercy.

REPENTANCE is a Sowre and austere Kind of Vertue, that was not created nor intended by GOD, but introduced by Sin, made fair by Mercy, in remitting the offence, and pardoning the Sin. It is a Strange Kind of off-spring, which flows from Parents so infinitely different, and has a mixture in its Nature, answerable to either an *Evil* which it derives from *Sin*, and a *Goodness* which flows from *Mercy*. Its Evil is that of Sorrow, Indignation and Shame, Its Goodness is the usefulness, and necessity of the thing, considering the Condition we are now in. It is highly ingrateful to Sence, but transcendently convenient and amiable to *Reason*; for it is impossible for him that has once been defiled with sin, ever to be cleansed, or to live after in a Vertuous manner, unless he be so ingenious as to lament his Crime, as to loath, acknowledge, and detest his Error.

THE Union of the Soul and Body is mysterious, but that Sin and Mercy should be united, as Causes so infinitely different, for the production of a Child so Black and so Beautiful, is the Greatest Wonder which the Soul can contemplate on this side Heaven; and will continue to be remembred for ever, and appear more Wonderful than before when the perfect Disparity and Opposition between them is clearly seen, in the Light of Glory.

THE *Efficient Cause* of Repentance is either Remote, or Immediate: Its immediate Efficient Cause is the Gracious Inclination, or the Will of the Penitent, its remote Efficient is GOD, the Father of Lights from which every Good and Perfect Gift descended. Its *Material Cause* is Sorrow. Its *Formal Cause*, which makes it a Vertue, is the Reason and Manner of that Sorrow, the Equity and Piety wherewith it is attended, containing many ingredients in its Nature too long a particular to be described here. Its *Final Cause* is either immediate, or ultimate, the first is Amendment, the last Salvation.

BEING thus bounded by its Causes, its Definition is Easie, Repentance is a Grace, or Christian Vertue, wherein a man confesses, hates and forsakes his Sin, with Grief that he hath been Guilty of it, and purposes of Amendment of Life in Order to His Peace and Reconciliation with GOD, that he may answer the Obligations that lye upon him, discharge his Duty, lay hold on the Advantages of GODS Mercy, escape everlasting Damnation, and be made a Partaker of Eternal Glory.

AMONG the Vertues some are *Purgative*, and some are *Perfective*. The Purgative Vertues are all Preparatory to Bliss, and are occasioned only by the Disorder of the Soul: the perfective are Essential to our formal Happiness, and Eternally necessary by the Law of Nature. Repentance is not in its own Nature, (If Simply and absolutely considered) necessary to Bliss: But, in Relation to Sinners, it is as necessary as Physick to the Recovery of Health, or as the *Change* it self is, by which we pass from the Distemper we are Sick of, to the right and Sound Estate which we had lost by the Disease. As the malady is accidental, so is the Cure. For the Nature of Man may be *well*, and perfect, without either this, or the other. He that is originally pure, has no need of a Purgative Vertue: but he that is faln defiled must needs rise, and wash away the filth, before he can be clean.

FOR this Cause, even among the Heathens themselves, the more Knowing and Learned have a Conscience of Sin; their Priests and Philosophers, devised several Rites and Manners of Purgation, which they taught, and imposed on their Disciples with much Circumstance and Ceremony, in order to their Reception. Nor was there any Temple, or Religion in the World, that pretended not something to Diviner Mysteries: Which were graced & beautified with Preparatory Washings, Humiliations, Fashions, Attirs, Watchings, Retirements, Shavings, Sprinklings, Anoyntings, Consecrations, Sacrifices, or some other Disciplines like unto these, to be endured and past thorow, before their Votaries could be admitted to their mysteries. All which Rites as they made a great shew, because they were sensible, so were they apt to put a magnificent face on their Religion to dispose the Persons *exercised* by them to a more complying Obedience, and to beget a Reverence mixt with Awful Admiration in their ignorant Spectators. All which nevertheless were but *Emblematical Ordinances*, signifying something invisible that was necessary to be done, of which the Priests themselves knew not the meaning. They had the name of *Pænitentia* in their Common Conversation, but applied it to profane and Trivial occasions: But *Repentance* in Religion, which is the Soul and substance of those mystical Observations, a broken and Contrite Heart, and internal sorrow for their sin, was a thing unknown; so that all their Appearances, how magnificent soever, were but Empty shells.

REPENTANCE alone though never so simple and short in its name, being of such value, that GOD accepts one contrite Groan above all the Ceremonies, even of his own Law. And therefore he saith,[1] *Thou desirest not sacrifice else would I give it; thou delightest not in Burnt offering. The Sacrifices of GOD are a Broken Spirit: A broken and a contrite Heart, O God, thou wilt not despise.*

FOR tho Repentance be not in it selfe a desirable Vertue, nor so much as a *Vertue*, till there be a sphere and Occasion for it, wherein to be exercised, tho Repentance in it selfe be far worse then obedience, yet upon the Account of our Saviours Merits, and GODS Love to Sinners, it is preferred above the Greatest Innocency and Purity whatsoever. *For there is more Joy in Heaven over one sinner that repenteth, then over Ninety and nine Just persons that need no Repentance.*[2] If the Soul be of greater value than the whole World, if the loss of any Thing we esteem, increaseth the sence of its excellency; if our Saviour justly and rationally compareth himself to a Shepheard, that leaveth Ninety and nine sheep in the wilderness, to seek one that is gone astray; if he rejoyceth when he hath found it, more for that one that was lost, then for the ninety and nine which he had in safety; if his Delight in the success of his Labours be answerable to their Greatness; if the frustration of all his Desires, and painful endeavours in seeking it, be infinitely Grievious; and the Vertues more Amiable and Wonderful, which sinners exercise after their Redemption; if their Love, and their joy, and their praise be increased, by the extreamity of their Distress and the multitude of the sins that are forgiven them; if their Communion with GOD be more sweet, and their Happiness more exalted, and the Kingdom of GOD it selfe made more sublime and Glorious thereby; *Repentance* hath something more in it then Perfection had before the fall, and as sinners have made themselves more infinitly Indebted, so are they infinity more subject to the Arbitrary Disposal of Almighty Power, infinitly more Capable of Obligations and Rewards, infinitely more Obliged for Pardon and deliverance, as well as infinitly more Obnoxious to Divine Justice, their Fear and Danger is infinitly Greater, they stand in need of infinite Grace, and Mercy, which when they receive and enjoy, their Love and Gratitude are proportionably greater, their Delights are more quick, and vigorous, and full, and so are their praises.

---

[1] Marginal gloss: P*sal.*51.16.17.
[2] Marginal gloss: Luke 15.

Christian Ethicks 131

BUT before a sinner can atchieve all this, or GOD enjoy the fruit of his Salvation, he must needs *repent*, for Repentance is the true and substantial Preparation of the Soul, the only Purgative Vertue, by which it is fitted for these Divine Attainments. It is, we confess in outward Appearance a slight invisible Act, but as Great within, as Wide and Comprehensive as the Heavens. It receiveth the Vertue of the Divine Essence of the whole Creation, of infinite Mercy, of the Blood of Christ, of his Humiliation, Merit, Exaltation, Intercession, and glory, of all the Work of Redemption into it self; and having fed it self, digested them, it receiveth strength by the Influence of these to dispence all their Vertue again, in the Production of those Fruits, for the sake of which GOD hath filled all the World with miracles, the Verdure, and Maturity, and Perfection of which shall with their beauty and sweetness continue in life and Florish for ever.

IF we respect Man alone, and the things that are done in himself by Repentance, it seemeth a Vertue of infinite value: It divests him of all his Rebellion, Pride, and vain Glory, strips him of all his Lust and Impiety, purges him of all his corruption, Anger, and Malice, pares off all his Superfluities, and excesses, cleanseth his Soul of all its filthiness and pollution, removeth all that is so infinitly Odious to GOD, and makes him amiable and Beautiful to the holy Angels. It fits and prepares him for all the exercises of Grace and Piety, introduces Humility and Obedience into his Soul, makes him capable of a Divine Knowledge, and makes way for the Beauty of his Love and Gratitude, inspires Fortitude, and Prudence, and Temperance, and Justice into his soul: renues his Nature, and makes him a meek and patient Person, restores him to that Wisdom and Goodness he had lost, cloaths him with righteousness and true Holiness, and seats him again in the Favour of GOD. By Repentance he recovers the Divine Image, and by Consequence it extends to all that Blessedness and Glory which is for ever to be enjoyed.

REPENTANCE is the Beginning of that Life, wherein all the sweat and Labour of the Martyrs, all the Persecutions and Endeavours of the Apostles, all the Revelations of the Prophets, all the examples of the *Patriarchs*, all the Miracles of old Time, all the Mysteries of the Law, all the Means of Grace, all the Verities of the Gospel begin to take full force and Effect, in obtaining that for which they were intended. Which sufficiently intimates the value of the Grace, and how highly well pleasing it must be to GOD: It is the *Conception* of Felicity, and the *New Birth* of the *Inward Man*, the Dereliction of the Old, and the Assumption of a New, and more cœlestial Nature. It is the Gate of

the Heavenly Kingdome which they that refuse to enter at, can never enjoy. It is one of the Keys of Death and Hell, by which the Gate of the Prison is unlockt, nay the very knocking off the Chains, and Manacles of Satan; the very Act wherein we regain our Liberty, and become the
5 Sons of GOD, and Citizens of Heaven. It was fitly Typified in the old Law, by the Laver that was set at the Door of the Tabernacle for the Priests to wash in, before they entred into the Sanctuary, to walk in the Light of the Golden Candlesticks, to offer their Devotions at the Incense Altar, and to partake of the shew bread on the Golden Table. In
10 the Outward Court they enjoyed the society of the visible Church, the sight of the Bloody Altar, (which answers our Saviors Cross erected in the World) and the Benefit of their Outward Profession, which consisted in their Admission to the Visible Ordinances, and exterior Rites of Religion: But that Court was open over head, obnoxious
15 to showers, in Token that a bare *Profession* is not Enough to shelter us from the Dangers and Incommodities that may be rained down in Judgments upon us from the wrath of GOD: whence the face of Heaven is overcast with Clouds, and Covered with black and Heavy Displeasure, till we wash and be clean, and enter by penitence into the
20 Invisible Church, of which the *Second Court* is a Figure, wherein we are illuminated by the Holy Ghost, and offer up the sweet Perfumes of our Thanksgivings and Praises; being admitted to feed upon the Heavenly Feast represented by the Shew-bread Table; we are never received into the Society of the Saints and Angels, painted out in the
25 *Cherubims* and *Palm Trees* round about on the inside of its *Walls*, nor Covered over head with a vail to protect us: A vail of *Blew* to represent the inferior Heaven, wherein *Cherubims* were interwoven to represent the *Angels* looking down upon us, a vail of *Goats-hair* concealed and unseen above that of Blew, to signifie the fruits of our Saviours Life,
30 and another of *Rams-skins* died *Red*, to signifie the Blood of Christ, by which we are secured from all the Displeasure which otherwise for Sin, was due to us. The Goats hair fitly resembles the Active Obedience, or the Righteousness of Christ; for as much as *Hair* may be clipped off, and a Covering made of it, while the Beast is *alive*: For so might Christ
35 have been perfectly Righteous, tho his Life had never been Taken away: But *red* is the Color of *blood*, the *Skin* importeth Death for as much as it cannot be fleyed off, without the destruction of the Creature. These vails therefore as they were above the other, were of higher and more mysterious importance: And spread over the inclosed, and invisible
40 Court, into which none but *Priests* and *Levites* entered, that *washed* at

Christian Ethicks 133

the *Laver*, to intimate the security only of those, that are washed in the Laver of Regeneration, and made *Kings* and *Priests* unto God, being purged from their old sins, and sanctified and illuminated, in a secret Spiritual manner. For as they only that tarried in their Houses, were under the protection of the *Paschal Lamb*, whose *Blood* was sprinkled on the *Lintils* of their *Gates* and *Doors*, when the destroying Angel past through the Land of *Egypt* to kill the First-born of Man and Beast: So onely they that keep within the *Pale* of the *Invisible Church*, are under the *Shaddow* of the Almighty, because they only dwell in the secret place of the most High, and they alone are under the Coverture of that Powerful *Blood*, which speaketh better things than the Blood of *Abel*, but pleads for the preservation of them onely, that repent and believe, and is therefore effectually spread over the *Invisible Church* alone. Which in another Type is exhibited by the mixture of the *Blood* and *Oyl*, which was sprinkled upon the Priests and Lepers that were cleansed: *Sanctification* and *Justification* moving alwayes together hand in hand, the Unction of the Holy One, or the Oyl of Love and Gladness annointing all those that are washed, and only those are washed in clean and pure water, they alone being effectually sprinkled with the *Blood* of Christ, *who of GOD is made unto us Wisdome, and Righteousness, and Sanctification, and Redemption*.

FOR if God should take Pleasure in us before we were *pure*, his Complacency would be *false*, and his Delight unrighteous. Till we are Delightful to him we can never be *Honorable* nor *Glorious* before him: Nor ever be pleasing to that *Goodness*, which is indelible (tho latent) in our *own* Souls, till we feel our selves clean and Beautiful.

IF any thing in the World can commend the value of Repentance, or discover the infinite use and necessity of it, this will certainly be a consideration Effectual: That tho GOD love us with an infinite and eternal Love, tho he magnifies his Mercy infinitely over all our Deservings, tho Jesus Christ loved us so, as to sacrifice himself in our places, tho he made infinite satisfaction to the Justice of God for our Sins, tho the Holy Ghost came down from Heaven for our sakes, nay tho we ourselves were taken up into Heaven, all this would be of little avail, and we should quickly be tumbled down again, if only Sin were Delightful to us, and our Wills so obstinate, that there was no place for Repentance in our Hearts, no sorrow, nor Contrition for the Offences we had committed. It is not the Love of GOD to us, so much as our love to him, that maketh Heaven. It may surprize you perhaps, but shall certainly instruct you, for the Love of GOD may be infinite, yet if it be unseen, breed no delight in the Soul: if it be sleighted and despised, it shall increase our Guilt, Shame, and Deformity, and make us the more Odious; which it must needs do, when we are impenitent. For so long, it is manifest that we are neither *Sensible* of his Love, nor *Just* unto it. The taste of its sweetness, and the Pleasure we take in his infinite Love, is the *Life* of Blessedness, and the *Soul* of Heaven. It is the *Concurrence* of our Love and His, when they meet together, that maketh Heaven.

HERE upon Earth we ought actually to grieve, and repent for our Sins: — But should GOD require a measure in our *Grief* answerable to its Causes, our Repentance it self would be an *Hell* unto us: For the Grief would be Endless and insupportable. Right Reason requires that we should be *infinitely* afflicted for the infinite folly and madness of Sin. But the Mercy of GOD dispenseth with our Grief so far, that it takes off the Pain, which its *infinite Measure* would inflict upon our sense, and accepts of an Acknowledgement made by our Reason that it ought to be infinite, if strict Justice were exacted at our Hands. Our intention is (in the Course of Reason,) to be infinitely and Eternally grieved for the Baseness of the Act, and the Vileness we have contracted, and so we should be, did its Effects continue and abide forever; for then we should be hated of GOD and become his Enemies World without End. But the Removal of that Hatred, and the infinite Mercy whereby we are forgiven, hath a kindly Operation on the Soul of every Penitent, and the Joy it infuseth restrains and limits the Excess of our Sorrow, it leaves the Intension of Grief, and its inclination in the Mind, yet stops the persecution, and relieves our Reason, by diverting the stream of its Operations and Exercises; it engageth its actual Resentments upon other Objects, which turn it all into Love and Adoration, Praise and Thanksgiving, Joy and Complacency. For the Love of God continued after our fall, and the Felicity to which we are called out of the Depth of our misery, all the Advantages we receive upon our Redemption, the Improvements of our miserable Estate, the Degrees and Ornaments that are added to the Beauty and perfection of Gods Kingdome upon so sad an occasion as Sin is, all these things take up our Thoughts in such a manner that while we are actually and fully Just to these, and Loving GOD, for his Eternal Love, infinitely more than we Love our selves, we live in him, and are all in raptures of Blessedness. Yet is there a *Vertual Sorrow* which Reason conceives as most due to Sin, which being expressed only in the Humility of our Souls, and seen as it were underneath the fruition of our Joys, in the lowly Conceit we retain of our selves (in the confession of our vileness and the deep Sence of our own unworthiness;) is far Greater, now we are restored to the favour and Love of GOD, far sweeter to be seen, and deeper to be understood; than the Grief for Sin would have been, had we been not redeemed, but Damned forever.

CHAP. XVIII.

Of Charity towards GOD. It Sanctifieth Repentance, makes it a Vertue, and turns it to a Part of our true Felicity. Our Love to all other Objects is to begin and End in GOD. Our Love of GOD hath an Excellency in it that makes it worthy to be desired by his Eternal Majesty. He is the only Supreme and Perfect friend. By Loving we enjoy him.

REPENTANCE without Love is so far from seating us in the Felicity of Heaven, that it is one of the Ingredients of the Torments in Hell, a natural Effect of Sin, and a great Part of the Misery of Devils. Love is a genuine Affection of the Soul, and so powerfully Sweet, when it is Satisfied and pleased, that it communicates the Relish of its own of *Delightfulness* to every Thing near it, and Transformes the most *Virulent* Affections into *Smooth*, Healing, *Perfective* Pleasures. Insomuch that in Heaven our Sorrow for Sin shall perhaps be infinite, yet the malignity of it so perfectly corrected, that tho we continue Eternally *Just*, in rendring our Sins that grief which is their due, it shall not discompose our peace, nor corrode our Delights, but increase our Repose in the Beauty of our souls, and make our Joys more full of Extasie, by those Melting, Lively, Bleeding, Resentments, which our Love will occasion in the very Grief, wherewith it perfects our Felicity. For as the falling out of Lovers is the Renewing of Love, so is the Mercy and Kindness of the one, even of him that was injured; and the calm and secure Indignation wherewith the other hates himself, for being guilty of so vile a miscarriage, the very Grace and Beauty of the Reconciliation; it is a great means of their mutual Endearment and Tenderness ever after: the Compassion of him that is Innocent, and the humble grief of the Guilty making the Joy of their future Correspondence more Deep and Serious, more Vigorous and Enflaming, more lasting.

LOVE is that which Sanctifies Repentance, and makes it pleasant bpth to him that is Beloved, and to him that is adored; Acceptable and Delightful to him that repenteth, as well as to him that had been injured. For the Sinners Restauration makes it as *Natural* to grieve for his *Fault* as to rejoyce in his *Felicity*, his sad and humble Resentments are his own Satisfaction, because he sees himself *Just* and *Rational* in them; he delights in his Sorrow, because it is *Honourable*, and finds a new Kind of pleasure in his *Abasement*, because it is relieved by the

Wonder of his Happy condition; and what he hath lost in himself is regained in the perfection and Goodness of his Object.

THAT GOD is the sovereign Object of Love I scarcely need to mention; all I shall observe upon this occasion, is; that we are more to Love him for his *Mercy* and *Compassion* towards us as *Sinners*, then for his *Goodness* and *Bounty* expressed at the first, as we were *Innocent Creatures*. The Bleeding Spectacle of his *Incarnate* Deity, and the Perseverance of his Miraculous and *Transcendent* Love after all our Offences, is another Kind of Motive to heighten our Charity of, and gives it another form, as much more Mysterious, so much more perfect and Delightful then ever. Our Sorrow for Sin infuses a New *Sense* into Nature, a New Beauty into Love, and gives as much unto it, as it receiveth from it. But this being better known by Experience, then by description I shall refer you to the Life of Heaven and Grace, for more ample satisfaction.

LOVE, as we have shewrd, may be extended to all Objects in Heaven and Earth; all that is Goodly and Amiable being capable of that Affection. Hereupon the Word *Love* is generally used for that Liking and Esteem we have for any thing, whether *Dead* or *alive*. We can Love Life, and desire to see Good Days; we can Love the Sun, and Wine; and Oyl, and Gold; Love our Dogs and Horses, fine Clothes and Jewels, Pleasures, Honours, Recreations, Houses, Riches, and as well as Love Men and Women, Souls and Angels. And evermore our Love expresseth it self in Tenderness and Care for the Preservation of what we Love, in Esteem of its Worth, and Delight in its Beauty, in endeavours also to promote its Welfare as far as it is capable. But there is another sort of Love towards *Living Objects*, Divine and reasonable, which we call *Charity*. This is that Vertue of which the Apostle saith, (after he had spoken of all the Miracles, Helps, Governments, Prophesies, Tongues, and other Gifts of the Holy Ghost, that were then in the Church) *And yet shew I unto you a more Excellent Way.* 1 *Cor.* 12. ult.[1] And in the next Chapter. *Tho I speak with the Tongues of Men and of Angels, and have not Charity, I am become as sounding Brass, or a tinkling Cymbal. And tho I have the Gift of Prophesie, and understand all mysteries, and all Knowledge, and tho I have all Faith, so that I could remove Mountains, and have no Charity, I am nothing, and tho I bestow all my Goods to feed the poor, and tho I give my Body to be burned, and have not Charity it profiteth me nothing.* It is that concerning which our

---

[1] Marginal gloss: 1 Cor. 13.1.

Saviour speaketh,[1] *The first of all the Commandements is, Hear O Israel, the Lord our GOD is one Lord, and thou shalt Love the Lord thy GOD with all thy heart, and with all thy Soul, and with all thy Mind, and with all thy Strength: This is the first Commandement: And the Second is like, namely this, Thou shalt Love thy Neighbour as thy self: There is none other Commandment greater then those.* Nay perhaps it is that of which he saith to his Apostles, when they had admired at his Miracles. *He that believeth on me, the works that I do shall he do also, and greater Works then these shall he do, because I go to the Father.* For Faith worketh by Love, Love is the Life of Faith, and without the Works of the one the other is Dead: The Works of Love are the End of all Miracles, and more Blessed then they. Nay Love is the End of *Faith* as well as it is of the *Law*: for the Apostle saith, The End of the Commandment is Charity, *out of a pure Heart, and of a good conscience, and of Faith unfeigned.* It is the End of the very Creation of the World, of all Gods Labors and Endeavours, of all his Ways in all Ages, all the faculties and powers of the Soul, the very End of the Redemption of Mankind, the End of the Jewish Oeconomy under the Law, the End of all the Dispensations of Grace and Mercy under the Gospel; the End of our Saviours coming down into the World, the End of all his Miracles, Tears, and Blood, the End of the Holy Ghosts appearing upon Earth, the End of all the Means of Grace, and in some sort the very last End of all Rewards and Punishments whatsoever. The everlasting Continuance of this Love is the End of Eternity it self in a manner, and if our Love be not the End of GODS Love, his is of ours. And if the Truth be deeply inquired into, the *Intermixture* is so sweet, that his is the End of ours, ours of his. For he Loveth us with the Love of *Benevolence*, that we may Love him; and he desires to be beloved of us, that he may Love us, with another Kind of Love, distinct from the former, even that of *Complacency*. Which Love of Complacency is the Crown of ours, and so Delightful to us, that it is the very End of our Desire, and begetteth in us a new Love of Complacency fitly answering his unto us.

NOW if Love be the End of all the laws, Works, and Ways of GOD, of all our Saviours Labours and sufferings, of our souls and Bodies, of the whole Creation, of all the Endeavours and Desires of the Deity, in all the Dispensations of his Grace and Providence, there must be something in its Nature Equivalent to all these Transcendent Undertakings, to justifie the *Wisdom* that selected Love for its Sovereign Object, for it is the office of Wisdome to suit the means

---

[1] Marginal gloss: Mark. 12.30,31.

and their End together, so that the Excellency of the one may be worthy of all the Cost and Difficulty of the other. For it is a foolish thing to pursue a base and feeble End by Glorious and Wonderful Methods, because its Vileness will Disgrace the Design, and with it their Beauty, their very Grandure will be absurd, where their Issue is but contemptible. The Apostle therefore telleth us that *Love is the fulfilling of the Law*, and that it is *the Bond of Perfectness*. And pursuing its properties a little more Ample, he saith, *Charity suffereth long, and is kind. Charity envyeth not, Charity Vaunteth not it self, is not puffed up, doth not behave it self unseemly, seeketh not her own, is not easily provoked, thinketh no evil, rejoyceth not in iniquity, but rejoyceth in the Truth, beareth all Things, believeth all things, hopeth all things, endureth all things. Charity never faileth, &c.*[1]

IT is one noble Effect of Charity, that it suffereth afflictions cheerfully and patiently for the sake of its Beloved: Another is its Kindness to its Object; its sweet and Courteous inclination to do all manner of Good: Another, for which it is highly valuable, is, that it envieth not the Felicity or Glory of its Beloved but taketh Pleasure to see it far higher and greater then its own: is not apt to vaunt and brag of its Perfections, but hath an humble Esteem of all its Atchievments: doth not behave it self in distasteful manner, but studies and designes the Honour Benefit and satisfaction of its Object. But that which of all other is its greatest Perfection, is, that *it seeketh not its own*: it is not Mercenary or self ended, but truly Generous and Heroick in its Performances. It Sacrificeth it self, and all its interests, to the Advantage of its Object; it preferreth the Person it Loveth above it self, desires its Exhaltation, and delights in its Glory more then its own, It *is not easily provoked*, because it puts the best sence upon all that is done by its Object: *Thinketh no evil*, is not suspicious, or malevolent, or censorious, but frameth honourable and fair *Ideas* of all that is thought or done by its Beloved: Hateth all Impurity that may displease its Object, all black and crooked Apprehensions, that may wrang and disguise it; *beareth all* with Hope and Equanimity, because it *believeth* its Object to be Good, and Wise, till it must of necessity change its Opinion, and entertain a Judgement tending to its condemnation. It is no longer Charity then, but dislike and aversion, when it ceaseth to think well of its Object: for it is another *Principle* or distinct in Nature from *Love*, as its Actions are from the Actions of Love; the diversity of the Effects evidently proving a Difference in their Causes.

---

[1] Marginal gloss: 1 Cor.13.4.5.&6.

THE Quality, by which Charity *rejoyceth in the Truth*, is an incomparable excellence and commendation of its Nature. Because the Truth is GODS infinite Goodness, and Love, and Providence, which are exercised in preparing Delights and Treasures for his Beloved. The truth is the Felicity and Glory of the Soul. And if it be *true* that all Eternity is full of Joys, and all the World enriched with Delights, that a man is infinitely beloved of GOD, and made in his Image on purpose, that he might enjoy all the Best of all possible Treasures in his similitude, he may well *rejoyce in the Truth*: because no ruth can be greater or more delightful, than that himself is exalted to the Throne of GOD, and ordained to live in Communion with him.

BUT that Quality, by which the Soul *believeth*, and *hopeth all things*, that concern the Honour and Fidelity of its Beloved, is yet more acceptable and delightful than the former. For a good opinion of the Nature and Intention of the Person with whom we are united, is the *Basis* and Foundation of all our Respect, the Cement of our Peace, and the Life and Soul of all that Honour that is paid unto him. The very Grace and Beauty of all our Conversation dependeth upon it, and if it be true, that we are more to love GOD for the intrinsick Perfections of his Essence, then for all his Gifts, the chief Business of our Knowledge is to Frame glorious Apprehensions of his Nature, and to Believe him in all things so Kind and Wise, that he is True and Faithful in all his Declarations, and most fit to be Honoured in all the Dispensations of his Providence, because he is ever mindful of his Protestations and Promises. For then we can believe, that all things shall work together for our Good, can safely trust our selves, and all that is ours in his hands; resign our selves up to his Disposal with Joy, and say *Thy Will be done*, for it is *Holy, Good, and acceptable*. Thy Will alone is of all other Wills most Perfect and Desirable. There are on Earth indeed more nice Emergencies, many Obscurities and Riddles, in the midst of all which to think so well of GOD as he deserveth, is the most acceptable thing in the World; for it argues a great confidence of his Worth, and a Love that is founded on *Substantial Causes* never to be removed. It feedeth the Soul with a lively hope, and fair Expectation of great Things from him: by which alone we do right to His GODHEAD, in acknowledging the Perfection of his Love and Goodness, and by which alone we are made able to adore him and to live in Union and Communion with him.

THERE is great Talk of Friendship, it is accounted the only Pleasure, in the World; Its Offices are highly magnified of all: Kindness of

Behaviour, a through and clear communication of Souls, a secure Reliance upon each others Fidelity, a perfect Discovery of all our Thoughts, Intentions, and Resentments, an ardent willingness to impart Lives and Estate for the Benefit of our Friend, the Reposing of all our Secrets in each others Bosomes, to do all services, and suffer all affliction, for each others sakes, to prefer the Concerns of our Friend upon all Occasions above our own, these are the *Magnalia Amicitiæ, & Arcana mutuæ Benevolentiæ*, the Great and mighty Effects for which Friendship is admired: But all these, without a good Opinion of our Friend, are nothing worth, they are but Externals of Friendship, the greatest Secret in its Nature is, the mutual agreement of Souls and Spirits, the Delight which either taketh in the other, the honour and esteem they give and receive, the Approbation and Love of each others Dispositions, the Sence and Admiration of each others Vertues, the continual Desire of being alwayes together, peculiar Extasie, which the Beauty of either occasioneth in the other, when of all other Treasures in the World their Persons are the greatest to one another. Either is the proper Element and *Refrigerium* of the others Soul. Their Bosoms are the mutual Receptacles and Temples of each others accomplishments, whereinto they are received in all their Desert, and have *Justice* done to every degree and Perfection in their Nature; their Hearts are the Thrones where they are exalted, and magnified, and live at Ease, are honoured and worshipped, extolled, and reign as absolute in each others Souls. There are some slight aims and Adumbrations of this Friendship on Earth; but the best and highest Degree of it here beneath is but a rude and imperfect shadow, only GOD is the *Sovereign friend*, all Adoration paid to any one beside is mere Idolatry. Our Hearts can be absolutely Sacrificed to none, but him; because he alone is immutable in Goodness. We cannot infinitely honour and delight in any but Him; it is he alone that can infinitely honour, and delight in us. All our Lives, Estates, and Services are Due to him, his Will alone is to be wholly ours, because no other Will is infallibly Right, Wise, Holy, but his alone.

   THE Union of our Wills is a Perfection of Love: but that at which he aimeth by all his Labours, and Gifts, and Benefits, is our Right and Good Opinion of his Excellencies and Perfections. That we should see and discern his interior Properties, admire his Graces, adore his Perfections, adore and magnifie his Beauty and Glory, this is the End for which he communicates himself in all his Works and Ways unto us; it is the End of the whole Creation, and of all the Excellent Things in the universe: for by this he establisheth his Empire in our souls and makes us Pleasing to himself in all our Operations. And for this Cause it is, that the Apostle plainly tells us that tho we give our Body to be burned, and all our Goods to feed the poor, without Charity it profiteth nothing. To render to GOD the Honour that is due to his Name, to receive and admire all his Bounties, to rejoyce in all his Operations, to adore him in all his Ways, to take pleasure in all his Works, to fill Heaven and Earth with our Joys and Praises, is a Work which cannot but be agreeable by its Nature, to his Eternal Essence. And if this be the Work of Love, it is that which is most Excellent, because he is therein both pleased and enjoyed; GOD and all his Creatures are united together by Love alone, and in the Eternal Exercise of pure and perfect Love all Blessedness and Glory consisteth.

IF you require what it is to love GOD, you will find it worthy of his Highest desire, because thereby all our souls, nay all his Creatures, and his whole Kingdome are perfected, for to Love GOD as we ought to do, is to Honour him as our Father, Benefactor, Bridegroom, and King, to contemplate him as our Cause with Complacency, and to rest in him as our End, to delight in him as our Creator, Preserver, Lawgiver, and Redeemer, to dedicate our selves, wholly to that Service, whatever it be, wherein he is chiefly pleased and delighted. It is to love him in himself, in all his Works, in all his Ways, in all his Laws, in all his Attributes, in all his Thoughts and Counsels, in all his Perfections; It implies the Knowledge of all Objects, the Use of all Means, the Attainment of all Ends: all Wisdome and Goodness, all Obedience and Gratitude, all Righteousness and Holiness, all Joy and Praise, all Honour and Esteem, all Blessedness and Glory. For it is to Love him with all our Heart, and with all our Soul, with all our Strength, and with all our Might, with all our Understanding, with all our Will, with all our Affection, with all the Power of our soul, with all our Inclinations and Faculties, in all his Creatures, in all his Appearances, in Heaven and Earth, in Angels and Men, in all Kingdoms and Ages. It is to see and desire, to Esteem and delight in his Omnipresence and Eternity, and in every Thing by which he manifesteth himself in either of these, so that all Enlargement, and Greatness, and Light, and Perfection, and Beauty, and Pleasure, are founded in it, and to Love him to Perfection implies all Learning and Attainment, because we must necessarily be acquainted with all Things in all Worlds, before we can thorowly and compleatly do it. Which here upon Earth to do by Inclination and Endeavour to the utmost of our Power, is all that is required of us;

And if we do it to our utmost, it shall be rewarded in the Beatifick Vision, with a full and Blessed Perfection with an actual Love exactly resembling his, and fully answerable to it in the Highest Heavens.

THERE are two common Motives of Love among Men, the one the Goodness and Excellency of the Person, the other his particular Kindness and Love to us: And both these are in the Highest Degree in GOD. He is of infinite Goodness and Excellency in himself, for there is nothing Good in the world, but what hath received all its Goodness from Him. His Goodness is the Ocean, and all the Goodnesses of Creatures little Streams flowing from that Ocean. Now you would think him a Madman that should say the Sea were not greater then a trifling Brook: and certainly it is no less folly to suppose that the Goodness of GOD doth not as much (nay infinitely more) exceed that of all the Creatures. The Sun is a lively Mirror of that Eternal Act of Love which is the Glory of his Essence, but it is infinitely less prone to communicate its Beams, and doth less Good to it self, and infinitely less to all other Creatures. It shines for their sakes nevertheless, and clothes it self with Glory, by the splendor of its Beams and is an Emblem of GOD, who exerteth his Power with infinite Pleasure, and by communicating his Essence in an infinite Manner, propagates his Felicity, and Glory, to the utmost Height and Perfection. By proceeding from himself to all Objects throughout all Worlds, he begets, and dwelleth in himself, he inhabits Eternity in a Blessed and more vigorous Manner, by establishing the Felicity of all his Creatures, and becomes their infinite and Eternal Glory. *Wherein* his particular Kindness and Love to us appeareth because he hath fitted us with Qualities and Powers adopted for so great an End, and as particularly appropriated all to us, as the Sun to the Eye of every Spectator. For our bodies and our Souls are made to enjoy the Benefit of all, and his Desire is that we should attain the End for which we are created. On his side all is prepared; on ours nothing is wanting but Love to embrace and take pleasure in his Goodness, which shineth in all these Things, and Created them on purpose, that being manifested by them, we might delight in it for ever.

HE that loveth not GOD with all his Heart, liveth a Life most contrary to Nature. For to Love is as natural for the Soul, as to shine for the Sun: and the more Lovely any thing is, the more prone we are to Delight in it: if any thing be infinitly Amiable, we are prone to Love it in an infinite measure, we prefer the Better above the worse, & cannot rest but in the best of all. Reason is the Essence of the Soul, and tends always to the utmost Perfection. The more Divine and Glorious any Thing is, the more high and Noble is the Love that we bear it: No Beauty less then the most Perfect, no Pleasure, no Wisdome, no Empire, no Learning, no Greatness, Wealth, or Honour, less then the most sublime can be our full Satisfaction: no little degree of Love, nothing less then the most Supreme and violent can content us: So that GOD being most truely perfect in all these, is the Adequate Object of all our Desires, and the only Person fit to be esteemed in an infinite manner. It is as natural for Man to Love him, as to desire and delight in any being, which supplies the ordinary and daily necessities of his Life.

TO Love him as we ought implies two things, that are agreable to the Nature of Love, yet very rarely to be found among the Sons of Men, a desire to please him, and a Desire to enjoy him. The Desire of *Pleasing* is a constant fruit and effect of Love. For he that Loves, is very desirous to approve himself, and to do whatsoever he thinks will be grateful to his Beloved. According to the Degree of Love, the desire is more or less. Where we Love Earnestly, we are extreamly Earnest and Careful to please: Where Love is remiss, there is little need or Regard of any thing: But *infinite* Love! It is impossible to declare what favour and Zeal it will produce. If we Love GOD, we shall keep his Commandements with a Tenderness and Desire so extreme, that no Joy will be so great as the Observation of his Laws; It will be with us, as it was with our Lord Jesus Christ, it will be *our Meat and Drink to do the Will of our Father which is in Heaven*. The measure of our Love will not infuse some slight and faint Endeavours of Pleasing, but put us on the most painful and costly Duties, make us willing to forsake our own Ease, Goods, Friends, yea Life it self, when we cannot keep them without offending our Creator.

THE desire of *Enjoying* is constantly seen in our Love to one another. If any man hath a friend whom he intirely loveth, he desires his Conversation, Wishes to be always in his Company, and thinketh the Time long till he and his friend be together. And thus will it be in our Love to GOD, if as great and Hearty as it ought to be. In this Life our Enjoyment of GOD is more imperfect, more compleat and perfect in the Life to come. Here upon Earth we desire to converse with him in his Ordinances, in Prayer, Meditation, hearing his Word, in receiving the Sacrament, which are intended all for this purpose, to bring us into a neerer Intimacy, and familiarity with GOD by speaking so to him, & hearing him speak, and shew himself to us. If we love him indeed, we shall highly Value these Ways of Conversing with him: it is all here upon Earth whereby we can enjoy him. It will make us with *David* esteem *one Day in his Courts better than a thousand.* We shall delight in all the Means of approaching to him as often as possible, and use them diligently, to the End of uniting us more and more unto him, who is the Object of our Desire and the Life of our Souls. And for as much as there is another Enjoyment of GOD which is more compleat and perfect, we shall groan earnestly, *desire to be dissolved and be with Christ*, where we may see no more in a Glass, but Face to Face, and Know as we are Known. For Love is strong as Death, many Waters cannot quench Love, neither can the floods drown it, Affliction, Persecution, Sickness, any thing that will bring us to Heaven, will be acceptable and Delightful.

IF you would know more fully, why GOD desires to be Beloved, you may consider, that Love is not onely the Motive, and Incentive to Vertue, the Cause of Obedience, but the form and Essence of every Grace, and the fulfilling of the Law, We shall chuse him for our GOD, and have no other GODS but him, no Delights, no Sovereign Enjoyment but him alone. We shall honour him with all our Souls, and adore him with every Power of our Will and Understanding: We shall not regard Images and shadows, but worship him immediately in Spirit and in Truth. We shall not take his Name in vain, nor contentedly stand by when others abuse it: But shall praise his Name, and desire to see it glorified throughout the World. For Love desires the Honour, and delights in the Glory and Advancement of its Beloved. We shall reverence his Sanctuary, and keep his Sabbaths, desiring Rest from other Avocations, that we may contemplate his Glory in all his Works. For his sake we shall observe the Laws of the second Table, and Love our Neighbour as our self. For to Love him is no Impediment, but a Strong Engagement, and incentive to the Love of all his Creatures. We shall honour our Parents for his sake, and preserve the Life of our Neighbour: We shall not rob him of his happiness in his Wife, nor wrong him in her Chastity and Fidelity towards him. We shall not steal from him, nor diminish his Possessions. We shall not defame him, nor hurt him by Lies; but vindicate and preserve his Reputation: it will be our joy and Satisfaction to see his honour clear and unblemished. We shall not injure him so much as in a thought, nor covet ought that is his, either for necessity or pleasure: but study to add to his Contentments.

WERE all the World as full of this Love as it ought to be, Paradice would still continue, and all Mankind would be the Joy and Glory of the whole Creation. The Love of GOD towards all would dwell and abide in every Soul, and the Felicity of all would be the particular Joy of every person. All the Earth would be full of Repose, and Peace, and Prosperity, nothing but Honour, and Kindness, and Contentment would replenish the World. Which leads me now to that other Branch of Love, which is Charity to our Neighbour.

CHAP. XIX.

Charity to our Neighbour most natural and Easie in the Estate of Innocency: Adams *Love to* Eve *and his children a great Examplar of our Love to all the World. The Sweetness of Loving. The Benefits of being Beloved. To Love all the World, and be beloved by all the World is perfect security and Felicity. Were the Law fulfilled all the World would be turned into Heaven.*

CHARITY to our Neighbour is Love expressed towards GOD in the Best of his Creatures. We are to Love GOD in all the Works of his Hands, but in those especially, that are most near unto him, chiefly those in which he manifesteth himself most clearly, and these are they that are most like him, most exalted by him, most loved of him, and most delightful to him.

ANGELS and Men, are so distinct from the residue of the Creation, that all the Works of GOD, as if they were Things of another Kind, are put in Subjection under their feet. They were made in his Image, and are often called *the Sons of GOD.* They are the Sovereign Objects of his Eternal Love, every one of them, considered apart, is so Glorious; as if he were the Sole individual friend of GOD, and King of the Universe, so that they are to be treated in another Manner, as High and Sacred Persons, elevated above the Race of ordinary Creatures, as a Progeny of Kings that are all of them friends to the King of Kings, Ambassadours representing his Person, in whom he is injured, or Obliged.

I confess there are many Disguises, that overcast the Face of Nature with a vail, and cloud these Sovereign Creatures: the Excellency, the Absence, and Distance, and unknown Nature of Angels; the Perversness of Nature, the Ignorance, and Unkindness, and Disorders of Men Darken, and Eclipse this Glorious Duty, and make it uncouth and difficult to us: But all these Disorders came in by Sin, and it is expedient to remove the Confusions that blind us, in our miserable Estate, and to look upon this Vertue of Charity, in the Naked Beauty which appeareth to us in the Light of *Eden.*

IN the Purity of Nature, Men are Amiable Creatures and prone to Love. Two great Advantages; of which Sin and misery hath bereaved us, and to which we are restored but in Part, even then when we are Sanctified. Where the Beauty of the Object is intire, and perfect, and the Goodness of the Spectator clear and undefiled, to Love is as Natural and Easie, as for fire to enflame when applied to convenient matter. For the Beauty of the Object is Oyl and Fuel to the affection of the Spectator. It is not more Easie to delight in what is pleasant, than it is to desire what is Good and Amiable. To be commanded to take pleasure in it is Liberty, not Constraint. To be forbidden would be hard. A Prohibition would be the Severest Law, and the most cruel Bondage. There was no Positive Law in *Eden*, that required a Man to Love his Neighbour, it was a Law of Nature. The Nature of the Object required it, and our Nature prompted it self thereunto. The Service that Law required was perfect freedome. *Adam* was commanded to Love *Eve*, by a silent Law, Suprized by her Beauty and captivated by the Chains of Nature. He was amazed at so fair a Creature, her Presence was so Delightful that there was no need of a Law; an injunction had imported some Sluggishness in the zeal of his Affection. His Appetite and Reason were united together, and both invited him to lose himself in her Embraces: She was as acceptable a Present of the Love of GOD, as Wisdome and Goodness could invent for him. He was too apt to admire her, had not her Soul been as worthy; as her Symmetry was transcendent. He admired the Bounty of the *Donor* in so Great a Gift, and Great Part of his Life was to be spent in the Contemplation of his Treasure. He had a Noble Creature made in the Image of GOD for him alone! Her soul was far more excellent in Beauty then her Face, a Diviner and more Glorious Object than the whole world. Her Intelligence and Vivacity, Her Lofty and clear Apprehensions, Her Honour and Majesty, Her Freedome of Action, her Kindness of Behaviour, her Angelical Affections, Her fitness for Conversation, Her sweet and Tender Principles, a million of Graces and Endowments conspiring to enrich Her Person and Perfection, made all the World to serve *Adam* with one Degree of Pleasure more in serving and pleasing her. The Universe seemed to be Nothing but the Theatre of their mutual Love, as if all the World were made for nothing else, but to minister to her for his sake, and to make him happy in the Enjoyment of Her. While the fruition was sanctified by a Just acknowledgement and Thanksgiving to the Author.

WE produce *Eve* only for a President; this first sweetness is but a Pattern and Copy of what follows, fair Prologue to a more magnificent scene, and used by us as a meer Introduction. *Adam* was able to Love Millions more, and as *She* was taken out of his *side*, so were *they* to spring from his *Bowels:* All to be as Great, and fair, and Glorious as she, as full of Soul, and as full of Love. As the Woman was the Glory of man, so were their Off-springs the Glory of both: I mean they had been so, by the Law of Nature, had not the due course of it been disturbed. Which Accident is wholy to be fathered on *Adams* fondness to please his Wife, and to be mothered upon her Lightness and Credulity. But we being here to disclose the Felicity which is hid in the fulfilling of GODS Laws and to justifie his Love in commanding this *Charity* to our Neighbors, must not regard the Malevolence of Men, but look upon the pure Intention of the Law; and the success that would have followed, had it been, as it might have been, perfectly observed.

ALL *Adams* Children had been himself divided, and multiplied into millions, and every one a Greater Treasure to him than the whole world. The Stars had not been by a thousand Degrees so great an Ornament to the skies, as they to the Earth, an offspring of Incarnate Angels, an assembly of corporeal Seraphims, a Race of Celestial Kings, every one loving and Honouring *Adam*, as the Fountain of their Being, and the Author of their Well being, of the one in begetting them, of the other by *Standing* and abiding in his Integrity. They had all been so many Pledges of his Wives Affection; Monuments of love, New and Powerful Endearments, Enlargements of their Parents, Being Mirrors and Memorials of both their perfections; For all had been made for every one; and every one had been the Joy, nay and the Beauty of all. All had been every ones Objects, and every one the Spectator of all, every one would have delighted in the Beauty of all, and all had conspired and strived together in the love of every one, their concurrence in fulfilling the Law would have banished all sin and Oppression, Discontentment and sorrow, Wrong and Injury, Theft and Murder, and Adultery, and Lying out of the World, there had been no noise of War or Contention, or anger, or Envy, or Malice, or Revenge, this accursed *the Black Guard* had never appeared; but all would have been Delightful to one another: Affections, Honours, Benefits, and Services, Pleasures, Praises, and Prosperities, these alone had filled the World, with Beauty, Security, Peace, and Glory, Wisdome, Goodness, Love, and Felicity, Joy, and Gratitude had been, all that had been Known, had Love been intirely and inviolably observed.

BUT where GODS Laws are broken there is confusion and every Evil Work. Which nevertheless does more highly commend the excellency of his Nature, and reflect a Praise upon that Authority, which must first be despised, before any Misery can come into the World. If the Duty which the Law requires be all sweetness, and Felicity, and Glory,

Compleatly good, and on every side Advantageous and Profitable; we that fail in the Discharge of our Duty may be condemned, but GOD is to be admired, and still to be confessed most Glorious and Holy, because he delights in the welfare of his Creatures, and makes Religion so desireable a Mystery, and enjoynes such admirable Things, as would make all transcendently Blessed, and Good, and Perfect were they perfectly observed. He designes that all should be amiable, whom we are commanded to Love, and that we should be not only prone to Love, but actually full of it, and the reason why he constitutes Love, as the Sovereign Law; is, because, as our Saviour saith, *There is none other greater Commandement*, none more Blessed, or Divine, or Glorious, none more conducive to our Bliss, his pleasure, the perfection of his Kingdome. Removing the Law of Love, it is impossible to put another Law in its Place, which can answer the Designs of his Wisdome and Goodness, or comply with the Exigencies of our Estate and condition. It is as easie to change the Nature of GOD, and devise another deity as Good and convenient, as to invent a better Law then this, which is plainly of all other the most Divine and Holy.

If we ascend up into Heaven, and take a perfect account of all the Operations and Effects of Love as they appear in Glory; we may first give our selves the Liberty of Wishing, and consult, what of all Things possible is most fit to be desired. Had we a Power to chuse, what Kind of Creatures would our selves be made? Could we desire to be any thing more great and Perfect then the Image of GOD? In the full extent and utmost height of its Nature it is the Resemblance of all his Blessedness and Glory. To have Beings without Power, or power without Operations, will never make us like GOD, because by an infinite and Eternal Act of Power he is what he is. Actions are so necessary that all Felicity and Pleasure is continually founded in some act or other, and no Essence is of any value, but as it employs it self in a delightful manner. What Law then would we have to regulate our actions by? Since Actions are of different Kinds, some good, some Evil, some convenient, some Hurtful, some Honourable and some Delightful, some Base and Odious, some are Miserable, and some are Glorious, we would chuse such a Law to guide our Actions by, as might make them honourable and delightful, and good and Glorious. All these are with Wisdome and Blessedness shut up in Love. And by Love it is that we make our selves infinitly Beautiful, and Amiable, and Wise, and Blessed, while we extend that Delightful and Blessed Affection to all objects that are Good and Excellent, so that on this side we have all we can desire, Essences, Laws and Actions that most tend to our full and compleat perfection. If on the other side, we look after objects for this Affection, and desire to have some Creatures most Excellent, and fit for their Goodness to be Beloved, what Creatures can we wish above all other, that can be made to satisfie and please us? Can any thing be more high and perfect then the similitude of GOD? GOD is LOVE, and his Love the Life and Perfection of Goodness. There is no *Living Goodness* so sweet and amiable as that alone, none so Wise, none so Divine, none so Blessed. What Laws can we desire those Creatures to be guided by, but the Laws of Love? By Love they are made Amiable and delightful to us; by Love they are made Great and Blessed in themselves. All Honour and Praise, Benevolence and Good-will, Kindness and Bounty, Tenderness and Compassion, all Sweetness, and Courtesie, and Care, and Affabilitie, all Service and Complacency are shut up in Love: It is the Fountain of all Benefits and Pleasures whatsoever. All Admiration, Esteem and Gratitude, all Industry, Respect, and Courage are shut up in Love, and by Love alone doth any object of ours Sacrifice it self to our Desire and Satisfaction. So that on that side our Wishes are Compleated too: while the most High, and Blessed, and Glorious Creatures love us as themselves. For thereby they are as much our Felicity as their own, and as much take pleasure and Delight therein. *As for GOD his Way is perfect*; like curious needle work on either side, compleat and exquisite.

ALL that we can fear, or except against, is his Omission, in forbearing to compell his Creatures to love, whether they will or no. But in that Liberty, which he gave them, his Love is manifested most of all. In giving us a Liberty it is most apparent: for without Liberty there can be no Delight, no Honour, no Ingenuity, or Goodness at all: No action can be Delightful that is not our Pleasure in the Doing. All Delight is free and voluntary by its Essence. Force and Aversion are inconsistent with its nature. Willingness in its operation is the Beauty of the Soul, and its Honour founded in the freedom of its Desire. Whatsoever it does not desire and delight in, tho the matter of the performance be never so excellent, the Manner is spoiled, and totally Blasted. Now can we compel another to desire or delight in any Thing? The Soul in it self hath an Inclination to, or an aversion from every object. The Ingenuity and Worth of the Soul is expressed in the Kindness of its own Intention, in the freedom of its Desire to do what is Excellent, in the delight it taketh to love, its Goodness is founded. Now tho GOD infinitely hated Sin, yet he gave us an irrevocable Power to do what we pleased, and adventured the Hazzard of that which he infinitely hated, that being free to do what we would, we might be Honourable and delightful in doing (freely, and of our own Accord) what is Great and Excellent. For without this Liberty there can be no Love, since Love is an active and free affection; that must spring from the Desire and pleasure of the Soul. It is the Pleasure of a Lover to promote the Felicity of his object. Whatsoever Services he is compelled to do, he is either meerly passive in them or Cross unto them, they are all void of the Principal Grace and Beauty that should adorn them, and make them pleasant and satisfactory: men may be Dead, and moved like stones; but in such causes there is no Love, neither do they act of themselves, when they are over–ruled, and forced by another. For this cause hath it pleased God, in order to our Perfection, to make the most Sublime and Sovereign Creatures all *Free*, wherein he hath expressed the greatest Love in the World. As we may see by all the Displeasures and Pains it hath cost him, through our Abuse of so illimited and great a perfection. But where his Love is most Highly and Transcendently expressed, there are we most prone to suspect it, Nature is so Cross and disorderly. There can be no Wisdom without a voluntary Act, for in all Wisdome there is Counsel and design. Where no consultation nor Election precedes, the best operation in all the World is Blind and Casual. Fortune and chance must have no hand in that which wisdom Effecteth: no more then Force and necessity must have in that Goodness, where all the kindness ought to be in the Intention of the Benefactor. There is something in it which I cannot explain. It is easily conceived, but will never (I think) in Words, be expressed. The *Will* has a mighty hand in all the Divinity of perfect Goodness. It is the *Mind* of the Doer that is the principal object of all our Desire and Expectation.

HAVING for these Causes made his Creatures free, he has for–feited their Choise, and secured their Determination, as far as was possible. He hath done all that can be devised to make them Love us, and left nothing undone but only that which was absolutely necessary that they might *Love*. They could not Love us, if they were not left to themselves to do it freely. And their *Ability* being provided for, nay an Inclination given to make them willing, he has strictly commanded & enjoyned them to Love, by Nature allured them, & ordered us so, that we might be fit to be Beloved, he hath made it sweet and rational to Love, given them his own Example, and solemnly protested that he will accept of no Love to himself, but what is accompanied with Love to his friends and servants, engaged them to Love, or be Eternally miserable. And if for all this they will not Love, the fault is none of his. All that he has done to let secure their Love to himself, he has done to secure their Love to us: and is as much or more concerned in their Love to us, then in that which himself requireth and Expecteth. Nay he hath made it impossible for them (truly) to Love themselves without doing of it: And if they will neither Love GOD nor themselves, we may well be despised for Company. He infinitely desires their Love, and would take infinite Pleasure in the Operation. There is no Way to make themselves Honourable and Delightful to GOD, but only by Loving us, as his soul requireth. And by all these Inducements and Causes, are we our selves stirred up to Love, freely to exert the Power of Love to others in like manner.

THAT which yet further commendeth this Vertue of Love unto us, is, that it is the only Soul of all Pleasure and Felicity *in all Estates*. It is like the Light of the Sun, in all the Kingdomes, and Houses, and Eyes, and Ages, in Heaven, in Earth, in the Sea, in Shops and Temples; in Schooles and Markets, in Labours and Recreations, in Theatres and Fable. It is *the Great Dæmon of the World*, and the Sole Cause of all Operations. It is evidently impossible for any Fancy, or Play, or Romance, or Fable to be composed well, and made Delightful, without a Mixture of Love in the Composure. In all Theatres, and Feasts, and Weddings, and Triumphs, and Coronations, Love is the Soul and Perfection of all, in all Persons, in all Occupations, in all Diversions, in all Labours, in all Vertues, in all Vices, in all Occasions, in all Families, in all Cities and Empires, in all our Devotions, and Religious Actions, Love is all in all. All the Sweetness of Society is seated in Love, the Life of Musick and Dancing is Love; the Happiness of Houses, the Enjoyment of Friends, the Amity of Relations, the Providence of Kings, the Allegiance of Subjects, the Glory of Empires, the Security, Peace and Welfare of the World is seated in Love. Without Love all is Discord and Confusion. All Blessings come upon us by Love, and by Love alone all Delights and Blessings are enjoyed. All happiness is established by Love, and by Love alone is all Glory attained. GOD Knoweth that Love uniteth Souls, maketh men of one Heart in a House, filles them with Liberallity and Kindness to each other, makes them Delightfull in presence, faithful in Absence, Tender of the Honour and Welfare of their Beloved, Apt to obey, ready to please, Constant in Trials, Patient in sufferings, Couragious in Assaults, Prudent in Difficulties, Victorious and Triumphant. All that I shall need to observe further, is, that *it compleated the Joys of Heaven*. Well therefore may Wisdome desire Love, well may the Goodness of GOD delight in Love. It is the form and the Glory of his Eternal Kingdome. And therefore it is that the Apostle saith, *Charity never faileth: but whether there be Prophesies, they shall fail; whether there be Tongues, They shall cease; whether there be Knowledge it shall vanish away. For we know in part, and we Prophesie in part, but when that which is perfect is come, then that which is in part shall be done away. For now we see through a Glass darkly, but then Face to Face; now I Know in part, but then shall I know, as also I am Known. And now abideth Faith, Hope and Charity, these three, but the Greatest of these is Charity.*

CHAP. XX.

Of Prudence. Its Foundation is Charity, its End Tranquillity and Prosperity on Earth, its Office to reconcile Duty and Convenience, and to make Vertue subservient to Tempora Welfare. Of Prudence in Religion, Friendship, and Empire. The End of Prudence is perfect Charity.

CHARITY is that which entereth into every Vertue, as a main Ingredient of its Nature and Perfection. Love is the fountain and the End of all, without which there can be no Beauty nor Goodness in any of the Vertues. Love to one self, Love to GOD, Love to man, Love to Felicity, a clear and intelligent Love is the Life and Soul of every Vertue, without which Humility is but Baseness, Fortitude but Feirceness, Patience but Stupidity, Hope but Presumption, Modesty but Simpering, Devotion but Hypocrisie, Liberality is Profuseness, Knowledge vanity, Meekness but a sheepish Tameness, and Prudence it self but fraud and Cunning. For as all other Vertues, so is Prudence, founded on Charity. He that is not Good can never be Prudent for he can never benefit himself, or others. For the Designes of Prudence are to secure one self in the Exercise of every Vertue, and so to order the Discharge of ones Duty, as neither to hurt a mans self in his Life, Estate, Honour, Health, or Contentment, nor yet to fail in the Attainment of that Worth and Beauty, which will make our Lives Delightful to others, and as Glorious to our selves, as Beneficial and Delightful.

PRUDENCE hath an eye to every Circumstance, and Emergence of our Lives. Its Designe is to make a mans self as Great and glorious as is possible, and in pleasing all the World, to order and improve all Advantages without incurring the least inconvenience: To reconcile our Devotion, Obedience and Religion, to our Interest and Prosperity in the World: To shun all extreams, to surmount all Difficulties, to overrule all Disadvantages, to discern all Opportunities, and lay hold on all Occasions of doing Good to our selves. Its Office is to consult, and contrive, and effect our own Welfare in every Occurrence that can befal us in the World, and so to mingle all Vertues in the Execution of our Duties, that they may relieve, and aid, and perfect each other, in such a manner as at once to be pleasing to GOD, profitable to his Creatures, and to our selves. To take heed that we do nothing out of Season, nor be guilty of any Defect, or Excess, or Miscarriage. All the Vertues are United by Prudence like several Pieces in a Compleat armour, and disposed all like Souldiers in an Army, that have their several Postes and Charges, or like the several Orders and Degrees in a Kingdom, where there are Variety of Trusts, & services to be done, and every Man has his Office assigned by the King, and knows his own work, and is fitted for the same.

FOR as no one man is sufficient for all; the same person cannot be chief Priest in the Temple, and General in the Army, and Admiral at Sea, &c. So neither can every Vertue serve for all purposes but there must be several Vertues for several Ends.

AS the King ordereth and directeth all his Officers and subjects in their several Places; if they do their duty in their own sphere, the Great End is attained by *all*, which no *one* of them alone, was able to Effect: so here, one Vertue supplies the Defects of another, and tho every one of them moves in his own Precincts, and does not at all intermeddle with anothers charge, yet the Work is done as effectually as if any one Vertue did all alone.

WHILE all the Vertues conspire to supply what is wanting in each other, Prudence is the general Overseer, and Governour of all, which while every single Vertue is ignorant of what the others are doing, fits and proportions the subservient Ends, to which every one of these Directeth its Care, and Labour, and Skill, to the Great and last End of all, the intire Perfection and Glory of the Kingdome. So that here upon Earth Prudence seemeth to be the King of Vertues, because we have such a Multiplicity of Concerns and Affairs to look after, that it is impossible for any one Vertue, but Prudence alone, to attend them all.

THIS discovereth the Excellency of [this] Vertue, & detecteth a very great Error to which we are liable, which we are prone imprudently to expect more from any Vertue than it is able to perform. We are apt to believe that in every Vertue there is an infinite Excellency. And this great Expectation of ours is a good opinion of Vertue, yet turneth (not seldome) to its Disgrace and Infamy. For when we look upon any single Vertue, and see it so Defective, that it scarce answereth one of many Ends, because we find our selves deceived in our expectation of its perfection, and the Service of that Vertue so Curt and narrow, which we thought to be infinite; we are distasted at its *Insufficiency*, and prone to slight it as a poor inconsiderable Business, infinitely short of our Hopes and expectations. Nay and to be discouraged from the practice of it, because we find it attended with many Difficulties and inconveniences, which it is not able to remedy or answer. Thus are we deterred from Liberality for fear of the Poverty to which it exposeth us; from Meekness because it encourageth all People to trample us under feet; from Holiness, because it is scorned and hated in the World; from Fortitude and Courage, because of the Perils and Hazzards, that attend it; from self–Denial, because of the Displeasures we do to our selves in crossing our Appetite. Nay sometimes men are so wicked as to hate to be obliged, for fear of the Inconveniences of Gratitude, and are much Prejudiced against Fidelity, and Love, and Truth, and Constancy. For all these Vertues can answer but one exigence, for which they are prepared (especially in our Daily Conversation with men) and a mistake in one of them doth expose us to more Inconveniences, then its Benefit is worth. M Fortitude

THIS is the Offence: and the Truth is, no Vertue is of any Value as cut off from the rest. We may as well expect all Beauty in a Nose divided from the Face, or an eye pluckt our of the head, all Perfection in an Ear, or a tongue cut off, all serviceableness in a Hand, or Foot dismembred from the Body; as a full and perfect Security from any one Vertue whatsoever. If one were sufficient, the rest would be Superfluous. Mans Empire and Dominion would be a very narrow Thing, (at least a very *Empty* and *Shallow* thing) if any one Vertue were enough for his Felicity. As his Exigencies and Concerns are Innumerable, so are his Cares and Endowments, his Honors and Pleasures, his Offices and Employments, his Vertues and Graces. His Offices and his Vertues must be at least so many, as will serve to regulate all his Concerns. And if any be so comprehensive as to cure many Exigencies at the same time, his Vertues are the Greater in force and Extent, but the fewer in Number. Their perfect sufficiency is to be measured by the ends for which they are prepared: and their Beauty Consists, (like that of an Army with Banners) in the Proportion and Symmetry of the entire Body, the mutual Supplies and Succors they afford to one another, the Unity of such a Great Variety of things in order to the Attainment of the same great and ultimate end, the full and compleat Number of Offices and inferior Ends, and the Extream Providence wherewith They are reducible to one supream End, which is most High and Excellent. It is enough for the Ear if it can hear well, tho it is no more able to See, or Taste, than a Stone. It is enough for the eye to see well, tho it is no more sensible of Noise, then a Rock or a Tree. The Office of the Tongue is to Tast well, of the Nostril to smell well, &c. and there is no Defect in any of these, because they are every one sufficient for its own immediate end, and also tempered and united together, that the rest are Supplies to make up the Defect of every single Sence and Organ, and altogether perfectly subservient to the whole Man, for whose sake they were prepared, that he might enjoy the benefit of them all. The eye sees for the Ear, and the Tongue, and all the rest of the Members of the Body: the foot supports and carries the eye, the hand defends and feeds the Eye, the Ear instructs and Counsels the Eye, the Nostrils smell for the eye, and the Tongue tasts and talks for the Eye, which the eye cannot do for it self, because it was made to need the assistance of the rest, the eye directs all these in Liew of their Services, and is of far greater Value, then if a man had no other Member, but an eye alone. For the Eye is the Light of all the members, and Great in its Relation to the whole man: It sees for the Ear, and the Hand, and for all, and is to all these after some manner Beneficial, but without these would be to no purpose. There is an infinite Excellency in every Vertue, but it is to be sought in its Relation to all the Rest. It is Good for nothing in its Place but for that Particular End to which it is assigned, in attaining that end it is subservient to all other Vertues; and while it serves all, is aided by all. The other Vertues remedie the inconveniences to which this doth expose us, and being all joyned together carry us safely and securely to our Last end: Because the Influence of every one passeth thorow all, every single Vertue is Pleasing to God, and a means in its place of our whole Felicity. The Beauty of all the Vertues is to be sought in Prudence, for there they meet in an intire Body: their Correspondence and convenience, their Symmetry and proportion, their Unity and Variety, their ful and perfect Harmony, makes up the features of the Soul, and compleats its Graces, just as the Diversity of Members perfects the Body. Knowledge gives Light to Love, but Love gives Warmth and Feeling to Knowledge. Love may, perhaps, like a Separate Soul, dwell in Heaven, alone; and yet even then it must include all Knowledge, and Righteousness, and Wisdome, and Holiness: for if Love know not how to guide it self, it will never attain its End, nor be a perfect Vertue. But here upon Earth tis like the Soul in the Body, it must Eat, and Drink, and see, and hear, as a thousand Works to do, and therefore standeth in need of many Vertues. Love without Goodness is perhaps a Thing impossible, because it always designs well. But Love without Wisdome is a Common Thing: for such is all that mistakes its End. Love without

Discretion is a mischievious Thing, Love without Prudence an Helpless Thing, Love without Courage a feeble and Cowardly Thing; Love without Modesty an impudent and Troublesome Thing; Love without the Fear of GOD is Lust and Wantonness; and if the most Great and Glorious of all the Vertues stands in need of all its Companions. The less and inferior must needs be lame and maimed without the residue, especially without the Superior.

UPON this account it is, that so much Care and Study goes to the making up of a Vertuous man. All kind of Vertues must concur to Compleat his Perfection. The Want of any one Denominates a Vice, and makes him Vicious. Nay the Want of any one destroys the form and Essence of the rest. Vertue is not Vertue but in order to felicity. If it hath lost its force, it hath lost its Nature. As a little Poyson turnes the best Meant from Nourishment into Poyson so doth one Vice cherished and allowed corrupt and viciate all the Vertures in the whole World. Hence it is that the Philosophers say, all the Vertues are linked together in the golden Chain of Prudence. And that a Thing is made Good by all its Causes, Evil by the least Defect. For as one Tooth wanting in a Clock, makes all the other wheels and Materials Useless; tho the frame be never so Elaborate and Curious; so doth the absence of the smallest Vertue make void and frustrate all the residue. A man of a Kind and Bountiful Disposition, that is loose and intemperate, may ruine his Estate, and dye like a Prodigal and vain–glorious fool. A stout Couragious person that is proud and debauched will be little better than a *Souldierly Ruffian*, and Live if not like a Thief for Want of Honesty, yet like a Swaggering Hector for Want of Discreetion. A Man endued with all Kind of Learning may be Morose and Covetous, and by one Vice lose all the Benefit of his Education. A Religious Votary that is Splenetick and Revengeful, brings a Disgrace upon his whole Profession. But he that is Wise, and Learned, and Holy, and Just, and Temperate, and Couragious, and Kind, and Liberal, and Meek, and Humble, and Affable, and Cheerful, and Prudent, and Industrious, shall be serviceable, and Honourable, and delightful to others, profitable to himself, and always Triumphant: Especially if he be so discreet and Prudent, as to make all these Vertues move like the Stars in their Courses, and knows how to apply and manage their Excellencies in their due and proper places upon all occasions: for they are so many different in nature that some of their Influences, will hit every business, and all of them together pass a Grace and Lustre upon each other, so Divine and Heavenly that they will make their owner

Venerable in the Eys of the World, and correct the Malignity of the most injurious and Censorious. Which moved our Saviour to exhort us to be *Wise as Serpents, Innocent as Doves*, to joyn many Vertues together: And occasioned that of the Apostle, *He that will love Life and see good Days, let him refrain his Tongue from Evil, and his Lips that they speak no Guile: let him eschew Evil, and do Good, let him seek Peace and ensue it, for the Eyes of the Lord are over the Righteous: And who is he that will harm you, if ye be followers of that which is Good?*[1] The only sure Way to live happily here upon Earth, is to joyn all kind of Vertues together, and to let them work in season according to their several Natures.

WHAT the efficacy of Prudence is may be seen in friendship, in the Regiment of States and Kingdoms, in the Rule and government of Private Famelies. He that is fitted for all these is an Excellent Person.

IT is the office of Prudence in all Estates, to find out the Temper of those with whom we are to deal; and so to suit the Exercises of all Vertues with their several Humours, as may make their Operation consistent with our own Repose, and their Benefit, without infringing our Duty.

IN Friendship it often falleth out by reason of the spiritual *Sickness* of those to whom we relate, that we must either make shipwrack of Fidelity and a good Conscience, or run the Hazzard of losing our Friend by displeasing, that we may be Profitable to him. There is no Duty so necessary, as that of free and faithful Reproof: no Duty so nice as this. A Good man Knows it is incumbent upon him, and yet is very Averse from the Discharge of it. It is as Troublesome to himself as to the Person that needs it. Tis difficult to be done well, and so unpleasant to both. Here Prudence comes in, and deviseth expedients for all Inconveniences, and with a strange facility scatters all Doubts and Fears. Three Things it discovers to be necessary in the foundation of the Business, Three in the Superstructure, and Three in the Conclusion. He that reproves well, must shew a great respect and Tenderness to the Person, a necessity of the Discharge of that Duty, his Averseness to it, and how Nothing but his Perfect Love could make him undertake it. The foundation of the Success is laid by these Provisions: In the Super–structure, he must consider whether it be Best to be done merrily or severely; by a Brief Hint or a strong Enlargement, according to the Temper and Degree of the Person. He must chuse out the best Opportunities, and consult the

---

[1] Marginal gloss: 1 Pet. 3:10.

Honour of him he reproveth. And if he be displeased and grow angry at the Liberty, he must in the Close of all bear it patiently, surmount it with Courtesie, and pursue him with Kindness. He that rules his own Passion is Master of another mans: He must needs win him and Melt him: For no man thus dealt with, is so very a Beast, as to be angry long. Or the mischief is, when he that reproveth miscarrieth in some of these Rules, especially the last: for there are few so prudent as not to be exasperated with the Affront that is put upon their kindness and Fidelity, when they are injured for their Good Will: few so discreet as to consider which way their patience and Meakness are to be made the Instruments of Amity and Happiness.

IN the Management of Empires, and Kingdomes Prudence hath a vast and Mighty Province to reign in. A Good King when he designs the extirpation of Vice, and the Establishment of Righteousness and pure Religion, meets with many Rubs and Obstacles in his Way, all which are sweetly and easily by Prudence removed. His Great encouragement is the Beauty of Religion, and the Assistance of GOD. For he Knows very well that Equity and Piety are such Glorious Things, that tho few practice them as they ought to do, yet all admire them.

GODLINESS, and Honesty, need nothing but to be maintained and assented by the Prince, when they are once countenanced by authority all the Enemies of Religion are confounded, and dare not lift up their face against it. Wise and Holy men may easily be exalted, and are more capable of Exaltation then others. As they are more faithful when they are in power, they will be more Grateful to the Prince, and more Obliging to the people; and in all Respects more able to serve them both. The Good will secure the Throne and exalt the Kingdome. Prudence in such a work Knows where to begin and where to end, by what steps and Degrees to proceed, what Instruments to use, how to Oblige, and how to Awe; whom to Oblige, and Awe; where to remit the Rigor of the Law and where to be severe. The Truth is, Prudence consists most in attempting the Business, for it will go on, and is ever waited with success when undertaken. A King that is so Wise as to design and endeavor, the Refurmation of his Nation, must needs be Prudent. GOD has assured him, *The Throne is established by Righteousness. When it Goeth well with the Righteous the City rejoyceth, and when the wicked perish there is shouting. By the blessing of the upright the City is exalted, but it is overthrown by the Mouth of the Wicked.*

IN Families the force of Prudence is prodigious. Some men by the assistance of this Vertue live more happily upon a mean state, then others upon Thousands, they have more respect among their Servants, more honour among their Neighbors, more plenty at home, more Authority abroad, more peace & comfort every where, then Men forty times above themselves in State & Grandure. Its first care is to be Wary in the Choise of Servants: For they that are good act well by Nature, and have little need of Force and compulsion. Its next Business is to oblige them, which is done by a religious example which instilles a Reverence, a strict prohibition of all Debauchery, a sweet and affable Behaviour, a plentiful Provision for their comfortable Subsistence, a prudent connivance at smaller faults, a Distribution of Rewards as well as punishments for the Encouragement of their Vertues, a meek and Gentle reproof of their Faults, a kind acknowledgment of their Good deserts; which is a cheap and easie kind of payment, yet more Obliging then any Dry gift of Gold or Silver. A prudent man will so demean himself in his Family, as to make himself cordially beloved of all: so order his affairs, that the Services of those about him shall be like Preferments. By which Means it will first come to pass, that he shall have his choise of servants, because it will be esteemed a Blessing to be with him: and in the next place their service will be mingled with respect and Love. They will be faithful as well for his sake, as their own. In the Midst of all this, his Prudence will guide him to take a strict account, and to make all his Servants see, it is impossible to cheat him. Thus in all Affaires Prudence happily demeans it self; and of this Gift especially is that of *Solomon* to be understood, *A gift is as a precious stone in the hand of him that hath it, whithersoever it turneth, it prospereth.*[1]

FOR the Foundation of all kind of Prudence you must remember, that he that winneth Souls is Wise. Mens Hearts are the stars by whose Influences the affairs of the World are regulated: they are as our Saviour calleth them Good or Evil Treasures; out of which proceeds Murders, Adulteries, Thefts, Slanders, &c. Or Praises, Honours, Preferments, Riches, Pleasures, all kind of Gifts, and Benefits: And the prudent mans main Business is to make himself intirely beloved by all the World, which can never be without great Fidelity, Courage, Goodness, Prudence and Dexterity. Flattery and Base compliances makes a man Odious.

THE Last End of Prudence is Eternal Happiness and Glory, to which it moveth by crooked Meanders and windings out as occasion requireth. It is a strange Vertue, for its Conversant amongst Terrene

---

[1] Marginal gloss: Prov. 17.8.

and inferior Objects, and yet a far more Difficult Vertue then Wisdom it self. Wisdome is a more High and Heavenly Vertue, but its Rules are always fixed, and its objects Stable, where as Prudence hath no set and Stated Rules, but in all occasions, is to mould and shape it selfe, it knows not which way, till it comes to Action. Its Paths are in the Deep and mighty Waters, among Storms and tempests.

CHAP. XXI.

Encouragements to Courage. Its Nature, Cause, and End. Its Greatness and Renown. Its Ornaments and Companions. Its Objects, Circumstances, Effects and Disadvantages; how Difficulties increase its Vertue. Its Ver[tues] and Triumphs. How subservient it is to Blessedness and Glory.

LOVE and Prudence are the Parents of Courage. A Feeble Hen, a Timerous Mother, will Sacrifice their Lives for their young ones. And he that forgetteth all his own Interests, divests himself (together with them) of his Fears, and despising Death first, easily slighteth all other Things. Even a Coward by Nature, is made more Bold and confident by Skill at his weapon. And he that is always assured of the Victory, can never be afraid of the Encounter, or the Enemy. He that is Dexterous at the use of all Vertues, and knows how to apply them so, as ever to come off more honourably, will laugh at the Trial of his own Innocence and make a Game of Difficulties and Terrors.

VALOUR is a right and strong Resolution of the Soul whereby it dare encounter with any Difficulty and Trouble, for Vertues sake. It is the Armour of the Soul against all Impressions of Fear, its Effect is an Equal and uniform stayedness of Mind, against all Dangerous and Terrible Accidents. It containeth Magnanimitie, Patience, Constancy, Invincible Resolution, Boldness and Industry in it Nature. Its cause is the Love of Vertue, and the sence of Honour, Indignation against any thing that is Base and vile, a High Ambition and desire of Glory. Its End is the preservation of a Mans person and Honesty, the Conquest of all Opposition in the Way to Bliss, the Destruction or Subjection of Enemies, Triumph and Conquest, the Establishment of Peace, the Attainment of Liberty and Glory. Its Attendants are Prudence, Justice and Temperance, the principal Ornament and Grace of valour is Worth and Goodness. its Aids and Encouragements are infinite, it groweth Great and High, by making use of all the Causes of Hope and Confidence. Conflicts and Dangers are the Element in which it lives, it owns its whole being to them; for without Causes of Fear, there could be no courage in all Nature. The Knowledge of GOD is the root of Divine Valour, and Fidelity to his Laws its Commendation. The Assurance of his Love, and all those Things that serve to beget and confirm it, are subservient to it. It draws in strength and Encouragements from all

Obligations and Rewards, from all Great and Holy examples, from the Knowledge of its own Sublimity, from the Greatness of Felicity, from the Omnipotence, and Omnipresence, and Providence of the Deity, from his Truth and Goodness, and from all those Things wherein he has manifested his Love above the Heavens.

OF all the Vertues in greatest Estimation, this is most renowned. For its Prerogative is so great, that it is simply called VERTUE. Vertue being the Word to express and signifie Valour among the Latines; because the Force and Efficacy that is in it, is most visible and Apparent, and by that all other Vertues are secured, vindicated, Exercised, and made Useful. It is stiled *Manhood* among the English, with a peculiar Emphasis: As if the Essence of a man was founded in Courage, because his Vigor is emasculated, and his Dignity lost, that is Effeminate and Timerous; for he is scarce a Man that is a Coward.

WHAT a Glorious and incomparable Vertue this is, appeareth from the Baseness and Ineptitude of its Contrary. A Coward and an Honest Man can never be the same; a Coward and a constant Lover can never be the same; a Coward and a Brave Man can never be the same: Cowardice, and Wisdome are as incompatible forever, as Love and Wisdom were thought to be of Old. A Coward is always despicable and Wretched; because he dares not expose himself to any Hazzards, nor adventure upon any Great Attempt for fear of some little Pain and Damage, that is between him and an Excellent Atchievment. He is baffled from the Acquisition of the most Great and Beautiful Things, and nonplust with every Impediment. He is conquered before he begins to fight. The very sight of Danger makes him a Slave; He is undone, when he sees his Enemy a far off, and wounded, before the Point of the Sword can touch his shadow. He is all wayes a Terror and Burden to himself, a Dangerous Knave, and an useless Creature.

STRANGE is the Vigour in a Brave Mans Soul. The Strength of his Spirit and his irresistible Power, the Greatness of his Heart, and the Height of his Condition, his mighty Confidence and Contempt of Dangers, his true Security and Repose in himself, his Liberty to dare and do what he pleaseth, his Alacrity in the midst of Fears, his invincible Temper, are advantages which make him Master of Fortune. His Courage fits him for all Attempts, renders him serviceable to GOD and MAN, and makes him the Bulwark and Defence of his King and Country.

LET those Debauched and unreasonable men, that deny the Existence of Vertue, contemplate the Reality of its Excellency here, and be confounded with shame at their Prodigious Blindness. Their Impiety designs the Abolishment of Religion, and the utter Extirpation of all Faith and Piety, while they pretend the Distinction between Vertue and Vice to be meerly feigned, for the Awing of the World, and that their Names have no foundation in Nature but the Craft of Politicians and the Tradition of their Nurses. Are there no Base fellows, nor Brave Men in the World? Is there no difference between a Lion and a Hare? a faint hearted Coward, and a Glorious Heroe? Is there Nothing Brave nor vile in the world? What is become of these *Rodomontadoes* wits! Where is the boasted Glory of their Personal Valour; if there be no Difference, but Courage and Cowardize be the same thing!

HOW empty these Self, but shallow-conceited Ranters are, is evident by their short and narrow measures. They place all Gallantry and Worth in Valour: all the Vertue of a man they think seated in this: They forget that Policy, and Learning, and Prudence, and Gratitude, and Fidelity, and Temperance, and Industry, and Compassion and Bounty, and Affability, and Courtesie, and Modesty, and Justice, and Honesty are Vertues, and that in every one of these there is something fitting a Man for the Benefit of the World. Nay they have lost the Notion of Vertue, and know not what it is. Those things by which a man is made serviceable to himself and the World, they think not to be Vertues, but imagine Chimeraes which they cannot see, & then deny they have any Existence. A Man is capable of far more Glorious Qualities then one of them: And his Courage it self may be raised to far higher Ends and purposes then Buffoons and Thrasonical Heroes can dream of.

IT is to be noted here, that any one of those Things that are called Vertue, being alone, is not a Vertue. It is so far from aiding and setting us forward in the Way to Happiness, that oftentimes it proveth a Great and intollerable Mischief, and is never safe, but when it is corrected and guided by the rest of its Companions. To stir no further then Courage alone: What is Courage in a Thief, or a Tyrant, or a Traytor but like Zeal and Learning in a pernicious Heretick.

YOU may note further, that Goodness is a principal Ingredient in the excellency of this Vertue, tho it be distinct in its Nature from the Being of Courage. A brave man will expose his Life in an Honest cause, for the Benefit and preservation of others, tho not for the Dammage or Destruction of any. He will slight his own safety, and despise his Repose to make himself a Saviour, and a Benefactor. A true Courage holdeth Vertuous Actions at such a Price, that Death, Imprisonment, Famine, Dishonour, Poverty, Shame, Indignation, all Allurements and Temptations are nothing, compared to the Performance of Heroick Deeds. He exceedeth all constraint, and walketh in the Glorious Liberty of the Sons of GOD.

THE last note which I shall offer to your Observation on this Occasion, is this, (for the Illustration of the Reason and excellency, of GODS Dispensations:) The Great End for which GOD was pleased not to seat us immediately in the Throne, but to place us first in an estate of Trial, was the Multiplication of our Vertues. For had we been seated in the Glory of Heaven at the first, there had no such Vertues as Patience, and Courage, and Fidelity been seen, no Faith, or Hope, or Meekness, no Temperance, or Prudence, or self Denial, in the World. Which Vertues are the very clothes and Habits of the Soul in Glory. The Graces and Beauties of the Soul are founded in the exercise of them. Actions pass not away, but are fixed, by the permanent Continuance of all Eternity, and tho done never so long ago, shall appear before the Eye of the Soul for ever in their places, be the Glory of their Author, the Lineaments and Colours of his Beauty, seen by GOD and his holy Angels, and Delightful to all that love and delight in worthy things. Our Life upon Earth, being so diversified like a Sphere of Beauty, so variously adorned with all sorts of Excellent Actions, shall wholly and at once be seen as an intire Object, rarely and curiously wrought; a Lively Mirror of the Nature of the Soul, and all the Elements of which it is compounded, all the Parts that conspire in its Symetry, all the Qualities, Operations, and Perfections that contribute to its Glory, shall afford wonder and pleasure to all Spectators. While every Soul shall be concerned more in its Actions then in its Essence; indeed its Essence, (how ever considerable) is of little or no Value in Comparison of its Operations. Every Vertue being the Natural Off–spring and production of the Soul, in which its Vigor principally appeareth, an effect discovering the Nature of the cause, and the sole occasion of its shame or Glory. For if the Essence of the Soul be all Power and its power exerted in its operation, the Soul must needs enter into its Actions, and consequently be affected with all that befalls its Operation. All Acts are Immortal in their places, being *enbalmed* as it were by Eternity, till the Soul revive and be united to them. Then shall it appear in its own Age, and in eternity too, in its last life enjoying the Benefit of its *first*. And in that sence is that voice from Heaven to be understood, which commanded the Divine to write

Blessed are they that die in the Lord, from henceforth, yea saith the Spirit, that they may rest from their Labours, and their Works do follow them.[1] For the Glory of the place is nothing to us, if we are not endued with those Glorious Habits, which will make our Souls *all Glorious within.* We must be Glorious and Illustrious our selves, and appear in Actions that will Beautifie the Throne to which we are exalted.

THAT these Actions may be Great and Amiable, manifold and Excellent, is the desire of every soul, the natural Wish and Expectation both of Reason it self and of self Love.

HOW Glorious the Counsel and Design of GOD is for the Atchieving of this Great End, for the making of all Vertues more compleat and Excellent, and for the Heightening of their Beauty and Perfection we will exemplifie here in the Perfection of Courage. For the Hieght, and depth, and Splendor of every Vertue is of great Concernment to the Perfection of the Soul, since the Glory of its Life is seated in the Accomplishment of its essence, in the Fruit it yeildeth in its Operations. Take it in Verse made long ago upon this occasion.

>   *For Man to Act as if his Soul did see*
>   *The very Brightness of Eternity;*
>   *For Man to Act as if his Love did burn*
>   *Above the Spheres, even while its in its Urne;*
>   *For Man to Act even in the Wilderness,*
>   *As if he did those Sovereign Joys possess,*
>   *Which do at once confirm, stir up, enflame,*
>   *And perfect Angels; having not the same!*
>   *It doth increase the Value of his Deeds,*
>   *In this a Man a Seraphim exceeds:*
>   *To Act on Obligations yet unknown,*
>   *To Act upon Rewards as yet unshewn,*
>   *To keep Commands whose Beauty's yet unseen,*
>   *To cherish and retain a Zeal between*
>   *Sleeping and Waking; shews a constant care;*
>   *And that a deeper Love, a Love so Rare,*
>   *That no Eye Service may with it compare.*
>   *The Angels, who are faithful while they view*
>   *His Glory, know not what themselves would do,*
>   *Were they in our Estate! A Dimmer Light*
>   *Perhaps would make them erre as well as We;*

---

[1] Marginal gloss: Rev. 14.13.

And in the Coldness of a darker Night,
Forgetful and Lukewarm Themselves might be.
Our very Rust shall cover us with Gold,
Our Dust shall sprinkle while their Eyes behold
The Glory Springing from a feeble State,
Where meer Belief doth, if not conquer Fate,
Surmount, and pass what it doth Antedate.

 THE Beatifick Vision is so sweet and Strong a Light, that it is impossible for any thing that Loves it self, (and sees the Face of GOD) to turn away to any vanity from so Divine and Strong a Blessedness. To Love GOD in the clear and perfect Light is a cheap and Easie Thing: The Love that is shewed in a more weak Estate to an absent Object, is more remiss perhaps, and Black in appearance; but far Deeper, if in the Lovers Weakness, and its Objects absence; it be Faithful to the Death; constantly Solicitous, and Careful to please, Laborious and Industrious, Wakeful and Circumspect, even and immutable, and freely springing from its own Desire, not out of bare pleasure; but humble Obedience to the Laws of its Benefactor. All the Courage which it shews in such Occasions is more full of Mystery and Divinity then is imaginable; far more Moving and full of Vertue, while it struggles with Impediments, Disadvantages, and Difficulties, then if without any such Occasion of shewing its Vertue, it did smoothly and Peaceably proceed in the Highest Rapture. Add to that the mysteriousness of its Beauty in all the varieties of its Operation, and the Different Sweetnesses that still appear in all its several Effects upon new occasions. The very Representation of Love upon the stage, in its Conflicts and Agonies, produces another kind of sence in the Spectator, then that of Embraces. It is more Tender and endearing, touches the Soul (of its Beloved especially) in a more Vigorous and lively manner, it makes all fruitions (afterward) more precious; by Fidelity, Courage, and Immoveable Perfection it maketh the Lover more Honourable, and Effects far more Serious Alterations in the Soul, solid Joys and tender Compassions, moving and Bleeding Resentments; all which, End in satisfactions heightened with more Perfect Complacencies.

 THUS you see Courage in the Root made more Glorious by a Persons Exposure and Abasement. In the fruit and Exercise it is otherwise to be considered. Where there is no Evil to be endured, or no Strength to be resisted, there can be no Courage or Vertue at all. Where the conflict is more sharp the Victory is more pleasant, and the success of the fight is far more Honourable. Where a Giant is to fight with a Gnat, or a Dwarf, the Disproportion of his Strength takes away the Pleasure of its Trial, and a Glory of the Combate. There is no Room, or occasion for its Exercise. And tho it might without any Trial be known by him that sees all things in their hidden Essences, yet without its Exercise it remaineth unexerted, is wholly vain, especially when there is no occasion for it in Nature. The Pleasure of the Spectacle springeth from its Operation.

TO see a Seraphim surmount one of our Difficulties, in the midst of all his Strengths and Advantages, is no more then to see a Giant destroy a Gnat, or subdue a Grass hopper. But in Man there is a certain Degree of strength, that makes him *a fit Match* for the appointed Encounter. In the Estate of Innocency indeed his Enemies and Difficulties were very few, just as many as were needful for the trial of his Obedience, Gratitude, Fidelity. All the Hardship he was to undergo, was to cross his Appetite in an Apple, and tho, he did not as yet see which way it was reserved for him, to be so Couragious as to hope well, so Grateful to GOD, as to dare to confide in him, rather let go the Knowledge he might gain by eating it, than break his Commandment. All other Duties were his Pleasure and Felicity: here lay his Trial, and his Obedience should have been crowned with infinite Reward. All which would in some Measure have risen out of the Duty discharged by him. For by this Resignation and Self-Denial he had manifested his Obedience, and acquitted himself, and shewed his Love, and his Prelation of his Makers Pleasure above all other Concernes, wherein he had been approved; and Wise, and Holy, and well pleasing to GOD, he would have put the Crown upon all Gods Works in accomplishing the End for which he was made, and been very Delightful to all the Angels: He had been crowned with Glory and Honour in all their Complacency. If that were too little, because he had then no enemy but his Appetite, the Dimness of his Sight maketh up the Mystery. If his Clarity was too Great and there was no Proportion between his Strength and the Temptation; that proceeded of the Tenderness of GODS Love, which feared to adventure him too far, and had rather something of Honour should be endangered, then his Soul lost, or thrust upon the Hazzard of too great a Temptation. When the Angels fell, the Devil was let loose upon man, for the increase of his Honour and Dominion: Yet like a Dog in his Chain so far, and no further. He had but one Way, and that was to perswade our first Parents to do what was forbidden: Perswade he might, and try his Skill to deceive, but could not compell, nor otherwise afflict, or hurt him in the least. He had not Power so much as to diminish the least Hair of his Head: yet so Gracious was Almighty GOD, that upon this Trial of his Prudence and Courage the Exercise of these Vertues had been infinitely pleasing to his Eternal Love, because he infinitely delighted in the Welfare and Preservation of what was so precious to himself, as a Soul is, that is infinitely Beloved. In that Complacency *Adam* had found little less then infinite Glory. It did not become the tenderness of GODS Love to expose him to any Severer Trial.

> *For there are certain Periods and fit Bounds,*
> *Which he that passeth, all his Work confounds.*

But when *Adam* fell, and brought more Hazzards and Difficulties on himself GOD might justly leave him to them, for his greater Trial and more perfect Glory. Now we are more blind and Weak by Nature, yet infinitely Beloved and more Precious: For the price of the Blood of the Eternal Son of GOD is laid upon the Soul as an Addition to its interior Value. We are even in our corruption to Grapple with Sin, and Hell, and Death, and Sickness, and Poverty, and Fear, and all the Devils, and Afflictions in the World; nay which is worse then all, with our own Errors, Lusts and Passions, more neer and Bitter Enemies: A poor Clod of Earth is to overcome all the World, to fight (as the Apostle speaks) *with Principallities and Powers, with the Rulers of the Darkness in this World, with spiritual Wickednesses in high places.* And to return laden with Victories and Trophies into the Kingdome of Heaven. Nor is the Combat so unequal, but that there is a mighty Hope and Assurance of triumphing, tho *Lucifer* and all his Angels are to be trampled under feet. For under the Disguise of this apparent Clod, there lies concealed a mighty Great and Cœlestial Personage, a Divine and Glorious Creature, Miraculous and Mysterious, even the Image of the Deity, that can derive Strengths and Succours from all eternity, and being aided by the Conduct of so great a Captain as our Lord *Jesus Christ* who has taught us by his example not to fear, because he has *overcome the World,* we may safely sing, *O Death where is thy sting? O Grave where is thy Victory!* And challenge all the powers of Heaven, Earth, and Hell to the combat, Which for one single person to do against all the Creation, is the most Glorious Spectacle which the universe affords. *Who shall separate us from the Love of Christ? shall Tribulation, or Distress, or Persecution, or Famine, or Nakedness, or Peril, or Sword? as it is written, for thy sake we are Killed all the day long, we are accounted as Sheep to the slaughter. Nay in all these things we are more then Conquerors through him that loved us. For I am perswaded, that neither Death, nor Life, nor Angels, nor Principalities, nor Powers, nor things present, nor things to come, nor Height nor Depth, nor any other Creature shall be able to separate us, from the Love of GOD which is in Christ Jesus our Lord.*

A REMARK.

To be Couragious is the Easiest thing in the World, when we consider the certain success, which Courage founded on Goodness must needs attain. For he that makes his Fortitude subservient onely to the excess of his Love, has all the Powers of Heaven and earth on his side, and the Powers of Hell that are already subdued are the only foes that are to be vanquished by him. To dare to be Good, is the Office of true and Religious valour. And he that makes it his Business to oblige all the world, he whose design it is to be delightful to all mankind, has nothing to overcome, but their error & bitterness, which by meekness, and Kindness, and Prudence, and liberality will easily be accomplished. For they all love themselves, and cannot chuse but desire those that are kind and Serviceable to them, and must so far forth as they love themselves, honor & delight in their Benefactors. So that Courage thus guided by Prudence to the works of Charity and goodness must surely be safe and prosperous on earth, its Admirableness and its Beauty being a powerful Charm, an Invincible Armour.

CHAP. XXII.

Of Temperance *in Matters of Art, as Musick, Dancing, Painting, Cookery, Physick, &c. In the works of Nature; Eating, Drinking, Sports and Recreations: In occasions of Passion, in our Lives and Conversations. Its exercise in Self-denial, Measure, Mixture and Proportion. Its effects and atchievments.*

PRUDENCE giveth Counsel what Measure and Proportion ought to be held in our Actions, Fortitude inspires Boldness and Strength to undertake, and set upon the Work; but it is Temperance doth execute what both of them design. For Temperance is that Vertue, whereby the actions of Prudence and Power are moderated, when they come to be exerted.

IT is the Opinion of some, that as Patience respects Afflictions, so Temperance is wholy taken up in moderating our Pleasures, and hath no employment but in the midst of Prosperities. But since there are certain bounds which Fear and Sorrow ought not to exceed, Temperance hath its work in the midst of Calamities, and being needful to moderate all our Passion, hath a wider sphere to move in, than Prosperity alone; its Province is more large and comprehensive, including all estates and conditions of Life whatsoever.

OTHERS there are that admit of its use in all Conditions, but confine it to one particular employment, even that of enlarging or bounding the Measure of every Operation: but in real truth it has another Office, and that more deep perhaps, and more important than the former. For Actions are of two kinds, either Mixt, or Simple. Where the work is single and but one, it is exprest in nothing else but the Measure of the Action, that it be neither too short, nor too long; too remiss, nor too violent; too slow, nor too quick; too great, nor too little: But where many things are mixt and meet together in the Action (as they generally do, in all the affairs of our Lives;) there its business is to consider what, and how many things are to enter the *Composition*, and to make their Proportion just and convenient. As in preparing Medicines, the skill whereby we know what is to be put in, and what left out is of one kind, and that of discerning how much of every *Ingredient* will serve the turn, of another. The skill of Mingling is like the vertue of Prudence, but the actual tempering of all together, exhibits the vertue of *Temperance* to the Life, because it reduces the Skill to its operation. Its End is the beauty and success of our Endeavours.

OF what use and value Temperance is in our Lives and Conversations, we may guess by its necessity, force and efficacy on all Occasions.

THE fit mixture and proportion of the four Elements in all Bodies, is that upon which their Nature, Form and Perfection dependeth. Too much of the Fire, too much of the Water, too much of the Air, too much of the Earth, are pernicious and destructive. There is an infinite wisdom exprest in the Mixture and Proportion in every Creature.

BEAUTY and Health, Agility, Repose, and Strength, depend upon the due Temperament of Humane Bodies. The four Humors of Choler, Melancholy, Flegm, and Blood are generally known: But there are many other Juyces talkt of besides, by the discreet and accurate mixture of which the Body of a Man, or Beast, is perfected. Some great inconvenience alwaies follows the excess or defect of these. Disorder and Disproportion go hand in hand, and are attended by Sickness, and Death it self.

IN matters of Art, the force of *Temperance* is undeniable. It relateth not only to our Meats and Drinks, but to all our Behaviours, Passions, and Desires.

> *All Musick, Sawces, Feasts, Delights and Pleasures,*
> *Games, Dancing, Arts consist in govern'd Measures;*
> *Much more do Words, and Passions of the Mind*
> *In Temperance their sacred Beauty find.*

A Musician might rash his finger over all his strings in a moment, but *Melody* is an effect of *Judgment* and *Order:* It springs from a variety of *Notes* to which *Skill* giveth *Time* and *Place* in their Union. A Painter may daub his Table *all over* in an instant, but a Picture is made by a regulated Hand, and by variety of Colours. A Cook may put a Tun of Sugar, or Pepper, or Salt in his Dishes: but Delicates are made by Mixture and Proportion. There is a Temperance also in the Gesture of the Body, the Air of the Face, the carriage of the Eye, the Smile, the Motion of the Feet and Hands, and by the Harmony of these is the best Beauty in the World either much commended, or disgraced. A Clown and a Courtier are known by their *Postures*. A Dancer might run into Extreams, but his Art is seen in the measure of his Paces, and adorned with a variety of sweet and suitable Behaviours. A Physician may kill a man with the best Ingredients, but good Medicines are those wherein every

Simple hath its proper *Dose*, and every Composition a fit admixture of good Ingredients. A Poem, an Oration, a Play, A Sermon, may be too tedious, or too dull, or too feeble and impertinent; but all its fault are avoided by a fit Temperance of Words and Materials. Temperance every where yields the Pleasure: And *Excess* is as destructive as *Defect*, in any Accomplishment whatsoever; Vertue being seated in the Golden Mean; It is by an Artificial limiting of Power that every Thing is made as it ought to be, Compleat and Perfect. All kind of Excellence in every sort of Operation springs from Temperance. A curious Picture, a melodious Song, a delicious Harmony by little invisible motions of the Pen or Pencil, or by Ductures scarce perceivable in the throat, or fingers, finisheth the Work, where Art is the only power of performing.

WE know that upon Mens Actions far more does depend, than upon Dancing and Painting: their Wisdom and Vertue, their Honour, Life and Happiness. And therefore more Care ought to be exhibited in the Actions of which their Conversation is made up and accomplished. In their Meats and Drinks, and Recreations, it is apparent, that without Temperance there can be no Success or Order. The best Wine in the World makes him that is lavish in the use of it a *Sot*. The most wholsom and delicious Meat upon Earth by excess in eating, may turn to a *Surfeit*. If Sports and Recreations take up all a mans Time, his Life is *unprofitable:* their End is lost, and their Nature changed; for instead of recruiting, they consume ones Strength; and instead of fitting a Man for it, devour his Calling.

AN exact hand over all our Passions, and a diligent Eye to extravagant Actions, tend much to our Welfare, Repose, and Honour. Loose and impertinent Laughter, excessive Cost in Apparel, a Lascivious wandering of the Eyes, an ungoverned Boldness which turns into Impudence, an extremity of Fear which degenerates into Baseness, a Morose and sour Disposition, Anxiety and needless Care, immodest and violent strivings after Things we too eagerly desire, inordinate Love, too keen and bitter Resentments, a fierce and raging Anger, a blockish Stupidity, a predominant Humour of Melancholy, too much Sloth and too much Activity, too much Talk, and too much Silence: all these are diligently to be ordered and avoided: for upon the right Temperament of these we are made Acceptable and Amiable, and being so, are full of Authority, and can do within the compass of Vertue and Reason, all that we desire, among our Friends and Companions, for our own good, or the benefit of others. And by this means also we shall be admitted to the society and friendship of Great men, where a Nod or a Word is able to prevail more, than the strength of Oxen and Horses among the dregs of the People. But for lack of tempering these Ingredients aright, and as we ought, we become odious and insupportable, lose all Esteem and Interest, are rejected, and trampled under feet, as vicious and deformed.

HERE you may observe, that all the qualities and dispositions in Nature, are ingredients and materials in our Lives and Conversations, and for the most part it is their Excess or Defect that makes the miscarriage, when we erre in the Measure. There is a certain mixture of Gravity and Chearfulness, Remisness and Severity, Fear and Boldness, Anger and Complacency, Kindness and Displeasure, Care and Carelesness, Activity and Idleness, Joy and Sorrow, Forwardness and Reservedness; nay of Envy, Pride, and Revenge in every Mans life, as well as of Selfishness and flowing Courtesie, Plainness and Policy; at least the grounds of these things, which are neither Vertues nor Vices in themselves, yet make *Conversation* transcendently Vertuous, when they are wisely tempered and united together.

I do not look upon Ambition and Avarice, nay nor upon Envy and Revenge, as things that are evil in their root and fountain. If they be, Temperance has a strange vertue in its Nature, for as Chymists make Antidotes of Poysons, so doth this vertue turn the Matter of all these into a Quintessential perfection. Nay Selfishness and Pride it self escape not its influence. A little touch of something like Pride, is seated in the true sence of a mans own Greatness: without which his Humility and Modesty would be contemptible Vertues. In all baseness of Mind there is a kind of folly and Cowardice apparent; and more veneration follows an humble Man that is sensible of his Excellency. An aiery Humor without something of the Melancholy to ballast it a little, would be light and trifling: And a melancholy Humor without something of Air and Jovialness in it, too sour and disobliging. Anger without Softness is like untemper'd Steel, brittle and destructive: and a plyant Humor without some degree of stiffness, too near to Flattery and Servility. Anger is the matter and fuel of Courage, and its appearance afar off puts a Majesty into Meekness, that makes it redoubted. A sorrowful Humor neatly allayed with a mixture of sweetness, begets a tenderness and compassion in the Spectator, that turns into a deeper and more serious Love: A little Selfishness puts our Companions in mind of our own Interest, and makes them perceive that we understand it: which adds a lustre to our Self-denial, and renders our Liberality more safe and precious. Plainness without Policy is downright Simplicity, and Policy without Plainness void of

Honesty. The one makes us Crafty, and renders us suspected; the other exposes us, and makes us *Ridiculous*; but both united are venerable and prudent. By the appearance of Revenge in its shady Possibility, a man that never does other than Actually forgive, does oblige for what is past, yet threaten and discourage from the like Offences. All these are the Subjects of Temperance. A little spice of Jealousie and Emulation are advantagious, in the midst of our Security and Resignation. They give a relish to our Confidence in, and Prelation of others; and make our Security and Civility taste of our Love to the Person we prefer, and of our Love to Vertue. There is not one Humor, nor Inclination, nor Passion, nor Power in the Soul, that may not be admitted to act its part, when directed by Temperance.

NOR is it unlawful to alter the Natural Complexion by Care and Study. I know very well, that the complexion of the Body can hardly be changed by the strongest Physick: and that Choler, and Phlegm, and abundance of Blood, will, where they are, have their Natural Course without any remedy. But the Humors of the Soul are more tractable things; they are all subject to the Will in their operations: and though they incline, yet they cannot act, but by consent and permission. I know furthermore that custom and Habit is a Second Nature: what was difficult at first, becomes at last as easie in its Exercise as if it were *innate;* and that the Soul of a Vertuous man does in process of time act by a new *Disposition*. I know further that all vertuous Operations are free and voluntary; and that the office of Vertue is to correct and amend an Evil Nature. Let no man therefore be disgusted, because a *Made-up man* is Artificial, and not Natural: for when the Conversation is sincerely guided to a good End, the more free and voluntary it is, it is the more Noble: the more Industry and Desire a man expresses in attaining all these measures and perfections, they are the more Vertuous: and the Probity of his Will is to be the more accepted. For Vertues are not effects of Nature, but Choice. Which how free soever it may appear, is as stable as the Sun, when founded on Eternal principles: it secures any Friend in the good and amiable Qualities he desires in his Beloved, as much as Nature it self could do, though they depend upon the Will, which is capable of changing every moment. This of Temperance in the Government of our *Humors*.

I shall add but one Note more, and that is, That a Wise man discards the *Predominancy* of all Humors, and will not yield himself up to the Empire of any: for he is to live the life of *Reason;* not of *Humor*. Nor will he have any Humor of his own, but what he can put off and on, as he sees occasion. He will cleave eternaly to the Rules of Vertue, but will comply in his Humor so far as to make his conversation sweet and agreeable to every Temper. Religion and Charity, as well as Courtesie and Civility, prompt to this; and where these concur with his Reason, and favour his Interest, he may well do what S. *Paul* taught him, *become all things to all men, that he might gain some.* And this encouragement he hath, A man by sacrificing his own, may comply with the satisfaction of all the World: and find his own far more great and honourable, and sweet and amiable in the End, far more high and blessed, in the Love and Esteem he shall obtain thereby, than if he had gratified his first inclination without any respect to the Prelation of others. It will bring him to the fruition of Pleasures, far greater than those he despised.

TEMPERANCE is the full composition and use of Vertues, is far more sublime, and more immediately approacheth the end of Vertue, than any Temperance in Meats and Drinks: It is resident nearer the Throne of Felicity, and seateth us by her. You may see its Task as it is prescribed in Prudence. But for Example sake we will instance it in Meekness, which of all the Vertues is the most weak and naked. A meek Spirit receiveth its Temper, its encouragement, strength, and facility, from the union and concurrence of all the Vertues. Knowledg is its light, and Love the principle of its life and motion. Wisdom guideth it to the highest End; Righteousness is a great incentive thereunto, while it teacheth us to esteem the favour of God, and the excellency of those Souls, whose value maketh us tender of their Repose, and prone to honour them with a due esteem, as well as to desire their peace and salvation. Holiness maketh us to delight in our Duty. Goodness inclines us to sacrifice our own, to the welfare of others. Mercy leads us to pity their Infirmities, and more to compassionate their Misery, than to be provoked with their Distemper. Justice makes us to pay our Saviours Love and Merits, what we owe unto *him*. All these establish the habit of Meekness in our Souls. Fortitude does several waies conspire thereunto, for it makes us to adventure upon any Trouble that we can fall into thereby, and puts a lustre upon us in the act of Meekness. Patience habituates the Soul to Afflictions, and makes our sence of Injuries easie. Repentance minds us of other employments than Anger and Revenge, even a contrite Sorrow for our own Offences. Humility gives us a sence of our own Unworthiness; and a willingness to be yet more low than our Enemies can make us. It inclines us also to confess, that we have deserved far worse, and more bitter Evils; and to despise our selves; which when we truly do, no Injuries or Wrongs can move us. Faith carries us up to higher Enjoyments. Hope hath respect to the promised Reward. Our Love towards GOD enflames us with Desire to please him, Charity to our Neighbour is prone to forgive him. Prudence teacheth us to expect no Figs from Thorns, nor better entertainment from Briars and Brambles: but rather to right our selves by improving their Wrongs, and to turn their Vices into our Vertues. Magnanimity despiseth the Courtship of Worms, and scorneth to place its rest and felicity in Trifles. Liberality is industrious to find out occasions of Obliging and Conquering: Contentment is fed by higher Delights, and beautifies our Meekness with a cheerful Behaviour. Magnificence carries to the most high and illustrious Deeds, and by very great and expensive Methods to multiply favours and benefits on our Beloved: for all are our Beloved whether Friends or Enemies. Temperance it self takes off the stupidity and sluggishness of our Meekness; puts activity and vigour into it, that it may not be a Sleepish, but Heroick Vertue; nay, adorns, secures, and perfects it by the Addition and Exercise of all these; and by giving to every other Vertue its Form and Perfection, makes them more fit and able to aid and assist us here. It moderates our Passions, and puts a better dose of Life into our Consideration. If there be any other Virtue, it is not so remote, but that it may lend us its helping hand, and be subservient to the perfection of our Love and Meekness. Which, however simple it may appear in Solitude, is very strong and irresistable, amazing, as far from Contempt as the Sun is from Darkness, when it is animated with Courage, and made illustrious by Love, enriched with Liberality, and made bright by Knowledg, guided by Wisdom to the highest End, and by Prudence to well-known and advantagious, tho inferiour Purposes. When the Soul appeareth neither foolish, nor Cowardly, nor base, nor soft, but High and Magnanimous in its Operation, Meekness is redoubted.

IN the Throne of Glory all the acts of Faith, and Hope, and Repentance shall be for ever perfected, or swallowed up in fruition. The fruit of all occasional and transient Vertues shall remain, the Divine Vertues shall be so firmly united, that in their Act and Exercise whey shall be *one* for ever. By Knowledg we shall see all that the light of Heaven and Eternity can reveal. By Love we shall embrace all that is amiable before GOD and his holy Angels. By Wisdom we shall use the most glorious Means for the attainment and enjoyment of the highest End; which is GOD in all his Joys and Treasures: in the use of those Means we must actually enjoy all Blessedness and

Glory. Righteousness and Holiness, and Goodness and Charity shall with all the rest be the Lineaments and Colours of the Mind, the Graces and Beauties of the blessed Soul: They shall shine upon its face, and it self shall be glorious in the perfection of their Beauty, as GOD is. Its Goodness shall make it a fountain of Delights to all the other Creatures. It shall be all Humility, yet all Enjoyment: Amazed at its own Nothingness and Vileness, yet ravished with wonder and the height of its Felicity: For the lower it is in its own Eyes, the more Great doth the Goodness of GOD appear, and the more transcendently Sweet is its Adoration and Satisfaction. By its Gratitude it sacrifice it self Eternally to the Deity, and taketh more pleasure in his Glory than its own. It is all Godliness and Contentment. All these Vertues are exercised together in the state of Glory, not so much by our own Temperance, as by the Infusion of his most Heavenly Grace, who fills us with his own Fulness and Perfection by way of Reward, and causing us to enter into his Eternal Rest, maketh us *to cease from our own Works, as he also did from his*, by inspiring us with his own Wisdom, Life and Strength, and actuating all our Powers by his own for ever: That we, by vertue of his Grace infused, may live in the Image of his Eternal Moderation, and attain that extremity of Bliss and Glory, which he hath (exceeding his Almight Power) by an exquisite and mysterious Temperance in all his Operations, Divinely attained.

CHAP. XXIII.

Of Temperance in GOD. How the Moderation of Almighty Power guided in its works by Wisdom its Works by Wisdom, perfecteth the Creation. How it hath raised his own Glory and our Felicity beyond all that Simple Power could effect by its Infiniteness.

IF Moderation hath such happy effects in Men, where the Strength is small, the Wisdom little, the Matter base, the Occasion low, as in divers Instances it is manifest it hath: how glorious must this Vertue be, where the Power is Almighty, the Wisdom Infinite, the Subject-Matter Perfect, the End, and the Occasion most Divine and Glorious!

IT would seem a strange Paradox, to say, That Almighty Power could not exist without Infinite Wisdom: but it is infinitely true: For the Wisdom and Power of GOD are *one*. No Blind Power can be Almighty, because it cannot do all that is Excellent. That Power would without Wisdom be Blind, is as evident as the Sun, the want of that being as great an impediment to its Operations, as the lack of Eyes is to a Man upon Earth: which so Eclipseth and darkneth his Power, that he cannot perform those excellent Works, to which Light is necessary. There is no Blind Power in GOD, and therefore no Power distinct from his Understanding. *By his Wisdom he made the Heavens, by his Understanding he established the Earth. By his Knowledge the Depths are broken up, and the Clouds drop down the Dew.*[1] Wisdom is the Tree of Life, which beareth all the fruits of Immortality and Honour. Inartificial Violence will never carry it: There is a Mark to he hit; and that is in every thing what is most fair and eligible. It may be miss'd as much by shooting over it, as by falling short of it. Naked Power cannot tell what to propose as its Aim and Object. Only that which is able to contrive, is able to effect its Desire, in the Work it conceiveth most fit and excellent for its Power to perform.

IT is a stranger Paradox yet, That Power limited is Greater and more Effectual, than Power let loose; for this importeth, that Power is more infinite when bounded, than Power in its utmost liberty. But that which solveth the Riddle, and removeth the Inconvenience, is our Assurance of this, That GOD can do nothing but what is Wise, and that his Wisdom therefore is all his Power. And of this it followeth,

---

[1] Marginal gloss: Pro. 3.19.20.

That nothing is possible with GOD, but what is infinitely Excellent: for to do any thing less than the Best is unwise; and being so, is contrary to the Nature of Wisdom which is his Power.

THE Will of GOD is his Wisdom: By the meer Motion of his Will he Created all things, and therefore it is his Power: his Power and his Wisdom meet in his Will and are both the same. By his Word he made the Worlds, and his Eternal Word is his Eternal Wisdom.

ALL this I speak because it is the Office of Wisdom to propose the most excellent End, and to pursue it by the most efficaious Means: And because the Wisdom of GOD will be found one with his Eternal *Moderation.*

THE utmost End of all that is aimed at, is indeed illimited: It is the Best and Greatest Thing that infinite and Eternal Wisdom could conceive: but being out of all measure High and Excellent, it includeth innumerable Varieties, that are shut up in bounds for their greater Perfection. Whereupon it followeth, that GOD hath attained a more excellent Effect, than if he had made any one Thing singly infinite.

HIS Love being Infinite and Eternal, in sacrificing it self in all its Works for its Objects welfare, became an infinite and eternal Act; which was not contented, unless in all its Works, it added Art unto Power, and exerted its Wisdom in all its Productions. Had it made one Infinite, some are of Opinion, it had exceeded it self; at least done all that was possible, both for it self, and for its Object, and that one Infinite, being so Created, must be its only Object. For more than Infinite what can be? We are apt to think that nothing can be beside. But to shew that GOD is infinitely more than what we conceive, while we think him infinite, and that we infinitely wrong him, while we limit his Essence to one single Infinity; Who is every way Infinite, in Himself, in all his Works, in all his Waies, in all his Counsels, in every one of his Perfections; He hath made every thing either Infinite, or better than so. For by variety of Effects he hath attained an End in the Beauty and Correspondence of all his Productions, far more Amiable and Divine than any one Effect is capable of being. All Things by a kind of Temperance are made and ordered in Number, Weight and Measure, so that they give and receive a Beauty and Perfection, every thing to and from all the residue, of inestimable value, in relation to the Goodness and Love of their Creator.

I doubt not but GOD (would his Wisdom have permitted such a thing) could have made an infinite Object. For whereever GOD is, he is able to Act; and his Omnipresence is infinite Wisdom and Power;

which filling Infinity is able to exert it self beyond all the bounds of Space in an infinite Manner all at once. If it so do, it cannot rest in a less Attainment, than one that answers the measure of its Operation: if it did, that Attainment would be infinitely defective: For infinite Wisdom could certainly conceive one infinitely Better. But this I will aver, that GOD hath wrought abundantly more, than if he had made any one single Effect of his Power infinite. He hath wrought a Work that pleaseth him infinitely Better, and so will it please us, when we are Wise as he is.

HAD he made any one single Infinite, it must be either Corporeal, or Spiritual: Be it either, there is room enough in his Understanding and Omnipresence to receive it. Empty Space is an Infinite Object in his understanding. But for the Glory of his Moderation, it is evident that he hath attained a far greater and more perfect End.

HAD he made an Infinite Object of a Spiritual Nature, it must be a Spirit Endued with illimited Power, to see his Omnipresence and Eternity. And had he made no more but only this, it is to be feared that the Spectator would be displeased for want of Objects, in preparing which the Love of GOD should have glorified his Wisdom and Goodness for its fruition.

If you say, the Omnipresence and Eternity of GOD had been filled with the Creature, it is evident that Spirits fill no Room, though they see all things: and that it had been much better if Objects had been prepared for its Enjoyment.

HAD he prepared any one Corporeal Object for the fruition of that Creature; any Corporeal Object if infinite in Dimensions, would be wholly useless: nay pernicious and destructive; for it would exclude all other Beings to which it might be serviceable, out of place, and have nothing whereto to be beneficial.

IF you say it would be Beneficial to GOD, or to that Spectator, or that Intelligible Power, that Spirit for whom it was made: It is apparent that no Corporeal Being can be serviceable to a Spirit, but only by the Beauty of those Services it performeth to other Corporeals, that are capable of receiving them: and that therefore all Corporeals must be limited and bounded for each others sake. And for this Cause it is, that a Philosophical Poet said;

> *As in a Clock,'tis hinder'd-Force doth bring*
> *The Wheels to order'd Motion, by a Spring;*
> *Which order'd Motion guides a steddy Hand*
> *In useful sort at Figures just to stand;*

Which, were it not by Counter-ballance staid,
The Fabrick quickly would aside be laid
As wholly useless: So a Might too Great,
But well proportion'd, makes the World compleat.
Power well-bounded is more Great in Might,
Than if let loose 'twere wholly Infinite.
He could have made an endless Sea by this,
But then it had not been a Sea of Bliss;
A Sea that's bounded in a finite shore,
Is better far because it is no more.
Should Waters endlesly exceed the Skies,
They'd drown the World, and all whate're we prize.
Had the bright Sun been Infinite, its Flame
Had burnt the World, and quite consum'd the same.
That Flame would yield no splendor to the Sight,
'Twould be but Darkness though 'twere Infinite.
One Star made Infinite would all exclude,
An Earth made Infinite could ne're be view'd.
But all being bounded for each others sake,
He bounding all did all most useful make.
And which is best, in Profit and Delight,
Though not in Bulk, he made all Infinite.
He in his Wisdom did their use extend,
By all, to all the World from End to End.
In all Things, all things service do to all:
And thus a Sand is Endless, though most small.
 And every Thing is truly Infinite,
 In its Relations deep and exquisite.

THIS is the best way of accommodating things to the Service of each other, for the fruition of all Spectators.

MODERATION is not so called from Limiting and Restraining, but from Moderating and Ruling. If Reason requires that a Thing should be Great, it is the part of Temperance to make it so. Where Reason requires, it is a point of Moderation to enlarge and extend Power: Nay to stretch it out to the utmost of its Capacity if Wisdom order it, is but equal. To moderate Almighty Power is to limit or extend it, as Reason requires. Reason requires that it should be so limited and extended, as most tends to the perfection of the Universe.

IF it be more Wise, and more tends to the perfection of the Universe, that Millions of intelligible Spirits should be Created, and every one of them be made infinite in Understanding, it shall be done: If not, Temperance forbears. If Sands and Atoms tend more to the perfection of the World than Angels; there where they do so, Sands and Atoms shall be made, and Angels there where they tend more to the perfection of the World. So that every thing is best in its proper place. Were there no Sands or Atoms there would be no *Universe*: For the Earth, the Sea, the Skie, the Air, all Bodies consist of these, either united or divided. If they had been left unmade, and Angels had been created in their Places, there had been no visible World at all.

TO make Visible Object useful it was necessary to enshrine some Spirits in Corporeal Bodies, and therefore to make such Creature as *Men*, that might see, and feel, and smell, and taste, and hear, and eat and drink by their Bodies, and enjoy all the Pleasures of the World by their Souls: And by their Souls moreover know the Original and End of all, understand the design of all, and be able to celebrate the Praises of the Creator. For by this means pure Essences abstracted from all Corporeity might enjoy the World, while they delight in the glory of its Uses, and especially in those compleat and amiable Creatures, for whom it was prepared.

IT was expedient also to make their Bodies finite, that they might converse together: but their inward Intelligences of endless reach, that they might see the holy Angels, delight in them, and by their Love be delightful to them: that they might also be able to search into the depth of all Things, and enjoy Eternity; Nay, that they might be fit Recipients for the infinite Bounty and Goodness of GOD, which is infinite in its Communications.

THAT they should be subject to his Laws, and depend upon him, was necessary in like manner. For by that distinction an infinite difference was between him and them; that disparity being laid in the foundation, though the benefits they receive are altogether infinite, the distance is still the more infinite between them: for the greater the Bounty is, the deeper is the Obligation. The Love and Service they owe is infinite, and so is the Gratitude.

TO see all his Glory is to be able to admire it, and to adore it with infinite amazement and joy, which is to be compleatly just unto it, and perfectly blessed.

There is but one thing more, wherein Almighty Power was by Wisdom infinite to restrain it self for the perfection of his Kingdom: And that is to create them free, that were made to enjoy it. Not to determine their Wills by a fatal Necessity, but to make their esteem and fruition of GOD and his Works their duty, and to leave them to themselves for the more free and voluntary discharge of their duty. For by that means, it wold make them capable of Rewards and Punishments, in the Righteous distribution of which the nature and the glory of a Righteous Kingdom consisteth.

THUS did GOD by infinite Moderation, and by sublime and transcendent Temperance prepare his Kingdom, and make every Thing exquisite in his whole Dominion, to the praise of his Glory, and the satisfaction of his infinite and Eternal Reason. The similitude of which Reason being the Essence of the Soul, all These things fall out for our glory and satisfaction also.

NOW if GOD himself acquired all his Joyes by Temperance: and the glory of his Kingdom is wholly founded in his Moderation: We may hope that our Moderation and Temperance in its place, may accomplish Wonders, and lead us to the fruition of his, by certain steps and degrees, like those that are observed in the Womb towards Manhood, and in the School of our Childhood towards perfect Learning.

TOO much Rain, or too much Drought will produce a Famine: the Earth is made fertile by a seasonable mixture of Heat and Moisture. Excess of Power may overwhelm, but moderation is that which perfecteth and blesseth the Creation.

ALMIGHTY Power is carried far beyond it self, or really is made Almighty, by vertue of that Temperance, wherein Eternal Wisdom is eternally Glorified.

IF any thing be wanting to the full demonstration of the perfection of GODS Kingdom, it is the consideration of his Delay: for we are apt to think, he might have made it Eternally before he did. But to this no other Answer is necessary thought many might be made) then that all Things were from all Eternity before his Eyes, and he saw the fittest Moments wherein to produce them: and judged it fit in his wisdom first to fill Eternity with his deliberations and Counsels, and then to beautifie Time with the execution of his Decrees. For were there no more to be said but this, his Empire is eternal, because all Possibilities, nay and all Impossibilities are subject to his Will. But if it be confessed that Eternity is an Everlasting Moment, infinite in duration, but permanent in all its parts, all Things past, present, and to come are at once before him, and eternally together. Which is the true Reason, why Eternity is a standing Object before the Eye of the Soul, and all its parts, being full of Beauty and Perfection, for ever to be enjoyed.

IF any man be disposed to cavil further, and to urge, that GOD might at the very first have placed Angels and Men in the state of Glory, the Reply is at hand: that GOD very well understandeth the beauty of Proportion, that Harmony and Symmetry springs from a variety of excellent Things in several places, fitly answering to, and perfecting each other: that the state of Trial, and the state of Glory are so mysterious in their Relation, that neither without the other could be absolutely perfect: Innumerable Beauties would be lost, and many transcendent Vertues and Perfections be abolished, with the estate of Trial, if that had been laid aside, the continual appearance and effect of which is to enrich and beautifie the Kingdom of GOD everlastingly: That God loveth Man far more than if he had placed him in the Throne at first, and designeth more Glory and Perfection for him, than in that dispensation he could have been capable of: all which springeth from the Restraint of his Power in some occasions, that it might more fully be exerted in the perfection of the whole, and of all things that where possible to be made, might end in the Supream, and most absolutely Blessed.

Therefore upon the whole Matter, we may conclude with *Solomon, Happy is the man that findeth Wisdom, and the man that getteth Understanding. For the Merchandize of it is better than the Merchandize of Silver, and the Gain thereof than of fine Gold. She is more precious than Rubies, and all the things thou canst desire are not to be compared with her. Length of Daies is in her right hand, and in her left hand Riches and Honour. Her Waies are waies of Pleasantness, and all her Paths are Peace. She is a Tree of Life to them that lay hold upon here, and happy is every one that retaineth her. The LORD by Wisdom hath founded the Earth, by Understanding hath he established the Heavens. My Son, let not them depart from thine Eyes: Keep sound Wisdom and Discretion.* Wisdom is the principal Thing: therefore get Wisdom, and with all thy Getting, get Understanding. For the same Wisdom which created the World, is the only Light wherein it is enjoyed.

CHAP. XXIV.

Of Patience. Its Original. How GOD was the first Patient Person in the World. The Nature, and the Glory, and the blessed Effects of his Eternal Patience. The Reason and Design of all Calamities. Of Patience in Martyrdom. The extraordinary Reward of ordinary Patience in its meanest obscurity.

PATIENCE is a Vertue of the Third estate; it belongs not to the estate of Innocence, because in it there was no Affliction; nor to the estate of Misery, because in it there is no Vertue: but to the estate of Grace it appertains, because it is an estate of Reconciliation, and an estate of Trial: wherein Affliction and Vertue meet together. In the estate of Glory there is no Patience.

THIS is one of those distastful Vertues, which GOD never intended. It received its bitterness from Sin, its life and beauty from GOD's Mercy. If we dislike this Vertue we may thank our selves, for we made GOD first to endure it. And if all things are rightly weighed, no Creature is equal of GOD in Sufferings. We made it necessary for the Eternal GOD-HEAD to be Incarnate, and to suffer all the Incommodities of Life, and the bitter Torments of a bloody Death, that he might bear the Penance of or Sins, and deliver us from eternal Perdition.

THE Corporeal Sufferings of our Saviour are not comparable to the Afflictions of his Spirit. Nor are there any Sufferings or Losses so great as those we cast upon the GOD-HEAD. He infinitely hateth Sin, more than Death: and had rather be Crucified a thousand times over, than that one Transgression should be brought into the World. Nothing is so quick and tender as Love, nothing so lively and sensible in resenting. No loss is comparable to that of Souls, nor any one so deeply concerned in the loss, as GOD Almighty: No Calamity more peircing, than to see the Glory of his Works made Vain, to be bereaved of his Desire, and frustrated of his End in the whole Creation. He had rather we should give him the Blood of *Dragons,* or the cruel Venom of *Asps,* to drink, than that we should pollute our selves, or his Kingdom with a Sin. Nay it were better (if without a Sin it could be done) that the whole World should be annihilated, than a Sin committed. For the World might be Created again with ease, and all that is in it be repaired with a word: but a Sin once committed, can never be undone; it will appear in its place throughout all Eternity: Yet is so odious. and so infinitely opposite to the Holiness of GOD, that no Gall or Wormwood is comparable thereunto. To see his Beloved blasted, his Love despised, and his Son rebellious; to see the most amiable Law in the World broken, his Kingdom laid waste, and his Image defaced; to see all his Labour marred and spoiled, his Benefits slighted; and his infinite Goodness abused and undervalued; all Obligations imposed, and all Rewards prepared, in vain: is worse than to see ones Palace on fire as soon as it is builded, or ones Wife smitten with Leprosie, and ones only beloved Son run mad. For a Child to trample on his Fathers Bowels is nothing in Comparison! He therefore that feels what he made GOD to endure, what Grapes of *Sodom*, and Clusters of *Gomorrah* he offered to his Teeth, how evil thing and bitter it is, to forsake GOD, how the Scripture saith, *He was grieved at the Heart*, when he saw the Corruption and Impiety of the Earth; and how the Sorrow inflicted was so sore, as to make him *repent that he had made Man* in the World: he surely will be more concerned at the Evil he hath *done*, than at any Evil he can otherwise *suffer*: and his Godly Sorrow (as *Moses*'s Rod did eat up all the Rods of the *Egyptians*) will devour all other Sorrows whatsoever.

   TO consider that GOD was the first *Patient* Person in the World, must needs sweeten the Bitterness of Patience, and make it acceptable unto us: to consider that we alone brought it upon our selves, and may thank our selves for the folly of its Introduction, must make us out of very Indignation against our selves contented to suffer, and in pure Justice, quietly to digest it: but to consider yet further, that *GOD*, by bearing our Offences with Patience, took off the trouble of them from us, and by refusing to ease himself of the greatness of his displeasure, in pouring it back again on our own heads, digested it so, as to turn our eternal Torments into transitory Woes, nay into his own Agonies and Pains on the Cross: this will help our Reason to rejoyce at *our light Afflictions which are but for a moment*; especially since they *work* out *for us a far more exceeding, and eternal weight of Glory*.

   The first Impression of that abominable Mischief, which occasioned Patience in *GOD*, made it a Calamity, but not a Vertue, Detestation and Grief in themselves are but Sufferings, and meer Sufferings have no Vertue, nor so much almost as Action in them. If his detestation and grief had broken out in Impatience, we had all been destroyed: Anger and Fury had been poured down upon us. That which made it a Vertue was the great and mighty Continence, whereby it was kept in, and governed for all our Benefit. For it was full of Goodness, and Compassion, and Mercy, and Love; and that was indeed the vertue of Patience, in which so much Magnanimity and Government did appear, so much Wisdom, and Stedfastness, and Immutability; and upon this vertue of that Act whereby he retained his displeasure, the whole Kingdom of Grace, and the glory of his Mercy and Love, and the blessedness and exaltation of his Church is founded, it depended upon it, and from his Patience it proceeded.

PATIENCE then is that Vertue by which we behave our selves constantly and prudently in the midst of Misfortunes and Troubles: That Vertue whereby we do not only forbear to break out in Murmurings and Repinings, or support our selves from sinking under Afflictions, or suppress our Discontentments, and refrain from Anger and Disquiet; but whereby we retain our Wisdom, and the goodness of our Mind, notwithstanding all the Confusions and Disorders that would disturb us, and demean our selves in a serene and honourable manner, surmounting the Pains and Calamities that trouble us, and that would otherwise overwhelm us. While we move in a quick and vigorous manner under our Burthen; and by a true Courage improve our Afflictions, and turn them into the *Spoils* of Invincible Reason.

IT is an easie Observation, that Troublous Times are the Seasons of Honour, and that a Warlike-Field is the Seed-Plot of great and Heroical Actions. Men that live in quiet and peaceful Ages, pass through the World as insensibly as if they had all their daies been asleep. Hazards, and Calamities, and Battles, and Victories fill the Annals with Wonder, and raise Great Men to an eminent degree of Fame and Glory. It is Saint *Chrysostoms* opinion, That a Man shews far greater Bravery, that grapples with a Disease, or surmounts his evil Fortune, or behaves himself with Courage in distress, bears the burning of his House, or the loss of his Goods, or the death of his Children with an equal Spirit, in the midst of all Calamities retains his Integrity with Humility and Patience, and Blesses GOD, chearfully submitting with Resignation to his Will, and shews himself Constant in all Estates: then he that in the midst of a prosperous Condition, buildeth Hospitals and Temples, shineth in the exercise of Bounty and Magnificence, and obligeth all the World without any other Expence than that of his Monies. A *Pelican* that feeds her young ones with her Blood, is a more Noble Bird than an Eagle, that fills her Nest with *Ravine*, though taken from the Altar: For though that of a Sacrifice be the more Sacred food, that of ones own Blood is more near and costly.

TIMES of Affliction are Seed-times for a future Harvest. *We are made perfect through Sufferings*: though the Way be mysterious, and the Manner almost incomprehensible, whereby the Sufferings we endure conduce to our Perfections. *Consider the Patience of* Job, how great a spectacle his Sufferings made him *to GOD, Angels, and Men*, and how glorious he became by his Patience to all *Generations*.

THIS Vertue has an Appearance, by reason of its Objects and Materials, so cross to its disposition, that if any thing be difficult in all Nature to be understood, Patience is one, it being a thing of the most deep and obscure value. Its Nature and Effect seem contrary to each other. It raises a Man by depressing him, it elevates by overwhelming, it honours by debasing, it saves by killing him. By making a Man little and nothing, it magnifies and exalts him. No Act of Love is attended with such bleeding Circumstances as that of Cruel Resolution, in exposing our selves to all Calamities that can befal our Souls, for our Beloved's sake. It is the glory of the good Shepheard that *He laies down his life for the Sheep*. And for this very Cause is our Saviour honoured by GOD and Men, *because being in the form of GOD he made himself of no Reputation, but took on himself the form of a Servant*, and died the most cursed *Death of the Cross*, for the sake of the World: *Wherefore*, saith the Text (that is, *For which very Cause*) *GOD also hath highly exalted him, and given him a Name which is above every Name, that at the Name of JESUS every Knee should bow, of things in the Heaven, things in the Earth, and things under the Earth*. Nor is this Gift of *GOD* so purely Arbitrary, but that it has a foundation in Nature. Angels and Men do not bow their Knees only because they are commanded; but because they see Reason to incline them to bow their Knees. There is something in our Saviours Nature, Action, and Merit, that deserves it at their Hands. The wonderful Love wherewith he loved us is the Root, the Soul, and Glory of his Passion. It is wonderful as it made him willing to become Death, and Sin, and a Curse for us. But the height of our Extasie is in the Reality of his Passion, and in the full accomplishment of all its Purposes.

IT is the Vertue of Love which is infused into Patience, and the chief Elixir of its Nature is founded in the Excellency of a Spirit, that Suffers for anothers sake. This therefore we ought ever to remember, That Patience when it is a Vertue springs from Love; and that this Love is chiefly towards *GOD*, and next that to our Neighbour. When we suffer any thing for *GOD*'s sake, or for our Neighbours good, we suffer in a Wise and Vertuous manner. And the Honour which follows such a Suffering is the Crown of Glory which it shall for ever wear. It is a vain and insipid thing to Suffer without loving *GOD* or Man. Love is a transcendent Excellence in every Duty, and must of necessity enter into the Nature of every Grace and Vertue. That which maketh the solid Benefit of Patience unknown, its Taste so bitter and comfortless to Men, is its *Death* in the separation and absence of its Soul. We Suffer, but Love not. Otherwise Love to the Person for whose sake we Suffer, is its own support and comfort; It makes the Action to be valuable; and infuses a sweetness into all the Affliction it can make us endure: A sweetness answerable to the Welfare and Pleasure, which is either caused or secured, to our Object thereby. Our own growth in the approbation and esteem of the Person we love, is the desirable Greatness which we covet to attain, which can no way be confirmed, and increased so perfectly, as by Suffering for him. For our Fidelity, Sincerity, Reality, Vigour, Life and Industry, can never be made so fair and apparent, as when we pursue our love, and are carried by it to the utmost extremities of Death and Misery, and labour through all disasters, Persecutions, and Calamities, to obey, and honour, and please, and glorifie the Object which in times of quiet we pretend to love. In an easie and prosperous Estate there is little difference between Friendship and Flattery: but he that sticks firm in Calamity is a Friend indeed. The Trial of Love consists in the difficulties it endures for its Beloved.

AND for this Cause it is, that *GOD* will expose us to so severe a Trial: himself ordaining some Trials in the beginning; but permitting more, when we brought them upon our selves: Many also he suffereth to come, which we daily bring upon our own heads by our own folly. Some he inflicteth perhaps himself, for the Chastisement of our Sins, or the Medicine of our Souls, to abate our Confidence, and to excite our Care; to awaken us out of our Lethargy, and to quicken our sence both of our Miserable Condition, and our need of his Favour: to humble our Rebellion, to heal and purge our Corruptions, to moderate our Passions, to heighten our Penitence, to abate our Pride, to increase our Ardour in Devotion and Prayer; to make our subjection to, and dependance on him Clear; to stir us up to a more strict Examination of our selves in our Thoughts, Words, and Deeds, least some *Jonas* or other should lie in the Ship, that continues the Tempest upon us; to enkindle our Compassion towards our afflicted Brethren, and to enflame us with more perfect Zeal, and Love towards *GOD*; It is like Wormwood that imbitters the Nipple, to wean us from the World, and augment our desire *to be dissolved and to be with Christ*; to make us groan after *our Eternal Rest*, and long for the *glorious Liberty of the Sons of GOD*. Sometimes he suffereth Tribulations and Trials to come upon us, by the Perverseness of Men, who being left at Liberty in their dominion over the World, are the principal Authors of all the Troubles and disorders in it. To know the several springs and sources of Affliction is very expedient; for our Patience and Contentment much dependeth upon it. A confused Apprehension makes us blind, but a clear Sight distinguisheth between the Will of *GOD*, and the Corruption of Nature; which in our selves and others is the principal Cause of all our disturbances.

BE it by which of all these Occasions it will, or for which of all these Ends it can befal us, it is evermore to increase our Conquest, and to make us like the King of Sufferings *pure* and *perfect*. And the Consideration of Gods over-ruling Power and Providence therein, which makes all these Things work together for our good, begetteth a grateful Admiration in us as well as a sence of our dependance on his Goodness, which increaseth the Fear of *GOD* in our Souls, and animates us with great Wonder, that he should put his hand to touch the vile and evil Off-spring of our Sin, and turn all into Good, and make it to rest in our Exaltation and Glory by his Wisdom and Mercy.

Concerning *GOD*'s End in bringing, and permitting all these Evils, the Scripture is very frequent: It was one of *Job*'s Contemplations,[1] *What is Man that thou shouldest magnifie him, and that thou shouldst set thine Heart upon him; and that thou shouldst visit him every Morning, and try him every Moment?* Man is magnified by his Trials. It was *David*'s Observation,[2] *The LORD is in his holy Temple, the Lords Throne is in Heaven: his Eyes behold, his Eye-lids try the Children of Men. The Lord trieth the Righteous; but the Wicked and him that loveth Violence his Soul hateth.* It was *Daniel*'s Prophesie,[3] *And some of them of Understanding shall fall, to try them, and to purge, and to make them White, even to the time of the End. GOD* himself expresseth his own Resolution,[4] *I will bring part of them through the fire, and will refine them as Silver is refined, and try them as Gold is tried: They shall call on my Name and I will hear them; I will say, It is my People, and they shall say, the LORD is my GOD.*

THE meaning of all which places is, not as if *GOD* did stand in need of all these Trials to know what is in us: for he knoweth what is

---

[1] Marginal gloss: Job.17.17,18.
[2] Marginal gloss: Psal.11.4,5.
[3] Marginal gloss: Dan. 11.35.
[4] Marginal gloss: Zech.13.9.

in Man from all Eternity: before these Trials come he *searcheth the Heart, and trieth the Reins*, and discerneth the thoughts, and purposes of the Soul: He seeth every Inclination in the seed, every Grace in the secret habit of the Mind, and every Vertue in the Root. They lie in the Seed, but yet he seeth a mighty difference between quiet Habits, and effectual Operations: for they differ as much as the Root and the Blossom, or the Blossom and the Fruit. For Vertues to lie asleep in the Soul, and for Vertues to be actually and fully perfected, is as great a difference, as for a Vine to be of a generous kind, and prone to bear, but to remain without Fruit; or for a Vine to bring forth, and to be really laden with all the bunches of Grapes that beautifie it. The Excellency of its Nature is vain, if its Fruit be never brought to perfection. There is a Glory in the Work which the silent Habit is uncapable of. It is the Life and Vigour of the Exercise in which all the brightness consisteth. Even Diamonds in the Quarry are dull and dim, they receive not their full lustre and Price till they are cut and polished. *GOD* hath placed our Trial in sharp and bitter Atchievments, because the Love that is exprest in Agonies and Conflicts, acquires other kind of Beauties, that produce more violent and strong Effects in the Mind of the Spectator, and touch the Soul of the Beloved with more quick and feeling Compassions, than any Love expressed in Ease and Pleasure can pretend to. And since all our Felicity consists in the violence of Gods Love, his great and perfect Sence of our Beauty and Honour, his full and compleat delight and Complacency, all that which affecteth his Soul with more feeling and tender Resentment, must be very dear and precious to us, because it maketh us more dear and precious to him. We live in him more effectually, and feel our selves rooted in his Love, and crowned with his Complacency more abundantly, by how much the more his Affection bleedeth, and his Piety (which enbalms Love) is stirred up to receive us. And therefore it is that St. *Peter* saith, *We are in Heaviness for a season through manifold Temptations, that the Trial of our Faith being much more precious than of Gold that perisheth, though it be tried with Fire, might be found unto Praise, and Honour, and Glory at the Appearing of Jesus Christ.*[1] For as we have before observed, Love is more effeminate in a condition of Repose, where all is sweet and easie to our selves: there can be no Fidelity, no Patience, no Fortitude, no actual Sacrificing of all our Contentments and Joyes to our Beloved; no Victory over Death, and Hell, and the Grave; no Self denial, no Endearments springing from the same, no Prelation of our

---

[1] Marginal gloss: 1 Pet. 1.6, 7.

Object above our selves; no loss of Honours, Riches, Liberties, and Lives for our Objects sake; and the more of this is Actually done, the more of Necessity must be the following Joy of Glory. And for this Cause doth St. *Peter* further exhort us, *Beloved, think it not strange concerning the fiery Trial which is to try you, as though some strange thing happened unto you: But rejoyce, in as much as ye are Partakers of Christs Sufferings: that when his Glory is revealed, you may be glad also with exceeding Joy. If ye be reproached for the Name of Christ happy are ye, for the Spirit of Glory and of God resteth upon you: on their part he is evil spoken of, but on your part he is glorified.*[1]

THIS he speaketh I confess of the Persecutions, Imprisonments, and Flames of the Martyrs, that were Gods Friends, and the Champions of his Truth in the World, that in vindication of his Glory endured the Brunt, and received all the Arrows of his Enemies in their Bosom: but no Man has cause to be discouraged. For where the greatness of the Cause is wanting, the apparent glory of the Consequence unseen, as for the most part it is in all our common and ordinary Afflictions; there to submit to the Will of GOD, where there is so much Baseness as in Poverty: in Sickness where there is so much Unprofitableness, in private Losses and Calamities where there is so much Obscurity; meerly because it is GODS pleasure, and because in other things he hath infinitely obliged us, and prepared infinite and eternal Joyes: this hath a peculiar Grace in its nature, that in ordinary occurrences makes our Patience more rare and extraordinary.

THERE are a thousand things that may be said on this Theme, which for brevity I must pass: All I shall observe further is this, that as the Scriptures open the design of Patience, and unvail the face of its mysterious Nature, so doth Reason shew its invincible height and magnanimity. Patience is a Vertue whose element is in Miseries: it owes its being to Pains and Calamites: were there no Miseries there could be no Patience. Evils are its Play–fellows, it feeds upon Sorrows, thrives by Disadvantages, grows rich by Poverties, it must needs surmount all Opposition, for the more it endures the greater it is. It is impossible for Calamity to hurt Patience: it is made perfect by Sufferings. The more Patient a man is, his Patience is the greater: and the greater his Patience is, the more strong and mighty his Soul is. Nothing can quell him, or discourage, or overcome him, that is compleat in Patience. He dareth all things, because he can endure them. All his Martial and Heroical Vertues are knit together in Patience. Fortitude it self cannot win the

---

[1] Marginal gloss: 1 Pet. 4, 12, 13, 14.

field without it. The most valiant Souldier is but useless if he cannot endure Hunger and Cold, and Heat and Rain, the Incommodities of a March, and lying on the Ground. While he that endures all things marches on, and gets into the Field where Fidelity, Love, and Loyalty are tried, and cannot be hindered from the full and perfect exercise of all these, because he can bear any thing that is Evil, he can do any thing that is Good: He will fight the good fight with alacrity, and at last most certainly attain the Crown of Righteousness, and the Kings favour.

CHAP. XXV.

The Cause of Meekness is Love. It respects the future beauty and perfection of its Object. It is the most supernatural of all the Vertues. The Reasons and Grounds of this Vertue in the estate of Grace and Misery. Its manifold Effects and Excellencies. Of the Meekness of Moses and Joseph.

MEEKNESS is a Vertue of the Third estate, as well as Patience. Patience regards Calamities, Meekness Wrongs. The Injuries that we receive from others are its proper Objects. It springs from Love, and tends to its Continuance and Preservation. It hath something peculiar in it nature, because it gives Immutability to Goodness, and makes our Worth not to depend on other Mens Deservings, but our own Resolutions. It is fed by Charity, and like a grateful Off-spring of a Parent so amiable, helps in it greatest extremity to preserve it from its extinction. For all Love by Nature dies into Distaste, when its Object hath offended: because Approbation which is the first step to Esteem, and Esteem it self which is a degree to Love, have no other Object but something that is Amiable and fit to be beloved. And again every thing that is divested of all its excellence, is common, if not odious; and lost to our Affection, till Meekness comes in to rescue and save both our Love and it from its dismal Period. Its End is the Recovery of what has offended, Hope and Possibility are the foundation of its exercise, Prudence is the Guide by which it is conducted to the satisfaction of our desire in the restitution of Amity between us and our Adversary.

WHERE there is no hope that the Beauty of what we love may be regained, Meekness hath lost its *Vertue*, and with that its *Existence*. For if it be impossible that an evil Person should ever be reclaimed, it is to no purpose to be Meek. He that can never be delightful more, is utterly useless: Meekness therefore which derives its solidity and Power from its End, is in such cases utterly abolished. For this cause it is that we are to esteem our Saviours Blood the ground on which it stands: since all Nature without his Incarnation, Death, and Passion, could never restore a Sinner to the possibility of becoming Just and Amiable. This Vertue of Meekness respects the future beauty and perfection of an Object that is now deformed; It must needs be of transcendent excellency, since the practice of Meekness is acquired by the price of our Saviours Blood, and the first step to its exercise did cost the death of the Eternal GOD.

IT is a transcendent Vertue, because the Means of introducing it are wholy Supernatural. It carries us above all the Rules of Nature, above all the Principles of Reason, and in that is Supernatural. For by Nature we are to be Just and Good towards all that are Innocent, and kind to all those to whom Kindness is due: but it is not by Nature either just or rational that we should love any Creature that is Evil: and how GOD came to do it first is an infinite Wonder. Though now since *he hath first loved us* who are so vile, nothing is more natural than that we should do as we are done unto, imitate him, and love those whom our Creatour loveth: With Pity and Benevolence at first, that we may hereafter do it, with full Complacency.

That Humane Nature is infinitely exalted by the Incarnation of the Son of GOD is confessed by all those, that believe the Article of our Saviours Incarnation: that the Earth how base soever it seem is the Bride of Heaven, its own quiet, and the embraces of the Skies, that make it the Centre of all their Revolutions, sufficiently demonstrate; though few have observed that the Sun, and Moon, and Stars dance attendance to it, and cherish it with their Influences, while the Earthly Globe is crowned with the fruits of all their secret Endeavours: That the Angels desire to look down into those things which are done upon Earth, the very Scriptures witness; and yet for all this, it would seem a New Doctrine, to affirm, that there are Works done here upon Earth, that are by Nature above the Heavens. Yet all the Operations of the Holy Ghost, and all the Good Works of Holy Men, especially the Meekness and Patience of the Saints, which are founded on the greatest Miracle in all Eternity, the Love of GOD to Sinners, and his stupendious Humiliation and Passion for them, are set upon a higher Basis than all Nature, except that of the Deity, can afford unto us. Which Note I make for our greater encouragement to the works of Meekness. They are all in Nature like the effects of our Saviours Love to the greatest Offendors. Reason it self is now exalted above all its former heights, and there is reason since our Saviours Death for the doing of that which no reason, before he designed to forgive, and Die for us, could lead us to do.

THAT GOD through the greatness of his Love may condescend to such Indignities as are infinitely unworthy of him, we see by the Examples of Kings and Queens, and other high and delicate Personages, that suffer their Children to play with their Beards, and the Tresses of their Hair; which other Persons dare not so much as approach, for the Reverence of their Majesty. I have oftentimes admired at the mean Offices to which Parents stoop, and the familiar boldness they permit to their little ones, to play with their Scepters, and Crowns, and Eyes, and Lips, with their Breasts and Jewels, and sometimes to pinch and hurt, nay and to defile them too, being unmindful of their State, and far from all Anger and Indignation. But the free Pardon, and desire of the Return of vicious and debauched Children, is a nearer instance and resemblance of GOD, in his gracious Dispensations, who suffers all Nature still to attend us, though we continually prophane his Name, and injure his eternal Goodness by our manifold Transgressions.

THIS Example of GOD, who died for Sinners, in the Person of his Son, and prayed for his Tormentors, in the very Act of their Cruelty and Rage against him, should prevail with us to esteem all those whom he owneth for his Children, as our own Bowels, and to be as Meek and Condescending to all Mankind, as Parents are to their Children. The Reasons of which Duty are thus variously offered to our Consideration.

TO labour after those Principles only that establish our repose in the estate of Bliss and Innocency, is utterly impertinent to our present Condition.—

> *Were all the World a Paradice of Ease*
>   *'Twere easie then to live in Peace.*
> *Were all men Wise, Divine, and Innocent,*
>   *Just, Holy, Peaceful, and Content,*
>   *Kind, Loving, True, and alwaies Good,*
>   *As in the Golden-Age they stood;*
>   *'Twere easie then to live*
> *In all Delight and Glory, full of Love,*
>   *Blest as the Angels are above.*
>
> *But we such Principles must now attain,*
>   *(If we true Blessedness would gain)*
> *As those are, which will help to make us reign*
>   *Over Disorders, Injuries,*
>   *Ingratitudes, Calamities,*
>   *Affronts, Oppressions, Slanders, Wrongs,*
>   *Lies, Angers, bitter Tongues,*
> *The reach of Malice must surmount, and quell*
>   *The very Rage, and Power of Hell.*

NO Man but he that came down from Heaven, and gave his Apostles power to handle Vipers, and drink any deadly thing without harm, was able to reveal the way of Peace and Felicity to Sinners. He, and only he that made them able to trample Satan under feet, and taught them how to vanquish all the Powers of Darkness, was worthy to make known this glorious mystery of Patience and Meekness, by which in despite of all the Corruptions and Violences in the World, the holy Soul of a quiet Man is armed and prepared for all Assaults, and so invironed with its own repose, that in the midst of Provocations it is undisturbed, and dwells as it were in a Sanctuary of Peace within it self, in a Paradice of Bliss, while it is surrounded with the howlings of a terrible Wilderness. Nothing else can make us live happily in this World, for among so many Causes of Anger and Distaste, no man can live well, but he that carries about him perpetual *Antidotes* and *Victories*.

THERE are two things absolutely necessary to Felicity, outward *Security*, and inward *Contentment*. Meekness is as it were the *Bulwark of Security*, which though it be as soft as *Wool*, is able with more success to repel the violence of a Cannon-Bullet, than the rough temper of a *Stone-Wall*. *Contentment* springs from the satisfaction of Desire in the sight and fruition of all Treasures and Glories: And as the Sun is surrounded with its own Light, the felicity of the Enjoyment becomes its own fortress and security. For he that is throughly Happy, has so much work to do in Contemplation and Thanksgiving, that he cannot have while to be concerned with other mens disorders, he loves his Employment too well to be disturbed, and will not allow himself the thoughts of Revenge or Anger.

IN two things Meekness is greatly profitable to a Mans self, *Possession* and *Triumph*. He that permits the Tumult of the World to enter into his Soul, and suffers the Temple of the Holy Ghost to be defiled with Rage and Anger, makes it an *unfit* habitation for the Blessed Spirit. Doves will not dwell in *Pigeon-Houses* disturbed, or haunted with Vermin: nor can Felicity be enjoyed but by serene and quiet Thoughts that are full of tranquillity. For *where Envying and Strife is, there is Confusion and every evil Work. But the Wisdom that is from above is first pure, then peaceable, gentle and easie to be intreated, full of Mercy and good Fruits. And the fruit of Righteousness is sown in Peace of them that make Peace.* Which must of necessity precede fruition, as Triumph followeth.

WERE I for my life to interpret that Text of our Saviour, *The Meek shall inherit the Earth*, I should in the first place say, that every Knowing man may enjoy the beauty and glory of the whole World, and by sweet Contemplations delight in all the abundance of Treasures and pleasant Varieties that are here upon Earth, especially since by the Ordinance of Nature all men are to be his peculiar Treasures. This he might do, I say, did all men love him, and fill the World with Glory and Vertue.

But since all is confounded by their perverseness and disorder, his Fruition is utterly lost, unless he will forgive all Injuries, and by the vertue of Meekness maintain the quiet of his own Soul in the midst of their distempers. The Meek man is not fretted nor disturbed, but may enjoy all Still: and the unspeakable Joy which all the Glories of Gods Kingdom do afford him, shall make him more meek, and able also to pacifie, and rule, and heal the minds of his Enemies, and even by the love of Sinners to recover his Right, and ancient Fruitions.

TO be able to live at quiet, and enjoy the felicity of Heaven and Earth, notwithstanding all the attempts of our Enemies, makes them mad when they see they cannot fret us, and so by Consequence a greater Revenge is seated in Meekness than in Revenge it self. For our Repose is their punishment and torment that hate us. Their vexation falleth on their own head, when they see they miss of their aim, and cannot molest us: but it is a joy to see our selves seated in a throne of Repose, clean out of their reach; it breeds a kind of triumph and ovation in the Soul. The secret Conscience of its own Power is a glory and satisfaction unimaginable.

HE that masters his own Passion is master of another mans, and seldom falls into those Broils and Inconveniencies that are the destruction of ungoverned and hasty Spirits. Which make *Solomon* to say, *He that is slow to Anger is better than the Mighty, and he that ruleth his Spirit, than he that taketh a City.*

HE that troubleth his own house shall inherit the Wind; he that is nice and exquisite in exacting all Faults shall never be beloved. They are disobliging, angry, testy men that are hated; and the Revengful that do frequently fall into mischief. But to be kind to the Unthankful and the Evil, and to deal with all men better than they deserve, is the way to be beloved by the worst of men, and admired by the best.

MEEKNESS is the retreat of Goodness, and the only force in the rear of Liberality. He that does one Injury afer forty Kindnesses, blots out the memory of all his Courtesies; and he that revenges an Injury seems to do one. For he that did the Wrong, seems innocent to himself, because he felt it not; and seeming innocent takes the Revenge as an undeserved Injury, and is lost for ever. Now some Injuries we must expect from our best Friends, which are alwaies lost for want of Meekness. So are all the Benefits we do, unless we will forgive as well as give. But an Injury forgiven is forgotten by him that did it, and the Friendship continues at the expence, and to the honour and comfort of the Pardoner, as if no Offence had ever been committed: Nay if afterwards he comes to see the Candor of his abused Friend, he that did the Injury loves him better than before, because he pardoned the Wrong.

MEEKNESS as it preserves Friendship between *two*, makes Goodness invincible and unalterable in *one*. He shall not be good long whose Goodness dependeth on others Merits. He is a miserable weak man, that is of an Exceptious humor; he is a trouble to his own flesh, and subject to the power of every Wasp, whether he shall be good or no. He is quickly stopt in his *Careir* of Vertue, and easily turned out of the way, that is apt to be infected with anothers Malice. He carries no Antidotes about him, and for want of a Preservative, is in danger of the Contagion. Meekness is a means of the health of the Soul: a Passionate man being all over *sore*, is covered with hot and angry Boils, which cannot be touched.

IT preventeth much mischief in Families. An occasion of Anger is like a spark of Fire, it is of great Consequence where it falleth. If it falls into barrels of *Gunpowder*, it blows up the World; if into green Wood or watery places, it does no harm. Penitent Tears, and the verdure of Humility prevent such flames, and extinguish the quarrel. If *Wild-fire* be thrown, I will put it out with my foot, and not by throwing it back, give my Enemy the advantage of retorting it upon me. *A soft Answer pacifieth much Wrath*, but virulent Speeches are a fireball tossed to and fro, of them that love Death.

BY Revenge a man at best can but preserve himself, by killing his Enemy: but Meekness well managed, destroys the Enmity, preserves the Person, and turns the enemy into an excellent Friend.

MEEKNESS is not the way to Peace, and Repose, and Victory only, but to Honour and Glory. As it is the strength, *it is the glory of a man to pass over a Transgression*: He that is lightly angered is quickly lost, and a fickle Friend is not worth a farthing. A straw and a feather shall forfeit all the Obligations in the World, in some Tempers. Nay he that is Revengful, is a dangerous Person: and *with an Angry man thou shalt not go*: He has the Plague upon him and is prohibited Company. All this is dishonourable. But a man that is a resolved and stable Friend, that cannot be alter'd, that will not change, though he be wronged, but forgive, and pity, and continue to serve and love his Friend, though he shews him some dirty Tricks; he that will surmount all by invincible Kindness, he is a solid and weighty Friend, a rare Treasure, and exceeding precious. Neither my Errors nor Misfortunes are able to change him that loveth me purely because he will love me. When his

Excellency is found out, he will more highly be esteemed, not only by his Friend, but by all that see him, and note his Fidelity.

INJURIES well forgiven are the highest obligations in the World: especially if a man has been injured after many Benefits. A Friend that will so oblige, is more to be preferred than the Gold of *Ophir*.

MEEKNESS brings a man into respect with his Servants, and into power with his Neighbours. *Anger resteth in the bosoms of Fools*, but Meekness hath alwaies this advantage, it is attended with Wisdom, and other Vertues, as Goodness and Courage. A man that is prudent in Affairs, and zealous of Good Works, faithful in retaining Secrets, and so full in Love, that he is prone to do all manner of Good with industry, and is couragious to expose himself to any Hazard, for the benefit of his Neighbours, shall keep his Servants in awe, and yet be beloved of them: He shall be able to do among his Neighbours what he pleaseth: He shall when known well, become the Father of all their Families, they will entrust their Wives and Children in his hands, as I have often experienced; their Gold, their Bonds, their Souls, their Affairs, their Lives, their Secrets, Houses, Liberties, and Lands; and be glad of such a Friend in whom to be safe, and by whom to be assisted. But though you have all the Vertues in the World, the way to the use of them is blockt up without Meekness: for your Neighbours are few of them Wise, or Good; and if you will be provoked by Injuries, you will upon forty occasions so distaste them, that they will never trust you. You will look as like a Trifle, a Knave, or a Fool, as one of them; and be as very a Mad man. He that will not do good but to deserving Persons, shall find very few to do good to. For he shall not be acquainted with Good men, and from doing good to others he excludes himself. But if all his other Vertues are beautified by Meekness, such a man will be like an Angel, and live above all his Neighbours, as if he were in Heaven. So that Meekness is his real exaltation. And this made our Saviour to cull out that Blessing for the Meek, *The Meek shall inherit the Earth*. Even here upon Earth the Meek are they that are most blessed.

TO do good to an innocent Person is Humane, but to be kind and bountiful to a man, after he has been Injurious, is Divine. *Philanthus*, gave Laws and Countries to the *Parthenians*, and was disgraced and banished: But he did them good after the Injury, and was made their God, as *Justine* recordeth.

THE very nature of the Work encourageth us to its exercise, because it is GOD-like, and truly Blessed. But there are many other Considerations moving us unto it.

Mankind is sick, the World distemper'd lies,
*   Opprest with Sins and Miseries.*
Their Sins are Woes; a long corrupted Train
*   Of Poyson, drawn from Adam's vein,*
*   Stains all his Seed, and all his Kin*
*   Are one Disease of Life within.*
*   They all torment themselves!*
The World's one Bedlam, or a greater Cave
*   Of Mad-men, that do alwaies rave.*

The Wise and Good like kind Physicians are,
*   That strive to heal them by their Care.*
They Physick and their Learning calmly use,
*   Although the Patient them abuse.*
*   For since the Sickness is (they find)*
*   A sad distemper of the Mind;*
*   All railings they impute,*
All Injuries, unto the sore Disease,
*   They are expresly come to ease!*

If we would to the Worlds distemper'd Mind
*   Impute the Rage which there we find,*
We might, even in the midst of all our Foes,
*   Enjoy and feel a sweet Repose.*
*   Might pity all the Griefs we see,*
*   Anointing every Malady*
*   With precious Oyl and Balm;*
And while our selves are Calm, our Art mprove
*   To rescue them, and shew our Love.*

But let's not fondly our own selves beguile;
*   If we Revile 'cause they Revile,*
Our selves infected with their sore Disease,
*   Need others Helps to give us ease,*
*   For we more Mad then they remain,*
*   Need to be cut, and need a Chain*
*   Far more than they. Our Brain*
Is craz'd; and if we put our Wit to theirs,
*   We may be justly made their Heirs.*

But while with open eyes we clearly see
*   The brightness of his Majesty;*

While all the World, by Sin to Satan sold,
    In daily Wickedness grows old,
    Men in Chains of Darkness lye,
    In Bondage and Iniquity,
        And pierce and grieve themselves!
The dismal Woes wherein they crawl, enhance
    The Peace of our Inheritance.

We wonder to behold our selves so nigh
    To so much Sin and Misery,
And yet to see our selves so safe from harm!
    What Amulet, what hidden Charm
    Could fortifie and raise the Soul
    So far above them; and controul
        Such fierce Malignity!
The brightness and the glory which we see
    Is made a greater Mystery.

And while we feel how much our GOD doth love
    The Peace of Sinners, how much move,
And sue, and thirst, intreat, lament and grieve,
    For all the Crimes in which they live,
    And seek and wait, and call again,
    And long to save them from the pain
        Of Sin, from all their Woe!
With greater thirst, as well as grief we try,
    How to relieve their Misery.

The life and splendour of Felicity,
    Whose floods so overflowing be,
The streams of Joy which round about his Throne,
    Enrich and fill each Holy One,
    Are so abundant, that we can
    Spare all, even all to any Man!
        And have it all our selves!
Nay have the more! We long to make them see
    The sweetness of Felicity.

While we contemplate their Distresses, how,
    Blind Wretches, they in bondage bow,
And tear and wound themselves, and vex and groan,
    And chase and fret so near his Throne,

  And know not what they ail, but lye
   Tormented in their Misery
    (Like Mad-men that are blind)
  In works of darkness nigh such full Delight:
   That they might find and see the sight,

What would we give! that they might likewise see
   The Glory of his Majesty!
The joy and fulness of that high delight,
   Whose Blessedness is infinite!
  We would even cease to live, to gain
   Them from their misery and pain,
    And make them with us reign.
For they themselves would be our greatest Treasures
 When sav'd, our own most Heavenly Pleasures.

O holy JESUS who didst for us die,
   And on the Altar bleeding lie,
Bearing all Torment, pain, reproach and shame,
   That we by vertue of the same,
   Though enemies to GOD, might be
    Redeem'd, and set at liberty.
    As thou didst us forgive,
So meekly let us Love to others shew,
  And live in Heaven on Earth below!

Let's prize their Souls, and let them be our Gems,
   Our Temples and our Diadems,
Our Brides, our Friends, our fellow-Members, Eyes
   Hands, Hearts and Souls, our Victories,
   And Spoils and Trophies, our own Joyes!
   Compar'd to Souls all else are Toyes!
    O JESUS let them be
Such unto us, as they are unto thee
  Vessels of Glory and Felicitie!

How will they love us, when they find our Care
   Brought them all thither where they are!
When they conceive, what terrour 'tis to dwell
   In all the punishments of Hell:
   And in a lively manner see,
   O Christ, eternal Joyes in thee!

> *How will they all delight*
> *In praising thee for us, with all their might,*
> *How sweet a Grace, how infinite!*

WHEN we understand the perfection of the Love of GOD, the excellency of immortal Souls, the price and value of our Saviours Blood, the misery of Sin, and the malady of distemper'd Nature, the danger of Hell, and the Joyes of which our sorest Enemies are capable, the Obligations that lie on our selves, and the peace and blessedness of so sweet a Duty, Compassion it self will melt us into Meekness, and the wisdom of knowing these great things will make it as natural to us as Enjoyment it self, as sweet and easie, as it is to live and breath. It will seem the harshest and most unnatural thing in the World to forbear so fair, so just, so reasonable, so divine a Duty.

NOR is it a small comfort, that the more vile our Enemies are, the more price and lustre is set upon our Actions. Our Goodness is made by their Evil, the more eminent and conspicuous: we improve their Injuries and turn them into Benefits, we make a Vertue of Necessity, and turn their Vices into Graces, make them appear more abominable and vile if they continue obstinate; and the greater their Perversness is, the more great and honourable is our Vertue. It was the praise of *Moses*, that *the Man Moses was the Meekest man upon all the Earth*, yet one passionate expression lost him so much in the esteem of GOD, that it hindered his entrance into the Land of *Canaan*. How great an Instrument he was nevertheless in the Conduct and Felicity of the *Jews*, and how much he profited the whole Nation by his Meekness Sacred story does record. How *Joseph* also dealt with his Brethren, how he saved all the Family of *Israel* in the Root by his Meekness, and by Meekness purchased an everlasting Name of Glory and Renown, all Christian Ages and Nations understand, where his Praises are celebrated to this day: And the benefit thereof is spread abroad, and propagated throughout all Generations for evermore.

CHAP. XXVI.

Humility is the basis of all Vertue and Felicity, in all Estates, and for ever to be exercised. As Pride does alienate the Soul from GOD, Humility unites it to him in Adoration and Amity. It maketh infinite Blessedness infinitely greater, is agreeable to the Truth of our Condition, and leads us through a dark and mysterious way to Glory.

MEEKNESS respecteth others faults; Humility and Penitence our own. But Humility is more large than Penitence, and is a distinct Affection of another nature. Penitence is an exercise of the Affection of Sorrow, and that only for Sin. Humility is an acknowledgment of all our Vileness; it respects our Original out of nothing as well as our Guilt, our Weakness and Unworthiness, our dependance upon anothers Will, our Debt and Obligation, the duty of Obedience and Allegiance which we owe, and all the naked Truth of our Condition. It confesseth our homage, and is sensible of our Smallness and Subjection. All that a man hath received it distinguisheth from what he is of himself: And its Fruits or Effects are suitable to its Nature. It is the Vertue by which we think basely of our selves, and behave our selves in a lowly and submissive manner. It makes us soft and pliant as Wax, susceptible of any form that shall be imposed on us by our Benefactour, and prone to Gratitude. It is accompanied with a high and mighty sence of Benefits received, and made Noble by the honour which it inclines us to return to GOD and Man for all the goodness which they shew unto us. It is of incomparable use in our Felicity, because it magnifies our esteem of all our happiness and glory.

IT is not through Ignorance, or want of good Will, that we speak nothing of Vices, the woful deformity of which being exposed to view, near the excellence of Vertue, would put a greater lustre on all their brightness: but the abundance of matter which Vertue it self doth afford, forbids us to waste our Time and Paper in the description of their Contraries. The glory of their nature being so full and perfect in it self, that it needeth not the aid of those additional Arts, which labour to set off the dignity of imperfect things by borrowed Commendations. And besides this, the mischief and inconveniency of every Vice is so great and manifold, that it would require a distinct and intire Volume to unfold the deformity of their destructive nature, so fully as their baseness and demerit requires. It is sufficient therefore here to observe, that Pride is of all other things most odious to GOD; because it puffeth up the Soul with Self-conceit, is forgetful of its Original, void of all Gratitude, and prone to Rebellion. Is it not an odious and abominable thing, for a Creature that is nothing in himself to flie in his Creators face, and to usurp a dominion over it self to the apparent wrong of its Soveraign Lord, to rob its Benefactor of all the glory of his Bounty, to renounce and deny all dependance on him, and to forswear its homage and allegiance, to ascribe all its Glories to it self, and abhor all sence of honour and gratitude, to look upon it self as the sole original and author of all its Greatness, and to be dazled so with the brightness of its condition, as to forget the true fountain of it, the goodness and the love of him that first raised him to all that Treasure and Dominion: to dote on its own Perfections without any reflexion on the Bounty of him that gave them! All this is to act a *Lie*, and to be guilty of apparent Falshood: It is as full of *Fraud* and *Injustice* as is possible: and as full of *Folly* as it is of *Impiety*. For Pride aimeth at the utmost height of Esteem and Honour; and is fed by its own beauty and glory: yet foolishly undermineth and blasteth the Person it would advance with the greatest baseness and shame imaginable, it devours the Beauty which ought to feed it, and destroies the Glory in which it delighteth. The higher, the greater, the more perfectly glorious and blessed the Person is that is exalted, his Ingratitude (which is the dregs of Baseness) is the more black and horrid, and provokes the greater detestation. It forfeits and renounces all the Delight which the goodness of its Lord and Benefactor affordeth, it cuts off the Soul like a branch from the root that gave it life and verdure, it tends all to division, alienation and enmity, it turns that Complacency, which is its only bliss, into wrath and indignation: And whereas it delights in nothing more than appearing highly amiable in the eyes of all Spectators, it falleth into contempt and extream disgrace before all the Creatures in Heaven and Earth, that look upon it, and behold its Unworthiness. No Toad has so much deformity, or poyson, or malignity as Pride, in its nature. It is the ruine of all that is great, and turns the brightest of the Seraphims into the most abominable of Devils.

NOW if Pride be so pernicious, and be by nature (though a meer Phantasie) so destructive: what shall Humility be which is full of truth and reality! How forcible, how divine, how amiable, how full of truth, how bright and glorious, how solid and real, how agreeable to all Objects, how void of errour and disparity, how just and reasonable, how wise and holy, how deep, how righteous, how good and profitable, how mightily prone to exalt us in the esteem of GOD and Man! How agreeable to all its Causes and Ends, how fit and suitable to all the circumstances of Mans Condition! I need not say more: It bears its own evidence, and carries Causes in it that will justifie our Saviours words, *He that humbeleth himself shall be exalted.* He that is puffed up has but a counterfeit glory, but Humility is full of solid glory. Its beauty is so amiable that there is no end of counting its proportions and excellencies. The Wise man that saw into the nature of all things very clearly, said long before our Saviour was born, *Pride goeth before a fall, but before Honour is Humility.* He that exalteth himself must needs be humbled, because the Colours are envenomed wherewith he painteth his face, which in a little time is discerned, and at the very first instant the Painting begins to turn into a Canker.

THE *Amiableness* of Humility appeareth by its *Excellency*; on these two the greatness of its beauty and success is founded. It is so agreeable to all the principles of Nature, and Grace, and Glory, to all the desires of Angels and Men, to all the designs of GOD himself, and to all the interests and concerns of the Soul, that it cannot but be the most advantagious Vertue in the whole World. It is strange that a man should look with the same Eye upon two Objects so infinitely distant and different from each other. But at the same time he seeth GOD and Nothing, Heaven and Earth, eternal Love and Dust to be his Original. Self-love and Justice, Wisdom and Goodness, Joy and Gratitude have the same Objects, but look upon them in a several manner: and are very differently affected with them. Humility regards all Objects high and low, Good and Evil: but with a peculiar remark and notice of its own. It takes them in another light, and discerns them all with another kind of sence. It is in some manner the taste of the Soul. Their Truth appeareth to the eye of Knowledge, their Goodness is apprehended by the life of Love, the perfection of their serviceableness to the most perfect End is discerned by Wisdom, the benefit which all Spectators receive is the delight of Goodness, the incomprehensible depth and mysterious intricacy of their frame and nature is the peculiar Object of our Wonder and Curiosity: they help our Faith as they shew a Deity, and the truth of all Religion and Blessedness. As they are the gifts of GOD they are the provocations of Gratitude, and as they are aggravations of Sin they are respected by Repentance. As they are the means of our Glory, and our proper Treasures, they are the Objects of Contentment; but

Humility looks upon them in relation to its Unworthiness, compares them with it self and its own deserts, and admires the disproportion that is between them. It useth them all as grounds of a deeper and profounder Lowness in the esteem which it ought to have of it self, and as the incentives to Love and Gratitude; which it paies in the depth of a more profound Acknowledgment and Adoration.

THIS habit or affection of the Soul is not inconsistent with its Joy and Glory (as by some foolish people, that are by Ignorance and Errors far from GOD, is generally supposed) but highly conducive and subservient to its perfection. It gives us the tenderest and greatest sence; it passeth *thorow* all things, embraceth the *Poles*, and toucheth all *Extreams* together. The *Centre* it self is but the middle of its profundity: it hath a *Nadir* beneath it, a lower point in another Heaven, on the other side opposite to its Zenith. In its own depth it containeth all the height of Felicity and Glory, and doubles all by a mystery in Nature. It is like a Mirror lying on the ground with its face upwards: All the height above increaseth the depth of its Beauty within, nay turneth into a new depth, an inferiour Heaven is in the glass it self; at the bottom of which we see the Skie, though it be not transplanted, removed thither. Humility is the fittest Glass of the Divine Greatness, and the fittest Womb for the conception of all Felicity; for it hath a double Heaven. It is the way to full and perfect Sublimity. A man would little think, that by sinking into the Earth he should come to Heaven. He doth not, but is buried, that fixeth and abideth there. But if he pierceth through all the Rocks and Minerals of the inferiour World, and passeth on to the end of his Journey in a strait line downward, in the middle of his way he will find the Centre of Nature, and by going downward still begin to ascend, when he is past the Centre; through many Obstacles full of gross and subterraneous Darkness, which seem to affright and stifle the Soul, he will arrive at last to a new Light and Glory, room and liberty, breathing-place and fresh-air among the *Antipodes*, and by passing on still through those inferiour Regions that are under his feet, but over the head of those that are beneath him, finally come to another Skie, penetrate that, and leaving it behind him sink down into the depth of all Immensity. This he cannot do in his Body, because it is gross and dull, and heavy and confined: but by a Thought in his Soul he may, because it is subtile, quick, aiery, free, and infinite; Nothing can stop or exclude it, oppress or stifle it. This local descent through all the inferiour Space and Immensity, though it brings us to GOD, and his Throne, and another Heaven full of Joyes and Angels, on the other side the World; yet is it but a real Emblem of the more spiritual and mysterious flight of Humility in the mind. We all know that the way to Heaven is through Death and the Grave, beyond which we come to another Life, in Eternity: but how to accommodate this to the business of Humility, few understand. By this Vertue we are inclined to despise our selves, and to leave all the garish Ornaments of Earthly bliss, to divest our selves of the splendors of Temporal prosperity, and to submit to all Afflictions, Contempts and Miseries, that a good Cause can bring upon us. In the eyes of other men we are beneath their feet, and so we are in our own, till we are gone a little further: but on the other side of all this Baseness, we find a better Life in Communion with the Deity. *Forasmuch then*, saith St. *Peter, as Christ hath suffered for us in the flesh, arm your selves likewise with the same mind: for he that hath suffered in the flesh hath ceased from sin: That he no longer should live the rest of his time in the flesh, to the lusts of Men, but to the will of GOD. For the time past of our life may suffice us to have wrought the will of the Gentiles, when we walked in Lasciviousness, Lusts, Excess of Wine, Revellings, Banquettings, and abominable Idolatries; wherein they think it strange that ye run not with them to the same excess of Riot.*[1] There is a motion from Vice to Vertue, and from one degree of Grace to another: by which we leave the phantastick World, with all its Shews and Gauderies; and through many Afflictions and Persecutions, come to the real and solid World of Bliss and Glory.

WHAT hand Humility has in leading us through all Afflictions, and in facilitating the way of Pressure and Calamity, I need not observe; I shall note the Errour which men incur, by their Weariness and Haste; who because they do not immediately see the Bliss of Humility and Patience, if they do not curse, yet they boggle at all Calamity. These men ought to be informed, that the middle of the Way is not the place of Rest and Perfection. They must pass thorow all these things to the further Regions of Clarity and Glory. Men are not to stick in Calamities themselves: but if Humility lead them to suffer all Indignities with Patience, it must lead them further to the bottom of their estate and condition; to the true light, and to the clear and perfect sight of their own Vileness: In which they shall see their Original, their Misery, their Sin, their Glory; their GOD and themselves, their Bliss and their Forfeiture, their Recovery and their Saviour, their Hope and Despair, their Obligations in the height of eternal Love and Bounty,

---

[1] Marginal gloss: 1 Pet. 4. 1, 2, 3, 4.

and their shame and confusion in the depth of their Apostasie and Ingratitude; their infinite demerit, and GODS infinite Mercy; the riches of free Grace, and their own Unworthiness: And in all these, *the length, and breadth, and depth, and height of the Love of GOD which passeth Knowledge, that they might be filled with all the Fulness of GOD.*

HUMILITY makes men capable of all Felicity. All deep Apprehensions and great Resentments, all extents and distances of things, all degrees of Grace and Vertue, all Circumstances that increase the guilt of Sin, all Adorations, Prostrations, Admirations, Debasements, Thanksgivings, Praises, Exaltations, are founded in Humility. All the Fulness of all Estates, all Honour and Obedience, all Devotion and Worship, all the beauty of Innocence, all the deformity of Sin, all the danger of Hell, all the cost of our Redemption, all the hatred of our Stupidity and Perverseness, all the hope of Heaven, all our Penitence and Grief, all our Fear and Expectation, all our Love and all our Joy are contained in Humility: there they are expressed, there they are exercised: There they are enlarged, and beautified in like manner: There they grow deep, and serious, and Infinite: there they become vigorous and strong; there they are made substantial and eternal. All the Powers of the Soul are employed, extended and made perfect in this depth of Abysses. It is the basis and foundation of all Vertue and Gratitude whatsoever. It is in some sort the very fountain of Life and Felicity it self. For as nothing is great but in comparison of somewhat less; so nothing is sweet but what is New and Eternal. All Life consists in Motion and Change. The pleasure of Acquiring is oftentimes as great, and perhaps alwaies greater than that of Enjoying. The long possession of that which we have alwaies had, takes away the sence, and maketh us dull: Old and Common things are less esteemed, unless we rub up our Memories with some helps, to renew them and our sences together. Gifts are alwaies sweeter in the coming, than in the abiding with us. And if what I observe in the course of nature be of any force, there is no possibility of enjoyment, at least no perfection in fruition, without some relation to the first Acquisition. Old things are apt to grow stale, and their value to be neglected, by their continuance with us. I have noted it often in the joy that young Heirs have, when they first come to their Estates, and the great felicity which Lovers promise to themselves, and taste also when they meet together in the Marriage–bed. The pleasures of all which pass off by degrees, not solely by reason of our dulness and stupidity, but far more from a secret in the nature of things. For all Delight springs from the satisfaction of violent Desire: when the desire is forgotten, the delight is abated. All Pleasure consists in Activity and Motion: While the Object stands still, it seemeth dead and idle. The sence of our want must be quick upon us to make the sence of our enjoyment perfect. The rapture proceeds from the convenience between us, the marvellous fitness that is in such Objects to satisfie our Capacities and Inclinations. The misery and vacuity must needs be remembred to make that Convenience *live*, and to inspire a sence of it perpetually into us. The coming of a Crown, and the joy of a Kingdom is far more quick and powerful in the *surprize* and novelty of the Glory, than in the length of its Continuance. We perceive it by the delight which Lovers taste in recounting their Adventures. The Nature of the thing makes the *memory* of their first Amours more pleasant, than the *possession* of the last. There is an instinct that carries us to the beginning of our Lives. How do Old men even dote into lavish discourses of the beginning of their lives? The delight in telling their old Stories is as great to themselves as wearisom to others. Even Kings themselves, would they give themselves the liberty of looking back, might enjoy their Dominions with double lustre, and see and feel their former Resentments, and enrich their present Security with them. All a mans Life put together contributes a perfection to every part of it, and the Memory of things past is the most advantagious light of our present Condition. Now all these sparkles of Joy, these accidental hints of Nature, and little raies of Wisdom, meet together in Humility. For an Humble man condescendeth to look into his Wants, to reflect upon all his Vices, and all his Beginnings, with far deeper designs than is ordinarily done.

WE recount these ordinary discoveries of the inclination of Nature, because Humility is (if I may so speak) the Rendezvous of their perfection. All the stirrings of Grace and Nature, all the acts of GOD and the Soul, all his Condescensions, and beginnings to advance us, all his Gifts at their first coming, all the depths and changes of our Condition, all our Desires, all our primitive and virgin Joyes, the whole story of our Creation, and Life, and Fall, and Redemption, in all the newness of its first appearance, all our Wants and Dangers, Exigencies and Extremities, all our Satisfactions and Delights are present together in our Humility; and are so infinitely near and present thereunto, so sweet and vigorous in their mixture, so strangely powerful in their influence, that they inspire our Hearts, enter our Thoughts, and incorporate with our Souls, and are as near and sweet, as our present condition, be it never so blessed: All put together is far more sweet than our present Condition, a great part of our felicity and glory is in it, while we take it in by our Conceptions here, and apply it to our Souls, in an humble manner; but it will be much more our felicity in Heaven. It is of so much concernment, that a Great Divine[1] in our *English* Zion said, *The greater part of our eternal happiness will consist in a grateful Recognition* (not of our Joyes to come, but) *of Benefits already received.*

NOW look into the office and work of Humility. I will not tell you how here upon Earth it shunneth all strife and contention about Places; and all the Mischiefs consequent thereto; nor of the Unity, and Peace, and Honour it produceth. These are all but Temporal Benefits. It has ten thousand other Walks and Circuits, and periods of Revolution. I will tell you how it behaves it self in Paradice and in Heaven.

HUMILITY by leading us to the bottom of our Condition, sets our Original before our eyes, considers that eternal abyss of Idleness and Vacuity out of which we were taken, that miracle by which we were made of Nothing. How destitute we should have been in our selves had not GOD created the World, had he not been pleased to communicate himself and his Glory to us. How weak and unable we were to devise or desire any Felicity, yet how infinitely necessary the preparation of it after we were created. How great our desires and expectations were, how sore and urgent our wants and necessities: how much we needed infinite Wisdom, and almighty Power to fill Immensity with the omnipresence of their Glory, and to fill their omnipresence with Effects and Treasures: How gracious and good GOD was to do all this for us, without our asking: and how justly *Davids* rapture may be taken up by the Soul, *The King shall joy in thy strength, O Lord, and in thy Salvation how greatly shall he rejoyce! Thou preventest him with the blessings of Goodness, thou settest a Crown of pure Gold on his head! His glory is great in thy Salvation, Honour and Majesty hast thou laid upon him. For thou hast made him most Blessed for ever; thou hast made him exceeding glad with thy Countenance!*[2] We might have been made, and put, in the condition of Toads; who are now created in the Image of GOD, have dominion over all his Works, and are made capable of all Eternity. The infinite condescention of GOD is the amazement of the Soul: The depth of its low estate increaseth the height of its exaltation. All that it wanted in it self it findeth in the goodness of its Benefactour, and the joy of being so Beloved, is greater than that of having all these things of our selves for ever. For the Love of GOD

---

[1] Marginal gloss: Dr. Hammond.
[2] Marginal gloss: Psal. 21.

alone, and his goodness in Giving, is our last, and best, and proper Felicity. Hereupon follows the extinction of all Envy, Regret, and Discontentment; the sacrificing of our selves, the annihilating of our selves, the lowliness of our selves; And the Exaltation of GOD, and the Adoration of GOD, and the Joy of adoring the Greatest of all other, The Amity and Friendship between GOD and his Creature, the Unity of both, and their happiness for ever. Without this Humility of looking into the *bottom* of our first Condition, all this is impossible: And for this cause is Humility an eternal Vertue, in all estates for ever to be enjoyed; (I might have said) exercised.

THUS in the estate of Sin and Misery, all the odiousness of our Guilt, all our despair and deformity, all our shame and misery, all the necessity of Hating GOD and being hated of him, comes before the eyes of an humble Soul, with all the mercies and condescentions of eternal Love in the work of Redemption.

AND in the state of Glory it self all the particular Sins, Neglects, Rebellions, Apostasies, and Villanies we committed against GOD after all his mercy and goodness in the Death of his Son; how infinitely base we were in despising all his Bounties and Glories; how infinitely those Offences made us unworthy of Heaven, and the eternal Glory we now enjoy; how marvellous and incomparable his Love was, in pursuing us with so much Long–suffering and Patience; how amiable he is, and how vile and unworthy we are in all this, it is the office of Humility to feel and ponder. Thus you see its work, and you may easily conjecture at its eternal Reward. All things are in it, in the utmost height and depth of Resignation and Contentment, enjoyed.

I need not observe that sweetness of Conversation, that Civility, and Courtesie, that springs from Humility. The Meek and Lowly are the same men: the Kind, and the Charitable, and the Affable and the good are all of them Humble, and so are all they that prefer others above themselves, and render themselves amiable by honouring their In Inferiours, and giving place to their Equals. At least they imitate Humility as Complemental Courtiers do, for their advantage. And it is no small token of its excellency, that the greatest enemies of Humility and Vertue, are forced sometimes to flie to it for succour: as those that well know they can never thrive, nor prosper in the World without Esteem, nor gain Esteem without covering their Vices under the mask of Vertue. All the advantages and effects of this will be enjoyed eternally.

CAP. XXVII.

That Contentment is a Vertue. Its Causes and its Ends: Its Impediments, Effects and Advantages. The way to attain and secure Contentment.

THOUGH we have not named it, in our first distribution of Vertue into its several kinds, yet the commendation which Contentment hath in Scripture, imports it to be a Vertue: so does the difficulty of attaining it, and the great and mighty force it is of in our Lives and Conversations. *Having Food and Rayment*, saith the Apostle, *let us therewith be content: For Godliness with Contentment is great Gain.* Where he fitly noteth, that Godliness is the original of true Contentment, and that the Gain of so great a Vertue is inestimable. The truth is, it is impossible to be happy, or grateful without it. A discontented Mind is exceeding prone to be peevish and fretful, and throws a man into all the indecencies of Avarice, Ambition, Envy, Treason, Murther, Contention, Turbulency, Murmuring, Repining, Melancholy and Sowrness, Anger, Baseness and Folly, into all the Malevolence and Misery which can disorder the Soul, or disturb the World. Suspicion, Unbelief, Enmity against GOD, Fear and Cowardice, Barrenness in good and praise-worthy Employments, Weariness and Complaint, hatred of Retirement, Spiritual Idleness and Ignorance are its Companions, followed by Debaucheries, and all the sorts of vile and wicked Diversions. For Man is an unwelcome Creature to himself till he can delight in his Condition, and while he hates to be alone, exposeth himself to all kind of Mischiefs and Temptations, because he is an active Creature, and must be doing something, either Good, or Evil.

TRUE Contentment is the full satisfaction of a Knowing Mind. It is not a vain and empty Contentment, which is falsely so called, springing from some one particular little satisfaction, that however Momentany it be, does for the present delight our Humour: but a long habit of solid Repose, after much study and serious Consideration. It is not the slavish and forced Contentment, which the Philosophers among the *Heathen* did force upon themselves; but a free and easie Mind attended with pleasure, and naturally rising from ones present Condition. It is not a morose and sullen Contempt of all that is Good. That Negative Contentment, which past of Old for so great a Vertue, is not at all conducive to Felicity, but is a real Vice: for to be Content without cause, is to sit down in our

Imperfection: and to seek all ones Blis in ones self alone, is to scorn all other Objects, even GOD himself and all the Creation. It is a high piece of Pride and stiffness in a man, that renders him good for nothing, but makes him Arrogant and Presumptuous in the midst of his blindness, his own slave and his own Idol, a Tyrant over himself, and yet his only Deity. It makes a man to live without GOD in the World, and cuts him off from the Universe. It makes him incapable either of Obligation or Gratitude, his own Prison and his own Tormentour. It shuts up the Soul in a Grave, and makes it to lead a living Death, and robs it of all its Objects. It mingles Nature and Vice in a confusion, and makes a man fight against Appetite and Reason. Certainly that Philosopher has a hard task, that must fight against Reason, and trample under foot the essence of his Soul, to establish his Felicity!

> Contentment is a sleepy thing!
> If it in Death alone must die;
> A quiet Mind is worse than Poverty!
> Unless it from Enjoyment Spring!
> That's Blessedness alone that makes a King!
> Wherein the Joyes and Treasures are so great,
> They all the powers of the Soul employ,
> And fill it with a Work compleat,
> While it doth all enjoy.
> True Joyes alone Contentment do inspire,
> Enrich Content, and make our Courage higher.
> Content alone's a dead and silent Stone:
> The real life of Bliss
> Is Glory reigning in a Throne,
> Where all Enjoyment is.
> The Soul of Man is so inclin'd to see,
> Without his Treasures no mans Soul can be,
> Nor rest content Uncrown'd!
> Desire and Love
> Must in the height of all their Rapture move,
> Where there is true Felicity.
> Employment is the very life and ground
> Of Life it self: whose pleasant Motion is
> The form of Bliss:
> All Blessedness a life with Glory Crown'd.
> Life! Life is all: in its most full extent
> Stretcht out to all things, and with all Content!

The only reason why a Wise and Holy man is satisfied with Food and Rayment, is because he sees himself made possessour of all Felicity, the image of the Deity, the great Object of his eternal Love, and in another way far more Divine and perfect, the Heir of the World, and of all Eternity. He knows very well, that if his honour be so great, as to live in Communion with GOD in the fruition of all his Joyes, he may very well spare the foul and feeble Delights of men: And though the Law be not so severe, as to command him to be Content without Food and Rayment: yet if for GOD's sake he should by the wickedness of Men be bereaved of both, he may well be Patient, nay and die with glory. And this indeed is that which maketh Contentment so great a Vertue. It hath a powerful influence upon us in all Estates; to take off our Perplexity, Sollicitude and Care, and to adorn our lives with Liberty and Chearfulness, by which we become acceptable and admirable to the Sons of Men. It makes us prone to be Kind and Liberal, whereby we become Obliging and full of good Works. For it delivers us from all servile Fear, and gives us Courage and Confidence in GOD. For well may we dare to trust him in such little Matters, who has manifested his Friendship and Bounty in such infinite good things, and made it impossible for us to be Miserable, if we are pleasing to him. An intelligent and full Contentment elevates the Soul above all the World, and makes it Angelical: it instills a Divine and Heavenly Nature, enflames the Soul with the love of GOD, and moves it to delight in Devotion and Prayer. The sweetness of his Thoughts, and the beauty of his Object draws a Lover often into Solitudes. And a Royal Man in a strange Country (especially when he has heard tidings of his Fathers Death, and the devolving of his Crown and Throne on himself) desires to be alone, that he may digest these Affairs in his Thoughts a little: He delights in being retired, because he can find nothing worthy of himself in Company. Magnanimous Souls are above Garlands and Shepherds: And there is no greatness of Soul like that which perfect Contentment inspires.

BUT that which above all other things makes me to note the Vertue of Contentment, is its great influence, efficacy, and power in confirming our Faith. For when I see the *Beauty* of Religion I know it to be *true*. For such is its excellency, that if you remove it out of the World, all the things in Heaven and Earth will be to no purpose. The business of Religion is the Love of GOD, the Love of Angels and Men, and the due esteem we owe to inferiour Creatures. Remove this Love, this Charity, this Due Esteem, this delight that we should take in all amiable Objects; Life and Pleasure are extinguished. I see Nature it self teaching me Religion: And by the admirable Contexture of the Powers of my Soul, and their fitness for all Objects and Ends, by the incomparable Excellency of the Laws prescribed, and the worthiness and Beauty of all the Objects for which my powers are prepared, see plainly, that I am infinitely Beloved: and that all the cross and disorderly things, that are now upon Earth, are meer Corruptions and depravations of Nature, which free Agents have let in upon themselves. All which since they are reducible to the Government of Reason, and may by Wisdom be improved to my higher happiness, I am sure I am redeemed, and that there is some eternal Power that governs the World with so much Goodness for my felicity, since I my self was not able to do it. That all Ages are beautified by his Wisdom for my enjoyment I hope in like manner: nay I see it plainly. And of all these Joyes the Cross of Christ is the Root and Centre.

I confess it is difficult to gain this high and divine Contentment, because its measure and value is infinite: Nay there are other causes both Temporal and Eternal that may seem to be impediments. One was a business which David did experience, *The prosperity of the Wicked.* They live in so much Splendour, Pomp, and Grandeur, have so much Respect and Reverence paid unto them, and reign as it were in the high Esteem of all that are round about them in such a manner, that a Poor good man is hardly lookt upon among them. His condition seemeth Servile, and he is little regarded. *David* carried the Temptation far higher, yet triumphed over it, *Psal.* 73.1, &c. *Truly GOD is good to Israel, even to such as are of a clean heart. But as for me my feet were almost gone, my steps had well nigh slipt. For I was envious at the foolish, when I saw the prosperity of the Wicked. For all the day long have I been plagued, and chastened every morning.* Whether it be through Nature, or its Corruption, I cannot tell (at least I will not stand to dispute it) but it is somewhat grievous, to see men of the same mould with our selves so highly magnified, and our selves slighted, and unable to appear with Equality among them: because the true Greatness of our Souls is hidden, oppressed, and buried as it were in the Meanness of our Condition. But yet we have excellent Company, *David* and the Prophets, *Christ* and his Apostles, and all the Martyrs, that are now so glorious. And if you please you may consider, what these Great men do when the *shew* is over: We when we come *abroad* are weak and despised, and they when they are *alone*. A Vertuous man is Great within, and glorious in his Retirements, is honoured also among men in Truth and *Reality*; the rest make an outward shew, and are honoured in *Ceremony*. We are accepted in the eyes of GOD and his holy Angels, and they are condemned: Their Life is a Dream, and ours is Eternal: We expatiate over all the World with infinite Joy and Pleasure in our Solitude, and they are nothing when they return to themselves. That wherein the greatest difficulty of all doth consist, is the boundless desire and ambition of the Soul, whereby we are tempted to envy any thing that is above us, and for ever to be displeased unless our glory and blessedness be Eternal; I do not mean Immortal only, but of everlasting Extent, and infinite Beauty. We soar to the Best and highest of all that is possible: And unless in all Ages and Kingdoms our Satisfaction be compleat, and our Pleasure exquisite; we are prone to be tormented with the perfection of our Desires. But GOD having given himself, and all his Kingdom and Glory to us, there is no room for Complaint. All his Power being glorified by his Wisdom and Goodness for our advancement, we need nothing but a clear sight of the face of Truth, and a lively sence of our Condition, to ravish and transport us into Extasies, and Praises.

THE happiness of a Contented Spirit consists not alone in the fruitions of its Bliss, but in the fruits and effects it produceth in our Lives. It gives us many advantages over Sin, Temptation, Fear, Affliction, Poverty, Sickness, Death, and all other Casualties to which we are obnoxious, by reason of our frail and fickle condition. But all these I shall pass over, and only mention two, which are worth our care and desire; *Security* and *Power*.

AS there is a vain and empty Contentment, so there is a rash and foolish Security. For a man to wink at all Hazards to which he is exposed, and without any consideration of what may befal him, to give himself up to his ease and pleasure, is as great a madness, as it is for a *General* environed with Enemies to sleep without his *Guards*, or be totally negligent of his *Camp*, and his *Army*. But when he has Conquered all his Enemies, then to be filled with *Melancholy* fears, and *Pannick* terrours, is as great a weakness, as a man of Worth can be capable of. Even in the midst of them, when he has surveyed all their strengths, and made full provision for their incursions; he may take his rest with liberty: provided he be moderate and wary in his proceedings. This last is our Condition. We must not live as if there were no Sickness and Death in the World. We must remember there are Calamities of every kind, and fortifie our selves with Principles and Resolutions against them all, *put on the whole Armour of GOD*, which is called sometimes *the Armour of Light*, and stand prepared for all Assaults whatsoever. When we have so done, as it is a terrible thing to be surprized, so it is a glorious thing with open eyes to see and know all the Evil that is in Death, Imprisonment, Persecution, Shame and Poverty, Famine, Banishment, Pain and Torment; and yet to be secure in the midst of our fruitions. There is a worthless, and there is a divine Security: It is a poor business for a man to be secure, that has nothing to lose. A Beggar sings upon the Road without any fear of Thieves. But to be full of Gold and Jewels, yet safe from danger; to be secure in a Palace of Delights; in the midst of a Kingdom, and in the possession of all its glory to rest with safety, this is a valuable and sweet Security, a safety enriched with solid Enjoyments, much more is it here upon Earth to have the bliss and security of Angels. Among Wolves, and Tygers, and Bears and Dragons; among Thieves and Murtherers, Bloody Men and Devils; among Dead-mens Bones, and Graves and Sepulchres, when showers of Arrows fall round about us, and Hell is beneath us; this is something more than to be secure where no danger is near, no Calamity possible. It is a kind of triumph in Security, and hath a peculiar glory in it which the very security of Heaven is incapable of. And yet poor frail Man obnoxious and liable to all these destructions is safe among them all, when he is once gotten into the heart of GOD's Kingdom, and surrounded with Felicity. Its very Beauties are its Strengths. He knows himself beloved of the eternal GOD, and that the King of Terrors is but a disguised Bug–Bear, a dark and doleful passage to the Ignorant, but to him a bright and transparent way to the King of Glory. This Blessedness is of a stable, incorruptible nature, which nothing can destroy. It digesteth all kind of Evils, and turneth them into nourishment. There is a Wisdom above us, and a Wisdom within us, that maketh *all things work together for good to them that love GOD*, and nothing is able to hurt us but our selves.

    Now for Power which Felicity giveth: There is an intrinsick power in the enjoyment it self, for which Felicity is to be admired: in comparison of which all other Powers are but poor and feeble. To speak with the tongue of Men and Angels, to move Mountains, or turn them into Gold, to raise the Dead, to command the Sun, are common things: The power of creating Worlds is but vain, without the power of enjoying them. All Honour, Pleasure and Glory are shut up in Felicity. Had we a power of Creating and enjoying all Worlds, it were infinitely short of the power of enjoying GOD, because he is infinitely greater and higher than all. The Creating Power is superfluous to us, because all is most exquisite and perfect already. The fools Wishing Cap, and the Philosophers Stone are but trifles: All things (that are not gold) are better than gold. Felicity giveth us the power of enjoying all, even GOD himself, all Angels and Men, and all Worlds, nay all their Riches, Splendors and Pomps in their places, which is the most amiable and desirable, the most sweet and profitable Power of all other.

BUT when we are Contented, there is another Power worth the having, which Felicity giveth us. It enables us to despise the Menaces and Angers of Men, it setteth us above their reach, and inspires us with a comely boldness to dare to do any thing that is good, as well as with ability to dare to suffer any thing that is evil. He that is secure, and he that hath enough, is independant, and *bold as a Lion*: And besides all this he has a certain lustre in his Actions, that gives him authority and power over others, to intercede and prevail in his requests, to live in honour and good esteem, and to make many subservient to his best occasions. He is great in Heaven, and whatever he asks of his eternal Father in his Sons Name, with Wisdom and Piety, shall not be denied him. He can touch the hearts of millions by his Fathers Mediation: *For the hearts of Kings are in the hands of the Lord, to turn them as the Rivers of water.* He made his people to be pitied of all them that carried them away Captive, and gave them favour in the sight of the *Egyptians*. And this secret alone is of more value then we can well describe.

To receive power from Heaven to be Vertuous, to delight in Vertue, to be irresistible and invincible in the practice of it, is a very divine and glorious Priviledge. Felicity it self is the fountain of this Power, and the knowledge of its greatness that which enflames us with the love of it. Felicity is excellent not only as it is the end of Vertue, but the encouragement of it. He that is Content has a great advantage above all other men, because he moves with greater ease, and passeth through all difficulties with greater pleasure. A general of an Army, that works with the Common Souldiers in the Trenches, does the same work, but with more honour and less labour. He is not servile in it as the rest are, but his pleasure is to do it for all their encouragement. He does it in the quality of a Prince, and with less molestation; he has higher Incentives, and more sublime Rewards. Yet he does it too with greater merit and acceptance. A man that sees and knows the glory of his high and heavenly Estate, does all things triumphantly. The sweetness of his Bliss alters the very nature of his Fights and Battles.

He does all things in the light, without groaning and reluctancy: He marches on with dancing and melody, and chearful looks, and smiles, and thanksgivings: whereas they that know not the glory of Felicity grop in the dark; they that are discontented move heavily, and are in all their proceedings lame and maimed.

THE way to attain the felicity of Contentment, is to attain Felicity that we may be contented. True Felicity is the source of Contentment, and of all Vertue. It is never to be gotten but by digging after Knowledge as for hidden Treasures. Praying for it is a good way, but Prayer without Industry is a meer mockery. Industry on the other side without Prayer is loose Presumption. For a man to pray to GOD to make his Field fruitful without ploughing and sowing is madness, and to expect all from his own labour, without GOD's Blessing, impiety. But GOD never yet said to any of the seed of *Jacob, Seek ye my face in vain.*

WHEN Contentment is gotten, it must be secured by the same means by which it was obtained. Care in fencing is as necessary as Care in ploughing, and there is Labour too but sweet and delightful even in reaping in the Harvest. But all the work is reduced into narrow room: Thou hast no charge over any other than thine own *Vineyard*. When thou has gotten the knowledge of Felicity and thy self, the grand means of Contentment is continually to enjoy it. With all thy getting get Wisdom, and with all thy keeping keep thy Heart; *For out of it are the Issues of Life and Death.* Nothing can waste thy Conscience but Sin, and nothing trouble thy Repose, but what disturbs thy Conscience. Let Vertue and Felicity be thy only good, and believe firmly that nothing can hurt thee but SIN alone. One evil action done by thy self, is more mischievous to thee, then all the Calamities and Sufferings in the World.

CAP. XXVIII.

Of Magnanimity, or Greatness of Soul. Its Nature. Its Foundation in the vast Capacity of the Understanding. Its Desire. Its Objects are infinite and eternal. Its Enquiries are most profound and earnest. It disdaineth all feeble Honours, Pleasures and Treasures. A Magnanimous Man is the only Great and undaunted Creature.

MAGNANIMITY and Contentment are very near allyed, like Brothers and Sisters they spring from the same Parents, but are of several Features. Fortitude and Patience are Kindred too to this incomparable Vertue. Moralists distinguish Magnanimity and Modesty, by making the one the desire of greater, the other of less and inferiour Honours. But in my apprehension there is more in Magnanimity. It includes all that belongs to *a Great Soul*: A high and mighty Courage, an invincible Patience, an immoveable Grandeur which is above the reach of Injuries, a contempt of all little and feeble Enjoyments, and a certain kind of Majesty that is conversant only with Great things; a high and lofty frame of Spirit, allayed with the sweetness of Courtesie and Respect; a deep and stable Resolution founded on Humility without any baseness; an infinite Hope; and a vast Desire; a Divine, profound, uncontrolable sence of ones own Capacity, a generous Confidence, and a great inclination to Heroical deeds; all these conspire to compleat it, with a severe and mighty expectation of Bliss incomprehensible. It soars up to Heaven, and looks down upon all the dominion of Fortune with pity and disdain. Its aims and designs are transcendent to all the Concerns of this little World. Its Objects and its Ends are worthy of a Soul that is like GOD in Nature; and nothing less than the Kingdom of GOD, his Life and Image; nothing beneath the Friendship and Communion with him, can be its satisfaction. The Terrours, Allurements and Censures of men are the dust of its feet: their Avarice and Ambition are but feebleness before it. Their Riches and Contentions, and Interests and Honours, but insignificant and empty trifles. All the World is but a little Bubble, Infinity and Eternity the only great and soveraign things wherewith it converseth. A Magnanimous Soul is alwaies awake. The whole globe of the Earth is but a Nutshell in comparison of its enjoyments. The Sun is its Lamp, the Sea its Fishpond, the Stars its Jewels, Men, Angels its Attendance, and GOD alone its soveraign Delight and supream Complacency. The Earth is its Garden, all Palaces its Summer houses, Cities are its Cottages, Empires its more spacious Courts, all Ages and Kingdoms its Demeans, Monarchs its Ministers and publick Agents, the whole Catholick Church its Family, the eternal Son of GOD its Pattern and Example. Nothing is great if compared to a *Magnanimous Soul*, but the Sovereign Lord of all Worlds.

Mistake not these things for arbitrary flourishes of Luxuriant fancy: I speak as I am inspired by Felicity. GOD is the Cause, but the knowledge of a Mans self the Foundation of Magnanimity. *Trismegistus* counteth thus, *First GOD, secondly the World, thirdly Man: the World for Man, and Man for GOD. Of the Soul that which is sensible is Mortal, but that which is reasonable Immortal. The Father of all things being full of Light and Life, brought forth Man like unto himself, whom he loved as his proper Off-spring: for he was all Beauteous having the Image of his Father.* This in his *Poemander*. Again he saith, *Man is a divine and living thing, not to be compared to any Beast that lives upon the Earth, but to them that are above (in the highest Heavens) that are called Gods. Nay rather if we shall be bold to speak the truth, he that is a MAN INDEED is above them!* He is infinitely greater than the gods of the Heathen: And a God like unto himself (as the Wise Man observes) he cannot make. *At least,* saith *Trismegistus, they are equal in Power: For none of the things in Heaven will come down upon Earth, and leave the limits of Heaven: but a Man ascends up into Heaven, and measures it. He knoweth what things are on high, and what below. And that which is the greatest of all, he leaveth not the Earth, and yet is above: so mighty and vast is the greatness of his Nature! Wherefore we must be bold to say, that an Earthly Man is a Mortal God, and the Heavenly GOD is an Immortal MAN.*

THIS is the Philosophy of the ancient Heathen: wherein though there be some Errors, yet was he guided to it by a mighty sence of the interiour Excellency of the Soul of Man, and the boldness he assumes is not so profane, but that it is countenanced here and there in the Holy Scripture. GOD himself said unto *Moses, Lo, I have made thee a God to* Pharoah. Again he telleth him concerning *Aaron, He shall be to thee instead of a Mouth, and thou shalt be to him instead of God.* And again concerning all the Great men of the World in general, *I have said ye are Gods, but ye shall die like Men.* But let us see the Reason of the Heathen a little, on which he foundeth his great Opinions. In one place he maketh his Son *Tatius* to say, *I conceive and understand, not by the sight o mine Eyes, but by the intellectual Operation, &c. I am in Heaven, in the Earth, in the Water, in the Air: I am in the living Creatures, in Plants, in the Womb: every where.* Whereupon he asketh him, *Dost thou not know (O my Son) that thou art born a God, and the Son of The One as I am?* And the ground of this Question he unfoldeth in another place thus; *Consider him that contains all things, and understand, that nothing is more Capacious than that which is Incorporeal, nothing more swift, nothing more powerful: but (of all other things) it is most Capacious, most swift, and most strong. And judge of this by thy self. Command thy Soul to go into* India, *and sooner than thou canst bid it, it will be there. Did it pass over the Ocean, and suddenly it will be there: not as passing from place to place, but suddenly it will be there. Command it to flie into Heaven, and it will need no wings, neither shall any thing hinder it; not the fire of the Sun, nor the Æther, nor the turning of the Sphears, nor the bodies of any of the Stars, but cutting through all it will flie up to the last and furthest Body. And if thou wilt even break through the Whole, and see those things that are without the World (if there be any thing without)* [i.e. if the World be confined,] *thou maist. Behold how great Power, how great swiftness thou hast! Canst thou do all these things, and cannot GOD? After this manner therefore contemplate GOD to have all the whole World in himself, as it were all Thoughts or Intellections. If therefore thou wilt not equal thy self to GOD, thou canst not understand GOD. For the like is intelligible by the like. Increase thy self to an immeasurable Greatness, leaping beyond every Body, and transcending all Time, become* ETERNITY; *And thou shalt understand GOD. If thou believe in thy self that nothing is impossible, but accountest thy self Immortal, and that thou canst understand all things, every Art, every Science, and the manner and custom of every living thing, become higher than all Height, and lower than all Depth, comprehend in thy self the qualities of all the Creatures, of the Fire, the Water, the Dry and the Moist, and conceive likewise that thou canst at once be every where, in the Sea, in the Earth; at once understand thy self not yet begotten, in the Womb, Young, Old, Dead, the things after Death, and all these together; as also all Times, Places, Deeds, Qualities, Quantities, thou maist, or else thou canst not yet understand GOD. But if thou shut up thy Soul in thy Body, and abuse it; and say, I understand nothing, I am afraid of the Sea, I cannot climb up into Heaven, I know not who I am, I cannot tell what I shall be; what hast thou to do with GOD? For thou canst understand none of those fair and good things, but must be a lover of the Body and Evil. For it is the greatest evil not to know GOD. But to be able to Know, and to Will, and to Hope, is the strait Way, and the divine Way proper to the Good. It will every where meet thee, and every where be seen of thee plain and easie, when thou dost not expect, or look for it. It will meet thee Waking, Sleeping, Sailing, Travelling, by Night, by Day, when thou speakest, and when thou keepest silence. For it is nothing, which is not the Image of GOD.* His Close is most Divine; *And yet thou sayest, GOD is Invisible; but be advised: for who is more manifest than he? For therefore he made all things, that thou by all things mightest see him. This is the Good of GOD, his Vertue is this, to appear, and be seen in all Things.* This is the bottom of all other Greatnesses whatsoever: GOD is infinitely communicative, infinitely prone to reveal himself, infinitely Wise, and able to do it. He hath made the Soul on purpose that it might see him: And if the Eye that was made for the World, being so little a ball of Earth and Water, can take in all, and see all that is visible, if the sight of the Eye be present with all it beholdeth; much more is the Soul both able to see, and to be present with all, that is Divine and Eternal.

I know very well that a Man divided from GOD is a weak inconsiderable Creature, as the Eye is, if divided from the Body, and without the Soul: but united to GOD a Man is a transcendent and Celestial thing. GOD is his Life, his Greatness, his Power, his Blessedness and Perfection. And as the Apostle saith, *He that is joyned to the Lord is one SPIRIT.* His Omnipresence and Eternity fill the Soul, and make it able to contain all Heights and Depths, and Lengths and Breadths whatsoever. And it is the desire of the Soul *to be filled with all the fulness of GOD.*

Magnanimous desires are the natural results of a Magnanimous Capacity. The desire of being *like Gods, knowing Good and Evil*, was the destruction of the World. Not as if it were unlawful to desire to be *Like GOD*: but to aspire to the Perfection in a forbidden way, was unlawful. By Disobedience, and by following our own Inventions, by seeking to the Creature, to the stock of a Tree, to make us *Like GOD*; that is erroneous, and poor, and despicable: but to know our selves, and *in the strait and divine Way* to come immediately to GOD, to contemplate him in his Eternity and Glory, is a right and safe Way: for the Soul will by that means be the Sphere of his Omnipresence, and the Temple of the God-head: It will become ETERNITY, as *Trismegistus* speaketh, or ONE SPIRIT with God, as the Apostle. And then it must needs be present with all things *in Heaven, and in the Earth, and in the Sea*, as GOD is: for all things will be in it, as it were *by Thoughts and Intellections*.

A Magnanimous Soul then, if we respect its Capacity, is an immovable sphere of Power and Knowledge, far greater than all

Worlds, by its Vertue and Power passing through all things, through the Centre of the Earth, and through all Existencies. And shall such a Creature as this be contented with Vanities and Trifles, Straws and Feathers, painted Butterflies, Hobby-horses and Rattles. These are the Treasures of little Children! but you will say a Man delighteth in Purses of Gold, and Cabinets of Jewels, in Houses and Palaces, in Crowns and Scepters. Add Kingly Delights, and say he delighteth in Armies and Victories, and Triumphs and Coronations. These are great in respect of *Play-things*. But all these are feeble and pusillanimous to a great Soul. As Scipio[1] was going up to Heaven, the Earth it self seemed but a Nutshel, and he was ashamed of all his Victories and Triumphs, amazed at his madness in Quarrelling, and fighting about Territories and Kingdoms contracted to a Star, and lost into nothing. The whole Earth is but one invisible Point, when a man soareth to the height of all Immensity, and beholdeth and compasseth its everlasting Circumference, which is infinite every way beyond the Heavens. It is the true and proper Immensity of the Soul: Which can no more be contented with the narrow confinement of this World, no more rest in the Childishness of all the noise of the Interests of Men, be no more satisfied with its Earthly Glories, than the SUN can be shut up in a *Dark-Lanthorn*. It is true indeed it would desire to see, as the Angels do, the least and lowest of all the Creatures full of the Glory and Blessedness of GOD, all Wisdom and Goodness in every thing, and is apt to complain for want of some eternal and Celestial Light wherein to behold them: but if all the expansions of Time and Eternity should be void, and all the extents and out-goings of Infinity empty round about them; though things upon Earth, nay and things in the Heavens, should be never so Rich, and divine, and beautiful, yet such is the Magnanimity of a Great Soul, that it would hugely be displeased: its loss and its distaste would be alike Infinite. Infinite Honours, infinite Treasures, infinite Enjoyments, things endless in number, value, and excellency are the Objects of its Care and Desire; the greatness of its Spirit leads it to consider and enquire, whether all the spaces above the Heavens, and all the parts of GOD's everlasting Kingdom be full of Joyes, whether there be any end or bound of his Kingdom; whether there be any defect or miscarriage, any blemish or disorder in it, any vile and common thing, any remissness or neglect, any cause of complaint or deformity? As also whether all the Ages of the World are Divine and Sacred; whether after they are gone, they abide in their places; whether

---

[1] Marginal gloss: *Tully* in *Somn. Scipion.*

there be any thing in them to entertain the Powers of the Soul with delight, and feed them with satisfaction? What end, what use, what excellency there is in Men? Whether all the waies of GOD are full of beauty and perfection; all Wisdom, Justice, Holiness, Goodness, Love and Power? What Regions eternal Blessedness is seated in? What Glory, what Reason, what Agreeableness and Harmony is in all his Counsels? Whether those durations of Eternity before the World is made, are full or empty, full of bright and amiable Objects, or dark and obscure? Whether the government of the World be perfect; whether the Soul be Divine in it self; whether it be conducive to its own felicity, or to the happiness of all those in whom it is concerned? Whether the World shall end? If it shall, after what manner; whether by Design or Accident? Whether all Ages and Nations shall rise from the Dead? Whether there shall be a general Doom, or a day of Judgment? Whether I am concerned in all the transactions and passages at that day? Whether all Mankind shall be united into one, to make up one compleat and perfect Body, whereof they all are the fellow-Members? What shall be after the End of the World? Whether we shall live for ever? Whether we shall see GOD, and know one another? Whether we shall reign in eternal Glory? Whether in the Confusions of Hell there be any Beauty, and whether in the Torments of the damned we shall find any joy or satisfaction? Whether all the Riches, Customs and Pleasures of this World shall be seen? Whether in the World to come any fruit shall appear and arise from them, for which they shall be esteemed to have been not in vain, but profitable in relation to all Eternity? What kind of Life we shall lead, and what kind of Communion and fellowship Angels and Men shall have with each other? Whether the Works of GOD were unworthy of his Choice, or the best of all that were possible? What his Laws are as to their nature and excellency? Whether his Love be really sincere and infinite? Whether there be any such thing as infinite Wisdom, Goodness and Bounty, Blessedness and Glory? Such things as these are the Concerns and Inquiries of a Magnanimous Soul. And if its expectations and desires are absolutely satisfied, it will easily appear, and break forth upon all Occasions, into the most high and Magnanimous Actions.

Trismegistus (or whoever else was the Author of that Book) saw the deep Capacity of his own Soul, but if a Conjecture may be made by the residue of the discourse, did not understand the end (at least not clearly) for which it was implanted. Some knowledge he had, that all the things in Eternity were the Objects of that Power, by reason

Christian Ethicks

of which he calls them *Fair and Good:* but that they were to be the *Treasures* and *Enjoyments* of the Soul I do not find him affirming. He that knows this must needs be of our Saviours mind, who when all the Kingdoms of the World, and the Glory of them were shewed him by Satan in a moment of time, despised them all. For the divine and Celestial Kingdom is infinitely greater, and in a far more perfect manner to be enjoyed.

HE that knoweth the Honour which cometh from above, will despise the Honour which men can pay, and in comparison of that Honouur which cometh from GOD only, esteem all the Honour of this World but false and feeble. Not as if Men were in the truth of Nature vile and despicable Creatures; a Magnanimous man knows all others to be by Nature like himself, and is apt to reverence all of his kind as sublime and Celestial Creatures. But he is a Man of a clear and discerning Spirit, and the Corruption of Nature makes him to slight all that is defiled. He sees that Men are generally Evil, deformed and blind, erroneous, perverse and foolish, poor and miserable: And that all the Honour which they generally give is irrational and feigned. A little colour in the face, a gay Coat, a fine Horse, a Palace and a Coach, an Exchequer full of Gold, or some such light and superficial Causes, are all the grounds of the respect that they pay us.

> *And if the Glory and Esteem I have,*
> *Be nothing else than what my Silver gave;*
>   *If for no other ground*
> *I am with Love or Praises crown'd,*
> *'Tis such a shame, such vile, such base Repute,*
> *'Tis better starve, than eat such empty Fruit.*

IF a King be dejected from his Throne, it is but a poor comfort that he is admired by Persons condemned to die, and praised by Beggars. The dignity and power of the Persons that admire us, is of great consideration, in the love and delight which they take in us. They all must vanish and perish as a Dream: no Honour is truly great, but that which is continual and endless too. A great and mighty Soul can care for no Honour but that which comes from wise and amiable Persons, that are themselves great and honourable, most rich and powerful, holy, just, blessed and glorious. Honour from GOD and his holy Angels, from the eternal Son of GOD and all his Saints, is marvellous and substantial. That Honour which is paid upon great and solid causes; because a Man is well-pleasing to GOD, and exalted to his Throne;

because he is the very true Image of GOD, and has dominion over all the Creatures; because he is infinitely beloved of GOD, and all Angels and Men are commanded to love him; because he is redeemed by the Blood of Christ, and made a Temple of the Holy Ghost; because he is a Priest and King to his Eternal Creatour, because he is full of Goodness and Wisdom, adorned with all kind of Vertue, and made an Heir of eternal Glory; because he is Faithful and True, and Just and Holy; because he hath conquered Death, and Hell, and Sin, and the Grave, and triumpheth over them, this is being paid by such Persons, Honour indeed: and to desire this Honour is the Property and the Vertue of a Magnanimous Soul.

An Eagle cannot stoop at Flies. An *Alexander*, or a *Cæsar* cannot debase or confine their Souls to the pleasures of a Cottage in a Wilderness. Infinite Hopes and infinite Desires, infinite Fears, and Despairs, and Sorrows, infinite Joyes, and Delights, and Glories, infinite Adorations, Praises and Thanksgivings, infinite and eternal Objects are the only fit and proper Concerns for the Affections of a Great and *Magnanimous* Soul. The very signification of the word is *Greatness of Soul*, or if you please, *of Mind*: For a distinction may be made between the *Soul*, and *Mind*. The Soul of Man is the immutable essence, or form of his Nature, unimployed. His power of Reasoning is alive, even then when it is quiet and unactive; and this is his Soul. It is one and the same in all men, and of it self equally inclined to all great and transcendent things: but in the most it is misguided, baffled and suppressed, and though it be never so great it is to no purpose. This greatness implanted by Nature is not *Magnanimity*: It is a Natural disposition, not an acquired habit, as all Vertue is. A Man is then said to be of such a *Mind*, when he determines, or thinks in such a manner. His mind is Good that intendeth well, his mind is Evil that designeth mischief. So that the Mind is the Soul exerting its power in such an act: and the greatest Soul in all the World is but *Pusillanimous* that mindeth little things. A great Soul is Magnanimous in *Effect*, a *Mind* applyed to mighty Objects. Some men have a Magnanimity infused by the power of Education, and are led by Custome to Great things, and in a manner by Necessity, for such is their Place and Calling, that they are frequently led to greater Objects than other men. Of this sort are the most eminent rank of Grandees, and Princes: Kingdoms, and Thrones, and Privy Councils, and Queens, and Armies are their natural Dialect. This is no Vertue, for though it be not innate by *Nature*, yet they are *born* to it, and it is given by *Fortune*. Others consider what they have to do, and make an election, and though they are born in a poor and despicable estate, are not Magnanimous by Nature, or Fortune, but by *Choice* and voluntary Election. Not to satisfie the humour of a high Blood, choler and fire, nor to answer the necessities of a higher Calling; but to discharge the office of Vertue and Wisdom. And this is the Offspring of the *Will*, the true and genuine *Vertue*. Which as it is far more worthy than any of the rest, is guided to far better and more glorious Objects, and more diffusively given by the Bounty of GOD to all kind of Men in all Conditions. In the Poor it is more marvellous than in the Great and Rich: It has such an undaunted property in its Nature, that though the disproportion between them and their Assurance, or Hope, or Desire seem infinite, and the end which they aim at by their Magnanimity is judged impossible: though their attempt appear a ridiculous madness to them to whom the Verities of Religion appear incredible, yet they are no whit discouraged or disheartened at the matter, but stoutly march on, being animated by the alarum of such a Trumpet, such a Drum as Magnanimity is. His Faith is more Divine by conquering the discouragements of the World, than if he met with no censure or opposition.

IF you would have the Character of a Magnanimous Soul, he is the Son of eternal Power, and the Friend of infinite Goodness, a Temple of divine and heavenly Wisdom, that is not imposed upon by the foul and ragged disguises of Nature, but acquainted with her great Capacities and Principles, more than commonly sensible of her interests, and depths, and desires. He is one that has has gone in unto Felicity, and enjoyed her beauties, and comes out again her perfect Lover and Champion: a Man whose inward stature is miraculous; and his Complexion so divine, that he is King of as many Kingdoms as he will look on: One that scorns the smutty way of enjoying things like a Slave, because he delights in the Celestial way, and the Image of GOD. He knows that all the World lies in Wickedness; and admires not at all, that things palpable and near, and natural, are unseen, though most powerful and glorious; because men are blind and stupid. He pities poor vicious Kings that are oppressed with heavy Crowns of Vanity and Gold, and admires how they can content themselves with such narrow Territories: yet delights in their Regiment of the World, and paies them the Honour that is due unto them. The glorious Exaltation of good Kings he more abundantly extols, because so many thousand Magnanimous Creatures are committed to their Trust, and they that govern them understand their Value. But he sees well enough that the Kings glory and true repose consists in the Catholick and eternal Kingdom. As for himself he *is come unto Mount Sion, and to the City of the living GOD, the Heavenly Jerusalem, and to an innumerable Company of Angels, to the General Assembly and Church of the Firstborn, which are written in Heaven, and to GOD the Judge of all, and to the Spirits of Just men made perfect, and to JESUS the Mediatour of the New Covenant:* And therefore receiving a Kingdom which cannot be moved, he desires to serve GOD acceptably with reverence and godly fear: And the truth is he can fear nothing else, for GOD alone is a consuming fire. He very well understands what the Apostle saith, and dares believe him: *I cease not to give thanks for you, making mention of you in my Prayers, that the GOD of our Lord Jesus Christ, the Father of Glory, may give unto you the Spirit of Wisdom and Revelation in the knowledge of him, the eyes of your Understanding being enlightened, that ye may know what is the HOPE of his Calling, and what the RICHES of the GLORY of his INHERITANCE in the Saints. And what is the EXCEEDING GREATNESS of his POWER to us-ward who believe, according to the WORKING of his Mighty Power: which he wrought in Christ when he raised him from the dead, and set him at his own RIGHT HAND in the HEAVENLY places: far above all Principality, and Power, and Might, and Dominion, and every Name that is named, not only in this WORLD, but in that also which is to come: And hath put ALL THINGS under his feet, and he gave him to be HEAD over all Things to the CHURCH which is his BODY, THE FULNESS OF HIM THAT FILLETH ALL IN ALL. Now to him that is able to do exceeding abundantly above all that we ask or think, according to the Power that WORKETH in us, Unto him be Glory in the Church by Christ Jesus, throughout all AGES, World without end. Amen.*

A great and a clear Soul knoweth that all these intimations must needs be true, for it is an amazing Miracle that they should be otherwise. *Infinite Love* and *Eternal Blessedness* are near allyed; and that these should cease, is contrary to all Nature, in GOD, in the Soul of Man, in Heaven, in Earth, in the order of the Universe, and contrary to all that VISIBLE GLORY which in the World appeareth.

CAP. XXIX.

Of Modesty. Its Nature. Its Original. Its Effects and Consequences.

MODESTY is a comely Grace in the Behaviour of a Man, by which he piously dissembleth his own Perfections, and blusheth at his Praises. It springeth from a certain fear and sence of his Imperfection. 'Tis the shadow of Guilt, and a beautiful cover of Original Corruption. It is sometimes Natural, and, which is contrary to all other Vertues, more truly vertuous for being so. For then it is Simple, Genuine, and Real; but studied Modesty is affected and artificial: yet where Nature has not been so obliging as to give the endowment, 'tis not altogether to be condemned, since it is agreeable to the best of our conditions in this World, and supplies a defect in his Nature, that is born without it.

IT is akin to Shame, yet increases the honour of him that wears it; it is the shade of Vertue, yet makes it brighter: It is a tincture of Humility, visible in a vermilion and deeper die; and the more natural and easie, the more sweet and delightful.

IT charms the Envy of those that admire us, and by seeming to extinguish our worth gives it a double beauty. It reconciles a man to the Enemies of his Grace and Vertue, and by a softness irresistible wins a Compassion in all Spectators. It is a Vertue which by refusing the honour that is due unto it, acquireth more; a real Counterfeit, and the only honest and true dissimulation. It is an effeminate, yet a laudable quality; a spice of Cowardice, more prevalent than Courage; a Vertue by which we despise all meaner Honours, while we are ambitiously carried to the highest Glory. It seemeth inconsistent with Magnanimity, yet is her youngest Sister.

IT hath not many Objects, nor are its Aims apparent, nor its Ends conspicuous. It is the Mother of fine and delicate Resentments; its strength consisteth in tenderness and fear. He that is Magnanimous in one respect, may be modest in another. Praises and Commendations are the fuel of its Nature, it feedeth upon them, while it grows by rejecting them. It delights in what it feareth; and is full of discords, but more full of harmonies. It is pleased in its displeasure, and alwaies fighteth with its own Repugnancies. It is a Vertue mixt of Sence and Reason; its region is in the Body more than in the Soul, and in all its Spiritual motions it is attended with Corporeal impressions. The

Blood and Spirits dance in the Veins, as if Nature were delighted with its own Confusions. By captivating the favour of Men upon Earth, it affecteth the very Angels in Heaven, with much of pleasure. It putteth us in mind of Guilt and Innocency at the same time, and by confession of the one adds lustre to the other. By making way for the acceptance of a mans Person, it giveth more esteem, success, and efficacy to his other Vertues. And by this means it hath much of excellency in a little.

HE that hath it not, must needs acquire something like it; and if he be elaborate in expressing it, must hide his Art under the vail of Nature. Though it be remote from the highest End, it may be guided to it, and when so directed, is alwaies innocent. It is very just, for while other Vertues make it a Vertue, it is a Grace unto them all. You may look upon it as a tangible flame and see it in others, but must feel it in your self before you can understand it. It is old in Children, young in middle Aged men, at last an Infant. It is greatest in the beginning of our life, it decayeth in Youth, in Old Age it vanisheth; at least changeth its dwelling, for it ceaseth to be in the Body of an Aged man, and turneth into Courtesie or Civility, in the Conversation. When it dieth, it is buried in Humility, and liveth in its Tomb, being empaled in as it were with Meekness, and waiting daily for its Resurrection. Much cannot be said of it precisely: but it is best commended, when left to your Practice. It is the only tender Infant of all the Vertues: like *Cupid* among the gods: it appeareth frequently, and is much exercised, in the School of *Venus:* but is capable of more high and more noble uses.

MODESTY in Apparel is commended in the Scriptures. It implies Moderation and Chastity together. It is sometimes opposed to Lasciviousness, sometimes to Excess, sometimes to Impudence: And is a great Vertue, if for nothing else, but the exclusion of these abominable Vices.

THE other Vertues seem to be the Members, and substantial parts of the Body of worth: Modesty like the Air, and Meen of them all. It is the guard of the Soul against Looseness and Pride, a Vertue repressing the fumes of Self–conceit, and a kind of silent restraint of all that Arrogance, that delights in pomps and superfluities.

THOUGH it be a little Vertue, its Reality is apparent: for unless it be made up with some other supplies, the want of Modesty is pernicious and destructive.

IT is exercised in small things, but is of long extent in the vertue of its influence; and because of the multiplicity of its uses and occasions, amounts to a considerable degree of *Goodness*. It hath something like Love in its nature, for it preferreth another above it self, and in that its magnetical and obliging quality much consisteth. *In honour preferring one another*. It fulfils that Law, wherein our most near and tender Interest is concerned. In preferring one another there is a lovely contest, more sweet and happy than the best Agreement. It is of all other the most friendly strife, and kind Contention.

CHAP. XXX.

The excellent Nature of Liberality. Rules to be observed in the practice of it. Regard to our Servants, Relations, Friends and Neighbours must be had in our Liberality, as well as to the Poor and Needy. How our external acts of Charity ought to be improved for the benefit of mens Souls. Liberality maketh Religion real and substantial.

LIBERALITY, in the common use and acceptation of the Word, differs from Magnificence, as Modesty from Magnanimity. There is much of liberty and freedom in its Nature. For Avarice is a strict and sour Vice, and they that are guilty of it are called *Misers*; but a Bountiful man hath a good eye and is as free from Anxiety, as he is free in disbursing. His Communicative humor is much his enlargement: he knows little of Confinement, Care or Bondage.

THERE are two Vertues that endanger a Mans welfare in this World; and they have all the *Temporal Promises*. Meekness seems to encourage our Enemies to trample us under feet, because it promiseth Impunity: And it is directly said *The Meek shall inherit the Earth:* nay be so far from having Enemies, that *the Meek shall inherit the abundance of Peace*. And concerning Liberality which makes a man a Beggar, at least threatens to make him so, by wasting his Estate, the Scripture saith, *The Liberal Soul shall be made fat. The Liberal Soul shall be made fat. The Liberal Heart desviseth liberal things, and by liberal things shall he stand.*

MEN are almost in all things contrary to GOD. For since they tumbled out of *Eden*, they have lost their wits, and their heads are downwards: They think it wisdom to keep their Mony *against a rainy day:* and to lay it up for fear of Poverty. But *Solomon* adviseth them to the direct contrary, and maketh it an Argument why they should be Liberal, *Becaus they know not what evil may come upon the Earth.* We cannot put our Treasures into safer hands, than into GOD Almighty's: Nor can we make any use of Gold and Silver, comparable to that of Charitable uses. By this it is that we *lay up a good foundation against the time to come*; and oblige others to receive us into Mansions here, into everlasting habitations hereafter.

MY Lord *Bridgeman*, late Lord Keeper, confessed himself in his Will to be but a Steward of his Estate, and prayed GOD to forgive him all his offences, *in Getting, Mispending, or not Spending it as he ought to do*: And that after many Charitable and Pious works, perhaps surmounting his Estate, though concealed from the notice and knowledge of the World.

I have heard of a smart obliging Calumny fastned on a Great Man of *France*, by one that had largely tasted of his Bounty: for having been in his House honourably entertained for some space of time, and observing how much the Palace was frequented by all kind of Learned Men: and how Liberal the Master of it was, especially to men of Worth and Vertue; he charges the Man with the greatest Covetousness in the World: *because he turned all his Riches into Obligations:* As if he had put all his Estate and Monies to Use: But to covet affections, and be rich in hearts is no deformity.

THE truth is, when the waies whereby Love is begotten in the Soul are well examined, and the happiness of being truly beloved, and delighted in, is known; no man is so wise as the Liberal man. He is his own end, while he thinks not of it. For nothing is more conducive to his ease and honour, than the bounty of Munificence which enriches his Soul. There are three things which beget Love, *Beauty, Benefits* and *Praises:* They are all three shut up in Goodness, which is the fountain of Liberality. The beauty of the face is a silent Oratory, a high stile of Commendation without an Epistle: yet by doing Benefits it prevaileth more, than by any of its Charms; and maketh it self great by enriching others. Love inspires it with an amiable Soul; and if others are delighted with their own Praises, he that is liberal in the acknowledgment of mens Vertues, and giveth Honour to the Worthy, is full of musick in his words, of a sweet and pleasing behaviour, agreeable in his deeds, and fraught with the Honour which he imparteth so freely. A Liberal man is cloathed like the Sun with the Raies of his own glory, and establishes himself in the hearts of his Neighbours, and reigns like a King by the sole interest of Vertue and Goodness. *Every man is a Friend to him that giveth many Gifts.* He may be as holy, and as temperate, and as wise as an Angel, no man will be offended at him, because he beautifies his Religion with so much goodness. He enjoys himself, and his Riches, and his Friends, and may do what he will (with perfect liberty) because he delights in the felicity of all that accost him. He puts embroideries on Religion by the chearfulness of his Spirit, and carries a light wherever he goes, that makes men to reverence his Person, and esteem his Censures. He moves in a sphere of Wonders, his life is a continual stream of Miracles, because he is alwaies sacrificing himself and his Possessions, to the benefit of the

World, and the comfort of others. Benefits and Blessings are his Life–guard, like his guardian Angels alwaies attendant on him. His House is the habitation of joy and felicity, and yields a spectacle of Contentment to every beholder. His Neighbours are his Security, not his Suspicion; and other mens Houses the forts and ramparts about his own. No man will hurt him, because they extinguish their own contentment and benefit in him. They tender him as the apple of their eye, because he is a greater comfort and advantage than that unto them. The ancient custome of *Paradice*, so long since lost and forgotten in the World revives in its Family, where all men are entertained as Brothers and Sisters, at the expences of GOD and Nature. He taketh care, because Thrift is the fuel of Liberality; and is Frugal, that he may be Bountiful. All his aim and labour is, that he may *maintain Good Works*; and *make his light so shine before men, that they seeing his good works may glorifie his Father which is in Heaven.* There is a generous Confidence discovered in all his Actions, and a little glimpse of Heaven in his Behaviour; for he lives as if he were among a company of Angels. All mens Estates are his, and his is theirs: If he had them all he would impart them, and restore them to supply their Wants: perhaps not with so much wisdom as GOD hath done, but with as much pleasure and contentment, as his goodness can inspire, in the exercise of power so kindly and well employed. But because the designs of GOD are infinitely deeper than he can well apprehend, and laid all in eternal Wisdom, he is pleased and delighted, that his Care is prevented; and that GOD hath done that for other men, to which his own inclination would readily prompt him were it left undone. If it were permitted him to wish whatsoever he listed, of all other things he would chiefly desire to be a Blessing to the whole World; and that he is not so, is his only discontentment. But for that too there are remedies in Felicity: when he knows *all*, his desire is granted. For a Life beautified with all Vertue is the greatest gift that can be presented to GOD, Angels and Men. And when all Secrets shall be revealed, all hidden things brought to light, his life shall be seen in all its perfection, and his Desires themselves be the enjoyments and pleasures of all the Creatures. There is a certain kind of sympathy that runs through the Universe, by vertue of which all men are fed in the feeding of one: even the Angels are cloathed in the Poor and Needy. All are touched and concerned in every one. Like the Brazen Pillars in the Temple of *Minerva*, if one be smitten all resound the blow throughout the Temple: or like the strings of several Lutes skrewed up to *Unisones*, the one is made to quaver by the others motions. If Christ himself be fed in the Poor, much more may Angels and Men. At the last day we find no other scrutiny about Religion, but what we have done or neglected in Liberality. *Come ye blessed of my Father, inherit the Kingdom prepared for you from the foundations of the World, for I was hungry and ye gave me meat, thirsty and ye gave me drink, naked and ye cloathed me, a Stranger and ye took me in; I was sick and ye visited me, I was in Prison and ye came unto me. Inasmuch as ye have done it to the least of these my Brethren, ye have done it unto me.* LOVE it seems will sit in Judgment on the World: and the Rule of Trial shall be the fulfilling of its Laws. *Love* shall be the glory too of all the *Assessors*. And every act of Cruelty and Oppression infinitely odious in all their eyes.

THERE was a certain King which would take account of his Servants: and when he had begun to reckon, one was bought unto him, that ought him 10000 *Talents. But forasmuch as he had not to pay, his Lord commanded him to be sold, and all that he had, and payment to be made. The Servant therefore fell down and worshipped him, saying, Lord have patience with me, and I will pay thee all. Then the Lord of that Servant was moved with Compassion, and loosed him, and forgave him the Debt. But the same Servant went out, and found one of his fellow-Servants which ought him* 100 *pence, and he laid hold on him and took him by the throat, saying, Pay me that thou owest. And his fellow-Servant fell down at his feet and besought him, Have patience with me and I will pay thee all. And he would not, but went and cast him into Prison till he should pay the Debt. So when his fellow-Servants saw what was done, they were very sorry, and came and told to their Lord all that was done.* Every neglect and contempt of our fellow-Brethren is injurious and grievous to GOD, Angels and Men: for there is one common Principle in all Nature, to hate evil Deeds, and especially those of Rigour and Severity, when we our selves stand in need of Mercy, and have received Favour. This common principle of Sympathy and Compassion intitles us to all the good, that is done to any Man in the World. The love of Equity and Reason, and the natural inclination that carries us to delight in excellent Deeds, gives us an interest in all that are performed. The beauty of the one is as sweet and blessed as the deformity of the other is odious and distastful. And if we our selves are infinitely obliged, and live by the bounty and goodness of another, after we have forfeited the Kings favour, have received it again with pardon and forgiveness, nay and with more and greater benefits; if we shall not be liberal to one another, it is a strange inequality. But the discharge of our duty will make us amiable and delightful.

That the King of Glory is so concerned in the welfare of his Subjects, were there nothing else in the Duty but that consideration, is an infinite encouragement. *He that receiveth you, receiveth me*, is such an obligation, that as it is all Goodness in it self, so is it all Motive unto us. Eternity will scarce be sufficient to fathom its depth. Do we feed GOD himself in feeding the Poor, and his eternal Son Jesus Christ? Are these Needy persons the Representatives of the GODHEAD, in whom we are to shew all our affection, love and gratitude to the fountain of all Life and Happiness? How infinite ought our Liberality to be, when we consider the excellency of our Bliss and Benefactour? Are they beloved, are they all his Sons, the very express image of himself; all disguised and concealed Kings; all Temples of eternal Glory? What measure can confine or shut up our bowels? Are the Spectators so innumerable, so divine, so blessed, so nearly allyed to our selves, so rich, and great, and beautiful, are they so deeply concerned in the welfare of others, and does every act of Charity extend to all; shall we appear in the very act it self eternally before them? What a vast ambition of pleasing all these glorious Persons, should be exprest in every operation of the Soul? As every Thought is seen throughout all eternity, and every Word (that is spoken here on Earth) heard in the utmost extents of immensity; so is there a kind of Omnipresent greatness in the smallest action, for it is vertually extended through all the omnipresence of Almighty GOD: even as every Centre, wherein it can be done is eternally near, nay and within him in the remotest part of his omnipresence. 'Tis dilated in a moment, and fills the immensity of GOD with its nature. According to its kind it affecteth all his Essence in all spaces whatsoever.

YET is there a Rule for the bounding of all external acts of Charity, and another for improving it. Intelligence is the light wherein Alms-deeds ought to shine, and attain their glory: Love is the soul of Compassion, and Zeal the fervour of Perfection: without which *though a man bestow all his Goods to feed the Poor, and give his Body to be burned, it profiteth nothing.* Where this great abyss of goodness is, Prudence may dispence it, as it seeth occasion. All other Vertues attending upon it, it is impossible to destroy it self here on earth, unless the case be so urgent, that it is better die, than to live in the World. *For a good man sheweth favour and lendeth*; but it is added, *He will guide his affairs with discretion.*

The first Rule is, to secure the life and growth of the tree, by causing it so to bear one year, that it may bring forth fruit another. It is no good husbandry to cut it down: nor any charity to make it wither and expire.

And on this very account a Charitable man must preserve himself, that he may do more good, by continuing longer able to do it.

HE that will examine the proportions and measures of his Liberality may take this Rule for the second: Let thy Superfluities give place to other mens Conveniencies, thy Conveniencies to their Necessities, thy Necessities to their Extremities.

A third Rule is this; Our Riches must be expended according to the several Circumstances and occasions of our lives. A Liberal man will not pinch and starve his Servants. For it is contrary to the nature of Bounty to oppress any, to hurt any, to trample upon any. He will be good to all, and to those most, that are near unto him. GOD hatheth robbery for burnt Offering, or that Strangers should eat the Childrens meat, or that Beggars or Riotous persons should devour the right of a mans Servants. He that does brave acts abroad, but is a Niggard within doors, has a glorious train spread abroad like a Peacock, but stands upon black feet; and may bear that unlucky bird for his Crest, which is the emblem of Pride and Vain-glory. So is it with young Prodigals that oppress poor Tradesmen, by defrauding them of their Debts, yet are lavish enough to the Poor and Needy. This is a defect with which Goodness is inconsistent, and it blasteth their Charity. It is better take off 100 pounds a year from ones benevolence to the poor, than wrong a Servant or Creditour of a shilling. The Rule therefore is this, First secure the works of Necessity; have food and rayment for thy self; keep out of debt. Next render to every man his due in point of Justice, and employ no man thou canst not pay; rather perish thy self than oppress another. If thou art able, and hast any thing to spare, then let the miseries of the Needy be supplied in the works of Compassion and Charity: but let not all be swallowed up here, thy Neighbours, and Acquaintance, and Friends, and Kindred claim a share; and thou must secure something for the works of Courtesie and Hospitality. So order all both in thy Estate and Life, that the kindness of GOD may shine in all. So doing thy Stewardship shall be acceptable to the whole World, and thy Memory blessed among men and Angels.

Our Saviour when he wrought his Miracles, as he opened the eyes of the blind, healed the sick, cast out Devils, raised the dead, gave food to the hungry, tongues to the dumb, ears to the deaf, and legs to the lame: so did he give advice to the ignorant, and interpret all his design, by those Parables and Sermons which attended his Cures. Good Counsel is often times, a greater gift than a Trunk of Mony. While the Iron is hot it is time to strike. Good Counsel is like a bitter Pill, that must be gilded with Liberality. If the Word of GOD be like *good seed*, the heart in which it is sown is softened by Sorrow, and ploughed up by affliction, and prepared to receive it by the husbandry of Providence. And the properest Season that can be chosen for Instruction is the time of Obliging. He that intendeth the welfare of the Soul by all the good works he doth to the Body, is deep and perfect in Charity. A wise man will improve his advantages, and enrich his Gifts with pious discourses. A Benefactour has authority to talk what he listeth, and bribes his Auditor to patience by his Bounty. Since *He that winneth Souls is wise*, a profound Liberality will not let slip a golden Opportuninty, nor suffer his Gift to be dark and insignificant. He will make mention of the glory of GOD, and the Love of Christ, the guilt of Sin, the danger of Hell, and the hope of Heaven, and alwaies endeavour to make hi Love apparent to that GOD, for whose sake he pities the Poor, and is kind towards all. Forasmuch as man hath two parts, and his Body is without the Soul but a putrid Carkass; he will put life into his Mony, and inspire his Munificence with all his Reasons, that his Bounty may consist of two parts in like manner, and have a Soul for its Interpreter. Liberality to the Soul is the Soul of Liberality. Paradice and Heaven are better to be given than Gold and Silver. And every Good man will imitate the Apostle, who was ready not to impart the Gospel of GOD only, but his own Soul to the benefit of those for whom Christ died.

THIS one thing further I desire you to note, *he that soweth sparingly shall reap sparingly, but he which soweth bountifully shall reap also bountifully.*[1] In the Kingdom of Heaven every man receiveth his Penny: because all their Joyes are common and equal. Their *Treasures* shall be the same, but they will differ in *Glory*. The same GOD, the same Angels, the same Men, all the same Objects shall be round bout every man. Every man shall see and enjoy all the Glory of his eternal Kingdom, because every ones life and felicity shall be perfect. But yet their works follow them; and every man shall be cloathed in the beauty of his own actions, Vertues and Graces. There may be twenty Children in the same family, yet all of several Features. There may be a thousand Trees in the same Orchard, yet all of different kinds. The same brightness and glory may be round about them, the same skie cover them, the same Earth support them, the same Stars serve them, the same Sun shine upon them, the same Sea, the same Dew, the same Air and Nourishment feed them, and yet the one be more fair, and honourable, and excellent than the other. All the World does know that

---

[1] Marginal gloss: 2 Cor. 9.6.

a Tree laden with Fruits and Blossoms is far more beautiful than a Tree that is barren and unfruitful. And the degrees of Beauty are according as the Fruits are, more or less. And as the fruits they bring forth adorn them, so do their own works praise them in the Gates. Heaven as it is a Kingdom of Light and Knowledge, is a Kingdom of Perfection; Righteousness and Justice flourish there in their fulness: and every several degree of excellence is entertained with an answerable degree of esteem: according to the number and greatness of their Vertues every one is honoured by Saints and Angels.

NOW least these Fruits should receive any impediment by the Vices and Corruptions of men, order is taken, *that we should love our Enemies, bless them that curse us, do good to them that hate us, pray for them that despightfully use, and persecute us.* By which means it is that a Liberal man surmounts all obstacles whatsoever, lives among Dragons as if he were surrounded with Doves, and though he be environed with Devils, is as if he were conversant with Angels: Because he takes no notice of any Vice in any man, to stop him, but is as Liberal as if all were full of worth and vertue. Nay he is more good and more miraculous. Their Vices, their Provocations, their Disorders cannot stain or imbitter his Nature: but he will be alwaies chearful, and bright, and fair, and free and perfect. To love the amiable, and be kind to the beautiful is natural and easie. It is not given to the Angels but to visit the Faithful and the Penitent. But to love the Evil, to be kind, and good and serviceable to the Deformed and the Odious, to the Injurious and Ungrateful, is somewhat more than Angelical. We learn it not of them but of GOD, and of his eternal Son: who hath commanded us *to be the Children of our Father which is in Heaven; for he maketh his Sun to rise on the Evil and on the Good, and sendeth rain on the Just and on the Unjust.* Even Publicans and Sinners do in some manner as much as Angels, love them that love them. In Heaven they have no malignity, or malice, or wrong to overcome, all that they love is Beauty and Goodness: unless they learn of Jesus Christ, and imitate him here on Earth towards us Sinners. But our duty is far greater, and our opposition more. Which is intimated also in our Saviours words: *For if ye love them which love you, what reward have you? Do not even the Publicans the same? And if ye salute your Brethren only, what do ye more than others? Do not even the Putlicans so? Be ye therefore perfect even as your Father which is in Heaven is perfect.*

In the Close of all, I beseech you to consider this one most cogent and weighty expostulation. It is the beloved Disciples, *If a man say,*

I love GOD, and hateth his Brother, he is a Liar: for he that loveth not his Brother whom he hath seen, how can he love God whom he hath not seen?[1] Our Neighbours are not only the representatives of GOD, but they are here upon Earth, are visible, are present with us, are Corporeal as we are, and alwaies near us, our actions among them are palpable, and our Conversation with them real. GOD is invisible, and absent from us, he is afar off in the highest Heavens, Incorporeal, and Incomprehensible: If we are remiss and careless in our duty towards our Neighbour, all our devotion towards GOD will be but imaginary, our Religion will degenerate into an idle and vain *Chimera*, become a weak and feeble shadow, be seated in the fancy, and dwindle away into an aiery Speculation. The reality of Religion consists in the solid practice of it among the Sons of men that are daily with us. The difficult and serious actions of our Lives abroad, feed our Meditation in all our retirements, and infuse a reality and strength into our Devotions, which make them solid and substantial.

---

[1] Marginal gloss: 1 John 4. 20.

CAP. XXXI.

Of Magnificence in GOD. Its resemblance in Man. The chief Magnificence of the Soul is Spiritual. It is perfectly expressed in the outward Life, when the whole is made perfect, and presented to GOD. GOD gives all his Life to us: and we should give ours all to him. How fair and glorious it may be.

GOD being proposed as the Pattern of our Liberality and Kindness by our Saviour, the nature of his Bounty is fit to be considered for our Information: which is great, and publick, and advantagious to many. In some of his private dispensations it walks under the notion and form of Liberality, as it giveth food and Rayment, Gold and Silver, Houses and Lands to particular persons: But in other effects of his eternal love, which are great and publick, its nature is changed into the highest Magnificence.

MAGNIFICENCE is a Vertue scarcely to be found, but in Kings and Emperours. It is busied in erecting Temples and Triumphal arches, Magnificent Theatres, Colledges and Universities, Aquæducts and Palaces, Royal Monuments and Pyramids, Marts, Havens, Exchanges, and all those other great and mighty things wherein the glory of Imperial Power is made conspicuous, and whereby whole Nations are benefited, and Kingdoms adorned.

GREAT Power, Riches, Wisdom and Goodness must concur in the effect which is truly Magnificent. It must be of great lustre and glory, as well as publick lustre and glory, as well as of publick use and benefit; and as it is wrought with great labour and expence, be imparted by a great Soul, and freely given to the good of the People. For Magnificence implies Greatness and Bounty united.

THE Creation of the Universe was a great and Magnificent work, because the lustre and beauty of the WORLD is a sublime and wonderful Gift imparted to millions. The bounty of GOD in adorning all ages with Cities and Empires, for the benefit and enjoyment of all the World is another piece of his Royal Magnificence. The infusion of a Soul so divine and everlasting into the Body of a Man is an act of love transcendently greater than all the Aquæducts and Trophies in the World. For such a Celestial presence, such a sublime and illimited power, such a vast and noble Workmanship, as that is, which can see and comprehend all Eternity and Time together, extend to all Objects in all Worlds, and fill Immensity with life and joy, and love and knowledge, with light, and beauty, and glory, with adorations and praises; though its essence be invisible, and all its splendour within, is next under GOD the highest Object of all the admiration of Men and Angels: It is a being as publick as the Sun, the great occasion of all the extasies of the Seraphims, the wonder and the rapture of all the Cherubims, the glory of GOD communicated to the World in so divine a Creature; a miraculous effect of his eternal Power, and the resemblance of his Godhead among all the Creatures.

THE Incarnation of his Eternal Son, and the giving of the Holy Ghost was another Magnificent effect of his almighty Power: so was the preparation of his Word, with the Gifts he gave unto Men in the Patriarchs, Prophets and Apostles, adorned with all the varieties of their Labours and Vertues, Wisdom, Courage and Patience, Lives and Examples, Deaths and Sufferings, Oppositions and Successes, Miracles and Revelations. The *Jewish* Nation alone is a Magnificent gift to the whole World. The Apostle phraseth the Regiment of it as a matter of Bounty: *Now if the Fall of them be the Riches of the World, and the diminishing of them the Riches of the Gentiles, how much more their Fullness!*[1] And again, *When he ascended up on high, and led Captivity captive, he gave Gifts unto Men, some Apostles, and some Prophets,* &c. When he presented all Nations and Kingdoms as a token of his love to the Angels; when he gave all those glorious Hosts in the Heavens to the vision, service and pleasure of Men; much more when he gave all these in their marvellous order and amity united, to every Soul: When he filled the Heaven of Heavens with Joyes; and gave all the glory of his Kingdom to one (and that one to every one) he manifested the glory of his Magnificent power, in that of his great and transcendent goodness. And in relation to this we may cry out with the Apostle (more than for the mysterious Regiment of a little Nation, as he doth upon the account of GODS dealing with the *Jews*) *O the depth of the riches both of the Wisdom and Knowledge of GOD! How unsearchable are his judgments, and his waies past finding out!*[2] *For all things are yours, Whether* Paul, *or* Apollos, *or* Cephas, *or the* World, *or Life or Death, or things present, or things to come, all are yours, and ye are CHRISTS, and CHRIST is GODS.*[3] Wherefore he saith, *My Thoughts are not your*

---

[1] Marginal gloss: Rom. 11.12.
[2] Marginal gloss: Rom. 11.33.
[3] Marginal gloss: 1 Cor. 3.21,22.

Thoughts, nor your Waies my Waies. For as the Heavens are higher than the Earth, so are my Waies higher than your Waies, and my Thoughts than your Thoughts.[1]

You give trifles, and give them but to one, I give Worlds and give them to every one. You divide and disperse your Gifts, and lessen by dispersing them, I communicate and unite my Gifts, and augment by giving them: You think it impossible for one man to enjoy all things, I think it possible for innumerable Millions. You think your interest is abated, and your fruition endangered by the communication of your Treasures to many, I know they are increased and multiplied by the number of the Enjoyers. You think Gold and Silver to be the greatest Gifts, and that nothing is yours but what is shut up within such Shores, and Walls, and Hedges, I know that Men are the greatest Treasures, and that your interest is extended through all Worlds, and your Possessions illimited. For according to the tenour of these words, and a little before he saith, *Thou shalt break forth on the right hand and on the left, and thy seed shall inherit the Gentiles, and make the desolate Cities to be inhabited. Fear not, for thou shalt not be ashamed: neither be thou confounded, for thou shalt not be put to shame: for thou shalt forget the shame of thy Youth, and shalt not remember the reproach of thy Widowhood any more. For thy Maker is thy husband, the Lord of Hosts is his Name, &c.*[2] And a little after he saith, *Thou shalt also be a Crown of Glory in the hand of the Lord, and a royal DIADEM in the hand of the GOD. Thou shalt no more be termed* Forsaken, *neither shall thy land any more termed* Desolate, *but thou shall be called* Hephzibah, *and thy land* Beulah: *for the Lord delighteth in thee, and thy Land shall be married. For as a young Man marrieth a Virgin, so shall thy Sons marry thee: and as the Bridegroom rejoyceth over the Bride, so shall thy GOD rejoyce over thee.*[3] For a Son to marry with his Mother is Incest: it is Confusion also for a Child to go in unto his Fathers Wife: And yet the Church of GOD shall be the lawful Bride of every one of all her Sons. Here is Magnificence! GOD giveth himself, and his eternal Son, and his Holy Spirit, and his Bride, and his Apostles and Prophets, and all the Universe to every Soul! Which justifieth that saying of St. *Chrysostome, GOD loveth every one with all the Love wherewith he loveth the whole World.* His Magnificence exceedeth all Limits, Laws, Imaginations, Wishes, Possibilities, and he maketh every one * *Heir of the World,* †

---

[1] Marginal gloss: Isaiah 55. 8, 9.
[2] Marginal gloss: Isaiah 54.3,4,5.
[3] Marginal gloss: Isaiah 62.3,4,5.

Coheir with Christ, * to inherit all things;[1] every one more than the sole end of all his Kingdom. For all the Ornaments and Riches of a Bride are given with her Person: her Palace and Attendants are her Lovers upon the Marriage, as well as she: and all things that magnifie, or make her amiable, are subservient to his enjoyment, and really his that is her Husband. So that GOD giving us his Church to be our Mother and our Bride, hath intended us in all the things whereby he benefited her in all kingdoms and ages: and hath loved us in all the Love which he hath exercised towards her: and all the fruit of all his Love to the whole World resteth in our Exaltation. This is the Magnificence of Almighty GOD to every Soul in his Kingdom. And for this it is that the Church is called, *The Assembly of the First-born*, because all her Children are the perfect Heirs, and Kings, and Bridegrooms, every one compleatly, and more to his satisfaction, than if he were so alone. For as GOD is wholly every where, and the more here for being in other places; and infinitely here because he is Omnipresent: So does he wholly see and intend every one, as if him alone; and love him far the more, by loving every one; for his Love being infinite, it is expressed towards him in all the parts of his Kingdom: and the more rich and glorious he maketh all things, the more great and happy he maketh *Him*, according to the immeasurable All-sufficiency of his infinite Wisdom.

THERE is in the Goodness of GOD an infinite Greatness that makes it Magnificent: for he gives Himself. When a Queen gives her self, whether it be to a Beggar, or to one of her Courtiers, or to another King, if it proceed from an ardent Love the Gift is full of sweetness within; but it is alwaies attended with great Magnificence without: together with her self she gives him her Palace, her Exchequer, Gardens of Pleasure, her Crown and Throne, her Soveraignty, her Nobles, Attendants, and all her Kingdom. GOD doth infinitely more. He gives himself by Loving, and with himself gives us all his Wisdom, Goodness and Power, by making them full objects of Complacency: by doing with them for us, all that we could devise, or desire, or effect with them, had they been our own and seated in our selves. His bounty in giving himself is attended with infinite advantages, innumerable wonders of love and goodness; a care to make himself (as a Bridegroom does) exceeding amiable and glorious, a care to purifie and fit his Queen for himself with all kind of greatness and beauty: a care to adorn his Palace with all kind of delectable things, Riches, Pleasures, magnificent Furnitures, Perfumes, Musicians, Pictures, Jewels, Dainties, Feasts,

---

[1] Marginal gloss: * Rom. 4.13; † Ro. 8.17; * Rev. 21.7.

Attendants, Nobles, &c. In all which he infinitely exceedeth all the Monarchs of the World. His Kingdom is celebrated by *David* with great Exultation, *Psal.* 145.

NOW if we would be Magnificent as GOD is, we must have a love within our Souls, that is willing to impart all these incomprehensible Treasures and Glories to every Soul, and to all his Hosts; and if it be possible, to out-do all this, to give all these Worlds, nay GOD himself, and every Soul to all with greater ardour, and joy and gratitude: Angels and Men, our selves to all, and all to every one. For that Love which is the fountain of all is greater than all, a greater Gift, and a greater Treasure. And that love which imitates the first is in its place the only desireable and excellent thing that is possible. GODS love in its place is infinitely better then all. Removing it you shake and abolish all. But in such a Creature he desires to be beloved. He made him free, that he might be capable of Loving, for it is impossible to love by constraint or necessity: and having made him free and left him to himself, infinitely desires to be beloved of him. All his own love unto him, and all the glories of Heaven and Earth which are prepared for him, are means for the obtaining of that end, Obligations, Motives, Allurements, Incentives of that Love which GOD desires. If he will not return Love, all are imbittered and made distastful. Infinite Love infinitely desires to be beloved, and is infinitely displeased if it be neglected. GOD desires to take Complacency in all, to see the beauty of his Bride, and the accomplishment of his design, in the Love of his Beloved. And nothing in all Worlds but the love of that Person can be his satisfaction. For nothing can supply the absence or denial of that Love which is his end. For in its place it is the only needful and proper thing, far more desired than all that went before: All that went before was but the Means, this is the thing designed and endeavoured by them. For upon this Return all the sweetness of the rest dependeth. All is made sweet and compleat, and delightful, if this Soul doth love GOD in all these things; if not, they are all made vain, and his love is turned into sour displeasure. All the other things are so far from *alleviating* that they increase his displeasure; the glory and abundance of them is so far from making him to despise this Love, that in respect of these things he the more desires it; because he would not have his labour vain; and his own infinite Love makes him more to esteem the love of this Creature, which is (in its place) his Soveraign object; and for that very cause so beloved and admired by all Angels and Men. Is not then the Love which a man returneth a Magnificent thing!

Certainly if it answers all these preparations and obligations as their end, and be lookt upon as that without which all the Creation is vain and frustrate, it is the most great and marvellous thing in all the World, and is *in its own place* of all other things most highly desired by all Angels and Men; and is the greatest Gift which (in, and by that Soul) can possibly be given. It is esteem of, honour paid to, and delight in, all these great and most glorious things. It contains in it self a *desire* to see GOD pleased with more than the fruition of all Worlds, and of becoming it self the greatest Treasure to his eternal essence of all that is possible. And if this *desire* be not satisfied, all the grandeurs of his eternal Kingdom are to no purpose. But *the desire satisfied is a Tree of Life*. What the Sun is to the Eye, that is Love to the Desire. GODS infinite desire of our Love makes it infinitely delightful to him. *Davids* purpose to build the *Temple* was more accepted than *Solomons* performance. And if one Contrite groan be better than all Sacrifices, to love GOD with all the Soul and Understanding is better than to give him all Worlds. We sacrifice all by Loving him as we ought. We see the Beauty and Glory of all, and offer it all up to him, with infinite Desire, our selves also with infinite Gratitude. Could we make millions of Worlds, infinitely greater and more perfect than this, they should all be his. No delight, no joy, no pleasure can be greater to us, than to see him reigning. He gives all to us, that we might give it all to him: In our Affection and with our Love it is most delightful. Our Affections are the flames and perfumes that enrich the Sacrifice. He is a Spirit to be served in a Spiritual manner: all that we *would* do, we do. Infinite desires and intentions of Pleasing him are real objects to his Eye. The goodness of the Soul, and the Greatness of his Goodness consisteth in them. A Will enlarged with an infinite Fancy is a prodigious depth of goodness when it is all Love. It would do millions of things for its Object! But GOD is incapable of more Worlds: and all that are possible he can make himself: our Magnificence must be shewn in something he cannot do, unless he were in our Circumstance, and which of all things in the World he knows most fit to be done, were he in our places. He cannot be the Soul of any of his Creatures: but would be the Soul of that Soul: the joy and delight of that Soul; the life and glory of that Soul: and that he cannot be, unless that Soul will delight in him, and love and honour him. It is not he must honour himself: but that Soul: His desire is, that that Soul would freely turn, and delight in him freely, of its own accord, would incline it self to consider his Excellencies, and dedicate it self to love and honour him. This is one way for the

Soul to be Magnificent towards Men too: who by Nature delight to see GOD beloved, and satisfied in a point of such infinite importance.

IT is true indeed, that GOD can be full of Indignation and punish: but for love to turn into anger is no compensation for the pleasure it lost by our miscarriage: and to punish is a strange and troublesome work, in which Love is extinguished, or else afflicted. Infinite Love puts an infinite value on the Gift. And I think it is Magnificence to give a Gift of infinite value.

OUR Magnificence towards Men must be laid on a deep and eternal foundation. We must be willing to give our selves to their comfort and satisfaction. And that we cannot do, but by imitating GOD in all his Goodness, studying their felicity, and desiring their love with the same earnestness to the utmost of our power: doing in all places, in all things, in all Worlds, the things they desire: supposing them to be what they ought to be, like Gods themselves.

THE best Principle whereby a man can stear his course in this World, is that which being well prosecuted will make his Life at once honourable and happy: Which is to love every man in the whole [504] World as GOD doth. For this will make a man the Image of GOD, and fill him with the mind and spirit of Christ, it will make every man that is, the Representative of GOD and of all the World unto him. It will make a man to reverence GOD in all Mankind, and lift him up above all Temptations, Discouragements and Fears. It will make him to meet the love of GOD, Angels, and Men, in every Person. It will make a man truly glorious, by making him pleasing to GOD, and universally good to every one; diffusive like the Sun, to give himself to all, and wise to enjoy their compleat Felicity. If there were but one, the Case is evident: supposing more than one, his duty is to love every one the more for all their sakes. For since he mst love all, and they are all to love one, and every one, he must please them all by gratifying their love to one, and by doing so to every one, they are all concerned in the welfare of one, and pleased in the love that is born to every one. This in the state of Glory will be clear, where every one like the Sun shall be clearly seen extending his love to all; though here upon Earth, where our estate is imperfect, by reason of the imperfection of our Knowledge it doth not appear. Our actions are limited: for being finite in our outward demeanour, they must needs be regulated by Justice and Wisdom. But two things come in here to the assistance of Magnificence, whereof the first is the interiour perfection of our Love to all, the second is the universal Satisfaction which the beauty of our outward life will afford at last. Concerning the last, two things are fit to be considered. First, that as GOD has communicated the Sun, by making it visible, to all; and there is not a Star but is seen by all Nations and Kingdoms: so has he communicated the Soul, by making it visible, to all; and there is not a Thought that shall remain uncovered; nor an action, but it shall be seen by all for ever. Secondly, that as GOD himself is admired for his *Inward Love*, so is he for the operations of his *Outward Life*, I mean for his *Works* and *Judgments*. When they saw his *Works* finished, *The Morning Stars sang together, and all the Sons of GOD shouted for joy*.[1] The Elders are represented before his Throne, casting down their Crowns, and saying, *Thou art worthy, O Lord, to receive Glory, and Honour, and Power, for thou hast created all these things, and for thy pleasure they are, and were created*.[2] Where the perfection of GODS Pleasure in the GLORY of the *Creation* is evidently discovered, to be one of the *Joyes of Heaven*; a great matter of their Contemplation, an eternal cause of their Praises. His infinite and eternal Love is that by which he is *All Glorious within:* all the sweetness of his Essence, and all the perfection of the Soul is there: but yet his Saints in the Church Triumphant, sing the Song of *Moses*, and the Song of the *Lamb*,[3] saying, *Great and Marvellous are thy WORKS, Lord GOD Almighty, Just and True are thy WAYES thou King of Saints!* His Works are the substantial Creatures in Heaven and in Earth: his Waies are his proceedings and dispensations among them in all ages. For all shall appear together for ever, the one being *Great* and *Marvellous*, the other beautified with *Truth* and *Justice*. So that neither of these doth swallow up the other, but both are distinct and perfect. Our Love may be infinite on the Inside, and yet our Life be diversified with many limited and particular actions. Now if our Life be like GODS, eternally to be seen; and our Actions in passing pass not away, but in the sphere of our life abide for ever, *our Life all at once* is a mysterious Object, interwoven with many Thoughts, Occurrences, and Transactions; and if it be to be presented to GOD like a Ring, or a Garland, we had need to be very choice in the mixture of our Flowers, and very curious in the Enammel of so *rare a Token*. Perhaps it is his Crown, nay our own; His and our Royal Diadem. It shall shine like a glory about our Souls for ever. That there should be any dirt or blemish in it, is inconsistent with our Felicity: but it is a Magnificent

---

[1] Marginal gloss: Job.
[2] Marginal gloss: Rev. 4.11.
[3] Marginal gloss: Rev 15.3,4,5.

Present if it be enchased with Jewels, well chosen and curiously set, I mean with the most pure and fit elections, the most Wise, and Just, and excellent Actions, the most bright and clear Apprehensions, the most divine and ardent Affections. The last are like Gold, the ground work of the Crown: but the work it self is a mixture of elaborate Distinctions that sparkle in their lustre like Gems of several cuts and colours. An imperial Crown is a Magnificent Present from a King to a King: But a Life like GODS in a sphere, for which Time was lent that it might be well wrought, and presented before him when made perfect, as far surpasseth the most glorious Crown that did ever sit upon Monarchs brows, as that can be supposed to excel a dull *Clod of Earth*, or a piece of *Rusty Iron*. There all Obligations, and Laws, and Duties, and Occasions are interwoven, all our Vertues, and Graces, and Vices, all our Tears, and Devotions, and Prayers, our Servants, the Poor, the Rich, our Relations, Parents, Friends, Magistrates and Ministers are set, and exhibited in their proper places; they appear to the life with all our Behaviors towards them: and though we did deny a Poor mans Request for the sake of another, and this and that, and the other particular action did not at present extend to all: but the Soul was feign to use much wisdom in contracting its operation for the greater advantage, in finding out its Duty, in moderating its Behaviour, in ballancing its occasions and accounts; yet in the result of all, it will be found full of Bounty and Goodness to all, by taking care to be just and pleasing to all in the beauty of its Conversation. When two things it desires to do, are incompatible to each other; it studies which of the two was more just, and fit, and necessary; which tends most to the full and final perfection of its Life; the interest of a Child sometimes carries it from another man, a debt of Necessity is paid with that we would give, for a work of Charity: yet when all is Obedience, Duty, and Love, that life is a most Magnificent Gift. A Wife, a Sister must be respected in her place, a Son, a Servant, a Friend, before a Stranger; if the case be such that one of them only can be relieved. All in the Family, being made in the Image of GOD, as well as the Beggars without doors, or Objects of our Charity. But so much *Goodness* being in the bottom of the design, and so much *Prudence* and *Justice* in the denial: Where his Gold and Silver faileth, his affection may be infinite, and the restraints he sets upon his Actions, be the several cuts and distinctions in the Work, the very true Engravings that make the Jewel, or the Crown *Glorious*. Its *Matter* is *Life* it self, yet the *Workmanship* far excels the *Matter*, when it is as *Accurate* and *Divine* as it ought to be.

This great and deep Thought makes every little act of Life magnificent and glorious, a better Gift to GOD in its place, than the Creation of all Worlds before him. While a mans Love is really infinite towards all, and he is ready to sacrifice himself with *Moses*, and St. *Paul*, for the good of the World: but is fain to set a restraint upon himself for the sake of others. The very grief which true *Goodness* conceives at the deficiency of is power, and the force that lies upon it in so *ungrateful* a Necessity, where it must be an Umpire and a Judge between its Bowels and its Children, is a molestation which he endures in the midst of his duty, filling all Spectators with as much pleasure as him with pain. All shall be remembered, and all these things which are now so grievous, shall themselves become a part of our future Glory.

REMEMBER alwaies thou art about a Magnificent work: and as long as thou dwellest here upon Earth lay every action right in its place. *Let not Patience only, but every Vertue have her perfect work.* Let Wisdom shine in its proper sphere: let Love *within* be infinite and eternal, in the light of true Knowledge it is impossible to exceed: be right in all thy Conceptions, and wise in all thine Elections, and righteous in all thy Affections, and just in all thy Actions; let the habits of Compassion and Mercy appear and break out fitly upon all occasions: and the severity of Justice too for the preservation of the World! Let all be underlaid with solid Goodness, and guided with Prudence, and governed with Temperance, ordered with Care, and carried on with Courage: lay hold on thy Incentives by a lively Faith, and on all the strengths of Eternity by a glorious Hope, let all be sweetened with a gracious Charity, fortified and secured with invincible Meekness, and profitably concealed, and vail'd over with Humility; let thy Contentment put a lustre and grace upon all: let Magnanimity and Modesty appear in thy actions, Magnificence and Liberality act their part; let Resignation to the Divine Will, and Gratitude, come in to compleat all these, and thy Life be beautified with the sweet intermixture of Obedience and Devotion: Thy GODLINESS will be so divine, that all Angels and Men will be perfectly pleased, especially when thou hast wiped out the Miscarriages by the bloud of the Lamb, which in a little chrystal Vial pure and clear thou ought'st alwaies to carry about with thee, when thou hast washed away the defilements contracted in the work, with the Tears of Repentance: Those Tears too he putteth in his Bottles, and they will turn into Jewels. There is not one drop so small, but it shall turn into a Precious Stone, and continue for ever as it were frozen into a Gem. *Many, O Lord my GOD, are thy wonderful Works which thou hast done, and thy Thoughts which are to us-ward: they cannot be reckoned up in order unto thee: If I would declare and speak of them, they are more than can be numbered:*[1] *how precious also are thy Thoughts O GOD; how great is the sum of them! If I should count them they are more in number than the Sand! When I awake I am still with thee!*[2] And with whom else can I be! for thou only art infinite in Beauty and Perfection: O my GOD, I give my self for ever unto thee!

---

[1] Marginal gloss: Psa. 40.5.
[2] Marginal gloss: Psal. 183.17.18; an obvious mistake; see instead Psalm 139.17–18.

CAP. XXXII.

Of Gratitude. It feeds upon Benefits, and in height and fervour answerable to their Greatness. It is impossible to be grateful to GOD without it. A hint of the glorious Consequences of so doing.

WHAT GOD has made us able to do by way of *Gratitude*, you must see in the Chapter of *Magnificence*. The Love wherewith all these things ought to be done, shall be so great in the estate of Perfection, our Charity and Wisdom so directly intend all Angels and Men, and especially GOD above all blessed for ever, our Gratitude and Goodness make us so zealous for their satisfaction, that no pleasure in the whole World shall be comparable to that of being Delightful to them. To receive all is sweet, but to communicate all (adorned thus within the sphere of our own lives) is infinitely beyond all that can be sweet in the reception, both for our glory and satisfaction. There is ever upon us some pressing want in this World, and will be till we are infinitely satisfied with varieties and degrees of Glory. Of that which we feel at present we are sensible: when that want is satisfied and removed, another appeareth, of which before we were not aware. Till we are satisfied we are so clamorous and greedy, as if there were no pleasure but in receiving all: When we have it we are so full, that we know not what to do with it, we are in danger of bursting, till we can communicate all to some fit and amiable Recipient, and more delight in the Communication than we did in the Reception. This is the foundation of real Gratitude, and the bottom of all that Goodness which is seated in the bent and inclination of Nature. It is a Principle so strong, that Fire does not burn with more certain violence, than Nature study to use all, when it hath gotten it, and to improve its *Treasures* to the acquisition of its *Glory*.

THE Holiness of all the work consists in the Fervour wherewith it is done, and if our Love shall in Heaven answer all its Causes, it will be equal to all its Obligations and Rewards, and as infinite in a manner as the excellencies of its objects, the very love of GOD towards all things will be in it, our Love shall be in all his, and his in ours. And if we love GOD, Angels and Men, all Vertue, Grace and Felicity as they deserve; we shall so delight in excellent actions, and in appearing amiable and glorious before them, that we would not for all Worlds miscarry in a tittle: And therefore every defect (even after pardon) will be an infinite *disaster* as well as *blemish*. This is one effect of *Gratitude* in Nature. And if it were not for the Satisfaction of *Jesus Christ*, and the efficacy of Faith and Repentance in his Blood, the least Sinner in all Nature would be eternally miserable, notwithstanding the advantages of *Christs* blood. It is the desire of the Soul to be spotless in it self. And if it be so prophane as to build upon these advantages, without taking care to be as excellent as it is able, it is the most ungrateful Creature in the World, and is too base and dirty, to appear in Glory.

TO talk of overflowing in the disbursments and effusions of Love and Goodness, till our emptiness and capacity be full within, is as impertinent and unseasonable, as to advise a Beggar to give away a Kingdom, or a dead man to breath, or one that is starving to give Wine and Banquets to the Poor and Needy. But when a man is full of blessedness and glory, nothing is so easie as to overflow unto others: to forbid, or hinder him, is to stifle and destroy him. Breath with the same necessity must be let out, as it is taken in. A man dies as certainly by the confinement, as the want of it. To shut it up and deny it are in effect the same. When a man hath the glory of all Worlds, he is willing to impart the delights wherewith he is surrounded, to give away himself to some amiable Object, to beautifie his Life, and dedicate it to the use and enjoyment of Spectators, and to put life into all his Treasures by their Communication. To love, and admire, and adore, and praise, in such a case are not only pleasant, but natural, and free, and inevitable operations. It is then his supream and only joy to be amiable and delightful. For the actions of Love and Honour belong in a peculiar manner to a plentiful estate: Wants and Necessities when they pinch, and grind us in a low condition, disturb all those easie and delicate Resentments, which find their element in the midst of Pleasures and Superfluities. Hence it is, that high-born Souls in Courts and Palaces are addicted more to sweet and honourable excesses, than Clowns and Peasants. The one spend their life in Toil and Labour, the other in Caresses and soft Embraces. Amities and Bounties, Obligations and Respects, Complements and Visits are the life of Nobles: Industry and Care is that of the meaner People. Honours and Adoration are fit for the Temple not for the Market. Soft and tender Affections are more in the *Court*, than in the *Shop* or *Barn*. There is some difference in this respect even between the City and Country. But *Heaven* is the Metropolis of all Perfection. GOD is a mighty King, and all his Subjects are his Peers and Nobles. Their life is more sublime, and pleasant, and free, because more blessed and glorious. Their very Palaces and Treasures are infinite Incentives to the works of honour and delight, and they cannot rest either day or night, but continually cry, *Holy, Holy, Holy, Lord GOD of Hosts, Heaven and Earth are full of the Majesty of thy Glory.* Their Beauties and Perfections enflame one another. Their very Joyes inspire them with eternal Love: and as all Care and Labour are removed, so are all delights and extasies established. Ravishments and Caresses, Adorations and Complacencies, all the force and violence of Love, Charms, Allurements, high Satisfactions, all the delicacies and riches of sweet Affection, Honours and Beauties are their Conversation. Towards GOD, towards themselves, towards each other, they are all Harmony, and Joy, and Peace, and Love: they flie upon Angels wings, and trample upon Spices. *Aromatick* Odours and Flowers are under feet; the very ground upon which they stand is beset with Jewels. Such you know were the foundations of the Walls of the *New Jerusalem,* and the pavement of the Street was beaten Gold. GOD and the Lamb were the Light, and the Temple of it.

THAT we are to *Enjoy* all Angels and Men by communicating our selves unto them, is a little *mysterious:* but may more easily be understood, than a thing so obscure as *The Enjoyment of GOD by way of Gratitude.* That we are to love GOD more than our selves is apparently sure, at least we ought to do it, but whether it be possible, is a question of importance. That we gain infinitely by his Love, is certain; but that we gain more by our own, is prodigious! It is our duty to love him more than our selves, but whether it be our Nature, or no, is doubtful. It is impossible to ascend at the first step to the top of the Ladder. Even *Jacobs* Ladder will not bring us to Heaven, unless we begin at the bottom. Self-love is the first round, and they that remove it, had as good take away all: For he that has no love for himself can never be obliged. He that cannot be obliged cannot delight in GOD: He that cannot delight in him cannot enjoy him: He that cannot enjoy him, cannot love him: He that cannot love him cannot take pleasure in him, nor be Grateful to him. Self-love is so far from being the impediment, that it is the cause of our Gratitude, and the only principle that gives us power to do what we ought. For the more we love our selves, the more we love those that are our Benefactors. It is a great mistake in that arrogant *Leviathan,* so far to imprison our love to our selves, as to make it inconsistent with Charity towards others. It is easie to manifest, that it is impossible to love our selves, without loving other things: Nature is crippled (or if it has her feet, has her head cut off) if Self-preservation be made her only concern: We desire to live that we may do something else; without doing which life would be a burden. There are other principles of Ambition, Appetite, and Avarice in the Soul: And there are Honours, and Pleasures, and Riches in the World. These are the end of Self-preservation. And it is impossible for us to love our selves without loving these. Without loving these we cannot desire them, without desiring cannot enjoy them. We are carried to them with greater ardour and desire by the love of our selves. Preservation is the first, but the weakest and the low'st principle in nature. We feel it first, and must preserve our selves, that we may continue to enjoy other things: but at the bottom it is the love of other things that is the ground of this principle of Self-preservation. And if you divide the last from the first, it is the poorest Principle in the World.

TO love another more than ones self is absurd and impossible. In Nature it is so, till we are obliged; or perhaps till we see it our interest, and find it our pleasure: It is a surprize to an Atheistical fool; That it should be ones interest to love another better than ones self: yet Bears, Dogs, Hens, Bees, Lions, Ants do it: they die for their young-ones. Nurses, Fathers, Mothers do it. Brides and Bridegrooms frequently do it; and so do Friends. All valiant Hero's love their Country better than them selves: *Moses* would have his Name blotted out of the Book of Life rather than the *Israelites* destroyed. St. *Paul* could wish himself accursed from Christ for his Brethren the *Jews:* and they both learnt it of their *Master, who made himself a Curse*, and even Sin *for us*. And it was his interest to do it! If we are immortal, and cannot but be blessed, it must needs be our interest to love him that is more blessed than we, better than our selves; because by that love we enjoy his blessedness, which is more than our own, and by that Love it is made ours and more than ours. Is not all our Glory, and Vertue, and Goodness seated in the excess of this perfect love! Do not all brave and heroical deeds depend upon it? and does not the man deserve to be burnt as an enemy to all the World, that would turn all men into Knaves and Cowards, and destroy that only principle which delivers them from being Mercenary Slaves and Villains; which is *the Love of others!* That alone which renders a man useful to the World is *the Love of others*. He that destroyeth this would pluck up all Gratitude by the roots: all Worth, Goodness, and Honour! No wonder therefore he should be an Atheist, since Nature is so base and abominable before him. But its Principles are oftentimes so generous, in Truth, that they are too great for themselves. Nothing is so ordinary in the false way, as that of loving others better than our selves. Even Dogs have starved themselves to death upon the absence of their Masters. How many Fathers have gone down with sorrow to their Graves, and lost all the comfort of their lives in the death of their Sons! How many Mothers have broken their hearts for the death of their Children! How many Widows have buried themselves alive for the loss of their Husbands; I mean, by sequestring themselves from all the delights and pleasures of the World! How many Lovers dote, and wax pale, and forget their Meat, Sleep, and Employment, and run mad for their Mistresses! Are there no such Examples; or is there no strength in such Examples as these? But to love GOD better than ones self seemeth more unnatural. Ah vile! the more base, and more wicked we! How we should love GOD better than our selves is easie to unfold by the principles of Self love, and Self exaltation. Take it in the manner following: (and when you have seen its possibility, consider the glory of doing it, the benefit, and felicity, and honour that is in it. For it is all worth and pleasure, goodness and beauty, Gratitude and Vertue, wisdom and security, perfection and excellency. We love our selves more in doing it, than it is possible to do without it.)

IT is natural to all them that love themselves, to love their Benefactors, and all those things that are conducive to their welfare, pleasure, satisfaction: And the more they love themselves, the more apprehensive they are of the benefit they receive, and the more prone to love that which occasions it. The more goodness we find in any thing, the more we are prone to love it; and the more we love it, the more to take pleasure in it. And if we find it highly convenient, and extreamly delightful, we had (not seldom) rather die than part with it: we love our selves only that we might live to enjoy that glory, or delight, or beauty, or convenience that we find so agreeable. It often falls out, for want of acquaintance with delightful things, that we think nothing so powerfully sweet, as to engage our Soul, beyond the possibility of retrieving it self: and that nothing can cleave so strangely to our minds, as to be nearer and dearer than Life it self. Yet oftentimes we find men of this opinion changing their minds, when they have chanced to taste some sweetness in Nature, they were not aware of, and then to become such miraculous Converts, that they love not themselves but for the sake of that delight which they have found in the World. I make it a great Question, would men sink into the depth of the business, Whether all Self-love be not founded on the love of other things? And whether it be not utterly impossible without it? Only the love of those things is so near and close to the love of our selves, that we cannot distinguish them, but mistake them for one and the same. If the Sun were extinguished, and all the World turned into a Chaos; I suppose there are few that love themselves so, but they would die, which plainly shews that the love of the World is inseparably annexed with the love of our selves, and if the one were gone, the other would be extinguished: especially if the sweetness of the Air, and its freedom and ease, were changed into fire and torment. For then we would surely desire to die, rather than endure it: which shews that the love of ease and repose is greater than the love of our very Beings, though not so perceivable, till we have examined the business. But if there be any pleasure, or goodness, or beauty truly infinite, we are apt to cleave unto it with adhæsion so firm, that we forget our selves, and are taken up only with the sence and contemplation, of it. The ravishment is so great, that we are turned all into extasie, transportation and desire, and live intirely to the object of our fruition. The power of infinite delight and sweetness is as irresistible, as it is ineffable. And if GOD be all beauty and delight, all amiable and lovely, truly infinite in goodness and bounty, when we see him, and taste the grace of his excellency, the blessedness and glory wherewith we are amazed, possesseth us intirely and becometh our sole and adæquate concern. After that sight it is better perish and be annihilated, than live and be bereaved of it. The fall from so great a height would fill the Soul with a cruel remembrance, and the want of its former glory and bliss be an infinite torment. Now if it loved nothing but it self, it could endure all this; rather than forsake it self, or lose, or be bereaved of its essence, it would endure any misery whatsoever. Or to speak more correct and accurate sence, it would be incapable of any Passion, Patience or Misery, but only that which flow'd from its abolition. Nothing could prejudice it but the change of its Being.

THAT is not likely to love it self after the way which some conceive proper to Self-love, which is willing to forsake it self upon any Misery, and apt to forget it self upon any great felicity. It loves it self that it might enjoy such a pleasure, but loves that pleasure so much beyond it self that it is ready to go out of it self, and is almost beside it self for the fruition of it. Loving it self only for that end, and that chiefly and for its own sake, it loves that far more than it loves it self. And there is no limit nor bound, when it once begins to love any thing more than it self, it may proceed eternally: and provided its Object be infinitely more excellent, it will easily and greedily love it infinitely more than it can it self, and value the continuance of its own life only for the sake of that which it so infinitely esteems and delights in. It is true indeed it presupposes its Capacity: but what would that capacity be worth, were it not for Objects.

WERE there no SUN it were impossible for so fair an *Idea* to be conceived in a Mirror, as is sometimes in a Glass, when it is exposed to the skie. The Mirror is in it self a dark piece of Glass; and how so much fire, and flame, and splendor should come from it while it is a cold Flint or piece of Steel, how it should be advanced by any Art whatsoever to so much beauty and glory, as to have a Sun within it self, and to dart out such bright and celestial beams no man could devise. Yet now there is a Sun, the Matter is easie, 'tis but to apply it to the face of the Sun, and the Glass is transformed. And if GOD dwelleth in the Soul as the Sun in a Mirror, while it looketh upon him, the love of GOD must needs issue from that Soul, for *GOD is love*, and his love is in it. The impression of all his Beauty swallows up the Being of the Soul, and changes it wholly into another nature. The Eye is far more sensible of the Day, and of the beauty of the Universe, than it is of it self, and is more affected with that light it beholds, than with its own essence. Even so the Soul when it sees GOD is sensible only of the glory of that eternal Object: All it sees is GOD, it is unmindful of it self. It infinitely feels him, but forgets it self in the Rapture of its Pleasure.

BUT we leave Illustrations, and come to the reason of the thing in particular. The Soul loving it self is naturally concerned in its own happiness, and readily confesseth it oweth as much love to any Benefactour, as its bounty deserveth. And if the value of the Benefit be the true reason of the esteem, and Reason it self the ground of the return, A little Kindness deserveth a little love, and much deserveth more. Reason it self is adapted to the measure of the good it receiveth, and for a shilling-worth of Service, a shilling-worth of Gratitude is naturally paid. For a Crown or a Kingdom the Soul is enflamed with a degree of affection that is not usual. Now GOD created and gave me my self; for my Soul and my Body therefore I owe him as much as my Soul and Body are worth: and at the first dash am to love him as much as my self. Heaven and Earth being the gifts of his Love superadded to the former, I am to Love him upon that account as much more as the World is worth; and so much more than I love my self. If he hath given all Angels and Men to my fruition, every one of these is as great as my self, and for every one of those I am to love him as much as that Angel or Man is worth. But he has given me his Eternity, his Almighty

Power, his Omnipresence, his Wisdom, his Goodness, his Blessedness, his Glory. Where am I? Am I not lost and swallow'd up as a Centre in all these Abysses? While I love him as much as all these are worth, to which my Reason, which is the essence of my Soul, does naturally carry me, I love him infinitely more than my self; unless perhaps the possibility of enjoying all these things makes me more to esteem my self, and increases my Self-love for their sake more than for my own. Thus when I see my self infinitely beloved, I conceive a Gratitude as infinite in me, as all its Causes. Self–preservation is made so natural and close a Principle, by all the hopes and possibilities to which I am created. Those Hopes and Possibilities are my tender concern: and I live for the sake of my Infinite Blessedness. Now that is GOD: And for his sake it is that I love my self, and for the glory and joy of delighting in him, I desire my continuance; and the more I delight in him, my Continuance is so much the more dear and precious to my self. Thus is GOD infinitely preferred by Nature above my self, and my Love to my self, being thoroughly satisfied, turns into the Love of GOD, and dies like a grain of Corn in the Earth to spring up in a new and better form, more glorious and honourable, more great and verdant, more fair and delightful: more free, and generous, and noble; more grateful and perfect. The Love of GOD is the sole and immediate Principle upon which I am to act in all my Operations.

NOW if you enquire what Advantages accrue by this Love, to the Soul of the Lover, we are lost again in Oceans of infinite Abundance. The strength, and brightness, and glory of the Soul, all its Wisdom, Goodness and Pleasure are acquired by it, founded in it, derived and spring from it: as we have before declared upon the Nature of Love. The solution of that one Question will open the mystery, Whether we gain more by his Love, or our own? All that we gain by his Love amounts to the *Power* of Loving, the *Act* of Loving we gain by our own, and all that depends upon it.

BY his Love he existeth eternally for our Enjoyment, as the Father of GLORY which is begotten by it self: but we do not gain all this by his Love; but by our own. Sone man would say, We gain our Souls and Bodies by the Love of GOD, all Ages and Kingdoms, Heaven and Earth, Angels and Men, infinite and eternal Joyes, because all these were without our care or power prepared by him, and his love alone. They were prepared indeed by *his* Love, but are not acquired, or enjoyed by it. *He so loved the World that he gave his only begotten Son*, and with him all the Laws and Beauties of his Kingdom: but unless we love him, unless we are sensible of his Love in all these, and esteem it, we do not enjoy our Souls or Bodies, Angels or Men, Heaven or Earth, Jesus Christ or his Kingdom: Rather we trample upon all, and despise all, and make our selves deformed. All these do but serve to increase our Damnation, and aggravate our Guilt, unless we love and delight in their Author, and his Love it self will eternally confound us. So that we gain and enjoy the Love of GOD by ours. Now Love returned for Love is the Soul of Gratitude. In that act, and by it alone, we gain all that is excellent: And beside all these become illustrious Creatures. It is more to our avail to be Divine and Beautiful, than to see all the World full of Delights and Treasures. They would all be nothing to us, without our Love. Nothing does so much alienate and estrange the Soul from any Object, as want of Affection. All the Kingdom of Heaven is appropriated and made ours by Love alone. The inferiour perfections of our own Essence are gained by Love, and by it we accomplish the end of our Creation. We receive and enjoy all the benevolence of GODS former Love by ours; are made excellent in our selves, and delightful to GOD, which can never be brought to pass any other way, but by our Love alone. By Loving him as we ought to do, we enable him to take pleasure in us! And this is of all other the greatest benefit. We cloath our selves with the similitude of all his Attributes, and shine in his Image by Love alone. Our Love, as it acquires, crowns our Perfections with his infinite Complacency. *This is my beloved Son in whom I am well pleased*, is a voice that can be directed to none, but him only that loveth GOD with an eternal Love. He cannot rest satisfied in any that hate, or despise him. The eternal complacency and delight of GOD, whereby we are crowned with eternal Glory is acquired, and receives its Being in a manner by Love alone.

NOW to love GOD is to desire Him and his Glory, to esteem him and his Essence, to long for him and his Appearance, to be pleased with him in all his Qualities and Dispositions, or (more properly) in all his Attributes and Perfections, to delight in all his Thoughts and Waies. It is to love him in all his Excellencies. And he that is not resolved to love every Excellency in him, as much as it deserveth, does not love GOD at all: for he has no design to please him. But he that purposes to do it, must of necessity love GOD more than himself, because he finds more Objects for his Love in GOD, than in himself; GOD being infinitely more excellent than he. But if this seem a grievous task, it is not a matter of *Severity*, but *Kindness*. We mistake its nature, the Duty does not spring from any disorder in GOD, not from any unreasonable or arrogant *Selfishness*, as base and foolish men are apt to imagine, but from his Excellency: it *naturally* springeth from the greatness of his *Worth:* And it is our *freedom*, when we see his infinite Beauty, to love it as it *deserveth*. When we so do, we shall infinitely love it *more* than our selves: because it is infinitely *better:* And indeed, shall find it so conveniently seated in the Deity for us, that could it be transposed or remov'd, it would no where else be fit for our fruition. It is that eternal act of Love and Goodness that made all the Kingdom of Glory for us: that Care and Providence that governs all Worlds for our Perfection, that infinite and eternal Act that gave us our Being. That Beauty is it self the Deity, and wherever it appeareth there GOD is. The GOD-HEAD is the Beauty in which we are all made perfect. And because we *were* nothing, we must be infinitely pleased that he *is* Eternal; because it is his eternal Act that gives us a Being: and the Act, Oh how Divine! It is his Beauty and Glory. Can we chuse but love that Act, which is all Goodness and Bounty! Which prepares for, and gives to, us, infinite felicity! If we love our selves we must needs love it, for we cannot forbear to love the fountain of all our delights, and the more we love it, the more ardently we delight in it, the sweeter and more transporting will all our Raptures be, the more feeling and lively, the more divine and perfect will our Souls and our Joyes be: When we know GOD, we cannot but love him more than our selves: and when we do so, his Blessedness and Glory will be more than ours; we shall be more than Deified, because in him we shall find all our Perfection, and be eternally Crowned. We must of necessity sit in his Throne, when we see him enjoying all his Glory, because his Glory is his Goodness to us, and his Blessedness our Felicity: Because in the acts of our Understanding we shall eternally be with him, and infinitely be satisfied in all his Fruitions. That Excellency which obliges us, will enable us to love him more than our selves: and while we delight in him for our own sakes, we shall steal insensibly into a more divine and deeper Delight, we shall love him for his. And even in point of Gratitude adore his Glory.

TO *Adore* and *Maligne* are opposite things: to *Envy* and *Adore* are inconsistent. Self-love is apt to leap at all advantages, and the more we love our selves, the more prone we are to covet and wish whatsoever we see Great and Excellent in another. But he hath conquered our Envy by his infinite Bounty: and made us *able* to adore him by the Perfection of his Essence. To covet the Perfections of him we adore, is impossible. It is impossible to adore him whom we would spoil, and rob of his Perfections. For Adoration is a joyful acknowledgment of the infinite Perfections of an *Adorable* Object, resting sweetly in them with acquiescence and rejoycing. It is prone to add and to offer more. An adoring Soul is in the act of sacrificing it self to the Deity, and with infinite Complacency admiring and adoring all his Glories.

HIS Glories will be inspired into the Soul it self, for the healing of that Envy to which it is otherwise addicted. And instead of Robbery, and Discontentment, and Blasphemy, and Covetousness, the Soul shall be full of Honour and Gratitude, and Complacency: and be glad to see its GOD the full and eternal act of Perfection and Beauty. It was from all eternity impossible there should be any other but he; and he from all eternity has so infinitely obliged us, that were it possible for any other to have been, it would not be desirable. He hath obliged us, and we love him better than any other. Should we fancy or conceive another, a Power from all Eternity acting, should we suppose it possible that a Power besides him might have bin; it mut be just such a Power as this is, and act just in such a manner as this hath done: or it would be displeasing. This hath done all that we can desire, all that all Powers infinite and eternal can do *well:* and therefore all possible Powers are conceived in him. He is the full and adæquate object of all Desire; because the Fountain of all the most Glorious things, and the sole perfect cause of all Enjoyment whatsoever.

CAP. XXXIII.

The Beauty of Gratitude. Its principal Causes. Amity and Communion the great effect of its Nature. The true Character of a Grateful Person. GOD's Incommunicable Attributes enjoyed by Gratitude. All Angels and Men are a Grateful Person's Treasures, as they assist him in Praises. He sacrifices all Worlds to the Deity, and supreamly delighteth to see him sitting in the Throne of Glory.

GOD having prepared the way to Gratitude by infusing generous and noble Principles into the Soul, beautified the Exercise of it by divers other provisions, that conspire to make it amiable and delightful. By the one he made it *Possible,* by the other desirable.

ONE of the greatest ornaments of this *Vertue*, is the *Grateful Sence* of Benefits received: For in it the Felicity of the Receiver consisteth; on it his Grateful behaviour dependeth; by it he is made *Grateful,* or *Acceptable;* and it is one of the great Ends intended in the Gift bestowed by the Donor, whose Satisfaction ought to be regarded highly by every honest and worthy Receiver. That Grateful Sence is the crown of the Gift, the Light wherein its Beauty appears, the Temple of its Honour as it were, the Womb wherein it is conceived, and findeth its life and value perfected.

SHOULD we stand upon the Explication of these, we should have little room for the Fruits and Effects of Gratitude, which are the principal things intended in this Chapter. But in short you may take this account. The greatest Benefits we can receive, are but *Abortive,* or rather turned into *Curses,* without a Grateful acknowledgment of them: All Gifts are but *Carkasses* devoid of Life, unless inspired with that *Sence,* which maketh them *Delightful.* For as Causes without Effects are not Causes; so Blessings, if they Bless not, are falsely reputed Blessings. No Benefit can be Blessings, unless they are *crowned* with our Complacency. They must be conceived the Mind before they can be transformed into Joyes before they can produce those Praises which are the musick of the Benefactors Soul, as well as of the Receivers. They are not *conceived,* unless they are *quickened* with the *Life* of the Receiver, not are they reputed Blessings, till they are had in *Reputation.* An *interior Sence* is the Life and Soul of every Blessing: without which a whole World of Delights would be but a

Chaos, the very Kingdom of Heaven but a Confusion to him for whom it is prepared, and a Soul among the Angels but a *Fool* in Paradice. An Ungrateful Person bereaves himself of the Pleasure, that should spring from his Enjoyment, for he stifles the enjoyment of the Gift he receiveth. He *Eclipses* and extinguishes his own blessedness by the *dulness* of his Soul, and the perversness of his Behaviour. He may be surrounded with *Causes* of Delight, but is not blessed, that is not full of the *Joyes* wherewith he is surrounded. When he is ful of Joyes he must needs overflow with Complacencies; which are the very element of Thanksgiving, the matter and fuel, as well as the Soul of Praises. Were there nothing in a Grateful Sence but this, Gratitude were an incomparable Vertue, because all the effects of infinite and eternal Bounty are by vertue of that Grace applyed to the Soul, and enjoyed thereby, but are lost without it. That certainly must be a great Vertue, by force of which we inherit all things.

AS for the Beauty of the Receiver, it is evident that a *dull* and *heavy* Complexion is the disgrace of his Nature. His Stupidity makes him a worthless piece of *Clay*, that cannot be improved to any advantage. A carelessness and contempt of Benefit springeth from his Sottishness, which maketh him *Ingrateful*, that is, *Odious:* because he cannot be won by Kindness, nor wrought upon by Gifts. But he is more deformed, because he acts in a bruitish manner, *against Reason*; while he faileth to do what is fit and proper on such occasions. It is a base and dirty Temper that cannot be enflamed with the Love of a Benefactor. It is incapable of high and generous *Sentiments*; is dull and dry, insipid and untractable, as dead as a Log of Wood, a crabbed and knotty piece of matter, that cannot be wrought, and only fit for the fire! But a quick and lively Perceiver, a tender Sence, and sprightly Intelligence, is all honour and delight upon the Reception, all activity, life, and vigour, Angelical in his nature, sweet and heavenly; apt to come up to the Benefactor, and answer his desires: He is rich and abundant in amiable Resentments, and prone to make Returns suitable to the Kindness wherewith he is affected. He has a strange kind of Beauty lodged in his Soul; there is a sweet Correspondence, and a delicate Convenience between his Nature and his Benefactors. All his Inclinations are Purity and Praise, he is a great encouragement to the Love of his Benefactor, an ornament to his Person, an admirer of his Worth, an appendix of his Honour, and a pleasure to his Disposition; all Life and Goodness. He is capable of Amity in the heights of its exercise.

A wise and worthy Benefactor designs the felicity and contentment of the Person, to whom he imparteth his Bounties: and if he were able, would do that for him, which above all other things is most to be desired; not *compel* him to be Grateful, whether he would or no; for that would but spoil the beauty of his Return, but make him capable of the best and highest Resentments; that he might have the Joy of seeing his Benefits work kindly. All which are lost and thrown away upon an ungrateful Person. This GOD hath done. He has put brave Principles and inclinations into the Soul of Man, and left him freely to exert them, with infinite desire to see him act freely but generously and nobly. For by this means only, is he made capable of Honour, and the essence of Gratitude consists in the freedom of its operation. Having so made him, and desiring nothing more than a lovely Behaviour, his Joy is as great as his Goodness can inspire, when he sees that sweetness which attends the Operation and the work of Reason, in a Grateful Person: and the Joy which he occasions is his own Joy, in the Soul of his Creature. Of which to rob GOD is a kind of *Spiritual Sacriledge*, and a cruel Murther committed on our selves. For we have an inclination to delight in the Joyes, of which we are the Authors, and by a kind of Eccho, or reflection, find the Pleasure doubled which we take, and which is taken in the communication of our Bounties. And in this there is founded a certain sympathy of Delight, which carries us to feel and be affected with anothers Joy, and makes *it* an Object, and a Cause of ours, nay almost the very Form and Essence of ours, when we are the Author of it. A grateful Soul holds Intelligence with GOD; as it receives his *Bounties*, it delights in his *Complacencies*.

THE great effect of obligation and Gratitude, is Amity and Communion. A Grateful soul is deeply concerned in the Honour of his Benefactor; in his Benefactors Pleasure, Life, and Safety, in all his Successes, Prosperities, Advancements; in all his Felicity and Glory! He is afflicted in all his Afflictions, he is delighted in all his Enjoyments, he is crowned in all his Promotions, he is wronged and injured in all his Affronts, he is touched with the least Displeasure that can befal him: Nay he is more tender of his Benefactors Repose than his own: The apple of his Eye is the tenderest part in himself, yet he had rather have it touched, than the Person of his Benefactor. No wounds can wound him more than those which his Benefactor receiveth, and he in him. His own wounds may kill his Body, but these destroy his Contentment. A thousand Injuries and Calumnies against himself he can forgive, and is never provoked but when his Friend is offended. He slights himself, and prefers his Benefactor: He would make his Face a Stepping stone to his Benefactors Glory. He exposes his body to Swords, and Spears, and Arrows, for his Benefactors safety; he would rather be torn to pieces, and suffer a thousand Deaths, than permit his Benefactor to be slain or dishonoured. Now all this in time of Trial and distress, would seem disadvantagious. But besides the Obligation, there is a Sence of Honour that compels a man thereunto; and a certain beauty in the act of Gratitude, distinct from the goodness of the Benefit, that is so naturally sweet to the goodness of the Soul, that it is better to die than renounce it. And a certain Baseness on the other side, an odiousness in *Ingratitude* (in the very act) so abominable, that it blasts any Safety and Repose that can be gotten by it.

WHERE the Benefits are small, the Vertue of Gratitude is less powerful and perfect: for its strength depends upon its food and nourishment. A thin and spare diet is not very healthful for it. Though all the benefits that are done upon the Earth by Men to Men are infinitely mean, if compared to those which the Godhead does to the least of his Creatures; yet the World is full of the praise of this Vertue, and an Ingrateful man is the most hateful Object living. Former Ages afford us many rare and glorious Examples of the power of Gratitude, and its sacred Zeal for, and tenderness of its Object. The union between the Body and the Soul is nothing comparable to the union of Love and its Beloved, though the Causes are but slight upon which it is founded. The Soul will often forsake its mansion to dwell with its beloved. It esteems all its beauties and Members only for its Beloveds sake. Yet Colours and Features, a little red and white, a sparkling Eye, a brisk Conversation, and a delectable Humor, are all that breed it, all that produce this mighty effect, this prodigy of Nature. There is something more, where the Life and Honour of a man has been saved, by the kindness of a Benefactor: especially if he be rich and amiable that has delivered us. If he be great and honourable that was the Author of the benefit, the obligation is the greater. For the Worth of the Person enter into the nature of the act, and enhances its value. Yet all this put together is exceeded by the Gratitude of a worthy Soul, because his own Worth inclines him to be more *Generous* than the Cause requires, and to magnifie the benefit, by the mighty addition of his own goodness. It is the natural property of Goodness to communicate it self, any occasion of doing it, is instead of a Cause. But when there is a Cause, it is like a spark to Powder, it enkindles a flame in his *Inclination*. All acts of Gratitude have a great deal of sweetness in their own nature, and for the sake of that beauty which is seated in themselves will not be rigorous and exact in their proportions, since it is a beautiful thing to exceed in Goodness. Its own disposition prompts it to do more than is deserved by the Kindness it receives, and if not to conceive it self more obliged than it is, yet to be more honourable in its Returns, than the meer goodness of its Benefactor can exact; because it conceives it self by its own Vertue obliged to be Noble and Munificent, in all its acknowledgments.

BUT however slow Gratitude may be in the Returns which it maketh for smaller benefits, it is infinitely prone to exceed all measure, when it is *infinitely* obliged. Praises are not fed by mean Contentments, but by sublime ones. The acknowledgment is cool, where the benefits are small; and the Contentments imperfect, where they are limited and restrained. Full Satisfaction hath another kind of influence on the Soul of Man, than single Kindnesses, or some few particular Supplies. An infinite Bliss produces more vigorous and joyful efforts, than bare Acknowledgments. Here upon Earth there are disquiets, and desires, expectations and Complaints, and defects, and imperfections fears and interests to be still secured, that lame and darken our Contentment and Gratitude. But in Heaven all these admixtures of alloy are remov'd. The glory of the light in which our Gratitude appeareth, adds lustre and beauty to the increase of its Perfection. In the utmost height of our Satisfaction there is such an infinite and eternal *force*, that our Gratitude breaks out in exulting and triumphing Effusions; all our Capacities, Inclinations and Desires being fully satisfied, we have nothing else to do, but to Love and be Grateful. An infinite and eternal Kingdom given to him that was taken out of Nothing, by a King that is infinite in greatness and beauty; all his Joyes, and all his Treasures! it makes the Soul a fountain of Delights, whose nature is to receive no more, but overflow for ever. When the Soul cometh once to love GOD so infinitely above it self, as the cause requireth, its only delight is to magnifie him and to see him blessed. The beauty and sweetness of its own Gratitude is as rich and divine as all *his* Gifts. It is tempted here infinitely more to exceed its Causes than ever before. Amazements, Admirations, Affections, Praises, Hallelujahs, Raptures, Extasies, and Blessings are all its delights: The pleasure of Loving is its only business; it is turned all into flame, and brightness, and transportation, and excess. It infinitely passees Light and Fire in quickness and motion: all Impediments are devoured, and GOD alone is its Life and Glory. The more Great, the more high, the more excellent he is; the more blessed is it self, the more joyful, and the more contented. Its Nature is to shine, and burn, and admire; to offer, and to sacrifice up it self to its Joyes: And GOD is its soveraign Joy, its perfect happiness. To suspend its beams were to act against Nature. All overtures of Pleasure, Beauty, Glory, Power, Exaltation and Honour it would have added to its happiness. The more Great, the more Good, the Wiser GOD is, the greater is its Happiness. The more he is admired and praised, the greater is its Happiness. The more he is magnified and pleased, the greater is its Happiness. All the Excellencies and Perfections in its Objective bliss, though they are not locally removed, are removed into the Soul of him that enjoyes it; and there express themselves far more powerfully and effectually, than if they were there alone. No joy can be like that of seeing its Creatour adored, no Service like that of magnifying its Beloved, no pleasure like that of delighting its Beloved, no melody like that of praising its Benefactor, no honour like that of obeying its Preserver. All Worlds are its Treasures, because they manifest his Power and Glory; all Angels and Men its Delights, because hey see and acknowledge the beauty of its Soveraign, and eternal *Perfection*; all Creatures the Instruments of its Joy, that celebrate his Praises! In him it enjoyes the glory of all Eternity, the infinite beauty of all Immensity, the innumerable riches of all Worlds, the pleasures and adorations of all the Angels, the state and magnificence of all Empires, the splendour and perfection of all Ages; all which it has in it self, by his infinite Bounty, as it own immediate and proper Possessions; but far more divinely and sweetly enjoyes them, by vertue of its Gratitude and Love, to him, whose they originally are, and from whom they proceeded. For the very true reason why it enjoyes *it self*, and all its *own* Treasures, is because it loves *it self:* And the more it loves *him*, the more it will be delighted with *his* fruitions. It is more concerned, it feels more, it sees more, it tastes more, it possesses more, it rejoyces more in its Object than it self. The imagination and fancy that is in Love frames all the thoughts of its Beloved, in it self; it has an exquisite and tender sence of every change and motion in the mind of its Beloved. *Stir not up, nor awake my Love, till he please*, is the song of a feeling and affectionate Soul. Every prick with a Needles point in its Object, is a stab with a Dagger to it self. Its heart bleeds in every drop of its Objects finger. It loves his Beloved ten thousand times more than it self: and is infinitely more pleased with its exaltation, than its own. True Gratitude is crowned in its Benefactor, enthroned in its benefactor, admired in its benefactor, adored in its benefactor. Nothing in all the World is so easily ravished as Love, nothing is so lively as Love, nothing so lovely! Nothing so violent in its grief or joy, nothing so capable of pain or pleasure: All the Victories and Triumphs of its Saviour are its own. My Joy, my Life, my Crown, my Glory; my exceeding great Reward, my Love, my Soul, my Idol, nay the GOD of my Soul! my All in all! This is the language of Love in it Rapture. Seraphick Love! It is Altar, Heart and Sacrifice, Angelical Love! It is Priest and Temple: All Service, Freedom, Duty, Reward, Desire, Enjoyment, Honour, Praise, Adoration, Thanksgiving, Extasie, Pleasure, Bliss and Happiness. It is all Goodness and Beauty, Paradice, Heaven; the life and Soul of Heaven! All that is incommunicable in GOD, Eternity, almighty Power, supream Dominion, independent Majesty, infinite Immensity, with all the adorations and praises of all the Creatures, are by such a Love and Gratitude enjoyed. Loving GOD more than it self, it is more happy in GOD, than if it were a GOD. Could his Deity be taken away, and seated in it self, the Soul of a Grateful Creature would be grieved at the exchange. Even GOD in his place is perfectly enjoyed. All Envy is by perfect Gratitude removed: All Discontentment at any thing in its Object, especially at its Objects Belessedness is abolished. It is carried above all Thrones, Dominions and Powers, and still ascends eternally higher, the higher its Object is exalted. Could it be miserable in it self, it would be happy in its Object: but the higher it is exalted, the more is its Creatour delighted. If the resentment be wholly Spiritual, the Soul perhaps may be transformed to Gratitude, as Gratitude is to Contentment, and Praise, and Thanksgiving. But it will have not Body, no frail and corruptible Flesh, no bones or members to look after. All its operations are of one kind, all its works and concernments are the same. It has no Fear, or Care to divert it; no impediment, or danger, or distraction. Pure Gratitude is so divine a thing that the Soul may safely wish to be turned *all* into Gratitude. Its Employment and Nature are all one, acknowledgment and benevolence united together. It sacrifices all Worlds to the Deity, and with infinite delight desires to offer all Honour and Glory to him. It is very sensible, that it can never pay so much Honour to GOD as is his due, unless it be assisted with all the Tongues of Men and Angels. It goes along with their Joyes, and consents to their Praises. In them it adores, and by them it admires, with them it conspires, and takes in all their powers and divine affections. It sees with all their Eyes, hears with all their Ears, speaks with all their Mouths, and useth all their Hearts in loving and adoring. All the tendencies and operations of

Universal Nature are subservient to its desires. It surmounts the Songs of *David*, and yet we know how earnestly he exhorted all Creatures to praise him. *Praise ye the Lord: Praise him in the Sanctuary; Praise him in the Firmament of his Power; Praise him in his mighty Acts; Praise him according to his excellent Greatness. Praise him in the Heights; Praise him all ye Angels; Praise him all his Hosts: Praise him Sun and Moon, Praise him all ye Stars of light. Praise him ye Heaven of Heavens!* And when all is done, it still confesseth, that *his Name is exalted far above all Blessing and Praise.*

HE that praiseth GOD only for his Health, and Food, and Rayment, and for his blessing on his Calling (as too many only do) either is very ignorant, or upon a strict scrutiny, will be detected for upbraiding GOD. for the meanest of his bounty. For his Love must infinitely be defective, that is able to bestow Gifts infinitely more, yet giveth us none but these. He that sees not more Causes of Joy than these, is blind and cannot see afar off: The very truth of Religion is obscure to him, and the cause of Adoration unknown. He wanteth ten thousand demonstration of the Love of GOD, and as many Incentives to enflame his Soul in the Return of Love, that is unacquainted with these high and mighty bounties. No man can return more Blessings than he receiveth: nor can his Praises exceed the number (and greatness) of his Joyes. A House is too little, a Kingdom is too narrow for a Soul to move in. The World is a confinement to the power, that is able to see Eternity, and conceive the Immensity of Almighty GOD! He that can look into infinite Spaces, must see them all full of delights, or be infinitely displeased. How like an Angel doth he soar aloft, how divine is his life, how glorious and heavenly; that doth converse with infinite and eternal Wisdom, intermeddle with all the delights of GOD, assume the similitude of his knowledge and goodness, make all his Works his Riches, his Laws his Delights, his Counsels his Contemplations, his Wayes his Joyes, and his Attributes his Perfections! He that appropriates all the World, and makes it his own peculiar is like unto GOD, meet to be his Son, and fit to live in Communion with him. The Kingdom of GOD is made visible to him to whom all Kingdoms are so many Mansions of Joy, and all Ages but the streets of his own City. The man that sees all Angels and Men his Fellow-members, and the whole Family of GOD in Heaven and Earth, his own Domesticks, is fit for Heaven. As he hath more encouragements to believe in GOD, and to delight in him, so hath he mor concerns to engage his fear, more allurements to provoke his desire, more incentives to enflame his love, and more obligations to compel his obedience: More arguments to strengthen his Hope, more materials to feed his Praises, more Causes to make him Humble, more fuel for Charity to others, more grounds of Contentment in himself, more helps to inspire him with Fortitude, more reward to quicken his Industry, more engagements to Circumspection and Prudence, more ballast to make him Stable, more lights to assist his Knowledge, more sails to forward his Motion, more employments in which to spend his Time, more attractives to Meditation, and more entertainments to enrich his Solitude. He hath more aids to confirm his Patience, more avocations from Injuries to Meekness, more wings to carry him above the World, and more Gates to let him into Heaven. He hath more *Withholders* to keep him from Sin, more aggravations to increase his Guilt, more odious deformities in every Vice, more waters to augment his Tears, more motives to Repentance, and more Consolations upon his Reconciliation: More hopes to relieve his Prayer, more bounds to secure his Prosperity, more comforts in Adversity, and more Hallelujah's in all Estates: More delights to entertain his Friends, more sweetness in his Conversation, more art to conquer his Enemies, more Feasts in abstemious Fasts, more and better sawce than other at his Feasts, innumerable Companions night and day, in Health, in Sickness, in Death, in Prison; at his Table, in his Bed, in his Grove, in his Garden, in the City, in the Field, in his Journy, in his Walk, at all times, and in all places. He hath more antidotes against Temptation, more weapons in his Spiritual Warfare, more balsom for his Wounds, and more preservatives against the contagion of Worldly Customs. From this Spring of *Universal Fruition* all the streams of Living Waters flow that refresh the Soul. Upon this Hing all a mans Interests turn, and in this Centre all his Spiritual Occasions meet. It is the great Mystery of Blessedness and Glory, the Sphere of all Wisdom, Holiness and Piety, the great and ineffable Circumstance of all Grace and Vertue, the Magazine and Storehouse of all Perfection.

An APPENDIX.

Of Enmity and Triumph: Of Schism and Heresie, Fidelity, Devotion, Godliness. Wherein is declared, how Gratitude and Felicity inspire and perfect all the Vertues.

I Should here have ended all my discourse on Vertue, had it not been necessary to speak something of our Enemies. Since there was never any man so Wise but he had some, it is not to be expected that the most Vertuous Man living should be altogether without them. *Moses*, and *David*, and *Elijah* and *Daniel* had Enemies, so had our Lord Jesus Christ himself. *Joseph* had some in his younger daies, and *Solomon* some in his Old age: Of all the Prophets I find *Samuel* the most clear and exempted from them. But this I observe, that Men of great and transcendent Principles, of staid and well-govern'd Passions, of meek and condescending Behaviours, highly kind and serviceable in their Age, free from the spots and blemishes of the World, have frequently arrived to an universal Applause and Honour, and moved in a sphere so high above the Nation in which they lived, that as if they had been Creatures of another World, they have enjoyed a Veneration above their Degree, and been surrounded with a repose, that makes them look like Angels in a kind of Heaven; that that Heaven which they enjoyed upon Earth, was the Work, and the Reward, and the Crown of Vertue. Thus *Moses* after his long Meekness, and invincible Fidelity to the *Jewish* Nation, was in the close of his life most exceedingly honour'd by all the People, and lamented after his death by a million of Persons, that felt the disastre of so great a loss. *Joseph* suffered much by the Envy of his Brethren in the beginning, and the Lust and Slander of his Mistress. But after he had once been the Saviour of the Land of *Egypt*, and of his Fathers Family, his Vertue being known, he enjoyed a long life of Glory and Honour, and of the abundance of his own peace and tranquility, communicated a repose and prosperity to his Nation. *Joshua* did run the hazard of being stoned for crossing the perverse humour of the *Jews*, when he returned from searching the Land of *Canaan*: but from *Moses*'s death, throughout all his life afterwards was an absolute Prince among his own People, and a glorious Victor over all their Enemies. *Samuel* was from his Infancy chosen of GOD, and from *Dan* even to *Beersheba* they knew he was established to be a Prophet of the Lord.

The honour of his Communion with Heaven joyned with his great Integrity and Gravity on Earth, gave him a Reputation that made him Greater than all the Elders in the Land. And it is very apparent, that the eminent Holiness, and Goodness, and great Wisdom of these Men made them to prevail, with GODS blessing on their Vertues, and to reign like Benefactors, and magnificent Patriots of their Country. *Solomon* was by his Wisdom exceeding glorious, till he revolted from GOD: and those Mischiefs with befel *David* after he came to the Throne did spring from his Fall in the matter of *Urias*. These things I note to encourage Men to Vertue. For though our Lord Jesus Christ, and his Apostles, were persecuted to the Death, yet two things are very considerable: First, that their Glory surmounted the Rage of all their Enemies, and continues immortally shining throughout all Kingdoms and Ages: Next, That they were born to troublesome Times, and were to break the Ice for all their Followers. For their business was extraordinary, to change the state and condition of Kingdoms, to alter the publick Rites of Religion both among *Jews* and *Gentiles*, and therein to shake and dissettle the Secular Interests of Millions, as well as to touch and offend the Conscience, in defaming that for which so many Ages had so great a Veneration. This created all the difficulty in their Lives. But where the publick Rites of Religion are approved, and a Man is born in peaceable and quiet Times, I do not see but the most Vertuous Men inherit all the Honour and Esteem of the People, and whatever estate and degree they are of, reign in the fullest and freest Prosperity. Nor has the Death of Christ so little prevailed upon Earth, but that all the World does now take notice of the Glory of his Doctrine, and far better understand the excellency of Vertue than they did before: They feel and admire its influences. Insomuch that as some Vertuous Men grow contemptible by their Vices; so do the most debauched and vicious Men, find a Necessity of appearing Vertuous, if they mean to be Honourable; for as all Errours receive their strengths from some Truths professed by Hereticks, so do all Vices and vicious Persons owe their supports to the powerful strengths of those Vertues on which they lean, and which they use (though in a wicked manner) for their own security. For they cannot rise and thrive in the World without some Vertue, or shew of Vertue at least, to cover and help out their Vices. Three things I desire you to note seriously, when you have first observed, that it is a very hard matter to hate an Excellent Man, or contemn him, when he is known. The one is, that Enmities and Disgraces are like the pangs and throws of the

New-Birth, they fall like Storms and Showers upon budding Vertues in their spring and greeness: When a Man first being to be Vertuous he is despised, suspected, unknown; it may be censured and hated: But when he has made himself eminent and conspicuous, is a man of tried and approved Vertue, well known for a Person of Honour and Worth; the first Envies and Censures abate; and if he constantly exercise all Honesty and Goodness with great activity, courage, and prudence, he shall conquer all his Enemies, and inherit the benefit of his own Vertues in the peace and tranquility of his happy Condition. Note also, that it is not so much the Malignity of the World, as some Vice of the Proficient, or some occasion that Religious men give the World to blaspheme Religion by some Infirmity or other, that makes them to be hated. And this I note, because I would have you not cry out of other Mens Corruptions, so much as of your own. There is a little Pride, or Covetousness, or Laziness, or Scorn, or Anger, or Revenge, some one Deformity or other, that gives Men advantage against us, when they deride at our Profession: but under the Name and Notion of Vertue no Man was ever yet upbraided. As a Fool perhaps, and a Coward (but not as a Wise and gallant Man) he may be scorned. Thirdly, Some Secular Interest may put People together by the Ears, but no Man is hated for being perfectly Vertuous. Misapprehensions, Slanders, Injuries, Quarrels about Estates and Possessions may arise; but where the Land is at peace, and the True Religion established, no Man is hated for being Wise, and Good, and Holy, and Chaste, and Just, and Liberal, and Honest, and Merciful, and Meek, and Couragious, but the more admired for being Holy and Blessed, when he joyns all GODS Vertues together. A man may be perverse and turbulent, a Schismatick and a Heretick, and by a rash and erroneous Zeal bring many Enemies and Penalties on himself, while he rails against the Magistrates, and reviles the Bishops and Pastours of the Church, breaks the Laws, and disturbs the Kingdom, prophanes and blasphemes GODS publick Worship, and endeavours to overthrow the established Religion and Discipline among us. But all the Troubles which a man brings on himself by any such means as these, are not to be fathered on Vertue, but rightly to be ascribed to their proper Causes. Had he that suffered them been more Vertuous, he had been less miserable. And truly this I may say for the glory of Christianity, Where it is freely and purely Professed in any Nation or Kingdom (as at present in Ours) a Man may be as divine and heavenly as an Angel. And if he be Liberal, and Kind, and Humble, and Cheerful, especially if withal he be Undaunted and

Couragious, most exceedingly Honest and Faithful in his dealings; the more Holy and Divine he is, the more he is commended and valued in the Land: but if he have any *flaw* the greater stir he makes in Religion, the more he is hated. He loses his Credit, and undergoes the Censure of a supercilious Hypocrite.

AS for the Enemies which Strife and Contention about Worldly Goods occasion to a Vertuous Man, he is no more liable to them than other persons: And yet when he meets them, he has far more advantages over his Enemies than other Men. For being full of Courage, he dares do any thing that is fit against them, and that sparkle of the Lion makes them to dread him: whereas a Coward is baffled and run over in a moment. Being full of Temper and Humility, he is not apt to exasperate them, and make them mad, as hot and angry Spirits are apt to do. By Kindness he obliges, and wins, and softens them: By Prudence he knows how to manage them, and all his other Vertues come in as so many strengths against them. Being Just he never quarrels but in a *Good Cause*; being Good and Merciful, he is not apt to make an Enemy: Being Wise and Holy his Soul is in another World, and it is no trivial Injury that can make him *contend:* Being Liberal and Magnanimous he is prone to do Heroical things, and to make himself Venerable to his very Adversary: And above all to tender and to love his Soul, and to steer all the Contention to both their benefit. We rail on the World when the fault is in our selves. The most of Men professing Vertue are but Children in Worth; very weak, and very defective: And too timorous too, GOD knows. They neither trust GOD enough, nor carry Vertue to the height. Vertue is base and not Vertue, while it is remiss: It never shineth gloriously and irresistibly, till it be acted almost in a *desperate* manner. He only is the *Great* Man, that contemns Danger, Life, and Death, and all the World, that he may be supreamly and compleatly Vertuous.

ENEMIES may sometimes spring from Envy. And indeed there alone lies the Core of the Matter: when some Men imperfectly Vertuous, abhor others for being more Excellent than themselves; at least for being more Honoured, and more Prosperous. Here again Temporal Interest is the ground of the Enmity. For thus our Saviour was hated by the Scribes and Pharisees. *Pilate* knew that they delivered him for Envy. But the main pretext and Cause of his Condemnation, was the Testimony of those that heard him say, *He would destroy the Temple*. Without which, and his imputed *Blasphemy* they could hardly have killed him. But he came to die, and was the less solicitous. Where these publick Cases are away: They that envy Vertuous Men are generally Men of equal rank and degree with themselves; but a Man truly Vertuous will out-strip them, as far as a Swallow will a Snail; all his Inferiours, and all his Superiours that understand him, and the most also of his Equals, and all they too, if he invents wayes and methods to oblige them, will at last be won to confess and acknowledge him. But in the mean time he grows, and thrives, and enjoyes their very Enmity. He never speaks ill of them behind their backs. He is not a jot discouraged, nor exasperated, he pities *their* Weakness, and is humble under the sence perhaps of his *own:* He is careful to give them no advantage against him: He confides in GOD, and strengthens himself in hope of Divine assistance: He rejoyces exceedingly that he has the opportunity of Forgiving, and considers how many Vertues he has to exercise upon that Occasion. It makes him to exult, when he considers that these Enemies are the Instruments and Materials of his greater Glory. He foresees the Victory, and delights in the Triumph. And besides all this, He is obliged by Jesus Christ to forgive greater Wrongs than these, and gladly yields some Trials of his Obedience: He has an infinite felicity in daily View, and remembers he is a Pilgrim in a strange Country. He is dead to the World, and alive unto GOD. The Moon is beneath his feet, and so are all fickle and transitory things. He is cloathed with the Sun, and walketh in the Light, environed with the beams of his own Enjoyments. If his Enemy be able to do him a Mischief; (which to a man perfectly Vertuous seldome happens) he turns it into Good, which a Foolish and a Vicious Man cannot do: He sinks not under it, but plunges out again, and surmounts it altogether: immediately forgives it, and can after cheerfully serve his Enemy. For his part he will be an Enemy to no man in the World. He knows his Duty and his Master: the value of Souls, and the excellency of Vertue: His very Gratitude to GOD and Jesus Christ is enough to make him go through a thousand greater and more terrible brunts than these.

I would not have Men ingrateful to Jesus Christ; nor blind to themselves. I know very well that the Age is full of Faults, and lament it: but withal I know, it is full of Advantages. As Sin abounds, so does Grace also superabound. Never so much clear Knowledge in any Age: Learned Ministers, multitudes of Sermons, excellent Books, translated Bibles, studious Gentlemen, multitudes of Schollers, publick Liberty, Peace and Safety: all great and eminent Blessings. There were many disorders in the Church of *Corinth*, and yet the Apostle tells them of their *Reigning*, and wishes, Would to GOD he did reign with them! after their City had a little flourished in peace, and received Religion:

and makes his Comparison between them and himself after such a manner, that when it is considered, it would make one apt to think the Reigning of the Saints, which is spoken of in the Book of the *Revelations*, were either now *present* or already *past. Now ye are full* (saith he) *now ye are rich, ye have reigned as Kings without us, and I would to GOD ye did reign*,¹ *that we also might reign with you. For I think GOD hath set forth us the Apostles last, as it were appointed to Death: for we are made a spectacle to the World, and to Angels, and to Men: We are fools for Christs sake, but ye are wise in Christ; we are weak, but ye are strong: Ye are honourable, but we are despised. Even to this present hour we both hunger and thirst, and are naked, and are buffeted, and have no certain dwelling place.* A small matter will make a Saint to Reign, by reason of the greatness of his interior Bliss. If he be not buffetted and cast out of doors; having Food and Rayment, with his Godliness it is *Great Gain*. Especially when Kings and Princes *yield a professed Subjection to the Gospel of Christ*. For then *all the Kingdoms of the World become the Kingdoms of the Lord, and of his Christ:* When the Cross is exalted above the Crown, and the Kings Palaces surmounted by the magnificence of our Saviours Temple, and there is no Idolatry or Poyson in the Church, but a pure publick worship, when the very Laws and Magistrates countenance Religion, and those Apostles that were once persecuted and cast out as Vile, are now glorified and admired for their Sanctity. Men may be Christians publickly and in the face of the Sun, it is horrible ingratitude to be unsensible of the advantage, to calumniate, and reproach, and disturb the Church, as if it were a sink of *Paganisme*. Rather we should admire and adore GOD Almighty, *that other men laboured, and we are entered upon their Labours.* We inherit the blood, and toyl, and sweat of the Martyrs, they bore the burthen and heat of the day, and we enjoy the victory and the peace they acquired. This is one, but not one of the least of GODS Mercies for which we should be Grateful.

THAT all the business of Religion on GODS part is Bounty, Gratitude on ours, and that this Gratitude is the sphere of all Vertue and Felicity, easily is discerned after the first intimation. Gratitude is all that is to be expressed here upon Earth, and above in Heaven. All our Complacencies in his infinite Highness, all our Delights in his eternal Praises, all our Adorations, Extasies, and Offerings, all our Joyes and Thanksgivings, are but the Feathers and the Wings of that Seraphim in Glory. All the Acknowledgment, and Faith, and Hope, and Repentance,

---

¹ Marginal gloss: 1 Cor 4.

all the Obedience and Resignation of a Sinner upon Earth, all his Care and fear to offend, all his Desire and Endeavour to please, all his Worship and Charity, all his Courage, and Perseverance, and Patience, all his Fidelity, Devotion, and Godliness, are but Gratitude in several dresses, as Time, Place, and Occasion require. Sermons are to inform and assist our Gratitude, Sacraments to revive and exercise its vertue. Vertues themselves are our Aids to bring us thereunto. Upon Sabbaths it enjoyes a Rest, that hath something in it of Heaven; and it is a hard matter to be wicked in the Sanctuary. But in ordinary Conversation, in Shops and Taverns, in the Camp, in the Navy, at a Feast, or in a Journey, to retain the Sence of all Mercies, and to carry all thee Vertues and Graces about a Man, is not ordinary for a Common Christian. But that which does realize our Gratitude, and make it perfect, is a true Fidelity to GOD and our selves, which is an acquired habit, or a Grace infused, by vertue of which we keep all those Promises which we made to GOD in our holy Meditations, and all those holy Resolves which in our best Retirements we put upon our selves to do his Will, even in the midst of all Assaults and Temptations. It is a Vertue by which we remain Constant in all Persecutions and Allurements; not warping, or moving aside on any Consideration; neither melting with Pleasures, nor flinching at Distresses; but continuing *faithful to the death, that we may obtain the Crown of Life*. He certainly that sees himself a King of all Worlds, and Brother to our Lord JESUS CHRIST (who hath said, *He that doth the will of my Father, is my Mother, Sister, and Brother:*) will not be wrought on to forsake or hazard so great a Bliss. His knowledge of its Perfection will animate his Soul with all *Fidelity*.

IT will draw him from the World too, and make him desire to be much alone, that he may be much with GOD. A Covetous man will be telling his Monies, an Ambitious man aspires to be alwaies near the Kings Person, an Epicure is for his Wine, or Women, or Feasts continually. A Vertuous man is more Covetous, more Ambitious, more prone to Celestial Epicurisme, if I may so speak, than all the World besides: And so art thou, if thou art really engaged in the study of Felicity. A Pious man has greater Treasures, higher Honours, more pure Pleasures, sincerer and truer Delights, a more glorious Friend than all the Earth beside. Why should we not enjoy him, why should we not retire to adore him, why not delight in Devotion and Communion with him? There a Man is to feed by sweet Contemplation on all his Felicities: He is there to pray for open Eyes, and a pure Heart, that he may see GOD. There thou art to exercise thy strengths, and acquaint thy self with him, to look into all Ages and Kingdoms, to consider and know thy self, to expaciate in the Eternity and Immensity of GOD, and to gain that GODLINESS, which with real Contentment is *Great Gain*. There thou art to stir up thy self, *by way of a pure Remembrance*, to recollect thy scattered and broken Thoughts, and to cloath thy self with all thy necessary Perfections.

FOR Godliness is a kind of *GOD-LIKENESS*, a divine habit, or frame of Soul, that may fitly be accounted *The fulness of the stature of the Inward Man*. In its least degree, it is an Inclination to be like GOD, to Please him, and to Enjoy him. He is *GOD-LIKE* that is high and serious in all his Thoughts, humble and condescending in all his Actions, full of love and good-will to all the Creatures, and bright in the knowledge of all their Natures. He delights in all the Works of GOD, and walks in all the Wayes of GOD, and meditates on all the Commandements of GOD and covets all the Treasures of GOD, and breaths after all his Joyes! He that hates all that *GOD* hates, and desires all the *GOD* desires, and loves all that *GOD* loves, and delights in all his delights, is *GODLY:* He that aspires to the same End, by the same Means, and forms himself willingly to the same Nature. Every Like in Nature draweth to its Like, the Beautiful, and the Wise, and the Good, and the Aged; but especially the *GOD-Like*. There is more reason why they should delight in each other. They have more Attractives and Incentives. *GODLINESS*, or *GOD-LIKENESS* is the cement of Amity between *GOD* and *MAN*. Eternity and immensity are the sphere of his Activity, and are often frequented, and filled with his Thoughts. Nothing less than the Wisdom of *GOD* will please the *GOD-LIKE Man*: Nothing less content him, than the Blessedness and Glory of his Great Creatour. He must enjoy GOD, or he cannot enjoy himself. That is, he must rest satisfied in him, as the Creatour, the Lawgiver, the Lord and Governour of the World; and for that end must be compleatly satisfied with the Glory and Perfection of all his Works, and Laws, and Wayes. He must delight in all his Counsels, that he may enjoy him as the Great Counsellour of all Nature; and see the Beauty of his Mind, that he may take pleasure in him as the Blessedness of the Angels, the Redeemer of Men, the Sanctifier of his Elect People, and the Soveraign End of all things. He must enjoy him as his own supream and eternal Object, his King, his Father, Bridegroom, Friend, Benefactour, All in all. Which he can never do, till he sees *GOD* to be the best Father, the best King, the best Benefactour, Bridegroom and Friend in all the World: Nor that, till he sees the Beauty of the whole Creation, the great and wonderful things of his Law, the marvellous glory of his All-wise dispensations, the Sacred perfection of his Decrees, and the nature of his Essence: And all these must be as sweet and satisfactory to himself, as they are to the Deity. To be GOD-Like is a very sublime and most glorious Perfection: which no man can attain, that is not either *curiously* satisfied in all these things, or *humbly* confident of their Beauty and Perfection. And for this Cause have we thus written upon all the Vertues, that all that need it, and read the Book may be elevated a little higher than the ordinary Rate, have something more erect and Angelical in their Souls, be brought to the Gates (at least) of GODS Kingdom, and be endued with GODLINESS a little more compleatly by their Care, than hitherto they have been; because they know, both *that GOD is, and is a Rewarder of them that diligently seek him.*

FINIS.

Textual Emendations and Notes

Emendations are recorded by page and line numbers. References to previous volumes of *The Works of Thomas Traherne*, ed. Jan Ross (Cambridge, 2005–) are given with volume and page numbers. References to Marks or the University of Illinois are to *CHRISTIAN ETHICKS*, eds. Carol L. Marks and George Robert Guffey (Ithaca, New York, 1968). References to *Christian Ethicks: or, Divine Morality* are to the 1675 edition printed for Jonathan Edwin.

To the Reader

6. 9   them, comma is followed by a colon in the Yale text; deleted to correspond to the complete section.
6. 16   Bounty, Traherne planned a topic for 'Bounty' in *CH*, Vol. II, p. 523.
6. 40   Atheism, see *CH* under 'Atheist', Vol. III, pp. 325–32.
7. 16   *Yet indeed it is not he*, printed as '*be*' in the Yale text.
7. 28   *Actions*, see *CH*, 'Action', Vol. II, pp. 188–97, as well as 'Activity', Vol. II, pp. 198–207.
7. 40   trample them under feet, see Matthew 7.6 and Hebrews 10.29; Traherne uses many biblical references which are not direct quotations but are interwoven into his prose as they fit his purposes; also he often quotes from memory.
8. 16   *Creation. for,* Yale text has a full stop after 'Creation'; WF, CUL (7.61.8 / Keynes T.4.10.), BCL, WCO, Union, University of Illinois have a comma. Corrected in WTN, BL, CUL and Union copies. Marks (p. 6) has a comma after '*Creation*'. It was Traherne's habit to use a full stop as a comma.

The Contents

10. IX   *attaineth the best*, printed as '*attaineth best*' in WTN, BL, CUL (7.61.8 / Keynes T.4.10), BCL, WF, WCO, Yale, Union, University of Illinois. Corrected by editor.
10. XV   *Of what Nature*, printed as '*Of Nature*' in Yale, WTN, BL, CUL (7.61.8 / Keynes T.4.10), BCL, WF, WCO, Union, University of Illinois. Corrected by editor.
10. XVII   *excellencies*, as in Yale; Guffey (p. 291) notes that Yale text reads 'excellenlenies' and corrects to 'excellencies'. The Yale text reads however 'excellencies'.

Chapter I

17. TITLE *Virtue is desired*, in the chapter summary 'is' is unclear; in The Contents it clearly reads 'is'.
17.   8   Acquisition, printed as 'Acquiston', in WTN, BL, CUL (7.61.8 / Keynes T.4.10,), BCL, WF, WCO, Yale, Union, University of Illinois. Corrected by editor.
17. 14   Means, Guffey notes (p. 291) that the Yale text printed as 'mean'; it printed however '*Means*' on the title page as well as in the chapter title in the text (p. 114); printed as '*Means*' in WTN, BL, CUL (7.61.8 / Keynes T.4.10), BCL, WF, WCO, University of Illinois.
18. 11   Means in Order, thereunto, Marks (p. 13) has a comma after 'thereunto'; WF, BCL, Yale, WCO, Union and University of Illinois have a semicolon after 'thereunto': 'order thereunto; and the'.
18. 36   Accident, see *CH*, 'Accident', Vol. II, pp. 109–23.
19.   3   under the Notion, printed as 'under Notion' in WTN, BL, CUL (7.61.8 / Keynes T.4.10), BCL, WF, WCO, Yale, Union, University of Illinois. Corrected by editor.
19.   4   in the Enjoyment, text is blurred and uneven in Yale. Corrected by editor.
20. 18   acquired and enjoyed, 'and' printed as 'an' in WTN, BL, CUL (Keynes T. 4.10 / 7.61.8), BCL, WF, WCO, Union, University of Illinois. Final 'd' added in ink to 'an' in Yale text. Corrected by editor.
20. 23   things unknown, comma inserted by editor.
20. 35   but puts Life, 'puts' printed as 'put' in Yale text. Corrected by editor.
20. 36   Felicity cannot, comma after 'cannot' in WTN, BL, CUL (7.61.8 / Keynes T.4.10), BCL, WF, WCO, Yale, Union, University of Illinois. Comma deleted by editor.

Chapter II

23.   4   Bliss, first letters of words are often printed in italics; I have omitted them because of the inconsistency within the text.
24.   5   thinking it impossible to be, 'impossible' printed as 'impossiable' in WTN, BL, CUL (7.61.8 / Keynes T.4.10), BCL, WF, WCO, Yale, Union, University of Illinois.
24.   7   Race set before us, see Hebrews 12.1.
24. 16   our perfection, both here, and hereafter, printed in the Yale text with no spaces between the words; this happens often throughout the text.
24. 18   we are to remember, that our, in the Yale text the comma comes after 'that'.
24. 25   trophies far, final 'r' in 'far' printed in superscript in the Yale text, 'fa^r' and may have been written by hand in ink. WF, CUL, BL WTN read 'far'.
24. 28   contemplate the Nature of the Highest Felicity, printed as 'contemplatetheNatureofthehighestFelicity' without spaces between the words.
25.   4   Relation, Use and, printed with no spacing between the words in the Yale text: 'Relation,Useand.'
25. 20   that is Lovely, printed as 'Louely' in WTN, BL, CUL (7.61.8 / Keynes T.4.10), BCL, WF, WCO, Yale, Union, University of Illinois. Corrected by editor.

26.	2	is a thorow, no comma after 'thorow' in WTN, BL, CUL (7.61.8 / Keynes T.4.10), BCL, WF, WCO, Yale, Union, University of Illinois. Corrected by editor; inserted by editor.
26.	18	the children of God … be glorified together, see Romans 8.16,17.
26.	20	our light Affliction … eternal Weight of Glory, see 2 Corinthians 4.17.
26.	22	beholding as in a glass … Spirit of the Lord, see 2 Corinthians 3.18.
26.	25	They are worthy … that have pleasure therein, see Psalm 111.4,2.
26.	40	and to patience, missing comma after 'patience'.
27.	1	'brotherly kindness' missing comma after 'kindness' in WTN, BL, CUL (7.61.8 / Keynes T.4.10), BCL, WF, WCO, Yale, Union, University of Illinois.
26. 34 –27.	3	He hath given … Saviour Jesus Christ, see 2 Peter 1.3–7,11.
27.	10	Breadth, and Length, and Depth, no spacing in the Yale text between words.
27.5–12		to the God … fulness of God, see Ephesians 3.14–19; the speaker is Paul, not Peter, which Traherne does not mention. There may be some confusion here.
27.	12	Fulness of God … Temple of the Holy Ghost; scripture references are as follows: filled with the fulness of God (Ephesians 3.19); to enter into his Kingdom and Glory (1 Thessalonians 2.12); to be translated into his Image (Romans 8.29); Heir of God, and a joynt Heir with Christ (Romans 8.17); Temple of the Holy Ghost (1 Corinthians 3.16,17).

Chapter III

28.	1	BEFORE, printed as 'BEfore' in WTN, BL, CUL, (7.61.8 / Keynes T.4.10), BCL, WF, WCO, Yale, Union, University of Illinois. Corrected by editor.
28.	21	we make them, printed as 'we making' in WTN, BL, CUL (7.61.8 / Keynes T.4.10), BCL, WF, WCO, Yale, Union, University of Illinois. Corrected by editor.
28.	29	and Art, has been, 'has' printed as 'have' in WTN, BL, CUL (7.61.8 / Keynes T.4.10), BCL, WF, WCO, Yale, Union, University of Illinois. 'Has' refers to 'Wisdom' so that 'has' is correct (see also Marks, p. 24).
30.	3	*Soul*, printed as 'Soul', S not in italics in WTN, BL, CUL (7.61.8 / Keynes T.4.10), BCL, WF, WCO, Yale, Union, University of Illinois. Corrected by editor.
31.	1	the parable of the unprofitable Servant, perhaps a reference to Matthew 14.30–34.
31.	27	orderd Habits alone, printed as 'orderd Habits alone' in WTN, BL, CUL (7.61.8 / Keynes T.4.10), BCL, WF, WCO, Yale, Union, University of Illinois. Traherne often omitted the final internal 'e' in words; the different renderings do not hinder understanding the text.
31.	32	Long Custom Inuring, 'Inuring' printed as 'in uring' in WTN, BL, CUL (7.61.8 / Keynes T.4.10), BCL, WF, WCO, Yale, Union, University of Illinois. Corrected by editor.
31.	35	we were created,] 'created' missing final full stop in WTN, BL, CUL (7.61.8 / Keynes T.4.10), BCL, WF, WCO, Yale, Union, University

		of Illinois. Corrected by editor. Bracket was not closed in the Yale text; supplied by editor.
31.	38	A vertuous Habit, printed as 'vertuous, habit' in Yale; missing comma in WTN, BL, CUL (7.61.8 / Keynes T.4.10), BCL, WF, WCO, Union, University of Illinois. Corrected by editor.
32.	20	Are made Vertuous, missing comma after 'Vertuous' in WTN, BL, CUL (7.61.8 / Keynes T.4.10), BCL, WF, WCO, Yale, Union, University of Illinois. Corrected by editor.
32.	21	in the Beginning, printed as 'Begnining' in Yale and WTN.
32.	21	Vertues in, the beginning, no comma after 'Vertues in' in WTN, BL, CUL (7.61.8 / Keynes T.4.10), BCL, WF, WCO, Yale, Union, University of Illinois.
32.	37	Whether it be Glory, 'Whether' printed as 'Wether' in WTN, BL, CUL (7.61.8 / Keynes T.4.10), BCL, WF, WCO, Yale, Union, University of Illinois. Corrected by editor.

Chapter IV

34.	6	Fear, comma missing in Yale, WTN, BL, CUL (7.61.8 / Keynes T.4.10), BCL, WF, WCO, Union, University of Illinois. Corrected by editor.
36.	31	Idle, printed with lower case as 'ɪdle' in some but capitalized in WTN, BL, CUL (7.61.8 / Keynes T.4.10) and Yale. Corrected by editor.
36.	40	to struggle, printed as 'strngl' in Yale copy.
37.	6	also, in relation, printed as 'also in [line break] in relation', in WTN, BL, CUL (7.61.8 / Keynes T.4.10), BCL, WF, WCO, Yale, Union, University of Illinois. Corrected by editor.
38.	39	for that Incarnation, printed with semi-colon 'Incarnation;' in WTN, BL, CUL (7.61.8 / Keynes T.4.10), BCL, WF, WCO, Yale, Union, University of Illinois. Printed with comma in the Yale text. Corrected by editor; comma inserted by editor.
39.	22	Atheism, being, printed with a comma after Atheism in WTN, BL, CUL (7.61.8 / Keynes T.4.10), BCL, WF, WCP, Yale, Union, University of Illinois. Marks deleted the comma (p. 34). Corrected by editor. See *CH*, 'Atheist', Vol. III, pp. 324–32.
40.	17	underneath, the Satisfaction, no spacing between words in Yale copy.
40.	22	his Laws are sweeter … Gold and Silver, see Psalm 19.8–10.

Chapter V

41.3–4		'obscure, Angels,' and 'unserviceable, Felicity' and 'impossible, were there no Knowledge,' in the Yale copy these phrases and lines run together: 'obscure,Angels'; 'unserviceable,Felicity'; 'impossible,were'.
41.	8	GOD is Light and in him is no Darkness at all, see 1 John 1.5.
41.	15	in the Soul, printed as 'in Soul' in WTN, BL, CUL (7.61.8 / Keynes T.4.10), BCL, WF, WCO, Yale, Union, University of Illinois. Corrected by editor.
41.	20	For all Powers, when transformed into Act, are Acts themselves, see *CH*, 'Act,' Vol. II, pp. 170–87.
41.	30	which to us, no spacing between words, 'whichtous', in WTN, BL, CUL (7.61.8 / Keynes T.4.10), BCL, WF, WCO, Yale, Union, University of Illinois. Corrected by editor.

Textual Emendations and Notes

41. 31   be perfect, as our Father … is perfect, see Matthew 5.48.
42. 6   WERE a Man a Seraphim by Essence, see *CH*, 'Angell', Vol. III, pp. 60–81; *CYB*, 'Meditations and Devotions on St Michael's Day', pp. 207–27, especially p. 216, where Traherne charts the 'Nine Orders among the Holy Angels'.
43. 33   'Dam' is a catch-word at the bottom of page 57 in the text and 'mage' at the top of the next page in the text. Corrected by editor.
45. 30   In his Presence there is fulness of Joy … for evermore, see Psalm 16.11.
45. 39   that Nature never made any Power in vain, a common notion in Traherne. *CH*, 'Human Ability', Vol. II, p. 29, and 'Angell', Vol. III, p. 67.
46. 13   Plato makes him the very Light of the understanding, and affirms, that as three Things are necessary to Vision, the Eye rightly prepared, the object conveniently seated, and Light to convey the Idea to the Eye; so there are three things required to compleat and perfect Intelligence, an understanding Eye, an Intelligible Object, and a Light intelligible in which to conceive it.
46. 20   In thy Light we shall see Light, see Psalm 36.9.
46. 23   For his Light is the Life of men, see John 1.4.
47. 23   Image of God: If his, printed in the Yale text as '*If his*'.
47. 25   Abilities, see *CH*, 'Human Abilitie', Vol. II, pp. 22–34.
47. 33   that he that overcometh … inherit all Things, see Revelation 21.7.
48. 2   when his essence and his Works; in the Yale, CUL (7.61.8 / Keynes T.4.10), BL, and WTN copies, the word is awkwardly printed at the beginning of a line at the inner margin as 'eslence' and may be a misprint of 'essence' or 'excellence'; WF, BCL, Union, and University of Illinois read 'essence'. Marks (p. 43) records 'essence' without note.
48. 7   infinitely, printed as 'in finitely' in WTN, BL, CUL (7.61.8 / Keynes T.4.10), BCL, WF, WCO, Yale, Union, University of Illinois. Corrected by editor.
48. 7   Adorations, see *CH*, 'Adoration', Vol. II, pp. 244–54.

Chapter VI

50. 31   an absent Good, see *C* 1.2.
50. 32   Attainment, see *CH*, 'Attainment', Vol. III, pp. 376–84.
51. 17   conformable, printed as 'comformable' in WTN, BL, CUL (7.61.8 / Keynes T.4.10), BCL, WF, WCO, Yale, Union, University of Illinois. Corrected by editor.
52. 6   all Beauty and Goodness, and Holiness, and that, printed as 'Goodness, and Bounty, and Holiness, and that' in WTN, BL, CUL (7.61.8 / Keynes T.4.10), BCL, WF, WCO, Yale, Union, University of Illinois. Corrected by editor.
52. 36   familiarly, printed as 'familiary' in Yale, BL, CUL, and WTN.
52. 38   can look into *Eden*, missing comma after '*Eden*' in WTN, BL, CUL (7.61.8 / Keynes T.4.10), BCL, WF, WCO, Yale, Union, University of Illinois. Comma inserted by editor. Marks inserts a comma (p. 48).
53. 39–40   *Video meliora proboque, Deteriora Sequor*, "I see the better way and approve, but follow the worse way," from Ovid, *Metamorphoses*, Book VI, 349–51.
54. 10   to all its Objects; when it is well understood, there may be a comma after

'Objects' but a semi-colon or full stop is necessary for clarity, printed with semi-colon in WTN, BL, CUL (7.61.8 / Keynes T.4.10), BCL, WF, WCO, Yale, Union, University of Illinois.

54. 12 Perfection, printed as 'Perfeon' in WTN, BL, CUL (7.61.8 / Keynes T.4.10), BCL, WF, WCO, Union, University of Illinois. Yale text reads 'Perfectio n'. Corrected by editor.

Chapter VII

55. 4 *GOD is Love*, see 1 John 4.8.
56. 23 Nor is it onely in GOD, printed as 'is onely it in' in WTN, BL, CUL (7.61.8 / Keynes T.4.10), BCL, WF, WCO, Yale, Union, University of Illinois. Corrected by editor.
56. 27 does it embrace, printed as 'embraces' in WTN, BL, CUL (7.61.8 / Keynes T.4.10), BCL, WF, WCO, Yale, Union, University of Illinois. Corrected by editor.
57. 13 Services, printed as 'Service', in WTN, BL, CUL (7.61.8 / Keynes T.4.10), BCL, WF, WCO, Yale, Union, University of Illinois. Corrected by editor.
57. 24 awaken, printed as 'a waken' in WTN, BL, CUL (7.61.8 / Keynes T.4.10), BCL, WF, WCO, Yale, Union, University of Illinois. Corrected by editor.
58. 9 one, printed with semi-colon 'one;' in WTN, BL, CUL (7.61.8 / Keynes T.4.10), BCL, WF, WCO, Yale, Union, University of Illinois. Marks has a semi-colon after 'one' (p. 53). Corrected by editor.
59. 10 in the Spirit, printed as 'in Spirit' in WTN, BL, CUL (7.61.8 / Keynes T.4.10), BCL, WF, WCO, Yale, Union, University of Illinois. Corrected by editor.
59.12–15 *every Creature ... and to the Lamb for evermore*, see Revelation 5.13.
59. 16 commanded, printed as 'commaned' in WTN, BL, CUL (7.61.8 / Keynes T.4.10), BCL, WF, WCO, Yale, Union, University of Illinois. Corrected by editor.
59. 16 *enter into the Joy of his Lord*, see Matthew 25.21,23.
59. 17 Saviour, printed as 'Savionr' in Yale WTN, BL, CUL (7.61.8 / Keynes T.4.10), BCL, WF, WCP, Union, University of Illinois.
59.18–19 *Lord will make his Wise Servant Ruler over all his Goods*, see Matthew 24.47.
59. 19 in one place, printed as 'in one-place' in WTN, BL, CUL (7.61.8 / Keynes T.4.10), BCL, WF, WCP, Yale, Union, University of Illinois. Corrected by editor.
59. 19 *and over all that he hath*, see Luke 12.44.
59. 19 hath, in another, missing comma in WTN, BL, CUL (7.61.8 / Keynes T.4.10), BCL, WF, WCO, Yale, Union, University of Illinois. Corrected by editor.
59. 40 *neither eye hath seen ... Heart of Man to conceive*, see 1 Corinthians 2.9.
61. 20 to feel its own Efficacy, there is an unnecessary comma in WTN, BL, CUL (7.61.8 / Keynes T.4.10), BCL, WF, WCO, Yale, Union, University of Illinois. Deleted by editor.
62. 8 the fruition of his Gifts), we are, missing comma after 'Gifts)' in WTN, BL, CUL (7.61.8 / Keynes T.4.10), BCL, WF, WCO, Yale, Union, University of Illinois. Inserted by editor.

Chapter VIII

- 63. 11   *Deus me solum dedit toti mundo* ... see *C* 1.15.
- 64. 9   Right, printed as 'Righ' in WTN, BL, CUL (7.61.8 / Keynes T.4.10), BCL, WF, WCO, Yale, Union, University of Illinois. Corrected by editor.
- 64. 18   Actors, printed with a comma in the Yale text. Corrected by editor.
- 64. 32   Knowledge, missing comma in WTN, BL, CUL (7.61.8 / Keynes T.4.10), BCL, WF, WCO, Yale, Union, University of Illinois. Corrected by editor.
- 64. 35   want, printed as 'wont' in WTN, BL, CUL (7.61.8 / Keynes T.4.10), BCL, WF, WCO, Yale, Union, University of Illinois. Corrected by editor.
- 65. 25   Felicity, printed with a semi-colon after 'Felicity;' in WTN, BL, CUL (7.61.8 / Keynes T.4.10), BCL, WF, WCO, Yale, Union, University of Illinois. Corrected by editor.
- 66. 5   Number, printed as 'Nunber' in WTN, BL, CUL (7.61.8 / Keynes T.4.10), BCL, WF, WCO, Yale, Union, University of Illinois. Corrected by editor.
- 66. 22   Actions)., printed as 'Actions;) with no full stop after parenthesis in WTN, BL, CUL (7.61.8 / Keynes T.4.10), BCL, WF, WCO, Yale, Union, University of Illinois. Corrected by editor.
- 66. 28   Thought of ours, comma printed after 'Thought' in WTN, BL, CUL (7.61.8 / Keynes T.4.10), BCL, WF, WCO, Yale, Union, University of Illinois. Corrected by editor.
- 67. 7   Apprehensions, printed as 'Apprenhensions' in WTN, BL, CUL (7.61.8 / Keynes T.4.10), BCL, WF, WCP, Yale, Union, University of Illinois. Corrected by editor.
- 67. 9   Conscience and please, printed as 'Conscience and and please' in WTN, BL, CUL (7.61.8 / Keynes T.4.10), BCL, WF, WCO, Yale, Union, University of Illinois. Corrected by editor.
- 67. 27   of the fall, printed as 'of fall' in WTN, BL, CUL (7.61.8 / Keynes T.4.10), BCL, WF, WCO, Yale, Union, University of Illinois. Corrected by editor.
- 67. 34   Neighbours, missing comma after 'Neighbours' (which comes at the end of the line) in WTN, BL, CUL (7.61.8 / Keynes T.4.10), BCL, WF, WCO, Yale, Union, University of Illinois. Corrected by editor.
- 68. 7   Acceptance, see *CH*, 'Acceptance', Vol II, pp. 77–84.

Chapter IX

- 69. TITLE   *attaineth the best*, printed as '*attaineth best*' in WTN, BL, CUL (7.61.8 / Keynes T.4.10), BCL, WF, WCO, Yale, Union, University of Illinois. Corrected by editor,
- 69. 2   whether, comma after 'whether' in WTN, BL, CUL (7.61.8 / Keynes T.4.10), BCL, WF, WCO, Union, University of Illinois. Corrected by editor.
- 69. 4   of the Soul, Yale text reads 'of Soul' as does Marks (p. 65).
- 69. 22   Allurement, see *CH,* 'Allurement', Vol. II, pp. 363–70.
- 70. 16   infinitely, printed as 'in finitely' in Yale, CUL (7.61.9 / Keynes T.4.10), WTN, BL.
- 71. 18   Power in every, Yale, CUL (7.61.8 / Keynes T.4.10), BL and WTN copies read 'very'.
- 71. 21   Willing, Decreeing, missing comma after 'Willing', 'Willing Decreeing' in

		WTN, BL, CUL (7.61.8 / Keynes T.4.10), BCL, WF, WCO, Yale, Union, University of Illinois. Corrected by editor.
71.	32	Treasures, printed as Treasnres in Yale.
72.	6	*For of him, and by him, and to him are all things*, see Romans 11.36.
72.	11	becometh an act, comma after 'becometh' in WTN, BL, CUL (7.61.8 / Keynes T.4.10), BCL, WF, WCO, Yale, Union, University of Illinois. Corrected by editor.
72.	12	inward, printed as 'in [line break] ward' in WTN, BL, CUL (7.61.8 / Keynes T.4.10), BCL, WF, WCO, Yale, Union, University of Illinois. Corrected by editor.
72.	28	Creatures, printed as Greatures in WTN, BL, CUL (7.61.8 / Keynes T.4.10), BCL, WF, WCO, Yale, Union, University of Illinois. Corrected by editor.
72.	28	prepared, final 'd' corrected in ink in Yale text.
73.	3	Wisdom, missing comma in WTN, BL, CUL (7.61.8 / Keynes T.4.10), BCL, WF, WCO, Yale, Union, University of Illinois. Corrected by editor.
73.	12	Beautiful, printed as 'Beatutiful' in WTN, BL, CUL (7.61.8 / Keynes T.4.10), BCL, WF, WCO, Yale, Union, University of Illinois. Corrected by editor.
73.	35	World, 'W' formed with two capital letters 'V'.
74.	20	Wisdome, 'W' formed with two capital letters 'V'.

Chapter X

75.	1	Wisdome, unclearly printed in Yale, CUL (7,61.8 / Keynes T. 4.10), and WTN copies and may be 'Wisnome'. Corrected by editor.
75.	3	It is Wisdome, 'W' formed with two capital letters 'V'.
75.	9	Righteousness of Esteem, printed as 'Right [line break] teousness,' 'Rightteousness', in WTN, BL, CUL (7.61.8 / Keynes T.4.10), BCL, WF, WCO, Yale, Union, University of Illinois. Corrected by editor.
76.	8	akin printed as 'a kin' in WTN, BL, CUL (7.61.8 / Keynes T.4.10), BCL, WF, WCO, Yale, Union, University of Illinois. Corrected by editor.
76.	25	*to fulfill all righteousness*, see Matthew 3.15.
78.	24	infinite, printed as 'nfinite' in WTN, BL, CUL (7.61.8 / Keynes T.4.10), BCL, WF, WCO, Yale, Union, University of Illinois. Corrected by editor.
78.	31	Expectation, printed as 'Expectations' in WTN, BL, CUL (7.61.8 / Keynes T.4.10), BCL, WF, WCO, Yale, Union, University of Illinois. Corrected by editor.
79.	6	contentment, printed as 'contentment;' in WTN, BL, CUL (7.61.8 / Keynes T.4.10), BCL, WF, WCO, Yale, Union, University of Illinois. Corrected by editor.
79.	26	Amiable and Delightful, printed as 'Amiable and [line break] and Delightful' (duplication probably due to the line break) in WTN, BL, CUL (7.61.8 / Keynes T.4.10), BCL, WF, WCO, Yale, Union, University of Illinois. Corrected by editor.
80.	3	not work; but, printed as 'not work but' in WTN, BL. CUL (7.61.8 / Keynes T.4.10), BCL, WF, WCO, Yale, Union, University of Illinois. Corrected by editor.
80.	4	ever in action and in indeed the Act it self, in the Yale text the 'r' in 'ever'

		and the 'f' in 'self' are in superscript; both come at the end of a line; the printer may have used the superscript to make the word fit into the line, although both lines are badly spaced.
80.	23	Goodness printed as 'Godness' in WTN, BL, CUL (7.61.8 / Keynes T.4.10), BCL, WF, WCO, Yale, Union, University of Illinois. Corrected by editor.
80.	39	*perfect, as our Father which is in Heaven is perfect*, see Matthew 5.48.
81.	1	*know as we are known*, see 1 Corinthians 13.12.

Chapter XI

82.	9	to which it is profitable, printed as 'it it profitable' in WTN, BL, CUL (7.61.8 / Keynes T.4.10), BCL, WF, WCO, Union, University of Illinois. Corrected in the Yale text to 'it is'. Corrected by editor.
82.	17	Nature of the Air, see *CH*, 'Air', Vol. II, pp. 354–61.
82.	28	to give Account of his Actions, see *CH*, 'Account', Vol. II, pp. 124–32.
83.	1	Will and Understanding, printed with full stop after 'Understanding.' in WTN, BL, CUL (7.61.8 / Keynes T.4.10), BCL, WF, WCO, Yale, Union, University of Illinois. Corrected by editor.
83.	25	Moral Goodness is an Alacrity, see *CH*, 'Alacritie', Vol. II, p. 362.
84.	36	All the Wonder is, awkwardly printed with 'All the' at the end of the line and 'Wonder is' at the beginning of the next; comma overlaps with the 'e' of 'the'. Printed as 'All the, Wonder is' in Yale, WTN, BL, CUL (7.61.8 / Keynes T.4.10), BCL, WF, WCO, Union, University of Illinois. Corrected by editor.
85.	8	fate in Nature., There is no full stop in Yale, CUL (7.61.8 / Keynes T. 4.10) and WTN. Corrected by editor.
85.	25	what he is for ever., missing full stop after 'ever' in WTN, BL, CUL (7.61.8 / Keynes T.4.10), BCL, WF, WCO, Yale, Union, University of Illinois. Corrected by editor.
86.	14	*Inasmuch as ye have done it to the least of these my Brethren, ye have done it to me*, see Matthew 25.40.
86.	24	to do our selves. because, Marks (p. 82) changes full stop to a semi-colon; Traherne however often used a full stop in place of a comma, colon or semi-colon. I have left it as it appears in WTN, BL, CUL (7.61.8 / Keynes T.4.10), BCL, WF, WCO, Yale, Union, University of Illinois.
86.	26	Which that we may do, 'Which' formed with two capital letters 'V'.
86.	35	Absence, see *CH*, 'Spiritual Absence', Vol. II, pp. 39–47.
86.	35	influences to them, printed as 'them!' in WTN, BL, CUL (7.61.8 / Keynes T.4.10), BCL, WF, WCO, Yale, Union, University of Illinois. Corrected by editor.
87.	22	all, as he is:, printed as 'all, as [line break] as he is' (as as) in WTN, BL, CUL (7.61.8 / Keynes T.4.10), BCL, WF, WCO, Yale, Union, University of Illinois. Corrected by editor.
87.	29	unspeakable and full of Glory, see 1 Peter 1.8.
87.	35	World, formed with two capital letters 'V'.
87.	38	also that they should, printed as 'also that, that they' in WTN, BL, CUL (7.61.8 / Keynes T.4.10), BCL, WF, WCO, Yale, Union, University of

87. 39   Illinois. Corrected by editor.
If we enter *Into his Eternal Glory*, perhaps a reference to 1 Peter 5.10.
88. 5   Sence and feeling, printed as 'Sence and [line break] and feeling' (and and) in WTN, BL, CUL (7.61.8 / Keynes T.4.10), BCL, WF, WCO, Yale, Union, University of Illinois. Corrected by editor.
89. 7   their own Consent.), missing full stop after 'Consent' in WTN, BL, CUL (7.61.8 / Keynes T.4.10), BCL, WF, WCO, Yale, Union, University of Illinois. The final parenthesis appears to have been inserted by hand in ink. Full stop inserted by editor.
89. 10   endeavoured as much as is, printed as 'much as [line break] as, in WTN, BL, CUL (7.61.8 / Keynes T.4.10), BCL, WF, WCO, Yale, Union, University of Illinois. Corrected by editor.
89. 15   that are possible, to be Good, comma after 'possible' missing in Yale, WTN, CUL (7.61.8 / Keynes T.4.10), BCL, WF, WCO, Yale, Union, University of Illinois. British Library has 'are possible'.
90. 26   *GOD is good to ... mercy is over all his Works*, see Psalm 145.9.
90. 33   is a far Greater. If it be, printed with comma after 'Greater' in WTN, BL, CUL (7.61.8 / Keynes T.4.10), BCL, WF, WCO, Yale, Union, University of Illinois. Corrected by editor.

Chapter XII

91.   At the bottom of the page, centered, is the signature M3. The M signature begins at Chap. XI, M1, p. 161, and in this text, p. 89, line 19; and it ends at Chap XII, M8, p. 175, and in this text p. 93, line 32. Because this signature is damaged in the Folger copy there are no references to WF in *CE* from this point on. See Introduction, p. xxi.
91. 4   all Beauty, and his Goodness, printed as 'all Beauty, his Goodness' in WTN, BL, CUL (7.61.8 / Keynes T.4.10), BCL, WCO, Yale, Union, University of Illinois. Corrected by editor.
91. 6   its own Holiness, and the Beauty of Holiness, printed as 'is all Beauty, and his Goodness' in Yale, CUL (7.61.8 / Keynes T.4.10), BL, BCL, WCO. WTN. Marks (p.87) prints as above, is its own Holiness, and the Beauty of Holiness.
91. 8   doth apprehend affect, missing comma after 'apprehend' in WTN, BL, CUL (7.61.8 / Keynes T.4.10), BCL, WCO, Yale, Union, University of Illinois. I have left it as it appears in the text because it does not hinder understanding.
91 27   Holiness of the Object., missing full stop in WTN, BL, CUL (7.61.8 / Keynes T.4.10), BCL, WCO, Yale, Union, University of Illinois. Corrected by editor.
92. 12   *The Beauty of Holiness*, see Psalms 29.2, 96.69; 2 Chronicles 20.21; 1 Chronicles 16.29.
92. 21   and is the real, printed as 'and the is real' in WTN, BL, CUL (7.61.8 / Keynes T.4.10), BCL, WCO, Yale, Union, University of Illinois. Corrected by editor.
92. 23   *Holy, Holy, Holy, Lord GOD of Hosts*. Traherne is perhaps quoting from the *Book of Common Prayer*, the communion service: 'Therefore with Angels and Archangels ... Holy, holy, holy, Lord God of Hosts, heaven and earth are full of thy glory'; it may also be a reference to Isaiah 6.3 and

Revelation 4.8. The Sanctus probably originated with Clement of Rome's (c. 96) first epistle to the Corinthians, quoting Isaiah 6.3: 'He exhorteth us therefore to believe on Him with our whole heart, and to bring no idle thing nor cares into every good work. Let our boasts and our confidence be in Him: let us submit ourselves to His will; let us mark the whole host of His angels, how they stand by and minister unto His will. For the scripture saith, Ten thousands of ten thousands stood by Him and thousands of thousands ministered unto Him: and they cried aloud Holy, holy, holy is the Lord of Sabaoth; all creation is full of His glory. Yea and let us ourselves then, being gathered together in concord with intentness of heart, cry unto him as from one mouth earnestly that we may be made partakers of His great and glorious promises. For he saith, Eye hath not seen and ear hath not heard, and it hath not entered into the heart of man what great things He hath prepared for them that patiently await Him.' 1 Corinthians 2.9 (J. B. Lightfoot, *The Apostolic Fathers*, edited and completed by J. R. Harmer (Grand Rapids: Baker Book House, 1973), p. 27); The Douay-Rheims Bible (1582–1610) also reads 'Holy, holy. Holy, the Lord God of Hosts'.

93. 32 *Dead flies corrupt the Apothecaries Oyntment, so doth a little folly him that is in Reputation for Wisdome and Honour*, see Ecclesiastes 10.1, *Oxford Dictionary of English Proverbs* (third edition, p. 270); and Morris Tilley, *A Dictionary of Proverbs in England in the Sixteenth and Seventeenth Centuries* (p. 224).

93. 35 Stain, printed as 'Srain' in WTN, BL, CUL (7.61.8 / Keynes T.4.10), BCL, WCO, Yale, Union, University of Illinois. Corrected by editor.

93. 36 the Rule of ours, printed as 'Ruled of ours' in WTN, BL, CUL (7.61.8 / Keynes T.4.10), BCL, WCO, Yale, Union, University of Illinois. Marks reads 'Ruler' (p. 90). The reading is uncertain.

94. 9 understand, printed as 'vnderstand' in WTN, BL, CUL (7.61.8 / Keynes T.4.10), BCL, WCO, Yale, Union, University of Illinois. The letter 'v' was often used for 'u' in the sixteenth and seventeenth centuries.

95. 11 the right use of their Liberty, printed as 'the right right use' in WTN, BL, CUL (7.61.8 / Keynes T.4.10), BCL, WCO, Yale, Union, University of Illinois. Corrected by editor.

Chapter XIII

99. 5 *for He that Loveth another hath fulfilled the Law*, printed as '*for the He that Loveth another hath fulfilled Law*' in WTN, BL, CUL (7.61.8 / Keynes T.4.10), BCL, WCO, Yale, Union, University of Illinois. See Romans 13.6–8, corrected by editor to agree with the AV.

99. 31 Justice, printed with semi-colon 'Justice;' in WTN, BL, CUL (7.61.8 / Keynes T.4.10), BCL, WCO, Yale, Union, University of Illinois. Corrected by editor.

99. 32 flourisheth, as the Laws, printed 'flourisheth,as' with no space between 'flourisheth' and 'as' in WTN, BL, CUL (7.61.8 / Keynes T.4.10), BCL, WCO, Yale, Union, University of Illinois. Marks has a semi-colon instead of a comma (p. 96). Corrected by editor.

99. 38 But where Tradesmen, there is an illegible mark after 'where', perhaps a semi-colon or exclamation mark; it has been omitted in the present text; printed without punctuation in WTN, BL, CUL (7.61.8 / Keynes T.4.10), BCL,

		WCO, Yale, Union, University of Illinois.
100.	5	Affections, printed as 'Affections' in WTN, BL, CUL (7.61.8 / Keynes T.4.10), BCL, WCO, Yale, Union, University of Illinois. Corrected by editor.
100.	13	Justice is a Severe Vertue, printed as 'is a [line break] a Severe' in WTN, BL, CUL (7.61.8 / Keynes T.4.10), BCL, WCO, Yale, Union, University of Illinois. Corrected by editor.
100.	24	*He that is faithful in a little … faithful also in much*, see Luke 16.10; Matthew 24.47.
100.	36	Seruant, as in, WTM, BL, CUL (7.61.8 / Keynes T.4.10), BCL, WCO, Yale, Union, University of Illinois, with full stop deleted by hand in ink in Yale text. The letter 'u' was often used as a 'v' in the sixteenth and seventeenth centuries.
100. 36 –101.	2	*Blessed is that Servant … gnashing of Teeth*, see Matthew 24.46–61.
101.	35	and feel the Wound, printed as 'feel. The' in WTN, BL, CUL (7.61.8 / Keynes T.4.10), BCL, WCP, Yale, Union, University of Illinois, with full stop deleted by hand in ink. Corrected by editor.
102.	4	Servants, printed as '*Seruants* in WTN, BL, CUL (7.61.8 / Keynes T.4.10), BCL, WCO, Yale, Union, University of Illinois. The letter 'u' was used for a 'v' in the sixteenth and seventeenth centuries. Corrected by editor.
102.13–15		and must in other Discourses more full and copious (on that Theme) be shewn. And to those we refer you. Traherne may be referring to his own works, such as *CH*, where he planned a topic 'Justice', see Vol. II, p. 524.

Chapter XIV

103.	19	Holiness of God, in Yale, CUL (7.61.8 / Keynes T.4.10), BL, BCL, WCO, Yale, Union, University of Illinois and Bodleian texts printed 'Holiness God'. Corrected by editor.
104.	8	cannot be saved, 'be' printed as 'he' in WTN, BL, CUL (7.61.8 / Keynes T.4.10), BCL, Union. University of Illinois. Corrected by editor.
104.	9	*took not upon him the Nature of Angels, but the seed of Abraham*, see Hebrews 2.6.
104.	16	forever. Amen., printed with a comma after 'Amen,' in WTN, BL, CUL (7.61.8 / Keynes T.4.10), BCL, WCO, Yale, Union, University of Illinois. Corrected by editor.
104.	20	*for it, that he*, printed as '*for it,; that he*' in WTN, BL, CUL (7.61.8 / Keynes T.4.10), BCL, WCO, Yale, Union, University of Illinois. Corrected by editor.
104.	23	For the church of God being his *Bride*, see 2 Corinthians 11.3; Ephesians 5.22–32; Revelation 19.7,8; 21.2,9.
105.	10	*In the Day that thou eatest thereof thou shalt die the Death*, see Genesis 2.17.
105.	29	THE Account, printed as 'Atcount' in Yale, WTN, BL, CUL (7.61.8 / Keynes T.4.10), BCL, WCO, Union, University of Illinois. Corrected by editor.
106.	1	continued against him, printed 'continued, against him, in Yale, CUL, BL, and WTN copies. The comma was placed after 'him' by editor for clarity.
106.	15	For GOD is love … he first loved us, see 1 John 4.10,18.

Textual Emendations and Notes

106. 18   to Love GOD and delight, Yale text prints 'to Love GOD. and delight; with full stop after GOD deleted in ink.
106. 36   by the Coming of, printed as 'by Coming' in WTN, BL, CUL (7.61.8 / Keynes T.4.10), BCL, WCO, Yale, Union, University of Illinois. Corrected by editor.
107. 2   adorning our selves, printed as 'adornig' in WTN, BL, CUL (7.61.8 / Keynes T.4.10), BCL, WCO, Yale, Union, University of Illinois. Corrected by editor.
107.8–10   *because our Father which is in Heaven Causeth his Sun to rise on the Just and the unjust and his Rain to descend on the Righteous and the Wicked.* Traherne is probably quoting from memory Matthew 5.45, which reads in the AV, 'That ye may be children of your Father which is in heaven: for he maketh his sun to rise on the evil and on the good, and sendeth rain on the just and on the unjust.'
107. 16   Heavens declare the Glory of GOD, and the firmament sheweth his Handy work, see Psalm 19.4.
107. 28   *GOD so loved the world, that he gave his only begotten Son, that whosoever believeth in him should not perish but have Everlasting Life*, see John 3.16.
108. 6   Angels, see *CH*, 'Angell', Vol. III, pp. 60–81.
108. 22   he was made a little lower than the Angels, that he might be crowned with Glory and Honour, see Psalm 8.5.
109.9–14   who being in the form of GOD … every Knee might bow, see Philippians 2.5–10.
109. 30   Sanctification, printed as 'Sanctificaton' in WTN, BL, CUL (7.61.8 / Keynes T.4.10), BCL, WCO, Yale, Union, University of Illinois. Corrected by editor.

Chapter XV

110. 5   without Faith it is impossible to please GOD, see Hebrews 11.6
110. 25   that GOD imputeth this Faith alone for Righteousness, see Romans 4.4–6.
111. 23   estate of Innocency, that he fell, missing comma after 'Innocency', in WTM, BL, CUL (7.61.8 / Keynes T.4.10), BCL, WCO, Yale, Union, University of Illinois. Corrected by editor.
112. 32   Try all Things … the hope that is in us, marginal gloss in Yale, BL, CUL, and WTN: 1 Pet. 3.15.
113. 19   face of the World, in LPL (Sion Arc A69.3 / T67) on page 211 there is an asterisk after 'World' with a manicule (☞) on the outer margin pointing to the phrase, 'face of the World'.
114. 11   enrich, printed as 'enriched' in WTN, BL, CUL (7.61.8 / Keynes T.4.10), BCL, WCO, Yale, Union, University of Illinois. Corrected by editor.
114. 13   for which it was prepared: printed as 'it was was prepared:' in WTN, BL, CUL (7.61.8 / Keynes T.4.10), BCL, WCO, Yale, Union, University of Illinois. Corrected by editor.
114. 18   Things that, printed as 'Thingsthat' in WTN, BL, CUL (7.61.8 / Keynes T.4.10), BCL, WCOr, Yale, Union, and University of Illinois texts. Corrected by editor.
115. 1   but never so much as Doubted, in the Yale text there are two insertions in

		ink, which appear to be twentieth-century: in the margin 'have' is inserted after 'never' and 'of' is written above the line after 'Doubted'; the reading would then be 'but never have so much as Doubted of'; both have carets to indicate insertion point. Both are unnecessary.
115.	29	Delightful Objects, printed as 'Delightful' in WTN, BL, CUL (7.61.8 / Keynes T.4.10), BCL, WCO, Yale, Union, University of Illinois. Corrected by editor.
117.	3	is sweeter still, printed as 'sweet' in WTN, BL, CUL (7.61.8 / Keynes T.4.10), BCL, WCO, Yale, Union, and University of Illinois texts. Corrected by editor.
117.	7	the fulness of Time, see Galatians 4.4.
117.	26	Volumne, printed as 'Volumen' in WTN, BL, CUL (7.61.8 / Keynes T.4.10), BCL, WCO, Yale, Union, University of Illinois. Corrected by editor. I have printed it as 'Volumne' to agree with the AV. See next note.
117.	26	the Volumne of the book in which it was written of him, see Psalm 40.7; Hebrews 10.7.
117.	35	Nation's being born at once, see Isaiah 66.8.
118.	13	And, printed with lower case 'a' in 'and' in WTN, BL, CUL (7.61.8 / Keynes T.4.10), BCL, WCO, Yale, Union, University of Illinois. Corrected by editor.
118.	16	the end of the Law, see Romans 10.4.
118.	29	that Jesus Christ might be known, perhaps an application of Jeremiah 29.9 to the Christian ministry (see for example passages like Colossians 1.23–27, or Philippians 3.7,8).
119.	9	Apostle Paul, marginal gloss: Heb. 11, not in the Yale text; see Heb. 11.7–17, 24–29 and 32–38.
119.	23	Resurrection. and, Traherne often used the full stop as a comma in his manuscripts; there is no reason to change it after 'Resurrection'. The printer may have been printing what Traherne's manuscript read.
119.	33	being an eternal Monument of his Wisdom, printed with comma after 'eternal' in WTN, BL, CUL (7.61.8 / Keynes T.4.10), BCL, WCO, Yale, Union, University of Illinois. Corrected by editor. Comma in Yale text appears to have been crossed out by hand in ink.
119.	35	more then conquerors in and thorrow Jesus Christ, who loved us, and gave himself for us, see Romans 8.37.

Chapter XVI

120.	9	Things past, present and to come, comma missing after 'past' in WTN, BL, CUL (7.61.8 / Keynes T.4.10), BCL, WCO, Yale, Union, University of Illinois. Corrected by editor. Comma in Yale text appears to have been crossed out by hand in ink.
122.	12	of him. for the, printed with a lower case 'for' in WTN, BL, CUL (7.61.8 / Keynes T.4.10), BCL, WCO, Yale, Union, University of Illinois. Corrected by editor.
122.	22	adapts us, printed as 'adopts' in WTN, BL, CUL (7.61.8 / Keynes T.4.10), BCL, WCO, Yale, Union, University of Illinois. Corrected by editor.
122.	23	wherein those things are, 'things' printed as 'thing' in WTN, BL, CUL

Textual Emendations and Notes 301

		(7.61.8 / Keynes T.4.10), BCL, WCO, Yale, Union, University of Illinois. Corrected by editor. See Romans 14.4.
122.	34	Harmony and sweetness, printed as 'sweetneess' in WTN, BL, CUL (7.61.8 / Keynes T.4.10), BCL, WCO, Yale, Union, University of Illinois. Corrected by editor.
123.	12	Antipodes, Yale text prints 'Antipodies'.
124.	32	the Length, and Breadth, and Depth, and Height, of the Love of God, which passeth Knowledge, see Romans 8.38, and Ephesians 3.18,19.
124.	36	Possible, printed as 'Possibles' in Yale, CUL, BL and WTN copies.
124.	36	*more then we are able to ask or think*, see Ephesians 3.20.
125.	12	and in touching the Possibility, printed as 'touching. The' in WTN, BL, CUL (7.61.8 / Keynes T.4.10), BCL, WCO, Yale, Union, University of Illinois. Corrected by editor.
125.	34	all these Enjoyments, printed as 'all, these Enjoyments' in WTN, BL, CUL (7.61.8 / Keynes T.4.10), BCL, WCO, Yale, Union, University of Illinois. Corrected by editor.
126.	10	with GOD, the Possession, printed without a comma after GOD in WTN, BL, CUL (7.61.8 / Keynes T.4.10), BCL, WCO, Yale, Union, University of Illinois. Corrected by editor.
126.	11	then the Bridegroom himself enjoys, printed with a comma after Bridegroom, in WTN, BL, CUL (7.61.8 / Keynes T.4.10), BCL, WCO, Yale, Union, University of Illinois. Corrected by editor.
126.	11	the Bridegroom himself, printed with no spacing as 'theBridegroom,himself' in WTN, BL, CUL (7.61.8 / Keynes T.4.10), BCL, WCO, Yale, Union, University of Illinois. Corrected by editor.
126.	15	Eternities, printed as Eterternities, in WTN, BL, CUL (7.61.8 / Keynes T.4.10), BCL, WCO, Yale, Union, University of Illinois. Corrected by editor.
126.	19	and Superior delights, printed as 'Supe–[line break] perior' in WTN, BL, CUL (7.61.8 / Keynes T.4.10), BCL, WCO, Yale, Union, University of Illinois. Corrected by editor.
126.	21	*are made like to his most glorious body, by that Almighty Power whereby he is able to subdue All Things to himself*, see Philippians 3.21.
126.	31	which some may, printed as 'so me' in WTN, BL, CUL (7.61.8 / Keynes T.4.10), BCL, WCO, Yale, Union, University of Illinois. Corrected by editor.
126.	34	abominable, Idolatrous, comma missing after 'abominable' in WTN, BL, CUL (7.61.8 / Keynes T.4.10), BCL, WCO, Yale, Union, University of Illinois. Corrected by editor.

Chapter XVII

129.	17	must needs rise, printed as 'musts' in WTN, BL, CUL (7.61.8 / Keynes T.4.10), BCL, WCO, Yale, Union, University of Illinois. Corrected by editor.
129.	39	a broken and Contrite heart, see Psalm 51.16.
131.	27	with righteousness and true, printed as 'right [line break] teousness' in WTN, BL, CUL (7.61.8 / Keynes T.4.10), BCL, WCO, Yale, Union,

302　　　　　*The Works of Thomas Traherne*

　　　　　　University of Illinois. Corrected by editor.
131. 31　　sweat and Labour, printed as 'sweat Labour' in WTN, BL, CUL (7.61.8 / Keynes T.4.10), BCL, WCP, Yale, Union, University of Illinois. Corrected by editor.
132. 8　　Devotions at the Incense, printed as 'at the [line break] the Incense' in WTN, BL, CUL (7.61.8 / Keynes T.4.10), BCL, WCO, Yale, Union, University of Illinois. Corrected by editor.
132. 29　　Saviours Life, printed as 'Saviour' in WTN, BL, CUL (7.61.8 / Keynes T.4.10), BCL, WCO, Yale, Union, University of Illinois. Corrected by editor.
133. 2　　and made Kings, printed as 'make' in WTN, BL, CUL (7.61.8 / Keynes T.4.10), BCL, WCO, Yale, Union, University of Illinois. Corrected by editor.
133. 9　　they only dwell in the secret place of the most High, see Psalm 91.1.
133. 20　　*of Christ who of GOD is made unto us Wisdome, and righteousness, and Sanctification, and Redemption*, see 1 Corinthians 1.30.
134. 16　　Acknowledgement, see *CH*, 'Acknowledgement', Vol. II, pp. 154–62.
134. 30　　Depth of our misery, all the, comma not printed after 'misery' in WTN, BL, CUL (7.61.8 / Keynes T.4.10), BCL, WCO, Yale, Union, University of Illinois. Corrected by editor.
134. 32　　miserable Estate, the Degrees, comma not printed after 'Estate' in WTN, BL, CUL (7.61.8 / Keynes T.4.10), BCL, WCO, Yale, Union, University of Illinois. Corrected by editor.
134. 37　　Blessedness. Yet is there, printed as 'yet' in WTN, BL, CUL (7.61.8 / Keynes T.4.10), BCL, WCO, Yale, Union, University of Illinois. Corrected by editor.

Chapter XVIII

136. 9　　so perfectly corrected, printed as 'correctd' in WTN, BL, CUL (7.61.8 / Keynes T.4.10), BCL, WCO, Yale, Union, University of Illinois. Corrected by editor.
136. 11　　nor corrode our Delights, printed as 'norcorrode our Delighs,' in WTN, BL, CUL (7.61.8 / Keynes T.4.10), BCL, WCO, Yale, Union, University of Illinois. Corrected by editor.
136. 28　　*Just and Rational* in them; semi-colon not printed in WTN, BL, CUL (7.61.8 / Keynes T.4.10), BCL, WCO, Yale, Union, University of Illinois. Corrected by editor.
136. 29　　he delights in his Sorrow, printed as 'delighs' in WTN, BL, CUL (7.61.8 / Keynes T.4.10), BCL, WCO, Yale, Union, University of Illinois. Corrected by editor.
137. 2　　in the perfection, printed as 'pefection' in WTN, BL, CUL (7.61.8 / Keynes T.4.10), BCL, WCO, Yale, Union, University of Illinois. Corrected by editor.
138. 13　　*Commandment is Charity*, printed as '*it*' in WTN, BL, CUL (7.61.8 / Keynes T.4.10), BCL, WCO, Yale, Union, University of Illinois. Corrected by editor.
139. 13　　1 Cor. 13.1, printed as '13 1' in WTN, BL, CUL (7.61.8 / Keynes T.4.10),

Textual Emendations and Notes 303

		BCL, WCO, Yale, Union, University of Illinois. Corrected by editor. This may have been intended to be a marginal gloss.
139.	21	in distasteful manner, Marks adds an 'a' after 'in' (p. 136), printed however as 'in distasteful' in WTN, BL, CUL (7.61.8 / Keynes T.4.10), BCL, WCO, Yale, Union, University of Illinois.
139.	21	and designes the Honour, Benefit and satisfaction, comma not printed in WTN, BL, CUL (7.61.8 / Keynes T.4.10), BCL, WCO, Yale, Union, University of Illinois. Corrected by editor.
139.	37	Object:, printed as 'Object.' in Yale, WTN, BL, CUL (7.61.8 / Keynes T.4.10), BCL, WCO, Union, University of Illinois. Corrected by editor.
139.	37	or distinct in Nature, printed as 'or distinct' in Yale, WTN, BL, CUL (7.61.8 / Keynes T.4.10), BCL, WCO, Union, University of Illinois. Corrected by editor. Marks changes to 'or is as distinct in Nature, as Love p. 13. The insertion of 'is as' makes a comparison with 'as its Actions …'; however, the 'as' in 'as its Actions …' could mean 'because'; it is not the same but a different principle because it has a different cause, as the last line explains: 'the diversity of the Effects evidently proving a Difference in their Causes'. The exact reading is uncertain. It makes sense however as in the Yale text; therefore I have left it unchanged.
140.	25	that all things shall work together for our good, see Romans 8.28.
140.	28	*Good, and acceptable.* printed as 'acceptable' in Yale, WTN, BL, CUL (7.61.8 / Keynes T.4.10), BCL, WCO, Union, University of Illinois. Corrected by editor. all other Wills, printed as 'Wilis' in Yale, WTN, BL, CUL (7.61.8 / Keynes T.4.10), BCL, WCO, Union, University of Illinois. Corrected by editor.
141.	30	in any but Him; printed with a comma after 'Him,' in Yale, WTN, BL, CUL (7.61.8 / Keynes T.4.10), BCL, WCO, Union, University of Illinois. Corrected by editor.
141.	40	whole Creation, 'whole' printed with an upside down final 'e' in Yale, WTN, BL, CUL (7.61.8 / Keynes T.4.10), BCL, WCO, Union, University of Illinois. Corrected by editor.
142.	3	give our body to be burned … it profiteth nothing, see 1 Corinthians 13.3.
142.	29	Inclinations and Faculties, in all, printed with a comma 'Faculties,' in Yale, WTN, BL, CUL (7.61.8 / Keynes T.4.10), BCL, WCO, Union, University of Illinois. Corrected by editor.
143.	2	Perfection, printed as 'pefection' in Yale, WTN, BL, CUL (7.61.8 / Keynes T.4.10), BCL, WCO, Union, University of Illinois. Corrected by editor.
143.	7	Goodness and Excellency, printed as 'Goodness and and Excellency' in Yale, WTN, BL, CUL (7.61.8 / Keynes T.4.10), BCL, WCO, Union, University of Illinois. Corrected by editor.
143.	9	Ocean, printed as 'Oeean;' in Yale, WTN, BL, CUL (7.61.8 / Keynes T.4.10), BCL, WCO, Union, University of Illinois. Corrected by editor.
143.	12	it is no less folly, printed as 'it no less' in Yale, WTN, BL, CUL (7.61.8 / Keynes T.4.10), BCL, WCO, Union, University of Illinois. Corrected by editor.
143.	24	all his Creatures, printed as 'all his [line break] his Creatures,' in Yale, WTN, BL, CUL (7.61.8 / Keynes T.4.10), BCL, WCO, Union, University

		of Illinois. Corrected by editor.
143.	25	and becomes their infinite, printed as 'become theirs' in WTN, BL, CUL (7.61.8 / Keynes T.4.10), BCL, WCO, Yale, Union, University of Illinois. Corrected by editor.
143.	27	and Powers adopted, printed as 'adopted' in WTN, BL, CUL (7.61.8 / Keynes T.4.10), BCL, WCO, Union, University of Illinois; Yale printed 'adapted'.
143.	38	we are prone, printed as 'weare prone' in WTN, BL, CUL (7.61.8 / Keynes T.4.10), BCL, WCO, Yale, Union, University of Illinois. Corrected by editor.
144.	17	to the Degree of Love, printed as 'Decree' in WTN, BL, CUL (7.61.8 / Keynes T.4.10), BCL, WCO, Yale, Union, University of Illinois. Corrected by editor.
144.	24	*our Meat and Drink to do the Will of our Father which is in Heaven*, see John 4.34, Matthew 7.21, and Romans 14.17.
145.	3	*one Day in his Courts better than a thousand*, see Psalm 84.10.
145.	8	*desire to be dissolved and be with Christ*, 'desire' printed as '*desired*' in WTN, BL, CUL (7.61.8 / Keynes T.4.10), BCL, WCO, Yale, Union, University of Illinois. Corrected by editor. The passage is from Philippians 1.3; Traherne probably quotes from memory, or, perhaps rearranges the words to fit his purpose; AV reads 'having a desire to depart, and to be with Christ'. See also *CE*, Cap XXIV, 'Of Patience', where Traherne quotes the same biblical passage 'to be dissolved and to be with Christ', p. 215.
145.	9	see no more in a Glass, but Face to Face, and Know as we are Known, see 1 Corinthians 13.12. Again Traherne adapts scripture to his purpose and prose; AV reads, 'For now we see through a glass, darkly, but then face to face; now I know in part, but then shall I know even as also I am known.'
145.	10	For Love is strong as death, many Waters cannot quench Love, neither can the floods drown it, see Song of Songs, 8.6,7.
145.	16	and the fulfilling of the Law, printed as 'fufilling' in WTN, BL, CUL (7.61.8 / Keynes T.4.10), BCL, WCO, Yale, Union, University of Illinois. Corrected by editor.
145.	40	the Joy and Glory, printed as 'the a Joy and Glory' in (u) UI; printed as 'the a Joy nd Glory' in CUL.

Chapter XIX

147.TITLE		*natural and Easie*, printed as 'an' in WTN, BL, CUL (7.61.8 / Keynes T.4.10), BCL, WCO, Yale, Union, University of Illinois. Corrected by editor.
147.TITLE		*into Heaven*, printed as '*in*' in WTN, BL, CUL (7.61.8 / Keynes T.4.10), BCL, WCO, Yale, Union, University of Illinois. Corrected by editor.
147.	11	considered apart, printed as 'a part' in WTN, BL, CUL (7.61.8 / Keynes T.4.10), BCL, WCO, Yale, Union, University of Illinois. Corrected by editor.
147.	14	elevated above the Race, printed as 'a [line break] above' in WTN, BL, CUL (7.61.8 / Keynes T.4.10), BCL, WCO, Yale, Union, University of Illinois. Corrected by editor.

Textual Emendations and Notes 305

147. 27 Two great Advantages, printed as 'To' in WTN, BL, CUL (7.61.8 / Keynes T.4.10), BCL, WCO, Yale, Union, University of Illinois. Corrected by editor.
149. 17 Author, see *CH*, 'Author', Vol. III, pp. 415–19.
149. 20 Enlargements of their Parents, printed as 'Parent,' in WTN, BL, CUL (7.61.8 / Keynes T.4.10), BCL, WCO, Yale, Union, University of Illinois. Corrected by editor.
149. 25 in fulfilling the Law, printed as 'infulfilling' in WTN, BL, CUL (7.61.8 / Keynes T.4.10), BCL, WCO, Yale, Union, University of Illinois. Corrected by editor.
149. 29 this accursed *the Black Guard*, in the Yale text 'the' is encircled in ink, as though questioning its appropriate place or perhaps indicating deletion, so that the sentence would read: 'All had been … the accursed *Black Guard* had never appeared'.
149. 34 Gratitude had been all that had been Known, printed 'been, all' in WTN, BL, CUL (7.61.8 / Keynes T.4.10), BCL, WCO, Yale, Union, University of Illinois. Corrected by editor.
150. 10 *There is none other greater Commandment*, see Mark 12.31.
150. 19 the Operations and Effects, printed as 'Op [line break] perations' in WTN, BL, CUL (7.61.8 / Keynes T.4.10), BCL, WCO, Yale, Union, University of Illinois. Corrected by editor.
150. 23 Could we desire, printed as 'could' in WTN, BL, CUL (7.61.8 / Keynes T.4.10), BCL, WCO, Yale, Union, University of Illinois. Corrected by editor.
151. 22 *As for GOD his Way is perfect*, see 2 Samuel 22.31.
151. 23 like curious needle work on either side, see Judges 5.30.
151. 36 hath an Inclination to, printed as 'Inclnation' in WTN, BL, CUL (7.61.8 / Keynes T.4.10), BCL, WCO, Yale, Union, University of Illinois. Corrected by editor.
151. 36 or an aversion from every object, printed as 'a version' in WTN, BL, CUL (7.61.8 / Keynes T.4.10), BCL, WCO, Yale, Union, University of Illinois. Corrected by editor.
152. 32 which was absolutely necessary, printed with a comma after 'which' in WTN, BL, CUL (7.61.8 / Keynes T.4.10), BCL, WCO, Yale, Union, University of Illinois. Corrected by editor.
152. 33 They could not love, printed as 'The' in WTN, BL, CUL (7.61.8 / Keynes T.4.10), BCL, WCO, Yale, Union, University of Illinois. Corrected by editor. In the Yale text it appears that a final 'y' was added to 'The' by hand in ink. Corrected by editor.
152. 33 if they were not left, printed as 'no left' in WTN, BL, CUL (7.61.8 / Keynes T.4.10), BCL, WCO, Yale, Union, University of Illinois. Corrected by editor. In the Yale text a final 't' appears to have been added to 'no'.
152. 35 to make them willing, he has, printed without a comma after 'willing' in WTN, BL, CUL (7.61.8 / Keynes T.4.10), BCL, WCO, Yale, Union, University of Illinois. Corrected by editor.
153. 21 the Composure. In all Theatres, printed as 'Composure. in' in WTN, BL, CUL (7.61.8 / Keynes T.4.10), BCL, WCO, Yale, Union, University of Illinois. Corrected by editor.
153. 22 and Coronations, printed as 'Goronations' in WTN, BL, CUL (7.61.8 /

306   *The Works of Thomas Traherne*

153. 23   Keynes T.4.10), BCL, WCO, Yale, Union, University of Illinois. Corrected by editor.
153. 23   in all Persons, printed as 'n all Persons' in CUL (7.61.8 / Keynes T.4.10), Yale (Guffey, p. 295), BL and WTN have 'in'. Corrected by editor.
153. 26   all in all, see *CH*, 'All in All', Vol. III, pp. 11–17.
154. 8   *but then shall I know*, 1 Corinthians 12.12. printed as '*but when*' in WTN, BL, CUL (7.61.8 / Keynes T.4.10), BCL, WCO, Yale, Union, University of Illinois. Corrected by editor. *Charity never ... of these is Charity*, see 1 Corinthians 13.8–10.12.13.

Chapter XX

155.8–10   Presumption ... and Prudence, in Yale, WTN, BL, CUL (7.61.8 / Keynes T.4.10) use italics for the first letters. Corrected by editor.
156. 18   so here, one Vertue, printed as 'Vertues' in Yale, CUL (7.61.8 / Keynes T.4.10), BL, WTN, BCL, WCO, Union and University of Illinois; however in the Yale text the final 's' on 'Vertue' has been deleted by hand in ink. Corrected by editor.
156. 24   others, Yale text has 'other' but leaves a space after it.
156. 31   detecteth a very great Error, printed as 'detected' in WTN, BL, CUL (7.61.8 / Keynes T.4.10), BCL, WCO, Yale, Union, University of Illinois. In the margin of the Yale text is written 'y', 'this'; the final 'ed' of 'detected' is crossed through with 'th' written over it by hand in ink. With the corrections it reads: 'THIS discovereth the Excellency of this Vertue, & detecteth'. Corrected by editor.
157. 6   trample us under feet;, printed with a comma instead of semi-colon in Yale, CUL (7.61.8 / Keynes T.4.10), BL, WTN, BCL, WCO, Yale, Union and University of Illinois. Semi-colon inserted to correspond to the punctuation within the series.
157. 17   the Truth is, no Vertue, printed without the comma in Yale, CUL (7.61.8 / Keynes T.4.10), BL, WTN, BCL, WCO, Union and University of Illinois. Corrected by editor.
157. 40   Stone. It is enough for the eye, printed as 'Stone. it' in Yale, CUL (7.61.8 / Keynes T.4.10), BL, WTN, BCL, WCO, Union and University of Illinois. Corrected by editor.
158. 4   end, and also tempered, printed as 'end, and also' in Yale, CUL (7.61.8 / Keynes T.4.10), BL, WTN, BCL, WCO, Union and University of Illinois. Corrected by editor. Marks (p. 155) changes it to 'to end, and all so', which somewhat changes the meaning. I have left it as it appears in the text.
158. 15   the Eye is the Light of all the members, see Matthew 6.22 and Luke 11.34.
158. 37   and hear, as a thousand Works to do, printed as 'as a thousand' in WTN, BL, CUL (7.61.8 / Keynes T.4.10), BCL, WCO, Union, University of Illinois. In the Yale text an 'h' has been inserted by hand in ink before 'as' (so 'has').
159. 5   Companions. The less, printed as 'Companions. The' in WTN, BL, CUL (7.61.8 / Keynes T.4.10), BCL, WCO, Yale, Union, University of Illinois. Marks inserts a comma after 'Companions' (p. 156), which is unnecessary, however, since Traherne often used the full stop as a comma in his

		manuscripts.
159.	39	all of them together pass a Grace, printed as 'past' in WTN, BL, CUL (7.61.8 / Keynes T.4.10), BCL, WCO, Yale, Union, University of Illinois. Corrected by editor.
160.	3	*Wise as Serpents, Innocent as Doves*, see Matthew 10.16.
161.	23	Wise and Holy men, printed as 'an' in WTN, BL, CUL (7.61.8 / Keynes T.4.10), BCL, WCO, Yale, Union, University of Illinois. In the Yale text a final 'd' is added to 'an' by hand in ink. Corrected by editor.
161.	35	*The Throne is established by Righteousness*, see Proverbs 16.12.
161.	36	*When it goeth well with the Righteous, the City rejoyceth ... overthrown by the Mouth of the Wicked*, see Proverbs 11.10–11.
162.	8	a strict prohibition of all Debauchery, printed as 'prohibitation' in WTN, BL, CUL (7.61.8 / Keynes T.4.10), BCL, WCO, Yale, Union, University of Illinois. Corrected by editor.
162.	16	so order his affairs, printed as 'ordered' in WTN, BL, CUL (7.61.8 / Keynes T.4.10), BCL, WCO, Yale, Union, University of Illinois. In the Yale text the 'd' is deleted by hand in ink and reads 'ordere'. Corrected by editor.
162.	30	our Saviour calleth them, printed as 'Savour' in WTN, BL, CUL (7.61.8 / Keynes T.4.10), BCL, WCO, Yale, Union, University of Illinois. Corrected by editor.
162.	30	Good or Evil Treasure, see Matthew 12.35.
162.	34	by all the World, which, written with a full stop in WTN, BL, CUL (7.61.8 / Keynes T.4.10), BCL, WCO, Yale, Union, University of Illinois. The printer was probably following Traherne's practice of using a full stop as a comma. Marks (p. 160) changes it to comma. I have left it as it appears in the text.

Chapter XXI

164.TITLE		The title of the chapter has many errors and is different from the title in the Contents page. The full, uncorrected title within the text reads: '*Encouragements to Courage. Its Nature / Cause, and End. Its Greatness and Re- / nown. Its Ornaments and Compani= / ons. Its Objects, Circumstances, Ef / fects and Disadvantages; how Diffi= / culties increase its Vertue. Its Ver- / and Triumphs. How subservient it is / to Blessedness and Glory*'. The title in the text has been taken from the Contents page, which also has errors: '*Encouragements to Courage. Its Nature, / cause, and end. Its greatness and renown. / Its ornaments and Companions. Its ob- / jects, circumstances, effects, and disad- / vantages; how Difficulties increase its / vertue. Its Victories and Triumphs. How subservient it is to Blessedness and Glo- / ry*'. Both have been corrected by the editor.
164.TITLE		*Nature*, missing comma in WTN, BL, CUL (7.61.8 / Keynes T.4.10), BCL, WCO, Yale, Union, University of Illinois. Corrected by editor.
164.TITLE		*Victories*, printed as '*Ver-*' without '*tues*' following. The line reads *Its Ver* [line break] *and Triumphs*. The title in the Contents reads '*Its Victories and Triumphs*'. '*Victory*' makes more sense than '*Vertues*' within the context. See page 334, line 12, 'And he that is always assured of the Victory can never be afraid of the Encounter, or the Enemy'; page 347, line 8, 'Where

		the conflict is more sharp the Victory is more pleasant', and page 351, line 7, 'O Grave where is thy Victory!'. '*Ver=*' is in WTN, BL, CUL (7.61.8 / Keynes T.4.10), BCL, WCO, Yale, Union, University of Illinois. Corrected by editor. Marks (p. 161) reads '*Victories*'.
164.	13	Armour, see *CH*, 'Armour', Vol. III, pp. 212–18.
164.	24	Goodness. its, printed as 'Goodness, Its' in WTN, BL, CUL (7.61.8 / Keynes T.4.10), BCL, WCO, Yale, Union, University of Illinois. Corrected by editor.
164.	26	lives, it, missing comma in WTN, BL, CUL (7.61.8 / Keynes T.4.10), BCL, WCO, Yale, Union, University of Illinois. Corrected by editor.
164.	31	from, printed as 'form' in WTN, BL, CUL (7.61.8 / Keynes T.4.10), BCL, WCO, Yale, Union, University of Illinois. Corrected by editor.
165.	20	were thought to be, printed as 'tos' in WTN, BL, CUL (7.61.8 / Keynes T.4.10), BCL, WCO, Yale, Union, University of Illinois. Corrected by editor.
165.	23	that is, printed as 'thatis' in WTN, BL, CUL (7.61.8 / Keynes T.4.10), BCL, WCO, Yale, Union, University of Illinois. Corrected by editor.
165.	29	Burden to himself, printed without a comma in WTN, BL, CUL (7.61.8 / Keynes T.4.10), BCL, WCO, Yale, Union, University of Illinois. Corrected by editor.
165.	29	useles, missing comma in WTN, BL, CUL (7.61.8 / Keynes T.4.10), BCL, WCO, Yale, Union, University of Illinois. Corrected by editor.
165.	30	Vigour in a, printed as 'Vigour in as' in WTN, BL, CUL (7.61.8 / Keynes T.4.10), BCL, WCO, Yale, Union, University of Illinois. Corrected by editor.
165.	32	Confidence, printed as 'Confiedence' in Yale, CUL (7.61.8 / Keynes T.4.10), WTN, BL. Corrected by editor.
166.	8	Is there Nothing, printed as 'Its' in WTN, BL, CUL (7.61.8 / Keynes T.4.10), BCL, WCO, Yale, Union, University of Illinois. Corrected by editor.
166.	11	Difference, printed as 'Defference' in WTN, BL, CUL (7.61.8 / Keynes T.4.10), BCL, WCO, Yale, Union, University of Illinois. Corrected by editor.
166.	23	Vertues, but imagine, printed as 'imagines' in WTN, BL, CUL (7.61.8 / Keynes T.4.10), BCL, WCO, Yale, Union, University of Illinois. Corrected by editor.
168.	5	Illustrious, Yale, CUL, BL, and WTN copies print the last two letters above the line in superscript. Corrected by editor.
168.	6	that will, Yale, CUL, WTN, BL print the last two letters of 'will' in superscript. Corrected by editor.
168.	8	Excellent, is, printed as 'Excellent, as' in Yale, WTN, BL, CUL (7.61.8 / Keynes T.4.10). Corrected by editor.
168.	28	yet unknown, printed as 'yet unknown.' in Yale, CUL, WTN, BL texts; changed to a comma by editor to correspond with other sentences within the series: 'To Act ... unknown,'; 'To Act ... unshewn,'; 'To keep ... unseen,'. The final 'n' of 'unknown' is in upper case; Marks (p. 165) reads 'unknown,'. Impediments, printed as 'Impediment' in Yale, WTN, BL, CUL (7.61.8 / Keynes T.4.10), BCL, WCO, Union, University of Illinois. Corrected by editor.
170.	16	Apple, and tho, printed as 'Apple', and [line break], 'and tho' in Yale, WTN, BL, CUL (7.61.8 / Keynes T.4.10), BCL, WCO, Union, University of

Textual Emendations and Notes

		Illinois. Corrected by editor.
171.	2	*diminish the least Hair of the Head*, see Matthew 10.30; Luke 21.18.
171.	11	*confounds*. Printed as 'confouds' in WTN, BL, CUL (7.61.8 / Keynes T.4.10), BCL, WCO, Yale, Union, University of Illinois. Corrected by editor.
171.	23	*places.*, printed as '*plaees*' in WTN, BL, CUL (7.61.8 / Keynes T.4.10), BCL, WCO, Yale, Union, University of Illinois. Corrected by editor.
171.22–3		*with Principalities … high places*, see Ephesians 6.12.
171.	33	*overcome the World*, see John 16.33.
171.	33	*O Death … where is thy Victory*, see 1 Corinthians 15.55.
171. 37 –172	6	*Who shall separate us from … Christ Jesus our Lord*, see Romans 8:35–39.
172.	2	*we are more then Conquerors*, printed as '*nore*' in Yale, WTN, BL, CUL (7.61.8 / Keynes T.4.10). Corrected by editor.

Chapter XXII

178.	5	*favour his Interest*, printed as 'Interest' with lower case in Yale, WTN, BL, CUL (7.61.8 / Keynes T.4.10), BCL, WCO, Union, University of Illinois. Corrected by editor.
178.	5	*become all things to all men, that he might gain some*, see 1 Corinthians 9.22.
179.	5	*Briars and Brambles*, see Luke 6.44.
180.	16	*to cease from our own Works, as he also did from his*, see Hebrews 4.10.

Chapter XXIII

182.	35	*a Beauty and Perfection, every thing to, and*, printed as 'a Beauty and Perfection every thing to, and, in Yale, WTN, BL, CUL (7.61.8 / Keynes T.4.10), BCL, WCO, Union, University of Illinois. Corrected by editor.
187.20–9		*Happy is the man that findeth wisdom. … Keep sound Wisdom and Discretion*, see Proverbs 3.13–19,21.
187.	30	*with all thy Getting, get*, printed without a comma after 'Getting' in WTN, BL, CUL (7.61.8 / Keynes T.4.10), Yale, BCL, WCO, Union, University of Illinois. Corrected by editor.

Chapter XXIV

188.	26	Blood of *Dragons*, or the cruel Venom of *Asps*, see Deuteronomy 32.33; Isaiah 34.14–15; Micah 1.8.
189.	13	*Sodom … Gomorrah*, two of the five 'cities of the plain' at the south end of the Dead Sea, destroyed by fire from heaven for their wickedness, see Genesis 10, 13, 14, 18 and 19 as well as other Old Testament passages, and Matthew 10.5, Mark 6.11, Romans 9.20, 2 Peter 2.6, and Jude 7.
189.	15	*He was grieved at the Heart … as to make him repent that he had made Man in the World*, see Genesis 6.6.
189.	20	*Moses' Rod did eat up all the Rods of the Egyptians*, see Exodus 7.12.
189.32–4		*our light afflictions … weight of Glory*, see 2 Corinthians 4.17.
191.	1	*We are made perfect through Sufferings*, see Hebrews 2.10.
191.	4	*Consider the Patience of Job*, see James 5.11.
191.	16	*He laies down his life for the Sheep*, see John 10.15.

191.18–24		*being in the form of GOD ... Servant ... Death of the Cross ... Wherefore ... GOD also hath ... and things under the Earth*, see Philippians 2.6–10.
191.	38	this Love is chiefly towards GOD, and next to our Neighbour; the first and greatest commandment and summary of the Decalogue; see Matthew 22.37, Mark 12.30, and Luke 10.27. See also Deuteronomy 6.4–5 and Leviticus 19. 17–18.
192.	35	*Jonas ... the Tempest upon us*, see Jonah 1.2.
192.	40	*to be dissolved and to be with Christ*, see Philippians 1.23.
193.	1	*glorious Liberty of the Sone of God*, see Romans 8.21.
193.	15	all these Things work together, printed as 'all these Things work to together' in WTN, BL, CUL (7.61.8 / Keynes T.4.10), BCL, WCO, Yale, Union, University of Illinois. Corrected by Editor. The 'to' is probably a printing error with the 'to' of 'together' printed twice. Marks (p. 190) reads 'work too together'. The exact reading is uncertain.
193.	15	all these things work together for our good, see Romans 8.28, 'all things work together for good to them that love God'.
194.	1	*searcheth the Heart, and trieth the Reigns*, see Jeremiah 17.

Chapter XXV

198.	8	since *he hath first loved us*, see 1 John 4.40.
198.	19	*That the Angels ... done upon Earth*, see Peter 1.12.
200.29–32		*where Envying and Strife is ... that make Peace*, see James 3.16–18.
200.	34	*The Meek shall inherit the Earth*, see Matthew 5.5 and Psalm 37.11.
201.	5	unspeakable Joy, see 1 Peter 1.7–8.
201.	19	Passion is master of another mans, printed as 'anothers' in WTN, BL, CUL (7.61.8 / Keynes T.4.10), BCL, WCO, Yale, Union, University of Illinois. Corrected by editor.
201.	22	*He that is slow to Anger is better than the Mighty, and he that ruleth his Spirit, than he that taketh a City*, see Proverbs 16.32.
202.	21	*A soft Answer pacifieth much Wrath*, see Proverbs 15.1.
202.	28	*it is the glory of a man to pass over a Transgression*, see Proverbs 19.11.
202.	32	*with an Angry man thou shalt not go*, see Proverbs 22.24.
203.	5	the Gold of Ophir, see 1 Chronicles 29.4; Job 22.24 and 28.16; Psalm 45.9.
203.	7	*Anger resteth in the bosoms of Fools*, see Ecclesiastes 7.9.
203.	10	Affairs, see *CH*, 'Affairs', Vol. II. pp. 267–73.
203.	31	*The Meek shall inherit the Earth*, see Matthew 5.5 and Psalm 37.11.
203.	37	as *Justine* recordeth, printed as 'recorderh' in WTN, BL, CUL (7.61.8 / Keynes T.4.10), BCL, WCO, Yale, Union, University of Illinois. Corrected by editor.
207.	9	so sweet a Duty. Compassion, printed with a full stop after 'Duty' in WTN, BL, CUL (7.61.8 / Keynes T.4.10), Yale. A full stop is needed after 'Duty' for clarity because of the long series within the initial clause. The printer may have been following Traherne's manuscript. Corrected by editor.
207.	21	*The Man Moses was the Meekest man upon all the Earth*, see Numbers 12.3.

Chapter XXVI

210.	6	*He that humbleth ... be exalted*, see Luke 14.11, 18.4.

210.	9	The Wise Man, King Solomon.
210.	10	*Pride goeth ... Honour is Humility*, see Proverbs 16.18, 15.33, and 18.12.
210.	28	them in another light, printed as 'them in in another light' in WTN, BL, CUL (7.61.8 / Keynes T.4.10), BCL, WCO, Yale, Union, University of Illinois. Corrected by editor.
211.	20	Divine, printed as '*Divine* in the Yale text.
213.4–5		*length, and breadth ... Fulness of GOD*, see Ephesians 3.18,19.

Chapter XXVII

217.	5	*Having food and Rayment*, saith the Apostle, *let us therewith be content: For Godliness with Contentment is great Gain*, see 1 Timothy 6.8.6.
219.	24	Devotion, printed in the Yale as '*Devotion*'.
220.	6	my Powers are prepared, printed as 'power' in WTN, BL, CUL (7.61.8 / Keynes T.4.10), BCL, WCO, Yale, Union, University of Illinois. Corrected by editor.
220.	20	*The Prosperity of the Wicked*, see Psalm 73.3.
220.26–30		*Psal. 73.1, &c. Truly God ... every morning*, see Psalm 73.1–3 and 14.
222.	1	*put on the whole Armour of GOD*, see Ephesians 6.11.
222.	2	*Armour of Light*, see Romans 13.12.
222.	26	Blessedness is of a stable, printed as 'of stable' in WTN, BL, CUL (7.61.8 / Keynes T.4.10), BCL, WCO, Yale, Union, University of Illinois. Corrected by editor.
222.	29	*all things work together for good to them that love God*, see Romans 8.28. See p. 224, note 4 (?), *things work together*, printed as 'things work too together' in WTN, BL, CUL (7.61.8 / Keynes T.4.10), BCL, WCO, Yale, Union, University of Illinois. Corrected by editor.
222.	33	*To speak with the tongue of Men and Angels*, see 1 Corinthians 13.1.
222.	40	than all. The Creating Power, printed as 'all. the' in WTN, BL, CUL (7.61.8 / Keynes T.4.10), BCL, WCO, Yale, Union, University of Illinois. Corrected by editor.
223.	13	*bold as a Lion*, see Proverbs 8.21.
223.	20	*For the hearts of Kings ... Rivers of water*, see Proverbs 21.1.
223.	32	through all difficulties, printed as 'difflculties' in WTN, BL, CUL (7.61.8 / Keynes T.4.10), BCL, WCO, Yale, Union, University of Illinois. Corrected by editor.
224.	9	hidden Treasures, perhaps a reference to 1 Corinthians 2.5–8.
224.	10	but Prayer without Industry, printed as 'Prayers' in CUL (7.61.8 / Keynes T.4.10), BCL, WCO, Yale, Union, University of Illinois. Corrected by editor.
224.	14	*Jacob, Seek ye my face in vain*, see Isaiah 45.19.
224.	14	*Seek ye my face in*, printed as '*ye me in*' in CUL (7.61.8 / Keynes T.4.10), BCL, WCO, Yale, Union, University of Illinois. Corrected by editor.
224.	19	Thou hast no charge over any other than thine own *Vineyard*, perhaps a reference to 1 Corinthians 9.7.
224.	22	*the Issues of Life and Death*, see Proverbs 4.23 and Psalm 68.20.

Chapter XXVIII

225.	23	Censures of men, printed as 'Ceusures' in WYN, BL, CUL (7.61.8 /

		Keynes T.4.10), BCL, WCO, Yale, Union, University of Illinois. Corrected by editor.
225.	26	World is but a little Bubble;, printed with a comma instead of a semi-colon in WTN, BL, CUL (7.61.8 / Keynes T.4.10), BCL, WCO, Yale, Union, University of Illinois. Corrected by editor.
226.	3	more spacious Courts, printed as 'Conrts' in WTN, BL, CUL (7.61.8 / Keynes T.4.10), BCL, WCO, Yale, Union, University of Illinois. Corrected by editor.
226.	14	*The Father of all things ... the Image of his Father*, The Divine Pymander, II.18; copied into the *CPB*, 'Man', f. 65.1.
226.	14	*Life and Light*, printed as '*Light and Life*' in WTN, BL, CUL (7.61.8 / Keynes T.4.10), Yale. Marks (p. 225) reads '*Life and Light*'.
226.17–19		*Man is a divine and living thing ... is above them*, from *The Divine Pymander*, 89–90; also copied in the *CPB* under 'Man', f. 65.1.
226.	24	*but a Man ascends*, printed as '*bur*' in WTN, BL, CUL (7.61.8 / Keynes T.4.10), BCL, WCO, Yale, Union, University of Illinois. Corrected by editor.
226.12–29		*At least*, saith *Trismegistus ... is an Immortal MAN*, from *The Divine Pymander*, IV, 90–3; also quoted in the CPB under 'Man', f. 65.1.
226.	34	*Lo, I have made thee a god to* Pharaoh, see Exodus 7.1.
226.	35	Aaron, he shall be to thee instead of a Mouth, and thou shalt be to him instead of God, see Exodus 4.10–16.
226.	37	I have said ye are Gods, but ye shall die like Men, see Psalm 82.6.7.
226.	40	
–227.	3	*I conceive and understand ... every where*, from *The Divine Pymander*, VII.47, also copied into the *CPB* under 'Man', f. 65.1, where there is a note in Traherne's script, 'Refer this to indwelling'. Marks (p. 363) notes that there is no such entry in the Commonplace Book; however, Traherne planned a topic, 'Indwelling', for the *CH*, see Vol. II, pp. 525 and 527.
227.	6	
–228.	8	*Consider him ... and be seen in all Things*, from *The Divine Pymander*, X. 119–37; quoted also in *KG*, Cap. XXXVII, pp. 463–4; also copied into the *CPB* under 'Capacity', f. 23.1.
227.	17	i.e. if the World be confined, printed as 'i.e.' in WTN, BL, CUL (7.61.8 / Keynes T.4.10), BCL, WCO, Yale, Union, University of Illinois. First bracket inserted by editor.
227.	25	If thou believe, printed as 'belive' in in WTN, BL, CUL (7.61.8 / Keynes T.4.10), BCL, WCO, Yale, Union, University of Illinois. Corrected by editor.
227.	29	the Dry, and the Moist, printed without a comma after 'Dry' in WTN, BL, CUL (7.61.8 / Keynes T.4.10), BCL, WCO, Yale, Union, University of Illinois. Corrected by editor. Marks (p. 227) reads 'the Dry, and the Moist'. The *Divine Pymander*, X. 120, reads 'the Dry, and Moist'; *KG*, Cap. XXXVII, p. 464, line 154 (LPL MS 1360, fol. 333), reads 'the Dry and the Moist' with no comma after 'Dry'. Under the topic 'Capacity', Traherne's amanuensis copied into the *CPB* 'the dry & moyst' (a seventeenth-century variant spelling of 'moist'). It appears that Traherne was neither using the passage as written by the amanuensis, nor quoting it directly from Everard's translation. He may have been using the *CPB* but correcting the spelling and wording, or the printer may have changed it. I see no reason

Textual Emendations and Notes 313

to change the 1675 printed text.

227. 36 cannot tell what, Yale, CUL and WTN texts print '*cannot what*'; taken from *The Divine Pymander*, tr. John Everard (London, 1650), *The Tenth Book*, 131; quoted in *CPB* under 'Capacity' (f. 23.1) and in *KG*, Cap. XXXVII, Vol. 1, p. 464, lines 161–2.

228. 2 *dost not expect*, printed as '*dost expect*' in WTN, BL, CUL (7.61.8 / Keynes T.4.10), BCL, WCO, Yale, Union, University of Illinois texts. From *The Divine Pymander*, X. 131, which reads 'when thou dost not expect to look for it'.

228. 20 *He that is joyned to the Lord is one* SPIRIT, see 1 Corinthians 6.17.

228. 23 *to be filled with all the fulness of GOD*, see Ephesians 3.19.

228. 26 *like Gods, knowing good and Evil*, see Genesis 3.5.

228. 31 *the strait and divine Way*, see Matthew 3.3, Mark 1.3, Luke 3.4, and John 1.23.

228. 36 or ONE SPIRIT with God, as the Apostle, see 1 Corinthians 6.17, as above.

229. 3 Vanities and Trifles, printed as 'TrIfles' in WTN, BL, CUL (7.61.8 / Keynes T.4.10), Yale. Corrected by editor.

229. 7 Crowns and Scepters: printed with a full stop instead of a colon in WTN, BL, CUL (7.61.8 / Keynes T.4.10), BCL, WCO, Yale, Union, University of Illinois. Corrected by editor.

299. 10 *Scipio*, see Cicero, *De Republica* (6.9–20), see Jean Porter, 'Virtue ethics in the medieval period', in *The Cambridge Companion to Virtue Ethics*, ed. Daniel C. Russell (Cambridge: Cambridge University Press, 2013), pp. 74–5: 'the Neoplatonist Macrobius (circa 4th c. CE) Scipio's Dream which is recounted near the end of the latter's *De Republica* (6.9–20) set for yet another analytic division of the virtues: political virtues, which are expressed within civil society; purgative virtues, which purify the soul and prepare it for contemplations; the virtues of the purified soul, which has overcome the passions; and the exemplary virtues that is to say, the divine exemplar of the virtues as they exist in God. This analysis too was popular among medieval authors.'

229. 11 Victories and Triumphs, printed as 'Triumhs' in WTN, BL, CUL (7.61.8 / Keynes T.4.10), BCL, WCO, Yale, Union, University of Illinois. Corrected by editor.

229. 13 nothing. The whole Earth, printed as 'nothing, the' in WTN, BL, CUL (7.61.8 / Keynes T.4.10), BCL, WCO, Yale, Union, University of Illinois. Corrected by editor.

229. 14 height of all Immensity, printed as 'of Immensity' in Yale, WTN, BL, CUL (7.61.8); printed as 'height of all Immensity' in CUL (Keynes T.4.10), BCL, WCO, Union, University of Illinois. Corrected by editor. Marks (p. 228) reads 'height of all Immensity'.

229. 19 noise and Interests, printed as 'noise of the Interests' in WTN, BL, CUL (7.61.8 / Keynes T.4.10), BCL, WCO, Yale, Union, University of Illinois. Corrected by editor.

234. 3–8 *is come unto Mount Sion ... New Covenant*, see Hebrews 12.22–24.

234.12–29 *I cease not to give thanks for you, making mention ... throughout all Ages, World without end. Amen*, see Ephesians 1.16–23 and 3.20–21.

Chapter XXIX

236. 26 MODESTY in Apparel is commended in the Scriptures, see 1 Timothy 2.9–10 and 1 Peter 3.1–5.
237. 3 *in honour preferring one another*, see Romans 12.10.

Chapter XXX

238. 11 *The Meek shall inherit the Earth ... the Meek shall inherit the abundance of peace*, see Psalm 37.11; see also Matthew 5.5.
238. 15 *The Liberal ... Heart deviseth liberal things, and by liberal things shall he stand*, see Proverbs 11.25.
238. 22 *Becaus they know not what evil may come upon the Earth*, see Ecclesiastes 11.2.
238. 25 *lay up a good foundation against the time to come*, see 1 Timothy 6.10.
239. 31 *Every man is a Friend to him that giveth many Gifts*, see Proverbs 19.6.
240. 7 They tender him as the apple of their eye, see Deuteronomy 32.10, Psalm 17.8. Proverbs 7.2, and Zechariah 2.8.
240. 13 *maintain Good Works*, see Titus 3.8.14.
240. 13 *light so shine ... Father which is in Heaven*, see Matthew 5.16.
241.3–8 *Come ye blessed of my Father ... done it unto me*, see Matthew 25.34–36,40.
241.12–25 *THERE was a certain King which ... Lord all that was done*, see Matthew 18.23–31.
242. 3 *He that receiveth you, receiveth me*, see Matthew 10.40.
242. 31 *though a man ... it profiteth nothing*, see 1 Corinthians 13.3.
242. 36 *For a good man ... with discretion*, see Psalm 112.5.
243. 11 GOD hateth robbery for burnt Offering, see Isaiah 61.8.
243. 38 which attended his Cures, printed as 'artended' in WTN, BL, CUL (7.61.8 / Keynes T.4.10), BCL, WCO, Yale, Union, University of Illinois. Corrected by editor.
244. 1 *good seed*, see Matthew 13.24.
244. 9 *He that winneth Souls is wise*, see Proverbs 11.30.
244.23–5 *he that soweth ... also bountifully.*, see 2 Corinthians 9.6; 2 Cor. 9.6. printed in marginal note with no full stop after 6 in WTN, BL, CUL (7.61.8 / Keynes T.4.10), BCL, WCO, Yale, Union, University of Illinois. Corrected by editor.
245.11–13 *that he should love ... persecute us*, see Matthew 5.44.
245.26–8 *to be the Children of our Father ... Just and on the Unjust*, see Matthew 5.45.
245.34–8 *For if ye love them ... in Heaven is perfect*, see Matthew 5.46–48.
245. 40
–246. 3 *If a man say, I love God .... God whom he hath not seen*, marginal gloss: 1 John 4.20, in Yale text.
246. 12 The reality of Religion consists in the solid practice of it among the Sons of men that are daily with us, see Marks, p. 369: 'Cf. Isaac Barrow in the sermon quoted in his *CPB*: 'It is indeed the special grace and glory of our Religion, that it consisteth ... in really producing sensible fruits of goodness' (*On the Duty and Reward of Bounty to the Poor*, p. 199). This does not appear in the *CPB*.

Chapter XXXI

247. 12 Monuments and Pyramids, printed as 'Momuments' in WTN, BL, CUL (7.61.8 / Keynes T.4.10), BCL, WCO, Yale, Union, University of Illinois. Corrected by editor.

248. 19 *Now if the fall of ... and some Prophets*, marginal gloss in Yale text: Rom 11.12.

248. 21 *when he ascended upon high, and led Captivity captive, he gave Gifts unto Men, some Apostles, and some Prophets*, see Ephesians 4.8.11.

248. 21 *when he ascended upon high, and led Captivity captive, he gave gifts unto Men* (Ephesians 4.8). Traherne often uses this verse; see for instance *KG*, Cap. IV (Vol. 1, p. 266, line 33); *CH*, 'Ambassadors' (Vol. III, p. 28, line 403) and 'Apostle' (Vol. III, p. 131, line 103); and *C* I.95 (Vol. V, p. 46, lines 22–3). See especially Volume IV, *CYB*, 'Meditations and Devotions upon the Resurrection of the Savior' (p. 9, lines 19–20), 'St Marks Day' (p. 46, line 4), 'Rogation Week' (p. 62, line 8), 'Ascension Day' (p. 95, lines 40–1, p. 96, line 6, and p. 106, lines 20–1), 'Of the Coming of Beulah', 'married', see Isaiah 62.4; 'the H. Ghost' (p. 116, line 28); and *Contemplation of the Mercies of God,* Thanksgiving for the Beauty of his Providence' (p. 396, line 12).

248. 37
–249. 3 *For my thoughts ... your ways my ways*, Isaiah 55.8.9, printed as '55. 8 9' in WTN, BL, CUL (7.61.8 / Keynes T.4.10), BCL, WCO, Yale, Union, University of Illinois. Corrected by editor.

249.22–9 *Thou shalt also be a Crown of Glory ... GOD rejoyce over thee*, marginal gloss in Yale text: Isaiah 62.3,4,5.

249. 19 *no more be termed*, printed as '*more termed*' in WTN, BL, CUL (7.61.8 / Keynes T.4.10), BCL, WCO, Yale, Union, University of Illinois. Corrected by editor.

249. 21 Hephzibah, 'my delight is in it', see Isaiah 62.4.

249. 21 Beulah, 'married', see Isaiah 62.4.

249. 26 *the Lord delighteth in thee*, printed as '*delighteth*' in WTN, BL, CUL (7.61.8 / Keynes T.4.10), BCL, WCO, Yale, Union, University of Illinois. Corrected by editor.

249. 29 Isaiah 62.3.4.5., printed as '62.3.4,5.' in WTN, BL, CUL (7.61.8 / Keynes T.4.10), BCL, WCO, Yale, Union, University of Illinois. Corrected by editor.

249. 37 he maketh every one * *Heir of the world ... to inherit all things*, marginal gloss in Yale text: * Rom. 4.13; Rom. 8.17; and * Rev. 21.7.

252. 12 *the desire satisfied is a Tree of Life*: this may be a variation of Proverbs 13.12, 'Hope deferred maketh the heart sick; but when the desire cometh, it is a tree of life'; it is repeated in *C* 1.43, Vol. 1, p. 22, *CH*, 'Angell' (Vol. III, p. 74), and *Contemplation of the Mercies of GOD*, 'Thanksgivings for the Beauty of his Providence' (Vol. IV, p. 388, line 112).

252. 14 *Davids* purpose to build the *Temple* was more accepted than *Solomons* performance, while Solomon built the temple, it was David's plan to be followed. David also made all the preparations and gathered the materials for the building of it. David was thought unworthy because he was a man of blood and war: see 1 Chronicles 22.2,14–19; 1 Chronicles 28.92–9.5; 2

		Chronicles 6.7–8; 1 Kings 5–6; 1 Kings 8.17–19; and Acts 7.45–47. See also 'Thoughts II' (Vol. VI, p. 66, lines 26–30); 'Inference II' (Vol. VI, p. 183, line 25).
253.	39	first is the interiour perfection, printed as 'inferiour' in WTN, BL, CUL (7.61.8 / Keynes T.4.10), BCL, WCO, Yale, Union, University of Illinois. Corrected by editor.
256.	14	*Let not Patience* only, but every Vertue *have her perfect work*, see James 1.4.
256.	37	Tears too he putteth in his Bottles, see Psalm 56.8.
257.	6	be!, printed as 'be!' in Yale, WTN, BL, CUL (7.61.8 / Keynes T.4.10), BCL, WCO, Union, University of Illinois. Corrected by editor.

Chapter XXXII

260.	4	*Holy, Holy, Holy, Lord GOD of Hosts. Heaven and Earth are full of the Majesty of thy Glory*, see Isaiah 6.3, Isaiah 24.14 and Revelation 4.8. See also the *Book of Common Prayer*, the Communion (pp. 310–11).
260.	15	*New Jerusalem*, see Revelation 21.2.
261.	16	cannot, printed as 'canot' in WTN, BL, CUL (7.61.8 / Keynes T.4.10), BCL, WCO, Yale, Union, University of Illinois. Corrected by editor.
261.	22	*Moses* would have … than the *Israelites* destroyed, see Exodus 32.32.
261.	23	St. *Paul* could wish … Christ for his Brethren, see Romans 9.3.
261.	25	*who made himself a Curse*, see Galatians 3.13 and 2 Corinthians 5.21.
261.	25	their *Master, who made himself a Curse*, printed as 'their *Master, who made himself a Curse'* in WTN, BL, CUL (7.61.8 / Keynes T.4.10), BCL, WCO, Yale, Union, University of Illinois. Corrected by editor.
261.	32	upon it? and does not the man, printed as 'upon it? and' in WTN, BL, CUL (7.61.8 / Keynes T.4.10), Yale. Marks (p. 262) corrects it to 'upon it. And'; I see no reason to change it: Traherne often punctuated sentences in this manner in his manuscripts.
262.	5	Sons!, printed as 'Sons!' in Yale, WTN, BL, CUL (7.61.8 / Keynes T.4.10), BCL, WCO, Union, University of Illinois texts. Corrected by editor.
262.	6	Children!, printed as 'Children!' in Yale, WTN, BL, CUL (7.61.8 / Keynes T.4.10), BCL, WCO, Union, University of Illinois texts. Corrected by editor.
262.	8	World!, printed as 'World!' in Yale, WTN, BL, CUL (7.61.8 / Keynes T.4.10), BCL, WCO, Union, University of Illinois texts. Corrected by editor.
262.	10	Mistresses!, printed as 'Mistresses!' in Yale, WTN, BL, CUL (7.61.8 / Keynes T.4.10), BCL, WCO, Union, University of Illinois. Corrected by editor.
262.	17	pleasure, goodness, printed in Yale without spacing: 'pleasure,goodness'. Corrected by editor
262.	21	welfare, pleasure, satisfaction:, printed as 'welfare,pleasure,satisfaction:' in Yale. Corrected by editor.
265.	39	*He so loved the World that he gave his only begotten Son*, see John 3.16.
266.	12	Love. Nothing, printed as 'Love .Nothing'. in Yale, WTN, BL, CUL (7.61.8 / Keynes T.4.10), BCL, WCO, Union, University of Illinois. Corrected by editor.

Textual Emendations and Notes 317

266. 24   *This is my beloved ... well pleased*, see Matthew 3.17, 17.5 and 2 Peter 1.17.
267. 29   and infinitely be satisfied, printed as 'and infinitely more than infinitely be', in Yale, WTN, BL, CUL (7.61.8 / Keynes T.4.10), BCL, WCO, Union, University of Illinois. Corrected by editor.
267. 32   should be any other but he, 'other' printed as 'ther' in Yale, WTN, BL, CUL (7.61.8 / Keynes T.4.10). Corrected by editor.
267. 32   he; and, printed as 'he;and' in 1675 Yale, WTN, BL, CUL (7.61.8 / Keynes T.4.10). Corrected by editor.

Chapter XXXIII

272. 6   the Obligation, there is a Sence, printed without a comma after Obligation in Yale, WTN, BL, CUL (7.61.8 / Keynes T.4.10), BCL, WCO, Union, University of Illinois. Corrected by editor.
272. 9   better to die than renounce it, printed as 'better to die than renounce it' in Yale, WTN, BL; CUL (7.61.8 / Keynes T.4.10) has 'better than renounce'. Corrected by editor.
272. 25   for its Beloveds sake, printed as 'Belo- [line break] loveds' in Yale, WTN, BL, CUL (7.61.8 / Keynes T.4.10), BCL, WCO, Union, University of Illinois. Corrected by editor.
273. 16   and joyful efforts, printed as 'effors' in WTN, BL, CUL (7.61.8 / Keynes T.4.10), BCL, WCO, Yale, Union, University of Illinois. Corrected by editor.
273. 28   Treasures! it makes the Soul, printed as 'it makes the Soul' in WTN, BL, CUL (7.61.8 / Keynes T.4.10), BCL, WCO, Yale, Union, University of Illinois. Marks (p. 273) changes 'it' to 'It', but this a common construction in Traherne's manuscripts.
275. 6   of my Soul! my All in all, printed as 'my All' in WTN, BL, CUL (7.61.8 / Keynes T.4.10), Yale. Marks (p. 275) changes it to 'My All'. There is no reason to change it. This is a common practice in Traherne's manuscripts.
275. 35   the Tongues of Men and Angels, see 1 Corinthians 13.1.
276. 3–7   *Praise ye the Lord ... Praise him ye Heaven of Heavens*, see Psalms 148.1–4, 150.1–2.
276. 8   *his Name is exalted far above all Blessing and Praise*, see Nehemiah 9.5.
277. 31   Storehouse, Marks (p. 277) reads 'Store-house'; the word however comes at the end of the line with a hyphen between 'Store' and 'house'. The *OED* spells 'storehouse' citing Pepys (1664) in the seventeenth century.

An Appendix

278. 4–7   *Moses*, and *David*, and *Elijah* and *Daniel*, so had our Lord Jesus Christ himself. *Joseph* had some in his younger daies, and *Solomon* some in his Old age, for Moses, see Exodus 5–19; David, 1 Samuel 18.29, 26.8; Elijah, 1 Kings 21.20; Daniel, Daniel 2.13; Joseph, Genesis 37 and 39.
278. 21–2   *Joseph* suffered much by the Envy of his Brethren in the beginning, and the Lust and Slander of his Mistress, see Genesis 37 and 39.
278. 26–8   *Joshua* did run the hazard of being stoned for crossing the perverse humour of the *Jews*, when he returned from searching the Land of *Canaan*, see Numbers 13.2.14.10; Deuteronomy 34.9; Joshua 1.1–2.

278.31–2		*Samuel* was from his Infancy ... from *Dan* to *Beersheba* they knew he was established to be a Prophet of the Lord, see 1 Samuel 10.24 and 1 Samuel 3.20.
279.	7	*Solomon* was by his Wisdom ... til he revolted from GOD, see 1 Kings 11.
279. 8–9		*David* ... the matter of *Urias*, see 1 Kings 15.5; see also 2 Samuel 11.
280.	4	when he has made himself, printed as 'when it' in WTN, BL, CUL (7.61.8 / Keynes T.4.10), BCL, WCO, Yale, Union, University of Illinois. Corrected by editor.
280.	22	Estates and Possessions may arise, printed as 'Possess [line break] sessions' in WTN, BL, CUL (7.61.8 / Keynes T.4.10), BCL, WCO, Yale, Union, University of Illinois.
280.	27	a Schismatic and a Heretick, Yale text has a marginal gloss at this point: '*Of Hereticks and Schismatics*'.
281.	34	For thus our Saviour was hated by the Scribes and Pharisees ... that heard him say, *He would destroy the Temple*, see Matthew 26.59–61; Mark 14.58.
282.	2	a Swallow will a Snail;, printed with a comma instead of a semi-colon, in WTN, BL, CUL (7.61.8 / Keynes T.4.10), BCL, WCO, Yale, Union, University of Illinois. Corrected by editor.
282.	18	Pilgrim in a strange Country, perhaps a reference to Hebrews 11.13.
282.	33	As Sin abounds, so does Grace also super-abound, see Romans 5.20.
282. 38 –283. 12		the Apostle tells them of their *Reigning* ... *Now ye are full* ... *dwelling place*, see 1 Corinthians 4.8–10.
283.	4	in the Book of the Revelations, see Revelation 5.10.
283.	14	Food and Rayment ... is *Great Gain*, see 1 Timothy 6.8.6.
283.	16	professed *Subjection to the Gospel of Christ*, see 2 Corinthians 9.13.
283.	16	*all the Kingdoms of the World ... and of his Christ*, see Revelation 11.15.
283.	27	*other men laboured, and we are entered upon their Labours*, see John 4.38.
284.	21	*faithful to the death, that ye may obtain the Crown of Life*, see Revelation 2.10.
284.	24	*He that doth ... Sister, and Brother*, see Matthew 12.50 and Mark 3.55.
285.	2	GODLINESS, which with real Contentment is *Great Gain*, see 1 Timothy 6.6.
285.	3	stir up thy self, *by way of a pure Remembrance*, see 2 Peter 1.13.
285.	7	*The fulness of the stature of the Inward Man*, see perhaps Ephesians 4.13, 'the measure of the stature of the fulness ot Christ'.
286.	6	And for this Cause, printed as 'for Cause' in Yale, WTN, BL, CUL (7.61.8 / Keynes T.4.10), BCL, WCO, Union, University of Illinois. Corrected by editor.
286.	12	*that GOD is, and is a Rewarder of them that diligently seek him*, see Hebrews 11.6.

NB: ITALICS ARE MAINTAINED AS IN THE 1675 TEXT.

Roman Forgeries

Roman Forgeries

Or a *TRUE*

ACCOUNT

OF

FALSE RECORDS

Discovering the

IMPOSTURES

AND

Counterfeit Antiquities

OF THE

CHURCH

OF

ROME.

*By a Faithful Son of the Church
of ENGLAND.*

LONDON.
Printed by S. and B. Griffin, for *Jonathan Edwin*
at the three Roses in *Ludgate-Street*, 1673.

1 Tim. 4.2

Speaking lies in Hypocrisie, having he Conscience seared with an hot iron.

2 Tim. 3.8, 9

Now as Jannes *and* Jambres *withstood* Moses, *so do these also resist the truth : men of corrupt minds, reprobate concerning the Faith.*

But they shall proceed no further : for their folly shall be manifest unto all men, as theirs also was.

TO THE
RIGHT HONORABLE
Sr *ORLANDO BRIDGEMAN*
KNIGHT and BARONET
One of
HIS MAJESTIES
Most Honorable Privy Council ;
The AUTHOR
Devoteth his best Services
AND
DEDICATETH
The VSE and BENEFIT of his
Ensuing Labors.

A Premonition.

THe Bishops of Rome, *in the persons of* Zozimus, Boniface, *and* Celestine, *Successively opposed* the Sixth Council of Carthage, *consisting of* 217 Fathers (*among whom the great* S. Augustine *is acknowledged to be one*:) *in the matter of* * Appeals:[1] *which was the first step made by that irregular Chair, to the Exorbitant* Supremacy *which they afterward claimed. In vindicating that Claim before the Council, they produced two counterfeit Canons, fathered upon the Oecumenical Synod at* Nice; *which were by the Records of* Carthage, Alexandria *and* Constantinople, *in the presence of all those Fathers, in the sixth Council of* Carthage, *detected to be forgeries, as well as by the Tenor of the undoubted Canons of the* Nicene Council *it self, which are contrary to those by the* Roman Church *pretended; and so they were esteemed by the Fathers in that sixth Council, who were startled at the sight of those New unheard of Monsters, at their first Publication, above* 1260 *years ago.*

Upon this Passage, I redoubled in the Book an observation (to make it more remarkable,) *which you will find cap. 2 pag. 9. to this purpose,* That in the first General Council of Nice it was ordered, that the chief in every Province should confirm the Acts of his inferior Bishops; And if any Trouble did arise which could not be decided by the Metropolitan, Provision was made *Can.* 5. (in words so clear and forcible, that none more plain can be put into their places) that the last Appeal should be made to Councils, and that the Person condemned in any Province should not be received, if he fled to others. *That Parenthesis* (In words so clear and forcible, that none more plain can be put in their places) *relates to the* CANON *it self: which here follows that you may see how forcible it is, and how much plainer then the very Words into which I had contracted it. It is worthy your Consideration, as one of the most Important Records in Antiquity, consented to by all the Popish Compilers of the Councils themselves.*

Can. 5.[2] *Concerning those that are Excommunicated, whether in the order of the Clergy or the Laitie, by the Bishops in every several province, let the Sentence prevail according to the Canon, that they who are cast out by some, be not received by others; But let it be required that no man be excluded the Congregation, by the Pusillanimitie, or contention,* or any such vice of the Bishop. That this therefore might more decently be inquired

---

[1] Marginal gloss: *viz* From all the world to the *Roman Church.*
[2] Marginal gloss: *This is the Canon opposed by the Forgeries.*

into, we think it fit, that Councils should every year throughout every Province twice be celebrated, that such Questions may be discussed by the Common Authority of all the Bishops assembled together. And so they that have evidently offended against their Bishop, shall be accounted Excommunicated according to reason, by all; till it pleaseth the Community of Bishops to pronounce a milder Sentence on such. But let the Councils be held, the one before the *Quadragesima* before Easter, that all dissention being taken away, we might offer a most pure Gift unto God: and the second about the middle of *Autumn*.

Had the Canon said, The last Appeal shall be made to Councils; *they that are accustomed to such shifts without blushing, might easily have evaded the Words, by affirming the Bishop of* Rome *to be particularly excepted, without any need of expressing the exception; because by the general and Tacit Consent of all, he is above the Limits of such Laws, and above the Authority of that, and all other Councils. Thus they might still render the matter doubtful by their Subterfuges and Pretences; as indeed they do, in evading one expression of the Canon it self. For whereas the Fathers say,* Let the Sentence prevail according to the Canon, that they, who are cast out by some, be not received by others: *Those Popish Hirelings make an exception of the* Bishop of Rome, *where the Oecumenical Synod maketh none*: and might as well except him here, though the Council had said in terms, The last Appeal shall be made to Councils. *For the last Appeal to any subordinate Authority, over which the Council had any Legislative Power, was ordered, they might say to be made to Councils: But the Bishop of* Rome *being the Head of the Church, and having the supreme Authority over all Councils, was not thought of in this Canon: nor was it fit he should be at all mentioned, because that would imply he was under their authority. The* Prodigious Height *of their* usurped Claim *being their sole* Defence, *and their incredible* Boldness *the amazement of ignorant People, which is their chief security.*

But the Council *adding to the former expression this clause,* That Councils should every year, throughout evry Province, twice be celebrated, *(for this very end)* that such Questions may be discussed by the common authority of all the Bishops assembled together: *it puts an end to the business: especially when they add, That* they who have evidently offended their Bishop, shall be accounted excommunicated according to reason, till it pleaseth the community of Bishops to pronounce a milder Sentence. *But that which renders it most plain and forcible, is this,* Let the Councils be held, the one before the *Quadragesima* before Easter, that all Dissention being taken away, we might offer a most pure

Gift unto GOD. And the second about the middle of *Autumn, All the wit in the world could not have invented a more clear and apparent* provision, *against the* Roman Bishops *absurd and impudent* Pretences. *No Evasion (I think) can possibly be made there from; when it is once noted and understood. For the Bar put in against the Pope, is not here in Words, but* Things. *It implies that the Controversie must* before Easter *be fully determined: The very end of calling such a Council, and holding it* then, *being the taking away of all dissention, that we might offer up a most pure Gift or Sacrifice to God: that is, That Unity being restored to the Church at that time, we might receive the* Sacrament *in Peace and Charity. Whereas, if after the Sentence of the* Council, *the business were to be carried to the Court of* Rome; *Suits and Quarrels could not be ended against* Easter, *but would be lengthened in many Provinces, beyond* Easter; *both by reason of the* Seas *and* Regions, *to be passed over by old and Crazy Persons, such as the venerable Bishops were, before they could come from their own Countries to the* Roman Chair; *and by those Prolatory delays they might find there, the matter being wholy referred to the Popes pleasure.*

The Variation *of the* Letter *in the Book, made my* Note *on this place look too like the* Text *of the* Council *it self; which for as much as it happened in a most weighty Place, I could not with a good* Conscience *let it pass, without acquainting the Pious Reader with the same. Though the* Letter *of the Canon it self (to prevent mistakes) is faithfully translated afterwards* page 26, *and* 27. *Yet without giving this* Gloss *upon the* Canon; *which was the occasion of this Præmonition, because so necessary to a clear and full understanding of all the procedure.*

This Note *is the more* weighty, *because the* Nicene Council *is confessed on both sides, (by us for its own sake and its conformity to the Scriptures, by the Papists, for the* Popes, *that have ratified it,) to be of* great Authority; *next to the* Holy Bible, *the very first, and most indisputable that is. Yet this* Canon *laid in the foundation, utterly overthrowes all the following Pretences and Forgeries of the* Roman Bishops. *Which I beseech the Reader to examine more perfectly. For though by many Arts and long Successes*, the Bishop *of* Rome *has ascended to an* Ecclesiastical Supremacy; *and a subtile* Train *of Doctrines, is laid, to make him the* Universal Monarch of the World, *as much higher then the Emperour*, as the Sun is greater than the Moon, *as they expresse it: Yet the Sentence of an* Eminent * Divine *well acquainted with these* Affairs *in a late Sermon preached before the* Lord Mayor *and* Court of Aldermen *in the City of* London, *and now published, is very true,* * The

Supremacy[1] of the Roman Church was a meer Usurpation, begun by Ambition, advanced by Forgery, and defended by Cruelty.

ERRATA.

THe Reader before he enters upon the Book is desired to correct these, as the principal Errata's, with his Pen. Page 35 line 15 dele *now* p. 43 l. 21 r. *love of the world that.* p. 55 for *Councils* r. *Statesmen* p. 66 l. 16 aft. *Magdenburg* r. *and.* p. 83 l. 21 for 1635 r. 1535. p. 104 l. 16 for *fit* r. *fift.* p 107 l. 10 for 1618 r. 1608. p. 109 adde in the Margin II. p 137 l. 7 r. *Right use of the Fathers.* p 157 l. ult. r. *Transeunt.* p. 172\pard fs22 Cap. 15. Contents: for *Falsify* r. *Falsely.*

---

[1] Marginal gloss: Dr. Still: Sermon Acts 24.17. *pag.* 45.

AN *ADVERTISEMENT.* TO THE READER.

Irenæus, one of the most Ancient Fathers, Scholar to S. *Polycarp*, S. *John*'s Disciple, in his Book against Heresies, giveth us four notable marks of their Authors: First, he sheweth how they disguize their Opinions; *Errour never shews* It Self, saith he, *lest it should be taken naked; but is artificially adorned in a splendid Mantle, that it may appear truer than Truth it self,*[1] *to the more unskilful.* 2. That *having Doctrines which the Prophets never preached, nor God taught, nor the Apostles delivered, they pretend unwritten Traditions: Ex non Scriptis legentes*, as he phraseth it.[2] 3. *They make a Rope of Sand,*[3] *that they may not seem to want Witnesses; passing over the Order and Series of Writings, and as much as in them lies, loosing the Members of the Truth, and dividing them from each other: for they chop and change, and making one thing of another, deceive many*, &c.[4] But that which I chiefly intend is the fourth;[5] *They bring forth a vast multitude of Apocryphal and Spurious Writings, which themselves have feigned, to the amazement of Fools; and that those may admire them, that know not the Letters* (or Records) *of the Truth.* How far the Papists have trodden the foregoing Paths, it is not my purpose to unfold, only the last, the Heretical pravity of *Apocryphal* and *Spurious Books*; how much they have been guilty of imposing on the World by *feigned Records*, I leave to the evidence of the ensuing Pages; which I heartily desire may be answerable to the *Merit* of so great a Cause.

Vincentius Lirinensis, another eminent Father, praised by *Gennadius*, died in the time of *Theodosius* and *Valentinian. He wrote a Book against Heresies* in like manner; wherein preparing Furniture and Instructions against their Wiles, he at first telleth us, that *the Canon of the Scripture is alone sufficient:* Then, that *the concurrence of the Fathers is to be taken in, for the more clear certainty of their sense and meaning.* Upon this latter point he saith afterwards, *But neither are all Heresies to be*

---

[1] Marginal gloss: Iren. *Pro-em.*
[2] Marginal gloss: *Lib.* 1, *cap.* 1.
[3] Marginal gloss: *Ibid.*
[4] Marginal gloss: *Lib.* 1. *cap.* 17
[5] Marginal gloss: *Ibid.*

assaulted¹ this way, nor at all times, but only such as are New and Green: to wit, when they first spring up, before they have falsified the Rules of the Ancient Faith, while they are hindered by straitness of time, and before (the Poyson spreading abroad) they have endeavoured to corrupt the Writings of the Fathers. So that Hereticks have inclination enough, where they are not *hindered by straitness of time*, to *corrupt* the most Ancient *Writings* of the Church: For which cause he further saith in the same place, *But Heresies that² are spread abroad, and waxen old, must not be set upon in this sort, because by long continuance they have had opportunity to steal away the Truth. Whatsoever Profanenesses there be therefore, either of Schismes or Heresies that are grown Ancient, we ought in no case otherwise to deal with them then either to convince them, if it be needful, by the Authority of the Scriptures only; or at least to avoid them, as convicted of old, and condemned by Universal Councils.*

In this Admonition the Father informs us of two things: First, that it is possible for *Errour to prevail and spread abroad*; to *continue long, and wax old*: Secondly, that having gotten possession of Books and Libraries, it may *falsifie the Rules of the Ancient Faith, and steal away the Truth, by corrupting the Writings of the Fathers.* In which case, he will not have the Controversie decided by the Fathers, but by the *Scriptures only*, or by old *Universal Councils*.

But if *Errour* proceed so far, as to corrupt the *Councils* too, then of necessity we must have recourse to some other remedy; either to the *Scriptures alone*, as he directeth; or else we must detect the *frauds*, whereby the *Councils* themselves are *falsified*: For that they are liable to the same inconvenience, is evident, both by the paucity of Ancient Records, and the many Revolutions that have been in the World: especially since Nature teacheth men to strike at the Root, attempts are more apt to be made upon *them*, because Hereticks are prone to be most busie in undermining the *Foundation*.

That it is possible for men so far to act against their Consciences, as to *corrupt the Ancient Records of Truth*, you see by the premises: and that it is an easie thing for them to effect it, that have gotten all kind of Books and Libraries into their hands, is apparent; because they that keep them, order them as they please: So that if Hereticks be the Lords and Masters of them, for many Ages together, we may not rashly adventure our Salvation upon their *own* Records: All the World knows, that the Church of *Rome* had all the Libraries of these *Western parts*,

---

¹ Marginal gloss: Vin. Lit. *cap.* 39.
² Marginal gloss: *Ibid.*

Roman Forgeries

for many Ages, in her power; & that the *Eastern parts* are swallowed up by the Deluge of *Mahumetanism*: *All that can seem harsh, is, that she that pretendeth her self the Catholick Church*, should be guilty of *Heresie*. But if the property of *falsifying the Fathers and Councils* may pass for a Badge of *Heresie*, there will no greater *Hereticks* be found in the world, than those who stile themselves falsly *Catholicks*. For as the sight of the possibility of such a thing made *Vincentius* talk more like a *Prophet* than a *Father*, the Church of *Rome* hath so behaved her self since his departure, as if she intended eminently to fulfil his Predictions: which will in the process of our Discourse be made evident to the pious and Christian Reader.

S. *Bernard* lived to see the accomplishment of that which *Lirinensis* feared; for he flourished in the Eleventh Age of the Church, when the Pope and his Chair were mounted up to the top of their Height and Grandeur; and bearing[1] an impartial Testimony, he wrote many things against their Enormities: The Vices of their Popes, with those of all other Orders and Degrees of men in the Church of *Rome*, he inveyeth against at large, in his 33. Sermon upon the *Canticles* smartly touching their *Vain-glory, Pomp, Luxury, Avarice, Simony, Usurpation*,[2] and *Incorrigibleness* so that for any *Piety* or *Conscience* in them, such *frauds* might easily be digested. He distinguishes the State of the Church into four several periods, or four different times; to each of which he annexeth one peculiar temptation: *Terrour* in the *Night* of Persecution, *Errour* in the *Morning* of her Peace, the heat of Lust, and the glaring splendour of Riot and Excess, beautified with Riches, and varnished over with *Hypocrisie* in the *Noon* of her prosperity, and the *Guile of Deception* in the *Evening*; where with great vehemence,[3] and impatient zeal, he speaketh *thrice* in little room, of a certain *business walking in the dark*. Now a little before his time, and not long after the second *Nicene* Council, that *Fardel of Forgeries* came forth under the Name of *Isidore, which seduced all the late Collectors* of the Decrees and Councils, which have risen up among the Papists (at lest if they have not been willful *corrupters* of the Records themselves, which is much to be feared) and discovered a design (probably) to S. *Bernard* also, that was then on foot in the Court of *Rome*, to alter and deface the *Monuments of Antiquity*:[4] For *Riculphus*, the Archbishop

---

[1] Marginal gloss: *Ibid.*
[2] Marginal gloss: *Ibid.*
[3] Marginal gloss: *Ibid.*
[4] Marginal gloss: Baron. *An.* 85, *nu.* 5, 6, 7, 8.

of *Mentz*, who first scattered those Forgeries abroad, and *Benedictus Levita*, who first put them into the *Capitular* Books of the Kings of the *Franks*, and *being conscious of their weakness, got them confirmed by the Authority of the* Roman Chair.[1] *Hincmarus Laudunensis* also, whom *Baronius* calleth *Novissimum usque ad hæc Tempora Collectorem, The last Collector of the Councils, till his own Age.* All these lived before *S. Bernards* time: So did *Hincmarus*, Archbishop of *Rhemes, who having a more sagacious Nostril than ordinary, as Baronius* observes, did first attempt the detection of the fraud, and was accused for the same, and that so roughly, that as *Baronius* further notes out of *Frodoardus* his History of *Rhemes*,[2] he was forced to recant; and though he did it, he was marked with Infamy, for having attempted to reprove them. *S. Bernard* therefore having such a Mirrour before his eyes,[3] speaking covertly for his own *preservation*, yet plainly enough for the Authors *Conviction*, among other notorious and open Abominations, seemeth to strike at this in particular: For shewing the State of the Church to be more miserable under the Pompous Hypocrisie of the *Popes*, than either in the night of persecution under *Heathen* Tyrants, or in the conflicts of *Hereticks* that sprang up in the morning, in the midst of the brightness of that *Glaring Noon*, he talks of, *a work going on in the dark*, a design privily carried on by the instigation and procurement of the[4] *Noon-day Devil, that should shortly after appear to seduce the rest, if there be any in Christ*, (saith he,) *abiding yet in their simplicity: For he hath swallowed up the Floods of the Wise, and the Rivers of the Mighty, and trusteth in himself: that he can take* Jordan *into his mouth, that is, the simple and the lowly that are in the Church.* Which immediately following that *business walking in the dark*, makes me to believe, that he looked upon that *business* as the *Engine* of their *Deception*; which gave him the Hint, to speak by way of Prophesie, concerning the *fourth Temptation* that was yet to come, in the Churches Declension; and which he expressly noteth to be the immediate means of opening the way for Antichrist to appear. His words are very Poinant and Emphatical:[5] *It was bitter at first in the Death of Martyrs, more bitter in the conflict of Hereticks, but now most bitter in the manners of Domesticks: She cannot put them to flight, she cannot fly them, they are so multiplied upon her: The Plague*

---

[1] Marginal gloss: *Ibid.*
[2] Marginal gloss: *Ibid.*
[3] Marginal gloss: S. Bern. *Serm.* 33. in Cant.
[4] Marginal gloss: S. Bern. *Ibid.*
[5] Marginal gloss: *Ibid.*

of the Church is in the Entrails, and incurable; therefore its bitterness is most bitter in its peace. But in what peace? It is peace, and it is not peace; peace from Pagans, *and peace from* Hereticks, *but truly none from her* Children: *The voice of weeping is in that time! I have nourished children, and exalted them, but they have despised me! They have despised and defiled me with their filthy life, their filthy gain, their filthy commerce; and finally, with* that business walking in darkness. *It remains now that the Noon-day Devil should appear to seduce the rest, if there be any in Christ abiding yet in their simplicity.*

That S. *Bernard* intended this, is only my conjecture; because whatsoever he spake against, under that Title of *Darkness,* he chose *obscure terms,* as it should seem on purpose: for that *business* is *Arcanum Imperii,* the Great *Mystery of the Roman Chair,* the Popes *Palladium,* not to be seen with profane eyes; nay, the very *Ark* of his *Most Holy Place,* to be lookt into by none but his own *faithful* Priests: It was Death to look into it with *suspitious eyes,* or to expose it to those of the people. Where we may further observe, that as a Serpent hideth her head, and exposeth any of her members, for the preservation of that, to the stroaks of her Enemy; so doth the Church of *Rome* desire more to conceal this *Grand Art of counterfeiting Ecclesiastical Antiquities,* than any other points less *Radical* and *Vital*: All other Controversies are but superficial blinds, more freely exposed to her Enemies debates, that mens eyes may be turned another way from this *Arcanum,* which is with all endeavour hidden from the people: And for this cause they find it better to buy up the *Editions,* than answer the *Discoveries;* which makes Dr. *James* his Treatise, and *Blondels Pseudo-Isidorus,* so rare among the people.

Matters of Fact may be manifest enough, where the means of contriving them remain unknown: a conjecture in a circumstance therefore destroys not the Foundation. You will find other kinds of Arguments in the subsequent *Epitome,* than bare conjectures. In the mean time, be pleased to remember, that the Papists have had all kind of Books, nay, and Libraries in their hands; that the Roman Clergy (especially those that attend the Chair) have Glory, Wealth, and Pleasure enough to tempt them to such endeavours; that the Pope hath Power enough to reward his *Creatures,* and that they have actually endeavoured to corrupt such Books by their *Indices Expurgatorii,* as also to put forth Apocryphal and Spurious Pieces; which Dr. *Reynolds,* Dr. *James,* Bishop *Jewel,* and the Learned *Crashaw,* as well as the *Indices* themselves, do evidently declare. It shall here appear more clearly, that they have adulterated all by *Counterfeit Records; the very places and things corrupted, being themselves produced, detected, and reproved.*

I shall not descend into the latter Ages, but keep within the compass of the first 420 years, and lay open so many of their *frauds,* as disguize and cover the face of *Primitive Antiquities,* which ought to be preserved most sacred and pure. It is sufficient to prove, that all the *Streams* are infected by the *Poyson* that is thrown into the *Fountain-head;* and to expatiate downwards, would over-swell the Book, which is intended to be little, for the use and benefit of all. Neither shall I talk of the Fathers at large: I will not meddle with their *Amphilochius, Abdias, S. Denis, &c.* but keep close to *Records,* and *publick instruments of Antiquity,* which have the force of *Laws:* Such as *Apostles Canons, Decretal Epistles,* and *Ancient Councils;* which they have either depraved by altering the Text, or falsified, as it were, by Whole-sale, in the intire Lump: And I shall concern my self in the latter, more than the former.

I desire the Reader to note, that I do not trust other mens information, but mine own eyes; having my self seen the *Collectors of the Councils,* and searched into all their *Compilers* for the purpose: Neither do I use our own, but their most affectionate and Authentick Writers, the circumstances of the things themselves (in their most approved Authors) detecting the Forgeries.

Before I stir further, I shall add one passage which befel me in the *Schools,* as I was studying these things, and searching the most Old and Authentick Records in pursuance of them. One Evening, as I came out of the *Bodleian Library,* which is the Glory of *Oxford,* and this Nation, at the Stairs-foot I was saluted by a Person that has deserved well both of Scholars and Learning, who being an intimate Friend of mine, told me there was a Gentleman his Cosen, pointing to a Grave Person, in the *Quadrangle,* a man that had spent many thousand pounds in promoting Popery, and that he had a desire to speak with me. The Gentleman came up to us of his own accord: We agreed, for the greater liberty and privacy, to walk abroad into the *New-Parks.* He was a notable man, of an Eloquent Tongue, and competent Reading, bold, forward, talkative enough: He told me, that the Church of *Rome* had Eleven Millions of *Martyrs,* Seventeen *Oecumenical Councils,* above an Hundred *Provincial Councils,* all the *Doctors,* all the *Fathers, Unity, Antiquity, Consent,* &c. I desired him to name me *One* of his *Eleven Millions of Martyrs,* excepting those that died for Treason in Queen *Elizabeths,* and King *James* his days: For the *Martyrs of the*

Primitive times, were Martyrs of the *Catholick*, but not of the *Roman* Church: They only being Martyrs of the *Roman Church*, that die for *Transubstantiation*, the *Popes Supremacy*, the Doctrine of *Merits*, *Purgatory*, and the like. So many he told me they had, but I could not get him to name one. As for his *Councils, Antiquities,* and *Fathers*, I asked him what he would say, if I could clearly prove, that the Church of *Rome* was guilty of *forging* them, so far, that they had published *Canons* in the *Apostles* names, and invented *Councils* that never were; forged *Letters* of the Fathers, and *Decretal Epistles, in the name of the first Bishops and Martyrs of Rome*, made 5, 6, 700 years after they were dead, to the utter disguizing and defacing of Antiquity, for the first 400 years next after our Saviour? *Tush, these are nothing but lyes,* quoth he, *whereby the Protestants endeavour to disgrace the Papists.* Sir, answered I, you are a Scholar, and have heard of *Isidore, Mercator, James Merlin, Peter Crabbe, Laurentius Surius, Severinus Binius, Labbè, Cossartius,* and the *Collectio Regia, Books of vast Bulk and Price, as well as of great Majesty and Magnificence: You met me this Evening at the Library door;* if you please to meet me there tomorrow morning at eight of the Clock, I will take you in; and we will go from Class to Class, from Book to Book, and there I will first shew in *your own Authors,* that you publish such Instruments for good *Records*; and then prove, that those *Instruments* are down–right frauds and *forgeries*, though cited by you upon all occasions. He would not come; but made this strange reply; *What if they be Forgeries? what hurt is that to the Church of* Rome? No! (cryed I, amazed) Is it no hurt to the *Church of Rome*, to be found guilty of *forging Canons* in the *Apostles* names, and *Epistles* in the *Fathers* names, which they never made? Is it nothing in *Rome* to be guilty of *counterfeiting Decrees* and *Councils*, and *Records of Antiquity? I have done with you!* Whereupon I turned from him as an obdurate person. And with this I thought it meet to acquaint the Reader.

AN ABRIDGMENT OF THE CHAPTERS.

Cap. 1. *OF the Nature, Degrees, and Kinds of Forgery.*

Cap. 2. *Of the Primitive Order and Government of the Church. The first Popish Encroachment upon it, backed with Forgery. The Detection of the Fraud in the Sixth Council of Carthage.*

Cap. 3. *A multitude of Forgeries secretly mingled with the Records of the Church, and put forth under the Name of* Isidore, *Bishop of* Hispalis: *Which Book is owned, defended, and followed by the Papists.*

Cap. 4. James Merlins *Edition of the Councils, who lately published* Isidore Hispalensis *for a good Record, which is now detected, and proved to be a Forgery.*

Cap. 5. *Divers Forgeries contained in* Isidores *counterfeit* Collection *mentioned in particular.*

Cap. 6. *A further account of* Merlins *design. How some would have* Isidore *to be a* Bishop, *others a* Merchant, *others a* Sinner; *no man knowing well what to make of him.*

Cap. 7. *Of* Francis Turrian, *the famous Jesuite, with what Art and Boldness he defendeth the Forgeries.*

Cap. 8. *Of* Peter Crabbe, *his Tomes of the Councils. Wherein he agrees with and wherein he differs from* Isidore *and* Merlin.

Cap. 9. *Of* Carranza *his* Epitome: *He owneth, and useth the Forgeries Forgeries for good Records.*

Cap. 10. *Of* Surius *his four Tomes, and how the Forgeries are by him confirmed. He hath the Rescripts of* Atticus *and* Cyril, *by which Pope* Zozimus *was convicted of Forgery, in the sixth Council of Carthage.*

Cap. 11. *Of* Nicolinus *his Tomes, and their Contents for the first 420 years How full of Forgeries. His Testimony concerning the sixth Council of* Carthage; *with his way of defending the Popes Forgery therein.*

Cap. 12. Nicolinus *his Epistle to Pope* Sixtus V. *His contempt of the Fathers. He beginneth to confess the Epistle of* Melchiades *to be naught. He overthroweth the Legend about* Constantines *Donation.*

Cap. 13. *The Epistle of Pope* Damasus *to* Aurelius, *Archbishop of* Carthage, *commanding the* Decretals *of the* Roman *Bishops to be preached and published, and Fathering those Forgeries on the H. Ghost.*

Cap. 14. *Counterfeit* Canons *made in the* Apostles *names, defended by* Binius. *A Glympse of his Pretences, Sophistries, and Contradictions. A forged* Council *of the Apostles concerning Images, defended by* Binius *and* Turrian.

Cap. 15. *A Book called the* Pontifical, *falsly fathered upon* Damasus, *an Ancient Bishop of* Rome. *How the most Learned of the Popish* Collectors *use it as the* Text *on which they Comment in their voluminous Books, yet confess it to be a* Forgery *full of lyes and contradictions.*

Cap. 16. *Of the Decretal Epistles, forged in the Names of Holy Martyrs and Bishops of* Rome, *for many hundred years together: The first was sent from S.* Clement, *by S.* Peters *Order, to S.* James *(as they pretend) Bishop of* Jerusalem, *seven years at least; and by the truest account, more than seven and twenty years after he was in his Grave. S.* Clements Recognitions, *a confessed Forgery; which detecteth the first Epistle of S.* Clement *to be a real fraud.*

Cap. 17. *Of* Higinus, *and* Pius. *A notable Forgery in the name of* Hermes: " \f D *Where you have the Testimony of an Angel concerning the Celebration of* Easter; *never cited while the matter was in controversie.*

Cap. 18. *A Letter Fathered on* Cornelius, *Bishop of* Rome, *concerning the removal of the Apostles Bones, about the year* 214. *It gives Evidence to the Antiquity of many Popish Doctrines, but is it self a Forgery.*

Cap. 19. *The ridiculous Forgery of the Council of* Sinuessa, *put into the* Roman Martyrologies. *How the City, and the Name of it, was consumed (no man can tell when) by an Earthquake,* &c.

Cap. 20. *Divers things premised, in order first to the Establishment, and then to the Refutation of* Constantines Donation; *the first by* Binius, *the latter by the Author. The Forgeries of* Marcellus, *Pope* Eusebius, *and* Binius *together, opened.*

Cap. 21. *The counterfeit* Edict of our Lord *Constantine* the Emperour: *wherein the* Western *Empire was given to the Bishop of* Rome.

Cap. 22. *The Donation of* Constantine *proved to be a Forgery by* Binius *himself. He confesseth the Acts of Pope* Sylvester *(which he before had cited for good) to be Forged.*

Cap. 23. *Pope* Melchiades *Epistle counterfeited.* Isidore Mercator, *the Great Seducer of all the* Roman Collectors, *confessed to be a Forger. The Council of* Laodicea *corrupted by the fraud of the Papists.*

Cap. 24. *Threescore Canons put into the* Nicene *Council after* Finis, *by the care and Learning of* Alphonsus Pisanus. *Epistles counterfeited in the name of* Sylvester, *and that Council. A* Roman Council, *under Pope* Sylvester, *wholly counterfeited. Spurious Letters Father'd on* Pope Mark,

Athanasius, *and the Bishops of* Egypt, *to defend the Forgeries that were lately added to the* Nicene Council.

Appendix. *Cardinal* Baronius *his Grave Censure and Reproof of the Forgeries. His fear that they will prove destructive and pernicious to the See of* Rome.

A TRUE ACCOUNT OF FALSE RECORDS;

Discovering

THE FORGERIES

OR

Counterfeit-Antiquities

OF THE

CHURCH of *ROME*.

CAP. I.

Of the Nature, Degrees, and Kinds of Forgery.

The Sin of *Forgery* is fitter to be ranked with Adultery, Theft, Perjury, and Murder, than to be committed by *Priests* and *Prelates*: One *Act* of it is a Crime to be punished by the *Judges*; what then is a whole *Life* spent in many various and enormous Offences of that nature?

If a *Beggar* forge but a Pass, or a Petition, putting the Hands and Seals of two *Justices of the Peace* to it, he is whipt, or clapt into the Pillory, or marked for a *Rogue*, though he doth it only to satisfie his Hunger.

If a Lease, a Bond, a Will, or a Deed of Gift be razed, or interlined by Craft, it passeth for a Cheat; but if the whole be counterfeited, the Crime is the greater.

If an Instrument be forged in the *Kings* Name, or his Seal counterfeited, and put to any *Patent*, without his privity and consent, it is High Treason.

If any Records of Antiquity be defaced, or wilfully corrupted, relating to the benefit of men, it is like the Crying Sin of *removing thy Neighbours Land-mark*, which *Solomon* censures in the *Proverbs*. But if those Records appertain to the Right of Nations, the Peace of Mankind, or the Publick Welfare of the World, the Sin is of more mysterious and deeper nature.

If Counterfeits be shufled in among good Records, to the disorder and confusion of the Authentick, and a *Plea* maintained by them, which without those Counterfeits would fall to the ground, upon the deposition of False Witnesses; *Theft* and *Perjury* are effectually couched, together with *Lying*, in the Cheat.

If the Records so counterfeited concern the Church, either in her Customs or Laws, her Lands, or the limits of her Jurisdiction, the Order of her Priests, or any other Spiritual or Ecclesiastical Affair, besides other sins contained in it, there is superadded the Sin of *Sacriledge*.

The highest degree of Forgery is that of altering the *Holy Scriptures*; because the Majesty offended being Infinite, as well as the Concernment, the Crime is the more heinous.

The highest, next under that, is to counterfeit *Rules* in the Names of the *Apostles*, *Oecumenical Councils*, most glorious *Martyrs*, and Primitive *Fathers*, that is, to make *Canons*, *Letters*, *Books*, and *Decrees* in their Names, of which they were not the Authors.

If the Church of *Rome* be guilty of this Crime, her *Antiquity* and *Tradition*, the two great *Pillars* upon which she standeth, are very *rotten*, and will moulder into nothing.

If *Money* be spent in promoting the Forgery, or any thing given, directly or indirectly, to its Fautors and Abettors, in order to the Usurpation of any *Spiritual* Priviledge or Power; he that doth it, is guilty of *Simony*: And in many cases, Simony, Lying, and Sacriledge, are blended together.

Finally, If they that make the Forgeries Father them upon GOD, or upon the *Holy Ghost*, the Sin of *Blasphemy* is added to Forgery; for it maketh God the Father of Lies; and being done *maliciously*, it draweth near to the unpardonable sin.

That some *Popes* have been guilty of *Simony*, cannot be doubted by them that are any thing versed in Church-Antiquity. *Hart*, in his Conference with *Reynolds*, noted out of Dr. *Genebrard*,[1] that the Popes, for the space of seven score years and ten almost, from *John* VIII. to

---

[1] Marginal gloss: *Confer. cap.* 7. *Divis.* 5.

Leo IX. about fifty Popes did revolt wholly from the vertue of their Ancestors, and were *Apostatical*, rather than *Apostolical:* and that some of them came not in by the *Door*, but were *Thieves* and *Robbers*.

That it is not impossible to *forge* Records for the Bolstering up of *Heresies*, those counterfeit *Gospels, Acts, Epistles, Revelations*, &c. that were put forth by Hereticks in the Names of the *Apostles*, do sufficiently evidence; which being extant a little after the Apostles decease, are pointed to by *Irenæus*, condemned in a *Roman Council* by *Gelasius*, and some of them recorded by *Ivo Cartonensis*, in a Catalogue *lib.* 2. *cap.* 27. The *Itinerary* of *Clement*, and the Book called *Pastor*, being two of the number.

I note the two last, because S. *Clement* in his first Epistle to S. *James*, is *made* to approve the one, and Pope *Pius* in his Decretal magnifieth the other. Which giveth us a little glympse of the Knavery by which those Ancient Bishops and Martyrs of *Rome* were both abused, having Spurious Writings fathered upon themselves; for had those *Instruments* been their *own*, they would never have owned such abominable *Forgeries*. But of this you may expect more hereafter, *Cap.* 16. and *Cap.* 17.

These aggravations and degrees of Forgery we have not mentioned in vain, or by accident. In the process of our discourse, the Church of *Rome* will be found guilty of them all, except the first, which is beneath her Grandeur; and in so doing, she is very strangely secured by the height of her impiety. For because it does not easily enter into the heart of man to conceive, that men, especially Christians, should *voluntarily* commit so transcendent a Crime, the greatness of it makes it incredible to inexperienced people, and renders them prone to *excuse* the Malefactors, while they *condemn* the Accusers.

But that the Church of *Rome* is guilty in all these respects, we shall prove not by remote Authorities, that are weak and feeble, but by demonstrations derived from the Root and Fountain. I will not be *positive* in making *comparisons*; but if my *reading and judgment* do not both deceive me, she is guilty of more Forgeries than all the Hereticks in the world beside: Their greatness and their number countenance the *Charge*, and seem to promise that one day it shall pass into a *Sentence* of *Condemnation* against her.

CAP. II.

Of the Primitive Order and Government of the Church. The first Popish Encroachment upon it, backed with Forgery. The Detection of the Fraud in the Sixth Council of Carthage.

It is S. *Cyprian*'s observation, that our Saviour, in the first Foundation of the Church, *gave his Apostles equal honour and power, saying unto them, Whose soever sins ye remit, they are remitted unto them; and whose soever sins ye retain, they are retained,* Cyprian. *Tract. de Simpl. Prælator.* The place has been tampered with, but unsuccessfully: For though they have thrust in other words into the Fathers Text, in some Editions of their own; yet in others they are left sincere: As Dr. *James* in his *corruption of the Fathers, Part.* 2. *Cap.* 1 does well observe. But the most remarkable attempt of the Papists is, that whereas they have set *a Tract concerning the Primacy of the Roman Church* before the Councils, containing many Quotations out of the *Bastard Decretals*, which they pretend to be extracted, *ex Codice antiquo, out of an Old Book*, without naming any Author; closing it with this passage of S. *Cyprian*, they leave out these words of Scripture, *Whose soever sins ye remit, &c.* as rendring the Fathers Testimony unfit for their purpose. You may see it in *Binius*[1] his Collection of the Councils, *&c.*

When the Apostles had converted Nations, they constituted *Bishops, Priests,* and *Deacons*, for the Government of the Church; and left those Orders among us, when they departed from the world.

It was found convenient also for the better Regiment of the Church, when it was much inlarged, to erect the Orders of *Archbishops*, and *Patriarchs*.

The *Patriarchs* being Supreme in their several Jurisdictions, had each of them many Primates and Archbishops under him, with many Nations and Kingdoms allotted to their several *Provinces*; every of which was limited in it self, and distinct from the residue: as appeareth in that first *Oecumenical Council* assembled at *Nice, An. Dom.* 327. where it was ordained, *Can.* 6. that *the ancient custom should be kept*; the Jurisdiction of the Bishop of *Rome* being expresly noted to be equal to that of the other Patriarchs.

---

[1] Marginal gloss: Bin. *Tom.* 1 *Tractat. de. Primat. &c.*

In the two preceding Canons they ordain: 1. *That in every Province Bishops should be consecrated by all the Bishops thereof, (might it consist with their convenience to meet together; if not) at least by three being present, the rest consenting; but the confirmation of their Acts is in every Province reserved to the Metropolitan.*[1] 2. *That the last Appeal should be made to Councils; and that the person condemned in any Province, should not be received, if he fled to others.*[2] Can. 4. and 5.

In the first of these Canons it was ordered, that the chief in every Province should confirm the Acts of his Inferiour Bishops, the Patriarch of *Rome* in his, and every other Patriarch in his own Jurisdiction. In the last, if any trouble did arise that could not be decided by the Metropolitan, provision was made (in words so clear and forcible, that none more *plain* can be put into their places) *that the last Appeal should be made to Councils.*

But the City of *Rome* being in those days Queen of the World, and lifted up above all other Cities, as the Seat of the *Empire*, the *Bishop* thereof began to wax *proud* in after-times, and being discontented with the former *Bounds*, invaded the Jurisdictions of his *Fellow-Patriarchs*.

For though the Foundation upon which the Government was laid was against it, yet when persons were *Immorigerous*, if any Bishop were censured by his Metropolitan, or Priest excommunicated by his Bishop, or Deacon offended with his Superiour, who chastised him for his guilt; though the Canon of the Church was trampled under foot thereby (which forbad such irregular and disorderly flights) the manner was, for those turbulent persons to flee to *Rome*, because it was a great and powerful City; and the Roman Bishop trampling the Rule under foot, as well as others, did (as is confessed) frequently receive them. Nay, their ambition being kindled by the greatness of the place, it tempted them so far, as to favour the Delinquents, and oftentimes to clear them, for the incouragement of others, invited by that means, to *fly* thither for relief, till at last the Cause of Malefactors was *openly* Espoused; and while they were excommunicated in other Churches, they were received to the Communion in the Church of *Rome*.

Hereupon there were great murmurings and heart-burnings at the first in the *Eastern Churches*, because *Rome* became an *Asylum*, or City of *Refuge*, for discontented persons; disturbing the Order of the Church, spoiling the Discipline of other Provinces, and hindering

---

[1] Marginal gloss: *Concil. Nicen.* 1. *Can.* 4.
[2] Marginal gloss: *Concil. Nic.* 1. *Can.* 5.

the Course of Justice; while her Bishop usurped an Authority, which neither *Scripture* nor *Canon* gave unto him.

It is recorded also,[1] that they sometimes acquitted Malefactors without hearing Witnesses, and sent Orders for the Restauration of those, who made such irregular flights, into the Provinces of other Patriarchs that were Subject indeed to the Roman *Empire*, but not within the *Province* of the Roman *Patriarch*.

Nay, when those Orders were rejected, (if some of their own *Collectors* may be believed) the Roman Bishops, through favour of the Empire, got Magistrates and Souldiers to see them executed by *plain force*: which grew chiefly scandalous in the times of *Zozimus*, and *Boniface*; of which you may read the three last and best *Collections* of the *Councils*, set forth by the Papists, *Binius*, *Labbè*, and the *Collectio Regia*, unanimously consenting in their Notes on the *sixth Council of Carthage*. And that this was the cause of calling that Council, they confess in like manner.

For to stop these intolerable Incroachments, and to suppress the growth of an Aspiring Tyranny, this seasonable Council was called at *Carthage*, consisting of 217 Bishops, among whom S. *Augustine* was one present in particular.

To this Council *Zozimus* the Roman Patriarch sent three persons, one of which was *Faustinus*, an Italian Bishop, to plead his Cause, with two *Canons* fathered upon the *Nicene* Council; designing thereby to justifie his Power of *receiving Appeals* both from *Bishops* and *Priests*, but by the care and wisdom of that *Council* they were detected and confounded, the Fraud being made a Spectacle to the whole world.

For first, the Copy which *Cæcilianus*, Archbishop of *Carthage*, brought from *Nice*, (he being himself one of the Fathers in that Council) was orderly produced, and the two Canons which the Roman Bishop sent were not there Next, because it might be pleaded upon the difference of the Copies, that the Copy of *Carthage* must give place to that of *Rome*, *Rome* being the greater *See*; they sent Messengers to the Patriarch of *Alexandria*, to the Patriarch of *Antioch*, and to the Patriarch of *Constantinople*, (and admonished the Bishop of *Rome* to do so too, that he might see sound and fair dealing) desiring the Records of the *Nicene* Council, from all the principal parts of the world, from the Patriarchs of *Constantinople* and *Alexandria* they received Authentick Copies, attested with their several *known* Authorities, which agreed exactly with the Copy at *Carthage*, but disagreed with that of *Rome;*

---

[1] Marginal gloss: *Concil. Carth. 6. Epist. ad Celestin.*

the Extract produced out of it, by the Name of a *Commonitorium*, being every word apparently forged.

Upon this the Bishop of *Rome* was condemned, his Arrogance and Usurpation suppressed by *Canons*, and his Pride chastised by *Letters*; the Letters and Canons being yet extant. This was done about the year 420.

Zozimus dying, *Boniface* and *Celestine* successively take up the Quarrel, without any Dissent appearing in the Roman Clergy: nay rather all the Interest of that *Chair* was imployed to uphold the Forgery; whereby it is evident, that it was not a *Personal* Act, but the *guilt and business of the Church of Rome*; as appeareth further by all their *Successors* persisting in the Quarrel, by the multitude of her *Members* defending it and the Forgery both; and by all the Popish *Collectors* conspiring together, to maintain the Spurious and Adulterate Canons.

Among other things which the Fathers wrote out of this Sixth Council of *Carthage* to Pope *Celestine*,[1] they oppose the true Canons of the *Nicene* Council, against the *false* ones, noting that, which is alone sufficient to overthrow the Forgery, that these two Popish Canons were really *contrary* to the Canons and Decrees of the *Nicene* Council: For desiring him *no more so easily to admit Appeals, nor to receive into Communion those that were Excommunicated in other Churches*; they tell him, he might easily find *this matter defined in the* Nicene *Council: for if it seemed fit to be observed in the inferiour Clergy, and Lay-men, much more in Bishops*. They tell him, that *he should chastise and punish such impudent* Flights, *as became him*: As also, that *the Canons of the* Nicene *Council had most openly committed both the inferiour Clergy, and Bishops themselves to their own Metropolitans; wisely and justly providing, that all businesses whatsoever should be determined in the places where they arose*; Nisi fortè est Aliquis, &c. *unless perhaps there be some one who will say, that God is able to give Justice of Judgment to* one, be he who he will, *but denies it to innumerable Priests assembled in a Council*. Which was in those days held so absurd and monstrous a thing to conceive, that (however the case is altered since) they thought no man impudent enough to affirm it. In these words they cut the Popes Arrogance sufficiently, for that he being but *One*, was so highly conceited of himself, at least so behaved himself, as if he had an extraordinary Spirit of Infallibility, and were fitter to determine the Causes of the Church, than a whole Council of Bishops assembled together. Finally, they charge him with bringing

---

[1] Marginal gloss: *Epist Concil Carthag. 6. ad Celestin.*

the empty puff of secular pride into the Church of Christ: And so proceed to their Canons against him.

Notwithstanding this, the *Roman Bishops* continued obstinate, contending so long, till there was a great Rupture made in the Church upon this occasion. And if some *Records* be true; namely, those *Letters* that past between *Eulalius* and another *Boniface*, the Bishops of *Rome* grew so impudent, as to Excommunicate the *Eastern Churches*, because they would not be obedient to an Authority founded on so base a *Forgery*. If they be not true, then there are more Forgeries in the *Roman Church* than we charge her with: for the Letters were feigned (as *Baronius* confesseth)[1] by some afterwards, that were zealous of the Churches welfare; to wit, for the better colouring of that *Schism* which was made by the pride and ambition of *Rome*.

These *Epistles* were set forth by the Papists, and were owned at first for good *Records*; but upon the consideration of so many *Saints* and *Martyrs* that sprung up in the Churches of *Africa*, during that 100 years, wherein it is pretended by those *Epistles*, that they were cut off from the *Church of Rome*, it was afterwards thought better to reject them as Counterfeits, because the *Roman Martyrologies* are filled with the names of those *African Saints:* And it is a stated Rule, that no *Saint* or *Martyr* can be out of the *Church*. Lest the *Eastern* Churches therefore should out-weigh the *Roman*, by reason of the Splendour, Multitude and Authority of these Eminent Saints, these Letters are now condemned by some among themselves; *vid*. Bellarm. *de Rom. Pont. lib.* 2. *cap.* 25. Baron. *In Not. Martyrol. ad.* 16. *Octobr. and* Bin. *in Concil. Carthag.* 6.

This unfortunate Contest happening so near to the Fourth Century, was the first *Head-spring*, or Root of the *Schism*, that is now between us: And the matter being so, on whose side the *fault* lay, I leave to the Reader.

How the *Roman Church* proceeded in this business, we may learn from *Daille*,[2] an able Writer of the *French* Nation: He tells us, *that the Legates of Pope* Leo, *in the year* 451, *in the midst of the Council of* Chalcedon, *where were assembled* 600 *Bishops, the very Flower and choice of the whole Clergy, had the confidence to alledge the sixth Canon of the Council of* Nice, *in these very words,* That the Church of *Rome* hath always had the Primacy: *Words which are no more found in any Greek Copies of the Councils, than are those other pretended Canons of Pope*

---

[1] Marginal gloss: Baron.
[2] Marginal gloss: *Daillé concerning the right use of the Fathers, lib.* 1. *cap.* 4.

Zozimus: *Neither do they yet appear in any Greek or Latine Copies, nor so much as in the Edition of* Dionysius Exiguus, *who lived about 50 years after this Council*: Whereupon he breaketh out into this Exclamation, *When I consider that the Legates of so holy a Pope, would at that time have fastned such a Wen upon the body of so Venerable a Canon, I am almost ready to think, that we scarcely have any thing of Antiquity left us, that is entire and uncorrupt, except it be in matters of indifferency, or which could not have been corrupted, but with much noise,* &c.

He further tells us, (in the place before-mentioned) *That whereas the* Greek *Code, Num. 206.*[1] *sets before us in the* XXVIII *Canon of the General Council of* Chalcedon, *a Decree of those Fathers; by which conformably to the first Council of* Constantinople, *they ordained, that seeing the City of* Constantinople *was the Seat of the Senate, and of the Empire, and enjoyed the same Priviledges with the City of* Rome, *that therefore it should in like manner be advanced to the same Height and Greatness in Ecclesiastical Affairs, being the second Church in Order after* Rome; *and that the Bishop should have the Ordaining of Metropolitans in the three Diocesses of* Pontus, Asia, *and* Thrace. *Which Canon is found both in* Balsamon *and* Zonoras; *and also hath the Testimony of the greatest part of the Ecclesiastical Historians, both Greek and Latine, that it is a Legitimate Canon of the Council of* Chalcedon, *in the Acts of which Council, at this day also extant, it is set down at large: Yet notwithstanding, in the collection of* Dionysius Exiguus *it appears not at all, no more than as if there had never been any such thing thought of at* Chalcedon. He hath other marks of *Dionysius Exiguus*, which sufficiently brand him for a *Slave to the Chair,* but omitted here, as out of our Circuit. However, I think it meet to lay down the Canon as I find it lying in the *Code* of the Universal Church.

'CCVI. Altogether following the Decrees of the H. Fathers,[2] and the Canon of those 150 Bishops, most beloved of God, which was lately read, which met under the Great *Theodosius* the Pious Emperour, in his Royal City of *Constantinople* [called] *New Rome*, we also define and decree the same, concerning the Priviledges of that most H. Church of *Constantinople* [that is] *New Rome*: For the Fathers justly gave priviledges to the See of Elder *Rome, Quod urbs illa imperaret*, because that City was the Seat of the Empire: And the 150 Bishops, most beloved of God, being moved with the same consideration, gave equal Priviledges to the most holy See of *New Rome*; rightly judging, that the

---

[1] Marginal gloss: *Concil. Chalced. Act.* 16. *Tom.* 2. *Concil.*
[2] Marginal gloss: *Concil. Calced. Can.* 28.

City which is honoured with the Empire, and the Senate, and enjoys equal priviledges with the Royal *Elder Rome*, ought in Ecclesiastical Affairs also, no otherwise then it, to be extolled and magnified, being the second after it, *&c.*'

Upon this advantage, the *Patriarch* of *Constantinople* advanced himself above the other Patriarchs; and his *See* being made equal to the See of *Rome*, by the Authority of the *Church*, upon the Interest he had in the Empire then setled in *Greece*, he arrogated the Title of *Universal Bishop*: Which *Gregory*, then Bishop of *Rome*, so highly stomacked, that he thundered out Letters against him, calling the Title a proud and prophane, nay, *a blasphemous Title*;[1] denying that *either himself, or any of his Predecessors had ever used it*; and plainly affirming, that *whosoever used that Title, was the forerunner of Antichrist.* And to this purpose, in the 34.[2] *Epistle of his fourth Book*, he asketh, *What else can be signified by this pride, but that the times of Antichrist are drawing near? For he imitates him* (says he) *who despising the Fellowship of the Angels in their common joy, endeavoured to break up to the Top of Singularity.* This he spake against *John* of *Constantinople*, because he brake the Order of the Patriarchs, and despised the Equality of his Fellow-Bishops. Now whether it does not hit his own Predecessors, *Zozimus*, and *Boniface*, and *Celestine*, and *Leo*, I leave to the judgment of the Reader: They were not contented with an Equality in Power, but aspired, and that some of them by the most odious way, that of Lying and Forgery, as well as Pride and Ambition, to the top of Singularity.

Whether this *Zeal of Gregory was according to knowledge*, that is, whether it proceeded from *integrity*, or *self interest*, I shall not determine. All that I observe is this which followeth, when the Tyde turned, and the Emperour next sided with the Bishop of *Rome*, the very next Successor of *Gregory* but one, took up the *Title*, a little before condemned for *blasphemous*, which is claimed by the *Roman Bishops* to this day.

The Emperour sided with the Roman Bishop, because the Roman Bishop sided with him: For when *Phocas* had murdered his Master, the good old Emperour *Mauricius*, and usurped the Throne in his stead, the Title of *Universal Bishop* was given to the Patriarch of *Rome* by this Bloody Tyrant, to secure his own; which had so great a Flaw in it, and needed the assistance of some powerful Agent.

---

[1] Marginal gloss: *Greg. lib.* 6. *Epist.* 30. *Lib.* 4. *Epist.* 32. *Lib.* 6 *Epist.* 30.

[2] Marginal gloss: *Greg. lib.* 4. *Epist.* 34.

Hereupon a Council was called at *Rome* by *Boniface* 3.[1] wherein the priviledge of the Emperour *Phocas* was promulged, and the Bishop of *Rome* made a POPE, upon the encouragement of the *Tyrant*, by the consent of the Council: but his own, *viz.* a *Roman Council.*

Thus *Boniface* and *Phocas* were great Friends: The Imperial and Triple Crown were barter'd between them: Connivance and Commerce soiling them both with the guilt of Murder, Simony, Treason; and if S. *Gregory* may be believed, with *Sacriledge* and *Blasphemy*: For being involved in a mutual Conspiracy, they became guilty of each others crimes; to partake with Adulterers, and comply with Offenders, being imputed as sin, in the H. Scriptures.

Platina, an Eminent Writer of the Lives of the Popes, and a Papist himself, informeth us sufficiently of this business, in these words, *Boniface* III. (saith he) *a* Roman *by Birth, obtained of the Emperour* Phocas, *but with great contention,*[2] *that the Seat of blessed Peter the Apostle (which is the Head of all the Churches) should be so called, and so accounted of all: which place the Church of* Constantinople *endeavoured to vindicate to it self, evil Princes sometimes favouring it, and affirming the first See to be due to the place where the Head of the Empire was.*

In the Life of *Zozimus the first Episcopal Forger* in the Church of *Rome, Platina* mentioneth the foresaid business at *Carthage*; but so briefly, that it is clear he did not like it. And to close up all, in the Life of this *Boniface* he endeavours to strengthen the Title of the *Roman* Bishop against the Patriarch of *Constantinople*, by the *Donation* of *Constantine*, another Forgery, of which hereafter.

The two counterfeit Canons contained in the *Commonitorium*, which the Roman Bishop sent to the sixth Council of *Carthage*, are these, as *Faustinus* the Italian Bishop delivered them in Greek, to be read by *Daniel* the Pronotary in the Council.

Ηρεσεν δὲ &c. *We are pleased, that if a Bishop be accused, and the Bishops of his Country being assembled together, have judged him, and deposed him from his Degree, and he thinks fit to Appeal, and shall fly to the most blessed Bishop of the Roman Church, and shall desire to be heard, and he shall think it just that the Tryal be renewed; then he* [the Roman Bishop] *shall vouchsafe to write to the Bishops of the adjoyning and bordering Province, that they should diligently examine all, and define according to the Truth. But if any one thinks fit that his Cause be heard again, and by his own Supplication moves the Bishop of* Rome, *that he*

---

[1] Marginal gloss: Helvic *Chronol.*
[2] Marginal gloss: Platin. *in vit.* Bonif. 3.

should send a [Legate or] Priest from his side; it shall be in his power to do as he listeth, and as he thinketh fit. And if he shall decree that some ought to be sent, that being present themselves might judge with the Bishops, having his Authority by whom they were sent, it shall be according to his judgment: but if he think the Bishops sufficient to end the business, he shall do what in his most wise counsel he judgeth meet.

Here the *Roman Bishop*, nay the meanest *Priest* he shall please to send as his *Legate*, is exalted above all Councils, Bishops, and Patriarchs in the world; he may do, and undo, act, add, rescind, diminish alter, whatsoever he pleaseth in any Council, when the Causes of the most Eminent Rank in the Church do depend in the same. All Bishops are by this Canon made more to fear the Roman Bishop than their own Patriarch, and are ingaged, if need be, to side with him against their Patriarch: the Gate is open for all the Wealth in the World to flow into his Ecclesiastical Court, which is as much above the Court of any other Patriarch, by this Right of Appeals, as the Archbishops Court above any inferiour Bishops, while we may Appeal to that from these at our pleasure. Thus Bishops and Patriarchs are made to buckle under the Popes Girdle, and the Decrees of Councils are put under his foot: And all this is no more but half a Step to the Popes Chair.

The other part of the Step in this *Commonitorium*, was the following Canon concerning Priests:

Οσιος ἐπίσκοπος, &c. *I ought not to pass that over in silence, that does yet move me: If any Bishop happen to be angry (as he ought not) and be suddenly or sharply moved against his Priest or Deacon, and would cast him out of his Church, Provision must be made, that he be not condemned being Innocent, or lose the Communion. Let him that is cast out have power to Appeal to the Borderers, that his Cause might be heard, and handled more carefully; for a Hearing ought not to be denied him when he asks it: And the Bishop, which hath either justly or unjustly ejected him, shall patiently suffer, that the business be lookt into, and his Sentence either confirmed, or rectified,* &c.

What is the meaning of this, *&c.* in *Binius, Labbè, Cossartius,* and the *Collectio Regia,* I cannot tell; but doubtless the Canon intends the same in the close with the former, that the last Appeal is reserved to the Roman Chair; which made the Fathers in the sixth Council of *Carthage* so angry as we find them, to see things so false and presumptuous, fastned upon the first most Glorious Oecumenical Council, which decreed the clean contrary, in the 4 and 5 Canons. The substance and force of which, as we gave you before, so shall we now the *words* of the Canons themselves.

Can. 4. Ἐπίσκοπον προσήκει, &c. *It is fit that a Bishop chiefly be ordained by all the Bishops that are in the Province: but if this be found difficult, either because of any urgent necessity, or for the length of the journey, then the Ordination ought to be made by Three certainly meeting together, the absent* [Bishops] *agreeing, and consenting by their Writs: but let the confirmation of the Acts be given, throughout every Province, to the* Metropolitan.

Can. 5. Περί των ακοινωνίτωιν, &c. *Concerning those that are Excommunicated, whether in the Order of the* Clergy, *or the* Laity, *by the Bishops in every several Province, let the Sentence prevail according to the* Canon, *that they who are cast out by some, be not received by others: but let it be required, that no man be excluded the Congregation, by the pusillanimity or contention, or by any such vice, of the Bishop. That this therefore might more decently be inquired into, we think it fit, that Councils should every year, throughout every Province, twice be celebrated: That such Questions may be discussed by the common Authority of all the Bishops assembled together: And so they, that have evidently offended against their Bishop, shall be accounted Excommunicated, according to the reason, by all; till it pleaseth the community of Bishops to pronounce a milder Sentence upon such. But let the Councils be held the one before the* Quadragesima *before* Easter, *that all Dissention being taken away, we might offer a most pure Gift unto God; and the second about the middle of* Autumn.

The last Appeal, you see, is ordered by the Canon to Councils; and, as they please, the Controversie is to be ended, without flying from one to another Bishop. These are the true and Authentick Canons of the *Nicene Council*, overthrown by the Forgery.

CAP. III.

A multitude of Forgeries secretly mingled among the Records of the Church, and put forth under the Name of Isidore, *Bishop of* Hispalis: *Which Book is owned, defended, and followed by the Papists.*

The *Roman Chair* being thus lifted up to the utmost Height it could well desire, care must be taken to secure its Exaltation. After many secret Councils therefore, and powerful Methods used for its Establishment; for the increase of its Power and Glory, (furthered by the Luxury and Idleness of the Western Churches) of which *Salvian* largely complains in his Book *De Providentiâ* (written to justifie the Dispensation of GOD in all the Calamities they suffered by the *Goths*, who sacked *Rome* in the days of the forenamed *Zozimus*)[1] there came out a *collection of Councils and Decretal Epistles*, in the Name of *Isidore*, Bishop of *Hispalis*, about the year 790. In which Book there are neatly interwoven a great company of forged Evidences, or feigned Records, tending all to the advancement of the Popes Chair, in a very various, copious, and Elaborate manner.

That the Bishop of *Rome* had a secret hand in the contrivance and publication of them, is *probable*, if not *clear*, from divers Reasons.

I. Before they were published, *Hadrian* I. maketh use of the *Tale* of *Constantines Leprosie*, Vision, and Baptism by Pope *Sylvester*; things till then never heard of in the world, but afterwards contained in the *Donation of Constantine*; a Forgery, which in all probability lay by this *Hadrian*, but of his own preparing, when he wrote his Letter to *Constantine* and *Irene*; which Letter was read, and is recorded in the 2. *Nicene* Council, on the behalf of Images:[2] being sent abroad like a *Scout*, as it were, to try what success it would find in the world, before he would adventure the whole *Body* of his Players to publick view: For if that were swallowed down without being detected, the rest might hope for the same good Fortune: if not, the first might pass for a *mistake*, and its Companions be *safely* suppressed, without any mischief following.

2. The Emperour and the Council having *digested* the first Legend, exposed by the Pope so craftily to publick view, the other *Forgeries*

---

[1] Marginal gloss: Platin. *in vit.* Zozim 1.
[2] Marginal gloss: *Concil. Nicen.* 2. *Act.*

were a little after boldly published in this Book of *Isidore*, together with the Legend and Donation of *Constantine*: which when *Hincmarus*, Archbishop of *Rhemes*, (upon its first publication) set himself to write against,[1] he was taken up so roundly for the same by the Authority of *Rome*, that he was fain gladly to acquit the Attempt for ever: And their *tenderness* over it, is, I think, a sufficient Indication of their *Relation* to it; every Creature being naturally affectionate to its own *Brood*, and prone to study its preservation.

The Church of *Rome* was so tender of *Isidores* Edition,[2] that, as some say, *Hincmarus* was forced to recant his Opinion; and to declare, that he believed and received the Book with Veneration.

3. It is recorded by *Justellus*, that the forementioned *Hadrian* was careful to give *Charles the Great* a Copy of the Councils[3] and Decretal Epistles, drawn up (as he affirmed) by *Dionysius Exiguus*. *Daillè* accuses the Book of many faults; but whether *Hadrian* or *Dionysius* were guilty of them, is little material; only 'twas done as a *Pledge* of Reconciliation, after several Bickerings between the Giver and Receiver. *Charles the Great* having several times invaded *Rome*, and now departing thence with *Friendship:* which makes me a little the more prone to suspect *Dionysius* too, for one of those *Danaum Dona*, which are given like *Nessus* his Shirt, when wounded by *Hercules*, to his Enemies Wife, for the destruction of her Husband.

Be if how it will, it shews that *Hadrian* I. was a busie man, that he understood the influence and power of Records, what force they would have upon the minds of *Lay-men*, and that his eyes and hands were sometimes busied in such *Affairs*.

But that which above all other Arguments discovers the Popes to have a hand, if not in the *Publication*, yet in the *Reception* of the Forgeries, is this; that the *Roman* Canonists, *Ivo*, *Gratian*, *&c.* have digested them into the Popes *Laws*; and they are so far countenanced by the Popes themselves, that almost from the time of their publication, throughout all Ages since, they have been received for *Authentick* in the Papal Jurisdiction, and are used as such in all the *Ecclesiastical Courts* under the Popes Dominion, as the chief of their *Rules* for the deciding of *Causes*: So that they are not only *fostered*, but *exalted* by the Authority of *Rome*. The Glory which they acquired in the Throne of Judgment, advancing them for a long time above the reach of

---

[1] Marginal gloss: Baron. *An.* 865. *nu.* 6.
[2] Marginal gloss: Baron. *ibid.*
[3] Marginal gloss: F. Tom. 2. Council [ ] Jus [ ]. *An.*

Suspition. The Veneration which is due to the Chair of Holiness was their best security.

By the influence of the Popes Authority they were received into the *Codes* of Princes, being (as we shall shew out of *Baronius*, in the next Chapter) introduced into the *Capitular* Books of the Kings of the *Franks* by *Benedictus Levita*; and at his instant request, confirmed and approved by the Papal Chair.

The Forgeries in *Isidore* being scattered abroad, it is difficult to conceive to what a vast Height the *Roman* See by degrees ascended: The Splendour of so many *Ancient Martyrs* Names, together with so many *Canons* and *Decrees* in her behalf, so far wrought, that her Bishop came at last to Claim all Power over all persons, *Spiritual* and *Temporal*, to have the sole power of *forgiving sins*, to be alone *Infallible*, to be Gods *Vicar* upon Earth, the only *Oracle* in the world, nay, the sole Supreme and Absolute *Monarch*, disposing of Empires and Kingdoms, according to the Tenour of the Doctrines contained in those Forgeries; wherein he is made the sole Independent Lord, without Controul, able to do what ever he listed.

Some few Ages after this first Publication of *Isidore*, there were other Records put forth, though lately seen, yet bearing the countenance of *Primitive Antiquitie*; which so ordered the matter, that (according to them) the *Evangelists* brought their *Gospels* to S. *Peter* to confirm them; and several books of S. *Clement*, S. *Peter*'s Successor,[1] were put into the Canon of the *Holy Bible*, the whole number of *Canonical books* being setled and defined by his sole Authority: In token (doubtless) of the Power Inherent in all S. *Peter*'s Successors at *Rome*, to dispose of the Apostles, and their Writings, as they please. S. *Clement*'s own Canon, for that purpose, being numbered among those of the *Apostles*.[2]

That the *Pope* was uncapable of being judged by any; that no *Clergyman* was to be Subject to *Kings*, but all to depend immediately upon the *Bishop of Rome*; that he was the *Rock* and *Head* of the *Church*, was the constant Doctrine of all those Forgeries, when put together, with many other Popish Points, of less concernment, sprinkled up and down in them at every turning.

Cui Bono? Among the *Civilians* 'tis a notable mark of Detection in a blind Cause, whose Good, whose Exaltation, whose Benefit is the drift and scope of things; and 'tis very considerable for the sure finding out of the first Authors. That they are Forgeries, is manifest: Now,

---

[1] Marginal gloss: *Apost. Ca* 1. 84.
[2] Marginal gloss: *Ibid.*

whose they are, is the Question in hand; and if Agents naturally intend themselves in their own Operations, it is easily solved.

How excessively the World was addicted to *Fables* about the time of *Isidore*'s Appearance, we may see by the Contents of the 2. *Nicene Council*, Dreams, Visions and Miracles being very rife in their best demonstrations; and among other Legends, a counterfeit *Basil*, a counterfeit *Athanasius*, a counterfeit *Emperour*, maintaining and promoting the Adoration of Images: As may perhaps in another Volume be more fully discovered, when we descend from these *first*, to succeeding Ages.

The *Counterfeits* in *Isidore* being mingled with the *Records* of the Church, like Tares among Wheat, or false Coyns among heaps of Gold, lay undistinguished from true *Antiquities*, and (after *Hincmarus* his ill success) were little examined by the space of 500 or 600 years. Some small opposition there was, made in particular by the Bishops in *France*, and perhaps by some Doctors and Bishops, now, more sincere than ordinary, or by some Learned Lawyer that rarely appeared:[1] but the general *Interest* of the Times, the Deluge of corrupted manners, the Ignorance of the Laity, the Luxury of the Priests, the Greatness of the Chair, and the Love of Superstition so far prevailed, that for a long time the *Court* of *Rome* luxuriantly flourished in the Light of her own Glory, and to this *Prodigious Sun-shine* owed much of its Splendour.

For the Pope having wrought himself by his first Arts into that high Reputation, the *Lustre* whereof dazled the world, it concerned him much to keep the Earth in a Profound Quiet, and to cherish *Ignorance*, (a Vertue highly praised in the Church of *Rome*) that as the *Tares* were *sown*, they might be permitted to *grow*, and be fruitful, *while men slept*: In which, the want of Printing much assisted him, Monks and Fryars being the only *Scribes*, or the chief ones, and all at his Devotion.

Written Copies were the only Books, which at most could be but *few*; enough indeed to preserve knowledge *by way of Record*; but being Chained up in Monasteries and Libraries, they came seldom abroad, unless by the report of such *well-affected* persons as had their Tutelage and keeping.

The Popes *Indulgence*, and the *sloth* ensuing, made way for the *Artifice* of *Priests* in after-ages; which were not *Bookish* ones, as this is, neither were *Lay-men* addicted much to *Reading*.

But upon the *Reformation*, occasioned by nothing more than the *nortorious* impiety and *excess* of Popes, (unless the impudence and security

---

[1] Marginal gloss: Baron. *An.*

of his Followers may contend for a share in it) when Libraries fell into the Protestants hands, Inquisition was made, *Archives* were entered, Books opened, *Records* searched and diligently compared: Whereupon much fraud and shufling was found, and exposed to the world.

For as the Copies were enough, had they been *sincere*; so, though they were not sincere, by the Providence of God, they contained *Indications*, wherby clear Judgments might easily discern between Records and Forgeries; as I found my self, to my great amazement, without any *Warning*! when I first set my self to read the Councils, and simply made use of none but Popish Compilers: For there is not more difference, for the most part, between a piece of Gold and an Oyster shell, than between a true Record and a Forgery.

Upon this Inspection the Popes Power began to be questioned, and his Throne to shake, as if it had been founded on a Quagmire: He therefore furnisheth himself with *Armies of Priests*, as S. *Gregory* phraseth it, new Orders of *Jesuites* and *Fryars*, (never before heard of) being erected for the defence of his Tottering Chair: men devoted against the Truth as those Conspirators were, that swore *they would neither eat nor drink till they had slain* Paul; for the Maintenance of whom, he is at great expence unto this day. Above all other arts, that of providing *Seminaries* being the most costly, and the most mysterious: wherein they are secretly trained up, like *Sappho's* Birds; of whom it is reported, that being ambitious to be thought a GOD, he privately cherished a multitude, and taught them by degrees to say, Μέγας Θεός ὁ Σάφω: Sappho *is a great God*: which being let loose on a sudden with their Lesson, all the other Birds in the Forrest were quickly instructed in the same *Ditty*: Whereupon (he withdrawing himself) the people thought him gone to Heaven, and a Temple was erected *to the God Sappho*. Whether the Story be true, I shall not determine; I am sure it may pass for an *Embleme* of the Popes Atchievement, who by this means has *made* the World to ring of a Doctrine which *makes* him a God; or if not that, at least Lord of all *Councils*, greater than Emperours, Head of the Church, *&c*. His *Emissaries* issuing forth from these *mysterious* Seminaries, and filling the Earth like Locusts, or like little fraudulent and simple Birds, chirping out the Ditty: and while all the Wood learning it one of another, the Earth is full of the *Miracle*.

All the late *Compilers* of the *Decrees* and *Councils* seem hence to flow; *James Merlin, Peter Crabbe, Laurentius Surius, Nicolinus, Carranza, Severinus Binius, Labbè* and *Cossartius*, the *Collectio Regia, &c*. being his sworn Adjutants for upholding the Chair. The last is a Book of such State and Magnificence, that it consists of 37 Volumes, and is in price about 50 pounds: More of less, they all carry on the Forgeries with one consent, which were at first published in the name of *Isidore* of *Hispalis*; though some had rather, upon mature deliberation, it should be *Isidore Mercator*, or *Isidore Peccator*, a *Merchant*, or a *Sinner*, rather than a *Saint*, and a *Bisho*p.

This Narrative of the Forgeries being thus nakedly, and by way of History plainly given, it remains now, that the *Forgeries* themselves be proved to be such: In the detection of which, much light will *reflect* upon the foregoing passages: All which, if you please, you may take only for a fair *Introduction*.

Howbeit, I must close with two or three Observations. First of all, I do not content my self with any single *Collector* of Councils among the *Papists*, lest they should say, This is but *one Doctors* Opinion; but I take the *Stream* of them together. Secondly, Detect not the Books of *private* men, but such as are adopted by the Church of *Rome*, being dedicated to Popes, Kings, Emperours, and coming out *cum summo Privilegio*. Thirdly, that the first of these *Compilers*, (excepting those that were imployed in the first publication and Promotion of *Isidore*) did begin with that Service not much above 130 years ago; all of them rising up since the times of *Martin Luther*, though their Names make a great noise and bluster in the world: For upon the Reformation of the Church, so happily wrought, and carried on by the Protestants, these *Armies* of *Collectors* were marshalled together, to help a little, and to uphold the Popes Chair by Forgeries: Which intimates a *Dearth* of *Antiquities*, since they are forced to *fly* to such *shameful* expedients.

Luther appeared in the year 1517. The first that appeared after him was *James Merlin*, in the year 1535. The next was *Peter Crabbe*, in the year 1538. After him *Carranza*, in the year 1564. Then *Surius*, in the year 1567. *Turrian* follows, not as a Collector, but as a *Champion* to defend them, in the year 1573. Whom *Nicolinus* succeeded as a *Compiler* of the Councils, in the year 1585. After him *Binius*, *Labbè* and *Cossartius*, and the *Collectio Regia* follow in their Order. So that it is an easie matter to discern what set these *Voluminous Writers* on work, to wit, the great and smart occasion they received by the *Reformation*.

Finally observe, that *Isidore* and *Merlin*, the first of the Compilers, whose Works are extant, lay down the Forgeries, simply and plainly, for good Records; but *Binius*, and his Followers, by reason of the Arguments which they cannot answer, begin to confess some of them to be Forgeries:

So do the most Grave and Learned Cardinals, *Bellarmine* and *Baronius*, though they still carry on the *Design* of the first *Inventers*, by some other Methods, which they hope will succeed better.

Nor is it any wonder, that a *Secular Kingdom* should make men more active than the love of *Heaven*; since we daily see, how the Kings of the world expend vast Treasures of Gold and Silver, and run through all dangers of Death and Battel, for their own preservation, and the Conquest of their Neighbours. The same care which they take in building *Forts* and *Cittadels*, being taken by the Bishop of *Rome*, in maintaining *Seminaries*, *Universities*, *Printing-Houses*, &c. which depend absolutely on him, for the securing of all that *Wealth* and *Empire*, which he hath by his *Wit* and *Policy* acquired: It standeth him upon; for if his Religion falls, his *Glory* vanisheth, and his *Kingdom* is abolished.

What men will do for *Secular Ends*, beyond all the belief and expectation of the *Vulgar*, we see in *Hamor* and *Shechem*,[1] the first and most Ancient *Myrrour* of that kind in the world: who for the accomplishment of their desires, introduced a new Religion, troubling themselves and their Citizens unto *Blood*, meerly to get possession of *Dinah*, *Jacob's* daughter.

Jeroboam's Policy[2] is about 2500 years old, though much more late. When the ten Tribes revolted from the House of *David*, for fear lest they should return to their Allegiance, if they went up yearly to *Jerusalem*, according to the Law, he set up two *Calves* for the people to worship, and underwent a great *expence* (besides the *Gold* in the Calves) in erecting a new Order of *Priests*, that the people might be kept at home in their *perverse* Obedience. He very well knew those Calves were no *Deities*, yet for secular ends he promoted their worship, and was followed therein by all the *Line* of the Kings of *Israel*, several hundred of years together.

What *Demetrius* the *Silver-Smith* did for *Diana of the Ephesians*, and what an uproar he made, purely for *Gain*, in making her *Shrines*, all the Christian World understandeth: But the *High-Priests*, Scribes and Elders of the *Jews*, in acting against all the *Miracles* of Christ, and against their *Conscience*; especially in giving Money to the Souldiers to hold their peace, when they brought the news of his Resurrection, their *resisting of the Holy Ghost* at his Miraculous *Descent*; these are a sufficient instance of the *incredible* obdurateness of mans heart, and his love of the world that allures his hopes, as the immediate crown of his Labours.

---

[1] Marginal gloss: Gen 34.
[2] Marginal gloss: 1 Kings.

The *Diana* of the *Romans* is much more *proficuous* than the *Diana* of the *Ephesians*: The *fattest places of the Provinces*, and the *greatest Empire in the World*, are the Game they Play. This *Dinah* animateth all their Strength to impose on the people: And for the easing of their own Charge, it is a usual thing with Popes, to permit their Priests and Fryers, for their better support, to deceive the people: which Dr. *Stillingfleet*, in his Book of *Popish Counterfeit Miracles*, does excellently open: in which, and in all other Arts and Tricks, they have a special connivance, provided they keep the poor simple Sheep within the bounds of their Jurisdiction, and contribute to the continuance of their Secular Kingdom.

This is the *truth* of the Story; and these are the circumstances of the whole procedure, which remains now to be proved.

CAP. IV.

James Merlin's *Editions of the Councils, who lately published* Isidore Hispalensis *for a good Record, which is now detected, and proved to be a Forgery.*

James *Merlin's* pains was to publish *Isidore*, with some Collections and Additions of his own. He positively affirmeth him to be that Famous *Isidore* of *Hispalis*, a Saint, a Bishop, and a Father of the Church: though as *Blondel* and Dr. *Reynolds* accurately observe, S. *Isidore* of *Hispalis* was dead 40, 50, 60 years, before some things came to pass that are mentioned in that Book of the Councils.

Blondel in a Book of his, called *Pseudo-Isidorus*, or *Turrianus Vapulans*, *Cap.* 2. observes, how the lowest that write of *Isidores* death, fix it on the year 647. as *Vasæus* in his Chronicle: Others on the year 643. as *Rodericus Toletanus Hist. lib.* 2. *cap.* 18.[1] Or on the year 635. as *the proper Office of the Saints of* Spain: or on the year 636. when *Sinthalus* entered his Kingdom, as *Redemptus Diaconus*, an eye-witness, *De Obitu* Isidori.

Brauleo Bishop of *Cæsar-Augustana*, *Lucas Tudensis*, *Baronius* the great Annalist, *Mariana*, *Grialus*, and others, agree with the last; which is eleven years sooner than *Vasæus*. So that the general prevailing Opinion is, that *Isidore* of *Hispalis* died in the year 636. However, that we may deal most fairly with them, we will allow them all they can desire, and calculate our affair by the last Account, which is most for their advantage.

Admit *Vasæus* in the right, that *Isidore* lived till the year 647. yet the Book which is Fathered upon him, can be none of his; for it mentions things which came to pass long after.

It is observed by *Blondel*, that *Honoratus*, who succeeded *Isidore* in the See of *Hispalis*, is found in the sixth Council of *Toledo*: whereas this pretended *Isidore* makes mention of the eleventh Council in the same place. He talks of the sixth *Oecumenical Council*, in the year 681. no less than 46 years after his own death, by the lowest account. He writes of *Boniface* of *Mentz*, slain as *Baronius* observes, in the year 755. which was threescore and sixteen years after *Isidores* death: Yet

---

[1] Perhaps intended as a marginal gloss: *Rodericus Toletanus Hist. lib.* 2. *cap.* 18.

Possevin, upon the word *Isidorus Hisp.* and *Hart* in his Conference with *Reynolds*, contend the Author of this Book to be the true *Isidore, Bishop of Hispalis*, as *Merlin* who first published *Isidore* in print, and others did before them.

Among his Witnesses produced against this Counterfeit, the first which *Blondel* useth, is the *Code of the Roman Church*; in which onely the Epistles of 13 Roman Bishops are contained, beginning with *Siricius*: Whereas there are in *Isidore* above 60. whereof five or six and thirty lived before *Siricius*, and were all unknown until the time of *Isidore*.

His next Testimony is that of the Bishops of *France*, about the year 865. who concluded, that *Isidore's* Wares *then newly beginning to be sold, could not have the force of* Canons, *because they were not contained in the* Authentick Code, *or Book of Canons formerly known*.

He next citeth the Council of *Aquisgranum, An.* 816. the Bishops of *Paris, An.* 829. *Henricus Caltheisensis, Erasmus, Greg. Cassander, Anton. Contius,* the famous Lawyer, *Bellarmine* and *Baronius*, the Learned Cardinals.

The Testimony of *Baronius* being more largely cited than the residue, I thought it meet to search the Author, and there I found these following passages.

Writing upon the Contest between Pope *Nicholas* and the French Bishops concerning Appeals, he beginneth to shew how they complained, *that the Causes of Bishops, which ought to be tryed in Councils by their Fellow Bishops, were removed to the Apostolick Chair: And they questioned in their Letters, whether those Epistles of the more Ancient Bishops, which were not inserted into the Body of the Canons, but were written in the Collection of* Isidore Mercator, *were of equal Authority with the residue?*[1]

For the making of which Controversie the more plain, and to shew what they mean by the *Body of the Canons*, he tells us,[2] *It is certain, that the more Ancient Collection of the Decretal Epistles of the Roman Bishops, and the Canons of divers Councils, acquired such a name, that the Volum was called,* The Book, *or* Code, *or* BODY *of* CANONS, *increased by the addition of other Councils, which were afterwards celebrated. But the more ancient and full collection of the Epistles of Roman Bishops, and Canons of Councils, was that of* Cresconius, *of which I have spoken before,* saith he: *Which being increased by the addition of many Canons and Epistles, went under the name of the Book, or* BODY *of* CANONS.

---

[1] Marginal gloss: Baron. *An. Christ.* 865. *nu.* 4.
[2] Marginal gloss: *Ibid. nu.* 5.

And whereas there were many other Collections of Canons *compiled, that which is the richest of all, made by* Isidore *sirnamed* Mercator, *containing the Epistles of the Ancient Roman Bishops, beginning from* Clement, *was* Longè recentior, *far younger than they all; as* Hincmarus, *Archbishop of* Rhemes, *does testifie: Forasmuch as it was not brought out of* Spain *into* France, *before the times of* Charles the Great, *by* Riculphus *Archbishop of* Mentz: *For so he testifies in a letter of his to* Hincmarus Laudunensis, *beginning,* Sicut de Libro, &c. *But he who first collected Canons out of the foresaid Epistles, published at first by* Isidore, *and inserted them into the books of the Kings of the* Franks, *was* Benedictus Levita, *as he testifieth of himself in his Preface before the fifth book of those Canons; who writ in the times of the Sons of* Ludovicus Pius *the Emperour*, Ludovicus Lotharius, *and* Charles, *as we shewed, where he saith, I have inserted these Canons, &c. to wit, those* WARES *of* Isidore Mercator, *which were brought, as thou hast heard of* Hincmarus, *into* France *out of* Spain *by* Riculphus. Nè quis calumniari possit, ab Ecclesiâ Romanâ aliquid hujusmodi commentum esse: *Lest any one should slander us, and say, the Church of Rome invented such a business as this.*

I think here is enough: He looks upon it as a *Commentum*, a meer *Fiction*, and is afraid lest any one should have the advantage of Fathering such a dreadful Bastard on the Church of *Rome*. He calls them *Isidore the Merchants Wares*; he does not refel the Bishops of *France*; he dares not affirm they were in the Ancient *Code* of Epistles and Councils; he acknowledgeth them *far younger* than the BODY of CANONS, and subscribes to *Hincmarus* Archbishop of *Rhemes*, citing him who writ against *Isidore*, as a good and Authentick Author. He confesseth that they were never known in *France* till the times of *Charles the Great*, that is 700 years after they first began to be written; and that they were introduced into the books of the Kings of the *Franks* by *Benedictus Levita*, in the times of *Ludovicus Lotharius*, which was about the year 850. So that the Church was governed well enough without them, and about 800 years after our Saviours Birth they were first hatcht as meer *Innovations*. This is too large a *Chink* for an Enemy to open; but he proceedeth further.

That the same Riculphus, *Bishop of* Mentz,[1] *did live in the times of* Charles the Great, *many Monuments of that Age do make it certain; especially the Testament of the same* Charles the Great, *to which this* Riculphus *is found to have subscribed among divers others. We find that he was President also in a Council at* Mentz, *held in the year of*

---

[1] Marginal gloss: Baron. *An.* 365. *nu.* 6.

our Redemption 813. &c. *Since therefore the French Regions, which are nearest to* Spain, *knew not the* Collection of Isidore *before the times of* Riculphus, *much less* Italy, *it is a conjecture, that this* Isidore *did live and write not long before; and so it was first published by* Riculphus, *who brought it thither; then by* Benedictus, *who put it into the Capitular books; and lastly, by* Hincmarus Junior, *Bishop of* Laon, *the last Collector unto this our Age*: *which* Hincmarus of Rhemes, *a man of a keener smell, reprehendeth in many things, defaming that collection of* Isidore *which the other used, for which cause he was accused. For* Frodoardus, *in his History of* Rhemes, *Cap*. 16. *near the end, saith of him, that being accused because he had condemned the Decretal Epistles of the* Roman Bishops, *he professed and protested otherwise, that he admitted, held, and approved them with the greatest honour. Upon this occasion, to wit, it appears, he was branded with a mark, because he had signified himself not to have approved that Collection of* Isidore *in all things.*

Baronius you see, who is one of the greatest Friends to the See of *Rome*, endeavours to remove the matter of *Isidore* as far as he can from the *Roman Chair*, being sore afraid, lest the guilt of so many *Forgeries* should too apparently be charged upon her: For which cause he will will not have the book so much as *known* in *Italy*, nay not in *France*, which is nearer unto *Spain*, for 800 years time, but that it came out of *Spain* first, being brought by *Riculphus*. Perhaps *Riculphus* was never there. He doth not tell us that he went into *Spain*, for ought I can find, nor upon what occasion, nor in what City, nor of whom he received *Isidore*: which putteth me in mind of *Cacus* his device, who being a strong Thief, and robbing *Hercules* of his Oxen, drew them all backward by the Tail into his Den, that the print of their heels being found backwards, they might not be tracked, but seem to be gone another way.

But he fails in his design: for as it is strange, that *Italy* should not know the Decretal Epistles of its *own* Popes for 800 years, till *Riculphus* brought them out of *Spain*; so is it more strange, that being such *Forgeries* as he would have them, *Hincmarus* Archbishop of *Rhemes* should be accused for condemning them, and ratled up, and branded in such a manner, and compelled to recant by so powerful an Enemy; for it seems he had no way to save himself, but by *renouncing* his Opinion. The jealousie of the *Roman Church*, and its tenderness over *Isidore*, appeareth most exceeding great in the *hard dealing* which *Hincmarus* met with, who though he did recant, was still *noted with infamy*; as if to speak against *Isidore*, were a Crime not to be washed off by the *Tears* of Repentance in the Church of *Rome*. Perhaps the poor Bishop was an Hypocrite in that forced Confession, and for this was branded, because he confessed a *lye*, as men upon the Rack are wont to do, for his own deliverance: for that he knew still that *Isidore* was a Counterfeit, and must therefore be reputed a rotten Member of the Church of *Rome*. This *Baronius* observes, while he ascribeth *Hincmarus* his reprehending *Isidore's* Collection, to his *keener scent*; whereby he was able, more readily than others, to *smell* a *Rat*, and discover the *Cheat*.

Baronius proceedeth further in condemning the *collection of Isidore*, thus; *But* Nicholas *the Pope seemed to abstain from it on purpose:*[1] *for though he was often ingaged in these Controversies, concerning Appeals to the Apostolick Chair, and there were in it many, and those most powerful, Testimonies of most holy Popes, and they Martyrs too, whose Authority might be of highest force in the Church; yet he wholly abstained from them (which that he knew to be doubtful at least, is not to be doubted) using only those, concerning which there was never any doubt in the Church of God; because the Church did not want those adventitious, and late invented Evidences, because it might receive them abundantly from other places: but* Benedictus Levita *himself also, though (as you have heard from* Hincmarus, *and as he himself testifies in the Preface before his books) he took many things out of that same Collection of* Isidore; *yet being conscious in himself, that the Authority of those Epistles was not so sure, but that it nodded exceedingly, he never cited any Author of them, as he did in the other Epistles of the Roman Bishops,* Innocent, Leo, Gelasius, Symmachus, *and* Gregory; *naming the Authors of those, whose Faith was clear and certain. But further yet, with great caution, because he knew the Evidences taken from them not to be so firm, he took care, as he testifies in the end, to have them confirmed by the Apostolick Authority.*

Is not here a merry passage? *Bendictus Levita* knew the Decretal Epistles to be *false*, and therefore he got them to be *made true* by the Popes Authority; at least to be *confirmed as true*, whereas they were *doubtful* before. It is the manner of [Statesmen] sometimes, to get others to propose the matters, which they themselves design to be done; that the business springing form the request of others, might appear more *graceful* in the eye of the people. We may justly enquire, whether *Benedictus Levita* were not *ordered* what to Petition, by private instructions from his Holiness, before he made his motion to the Chair: for it had otherwise been an *extravagant impudence* to have assaulted

---

[1] Marginal gloss: *An.* 865. *nu.* 7.

the Chair with such a request as that is, of craving a Confirmation of new-found Records, so feeble and suspected. Whatever the *Intrigue* was, the *event* is clear, *Benedictus Levita* got them *confirmed*, and so they were adopted for his Holiness Children, though Pope *Nicholas* was shy a little out of shame and modesty, and blushed to acknowledge his poor Kindred.

It is further observable, that these counterfeit *Epistles* were first brought in into the Records of the *Franks*, without naming their Authors: and that a little after their *quiet* publication, some Favourite of the Chair grew more bold, and added their *names* unto them; this of *Clement*, that of *Anacletus*, &c. And that the work was thus perfected by degrees, *Baronius* shews us in the following passage.

But he who first published the Decrees extracted out of those Epistles,[1] *with the Title of the* Roman Bishops, *in whose names they are recorded, was that* Hincmarus *we mentioned, the Bishop of* Laon, *as appears by an Epistle or book written against him by* Hincmarus *of* Rhemes; *who receiving that work of the Bishop of* Laon, *read it not without indignation, and in very many things reproved it. But others have followed the Bishop of* Laon, *as* Burchardus, *who writ in the following Age, and others after him, who prefixed the names of the very* Roman Bishops *before all the Chapters, which* Gratian *also did the last of all.*

But that those Epistles are rendered suspitious, by many things which we have said in the second Tome of our Annals, while we mentioned each in particular, is sufficiently demonstrated: Where we shewed withal, that the holy Roman Church *did not need them, so as (if they should be detected of falsity) to be bereaved of its Rights and Priviledges, since (though she wanteth them) she is abundantly strengthened and confirmed by the Legitimate and Genuine Decretal Epistles of other Popes. But that the Chapters taken out of them by* Benedictus Levita, *were at first approved, as agreeable to the* Canons (*as himself testifies*) *by the Authority of the* Roman Bishops, (*which was done also by the latter Collectors*) *it happened rather by long use, than for any strength or firmness in themselves.*

Thus *Baronius* in his *Annals, An.* 865. *nu.* 5, 6, 7, 8. all together.

In Notis Martyrol. ad. 4. *April.* he saith, Vasæus *is convicted to have erred, who thought this* Isidore Pacensis *that* Isidore *who collected the Epistles of the* Roman Bishops, *and the Councils, &c.* Hincmarus Laudunensis *also, and* Trithemius, *and others err, who ascribe that collection to* Isidore *of* Hispalis: *That Opinion is refelled; first, because* Brauleus *and* Ildephonsus, *who lived in those times, drawing up a*

---

[1] Marginal gloss: *Ibid. nu.* 7.

Catalogue of his Writings, make not the least mention of that work. But further, all doubt is taken away concerning this matter, while the Author of that work, speaking there concerning the manner of holding a Council, *recites the words of the first* Canon *of the eleventh Council of* Toledo, *and mentions* Agatho *the Pope in his Preface, since* Isidore *of* Hispalis *departed this life, long before the times of that* Council, *and Pope* Agatho.

Had we time, we might make many curious reflexions upon these passages of *Baronius*: He afterwards talks of another *Isidore*, called sometimes *Mercator*, and sometimes *Peccator*; but of what Parents, what Calling, what City, or what Country he was, he mentioneth nothing. So that this *Child*, among all those *Isidores* and *Fathers* that are found out for it, must rest at last in one that is *unknown*.

All that can be gathered from this whole discourse of *Baronius*, is this, That a new Book of Councils, richly fraught with Evidences for the *Roman Church* and *Religion*, came abroad under the name of *Isidore*, containing Decrees and Decretal Epistles that were never before heard of in the world: that this Book was *falsly* Fathered upon *Isidore* of *Hispalis*; and that all those ancient Epistles of the Roman Bishops, from S. *Peter* down to *Siricius*, are justly suspected: Nay, he confesses them to be *infirm, adventitious,* and *lately invented,* or *newly found,* and to *nod exceedingly*: He opposeth them to those Records which are *Legitimate* and *Genuine*, though they are of late magnified, and followed by all the Collectors of the Decrees and Councils, being, though waved by some, cited and *approved* by other Popes, as well as Doctors, Jesuites, Cardinals, &c.

This is the last and best Story that can be made on the behalf of that *Book*, the Counterfeits in which, as we observed before, were, because they extol and magnifie the Popes Chair, received for good and Authentitck *Laws* in the Church of *Rome*: For *Baronius* died not long since, about the year 1607. in this last Century; and when he had seen the truth of those Arguments that are urged against the Forgeries, endeavours so to handle this matter in his History, as to clear the Church of *Rome* from the imputation.

Bellarmine, that saw not into this Mystery so clearly, takes another course; which when we have intimated one or two Marginal Notes in *Baronius*, we shall declare. *Baronius* deals more fairly with us than *Binius*; for the one in his Marginal Notes contradicteth his Text, sometimes to delude the Reader; but *Baronius* fairly notes in the Margin, Isidori *collectio vulgata in Galliis.* Isidori *collectio ab Antiquis non adeo probata.* Isidori *collectio ut minùs sincera notata, &c.* Soft words for a Treatise rejected, but strong Indications of a Desperate Cause. *The Ancients approved not the collection of* Isidore. *It was not so sincere as it ought,* &c.

Cardinal *Bellarmine,* to prove the Popes Supremacy, draweth one Argument from the Popes themselves; whose Testimonies he casteth into three Classes.[1] *The first,* saith he, *contains the Epistles of Popes that sate from* S. Peter *to the year* 300. *in which* Calvin *and the Magdenburgenses confess the Primacy to be plainly asserted; and that those Bishops were holy men, and true Bishops; but they say the Epistles are forged and new, and falsly Fathered on those Bishops.* In this Class he affirmeth, *These Holy Fathers do clearly assert the Primacy*; Clemens *in his first Epistle,* Anacletus *in his third,* Evaristus *Epist.* 1. Pius *Epist.* 1, *and* 2. Anicetus *Epist.* 1. Victor *Epist.* 1. Zephirinus *Epist.* 1. Calixtus *Epist.* 1. Lucius *Epist.* 1. Marcellus *in Epist.* 1. Eusebius *Epist.* 3. Melchiades *Epist.* 3. Marcus *Epist.* 1.

After this he saith, *Quamvis aliquos Errores, &c. Though I cannot deny, but that some Errours are crept into them, and dare not affirm that they are indubitable, yet I doubt not at all, but that they are very Ancient.* As if an old Deed being called into question, and the matter of Fact made certain, that it was a real Forgery; he that holds his possession by it, should say, It has been *interlined* indeed, and *corrupted* in may places, but 'tis very *old*. Let us see however what his reason is for the Antiquity of it: He is rough with his Opponents, and telleth us, *The* Magdeburgenses *do lye, when they say* Cent. 2. Cap. 7. *near the end, that no Author worthy of credit ever cited these Epistles before* Charles the Great: *For* Isidore, *who is* 200 *years older than* Charles the Great, *in the Proem of his collection of the Holy Canons,* saith, *that by the advice of* 80 *Bishops, he collected* Canons *out of the Epistles of* Clement, Anacletus, *&c.*

Isidore did indeed begin to flourish near to the year 610. So that *Bellarmine* takes him right for the same *Isidore* Bishop of *Hispalis*. But had he well examined the matter, he would have forborn to give the Lye to men more in the right than himself, confiding in the *rotten* Antiquity of this Counterfeit *Isidore*. For *Isidores Preface* is a Counterfeit too, made on purpose to countenance the Forgeries; not 200 years older than *Charles the Great*, things after the Death of *Isidore,* its pretended Author, being mentioned in the same.

Dr *Reynolds* in his Conference with *Hart,*[2] having smartly checked him for his *fourscore Bishops* out of one *Isidore,* asked him, *About what*

---

[1] Marginal gloss: Bellarm. *de Rom. Pont. lib.* 1, *cap.* 14.
[2] Marginal gloss: *Confer. Cap* 8. *Divis.* 3.

year of Christ Isidore *did die? How doth* Genebrard *write?* (because Genebrard was *Hart*'s most admired Author.) He answereth, *About the year* 637. as he proveth out of *Vasæus.* Asking him, *When the General Council of* Constantinople, *under* Agatho, *was kept?* He answereth, *In the year* 681. *or* 682. *or thereabout. Then* Isidore *was dead above* 40 *years,* saith Reynolds, *before that General Council. He was,* saith Hart, *but what of that? Of that it doth follow, that the Preface written in* Isidores *name, and set before the Councils, to purchase credit to those Epistles, is a counterfeit, and not* Isidore's: *For in that Preface there is mention made of the General Council of* Constantinople, *held against Bishop* Macarius *and* Stephanus, *in the time of Pope* Agatho, *and the Emperour* Constantine: *which seeing it was held above* 40 *years after* Isidore *was dead, by* Genebrard'*s own confession, by his own confession* Isidore *could not tell the fourscore Bishops of it. And so the* 80 *Bishops which* Turrrian *hath found out in one* Isidore, *are dissolved all into one Counterfeit, abusing both the name of* Isidore, *and fourscore Bishops.* Hart was unable to answer him, and fled from the Point.

Harding, in his Book against Bishop *Jewel,* citeth these Forgeries frequently and briskly: Upon the failure of which, though *Baronius* pretends an abundant number of other *Evidences*; yet in the loss of 30 or 40 *Primitive* Bishops and Martyrs, that were so long time, for the first 300 years after Christ together, thought to speak for the Supremacy of the Church of *Rome,* one of the fairest Feathers in the Popes Crown is plucked away; and the younger Evidences, in which *Baronius* trusts, being none but the Malepert and Arrogant Testimonies of *Junior Popes,* in their own Causes, will make but a slight impression in the minds of men, that have found themselves deluded with more ancient pretences, of the grave and unspotted Authorities of Holy Men, that Sacrificed themselves for the Glory of God, and the good of the World, and sealed their Testimony with their latest blood: which the latter Bishops of *Rome* have been more Secular and Pompous, than to be doing like their Predecessors.

CAP. V.

Divers Forgeries contained in Isidore's *Collection, mentioned in particular.*

Isidore, as he now standeth set forth by *Merlin*, has 50 *Canons of the Apostles* for pure and good Records; many Decretal Epistles, made, as he pretends, by the first Martyrs and Bishops of *Rome*; very long, and full of Popery.

He has two Epistles of S. *Clement* written to S. *James* Bishop of *Jerusalem*, that was dead before S. *Clement* came to the Chair: one to the Brethren dwelling with S. *James*, and two others in his name.

He has four Epistles in the name of *Anacletus*, who lived in the time of *Trajan*, and sate in the Roman Chair, *An.* 104. In the last of which the Counterfeit *Anacletus* feigneth, 'That all the Primacies and Archbishopricks in the World were divided and setled by S. *Peter*, and S. *Clement*; that the Church of *Rome* is the Head and Hinge of all the Churches; and that all the Patriarchal Sees were made such by vertue of S. *Peter*: *Antioch*, because he sate there, before he came to *Rome*; *Alexandria*, because S. *Mark* came to sit there from S. *Peter*: but *Rome* especially the first See, because it is sanctified by the death of S. *Peter*, and S. *Paul*. As if our Saviours Death were nothing able to sanctifie *Jerusalem*, as S. *Peter's* death was to sanctifie *Rome*: though besides the Death of Christ, *Jerusalem* hath this advantage, that it is the *first Church*, and the *Mother of us all.*'

That you may a little discern the dealings of the Papists, note here, that *Anacletus* his first and second Epistles are cited by *Bellarmine* for good Records, in the very same book[1] where he confesseth them to be Counterfeits: For though in one *little* passage they be confessed for the present satisfaction of a stiff *Opponent*; yet where men are minded to be corrupt, they may serve the turn in an hundred other places, by a *Pious Fraud*, and the Confession being over-skipped, they may still seem Authentick, especially if the place happen to be unseen where the Confession was made, as it often cometh to pass in voluminous writings.

Isidore has besides these, 2 counterfeit Epistles of *Evarisius*, 3 of *Alexander*, two of *Sixtus*, 1 of *Telesphorus*, 2 of *Higinus*, 2 of *Pius*, 1 of *Anitius*, 2 of *Soter*, 1 of *Eleutherius*, 2 of *Victor*, 2 of *Zephirinus*, 2

---

[1] Marginal gloss: Bellarm. *de Rom. Pont. Lib.* 1 *cap.* 23.

of *Calixtus*, 1 of *Urbanus*, 2 of *Pontianus*, 1 of *Anterus*, 3 of *Fabian*, 2 of *Cornelius*, 1 of *Lucius*, 2 of *Stephen*, 2 of *Sixtus*, 2 of *Dionysius*, 3 of *Felix*, 2 of *Eutychianus*, 1 of *Gaius*, 2 of *Marcellinus*, 2 of *Marcellus*, 3 of *Eusebius*, 1 of *Melchiades*. All laid down without the least note of any *Fraud*: though the letter Compilers of the Councils, having their eyes opened by the Century-Writers of *Magdenburge*, and the care of other Protestants, begin to acknowledge several of them to be Forgeries.

These *Epistles* have one common blast upon them: they were first seen in a *counterfeit book*, and never known to the World, till many hundred years after their *pretended* Authors were set in their Graves. They cannot *all* be confuted at once; the Reader therefore must have patience, till we meet with them in their places. In the mean time see what Bishop *Jewel* saith concerning them, a man never answered by any, especially as to these points, wherein he chargeth them with Forgery. '*Gratian* sheweth, that[1] the Decretal Epistles have been doubted of among the Learned. Dr. *Smith* declared openly at *Paul's-Cross*, that they cannot possibly be theirs whose names they bear: And to utter some reasons shortly for proof thereof, these Decretal Epistles manifestly deprave and abuse the Scriptures, as it may soon appear to the Godly Reader upon sight. They maintain nothing so much, as the State and Kingdom of the Pope; and yet there was no such State erected in many hundred years after the Apostles time. They publish a multitude of vain and Superstitious Ceremonies, and other like fantatsies, far unlike the Apostles Doctrine. They proclaim such things as Mr. *Harding* knoweth to be open and known Lies. *Anacletus*, that[2] was next after *Peter*,[3] willeth and straitly commandeth, that all Bishops, once in the year, do visit the Entry of S. *Peter's* Church in *Rome*, which they call *Limina Petri*; yet was there then no Church as yet built there in the name of *Peter*. Pope *Antherus* maketh mention of *Eusebius Alexandrinus*, and *Felix*, which lived a long time after him. *Fabrianus* writeth of the coming of *Novatus* into *Italy*; yet 'tis clear by S. *Cyprian*, and *Eusebius*, that *Novatus* came first into *Italy* in the time of *Cornelius*, who was (next) after *Fabianus*. One *Petrus Crab*, the Compiler of the Councils, complaineth much, that the examples from whence he took them, were wonderfully corrupted, and not one of them agreeing with another. *Gratian* himself upon good advice, is driven to say, that all such Epistles ought to have place, rather in

---

[1] Marginal gloss: D*ist*. 19. De. *Epistolis*. in copies: D*ist*. 19. De *Epistolis*.
[2] Marginal gloss: Dist. 9. Juxta Sanctorum.
[3] Marginal gloss: Dist. 97 Juxta Sanctorum.

debating matter of Justice in the Consistory, than in determining and weighing the truth of the Scriptures. Besides this, neither S. *Hierom*, nor *Gennadius*, nor *Damasus*, nor any other Old Father, ever alledged these Epistles, or made any account of them; nor the Bishops of *Rome* themselves at the first, no not when such Evidences might have stood them in best stead, in their ambitious contention for Superiority over the Bishops of *Africa*: The Contents of them are such, as a very Child of any judgment may soon be able to descry them. Here he nameth St. *Clement*'s writing to St. *James* when he was dead, *Marcellus* charging the Emperour *Maxentius*, an Infidel and a Tyrant, with the Authority of *Clement*; with several things of this kind. In his *Reply to* Harding's *Answer*, *Artic.* 1. and 4. But I proceed with *Isidore*, or rather *Merlin*, that first printed him.

He has, besides all these Epistles, certain counterfeit Decrees of *Sylvester*, Bishop of *Rome*, in the time of *Constantine* the Great, and the *Epilogus brevis Romani Concilii post Nicænum celebrati*; which *Hincmarus*, Archbishop of *Rhemes*, is reported particularly to have excepted against, as absurd, because it ordaineth, 1. *That no Lay-man ought to accuse a Clergy-man.* 2. *That no Inferiour Priest may accuse his Superiour.* 3. *That a Prelate may not be condemned without 72 Witnesses, a Cardinal Priest not without 43, a Cardinal Deacon of the City of* Rome *not without 27, a Sub-Deacon, an Acolythite, a Reader, a Door-keeper, not without 7 Witnesses.* It is further provided, that every one of these Witnesses must be *without any spot of infamy*: no Lay-man at all, nor any inferiour Clergy man. So that upon the matter a safe Indemnity is prepared for all kind of Priests, especially the great ones, to swim in any Excess as himself listeth, provided he be not guilty of the Protestants faults; that is to say, that he doth not touch the Popes Crown, or the Monks Belly.

This *Decree* is most solemnly put among the Councils by *Isidore*, and *Merlin*, by *Peter Crabbe*, *Surius*, *Binius*, *Labbe*, and *Cossartius*, and the *Collectio Regia*; and as solemnly put among the Popes Laws, by *Ivo* an ancient Bishop, a great Civilian, and one of the Eldest Digesters of the Canon Law, before *Gratian*.

This brief *Epilogue* set *before* the Council, giveth you to wit, that there were Cardinals in *Rome* in the time of *Constantine*,[1] the first Christian Emperour. But if you please to examine Antiquities, you will hardly find Cardinals so ancient.

Isidore in his Preface directed to one, whom he calls his *Fellow-servant and Father of the Faith*, mentioneth 70 Canons of the *Nicene*

---

[1] Marginal gloss: *An.* 320.

Council, somewhat too affectedly: 'You 80 Bishops, *saith he*, who have compelled me to begin and perfect this work, ought to know, and so ought all other Priests of the Lord, that we have found more than those 20 Canons of the *Nicene* Council, that are with us: And we read in the Decrees of *Julius* the Pope, that there ought to be 70 Chapters of that Synod.' Yet when he cometh to the Council it self, he forgets himself so far, as to lay down but 20; the 50 forged Canons receiving a fair Countenance only, by that Preface or Epistle, set for *shew* before the work.

He has an Epistle of *Athanasius*, and the Bishops of *Egypt*, to Pope *Mark*; wherein they tell him, that there were 70 Canons of the *Nicene* Council, and desire him to send them into *Egypt* from *Rome*, since all their own were burnt at *Alexandria* by the *Arrians*. *Mark* was dead 9 years before the Burning happened;[1] howebeit, he sent them a Gracious Answer, with the 70 Canons. The first of these was seriously cited to me by a Learned Son of that Church, to prove the Bishop of *Rome* was called Pope (to wit, by *Athanasius*, and all the Bishops of *Egypt*) within the first 400 years: But some of their latest Authors begin to blush at it, as *Binius* and *Baronius* do in particular.

Next to these he has three Epistles of *Julius* the Pope, as very Counterfeits as the former, yet generally cited by the Pseudo-Catholicks, as good Records.

After these, *an Epistle of* Athanasius, *and the Bishops of* Egypt *to* Liberius; the oppression of the Church by the *Arrians* being the pretended Theme, but its real design is to magnifie the Popes Chair.

Liberius *his Answer. Ejusdem farinæ.* A lofty Brag like the residue.

An Epistle of the Bishops of Egypt *to Pope* Felix, *concerning the cruel Persecutions of the Arrians*: An humble Address, and very Supplicatory. Though *Felix* was an *Arrian* himself, and an Usurper of the Chair, thrust in by an *Arrian* Emperour, while *Liberius* the true owner of it was banished for the Faith; yet the stile of the Epistle runneth thus, *Domino beatissimo,* &c. *To our must blessed and most honourable Lord, the Holy Father* Fælix, *Pope of the Apostolical City,* Athanasius, *and all the Bishops of* Egypt, Thebais *and* Lybia, *by the Grace of God assembled in the Holy Council of* Alexandria. A stile too too lofty for those purer times of humble simplicty: The usual Compellations of those days (as may be seen by S. *Cyprian*'s Letters to the Bishops of *Rome*, and some other good Records) being far more *short* and *familiar*; such as *Julio Urbis Romæ Episcopo,* or, *Stephano fratri,* or, *Cornelio Collegæ &*

---

[1] Marginal gloss: Bin. *Tom.* 1 *in vitâ* Marc.

Coepiscopo; that is, *to* Julius *Bishop of the City of* Rome, or *to* Stephen *my Brother*, or *to* Cornelius *my Associate and Fellow-bishop*: Nor can we find any other, in undoubted instruments, for the first 300 or 400 years: But for an *Usurper* to be called *Most blessed and honourable Lord*, an *Heretick, Holy Father and Pope of the Apostolical City*; and that by a man who had rather die than be guilty of such a Flattery, was little suitable to the Spirit of *Athanasius*, that Great and Couragious Champion of the Church, being (as God would have it) one, that of all others was the most mortal hater of the *Arrians*.

Isidore and *Merlin* dote so exceedingly, as to make this Usurper a *Pope*, and to record his Decrees as *lawful Canons*.

After a little time *Liberius* was restored, but on very base and dishonourable terms, as *Bellarmine* himself testifieth[1] out of S. *Hierom*, and *Athanasius*. He fainted in his Persecution, and was restored by an Arrian Emperour, *upon his Subscription to the Heretical Pravity*. After this he writeth more Decretals; and the Title of his Epistle is in *Isidore* thus, *Epistola* Liberii *Papæ, ut nullus pro Persecutionibus dum durare potestatem suam relinquat Ecclesiam*. It is Nonsense, and false Latine: but *Binius*[2] about a thousand and three hundred years after Liberius his death, mendeth it thus: *Epistola* XII. Liberii *Papæ, ad omnes generaliter Episcopos, ut nullus pro persecutionibus dum durare potest suam relinquat Ecclesiam: That no man should forsake his Church, for persecution sake, while he was able to bear it*. By the Title it should be a compassionate Letter: For if any one be wearied with persecution, as *Liberius* was, by a tacit intimation, it seemeth to permit him to renounce the Faith, as *Liberius* did: for *Bellarmine* and *Platina* consent to this,[3] that he subscribed to the Arrian Creed; only the one saith, he did it in the external act, *through fear*; and the other *Sentiens*, that he thought, or *consented with them in all*. Platin. *in vit*. Liberii.

Damasus *his Epistle to* Paulinus *Bishop of* Antioch *follows*. I fear an Imposture: *Isidore* and *Merlin* were not aware there was no such man: Their followers are fain to mend it thus; Paulinus *Bishop of Thessalonica*. As *Binius, Labbe*, &c. *In vitâ Damasi*.

Next the Epistle of *Damasus* to *Hierom*, and *Hierom*'s Answer,[4] both confessed to be a Forgery, there is *an Epistle of* Stephen *the Archbishop*,

---

[1] Marginal gloss: Bell. *de Rom. Pont. lib. 4. cap. 9*. Baron. *An. Christ.* 357. Liberii 6, *nu*. 32, 33.
[2] Marginal gloss: Bin. *in vit*. Liberii.
[3] Marginal gloss: Bellarm. *ut supra*.
[4] Marginal gloss: Bin. *Not. In Epist. 3*. Damasi. *&c in Epist*. Hieron. *ad* Damas.

and of three Councils in Africa, to Damasus the Pope, concerning the priviledge of the Roman Chair. Doubtless the Bishops in *Africa* were very zealous for the *priviledge of the Roman Chair*, ever since the Oppression, and Cheat of *Zozimu*s. The Title is somewhat suspitious: *Beatissimo Domino, &c. Apostolico Culmini sublato, &c. Stephanus Archiepiscopus Concilii* Mauritanii, *&c*. In English thus; *To our most blessed Lord, and the Apostolical Top highly lifted up, the Holy Father of Fathers, and the Supreme Bishop over all Prelates, Stephen Archbishop of the Council of Mauritania, and all the Bishops of the three Councils in the Province of Africa*. Many men have stiled themselves Archbishops of *Provinces*, but no man (as I remember) *Archbishop of a Council*. There may be Archbishops in a Council, but not an Archbishop of the Council. *Three Councils at once in the same Province* were never heard of: One and the same *Letter sent from three Councils* is a strange thing: So is a Letter sent in the name of one Archbishop, as *President of three Councils* at a time.

After this we have 6 Epistles of *Siricius*, 2 of *Anastasius*, 19 of *Innocent*, 2 of *Zozimus*, 3 of *Boniface*, with several Answers: Among which there is inserted a *Constitution of* Honorius *the Emperour* sent to *Boniface, That if there were two Bishops of* Rome *made any more, they should be both driven out of the City*: Which shews how subject the Roman Chair is to Schisms, and the Power that did of old belong to the Emperour.

There are other Epistles of *Celestine, Sixtus, Leo, Hilarius, Simplicius, Felix, Gelasius, Anastasius, Symmachus, Hormisda, &c.* the most of which do much exceed our compass of the first 400 years, and are too late for our Cognizance: For since the Forgery of *Zozimus*, much credit is not to be given to the Roman Bishops: Not as if one mans fault had blasted them all; but he leads up the Van of Forgers, and they have all persisted in his Guilt, no one of them making acknowledgment or restitution, and almost all of them guilty of the like, either by doing, or suffering.

Among the rest there is an Instrument, which the Collector calleth, *Sacra* Justini *Imperatoris ad* Hormisdam *Papam*: The Sacred Writing of the Emperour *Justinus* to *Hormisda* Pope. But the word POPE is not in the superscription: The Letter it self is, *To the most Holy and blessed Archbishop and Patriarch of the Venerable City of* Rome, Hormisda. Archbishop and Patriarch we allow him; but not that *Typhus* wherewith the Fathers in the sixth Council of *Carthage* charge Zozimus, that *blasphemous Title* which *John* assumed at *Constantinople*, and S. *Gregory* so declaimed against at *Rome*.

This Letter of *Justin* the Emperour was written more than 500 years after our Saviours Birth, yet I never saw true Record, in all that time, give a Title so high to the Bishop of *Rome*. But *Justin* was a man of low Descent, a Swineherd at first, a Carpenter afterwards, then a Souldier of Fortune, and at last an Emperour: He was the more solicitous therefore to complement so Mighty a Bishop with accurate expression.

Note well. *Isidore* has suppressed all the Canons of the sixth Council of *Carthage*, as too bitter and sharp for the Popes Constitution. And so has *Merlin*, though very foolishly: for in the beginning of the Book he hath a Preliminary Tract, called, *An Annotation of Synods, the Acts whereof are contained in this book*. In which he giveth us this account: in the *Aquitan* Council, 18 Fathers made 24 Canons: in that of *Neocæsarea*, 16 Fathers made 14 Canons: in that of *Gangra*, 16 Fathers made 21 Canons: in that of *Sardica*, 60 Fathers made 21 Canons: in that of *Antioch*, 30 Fathers made 25 Canons: in that of *Laodicea*, 22 Fathers made 59 Canons: in the Council of *Carthage*, 217 Fathers made 33 Canons. I had a long time coveted a sight of these Canons, and finding them numbred in such *an Annotation of Synods, the Acts whereof are contained in this book*, I was much comforted with hope of seeing them: But when I turned to the place, I found them not! Surely to slip out 33 Canons at a time, made by more Fathers than were in all the other Councils put together, is a lusty *Deleatur*: There was never *Deed* of more importance imbezelled in the World.

The *Nicene Council* had 318 Fathers, that made 20 Canons: for what secret cause therefore he skippeth over the account which he ought especially to give of this, is worth the enquiry. He mentions it by the *by*, and shuffles it off without an account, (perhaps) because he was loath to say, or unsay the story of 70 Canons in the *Nicene* Council. However he dealeth fairly with us in this, that having noted *Aurelius* to have been President in the sixth Council of *Carthage*, he confesseth, *that S.* Augustine, *Bishop of* Hippo, *is recorded to have been in that Council, in the Reign of* Honorius. *Ibid.*[1]

Binius, and all the Popish Compilers I could ever meet with before, clipped off that Council in the midst, without so much as signifying the *number* of its Canons. I was glad I had a sight of their number *here*, though I mist of themselves: and was confident, that however cruelly the Pope dealt with *Aurelius* Archbishop of *Carthage*, S. *Aug.* Bishop of *Hippo*, and other holy Fathers, in cutting out their Tongues,

---

[1] Intended marginal gloss: *Ibid.*

I should at last meet with them: And the Learned *Justellus* with much honesty and honour has made us satisfaction.

We acknowledge some *true* Records among these *Spurious* Abominations: but a little *poyson* spoileth the greatest Mess of the most wholesom Meat; much more doth a Bundle of Forgeries that over-poyseth the true Records in *size* and *number*.

The method which he useth in the *mixture* of the Records and Forgeries is remarkable: For beginning with the Counterfeit Epistles of *Clement, Anacletus, &c.* he first seasoneth the Readers spirit with Artificial *Charms*, and *prepossesseth* him with the high Authority of the Roman Patriarchs; and after he has given him those strong Spells and *Philtres*, composed of *Roman Drugs*, permits him boldly to see some true Antiquities, his eyes being dazled in the very *Entry*, with Apparitions of Popes, and such other *Spectres*.

Lest the *Tincture* should decay, he reserves some of the Forgeries till afterwards; that the *true Records* might be compassed in with an *Enchanted Circle*, and the last *Relish* of Antiquity go off as strong as the first, and be as successful as the *prepossession*. Thus he cometh down with Forgeries to *Melchiades*; and then he breaketh off the *Decretal Epistles*, to make room for the *Councils*, beginning with the *Nicene*, under pretence of its Excellency, and putting the Councils before it in time, after it in order, that he might get a fit occasion to introduce them here, so running down in a disorderly manner, from *Ancyra* to *Neocæsarea, Gangra, Sardica, Antioch, Laodicea, Constantinople, Ephesus, Chalcedon*, among the *Greeks*, and then up again to the *Latine Councils*, many of which preceded divers of the other; as the first, second, third, fourth, fifth, sixth, Council of *Carthage*, all which were before the Council of *Constantinople, Ephesus*, and *Chalcedon*: From the seventh Council of *Carthage*, he runneth down to the thirteenth Council of *Toledo*, which happened long after *Melchiades, Silvester*, Pope *Mark Liberius, Felix*, &c. were dead: Then he cometh (in the second part of his Work) up again to *Sylvester*, and so downwards with more Decretals, that he might Husband his Forgeries well, and not glut us with them altogether.

And remarkable it is also, that he doth not give us the least syllable of notice of any Fraud among them: Nay, even *Constantine*'s *Donation* set in the Front before the *Nicene*, and in the midst between the first Order of Counterfeits and the Councils, passeth with him silently and gravely for a true and sacred Instrument, which is of all other the most impudent Imposture.

Let *Baronius* say what he will, it was impossible to *debauch* all Antiquity and Learning with so much *Labour* and *Art*, without some deep *Counsel* and *Design*. What use *Merlin* puts all these things to, and how much he was Approved in the Church of *Rome*, you shall see in the next Chapter, and how highly also he extolleth this Book of Forgeries.

How plainly he fathereth it upon S. *Isidore* Bishop of *Hispalis*, is manifest by the *Coronis* of the first Part, wherewith it endeth.

Give thanks to industrious and learned men, studious Reader, that now thou hast at hand the Acts of the Councils, *as well as of the* Popes; *which* Isidore *the Bishop of* Hispalis *collected into one Volume*, &c. What shall we believe? The *first* Edition of the Book it self, or *Baronius* his Testimony? Old *Merlin* fathers it upon *Isidore* before *Baronius* was born, and all the World was made to believe the Bishop of *Hispalis* was the Author of it; though now for shame, and for a shift, they fly to another *Author*. Now if *Isidore* were dead before the Booke was made, it must needs be a Cheat; which, as * *Merlin* saith,[1] *honest* Francis Regnault, *the cunning Printer, ended at* Paris, *in the year of our Lord* 1535, which unusual form of *Concluding*, instead of allaying, increaseth the suspicion.

---

[1] Marginal gloss: Ibid. *Clausulæ insuetæ suspicionem pariunt* [an unusual way of conclusion raises suspicion].

CAP. VI.

What use Merlin *makes of* Isidore, *and the Forgeries therein. How much he was approved in the Church of* Rome. *How some would have* Isidore *the Bishop to be a Merchant, others, a Sinner.*

How false and fraudulent soever the Collection of *Isidore* be, yet its Title is very Splendid, and its Authority Sacred in the Church of *Rome*.

JAMES MERLIN'S
COLLECTION
OF THE
Four General Councils ;

The NICENE, *the* CONSTANTINO-
POLITAN, *the* EPHESINE, *and
the* CHALCEDONIAN:

Which S. Gregory the Great *does Worship and Reverence as the Four Gospels.*

TOM. I.

Of 47 *Provincial Councils also; and the Decrees of* 69 POPES.
From the APOSTLES *and their* CA-
NONS, *to* ZACHARIAS.

ISIDORE *being the Author.*

ALSO

The GOLDEN BULL *of CHARLES IV.*
Emperour, concerning the Election of the KING *of the* ROMANS.

PARIS :

At Francis Regnault. 1535.

All we shall observe upon this Title, is this; If *Gregory the Great* did Worship and Reverence the *Four General Councils*, as the *Four Gospels*, they were the more to blame that added 50 Canons to one of them; and they much more, that stain them all with the Neighbourhood, and Mixture of such hateful Forgeries.

But who could suspect that so much Fraud could be Ushered in with so fair a Frontispiece? or so much Sordid Baseness varnished over with so much Magnificence! I have heard of a Thief that robbed in his Coach, and a Bishops *Pontificalibus*; of the *German Princess*, and of *Mahomet's Dove*: But I never heard of any thing like this, that a *Patriarch* should trade with Apostles, Fathers, Emperours, Golden Bulls, Kings, and Councils; under the fair pretext of all these, to Cheat the World of its Religion and Glory.

His *Grandeur* is rendered the more remarkable, and his *Artifice* redoubted, by the Greatness of his *Retinue*: *Riculphus* Archbishop of *Mentz*, *Hincmarus Laudunensis*, *Benedictus Levita*, the Famous *Isidore*, and his fourscore Bishops, *Ivo Cartonensis, Gratian, Merlin, Peter Crab, Laurentius Surius, Carranza, Nicolinus, Binius, Labbè, Cossartius, the* COLLECTIO REGIA, *Stanislaus Hosius*, Cardinal *Bellarmine, Franciscus Turrianus*, &c. Men that bring along with them Emperours and Kings for Authority, as will appear in the Sequel: Men who think it lawful to Cheat in an *Holy Cause*, and to lye for the Churches Glory: These augment the Splendour of his Train. Their Doctrine of *Pious Frauds* is not unknown: And if we may do evil that good may come, certainly no good, like the Exaltation of the *Roman Church*, can possibly be found, wherewith to justifie a little evil.

The *Jesuites Morals* are well understood: Upon their Principles to do evil, is no evil, if good may ensue. Perjury it self may be dispenced with by the Authority of their Superiour. An illimited Blind Obedience is the *sum* of their Profession. To equivocate and lye for the Church, that is, for the advancement of their Order, and the Popes benefit, is so far from sin, that to murder Heretical Kings is not more Meritorious.

It is a sufficient Warrant, upon such grounds, to *James Merlin* our present Author, that he was commanded to do what he did, by great and eminent Bishops in the Church of *Rome*: as he sheweth in his Epistle Dedicatory, *To the most Reverend Fathers in Christ, and his most excellent Lords,* Stephen *and* Francis, *&c.* the one of which was Bishop of *Paris*, and the other an Eminent Prelate, who ordered all his work by their care, and made it publick by their own Authority.

Conceiving nothing (saith he) *more profitable for the Commonwealth, I have not dissembled to bring the Decrees of the Sacred Councils and Orthodox Bishops, which partly the blessed* Isidore *sometime since digested into one, partly you, most Reverend Fathers, having confirmed them with your Leaden Seal, gave me to be published in one Volume: For every particular appeareth so copiously and Catholickly handled here, which is necessary for the convicting of the Errours of mortal men, or for the restoring of the* now almost ruined World, *that every man may readily find wherewith to kill Hereticks and Heresies.*

The *Protestants* being grown so dangerous, that they had almost ruined the *Popish World*, by reforming the Church; nothing but this *Medusa*'s Head of Snakes and Forgeries was able to affray them. The nakedness of the *Pontificians* being discovered, they had no Retreat from the Light of the Gospel, but to this Refuge of Lies: *Where every one may readily find*, saith Merlin, *wherewith to kill Hereticks and Heresies, to depress the proud, to weary the voluptuous, to bring down the ambitious, to take the little Foxes that spoil the Vineyard of the Church.* By the proud and ambitious, he meaneth Kings and Patriarchs, that will not submit to the Authority and Supremacy of the *Roman Church*; and by the *little Foxes*, such men as the Martyrs in the *Reformed* Churches; the driving away of which was the design of the publication. That he meaneth *Kings* and *Patriarchs* in the former, you will see in the Conclusion.

And[1] if any one shall hereafter endeavour to fray, and drive away these Monsters from the Commonwealth, what can be more excellent, saith he, *than the stones of* David, *which this* Jordan *shall most copiously afford? If any one would satisfie the desires of the Hungry, what is more sweet and abundant than the Treasures which this Ship bringeth from the remotest Regions? but if he desires the path and splendour of Truth, by which the clouds of Errour (with their Authors) may best be dispelled, and driven far away; what is more apparent than the Sentences of the Fathers, which they, by the Inspiration of the Holy Ghost,[2] have brought together into this Heap? For here, as out of a Meadow full of all kind of Flowers, all things may be gathered with ease, that conduce to the profit of the Church, or the suppressing of Vices, or the extinguishing of Lusts. Here the most precious Pearl, if you dig a little, will strait be found, &c. Here the Tyranny of Kings and Emperours, as it were with a Bit and Bridle, is restrained. Here the Luxury of Popes and Bishops is repressed: If Princes differ, here peace sincere is hid: If Prelates contend about the*

---

[1] Marginal gloss: *Ibid.*
[2] Marginal gloss: The Forgeries Fathered on the Holy Ghost.

Primacy, here THE ANGEL OF THE GREAT COUNCIL *discovers who is to be preferred above the residue,* &c.

Are not the *Roman Wares* set off with advantage here? How exceedingly are these *Medicines* for the Maladies of the Church boasted by these Holy *Mountebanks?* The stones of *David* that kill *Goliah,* the River that refresheth the City of God, the Food of Souls, the Ship, the very *Argonaut* of the Church, that comes home laden with *Treasures* from unknown Regions, are but mean expressions; the Inspirations of the Holy Ghost, the Pearl of Price, *Angelus ille Magni Concilii,* the Angel of the Covenant are hid here; and all (if we believe this dreadful Blasphemer) declare for the Pope against all the World. Here is a Bit and Bridle for Kings and Emperours, a Rule for Patriarchs, and what not?

The *Councils,* and true Records, we Reverence with all Honour due to Antiquity: And for that very cause, we so much the more abhor that admixture of Dross and Clay, wherewith their Beauty is corrupted. Had we received the Councils sincerely from her, we should have blest the Tradition of the Church of *Rome* for her assistance therein: But now she loveth her self more than her Children, and the Pope (which is the Church Virtual) is so hard a Father, that he soweth Tares instead of Wheat, and giveth Stones instead of Bread, and for Eggs feedeth us with Scorpions: We abhor her practices, and think it needful warily to examine, and consider her Traditions.

What provisions are made in *Merlin*'s *Isidore* for repressing the Luxuries of Popes and Bishops, you may please to see in *Constantines Donation,* and the *Epilogus Brevis.* In the one of which so many Witnesses are required before a Bishop be condemned; and in the other, care is taken for the *Pomp* of the *Clergy,* even to the *Magnificence* of their *Shooes,* and the *Caparisons* of their *Horses.*

As *Merlin,* (who was a Doctor of Divinity of Great Account) so likewise all the following *Collectors* among the Papists, derive their Streams from this *Isidore,* as their Fountain. And for this cause I was the more desirous to see the *Book,* which is very scarce to be found; and the more scarce, I suppose, because if the Fountain be unknown, a greater Majesty will accrue to the Streams. The Booksellers-Shops afforded me none: but at last I met with two of them; the one with the Learned Dr. *Barlow, Margaret Professor,* and *Provost of Queens Colledge* in *Oxford,* the other in the *Bodleian* Library: The one was Printed at *Collein, An.* 1530. The other at *Paris* before-mentioned. Either had all, and both affirm *Isidore Hispalensis* to be the Author.

Though some afterwards are careful to distinguish *Isidore Hispalensis* from *Isidore Mercator*. The one failing, the other is obtruded as the Author of the Work: the latter *Collectors* unanimously leaving out *Hispalensis*, and calling him only by the Name of *Mercator*. But how the Name of *Isidore Mercator* should come before the Book, the Wisest Man in the World, I suppose, can scarcely *Divine*.

It is said, that Eulogius *Bishop of* Corduba *had a Brother*,[1] *whose Name was* Isidore, *whose condition of Life Banishment, whose Nation* Spain, *whose Trade was Merchandize: And that this Spanish Merchant flying out of his Country, upon the account of Religion, chose rather to intrust this most precious Treasure, which he had saved from the Lust of Barbarians, to the care of the Germans, than to expose it to the Rage of those Wasters and Destroyers wherewith* Spain *was at that time infested, as the Monks of* Mentz; *at least, who, upon his having sojourned there, took occasion to put his Name before the Book that was then in their hands,* would have the World really to believe. This is *Blondel*'s conjecture, which he raiseth from the real existence of such an *Isidore*. But he excuseth himself for *conjecturing barely* in such an affair, because the Work is a *Work of Darkness*, and they that did it, hated the Light, because their Deeds were evil: *And the Patcher up of those Epistles coming forth in the Vizor of another Name*, in such *a business* a conjecture may suffice. Let them that imposed the Name, give us a Reason why they did it: it is not incumbent on us to render an account of what other men are pleased without reason at any time to do.

Is it not impossible, but a Knave, called *Isidore*, might be sent abroad with the Book, being pickt out on purpose, that the Famous *Isidore*, Bishop of *Hispalis*, might be believed to be the Author. He might come to *Mentz*, and sojourn there under the notion of a *Spaniard*, and give *Riculphus*, or the Monks, a sight of the Book, as a rare inestimable Treasure: For *Sinon* was let loose, with as little Artifice as this, to the Destruction of *Troy*. Thus, whence it came really, could hardly be discovered; and the Thing too would be the more admired, because it came from the *farthest Regions*, as *Merlin* speaks, being saved so Miraculously from the hands of *Barbarians*. But where did this Traveller find it? this Merchant, of whom did he receive it? For *morally* speaking, it is impossible, that a Merchant should be the Author of it; especially at that time, when the Records lay scattered perhaps in an hundred Libraries, and were all to be sought in obscure *Manuscripts*. An Ass may be expected to meddle with an Harp, as soon

---

[1] Marginal gloss: Blondel, *cap.* 6.

as a Merchant with the Mysterious Records of the Church. How come *Lay-men* to be so Judicious? Had any Merchant so great a Skill as this imports? It is improbable *fourscore Bishops* should know it, much more that they should urge him to do that, which their own Learning and Function fitted them to do far better: Yet *Isidore* in his Preface writeth thus, *You Eighty Bishops, who urged me to begin and perfect this Work, ought to know, as ought all other Priests of the Lord also, that we have found more than these* 20 *Chapters of the Nicene Council, &c. It is a shame to the Church of Rome, that a Lay²man should* be the Fountain of all her Records; and that in very deed, the greater part of them should be in no Manuscript nor Library in the World, being never seen, nor heard of, till *Isidore* brought them out of *Spain*: That no man can tell what *Isidore* made the Book, which is now the President, and the sole Storehouse of all their Collections, is a little infamous; especially since they believed of old unanimously, that the Bishop *Isidore* of *Hispalis* was its ancient Author.

Baronius when he had irrefragably disproved *him*, puts nothing certain in his stead: but having a Wolf by the ears, and being willing to say something, raises a dust. and goes out in the Cloud.

In the ancient Manuscripts,[1] saith he, *we find this* Isidore, *the Collector of the Councils, sirnamed* Mercator; *as in those which we have in our Library: but in the Inscription of the Books lately Printed, he is stiled not* Mercator, *but* Peccator, *according to the manner of some of the ancient Fathers, who for Humility sake were wont to superscribe, and subscribe themselves so. I conceive it crept in by a mistake, that* Mercator *was written for* Peccator; *but since the Author of that Collection, reciting the General Councils in his Preface, endeth with the sixth, it is evident that he lived after the sixth Council, and before the seventh.*

What Hypocrisie is here? He had before sufficiently detected the Collection for a Cheat, and yet he now gravely troubles his Brains, to know what *Isidore* this might be. It is a blind *Isidore*, that has left no mark of his Life behind him, but only that which lies in this counterfeit Preface; an *Isidore* that can no where else be found, *by the great Annalist, Baronius*. He has no other help to know the time about which he lived, but the Preface: Whether *Peccator*, or *Mercator*, is but a superficial Controversie; whether any *Isidore* made the Book, is a deeper enquiry: The old Manuscripts of *Baronius*, are Books of yesterday, all written since the counterfeit *Isidore* was published. The variety shews, that the Papists can rest no where: And the liberty they

---

[1] Marginal gloss: Baron. *in Nat. Martyrol. ad* 4. *April.*

take to alter what they see in *Manuscripts*, as they please, is an ill sign of a large Conscience, which studies not what is *faithfully* to be published, but *conveniently*. For because the Name of *Mercator* did smell too strong of the *Wares*, lest the World should wonder how the Inscription of a *Merchant* should come out before the Councils, they thought it fit to strain the courtesie of a Letter, and (because *Peccator* is an humble Name) to turn the Merchant into a Sinner. That it was a *Sinner*, I dare be sworn, and a sly *Merchant* too; lucky Names both of them: but the last is capable of a finer pretence, no Cheat being so vigorous and unavoidable, as that of a penitent weeping Sinner. The Pride of *Rome* comes cloathed in Humility, after the example of her Supreme Head, who stileth himself *the Servant of Servants*, while he aspires (by these very Records) to be the *King of Kings*.

    Isidore and *Merlin* being two of the first Collectors of the Councils among the Papists, I have taken the more liberty to be somewhat copious in them, that I may conveniently be more brief in perusing the residue.

CAP. VII.

Of Francis Turrian *the Jesuite*: *With what Art and Boldness he defendeth the Forgeries.*

Notwithstanding all the weakness and uncertainty of *Isidore*, *Francis Turrian*, the Famous Jesuite, appears in its defence, about 40 years after the first publication of it by *Merlin*. The *Centuriators of Magdenburg* having met with it, to his great displeasure, he is so Valiant, as not only to maintain all the Forgeries therein contained, but the whole Body of Forgeries vented abroad by all the *Collectors* and *Compilers* following, till himself appeared.

His Book is expresly formed against the Writers of the *Centuries*, and is a sufficient Evidence, that as soon as *Isidore* came abroad by Dr. *Merlin*'s *Labour*, and the Bishop of *Paris Command*, it was sifted by the Protestants.

It is dedicated to *the most Illustrious and most Reverend D. D.* Stanislaus Hosius, *Cardinal of the Holy Roman Church, and Bishop* of Collein. Printed by the Heirs of *John Quintel*, and approved by *Authority, An. Dom.* 1573.

He defends all the Canons of the Apostles which are recounted by other *Collectors*.[1] That you may know the *Mettal* of the Man, I will produce but two Instances.

The last of those Canons, which he maintaineth to be the Apostles, is this which followeth.

Qui Libri sunt Canonici, &c. *Let these Books be Venerable and Holy to you all:*[2] *Of the* Old Testament, *five Books of* Moses, Genesis, Exodus, Leviticus, Numbers, Deuteronomy; *one of* Joshua *the Son of* Nun, *one of* Judges, *one of* Ruth, *four of* Kings, *two of* Chronicles, Hester *one, three of the* Macchabees, *one of* Job, *one Book of* Psalmes, *three of* Solomon, Proverbs, Ecclesiastes, *and the* Song of Songs; *one of the* 12 Prophets, *one of* Isaiah, *one of* Jeremiah, *one of* Ezekiel, *one of* Daniel: *And without, let your young men learn the Wisdom of the Learned* Syrach.

But of ours, that is, of the New Testament, *there are four Gospels*, Matthew, Mark, Luke, *and* John; *fourteen epistles of* Paul, *two Epistles of* Peter, *three of* John, *one of* James, *one of* Jude, *two Epistles of* Clement,

---

[1] Marginal gloss: *Vid.* Turrian.
[2] Marginal gloss: *Can.* 84.

and the Ordinations of Me Clement, *set forth in Eight Books to you Bishops, which are not to be published to all, because of the Mysteries contained in them; and the Acts of our Apostles.*

This is the eighty fourth Canon, and in some Accounts the eighty fifth; where you see the *Epistles of Clement,* and *Eight Books of his Ordinations,* put into the Body of the Bible: As for the difference of the Accounts he sheweth you the way how to reconcile them.

If this be one of the Apostles Canons, then *Clement* was an Apostle, or had Apostolical Power: but if it be a Forgery, then not only the Apostles Canons, but the very Text of the Holy Scriptures is interlined and forged by the same.

He maintains all the *Decretal Epistles,* and among the rest S. *Clement*'s: Whose genuine *Epistle to the Corinthians* they leave out, as making nothing to their purpose: but five *Spurious* ones they record; the two first of them being written to S. *James,* and the last *to the Brethren dwelling with him at Jerusalem.*

It is good sport to see how like the *shot* of a great Gun, the Discovery of the Protestants comes in among them: Their keenness in detecting *the time of* S James *his Death,* shatters the Knot; and whereas before they were all united, they now fly several ways, every man shifting for himself, as he is best able.

Baronius dislikes such Arts of upholding the Church,[1] not as impious and unlawful, but as inconvenient and pernicious. *Bellarmine* affirms the Epistles to be Old, but dares not attest them; *Isisdore, Merlin, Peter Crabbe, Nicolinus, Carranza,* and *Surius,* own them freely without any scruple: For saying nothing of the Quarrel, they lay them down simply as good Records. *Binius, Labbè,* and the *Collectio Regia,* confess some of them to be false; and in particular, that S *James* was dead seven years before S. *Clement* could write his first Epistle to him. And to salve the sore, they say, that it was not written to *James,* but to *Simeon,* who was also *Bishop of Jerusalem,* and *Brother to our Lord*; and that the Name of *James* crept into the Title *Mendosè,* by Errour and Mistake, for that of *Simeon.* But honest *Turrian* maintains plainly, that S. *Peter* and S. *Clement* knew very well that S. *James* was dead before they wrote unto him; yet nevertheless they did very wisely, both S. *Peter* in ordering the Epistle, and S. *Clement i*n writing it. And his Reasons, as he bringeth the matter about, are pretty specious.

For my part, I protest, that such a High Piece of Impudence was to me incredible: But that you may see the rare Abilities of a *Jesuite*

---

[1] Marginal gloss: *In Not. Martyrol. ad* 6. *Octob.*

to argue well for the *absurdest Cause*, turn to his Book, and read his Comment on S. *Clement's first Epistle*, and there you shall see *Wit* and *Folly* equal in their height: Wit in *managing*, but Folly in *attempting* so mad a business.

For the sake of those who are not able to read, or get the Book, I will give you a Glympse of his Demonstrations. First he observeth, how *Reason it self compelleth us,*[1] *especially being confirmed by so many and so great Testimonies of the Ancients, to confess the Epistle to be S.* Clement's, *whose it is reported to be.* He sophistically pretendeth here, that there were great Authorities of the Ancient Fathers extant to prove it: *Whence,* saith he, *it began to be had in every mans hand, to be read by the Catholicks, to be put among the Decretal Epistles, and produced and cited in Ecclesiastical Causes and Judgments.* The latter part of which Clause is true: For (as we before observed) *Gratian, Ivo,* and the rest of the Popes Ministers, have brought the *Decretals* into the Body of the *Canon-Law,* which maketh the matter more *fatal* and abominable; for being really cited in their *Ecclesiastical Courts,* and used both in matters of Controversie, and in cases of Conscience, they are forced either to defend them, or to pluck up their Customs by the very Roots; and so further expose the Church of *Rome* to the shame of Levity or Fraud; yet for this very cause, it is far more impious and wicked to retain them: So that not knowing which way is best, some of them retain them, and some of them renounce them. But you must wink at all this, and believe what *Turrian* says, for the Authority of the Roman Church (which hath seated the Forgeries in the Chair of Judgment) is a greater Argument, to them that believe her Infallible, than any one Doctor can bring against them: *Neither was blessed* Peter *ignorant, when he commanded to write to the Dead, nor* Clement, saith he, *when he wrote by the Commandment; but that the Readers would presently see, the Epistle to be written to him, whom all men knew to be dead before* S. Peter; *they being about thereupon, to enquire diligently into the cause thereof, and seeking to find it: Nay, this was the design of the blessed* Peter, *and therein he imitated the Holy Scripture.* Whether to *counterfeit,* or *blaspheme* the Scriptures, be the worse, I cannot tell: but of this I am sure, that they who think such courses lawful, (as this fastned on S. *Peter,* and the Holy Scripture here) will stick at nothing which they take for their advantage. For that it was lawful to counterfeit S. *James* his Name, he proveth afterwards very largely; and now he is giving the reasons of it: One intention was to stir up all people to Enquiry;

---

[1] Marginal gloss: Turrian *in* Clement *Epist.* 1.

their admiration at so strange a thing, being very prone to make them diligent to learn the cause of it: Another was, that all Bishops might see the more clearly, that they were taught in the person of *James*: for *James* being dead, and uncapable of receiving the instruction, it is evident, that he was not intended thereby; and therefore it must be for others in his capacity. A third reason was the preventing of envy: for had S. *Peter* vouchsafed (being our Saviours *Vicar*, and *Head* of the *Church*) to write to any Bishops alive, the Honour done unto that Bishop had been so great, that all the rest had been tempted to maligne him shrewdly for that advantage: *His intention was, saith he, to transfigure these things in the person of* James,[1] *after the manner of the Holy Scripture; and that as well for other Bishops, as especially those that should succeed him in the Church of* Jerusalem, (*whence the preaching of the Gospel began, according to the Prophesie of* Isaiah) *that they might thus think with themselves; If the Prince of the Apostles commanded* Clement *to write these things to* James *the Brother of our Lord, whom* Peter, James *and* John *did first of all ordain, who now ceased to be a Shepherd, and was rewarded with his Crown; he certainly did not command him to write for his sake, but for us, to whom* Solomon *saith, Look diligently to the face of thy Cattel and consider thy Herds, &c. Let this*, saith he, *be one cause of the Transfiguration, or counterfeiting a person in this Epistle.* Having noted how S. *Paul* transferred a certain business on himself and *Apollos* by a Figure, he concludeth thus: *Why therefore may we not think, that* S. Peter *for the same reason commanded* Clement *to transfer his Epistle concerning his Death and Doctrine, pertaining in common to every Bishop, by a Figure to* S. James *already dead? lest if he should have commanded him to have written to* Simon *the Bishop of* Jerusalem, *who succeeded* S. James, *or to any other, as to* Mark *the Bishop of* Alexandria, *or* Ananias *of* Antioch, *or any other, he should then perhaps seem to love him, or honour him, more than the residue?*

Much more he saith to this purpose but all made vain, with one small observation. Whereas he pretends that *Clement* knew S. *James* to be dead, there is a fifth Epistle written by the same *Clement*, *To his most dearly beloved Brethren dwelling at* Jerusalem, *together with his dearest Brother* James, *his Fellow-Disciple.* So that S. *James* after all, was still thought to be alive, by those that *transferred* this Epistle on S. *Clement* by a *Figure*.

S. *Peter*'s influence over the Bishop of *Jerusalem*, and *our Lords Brother*, was thought a considerable Circumstance for the Establishment

---

[1] Marginal gloss: *Ibid.*

of the following Popes: And till the Protestants discovered the *Fraud*, let *Turrian* say what he will, there was scarce a person in the World, that thought not the Letter *timed* well enough for the purpose.

And whereas he pretendeth *so many and so great Testimonies of the Ancients, confessing the Epistle to be S.* Clement's; he is not able, nor does he so much as attempt to name one, from S. *Clement* downward, till this *Spurious Isidore*, that affirmed any such matter. Howbeit, he quotes *Origen, Theodoret, Gregory Nazianzen*, &c. to prove the lawfulness of a Transfiguration, and makes great Ostentation of the Fathers, in shewing that S. *Peter* and S. *Clement* did wisely in the business.

CAP. VIII.

Of Peter Crabbe's *Tomes of the Councils: Wherein he agrees with, and wherein he differs from* Isidore *and* Merlin.

Besides the Forgeries that are in *Merlin* and the Bastard *Isidore, Peter Crabbe*, whose Tomes of the Councils were published eight years after the *first Edition of Merlin*, published more, of as great importance as the former; not omitting those of *Isidore* and *Merlin*, but recording and venting them altogether.

He pretends to give an account of all those councils that have been from S. *Peter* the Apostle, down to the Times of Pope *John* 11.

He wrote before *Turrian*, as *Carranza* and Surius did, whom it is Turrian's business to defend.

The End being proposed before the Means, with what design these Editions of the *Councils* are so carefully multiplied, we may conjecture by a *Treatise* that is set in the Front of them, *concerning the Roman Primacy*. Almost all the Compilers, after *Peter Crabbe*, having prefixed the same with one consent before their Work, as the Aim of their ensuing Labours.

It is extant in *Crab, Surius, Nicolinus, Binius, Labbe* and *Cossartius*, and the *Collectio Regia*. *Carranza* hath it not nor *Paul* v.

Paul V. in his own Work, published at Rome, *Anno Dom.* 1608. touches the Forgeries but very sparingly. It does not become the Majesty of a Pope in his own Name to utter them: It is moreover a thing of hazardous consequence for *him* to appear in Person in such a disgraceful business: It befits his Holiness to act rather by Emissaries and Inferiour Agents, as all great Statesmen and Polititians do, being unseen themselves in matters that reflect too much upon their safety: that Method (you know) is more stately, as well as more Honourable and secure. Yet he approveth others at a distance, as his dear Son *Severinus Binius* in particular, who dedicated all his Tomes to Pope *Paul* v. in the year 1608. and has a particular Letter of Thanks from Pope *Paul* himself, as a Badge of his Favour before the Work. As for *Carranza*, he is but an Abstract, or brief *Compendium*.

This *Treatise of the Primacy*, thus put before the Councils, containeth a Collection of Testimonies out of Counterfeit epistles of the Primitive Bishops and Martyrs of *Rome*, proving under the Authorities of most

Glorious Names, *that the Holy Apostolical Church obtained the Primacy, not from the Apostles, but from our Lord himself: that it is the Head and Hinge of all the Churches; that all Appeals are to be made thereunto; the greater causes, and the contentions of Bishops, being to be determined only by the Apostolical See: that she is the Mother of all Churches; and as the Son of God came to do the Will of his Father, so ought all Bishops and Priests to do the Will of their Mother: that all the Members ought to follow the Head, which is the Church of* Rome: *that the first See ought to be judged by no man, neither by the Emperour, nor by Kings, nor by the People: that it was granted to the Church of* Rome, *by a singular priviledge, to open and shut the Kingdom of Heaven* to whom she would: *that none may Appeal from her to any other: that the Apostolical See may without any Synod unbind those whom a Synod or Council hath unjustly condemned.* Of which Sentence she is to be the Judge, whether it be just; for she may judge all, but none her: *that the Church of* Rome *is the Foundation and Form of all the Churches;* so that no Church hath its Essence without that of *Rome: that from her all the Churches received their beginning.* Doctrines as true, as the Authorities by which they are confirmed; and to say no more, as true as the last: For the Christian Churches received their beginning from *Jerusalem*, before the Church of *Rome* had any Being.

Consider it well, and you shall find this the removing of a *meer stone* of highest importance, an Encroachment upon the Territories of other Patriarchs, an Usurpation of all Spiritual and Secular Power, to the subversion of Emperours, Kings and Councils.

For if all are to obey her, as Jesus Christ did his Eternal Father; if it be granted to the Roman Church, by a singular Priviledge, to open and shut the Kingdom of Heaven to whom she will; if no King, Emperour or Council, hath power to judge the Pope, while he hath power to judge all; Kings, Emperours and Councils are made Subject to him, and nothing can escape the Sublimity of his Cognizance.

Besides this *Treatise of the Primacy, Peter Crab* has 34 *Canons of the Apostles* more than *Isidore* and *Merlin*: So that Antiquities are daily increasing in the Church of *Rome*, and Records are like Figs, *new* ones come up instead of the *old* ones.

The last of these Canons is that of *Clement*, about the *Canon* of the Bible: a Forgery of more *Scriptures*, added to the former, in the names of the Apostles; defended by honest *Turrian* zealously, and magnified by *Nicolinus* as the *Coronis* of the Apostles Canons.[1]

---

[1] Marginal gloss: *Vid. Cap. 11.*

He has the *Roman Pontifical,* a Treatise of the Lives of Popes, fitted exactly to the *Decretal Epistles,* and accordingly, most richly stored with all kind of Forgeries and Lyes. It is a *new* Book Fathered upon Pope *Damasus*; which *Isidore* and *Merlin* (I think) were ignorant of, for it is not in them; and I admire where he had it. It is the Text on which he commenteth, as a Great Record; he useth it as a great proof in doubtful matters, and according to it the Method of his *Tomes* is ordered. You will see more of it hereafter.

He has the counterfeit *Council of Sinuessa,* a new Piece, which I find not in *Merlin*: But I verily believe, he scraped it up some where else, and 'tis not his own, 'tis so full of nonsense: A Council sitting in the year 303. and defining from that Text, *Ex ore tuo justificaberis, & ex ore tuo condemnaberis,* that no Council can condemn a Pope, nor any other Power, but his own mouth: For because our Saviour has said, *Out of thine own mouth thou shalt be justified, and out of thine own mouth thou shalt be condemned*; therefore no body can condemn the Pope but himself alone: for which purpose they repeat the Text over and over again, very feebly and childishly, even unto nauseating: And the example of *Marcellinus* is made an instance in the case; who being called to an Account for offering Incense to an *Idol,* could not be condemned by this Council, and was therefore (because he was Pope) humbly implored to condemn himself.

It is a Council of great value, because of the President we have in it, how Scriptures may be applied to the Bishop of *Rome*; and how places that belong to all the World, must peculiarly be ascribed to him alone: Howbeit *Crab* makes a sowre face on't, and is fain to premise this Premonition to the Reader.

By reason of the intollerable difference and corruption of the Copies, whereof the one was old and faulty, though written in the best Parchment and Character; the other more old, but equally depraved (as the Beholders might discern with their eyes) so far, that what they mean sometimes cannot be understood, we have set both the Copies, without changing a syllable of them, in two Columns; setting the Letter A *over the first, and* C *over the other: but the middle Column over which* B *is placed, for its capacity, or rather conjecture, endeavours as much as it is able, to reconcile the other two so very divers, and bring them to some sense.*

He does not tell you plainly, that he made the middle Copy; but 'tis easie to conceive it, since he found but *two,* and they were so full of nonsense, that he added one, which is the third, to reconcile them. Yet *Crabbe's* Invention is now recorded by the *Collectio Regia,* and the two old ones, for their horrid *Barbarismes*, are thrown out of the Councils, and (for very shame) are cast away: for proceeding in his Apology, *Crab* a little after saith, *Nemo ergo caput subsannando moveat*, &c. *Let no man therefore wag his Head in derision, who having either gotten more correct Exemplars, or being of a more Noble and clear apprehension, is able to mend these: but rather let him patiently bear with what is done, and reduce it himself into better form.*

This is a sufficient Light, wherein to see the dissimilitude between Forgeries and true Records: For whereas the *undoubted* were made in great Councils of Holy Men, and are all of them clear and pure, and well-advised, full of Uniformity, Sense, Gravity, Majesty, Smoothness, Order, Perspicuity, Brevity, Eloquence and Verity; it is the common Fate of these Instruments which we accuse as *Forgeries*, being made in a *Dark* Age by men not so Learned as the Church of *Rome* could desire, (and sometimes in a Corner by some silly Monk) to swarm with Absurdities, Errours, Tautologies, Barbarismes; to be rude and tedious, empty and incoherent, weak and impertinent: yet some of them we confess to be more pure in Language, and better in sense than others.

This Council of *Sinuessa* is more ridiculous than it is possible well to imagine, before you read and consider it.

He has the Counterfeit *Edict of the Emperour Constantine* for a good Record. It is more warily made than the other, and better Latine, but of *Swinging Importance*: 'Tis but a Deed of Gift, wherein the first most Christian Emperour is made to give all the Glory of the Western Empire, with its Territories and Regalities, to the Bishop of *Rome*. We shall meet with it in others: for the Collectors of the *Decretal* Epistles, all of them, harp upon this String most strangely.

As Pope *Paul* V. so *Peter Crab* has but 20 Canons of the *Nicene Council*; wherein he agrees with *Isidore* and *Merlin*, and differs much from some that follow him: Nay, he agrees and disagrees with *Isidore* at once, in this very thing: He agrees with *Isidore* in his Book it self, (on the *Nicene* Council) but disagrees with him in his *Preface*.

But then he maketh amends for the Omission; for he hath the Synodical Epistle of the *Nicene* Council, a *new* Record, which I find not in *Isidore*, or in any before him: It is an humble Address of the *Nicene* Council to Pope *Sylvester*, beseeching his Holiness to *ratifie* their Decrees: To shew that no Council is of any value, unless it be approved by the Bishop of *Rome*: And he has a Gracious Answer too by the same Pen, or I am sorely deceived; for they are both alike so full of Barbarismes and false Latines, that another Dunce can hardly be found like the first to imitate them. In good earnest, they are the most feculent Forgeries that ever I saw. To speak much in little, is, they are worse than the *Sinuessa* Council.

They are without Greek Copies, which (where all the rest is in Greek) is an evil sign: But as they are, you shall have them, when we come to *Binius*, that the more Learned may judge of their Excellency.

He has a *Pseudo-Catholick* Council at *Rome* under Pope *Sylvester*, with the same *Premonition to the Reader*, word for word, which he set before the *Sinuessa* Council, *Propter Exemplariorum intolerabilem nimiamque & Differentiam, & Depravationem*, &c.

He has the other Forgeries of *Isidore Mercator*; and among the rest, the *Epilogus brevis* concerning the number of Witnesses.

He defaces and suppresses the sixth Council of *Carthage*, as well as his Predecessor.

What with blotting out, and putting in, he so disguizes the Face of Antiquity, that unless it be to very clear eyes, the Primitive Church appeareth not the same.

Yet are his Voluminous Tomes dedicated *to the Invincible Emperour* Charles V. being Printed in the year 1538. by Peter Quintell. *Cum Gratiâ & Privilegio tam Cæsario quam Regio Colloniæ*. That is, *At* Collein *by the consent and Authority both of the King and Emperour*. So far even Monarchs are deluded sometimes with a shew of Piety, and the Light of Depraved and Corrupted Learning.

CAP. IX.

Of Carranza: *his Epitome of the Decrees and Councils. He owneth the Forgeries.*

Carranza, being but a short *Compendium,* was Printed at *Paris, An.* 1564. to wit, very fitly, for the more general spreading of the corrupted Councils: All the other *Collections* being great Volumes, but this a little Informer, or Companion for the Pocket.

It was dedicated *to the Illustrious* Diego Hurtado Mendoza, *Orator in the State of V*enice, *and his Imperial Majesties Vicegerent in the Holy Council of* Trent.

He lays down all the *Apostles Canons* for good Laws, even the last it self being not excepted; and selects Decrees out of the *Decretal Epistles* for good and Catholick *Canons.*

The Decretal Epistles themselves would be too long for so short a Compendium; and therefore he has not the Decrees themselves, but Excerptions.

He has the *Pontifical* of the Popes Lives, but more modesty than to ascribe it to *Damasus*: It is a part of his Text however.

He has but 20 Canons of the *Nicene* Council, and skippeth over the Council of *Sinuessa*.

He omits the *Epilogus Brevis*, but owns the Council to which it is annexed.

He followeth *Isidore,* and exceeds him a little.

CAP. X.

Of Surius *his four Tomes, and how the Forgeries are by him defended. He hath the Rescripts of* Atticus *and* Cyril, *by which Pope* Zozimus *was condemned of Forgery in the sixth Council of* Carthage.

Laurentius *Surius* was a Monk of the Order of the *Carthusians*: He wrote four Tomes: He pretends to have all the Antiquities of the Church at large, and to *mend* and *restore* the defects of the Ancient Manuscripts. What their *mending* and *restoring* is, you begin to discern. He dedicates the whole Work to *Philip* King of *Spain, Sicily,* and *Neapolis,* &c. and directeth it in another Epistle *to the most August and Invincible Emperour* Charles V. It was *Printed at* Collein *by* Geruvinus Galenius, *and the Heirs of* John Quintell, *in the year of our Lord* 1567.

He has the counterfeit Preface of *Isidore Mercator,* before detected; *The Treatise of the Primacy of the Roman Church,* all the 84 *Canons of the Apostles,* and the *Apostolical Constitutions* of Pope *Clement* (newly added to the Tomes of the Councils) for good Records; though *Isidore Mercator,* some of the *Apostles Canons,* and *Clement's Constitutions,* are rejected by some of the best of his most able Followers, (as you shall see hereafter:) not I suppose upon mature deliberation, but inevitable necessity.

The *Liber Pontificalis* of Pope *Damasus,* that notorious Cheat, is the groundwork upon which he commenteth. It so exactly containeth the Lives and Acts of the Bishops of *Rome,* that when I first approached it, I apprehended every *Life* to have been recorded by some person contemporary with the Pope, of which he was writing: for it nominates the time of their Session to a Year, a Moneth, a Week, and a Day, from S. *Peter* downward: Which being done for no Episcopal Chair beside, it made the *Roman See* seem of more Eminent Concernment than the residue from the very first beginning; such a peculiar and extraordinary care being no mean Indication of its High Exaltation above all other Chairs, that were not for a long time together so accurately regarded. But a little after, I found *a shrewd sign*; for beside the errours and contradictions noted before, in the midst of all this exactness, he misseth sometimes 3, 4, 5, 6, 9 years together. This shall be proved hereafter, with more than we yet say, when we come to *Binius*.

He has all the *Decretal Epistles,* and the *Donation of Constantine* for good Records. *The Epistle of* Melchiades *concerning the Munificence of*

Constantine; the Spurious *Roman Council under Pope* Sylvester, with the *Epilogus Brevis*; *the Letters between* Athanasius *and Pope* Mark, concerning the number of the *Nicene* Canons: Those Letters tell us the Canons of the *Nicene* Council are 70. and yet he records but 20 of them.

The most of these Great Appearances are rejected afterwards, by *Baronius, Binius, Labbè*, and the *Collectio Regia*.

By good fortune he has the *Rescripts* of *Atticus*, and S. *Cyril*, the Patriarchs, concerning the *true Records* of the *Nicene* Council, sent to the sixth Council of *Carthage*, upon the occasion of *Zozimus* before related.

The Letter of that Council to *Celestine* the Bishop of *Rome* concerning that Controversie.

And a Scrap of the Council it self: but he omits the Decrees.

Did I follow them throughout all Ages, my work would be endless. We should find much foul Play in following Councils and Records of the Church: but for several weighty Reasons I have at present confined my self within the compass of the first 400 years next after the Death of our Lord, whose Name is not to be mentioned without praise and glory.

Note well: I go on thus, to observe particularly what Forgeries every Collector of the Councils owneth, and what Emperours, Kings, and Popes, their Books are dedicated to; and what priviledge, in all the principal parts of the Popes Jurisdiction, they come forth withal; and especially what a multitude of men have been encouraged to carry on this Design, that you might see the Conspiracy of the Members with the Head, and the general Guilt of that Church in so Enormous an Affair. To which we might add the innumerable *Armies* of Learned men that have cited them in that Church, and the Company of Captains that have defended them: But it had been better for them that they had never medled with the Protestant Objections, for they have made the matter worse than they found it, and bewraid themselves in all their Answers; nay, they have made the *Frauds* more eminent and notorious, by disturbing the Reader, while they give him Warning by their *Notes*, though the intent be to defend them. This I speak especially upon the last, from *Binius* downward.

CAP. XI.

Of Nicolinus *his Tomes, and their Contents for the first* 420 *years. His Testimony concerning the sixth Council of* Carthage.

Nicolinus is printed in five Volumes, *Sixti V. Pont. Max. fælicissimis Auspiciis*, as himself phraseth it: I think he means, *By the favourable Permission and Authority of Pope* Sixtus V. He dedicates his Tomes *to the* same *most Holy Lord* Sextus, *&c.* which were printed at Venice, *An.* 1585.

Among other things in which I should say he is peculiar, had not *Merlin* in his *Isidore* done the same, he sets a counterfeit *Epistle of* Aurelius, *Archbishop of* Carthage, *to* Damasus *the Pope*, and the Popes *Answer*, in the Front of his Work. The Epistle requesteth a Copy of all the *Decretals* that were made by the Bishops of *Rome*, from S. *Peter* downwards. The Answer intimates a Copy, commanding him to preach and publish the same.

In both these *Collectors* the Epistles are displaced above 300 years out of their due order, meerly that they might face the Forgeries with the great Authorities of *Aurelius* and *Damasus*, who were both dead 300 or 400 years before the Counterfeits were made: Howbeit, the Pageant does well to adorn the Scene; it entertains the Spectators as a fit *Præludium*, to make the way more fair for these disguized *Masquers*.

In the last of these Epistles, the Counterfeit Decrees are Fathered on the *Holy Ghost*, and whosoever speaketh against them, is charged with *Blasphemy*.

Yet for all this, though the Epistles were desired by *Aurelius*, and sent by *Damasus*, and commanded to be preached and published throughout the world, they were never heard of by the space of 700 or 800 years after their first Authors, nor for 300 or 400 years after this *Damasus* and *Aurelius*; though pretended to be the Canons of the Holy Fathers, so Sacred, and so Divinely inspired by the Holy Ghost.

This is that *Damasus* upon whom the Famous Pontifical is Fathered: He sate in the Chair *An.* 370. The Forgeries were unknown till about the year 800.

This *Aurelius* is he who tasted the Decrees of *Zozimus*, and had experience of their sincerity, when he resisted the Encroachments of the Roman Chair.

But to return to *Nicolinus*; he has *Isidore*'s Preface, *The Treatise concerning the Primacy of the Roman Church*, containing so many Testimonies out of forged Bishops, Martyrs, and Fathers: *All the Apostles Canons*, of which he maketh S. *Clement*'s the Top and *Coronis*, concluding that Impious Counterfeit with this affected phrase, *Coronidis ipsorum Canonum Apostolorum finis: The end of the Coronis of the Apostles Canons.*

Francis Turrian is in so much esteem with him, that he hath Eight Books of *Clement*'s Constitutions, with *Turrian*'s *Proem*, and *Explanatory Defences* upon them.

The *Liber Pontificalis*, drawn from the beginning like a *Vein* of Lies, through the tedious length of 800 years, infecting all these Ages with Forgery: It is his Text in like manner.

He has all the *Decretal Epistles* without Exception; *the Council of* Sinuessa, *or condemnation of Pope* Marcellinus, with the same *Premonition* you saw in *Peter Crab* to the *Reader*; *The Donation of the Emperour* Constantine, which by this time one would think to be a sound and admirable Record, having so many Hands subscribing it, and so many Pens inserting it among the *Councils*, without the least note of any *dubiousness* or *blemish* in it.

He has *threescore and eighteen Canons* of the *Nicene* Council,[1] and professeth himself to be the first which added them thereunto: And he had them of *a certain man* that brought fourscore of them in *Arabick* to *Alexandria*, as his *Printer* does witness for him to the Reader. But surely had there been so many, Pope *Paul* V. and all the Collectors before him, had not omitted them.

Some 40 years hence we may expect fourscore more: for as for those *naked and vulgar Canons*, (as he calleth the Old and Authentick Records) they will not serve the turn; nor yet the old *Seventy* mentioned by *Isidore*, *Athanasius*, and Pope *Mark*: by which you may see they are always growing, and may come to a *Million*, if the continuance of the World permit it, and their need require it.

What say you? In good earnest, methinks, the year 1585. is very late, for the finding of *eight and fifty Canons of the Nicene Council*:[2] That Council was assembled in the year 327. and made its Canons

---

[1] Marginal gloss: Nicol. *Epist Dedicat. ad* Sixt. *V.*
[2] Marginal gloss: Nicol. *Ty-pogr. Lecto.ri*

above *one thousand and two hundred years* before *Nicolinus* time: They were written in *Greek*, and these lay dormant in *Arabick*, so many Ages, no man can tell where. But the *blessed* Jesuites, or *one of the same Society*, luckily found them the other day.[1]

Here and there he has a true Record, and among the rest a piece of the sixth Council of *Carthage*, though mangled too: where concerning the two Counterfeit Canons of Pope *Zozimus*, he saith, *The African Fathers not finding any such* Canons *as these, in the* Codes *which they had of the* Nicene Council, *both in* Greek *and* Latine, *promised that they would keep them only so long, as the time would be, that they might get the true* Copies *out of* Greece: *Which when they had been sent for, and were brought from* Cyril *of* Alexandria, *and* Atticus *of* Constantinople, *they were found imperfect, as not containing but only those* 20 Canons, *which were extant also among the* Latines; *in which nothing is contained concerning Appeals to the Roman Bishop: Nay, those African Fathers from the fifth and sixth of those* Canons *gathering the contrary, did earnestly beseech* Celestine *the Pope, that succeeded* Boniface, *who was the Successor of* Zozimus, *that he should not admit Appeals: which (they said) as it was most prudently and justly provided for by the* Nicene Council, *so they found it in no* Synod *of the Fathers, that any should be sent from the side of his Holiness.*[2] *What* Boniface *and* Celestine *answered, it is not certain*: Acta enim illa valdè concisa sunt, & mutila, *For those Records are cut very short, and maimed; and therefore the matter is the more obscure.*

Who maimed those Records is worth the Enquiry: Some-Body that was concerned in them, and whose influence must be exceeding great for the attempting of such a thing, hath *cut them short*, that Records so offensive and pernicious to him, might be made *obscure*. But as Thieves, by dropping some of the Goods by the way, are oftentimes detected, or Murderers by forgetting the Knife behind them; so doth the Great and Just GOD infatuate the Pope of *Rome*, against whom this Council was assembled, and smite his Agents with blindness here; and at other times their heart faileth them, because of *Guilt*: so that not daring to make *thorow work* with the Councils, they faulter, and are detected.

Here is a rare case, all the Copies of the *Nicene Council*, throughout the World, were *imperfect* 1200 years ago, both among the *Greeks*, and among the *Latines*, only those at *Rome* were valid and Authentick. For the Councils of *Carthage* were reckoned among the *Latines*, as you may

---

[1] Marginal gloss: Nicol. *Ty-pogr. Lecto.ri.*
[2] Marginal gloss: *No Legatus à Lætere.*

see by *Isidore*, and *Merlin*, placing them in that number, and that justly; for the *African* Fathers that pertained to *Carthage*, wrote in *Latine*, as S. *Augustine, Fulgentius, Tertullian, &c.* They were Naturalized so far, that *Latine* was almost their Mother-Tongue, as *Justellus* observes out of S. *Augustine*: and yet these that were Allied to the See of *Rome* so near, were at one with the *Greeks* in the Records controverted: None were good at *Carthage, Constantinople,* or *Alexandria,* &c. but only those which the Pope produced in his own Cause: Nor were any like his upon the Face of the whole Earth besides.

At first I admired to see those Canons of *Carthage* so abruptly cut off by *Binius*, where I happened first to miss them: but when I afterwards found them, by the help of *Justellus*, I saw the reason: The *Roman Bishop* was curbed; though that of *Anacharsis* concerning Laws proved true; *Laws are like Spiders Webs, they detain Flies, but Hornets break through them.*

Nicolinus having intimated the lameness and obscurity of the Narration, goeth on thus: *It is probable that* Celestine *wrote back sharply, and would have the Appeals of Priests, from their own, to the bordering Bishops, and of Bishops themselves to the* Roman Chair *established and valid.* The Pope would have it so, notwithstanding all contradiction: *For as much as they were founded on Right and custom, and upon the* Nicene Canons, *which were kept entire (it is credible) in the Roman See, as they were extant in the time of* Mark.[1]

It is credible: Was ever such Impudence known before! They were not able to urge one Argument why it should be *credible*, and yet this *credibility* must overthrow all the Evidence in the whole World.

But they were kept entire *in the Roman See, as they were extant in the time of* Mark. This spoileth all! for by referring you to *Mark*, he appeals to the Epistles of *Athanasius* to *Mark*, and of Pope *Mark* to *Athanasius, concerning the number of the Nicene Canons.* Which Epistles of *Mark* and *Athanasius*, by invincible reasons urged by *Binius*, as well as the Authorities of *Baronius, Labbè,* and the *Collectio Regia*, are evidently proved to be very Forgeries.

He gives you more of these audacious *Guesses*; He says *it is credible, that they were contained also among the Canons of* Sardica *which* Celestine *sent, it is probable, unto them: But that the Africans rested not satisfied, either because they suspected those Canons to be corrupted, or for some other cause; it is shewn in the Epistle of* Boniface *the* II. *to* Eulalius *of* Alexandria, *concerning the Reconciliation of* Carthage, *which happened about* 100 *years after.*

---

[1] Marginal gloss: Nicol. *Ibid.*

The more you stir this business, the more it stinks. The *Epistles* made in the name of *Eulalius* and *Boniface*, concerning the *Excommunication of the Churches of* Africa *for* 100 *years*, past down so fair to *Nicolinus*, that he took them for good Records; and doubtless he thought it well enough, that the African Fathers were Excommunicated for opposing the Popes Opinion: So that the Quarrel rose very high, or, what we before observed was very true, these Epistles of *Boniface* and *Eulalius* were invented to colour the Popes Cause, and disgrace the Fathers. Take it which way you please, it smells ill: *Baronius* and *Bellarmine* had rather they should be Counterfeits.

His *probability* about *Celestine's* sending the Canons of *Sardica* to *Carthage* fares little better: *Celestine* knew very well the Canons of *Sardica* would not do in that Council: *Nicolinus* cannot produce one syllable in proof, to make it *probable*, that he sent them thither; and his flying to *Sardica* is in an evil hour; for it is opposed by 217 Bishops, so great, that they have frighted *Rome* out of her Excommunication, who altogether testifie, no less than twelve hundred years ago, *that no Synod of the Fathers made any such Canons.* And if *Sardica* were no Synod, what will its Canons signifie? The Popes then living and concerned, never attempted so vain a shift, but positively affirmed and maintained still, that they were the *Nicene* Canons: only the Council of *Sardica* is pretended of late, and some *new* men, now the business is over, perswade us they did all mistake while the *matter* was in agitation, both at *Rome* and *Carthage*; and that themselves have more clear and piercing judgments (to see into a business so far off better) than all the Fathers.

Admit those Canons were made at *Sardica*, it was a gross Errour to Father them upon the *Nicene* Council: for the Authority of *Sardica* is not to be compared with that of *Nice*. *Sardica* was unknown to all the Council at *Carthage*. S. *Augustine* thought it an Arrian Council; as *Binius* in his Notes upon it observeth: and *Bellarmine* puts it among *the partly Reprobated*.[1] And that which induceth me to believe those Canons now extant in the name of *Sardica* to be forged, is, that they were first produced in *Zozimus* his Counterfeit, and Fathered upon *Nice*. And there being a *Council* once, it is now pretended that there were two there; that these Bastards disowned at *Nice*, might have a Sanctuary somewhere, and find some Fathers. My conjecture is made considerable, because the Canons now Fathered upon *Sardica* are *contrary* to those of *Nice*: And it is not probable, that two *Catholick Councils* so near, should so suddenly Decree things contrary to each other; nor that the *same Fathers* that were

---

[1] Marginal gloss: Bell. *de Council & Eccles. lib I cap.* 7.

at *Nice*, when they came to *Sardica*, should change their minds with the place of their Session. That there were no Canons of *Sardica* known till the time of *Dionysius Exiguus*, is very probable, because they were not in the *Code of the Universal Church*, nor in the *African Code*, till *Dionysius Exiguus* put them in; as *Jacobus Leschasserius* most excellently proveth.

Whether *Dionysius* or *Hadrian* put them in, is to me uncertain: But *Hadrian* I. first gave the Copy of *Dionysius* to the Emperour *Charles*, whence the *old Manuscripts were transcribed, which are now extant in several Libraries; and in which* the Dedication of Pope *Hadrian* is contained in Verse, *To his most Excellent Son King Charles, &c.* The first Letters of the Verses being put together, make this Acrostick, EXCELL. FILIO. CARULO. REGI. HADRIANUS. PAPA. The Verses are found in the Copies yet extant of *Dionysius Exiguus*.

This shews that some *New* Thing was put into the Book, and that *Hadrian* had a finger in it, which reached perhaps farther than the beginning. If the Book was as new as the Acrostick, *Dionysius* was far enough from being its Author. What Faith we are to have in the Papists, when they tell us who were the Ancient Compilers of the Councils, you may see by *Baronius*, who giving us an Account of their Order,[1] reckons *Isidore* (a known Counterfeit) for *one*; *Dionysius Exiguus* for the *first*, *Ferdinandus Diaconus* for the *second*, *Martinus Bracarensis* for the *third*, *Cresconius* for the *fourth*; and after all these, *Isidore* for the fift. As certain as *Isidore* was a Collector of the Councils, so certain is it that *Dionysius* was one, but further certainty yet I can see none.

Charles the Great, perhaps having never seen the like before, was pleased with the Acrostick; and the putting of his Name in Capital Letters before the *Councils* was delightful to him. *Syrens* sing sweetly, while they deceive bloodily. *Hadrian* I. knew well, what was a Gift fit for a *Scholar*, and a *Pope of Rome*.

If I should produce but one passage which I found in it, the matter would be more effectual: For after he has done with the Councils, he lays down the Decretal Epistles of 13 Roman Bishops, beginning with *Syricius*, who lived in the year 385. In his Epistle to *Himerius*, there is this passage: *Such is our Office*, saith he, *that it its not lawful for us to be silent, for us to dissemble, upon whom a Zeal greater than that of all others, of the Christian Religion, is incumbent: We bear the burdens of all that are oppressed; nay rather the blessed Apostle* Peter *beareth them in us: who as we trust, protecteth and defendeth us his Heirs in all the things of his Administration.*

---

[1] Marginal gloss: *In Not. Martyrol. ad. 4. April.*

Of GOD he saith nothing here, but his confidence is all in *Peter*. There is not a word like it in all Antiquity: and those words *protecteth and defendeth us*, seem to relate to those Jars that had been before between *Hadrian*, and *Charles* the King, or Emperour.

These observations carry me to believe what I met with in *Daille*, since *Dionysius* is gone from under my hands: and having searched into the Book since, I am further confirmed.

About 74 *years after the Council of* Chalcedon,[1] Dionysius Exiguus, *whom we before-mentioned, made his collection at* Rome, *which is since Printed at* Paris, cum Privilegio Regis, *out of very Ancient Manuscripts.* Whosoever shall but look diligently into his collection, shall find divers alterations in it; one whereof I shall instance in, only to shew how Ancient this Artifice hath been among Christians. The last Canon of the Council of Laodicea, which is the 163 of the Greek Code of the Church Universal, forbidding to read in Churches any other Books than those which are Canonical, gives us withal a long Catalogue of them. Dionysius Exiguus, although he hath indeed inserted in his collection, Num. 162. the beginning of the said Canon, which forbiddeth to read any other Books in the Churches, besides the sacred Volumes of the Old and New Testament; yet hath ne wholly omitted the Catalogue, or List of the said Books; fearing, as I conceive, lest the Tail of this Catalogue might scandalize the Church of Rome, *&c*. A little after he saith, *the* Greek Code *represents unto us* VII *Canons of the first Council of* Constantinople, *which are in like manner found both in* Balsamon, *and in* Zonoras, *and also in the* Greek *and* Latine *Edition of the General Councils, Printed at* Rome. *The three last of these do not appear at all in the* Latine Code *of* Dionysius, *though they are very considerable ones, as to the business they relate to, which is the order of proceeding, in passing judgment upon Bishops accused, and in receiving such persons, who forsaking their communion with Hereticks, desire to be admitted into the Church.* It is very hard to say, what should move the Collector to Gueld this Council thus: But this I am very well assured of, that in the sixth Canon, which is one of those he hath omitted, and which treateth of judging of Bishops accused, there is not the least mention made of Appealing to Rome; nor of any Reserved Cases, wherein it is not permitted to any, save only to the Pope, to judge a Bishop: The power of hearing and determining all such matters being here wholy and absolutely referred to the Provincial Synods, and to their Diocesans.

Another instance which he hath is this, *After the Canons of* Constantinople, *there follow in the* Greek Code VIII *Canons of the*

---

[1] Marginal gloss: Daille *pag*. 45. *&c.*

General Council of Ephesus, *set down also both by* Balsamon *and* Zonoras, *and Printed with the Acts of the said Council of* Ephesus, *in the first Tome of the Roman Edition: but* Dionysius Exiguus *hath discarded them all,* &c. Daille in his *Treatise of the Right use of the Fathers.* Cap. 4. pag. 45, 46, 47.

This being true, the Authority of *Dionysius* is very small, relating to the matter of the Council of *Sardica*. If any man hath any thing to say against it, let him, when he answereth this Charge of ours, produce what he is able in Defence of *Dionysius*, as to the points whereof he stands accused by *Daille*; but we proceed to *Nicolinus*.

CAP. XII.

Nicolinus *his Epistle to Pope* Sixtus. *His contempt of the Fathers. He beginneth to confess the Epistle of* Melchiades *to be dubious, if not altogether Spurious. He overthrows the Legend about* Constantines *Donation.*

That you may know the *Genius* of the Man a little better, how much he was devoted to the service of the Pope, and how little he valued the Authority of Councils and Fathers, I have thought it meet to give you his *Epistle,* and his *Admonition to the Reader,* recorded by him in the words following.

To our Most Soveraign Lord, *Sixtus V.* High-Priest.

'It fell out conveniently for me, Most Blessed Father, in the Universal Joy of the Christian World, for your Elevation to the Sublimity of the Apostleship, that in so great a multitude flowing from every place to honour you, I also, among the Oldest Servants of your Holiness, had something near at hand, which is unworthy neither of the Ma[je]sty of your Name, or Authority; and yet very fit for my Occasions to offer at your feet, as suitable to the Office of my Gratitude and Veneration. It is a new Edition of the Councils: for the remarkable addition of two Councils especially,[1] the *Nicene* and the *Ephesine,* never published so entire and full, as now.

'For to whom may the Councils of the Church, aided by the Inspiration of the H. Ghost, according to the seasonableness of various times, for the repairing of her Ship, more fitly be Dedicated, than to her Chief Master, to whom it is given from Heaven to call and confirm them? especially him, who is so well versed in all Scholastical Disciplines, and Ecclesiastical History!

'I have used all diligence, according to my weak ability, sparing no cost, omitting no labour; the most Catholick and Learned Divines of our Age, being assembled also from every Quarter, especially the most Excellent Father *Dominicus Bollanus,* a Noble-Man of *Venice,* of the Order of Preachers, never enough commended for his excellent parts;

---

[1] Marginal gloss: Things put into the Councils of *Nice* and *Ephesus* by *Nicolinus.*

who by his Industry, Care, and Learning, was a vast help both to me, and to the Work.

'And that I may in one word signifie my study and pains bestowed thereupon, lest I should seem to draw the Saw backward and forward too often upon the same Line, I have taken care to perform whatever could be done by one man, and he a private person, that this Edition might come forth from me, and be offered to you, more Copious and Illustrious than any other Publications hitherto sent abroad: In which I trust, that as a just and knowing Judge, you will discern some Accomplishment: Wherefore I suppose I may affirm, that nothing is perversly, or too concisely exprest; but all things most rightly and clearly, as far as was possible, according to their Primitive Candour.

'This my Gift therefore, from which men may receive so great profit and benefit, since both those things that before were wanting, and those that have hitherto been dispersed, may be had together in it; and this Work of mine, not of less cost in Printing (the great expences of which may easily be proved by the magnitude of the Volume) than labour: to which I was not so much present, as presiding; earnestly desiring that it should come forth most free from Errour and Faults, for the benefit of the Studious, I doubt not but according to your Humanity, you will accept it with a willing mind, as some kind of Token of my will to serve you; even as I desire with all my Soul, and humbly pray, that your Holiness may receive it. In the mean time, Holy Father, I desire that all things may fall out prosperously to your Blessedness: And I pray, that you may long be preserved in health, and more plentifully adorned with Heavenly Gifts, for the good of the whole Church. *Venice* VI. Kal. *Octob.* M.D. LXXXV.'

Here you see one of the Popes Old Servants laying down all the Councils at his Holiness Feet, boasting of additions to the *Nicene* and *Ephesine* Councils, never before published, ascribing the Councils to the Inspiration of the Holy Ghost; and yet adding, for the good of the *Roman* Church, eight and fifty Canons to the most glorious of them all, ascribing the power of calling and confirming Councils, to the Pope, sparing no cost (though he draws the Saw too often upon that point, which as if he were enchanted, he cannot leave, throughout all the Epistle) assisted, as himself confesseth, with a confluence of the best Popish Divines, permitted to come forth under the Popes Nose, with all these Abominations. By which you may perceive, it is not the work of a private Doctor, but the Disease of the Church of *Rome*.

    His *Typographus Lectori*.

His contempt of the Fathers appears in his *Printer to the Reader*: for by one *of Turrian's Transfigurations*, he covers that *Admonition* with the Printers Name, though too Learned for any Printer, and evident enough to be his *own*: for he there unfoldeth the matter, order and use of the Work, far above a Printers reach; and especially notes its *Corrections and Emendations* to us: which he reduceth to four Heads.

1. *To the observation of the time wherein Councils were held, and under what Pope.* Whereupon we note, the manner of ordering the Councils *under such and such a Pope*, seemeth a new thing: *Nicolinus* else arrogates too much to himself, in ascribing this to his own Invention. Certainly the custom of *computing times by the Popes Lives*, is of no long standing, but an Artifice lately taken up by his Flatterers, to dazle the eyes of their Readers; for it adds much to the Splendour of the Chair, to see Kings and Councils marshalled under the *Reign*, as it were, of this, and that, and the other Pope, down from S. *Clement*, throughout all Ages. But from the beginning it was not so.

2. *To the truth of History and Actions: As when various Authors are often cited, either for the confirmation of Sentences, or to shew the variety that is among Writers, or to reprehend some falsity, Quod interdum, parcè tamen, &c. timidé fecimus.* In his Dedicatory Epistle he told the Pope, *that he did nothing perversly, but all things most rightly and clearly, as far as was possible, according to their Primitive Candour:* As you see before. But here he confesseth, the business of reproving falshoods to be a tender work, which he went about with great caution and trembling. Some he detected, but *timerously and sparingly:* he durst not meddle with them all.

3. *To the confutation of some contumacious and rebellious persons; who lay hold on the lightest occasions, and oftentimes wrest the plainest matters, to the disgrace of the H. Roman Church. As when from a slight contention of the African Fathers, about Appeals to the Church of Rome, they forcibly conclude against the very truth of the Acts, and the Faith of the History, that those Fathers did not acknowledge, but refuse its Primacy over them.* In the Body of his Tomes, he citeth the Epistles of *Boniface* and *Eulalius*, as good Records, testifying the Excommunication of all the African Churches by the Pope; yet here he calleth it a light contention: Himself wresteth the plainest matters forcibly against the very truth of the Acts, and chargeth the fault on the Protestants: For in this very place he pretendeth that the African Fathers did not refuse the Primacy of *Rome*, but acknowledge its Supremacy, or its *Primacy over them*. Yet is all this but a Copy of his countenance, a common flourish in the Frontispiece of their work: For if they submitted to

the Popes *Primacy over them*, why should they be Excommunicated? He knows well enough, when we come close to the matter, that these *Rebellious Protestants*, and those *Catholick Fathers*, were of the same judgment, and acted the same thing. By way of provision therefore he addeth, that *this was far from the mind of those Fathers; but if they had conceived so, it would have redounded to their Infamy, and not at all have tended to the lessening of the Supreme Authority of the Roman Church, ordained and established by God.*

Two hundred and seventeen Bishops in an ancient approved Council, even the *sixth Council of Carthage*, protested against the *Popes* Supreme Authority, *to their perpetual Infamy*; as *Nicolinus* would have it: for should all the Bishops in the World joyn together, they would but dash themselves against that *Rock*, and do things *to their Infamy*, and there's an end. This is the value which Papists have for the Councils and Fathers, when they stand in their way: And this Impudence comes abroad by the consent of *Nicolinus*, and the Pope, without *Blushing*.

His fourth Head is Addition. His Emendations are referred *lastly to Addition, either by making those things perfect and entire, that before were imperfect and maimed: as when for* 20 *vulgar and naked Canons of the* Nicene Council, *all the Acts of that Council are put together, out of a Greek Book in the* Vatican *translated into Latine by* Alphonsus Pisanus *a Jesuite; and fourscore Canons turned into Latine out of an Arabick book brought to* Alexandria *by another man of the same Society.*

I once thought a certain man had *had* the Book at *Alexandria*; but now it seems a Jesuite brought it thither. He does not tell you *who*, nor *from whence*. Jesuites are the Popes *Janizaries*, and fit to be so imployed: And the *Vatican* is an admirable Storehouse doubtless for the Greek too, a very Pit of Witnesses for the Popes Supremacy. As if *Perkin Warbeck* should have brought Evidences out of his own Closet to prove himself King of *England*. If no body but he must be believed, the veriest Cheat in the World must needs prevail. *Greek* and *Arabick* are strange amusements: else a Book out of the *Vatican*, in its Masters own Cause; or *another man* without a name, that *brought an Arabick Book to* Alexandria, *with fourscore Canons of the* Nicene *Council in it*, would scarcely be regarded against the Evidence of the whole World; especially in a matter so upheld by Forgeries.

Two things there are wherein he adventures to be a little cordial; *Licèt parcè &c timidè*: though *seldom*, and with *fear*.

1. Whereas *Isidore*, and *Merlin*, and *Peter Crab*, and *Surius*, &c. have the Epistle of *Melchiades* without any Note of its dubiousness,

he confesseth it can be none of *Melchiades, because mention is made therein of the* Nicene Council, *and of other things that were done after* Melchiades *Death.*

2. Whereas *Binius* lays a Dreadful Reproach upon *Constantine*, the first most Excellent Christian Emperour, as if after all his Glorious Acts done for the Church and State of *Christendom*, he were an Apostate, a Murderer, a Tyrant, a Persecutor, a Parracide, smitten with Leprosie for notorious Crimes, for killing *Licinius* unjustly, and his own Son *Crispus*: And all, that he might uphold the *Counterfeit Donation*, *Nicolinus* begins the first Book *of the Acts preceding the Nicene Council, (translated out of an Ancient Greek Book in the Vatican)* thus.

De Gestis post Sublatum impium Licinium,
& de Imperio Regis Constantini,
& de Pace Ecclesiarum Dei.

'*Constantine*, when he had conquered his Enemies, shewing himself an Emperour by the Wisdom given him of God, took care to better the Affairs of the Christians day by day, more and more. And this he did several ways, having a most flaming Faith, and faithful Piety towards the God of all: And the whole Church under Heaven lived in profound peace. Now let us hear what *Eusebius*, that most excellent Husbandman of the Churches Agriculture, sirnamed from the most Famous *Pamphilus*, speaketh here. In his tenth Book he saith, What *Licinius* saw long ago to befall wicked Tyrants with his eyes, he now suffered himself, like to them; and that deservedly: for he would neither receive Discipline, nor be admonished at any time to learn wisdom by the punishment of his Neighbors, *&c*. But *Constantine* the Conqueror being adorned with all kind of Piety, together with his Son *Crispus*, the Emperour beloved of God, and in all things like his Father, reduced all the *East* into his Power, and brought the Empire of the *Romans* into one, as it had been of old, and obtained an Universal Kingdom, from the rising of the Sun, to the utmost borders of the *West*, and to both the other Regions of the *North* and *South*, in perfect peace: Then the fear of Tyranny wherewith men were before oppressed, was utterly taken away from the life of men, then frequent Assemblies were held, and Festivals kept; then all things abounded with gladness and joy; then they that were before of a dejected countenance, and sorrowful, looked with a pleasant face, and with joyful eyes; then with Dances and Hymns, throughout all Cities and Fields, they proclaimed first, that God was truly God, and the Highest King of all: next, they magnified the Emperour and his Children, most dear unto God. Then there was no remembrance of the former evils; then all Impiety was forgotten; then there was a sweet enjoyment of present goods, and a joyful expectation of future: Then finally, not only the Decrees of the Emperour, the most Illustrious Conquerour, full of Humanity and Clemency, but his Laws also glorious in Magnificence, and fraught with Tokens of true Piety, were published in all places: So the Pestilent Spot of all Tyranny being purged away, and wholly blottted out, *Constantine* alone, and his Children, thenceforth possessed the Helm of the Empire, which by Right pertained to them; it being made secure by his Authority and Government, and freed from all envy and fear. Hitherto *Eusebius Pamphilus*, of all Ecclesiastical Writers most worthy of belief.'

Thus their own Record in the *Vatican* justifieth *Eusebius*: and thus *Nicolinus* produceth it, who also defendeth *Eusebius*, though himself holdeth the *Donation of Constantine* firm; not discerning how that History overthroweth the same. But *Binius* who saw the inconsistence better, crys out of *Eusebius* for a Lyar, a Flatterer, an Arrian, because he stands in his way. Thus all of them, here and there, serve the Fathers: For *Eusebius* lived in the time of *Constantine* himself, and was Honourable in his eyes: He was Bishop of *Cæsarea-Cappadocia*, and an individual Friend of *Pamphilus* the *Martyr*, a Father in the *Nicene Council*, and one of those that disputed there, in person, against *Phædo* the *Arrian*: As *Binius* also himself recordeth in the Disputation, extant in his *Tomes*. But of such Legends as this, and the Tragical Story of *Constantine*, we have more than good store in Popish Writers: As you may see at large in Dr. *Stillingfleet* his Book of *Popish Counterfeit Miracles*.

CAP. XIII.

The Epistle of Pope Damasus *to* Aurelius, *Archbishop of* Carthage, *commanding him to take care, that the Decretals of the Roman Bishops be preached and published abroad: Wherein the Forgeries of the Church of* Rome *are Fathered on the Holy Ghost.*

D amasus, *to his most Reverend Brother, and Fellow-Bishop* Aurelius. We have received the Epistle of your Holiness with due Veneration: Wherein we understand how your Reverence and Prudence thirsteth, as is fit, for the Apostolical Decrees. Concerning which Affair, we have sent some of those which you desired, and desire to send more when you shall send unto us. Yet we have past by none of our Predecessors, from the Death of Blessed Peter, *Prince of the Apostles, of whose Decrees we have not sent somewhat to you under our certain Seal by* Ammonius *the Priest, and* Fælix *the Deacon: Which we both desire you to keep, and command to be preached and published to others; that they may inviolably be kept with due Veneration of all, and inviolably observed, and diligently reverenced by all future Ages.*

Because the voluntary Breakers of the Canons are heavily censured by the H. Fathers, and condemned by the H. Ghost, by whose Gift and Inspiration they were dictated: Because they do not unfitly seem to blaspheme the H. Ghost, who being not compelled by any necessity, but willingly (as was before said) either do any thing perversly, or presume to speak against the same Holy Canons, or consent to them that will; for such a presumption is manifestly one kind of blaspheming the H. Ghost: Because (as was even now promised) it acteth against him, by whose grace and impulse the same Holy Canons were set forth. But the wickedness of the Devil is wont to deceive many, and so doth very oftentimes delude the imprudence of some by a similitude of Piety, that he perswadeth them to take hurtful things for healthful.

Therefore the Rule of H. Canons which are made by the Spirit of God, and consecrated by the Reverence of the whole World, is faithfully to be known, and diligently to be handled by us; lest by any means the Decrees of the H. Fathers should without inevitable necessity (which God forbid) be transgressed:[1] but that we walking most faithfully in them, may by

---

[1] Marginal gloss: 'A loop-hole for the Popes'.

their Merits, God assisting, deserve the glory of a reward, and the heap of our labour.

These therefore being rightly considered, and upon our deliberation brought to the knowledge of your Churches, it most highly becometh you to obey the Rules of the same H. Canons, lest the sloth of some should make them in any thing to walk contrary to them. But let your wise and wholesome Doctrine, which desires you in all things to please God, shew them these faithful Fellow-workmen in their Thrones, the coheirs and partakers of the Cælestial Kingdom. Dated XVI. *Kal. Jun.* Gratian *and* Cyricius *being Consuls.*

The close of the Epistle (if not clear nonsense) is very obscure. The meaning of it is, that *Aurelius* should shew men the Decretal Epistles of *Clement, Anacletus,* &c. *those faithful Fellow-workmen in their Thrones, the coheirs and partakers of the Cælestial Kingdom,* that are now in Heaven, to the intent they may obey them, and come to the same Eternal Glory. A goodly design doubtless. But we have a cross Proverb, *Woe be to the Sheep, while the Fox Preacheth.* This piety in the Close is but the Sheep-skin to cover the Fox, who needs not more cunning in Preaching, than concealing himself. We have a more sacred saying, *In the Pit which he made for others, is himself fallen.* And it is not impertinent: for while he chargeth others with the unpardonable sin, himself *blasphemes the Holy Ghost.* For to make the Holy Ghost the *Father of Lies,* is (I think) to blaspheme him.

Damasus, we confess, never made the Epistle; but that makes the matter worse. Some other in *Damasus* his Coat, is guilty of this accursed business; that while he Fathers the Frauds, which himself invented, on the H. Ghost, has not *ignorance* to *excuse,* but *malice* to *condemn* him. And whether the Forgeries are not so Fathered still on the Holy Ghost, may be a proper Question. *Binius,* I think, was afraid of these Epistles.

Nicolinus in his *Printer to the Reader,* pretendeth an exact *observation of the time, under what Pope* things were done: but for once he varies the method, and sets this in the Front of the Forgeries, to countenance all.

He knows them perhaps to be what they are, yet clearly owns them.

There is some Errour in the date of these Epistles; an usual Symptom of the Disease in such Instruments. Instead of the XVI. *Kal. Jun. Nicolinus* putteth it the XI. Some hidden reason compels him, or he would never be so nice: for *Cyricius, Siricius* a small mistake: But the next is greater, for *Gratian, Equitius.* As if *Damasus* the Pope could not tell who was *Consul at Rome* when he wrote his Letter.

I wonder at *Damasus* for one thing much; he tells us of the *wickedness of the Devil, who deludes men with a shew of Piety*, and forces in that expression of the *Devils perswading men to take hurtful things for healthful* so affectedly, that it would make one to think his Guilt put him in memory of such a saying. But his design in charging all that impugn them, with the dreadful and unpardonable sin of blaspheming the Holy Ghost, was more clearly to deter men from writing or speaking against these pretended Canons. And perhaps he declaims against *the wickedness of others, that delude the imprudence of some with a similitude of Piety*; and so loudly inveigheth against the Guilt of *perswading men to take hurtful things for healthful*, to remove the suspition from himself. Whatever 'tis, no man is more guilty of the Fraud in the World.

You may note a contradiction in the Letter: The Canons of the H. Fathers, and Bishops of *Rome*, were *consecrated by the Reverence of the whole World*; and yet upon *Aurelius* his desire, were newly *brought to the knowledge of the Churches*, and now first ordered to be *published and preached*.

They past the *deliberation* of our present *Damasus* before they came aboard, *being rightly considered, and upon due deliberation brought to the knowledge of the Churches*. Doubtless they were well weighed, and what was most agreeable to the *Roman Chair* was pickt out, and chosen for the purpose.

CAP. XIV.

Counterfeit Canons of the Apostles defended by Binius. *A Glympse of his Pretences, Sophistries, and Contradictions. A Forged Council of Apostles concerning Images, defended by* Binius *and* Turrian.

Severinus Binius, a late Collector of the Councils, is grown so famous, that his Voluminous Tomes have been Printed thrice; he is approved by an Epistle of Pope *Paul* v. inserted among other Instruments before his Work, and so highly esteemed, that he is exactly followed by *Labbe* and *Cossartius* in 17 Volumes, and taken in, word for word, by the COLLECTIO REGIA; lately published by the care of a King in 37 Tomes.

The reason why they follow *Binius* so exactly, the *Collectio Regia* giveth in these words, set next to the Title-page of the Book, for our better information. *We thought fit to follow the last collection of the Councils put forth by* Binius, *and illustrated with his Notes; and to Print it wholly, as that which of all others is most richly stored.* Wherein they have done *Binius* as great Honour as one can well imagine: for it shews his Notes to be the best and most convenient that can be gotten in the Church of *Rome*, and that all the Collectors since (which were very many) have not been able to devise better.

Hereupon it followeth, that in one Work we may the more concisely treat of *Binius, Labbe, Cossartius,* and the *Collectio Regia* together.

I once intended to give you a Copy of the Popes approbation, with the other Authorities by which *Binius* is approved; but as the case standeth it is superfluous.

He pretendeth in *Prefaces and Promises*, to justifie all the Canons, Councils, and Decretal Epistles, and maketh a glorious shew, setting them down afterwards with great *Titles* of Splendour and Majesty; in such sort, that a man would take them all for Authentick Records: But when he cometh to his *Notes*, he many times deserteth his design, and confesseth the Imposture. But his *Notes* are Pen'd in more obscure and inconsiderable Letters, and those his acknowledgments hidden from a [Transeunt] Eye in little room.

In his Letter to *Paul* V. he layeth all his Labours at the Popes Feet. So that we are like to have good on't, when the Malefactor (accused) is made sole Lord and Judge of the Witnesses.

He hath several Prefaces to the Reader, and to Persons of the Highest Rank and Splendour: in which he pretends to magnifie the Decrees and Canons following, as good Records.

He prefixeth *Isidore*'s Counterfeit *Preface* before his Collection.

Over the Canons of the Apostles, in a Splendid manner, he sets this Title.

THE CANONS
OF THE
HOLY APOSTLES
WITH ALL VENERATION
TO BE FOLLOWED.

According to

The Ancient Edition

OF

DIONYSIUS EXIGUUS.

A man would think now there should no more *Canons* be laid down, than *Dionysius Exiguus* hath in his Ancient Edition: But as if he intended to bear the Mark of the Beast in his Forehead, he puts under this Title *eighty four Canons of the Apostles*, whereas *Dionysius* hath but 50. Certainly 'tis not well done so to Cheat his Reader with a Lye; but in some blind Corner or other he will make us satisfaction.

Over against this he puts a Note in the Margin, thus: Francis Turrian, *of the Society of* Jesus, *hath published a very clear Book in Defence of the Apostles Canons.* He approveth the Book, yet rejecteth two of the Canons which *Turrian* defendeth: but that is concealed till afterwards.

It is his custom, in the top of his Pages, Chapters and Margins, eminent and conspicuous places, to put Notes or Titles, defending those Counterfeit Antiquities, which in some little Gloss hidden in the Text, he really slighteth: For the Potentates of the World, with their Lords and Councellors, not having time enough to search into the bottom, may by such means as these neatly be deceived; while they think no man so impudent, as in the same Leaf, to contradict his *pretences*. So that the very greatness of the Crime is their greatest security.

Another Artifice like this, is that of putting the Preface of *Dionysius Exiguus* before these Tomes of his own, the better to countenance the ensuing Frauds. Though *Dionysius* were dead 1000 years before he wrote them, and never intended, nor thought of the greater part of them.

But Lyars are intangled always in the Bryers: what is convenient in one respect, being inconvenient in another.

For in that his Preface, *Dionysius* speaking for himself, saith only this: *In the beginning we have placed those Canons which are said to be the Apostles, translated out of* Greek: *which because the most do not easily acknowledge, I thought meet to acquaint your Holiness with the same.*

He doubts them all you see; yet speaketh only of his own fifty, which he hath in the Code which himself digested: He does not meddle with those that make up the number of 84. no more than *Isidore* and *Merlin* do: Howbeit *Binius*, when he comes to his Notes upon the word *Canones Apostolorum*, speaketh thus, after his large Copy in three Columns of all the 84. *These* Canons *made by the Authority of the Apostles, and by Tradition from them delivered to us,* Clement *of* Rome, *S.* Peter's *Disciple, wrote in Greek; and* Dionysius Exiguus, *an Abbot of* Rome, *translated them into Latine, in the time of* Justinus *the Emperour.*[1]

He does not prove that *Clement* wrote them, unless by the last Canon, which hath *Per me Clementem* in it: nor by that neither; for that he confesseth to be a Forgery. *Dionysius* that lived 1000 years before *Binius*, does not say that *Clement* wrote them, but rather the contraary: He suspects them all, and knows *Clement* could not write them all; since himself has but fifty, and those only by rumour, not Tradition.

Nay *Binius* himself, you will see presently, rejected some; and yet here he pretendeth the whole number to be written, both by *Clement* in Greek, and by *Dionysius* in Latine: For of all his Catalogue, he saith, *These Canons,* &c. Clement *of* Rome, *S.* Peter's *Disciple, wrote in Greek, and* Dionysius Exiguus, *an Abbot in* Rome, *translated them into Latine*; as if it were not sufficient to write a Lye in the Front, unless he closed up the Canons with a Lye in the Tail.

It would be worth the Enquiry to know where they had the 34. which were unknown to the Ancient *Dionysius*? For after all this, he seems to reject them in the passage following.

Horum quinquagint a priores, &c. saith he, *Only the first fifty of these (the last of which is of dipping thrice in Baptism) containing nothing but sound Apostolical Doctrine, and approved by Ancient Bishops, Councils, and Fathers, are received as Authentick,* Cap. 3. Dist. 16. *And according to that common Rule of the Holy Fathers, because the Author of them is unknown, they are rightly believed to flow unto us by Apostolical Tradition. The residue by Pope* Gelasius, Can. Sanct. Dist. 15. *are accounted Apocryphal; both because their Author is unknown, as also because by the*

---

[1] Marginal gloss: *An.* 520.

65. *and the last Canon, it is evident, that some of them are craftily put in by the Grecians, and some of them corrupted by Hereticks.*

This passage deserves one or two remarkable Observations.

1. If the Tradition of the Apostles, though committed to *writing*, be capable of corruption; what security can we have of *Oral Traditiion*, which is far more loose, and liable to danger?

2. If the Church of *Rome* were unable to secure the *Apostles Canons* from the Leven of the *Grecians*, and other *Hereticks*; or so careless, as not to keep one Copy, or Record *sincere*; what assurance can we have of her care and ability in the residue? This shews the weakness of these inconvenient Shifts, and pitiful Answers.

But the reason why some are *received as Authentick*, and others *accounted Apocryphal*, is most fit to be marked. The reason why it is highly to be presumed, that the first 50 Canons should be Apostolical, is, *Because the Author of them is unknown*: And the reason why the residue are rejected, is, *Because the Author of them is unknown*. So that the same reason (as Fire hardens Clay, and softens Wax) will prove contrary things. And by reasoning in such a Latitude, it will be easie to prove the Sun *black*, and the Sky a Molehill.

Howbeit for these reasons, *Gelasius* an Ancient Pope rejecteth some of them: But *Binius* takes the liberty to put his judgment in the other end of the Scale; and outfacing us with a Counterfeit *Clement*, and Pretended *Dionysius*, will have all but two, to be Authentick Canons: All but two; namely, *the 65. and the last Canon; by which it is evident, that some of them are craftily put in by the Grecians, and some of them corrupted by Hereticks*. Some of them *put in* by the Grecians, must at least be two; and some of them *corrupted* by Hereticks, must at least be two more; yet they are all of them, except two, Authentick.

Let his reason be what it will, we observe, 1. That the Church of *Rome* is in a tottering condition, when a poor Canon of *Collein* shall take upon him to refel the Sentence of an Ancient Pope, and fourscore Bishops: for so many did *Gelasius* use in discerning the *Apocyrphal* from *Genuine* Books; and this Sentence was Definitive by a Pope in his Council: So that 2. A Pope in his Council is not Infallible. 3. If *Binius* be right, *Gelasius* and fourscore Bishops did err exceedingly in condemning the Code of 84 Canons, which S. *Clement* wrote from the mouth of the Apostles. 4. The Church of *Rome* is divided, the New and the Old Church of *Rome* are against each other. The New is all for Additions, and the very Apostles Canons, allowed in *Gelasius* his time, which was 1260 years ago, are not sufficient, unless more be added.

But let us now consider *Binius* his reasons. *Quia tamen ex his posterioribus ferè omnes præter prædictos duos, &c.* But because all these latter almost, besides the two forementioned, are either by the Authority of the Roman Bishops, or by the Decrees of other Councils, or by the Sentences of some Fathers, confirmed and approved, as is manifest by these our Marginals and Annotations: (So that it may not lightly or rashly be doubted, whether they were taken hence by the Bishops, Councils, and Fathers, or rather translated hither, and put here out of their Writings:) Hereupon they may and ought rightly and deservedly all, except the two excepted, to be taken for Authentick.

How perplexed his discourse is, I suppose you see. His courage fails in the midst, and it becomes thereupon so rough and difficult, that it is scarce intelligible. The occasion of its Incoherence is that Parenthesis (thrust into the middle.) For *Binius* foreseeing a strong Objection to the Discourse he was going to make, claps it Sophistically into the midst of his Argument; hoping thereupon, that it would never more be retorted upon him: Which you may easily see, both by the Nature of his Argument, and by the resolution of his words. For his Argument is this; which if you lay aside the Answer to it, runs smoothly. *Almost all these latter Canons, besides the two forementioned, are either by the Authority of Roman Bishops, or the Decrees of other Councils, or the Sentences of some Fathers, confirmed and approved (:) hereupon they may and ought rightly and deservedly, all except the two excepted, to be taken for Authentick.* Now the Answer is the *Parenthesis* in the midst. Certain Sentences like to these Canons are in the Fathers writings, but so contained there, *that it may not lightly or rashly be doubted, whether they were taken hence by the Bishops, Councils, and Fathers, or rather translated hither, and put here out of their Writings.* To doubt a thing rashly is nonsense; but it may justly be feared, that these Canons are Sentences pickt out of other Books, and packt into a Body, bearing the name of the *Apostles Canons*. His Conscience did convict him, and he replieth not a word, though it be an important consideration in the case.

But there is a worse fault in his *Logick*; he argues from *Particulars* to *Universals*: for having said, *Ferè omnes præter prædictos duos*, he comes to conclude, *Omnes præter prædictos duos*. Almost all except two are approved; therefore all except two are Authentick.

Such Tricks as these he hath often: And sometimes affects an obscure kind of speaking, on purpose to blind the Reader; especially when he is intangled with some difficult Argument: He then Clouds himself, like the *Cuttle*, in his own *Ink*, that he might vomit up the *Hook* in the dark, and scape away.

He might have produced a General Council, if he pleased, to confirm all the 84 Canons, and that *under the Name of the Apostles too*, which had been more to the purpose: but then he must have confessed the last Canon of *Clement* to be true, and consquently that his eight Books of Constitutions, and his two Epistles, are part of the Bible; or else that the Decree of the Council, confirming these, was *Spurious*; or else of necessity, that the Pope and Council did *err*. But he had more kindness for the Pope than so, and therefore perhaps let the Council alone.

He would inure you by his words to believe that Popes are equal to Councils. *Because they are,* saith he, *either by the Authority of Roman Bishops, or other Councils, or some Fathers confirmed, they may and ought to be taken for Authentick. Some Fathers* is a dwindling *expression*: He very well knows that 217 were rejected together in the sixth Council of *Carthage. Roman Bishops,* and *other Councils,* are words of some weight: But what can *other Councils* do, if the *Roman Bishops* please to reject them? The *Roman Bishops,* and *other Councils,* are so put in contradistinction, that the Authority of *Roman Bishops* is set before that of *other Councils*: And perhaps the proportion being observed, the *Roman Bishops* must be thought as far above *other Councils,* as *other Councils* above *some Fathers*.

In other places they affirm a Pope with his Council to be Infallible: Here, that *the Roman Bishop is a Council*: Otherwise it is nonsense to say, *The Roman Bishops, or other Councils*. The Roman Bishop hath a Council in himself: And indeed it is requisite, that he of all other should be the greatest Council, when standing alone, he is to judge of a Council, and to determine, even whether an Oecumenical Council shall be approved, or disapproved.

This is a Tast of *Binius,* an Elephants Clee, a Scrap of five large Volumes, full of the same integrity and perverseness.

The swelling words which they talk of, *approved* and *disapproved Councils*, are all to be understood, of Councils approved, or disapproved by the Roman Bishop.

From his Canons we proceed to his Council: for *Binius* hath a Council of Apostles too, on a Prodigious Theme! the setting up of Images. It is but a short one, and hath but one Canon, and that is the *eighth*. It is set forth in this form.

ANTIOCHENA SYNODUS APOSTOLORUM.

Canon. 8. *Nè decipiantur Salvati ob Idola: sed pingant ex Opposito Divinam Humanamque manufactam impermixtam Effigiem Dei veri ac Salvatoris nostri Jesu Christi, ipsiusque Servorum, contra Idola & Judæos. Neque errent in Idolis, neque similes fiant Judæis.*

This is all: and sure it is old, for the Latine is very bare. If you construe it, it speaketh thus, but hath no Greek Copy.

A COUNCIL of the APOSTLES at ANTIOCH.

Canon. 8. *Let not the Saved be deceived for Idols: but let them paint on the Opposite, the Divine and Humane unmingled Image of the true God, and of our Saviour Jesus Christ, made with hands, and of his Servants. Neither let them err in Idols, nor be made like the Jews.*

The first Authority he hath to prove it, is the 2 *Nicene* Council, 800 years almost after the Apostles. And he collecteth it thence by a blind conjecture, not by any evident Assertion of theirs.

Besides this he citeth one *Pamphilus*, who testifieth that he found it in *Origen*'s Study, as *Turrian* saith against the Writers of *Magdenburg*. So that all this resteth upon *Turrian*, an impudent Corrupter, as the World hath any. Where we first observe, that *Origen* had no Images himself, neither adored any. 2. That Images were fobidden in the H. Scripture, especially in the Old Testament. 3. The Apostles were wont to allure the Jews, and not to offend them. *To the Jews*, saith S. Paul, *I became as a Jew that I might gain the Jews*. Whereas to set up Images, was the only way to drive them out of the Temple. 4. That all other Councils, *Nice, Constantinople, Ephesus, Chalcedon, Arles, Eleberis, Antioch, Laodicea, Sardis, Jerusalem, Alexandria, Rome*, &c. during all the time of 800 years, were silent of this Apostolical Canon.

Concerning which, I beseech you to consider further: 1. That admitting it were in the 2 *Nicene* Council, that was an Idolatrous Council, addicted to Fables, and full of Forgeries; for which it is rejected by all the knowing and sounder part of the World. 2. The Apostles were not obeyed in this Commandment, neither in their own Age, nor in divers Ages after. 3. *Binius* himself seemeth conscious of its unsoundness, for he putteth it not among the Councils of the Apostles, which are before their Canons altogether, but in another place straggling by it self, in his own Notes, and after the Apostles Canons. 4. Since the Apostles wrote in Greek, this is rendered suspitious by wanting a Greek Copy. 5. No Collector produceth one word besides himself, in the whole Circuit of the first 400 years, on the behalf of Images. 6. The Fathers unanimously write against Images in the Church of GOD. 7.

You may perceive by the dulness of the Sense out of what Storehouse this Fragment came, and by the horrid incongruity of *making a Divine and Humane Image unmingled with hands*: The Divinity and Humanity being Natures infinitely distant, cannot be painted in the same Picture. But for want of a better, this Musty Evidence must serve the turn.

CAP. XV.

Of the Pontifical Falsely Fathered upon Damasus, *Bishop of* Rome, An. 397. *How the Popish Collectors use it as their Text, yet confess it to be a Forgery full of Lyes and contradictions.*

The *Liber Pontificalis* is a Legend so stuffed with Lyes, that the very *Title* of it is notorious: The very first Inscription of the Book miscarries; not so as to need, like the former Counterfeits, either those of the *Apostles Canons*, or their *Council*, or the *Preface of Isidore*, a long Circuit of Deductions to prove the Forgery; *Binius, Labbe,* and the *Collectio Regia*, immediately confess it. It beginneth thus.

> THE BOOK OF POPES,
> *From Pope* Peter *down to Pope* Nicholas *of that Name the First; in which their Acts are described: The Acts of the first Popes by Pope* Damasus: *The rest by other* * *Ancient Men and* * *worthy of credit.*[1]

Upon this Title *Binius* noteth, *Hujus libri Pontificalis* Damasus *Auctor non est, &c.* Damasus *is not the Author of this Pontifical: but rather it is patched up of two divers Authors; as may be proved by this, that almost in every Popes Life, it contains things fighting with themselves: And so no account can be given of Things and Writings clashing with one another.* And for this be cites *Baronius, An. Christ.* 69. *nu.* 35. *An.* 348. *nu.* 16 *&c* 17. *Anton. Possevin. Apparat. Sac. on the word* Damasus.

Now a man would expect he should lay aside the Book, and refuse to make use of such an odious Pamphlet: But for want of a better he takes it in, as his most Learned Companions do; and so they labour all under the miserable Fate of making a Forgery, the Text upon which their Notes and Volumes are the Commentary.

It is meet before I pass, to make some use of what is given us: for Observation is the Life of History, Reflexions digesting the Objects that are before us, and turning them into nourishment.

What is here said, concerneth not a Page, but a whole Book, stuffed with Legends, and Lives of Popes.

---

[1] The asterisks refer to marginal gloss: **Cunning honest men, like *Merlin*'s Printer.

It was set forth as a Book made by *Damasus*, a Learned, Grave, and Ancient Bishop of *Rome*, that his name might give colour and Authority to the same.

Because it could not be believed that *Damasus* should write of Popes that followed after he was dead, part of it is ascribed to *other ancient men, and worthy of credit*; naming no body, for the greater Reverence, and shew of Antiquity, and the more pious estimation of unknown persons.

How ancient, and how worthy of credit they are that use such Cheats, and what a Mystery of Iniquity they make of Antiquity, you may easily conjecture.

Sometimes Forgeries are thrown upon the Greeks and Hereticks: but here is one made and compiled by the more Famous *Romans*.

Binius knew it to be a Forgery by the baseness of the Stile; *Consarcinatus est, It was patched up.* That is his word; a Metaphor implying, the Taylors were but Botchers that made it. Secondly, by the contradictions that are in it, he knew they were divers Authors, because they jangle, and cannot agree. The parts of it are so irreconcileable, that the Story will by no means hang together.

It is a Vein of Lyes, reaching from S. *Peter* to *Damasus*, and from *Damasus* to *Nicholas* I. containing the Lives of above 100 Popes, from S. *Peter* to the year 860.

About the time of this *Nicholas* I. the Popedom was exalted above the Clouds, and was (of necessity) to be secured by as evil means, as it was gotten: When loe the Witch of *Endor* raises up *Samuel* in the good old *Damasus*, to tell the World that *Peter* was a Prince, and all his Successors *Universal Heads* of the *Catholick Church*.

Nicholas I. began to sit about 50 years after the death of *Hadrian* I. the Pope that is suspected by us to be the Father of the Forgeries. So great an Impression therefore being made by the Publication of *Isidore*, a little before, it was thought good to follow the Blow by this *Pontifical*: and a more ancient Father than *Isidore* must be awakend out of his dust to justifie *him*. For as Light answered Light in *Solomons Buildings*, so do the *Lives* and *Letters* of the Popes; their Lives in the *Pontifical*, and their letters in the *Decretal*.

The Artifice shews contrivance, and the design of it a deep and hidden Correspondence.

The World has been cheated for so long a time, by the attempt of wicked and deceitful men.

Peter Crab, Carranza, Surius, Nicolinus, the Elder Compilers of the Councils, use it boldly and freely, without warning their Readers to suspect it, or confessing it to be a Forgery; though *Binius*, and the last Compilers, upon necessary Conviction, are forced to do it.

Isidore and *Merlin* have it not at all: we may justly wonder therefore where these latter Collectors got it.

The Forgery is not about mean matters, but things most Sacred, the Rights of the Church, and the Souls of men.

Here the Papists are detected by their own confession; and he that is once taken, is still suspected.

The Works of Darkness are seldom discovered, so that more are committed than are known.

All these Forgeries that are now acknowledged, did pass about 290 years ago for good Records, excepting some perhaps that were since invented: And if the last two Ages brought so many to light, an Age or two more may, through Gods blessing, accomplish Wonders.

The Secular state and security of the Pope, with his Adherents, which *Binius* in his Epistle to Pope *Paul* v. calls *Honor & Augmentum Ecclesiæ*, was the end of all. And if men excogitate Titles to Crowns, and patch up Genealogies with some Flaws, yet serviceable enough with the help of a Long Sword; then a Chair so Politick is able to do it more neatly, having had the strong Holds of the Church so long in their hands.

Now we shall note some few of those many Errours that are in the *Pontifical*; which, though it be a dirty circumstance to have such a Text to gloss on, is the Basis of their Discourses, and the Rule of their Method, both in the Popes and Councils. It beginneth thus.

Peter *the blessed Apostle,*[1] *and Prince of the Apostles, the Son of* John, *of the Province of* Galilee, *of the City* Bethsaida, *the Brother of* Andrew, *sate in the Chair of* Antioch *seven years.* In the end it telleth us how long S. *Peter* Reigned, just *twenty five years, two moneths, and three days.* *Binius* tells us with the consent of *Baronius*, it was rather twenty four years, five moneths, and eleven days.

The Pontifical saith, Peter *was Martyred with* Paul *on the same day*: though *Prudentius* and S. *Augustine* say, *It was not the same year.* *Binius* reconcileth them, *They* were slain the same *day* indeed, but not the same *year*: Therefore say we, *Peter* was not Martyred with S. *Paul*.

The Pontifical says, *It was 38 years after the Passion of our Lord.* More truly the 35. saith Binius, *in the 13 year of* Nero, *and the 69 after the Birth of Christ*.

S. *Peters's Name* is the Patron and Bulwark of the Roman Church; and therefore inserted like a Shield in the Front. Next his Notes on S.

---

[1] Marginal gloss: *An.* 15.

Peter's Life. *Binius* inserts *the Treatise of the Roman Churches Primacy*, Ex antiquo Codice: *out of an Old Book*, without any name at all: Which puts me in mind of the *Gibeonites old Bottles, clouted Shooes, and mouldy Bread,* and the notable Cheat which thereby they put on the Israelites. All is Old and Ancient in the Church of *Rome*: and this *Old Book* of the Primacy set before the Councils according to the Rules of Art, because the *End* is to be proposed before the *Means.*

After this *old Treatise* of the *Primacy*, he cometh to S. *Linus, Pope and Martyr.* He is pleased to call him *Pope,* as well as *Pope Peter*; not as if his Contemporaries called him so, but because the Modern Title will not fit well on the present Popes, unless it be given to S. *Peter,* and the first Bishops of that *See.* And ever and anon he begins with a known Lye in the top of the Chapter, formally set by it self, the more pleasingly to take the eye, after the manner of a Title, *Ex Libro Pontificali* Damasi *Papæ*;

OUT OF THE PONTIFICAL OF POPE *DAMASUS.*

This course he continues from Life to Life throughout all the Popes, so far as the Pontifical lasteth, intermixing the *Decretal Epistles* first, and then the *Councils,* in the Lives of the several Popes: or to use his form, *under the Pope* in whose Life they happened. And all his Tomes being moulded into that form, it makes every Pope seem, to him that is not aware of the fetch, the Supreme over all Councils from the beginning. And with this Method he always goes on, *Ex libro Pontificali* Damasi *Papæ,* hoping perhaps that in long tract of time, he should be at last believed.

In all the Book, there is scarce a Life, wherein there are not as many Errours, as in S. *Peter*'s. As in example.

Linus *sate eleven years, three moneths,*[1] *and twelve days,* saith the Pontifical: *Binius* saith, *It was eleven years, two moneths, and twenty three days.* A days difference, where the exactness is pretended to be so great, shews all to be Counterfeit.

He saith, Cletus *sate twelve years,*[2] *one moneth, and eleven days*: *Binius* rails on him for the mistake; though he agrees with him in the main, *that* Linus *and* Cletus *sate some twenty three years between* Peter *and* Clement. So that on this account, S. *James* was dead above 27 years before S. *Clement* (who wrote a Decretal Epistle to him) came to

---

[1] Marginal gloss: *An.* 70.
[2] Marginal gloss: *An.* 83.

the Chair: For before he was Pope he might write an *Epistle*, but not a *Decretal Epistle*.

Cletus (saith *Binius*) *was by* S. Irenæus, Ignatius, *and* Eusebius, *called* Anacletus, *which* Baronius *thinks was a mistake among the Greeks, occasioned by the Errour of Writers and Libraries.* What shifts will a man be driven to by a desperate Cause! Three of the best and most Ancient Fathers were cheated *with the Errour of Writers and Libraries*, concerning a mans *Name* that was alive, either not long before, or together with themselves. S. *Irenæus* and *Ignatius* are extremely Ancient. *Ignatius* lived before *Anacletus* was Bishop of *Rome*, much more before his Name was put into *Libraries*, and much more yet, before it could be corrupted there by the *mistake of Scribes and Writers*. But such *Errours of Writers and Libraries* are a good hint, how capable they are of them, and how much the Church of *Rome* is acquainted with them.

Binius is at last terribly provoked with the nonsense of the *Pontifical*: for whereas it saith, Cletus *was in the Church from the seventh Consulship of* Vespasian, *and fifth of* Domitian, *to the ninth of* Domitian, *and the Consulship of* Rufus; that is, from the 78 year of *Christ*, to the 85. *Binius* speaking as if he were present, takes him up smartly, *Errorem igitur Errori addis, quisquis hujus Pontificalis Author es*, &c. *Whoever thou be that art the Author of this Pontifical, thou addest Errour to Errour: For if* Cletus *began to sit in the forementioned Consulship, in the* 78 *year of Christ, how did he immediately succeed* Linus, *dying, as thou saidst, in the* 69 *year of Christ,* Capito *and* Rufus *being Consuls? How wilt thou excuse a* 9 *years Interregnum in the Chair, made only by thy Authority contradicting it self? How sayest thou that* Cletus *sate twelve years, whose continuance thou doest circumscribe by two Consulships, in the space of* 7 *years distant from themselves? How, which is more intollerable and absurd, doest thou say, that* Clement *sate from the Consulship of* Trachilus *and* Italicus, *even to the third year of* Trajan; *which is from the 70 year of Christ to the* 102. *and so to have administred the See* 33 *years, whom in his Life thou affirmest to have continued only* 9 *years?* Thus far *Binius*.

When *Cato* saw the Southsayers saluting one another in the *Roman* Market-place, he said, I wonder they can forbear laughing, to think how delicately they cheat the people! *Hence therefore*, saith Binius, *O Reader, thou mayest perceive on what Rocks he shall dash, whosoever shall suppose the writings of this Book to be taken upon Trust, without any Inquisition!* Yet when the fit is over, in the very next line, he is at it again, THE LIFE, EPISTLES, AND DECREES OF CLEMENT,

EX LIBRO PONTIFICALI DAMASI P. The Pontifical is (afresh) ascribed to *Damasus*: For Friends may quarrel, without falling out eternally. But if they are so angry, what make they together? What have Scholars to do in so scandalous a Fellows Company? Why of all Books in the World do they take this to follow? All of them from *Peter Crab* to the *Collectio Regia?* Why not the Grave, Sincere, and Learned? Why not a true Record? Why do they chuse a Counterfeit so *full of lyes and contradictions*? It is the highest Symptom of a deadly cause, that they take such a Fellow to be their Copy to write after, their Text to gloss on, their Guide to follow. For all these Gross mistakes are committed within the compass of some 30 or 40 lines, in four Lives of *one hundred and six*: And in every Life almost throughout, they are exercised in the same manner. If this be the best Record they can find for the purpose, and all their Antiquities be like this, they are as mouldy and rotten as can well be desired.

CAP. XVI.

Of the Decretal Epistles forged in the Names of the first holy Martyrs and Bishops of Rome. *The first was sent (as they pretend) from S.* Clement, *by S.* Peter's *order, to S.* James *the Bishop of* Jerusalem, *seven years after he was dead; and by the best Account* 27. *S.* Clement's *Recognitions a confessed Forgery.*

To stumble in the Threshold is Ominous: If the first of all the Decretals be a Forgery, it is a leading Card to the residue. *Binius* his Title, and the Text of the *Pontifical,* is represented thus.

THE LIFE, EPISTLES, AND DE‑ CREES OF POPE *CLEMENT* I.
Out of the *Pontifical* of Pope
DAMASUS.

He made two Epistles that are called Canonical. *This man, by the Precept of* S. Peter, *undertook the Government of the Church; as by Jesus Christ our Lord the Chair was committed to him. In the Epistle which he wrote to* S. James, *you shall find after what manner the Church was committed from* S. Peter. Linus *and* Cletus *are therefore recorded to be before him, because they were made Bishops by the Prince of the Apostles himself, and ordained to the Priest=like Office before him.*

NOTES.
(After the Method of *Binius.*)

He made two Epistles called Canonical.] These words are adapted to the 84th Canon of the Apostles, where two Epistles of *Clement,* and his eight *Books of Ordinations,* are made parts of the Canonical Scripture.

In the Epistle which he wrote to S. James.] Here the Pontifical openly voucheth his Epistle to S. *James*; which *Binius* afterwards tells you was written to *Simeon.* If the *Pontifical* be right, *Binius* was overseen, in saying, the name of S. *James* crept by corruption into the Title of the Epistle, for that of *Simeon.* The Tales do not hang together.

They were made Bishops by the Prince of the Apostles, &c.] You understand here, that S. *Peter* out of his superabundant care for the Church, made three Bishops of *Rome* in his own life time: So that *Rome* had four Popes at once, S. *Peter,* S. *Clement,* S. *Linus,* and S. *Cletus.* Some think that *Linus* and *Cletus* were S. *Clement's* Adjutants in External Affairs: Some, that they succeeded each other in order: Some, that they presided over the Church together. Some say, that *Clement* out of modesty refused the Chair, till he was grown older belike. It is a world to see, what a variety and puzzle they are at in this matter: The confusion springeth from two causes: The first is the obscurity of the State of *Rome* in the beginning: The second is the ignorance of the Forger that made S. *Clement's* Letter to S. *James*: For happening so heedlesly to Father it on S. *Clement*, he has made all the Story inconvenient. S. *Clement* saith not one word of refusing the Chair in his Epistle, nor of *Linus* and *Cletus* coming between him and it; but with a very fair Hypocritical shew, pretendeth in his Epistle to S. *James*, that he was chosen by S. *Peter*, and succeeded him accordingly. Whereupon, they that will have this Epistle to be a good and true Record, are forced of necessity to say, that S. *Peter* did himself ordain *Clement*, though they very well know that *Linus* and *Cletus*, or *Anacletus*, were both in their Order Bishops before him: For a sure Token, either that the Church of *Rome* was little considered in the dawning of the Gospel, or that their ignorance marred her Officious *Impostors*, nothing is more obscure and doubtful than the order and manner of her first Bishops. The Pontifical undertakes to reconcile all; and does it luckily, were it not that it contradicts it self: For he saith of *Clement*, that *he undertook the Government of the* Church *by the precept of* Peter. And yet of *Linius* and *Cletus* it saith, they *are recorded to be before him, because by the Prince of the Apostles they were made Bishops before him.*

Be that a contradiction or no, it was neither *Linus* nor *Cletus* it seems, but *Clement* who writ the Epistle to S. *James* about the death of *Peter*.

He made many books.] *Binius* upon those words observes, that *before his Epistles he wrote the Constitutions of the Apostles, &c. He did not make, but write the Apostles Canons in Greek,* &c. It is much he did not make them, for the *Coronis* of them, as *Nicolinus* calleth it, hath *by me Clement* in it; and for ought I know a *Pope* that hath the *fulness of power Apostolical*, may make Apostles Canons at any time. It is an odd observation, *He did not make, but write the Apostles Canons.*

Among his other Monuments (saith Binius) *there are ten books of the circuits of* Peter; *which by some are called,* The Itinerary of Clement, *by others his Recognitions: Which since they are stuffed with* Loathsome Fables, *and the* Fathers *abstained from the use of them, as* Gelesius *also in a* Roman Council *rejected them for Apocryphal; all wise men will advisedly abstain from reading them. It is a Tradition, that* Clement *left the Rite of offering Sacrifice to the Church of* Rome *in writing. It is reported also, that many pieces are falsly published under the Name of* Clement.

Forgeries are (you see) thick and threefold in the Church of *Rome*: but this of *Clement*'s Itinerary, which *Binius* disswadeth all men from reading, even ten Books, *Cum insulsis fabulis referti sunt, since they are stuft with loathsome Fables*, I desire you to take special notice of; because this Confession of his will discover him to be either a false man, or a Fool. It is a delicate Snare, and will detect S. *Clement*, and S. *Binius* together.

As for *Binius*, who defendeth *the first Epistle of* Clement *to S.* James for a good Record; if he did read the Epistle, and note what he read, he was a false man for defending it against his Judgment and Conscience. He that so mortally hated *the Itinerary of Clement*, could not but know the *Epistle* to be Forged, if he read it with any diligent observation: If he trusted others, he was an unwise man, to be so confident in maintaining it, upon the report of those that read and transcribed it for him: For their inadvertency hath deceived him.

For S. *Clement* himself (if that Epistle be his) owneth the Forgery of S. *Clement*'s *Itinerary*, which *Binius* so extremely abhorreth. It must needs be a Forgery therefore, because in this case, nothing but a Forgery can defend a Forgery: no Author (if a Saint) acknowledging those Forgeries for his, which he never made.

After a long Oration which S. *Clement* sendeth to S. *James*, in that Epistle out of S. *Peter*'s mouth, concerning the Dignity and Excellency of the Roman Chair, he has these words, speaking of S. *Peter*.

When he had said these things in the midst before them all, he put his hands on me, and compelled me (wearied with shamefacedness) to sit in his Chair. *And when I was sate, again he spake these things unto me: I beseech thee, O* Clement, *before all that are present, that after (as the Debt of Nature is) I have ended this present life, thou wouldst briefly write to* James, *the Brother of our Lord,*[1] *either those things that relate to the beginning of thy Faith, or those thoughts also which before thy Faith thou hast born; and after what sort thou hast been a companion to me from the beginning, even to the end of my Journey, and my Acts; and what, being a Solicitous Hearer, thou hast taken from me disputing through all the* Cities; *and what, in all my preaching, was the order either of my words or actions: as also what End shall find me in this* City, *as I said; all things being (as thou art able) briefly comprehended, let it not grieve thee to destine unto him: Neither fear, that he will be much grieved at my End,*

---

[1] Marginal gloss: *S.* Peter's order about the *Itinerary*.

since he will not doubt but I endure it for piety. But it will be a great solace to him, if he shall learn, that no unskilful man, or unlearned, and ignorant of the Discipline of Ecclesiastical Order, and the Rule of Doctrine, hath undertaken my Chair: *For he knows, if an unlearned or an unskilful man take upon him the Office of a Doctor without, the Hearers and Disciples being involved in a Cloud of Ignorance, shall be drowned in destruction.*

Wherefore I my Lord James, *when I had received these precepts from him, held it necessary to fulfil what he commanded, informing thee both concerning these things, and briefly comprehending, concerning those, which going through every* City, *he either uttered in the word of preaching, or wrought in the vertue of his deeds. Though concerning these things I have sent thee more, and more fully described already, at his command, under that very Title which he ordered to be prefixed; that is,* Clementis Itinerarium, The Itinerary of Clement, *not the preaching of* Peter.

In these words he telleth us, how S. *Peter* taking his leave of the World, placed him *in his Chair,* and by that Ceremony installed him in the Episcopal Throne in the presence of them all: What a charge he gave him in that moving circumstance of time, just before his piercing and bitter Passion, to write to S. *James*: How he ordered him to make an *Itinerary* of his Circuits throughout the World, and furnished him at the same time with the *Materials* and *Title* of the Book; *The Itinerary of* Clement, *not the preaching of* Peter. S. *Peter*'s modesty (as is to be supposed) giving the Honour of the Title, not to himself that was the *Subject,* but to the *Author*: How S. *Clement,* according to this *commandment,* had sent to S. *James,* not only this Epistle, but the Book it self long before it; wherein the *Journeys and the Acts of* Peter *were more fully described*: And the great care which S. *Peter* took, lest the dead man should be grieved, by the Solace he provided in the Tydings sent unto him, concerning the perpetual certainty of *Skilfulness* and *Learning* in all his Successors, securing at once both the Church, and *his* Chair, is very remarkable. All these things, out of the very Bowels of the Epistle, disgrace the Chimera's of *Binius* and *Turrian.* For what Saint being well in his Wits, would tell the World, that S. *Peter* commanded him to make a *Forgery,* nay a putid Forgery, *stuffed with loathsom Fables!* S. *James* his Name is over and over in the *body* of the Epistle, not only in the *Title.* The Epistle was not sent to S. *James* by a *Figure,* but it plainly tells S. *James,* that he had sent him the *Itinerary* before; which consisting of *ten books,* must be some considerable time after S. *Peter's* Death in making, some time in going from *Rome* to *Jerusalem,* and some time must be spent in coming back with the

Answer, that certified him of S. *James* his receiving it. After all which, this new Letter was written to S. *James*, impertinently giving him an account of the same business: And yet all this while S. *James* was dead before S. *Peter*. For as *Binius* observes, S. *Peter* was put to Death in the thirteenth year of *Nero*, and S. *James* in the seventh.

The compiler of this Epistle, finding S. *Clement*'s *Itinerary* extant in the World, several hundreds of years before himself, and being not aware of its unsoundness, took it up as a good Record, and so fitted the Epistle and Fable to the purpose in hand, being himself cheated with a Forgery, as many others are, and not expecting to be detected so clearly, as it hath since happened.

But to make the matter more absurd, they have a second Letter to S. *James, De Sacratis vestibus, vel vasis*. Wherein he divides the *Priesthood* (as *Pius* in his Decretal afterwards does) *into three Orders, of Presbyter, Deacon,* and *Minister*: With what design I cannot tell, unless he would have us think *the Pope the only Bishop*. Wherein he also takes care about the *Lords Body*; orders the Priests with what Ceremony of *Fasting* and *Reverence* it shall be *consumed*: Gives Commands about the *Pall*, the *Chair*, the *Candlestick*, and the *Vail:* speaks of the *Altar*, the *Worship of the Altar*, the *Doorkeepers*, the *Vails for the Gates*, the *covering of the Altar*, &c. As if there were stately Temples, Attires, Ornaments, and Utensils, in those early days of poverty Persecution, when a Den or a Cave was both *Sanctuary* and *Temple*. Among other things, he orders that no man should *through ignorance believe a dead man ought to be wrapt in a *Fryers Coul;*[1] a Novel, superstitious Errour. All which he speaks out of the mouth of S. *Peter*, whom he calls the *Father and Prince of the Apostles*. In the end of the Letter, he denounces a Curse against all them that will not keep S. *Peter's Commandments*. So that *Peter*'s Name, and *Peter*'s Authority, is used for every thing appertaining to the Chair, and all the Apostles to be ordered by S. *Peter*'s Successors, as S. James *the Brother of our Lord* was.

---

[1] **Fryers Coul*, marginal gloss: *Clerks.

CAP. XVII.

Of Higinus *and* Pius, *as they are represented in t*he Pontifical; *and of a notable Forgery in the name of* Hermes: *Where you have the Testimony of an Angel, concerning the Celebration of* Easter, *cited by no body, while the matter was in controversie.*

Higinus sate, saith the Pontifical, *four years, three moneths, and four days.*[1] Binius saith, *He sate four years, except two days*; counterfeiting as much exactness as the other. *If we should follow him in his Consuls*, saith he, *we should make* Higinus *sit twelve years.*

5   But the Pontifical is guilty of a more arrogant and *ambitious* errour: *the Hierarchy of the Church,* it saith, *was made by* Higinus, *to wit, the Order wherein Presbyters were inferiour to Bishops, Deacons to Presbyters, the people to Deacons.* Binius mendeth it as well as he is able, interpreting it only of a Reformation of Collapsed Discipline. But it
10 suiteth so exactly with the distinction before made in S. *Clement's* second Epistle, who will have the Priesthood divided into *the Order of Presbyter, Deacon, and Minister,* that the design seemeth deeper than so. He doth not say, the Hierarchy of the Church was *corrected*, but *made* by *Hyginus*: which strikes at the Root of Episcopacy; as if it were not
15 of Divine, but Humane Institution: and being *made* by the Pope alone, depended only on the Popes pleasure.

Binius is not able to name the time wherein the Discipline of the Church was (in this respect) corrupted so, as to need the Reformation pretended.

20 Next after *Hyginus*, the Pontifical bringeth in *Pius,*[2] *an Italian, the Brother of a Shepherd. He sate nineteen years, four moneths, and three days, in the times of* Antoninus Pius. Hermes *his own Brother wrote a book, in which a Commandment was contained, given him by an Angel of the Lord, coming to him in the Habit of a Shepherd, that* Easter *should be*
25 *observed on the Lords Day. This man ordained, that an Heretick, coming from among the* Jews, *should be baptized*, &c.

This *Hermes*, saith *Binius*, in his Notes on the place, *is the same whom S.* Paul *mentioneth in his Epistle to the* Romans. *Salute Asyncritus, Phlegon, Hermas, Patrobus, Hermes*, &c. He was at Mans Estate when

---

[1] Marginal gloss: *An.* 184.
[2] Marginal gloss: *An.* 158.

S. *Paul* saluted him, and a very old man sure for a Writer of Books in the time of *Pius*.

Binius is not willing to have him so obscure as a Shepherd, but saith, *He was called* Pastor, *either because he was of the Family of* Junius Pastor, *who in the third year of* Aurelian *was Consul, or more probably, because the Angel appeared to him in the form of a Shepherd*. In this his Guess he is upon the brink of rejecting the Pontifical. Howbeit he quits it not of a Lye: for instead of nineteen years which the Pontifical giveth him, *Binius* saith, *he sate but nine years*. A small mistake in this Learned Pontifical.

Concerning the Book which *Hermes* the Shepherd wrote, he saith, *It was almost unknown among the Latines, but very famous among the Greeks*: Which was very strange, considering he was the *Popes Brother*: A Book made by so eminent a person, and so near home, *unknown among the Latines*! But his meaning is perhaps, it was better known than trusted. For a little after he saith, *The Latines esteemed it Apocryphal, as* Tertullian, Athanasius, *and* Prosper *witness, and as* Gelasius *decreed*; Can. Sanct. Dist. 15.

Now because their unmannerliness doth reflect a little upon the Pope himself, who in his Decretal Epistle annexed, owns his Brother with an Honourable mention of the Angelical Vision; *Binius* to display more Learning on the behalf of the *Pontifical*, and *Pius* his *Decretal*, tells you; that *the Book of the true* Hermes Pastor, *praised so much by* Tertullian, Origen, Athanasius, Eusebius, Jerome, &c. *is not now Extant. Which is evident* (he saith) *because in that we now have, there is no Mention at all of Easter. Nay the Author of it saith, he was admonished to deliver it to* Clement *the Pope, by whom it was to be sent to forreign Cities*. They have as good Luck at *Rome*, as if they held Intelligence with *Purgatorie*. The *Dead* and *they* have as intimate a Correspondence, as if the Pope knew the Way to send his *Bulls* thither. Here is another Forgerie detected, by its Dedication to *S. Clement* who by no unusual Providence is served just in his own kind, for he disturbed *S. James*, and another disturbes him, in his *Grave*. Yet *Binius* is very much inclined to this Opinion, for from hence he gathereth, it was *longè ante hæc Tempora Scriptus, a Book written long before the time of* Pius. As no doubt it must, if it be not the same that was praised by *Tertullian, Origen, Athanasius, &c.* For all Forgeries must be old and True, or they are not worth a farthing.

But how comes *Tertullian* and *Athanasius, &c.* to esteem it Apocryphal, and yet to praise it so much, in the same Breath? It is

Binius his Breath, not theirs. They poor men are made like *Stage players* to say whatsoever the Poet listeth. Or else as *Binius* observes there were two Books of *Hermes* (though it be double dealing thus to have two of a Sort:) the one right, and the other *Apocryphal.*

But then *Gelasius* did very ill, there being two of a Sort, to condemn the one, and not tell us of the other. And so did *Ivo.* For this *Pastor* is one of the Catalogue we told you of in the Beginning.

But *Binius* has a fetch beyond this; He teaches you a way, how to take *both* these persons for the *same* man: and what you may say in defence of your self, if you so do. *However* (saith he) *if any one be disposed to take them for the same Author, Ex Sententiâ Illustriss. Card.* Baronii *dicendum est,* &c. He must necessarily say, as Baronius *gives his Opinion, that they were two commentaries, written at divers times, whereof the first was more famous among the Greeks the later more obscure among the Latines.* A brave Antithesis! So that upon the point the *Latines* had none. *The more obscure among the Latines* was *obscure* every where: *the more famous among the Greeks* and *the more obscure among the Latines!* The *Antithesis* makes a shew of giving you some Solid matter, but when you grasp it in your hand, it turnes to Air. Unless perhaps you will learn thereby, that the more obscure among the Latines was a Book made in an instant, by a meer Conjecture and a pretty Mockery to gull the Reader, as a shadow at least of some proof that the Pontifical and the Decretals are not Lyars.

Among other Things their Allowances are considerable: for they are good honest reasonable men, and will let you think what you will of the Book, so you consent to the main, and believe *the Popes Supremacy*. And next that, their Art of Instruction is to be weighed, Whether it be true or no, no matter: If the *Disciple* can but defend himself by a Distinction, and escape the Conviction of an Absurdity, it is enough; *Bellarmine* is at such *Dicendums* often. Though 'tis a Secret among themselves, they teach their Disciples *What to say,* not *What is* True. But I thought we had been agreed before, that of these *Hermes* [one] at least was a Forgerie.

It seems by Pope *Pius* his Letter, that *Hermes* was a *Doctor*, and not a *Shepherd, for in these Days,* he saith, *Hermes a Doctor of the faith, and of the* H. *Scriptures shined among us.* Not of old, but *in these Days.* Yet it is pretended, that the Book of old was by some order from on high, to be *delivered to Clement the Pope, by whom it was to be sent to forreign Cities.* Notwithstanding all their contrivance, there Wit failes them sometimes, that are so accustomed to Lying. They have so many Irons in the fire that some of them miscarry, whether they will or no.

Nevertheless *that Hermes received this Commandment from the Angel Tertullian witnesseth, in his third Book of verses against Marcion* saith *Binius.* I have not heard much of *Tertullian's Poetrie.* I have his Works, put forth with the Notes of *Beatus Rhenanus,* and cannot find any such *verses* among them. If he hath, all that *Binius* pretendeth out of them, is that *Hermes spake Angelical Words*; Therefore he saw the Angel.

Pius in his Decretal Epistle applieth this Scripture, *Not holding the Head from which all the body by joynts and bands having nourishment ministred, and knit together, increaseth with the increase of God,*] to the Pope of *Rome. Whereupon,* he saith, *We instruct you all by our Apostolical authority, that you ought to observe the same Commandments, because we also observe the same. And ye ought not by any means to divide from the Head.*

The Commandment was given to *Hermes* by an Angel. Whereupon Pope *Pius* after the first complement, beginneth very unluckily with *forbidding the Religion or worshipping of Angels.* Whereas upon this occasion some eminent matter ought to have been spoken concerning Angels. But because of the words following, he puts them together. *Let[1] no man beguile you of your reward in a voluntary humility of worshipping Angels,* &c. *Not holding the Head from which all the body by joynts and bands,* &c. Where he taketh off the *Eternal* Head, and puts a *New* one on the Churches shoulders. *For in these dayes* Hermes *a Doctor of the Faith and of the Holy Scriptures shined among us: And though we observed Easter on the foresaid day, yet because some doubted, for the confirming of their Souls, an Angel of the Lord appeard to the same* Hermes *in the shape of a Shepheard, and commanded him that the Passeover should be celebrated by all on the Lords day: Whereupon we also instruct you all by our Apostolical authority, that you ought to observe the same Commandments.* (Not because an Angel brought them, or GOD sent him; but) *Because we also observe the same, and ye ought not by any means to divide from the Head.* And because the business is to promote the Apostolical Authority above all the Angels, instead of extolling and magnifying them, which had been the natural method on such a Topick: as if he would enervate the evidence of the Angel, he biddeth them *take heed,* and that *diligently, least any one seduce you, by any Astrology, or Philosophy, or vain Fallacy, according to the tradition of men: after the Rudiments of this World, and not after Christ's and true Tradition.* As if no more heed were to be given to an *Angel,* than to an Asse, unless the *Pope* first approved the Vision: Nor is Philosophy, nor

---

[1] Marginal gloss: Colos. 2.18,19.

the Tradition of men, nor any thing else to be valued in opposition to him, and his *true Tradition; for in him dwelleth all the fulness of the Godhead bodily: that ye may be repleat in him, who is the Head of all Principality and Power, and who hath commanded this Apostotlical See, to be the Head of all Churches, saying to the Prince of the Apostles, Thou art Peter, and upon this Rock will I build my Church.*

What it is to walk *after Christ and true Tradition*, you may see Cleerly, by this Gloss upon our Saviours Text. They that do not *hold the Head, from which all the Body by Joynts and Bands having nourishment ministered, and knit together, increaseth with the increase of God*, are in extream peril of damnation. And our Saviour who is *the Head of all Principality and Power*, hath commanded this Apostolical See to be the Head of all Churches; Therefore, Whosoever holdeth not to this Head is in extream peril of damnation. For the Pope is not the Head of all Principality and Power *in himself*, but only by Derivation he is made the Head, &c. And consequently, 'tis as necessary to cleave unto him as to *Christ* himself. Since he *in whom all the fulness of the Godhead dwelleth Bodily*, dwelleth in his *Vica*r, even as *S. Peter* does in like manner. So that all Angels and Traditions of men, Reason, Philosophy *&c.* are but feeble Threeds for him that hath *Plenitudinem Potestatis, the fulness of Power*, and *may open the Kingdom of Heaven to whom he will.*

It is a Cross observation to note the little Authority of the Popes *Custome. For* though it was the Practice of all the Roman Church to Keep Easter in such a manner before, yet *some doubted*, that is, all the *Eastern Churches* were of another Opinion; till an Angel came to teach them otherwise.[1] Yet when he came, he must not be believed for his own sake, but the Popes: nor be obeyed for himself: so jealous was the Pope of his Apostolical Authority.

How weak both the Popes Authority and the Angels were, (which thus mutually needed each others assistance) appeareth by the Event, for notwithstanding the Testimony of *Pius* and the *Angel*, this Controversy was left undetermined till the *Nicene* Council.

It continued above 150 years after Pope *Pius* his days. Yet through all that considerable Tract of time, this *Testimony* of the *Angel* was cited by no Body. Only as *Ovid* makes use of the *Cock*, and his *Crowing* in the Morning, to introduce the fable of *Alector*; this wicked *Pius* maketh use of this Controversy, for the sake of the Angel. But it was a little Suspicious that the *Angel* should appear to no body but the *Popes*

---

[1] Marginal gloss: *Euseb.*

Brother, and the matter be published by no body but the Pope himself. It smelleth of the Forge out of which it came, being proved by the Pontifical of Pope *Damasus*.

CAP. XVIII.

A Letter fathered on Cornelius Bishop of Rome in the year 254. *concerning the Removal of the Apostles Bones: giving Evidence to the Antiquity of many Popish Doctrines, but is it self a Forgery.*

The forgery made in the Name of *Pius*, is fitted to the year 158. You shall now see one made in the Name of *Cornelius* Bishop of *Rome* in the year 254. 100. years after the former excepting four. Not as if there were no forgeries between this and that, there is scarce a year upon which they have not fastned some thing, but should we trace them all, through the weary length of so many Ages, our Travail would be Endless. We have chosen one, or two, as Exemplars of the residue.

THE FIRST EPISTLE
Of Cornelius *the Pope*

Concerning the Translations of the Bo–
dies of Peter *and* Paul, &c.

Cornelius the Bishop to his Dear and most Beloved Brethren, the Sons of the Holy Church of God, and to all them that Serve our Lord in the right Faith.

'Considering the Benevolence of your Charity, because ye are Lovers of the Apostles and hold their Faith and Doctrine, I determined to write unto you, (the Lord being the Author) some of those things which are at this time necessary to be Known, and which the Lord assisting, by the Merits of the Apostles, were lately done among us in the Church of *Rome*, or are now in Doing. Because Charity patronizing, I believe with fatherly Grace, ye willingly receive the Writings of the Apostolical See, and preform the Commandments of the same, and rejoyce in the Increases thereof. Because whosoever engraffes himself in the root of Charity, neither failes of Greatness, (nec a fructibus inanescit) nor waxes vain from fruit, neither does he by Love lose the Efficacious Work of fruitfulness. For Charity it self does exercise the Hearts of the faithful, corroborates their Senses, that nothing seemeth Grievous, nothing difficult, but all is easy which is done; while its property is to nourish Concord, to keep the Commandments, to joyn things dissevered, to correct Evil things, and to consolidate all other vertues by the Bulwark of its perfection.

'Wherefore I beseech you to rejoyce with us, because by the Entreaty of a certain devout Woman, and most noble Matron *Lucina*, the bodies of *Peter* and *Paul* were lifted out of the Catatumbæ. And first of all, the Body of the Blessed *Paul* was carried with Silence and put in the Grounds of the foresaid Matron, in the Ostiensian Way, neer to that Side where he was beheaded. But afterwards we received the Body of the Blessed *Peter*, the Prince of the Apostles, and decently placed it neer the place where he was crucified, among the Bodies of the H. Bishops, in the Temple of *Apollo*, in the golden Mountain, in the Vatican of *Nero*'s palace; the third day of the Calends of *July*: praying God and our Lord Jesus Christ, that these his holy Apostles interceding, he would purge away the Spots of our Sins, and keep you in his Will all the dayes of your Life, and make you perseverable in the Fruit of Good works. But see that ye rejoice together for these things: Because the Holy Apostles themselves also rejoice together for your joy. Praise ye God alwaies, and he shall be glorified in you. For it is written, What shall I return unto the Lord, for all he hath returned to me? I will take up the Cup of Salvation, and call upon the Name of the Lord.'

In this first part of the Epistle *concerning the Translation of the Bodies of the B. Apostles*, Peter *and* Paul, the Pope does you to wit of his wonderful kindness and charity to the Dead, as also of his devotion and reverence towards the Relicks of such glorious Saints.

Wherein first of all, he would have his gratitude towards those blessed Founders of the *Roman See* made conspicuous, it being a thing meet to be published all the World over, as it is in most solemn manner here, by *Decretal Epistle*. 2. He does intimate the veneration due to Relicks, especially those of such glorious Saints as *Peter* and *Paul*. 3. He gives us to know that the Translation of their Bodies from one Grave to another was a matter of such moment, that it was *Quædam ex his quæ nunc temporis necessaria sunt scire, A thing, in these dayes, necessary to be known.* 4. That the merits of the Apostles moved God to assist and bless the Church of *Rome* in all her Doings. 5. That God was the Author of those things which he wrote unto them: According as he saith, *Decrevi vobis scribere, Domino Authore.* 6. That all the World did even in *Cornelius* daies, and upward, to the time of S *Clement* and S. *Peter, Scripta sedis Apostolicæ libenter suscipere, Willingly receive the Writings of the Apostolical See,* obey its commands, and *rejoice in its increases.* For the *Roman* Church is alwaies *increasing* in Tradition,

Doctrine, Wealth, &c. 7. That Love is so excellent an ingredient, that like Salt it must season all things, especially this Epistle, Because it covereth a multitude of faults: The Contemplation of it otherwise comes in very boisterously, as little pertaining to the Story of removing the Apostles bones.

The Epistle affords many other Notes, even in this little part of it: As that all Saints are to rejoice for any benefit done to the Church of *Rome*: That the bodies of the most blessed Apostles being too dishonourably buried before, turned to the greater joy of the Church, which otherwise had lost this occasion of Festivity. If you ask, how it was possible they should be *interred so gloriously* in the days of *Decius* a bloudy Persecutor? It was at the intreaty of *Lucina*, a noble Matron, of which kind there are some alwayes that have a great influence in the Church of *Rome*. That *Peter* was buried in the *Golden Mountain* as a presage of his Successors glory. That the Bishops of *Rome*, were even in the Height of Paganisme (and Idolatry) buried in *the Temple of Apollo*: That *Peter* was buried in three or four places at once: *among the Bishops of* Rome, *in the Temple of* Apollo, *in the* Golden Mountain, *and in the Vatican of* Nero's *Palace*; a little before *Cornelius* his Martyrdome, on the 3. of the Kalends of *July*.

If you will not believe this, consider yey further, the holiness of *Cornelius* affirming it. For while he was settling these Holy Bodies, he, and the Saints of the Church of *Rome* with him, prayed God and our Lord Jesus Christ, that upon the Intercession of those Holy Apostles, he would purge away the Sins of all them to whom he wrote; the Merits of the Apostles, and especially the Intercession of those that sate in the *Roman Chair* being established 1450 years ago, by the Decretal Epistle of *Cornelius*: The Vision of the Apostles, and their knowledge of things done upon Earth is intimated sufficiently, together with the Principality and Piety of the Church of *Rome*, that was ever a Lover of the Saints, and a Worshipper of their Relicks. Way is made too for Praying to Saints departed:[1] this Part of the Epistle ending with that notable Passage of David, *What shall I give unto the Lord for all his Benefits towards me? I will take up the Cup of Salvation, and call upon the Name of the Lord*. Which shews the honourable use they make of the Scriptures.

Now if you enquire, Whether this Epistle be Authentick? you sin against the Doctrine of *Implicit faith*, and highly Scandalize the Church of *Rome*. For can any man be so wicked, as to believe that *Cornelius*,

---

[1] Marginal gloss: *An.* 158.

or any other Pope should counterfeit GOD to be the Author of a Counterfeit; or return such Solemn praises for a feigned Deliverance; or write Publick Admonitions to all the Churches in the World concerning a Lie; or abuse the Holy Scriptures; and make nothing of Love, but a pretext to patch up, and cover Forgery? Yet let us hear what *Binius* and *Baronius* say concerning these Matters. For though the Epistle be never so formally set down, and a Lie written in the Top, both of the Epistle, and the Page, *Cornelii Papæ Epistola* I. And again, *The first Epistle of Pope Cornelius*: yea, though *Binius* saith in his *Notes* on this Epistle, that *S. Jerom witnesseth* Cornelius *to have written many Epistles; and that this therefore is undeservedly taxed for its faith and authority, which has gotten so famous a Witness as Jerom.* Yet after all this, (though (among other Circumstances of Importance) it hath been laid down as a Good Record by *Binius* his Ancestors) he saith, *That it doth attribute to* Cornelius *the Translation of the H. Bodies of* Peter *and* Paul *from the Catatumbæ,* (which is, if I mistake not, from the meaner Graves of the Common people) *Id ex livri Pontificalis Erroribus in Epistolam irrepsisse, probabile, &c.* That *that crept in into this Epistle, from among the Errours of the Pontifical, seemeth probable. For more truly that Translation happened in the first Age, a little after their Passion: As by the testimony of S. Gregory the Pope we demonstrated above.*

Surely the feet upon which this Peacock stands, are very Black. The pride of *Rome* is founded like that of the great Whore, on the waters at least, if not in the mire.

If you examine What, or Where this Testimony of S. *Gregory* is, that overthroweth this Epistle of *Cornelius,* a Person much more Ancient and Authentick than himself; and with what Circumstances, or with what form of words *Binius* maketh use of the same? Let your patience turn to *Binius* his Notes on those Words in the Pontifical, *Hic Temporibus,* &c. in the Life of *Cornelius,* and there it shall be satisfied.

CAP. XIX.

The ridiculous Forgery of the Council of Sinuessa, put into the Roman Martyrologies. How the City, and the name of it was consumed, (though when, no man can tell) by an Earthquake.

MARCELLINUS the Bishop of *Rome*[1] entered on his See about the year 296 in the dayes of *Dioclesian*. The Pontifical in the Life of *Marcellinus* telleth us, that *he offered incense to an Idol,* to escape the wrath of the Emperour.

Binius saith, *When* Marcellinus *the* Roman *Pontifex was therefore accused, because in the Temple of* Vesta *and* Isis, *he burnt incense, and offered Sacrifice to Heathen Images and Idols, to wit, that of* Jupiter *and* Saturn; 300 *Bishops came together in the City* Sinuessa, *to pass their Sentence on the Fall of* Marcellinus. *The place of meeting was the* Crypta Cleopatrensis, *which fifty, one after another could enter, it not being able to contain them all, by reason of its straitness. After the discussion of the Cause, and condemnation of certain Priests,* Marcellinus *the chief Bishop, publickly confessing his Sin, cloathed with Sackcloath, sprinckled with ashes, prostrate on the ground, acting Repentance, said, I have sinned before you, and cannot be in the Order of Priests: and so condemned himself by his own Sentence.*

After those of Magdenburg, *the English Innovators reject this Convention of* 300 *Bishops, as if it were feigned by the Donatists. Because they think it improbable, that in this* 20. *year of* Dioclesian, *wherein the fiercest Flame of Persecution burned, and the Anger of the Emperours did rage more bitterly against the Christians, throughout all the* Roman *world,* 300 *Bishops should be assembled together,* Bin. Not. in Vit. Marcellin.

By the way I must tell you, that the *English* do upon several accounts, besides that of the *Persecution* reject this *Council of Sinuessa,* however it pleaseth *Binius* to ease himself of labour, by mentioning only that. Neither do they fasten it on the *Donatists,* but the *Papists.* For though *Marcellinus* be made a *Donatist* in opinion, his Confession being founded on that Doctrine, that no man guilty of mortal sin, can (though penitent) continue in the Order of Priests: *Binius* himself puts the Doctrine into his mouth: while other *Doctrines* relating to

---

[1] Marginal gloss: *An.* 296.

Roman Forgeries 445

the Popes Supremacy, and other *Persons* defending this Council, shew plainly enough whose it is, notwithstanding the present *Mist* which *Binius* putteth before our eyes. Hear him on.

But if no fear of the Persecution of Decius, saith he, *could hinder them, but that about fifty years before this, as we said in our Notes of the* Roman *Council held in the Interregnum, many Bishops of the Remoter Provinces, and many others neighbouring on* Italy, *and living in banishment, came together upon the Letters of the* Roman Clergy, *at* Rome, *and holding a Council there, ordained those things, which the present necessity of the Church did require: why should it seem more distant from the truth, that by the most vigilant care of the* Roman *Clergy, the Bishops of Forreign Churches should be called together by Circular Epistles, and no fear or Danger of Life deterring them, meet at the time and place appointed, to transact and decide that cause, of all other the most deplorable, in which not only the* Roman *Church, but the whole Christian Religion was brought into the greatest Hazard, wherein the whole Foundation of the Church was shaken, in the first Bishop of the Catholick Faith, and almost utterly overthrown?*

Binius you see confesseth the Truth, that *Mercellinus* did offer *Incense to an Idol*: and that the Gates of Hell had well nigh prevailed against S. *Peters* Chair, in the Idolatry of his Apostate Successor. That therefore they might imitate God, *though the perverse way*, in bringing Good out of Evil: the matter is so neatly ordered, that the Ball reboundeth higher by its Fall; the Weakness of *Marcellinus* increases the Popes power, and his Disgrace is turned to his Greater Glory. His slip is made the establishment of all his Successors. For a Council of 300. Bishops is raised up, by the Invention of the Papists, which do all of them most humbly beseech the *Guilty Pope* to condemn himself, and Decree with one Consent, that the Sovereign Bishop of the City of *Rome* can be condemned by no body. For *out of thine own mouth thou shalt be justified, and out of thine own mouth thou shalt be condemned*. It is an important Point: and no witness fit to be lost, that giveth Testimony thereunto.

Concerning this Council therefore, on the Words *Act a Omnia*.] he saith, *Though exceeding many among the most learned of men, have endeavoured to prove those Acts to be Spurious, and of no weight*, truly *by Strong Arguments, and would esteem it as no other than a Device of the Donatists, cunningly contrived that the Name of Marcellinus, well accepted of among all the Ancients, and had in great Esteem, should be defamed: We nevertheless conceive the same Acts, to be not only not Commentious, or forged, to be ascribed to the Donatists; but rather to be had in great Veneration, both because venerable Antiquity it self fighteth*

Sharply for them, compelling a Reverence even from the unwilling by its majesty: and because, by the Common Assent of all, being believed, it hath hitherto been received, and without all Controversy maintained in the Ancient Martyrologies and Breviaries both of the Roman, and other Churches. Baron. *In Append. Tom.* 10. *Ad hunc Annum.*

Note here, that as *Surius,* and *Binius* and *Baronius,* so even the *Roman Church* hath it self received this Council into her purest Records, her sacred *Martyrologies,* and *Mass-books,* or *Breviaries.* Which is a reason above all other reasons, compelling *Binius* and his fellowes, *Baronius, Labbe,* and the *Collectio Regia,* to embrace this Council. For it cannot be rejected without Prejudice to the Authority of the *Roman Chair.* Which as it clears the *Donatists* from the pretended imputation, discovers plainly who are the true Authors of this *Council.*

For though it be more than probable, that some pitiful barren Head, void of all Sence and Learning, did at first compose it, out of the affection he had to the See of *Rome*: Yet as in Treason all are Principals, so here *the Receiver is as bad as the Thief.* The *Roman* Church by aiding and abetting this Abomination, hath made it her own: Be it forged in what empty Shop it will, she hath magnified it to the Stars, by fixing it in her *Martyrologies*: The Chair is defiled with the Forgery it hath adopted: and the Pope hath made it as much his, as if it had been the issue of his own Brain.

Being therefore it cannot now be deserted, without discovering the *shameful Secrets* of the *Roman Church*; *Binius* like a good Son endeavours to maintain it: but with such ill success, that he shames her more by miscarrying in the enterprize.

First he saith, *Exceeding many among the most learned of men, have endeavoured to prove those Acts to be spurious.* By these *most learned of Men* he means the Papists, not the Protestants: So that exceeding many of the most learned Papists have rejected that Council; lest the Chair should be too much disgraced with the reproach of *Marcellinus.* 2. He saith, *They have endeavoured to prove these Acts to be spurious, truly by strong Arguments.* He confesseth the Arguments to be strong against it. And here he varies a little from himself: for besides the Persecution of *Decius,* there are Arguments and Strong ones too, against this Council; which he before concealed. Nor do the *English Innovators* only, but the Papists also, and the most learned among them write against it. What Arguments doth *Binius* bring to defend it? His Opinion, Antiquity, General Consent, and all resolved into the *Roman Martyrology.* As for the first, his *Nevertheless I conceive,* will not do, against *strong*

Arguments. Antiquity, which is the second, stands upon other mens Legs, and speaks by other mens Mouths: She may be painted like a Woman, but is of neither Sex: And though *Binius* would perswade us, that She fighteth in person very *sharply* for the Council, you can see nothing but her *Name*, and his Talk of her Majesty. She wanted the tongue of the Learned, and is a *dumb Champion*. His *General Consent* is disturbed by those *exceeding many most Learned men*, of which he had spoken before, *that endeavoured to prove these Acts to be spurious*. They come out of their Graves with *strong Arguments*, to disorder the *common Assent of all, by which it is beleived;* to defile the *Majesty of Antiquity*, by which it is asserted, and to reprove *Binius* for a Lyar, who saith, that *it hath hitherto been received, and without all Controversie maintained*. Nor is he a Lyar onely, but contradicteth himself, and foolishly bewrayeth his design, while he shufles and cuts upon all occasions.

But perhaps you will say his meaning is, *It is without all Controversie maintianed in the Roman Martyrologies and Breviaries*. That reserve he keeps for a *Startinghole* then, but it will not do. He might say, it was *put in* without all controversie, because the *Roman Martyrologies* and *Breviaries* were works of Darkness, made in Secret by the Popes Authority: But is it *maintained* without all controversie, when *exceeding many of the most Learned Men endeavour to prove its Acts to be Spurious by strong Arguments?* Does *venerable Antiquity it self fight sharply for them, compelling a Reverence from the unwilling by its Majesty; or is it by the common Assent of all believed*; when *exceeding many* endeavour to refute it? As for the *Roman Martyrologies*, it is no wonder it should lie quiet in them. None were by but the Actors only, when the Council was put in; and if by dissembling the fraud, it be *maintained there*, it is no great business. But there it is, and that is sufficient.

For my part I could not have believed, that *Binius* or any other Sober man, could ever reckon such an horrid piece of Barbarism for a *Council*; had I not seen it with my own eyes in the Author. It is so much against all reason, that a thing so absurd should be owned, to the disgrace of all Martyrs, Synods, and Councils. And were it not for the *Clavis* of the wonder, the *Roman Martyrologies*, whose credit must be saved, it would be my lasting amazement.

Binius is so stiffe in defending this Council, that in the next words he chargeth ignorance on S. *Augustine* for not understanding it.

Love and Hunger will eat through stone walls. His Zeal for the Church of *Rome*, and its Direful necessity, makes him to defend this Council in the *Roman Martyrologies*, against an apparent falsehood in the bottom of it, against very many most learned men, against all the barbarous and intollerable Nonsence and Tautologies therein, against the Killing Circumstance, that there was no such City or *Crypta* at least in the World, as well as against the Impossibility of calling it, *on his own Principles*; Besides all which, the vanity of its Design, and the Absurdity of its meeting on such an occasion, is sufficient to detect it.

The Lye in the bottom of it is in those Words, *Cum esset in Bello Persarum*. This Council was convened, as the Title sheweth, *when Dioclesian was in his War with the Persians*. Upon these words *Binius* saith, *Hæc nisi emendentur falsa sunt, &c.* 'These Words be false unless they be mended: for since Eusebius, and divers others witness, that Dioclesian in this 20. Years of his Reign devested himself of the Empire, and which is more, two years before triumphed at Rome with his Collegue *Maximianus*, for having conquered the Persians; how I pray you could he this year be going forth with his Army against the Persians.'

This is one reason more, for which the *Writers of Magdenburg*, and the *English Innovators*, as he is pleased to stile them, reject that Council. Another is contained in *Binius* his Notes on the word *Sinuessa*, 'So called from the City *Sinuessa*, in a certain *Crypta* whereof, called *Cleopatrensis*, they came together secretly to shun the Sword of the raging Gentiles. For whereas men doubt whether any such City was ever in the World, he proceedeth to tell us, that it is not to be admired at all, that there is no mention made either of this City, or such a *Crypta*, in any other Writers, nor at least the smallest memory of this Place to be found: Since we know that by great Earthquakes, not only mountains and plains have lost their Situation and Name, but the Desolation of some most ample Cities hath bin also made.'

It is an unlucky Chance that this City should be swallowed up by an *Earth-quake*: As ominous almost as the *Burning of the Nicene Canons* by the *Arrians*. That other Place[s] have been lost we know: but no man knoweth that this City was lost, nor is *the least memory of it to be found*. Whereas such Strange Accidents being the fittest Themes for the Trumpet of the famous, such a Rarity had made it more remarkable, than if it had continued until this Day: Since *Marvels* chiefly busy the Pens of Historians. That they should be Silent, or its Name be shaken out of all Books by an Earthquake, is the greatest *Miracle* Story doth afford.

Inserting the *Notes* of *Peter Crab* and *Surius*, he giveth us another reason for which we reject that Council. Be pleased to look back on *Peter Crab*, and there you shall see his Premonition beginning thus, *Because of the intolerable and too too grievous Depravation of the Copies,*

&c. The *Collectio Regia* hath rejected the old ones, and for the smoother Conveyance of that Council hath left them both out, and recorded only the false one that was made in their Stead. So may it come to pass in time, that all the Barbarismes shall be forgotten, and the well-mended but Spurious Copy be taken for the true Record. *They* reject the old one for their *Nonsence,* and we *theirs* for its *Novelty.*

Surius, whose *Premonition to the Reader* Binius reserveth till after the Council, yieldeth us another reason whereupon we refuse it. It is pretty to see the Hypocrisy wherewith he admires *the Care and Diligence* of its first Compilers, notwithstanding the *Depravations* and *Corruptions* of the same. For he telleth us, *It seemed not good to the* Collector,*[1] *to pass over these things for the forementioned Trifles, which our forefathers have with so much Labour and Diligence left us.* That is (when you pull off the mask, which *Peter Crab* the Collector, out of some idle Monk or other set on work by the *Church of Rome,* was pleased to record, for the interest of that Chair) though those little *Trifles,* The intolerable *Difference and Depravation of the Copies* would otherwise have hindered him. The reason why he defendeth it, moves us to reject it. *For they, who being Zealous for the Bishop of Rome, conceit these things to be feigned by those who rival the Apostolical See, as if it were unworthy of the Apostolical Chair, that so great a Bishop should be brought to so strait a Pass, as to Sacrifice unto Idols; seem little to remember how* Peter's Denial did not hurt him; *or that, there is joy among the Angels over one Sinner that repenteth; or that this very* Marcellinus *afterwards constantly met his Death for the sake of Christ; and according to the Proverb, fought manfully after he ran away. However it be, O Reader, we would not have that concealed from thee, which we have found in the Monuments of the Ancients, leaving the Truth of this to the Records themselves, and not prejudicating any mans Sentence by our Opinion.* His Reason why it may be held for a good and true Record, is the safety of the Roman Chair notwithstanding it should be thought so. And one of the Reasons why we so greatly suspect them, is that very behaviour: The advantage of the *Roman* See being the only Touchstone among them, of Records and Forgeries. By this very example you see, that men as wise as *Binius l*eave the Council Doubtful; and by his Testimony you find that many *Romanists* renounce it: So may you discern by the Crookedness of their Rule, that they are fit to be suspected. It is a very great Secret and warily to be discovered, and that to none but friends! but *they that are zealous for the Bishop of* Rome, *shape their Opinions by their Affections.* Some

---

[1] The asterisk refers to the marginal gloss: *Peter Crab.*

that are zealous, *conceit those things to be feigned, because they think it unworthy of the Apostolical Chair, that so great a Bishop should sacrifice to Idols.* While some of them, that are *zealous too for the Bishop of* Rome, because they remember *how* Peter's *denial did not hurt him*, and know that the fear of the former might easily be removed with pretences enow, think it better to retain this Council. For *there is joy among the Angels for a Sinner that repenteth;* and *Marcellinus*'s Martyrdome is as glorious to the *Chair*, as his Fall was disgraceful. The one are afraid of the Popes Infallibility, and because they think the Fall of *Marcellinus* in that respect too dangerous to be recorded, would suppress the Council: The other are zealous of the Popes Supremacy, and because they would exempt him from all Superiours, and make him uncapable of being judged by any, record the Council. And which is the Wisest, that is the Question: Not what is true, but what is expedient? While their Judgments are formed not according to *Things*, but conveniencies.

Another reason why we reject this Council is because it containeth a Doctrine, which no true Record of Antiquity teacheth: but wherewith the Forgeries before laid open do extreamly abound. And here the behaviour of *Surius* is a little further to be noted. He avers that *he found these things in the Monuments of the Ancients*, and yet is so dasht, *that he leaves the truth of them to the Records themselves.* What Records, what Monuments, what Ancients can these be, that are fit to be suspected? He will not *prejudicate any mans Sentence by his Opinion.* Which is a piece of Liberality in a Papist, that implies some extraordinary Cause not to be uttered.

Another reason of our opposing it, is because it so notoriously wresteth the H. Scriptures. That Place which is spoken of the *general* Account, which all men must give at the Day of judgement, being applied in *particular*, to shew that no man may condemn the Pope. *Out of thine own Mouth thou shalt be justified, &c.* Which being the Sole foundation on which they lay any stress, is with so much ridiculous Babling repeated, that it would turn a mans Stomack, and make him sick to peruse it.

But the Impossibility of the Thing is an Argument *ad Hominem*, that may perhaps be more convincing. For as they hold that no man may condemn a Pope, So do they hold that no man, but he, can call a Council. And though for *Form-sake* they ascribe the Power of Calling Councils, in the Vacancy of the See, to the Roman Clergy; yet when a Pope is *Alive*, they utterly deny it to them, or any else: Because the Pope is supreme, and be he Good or Bad, *can be judged by none.* By what Authority then did the Roman Clergy call this Council, before the Pope was judicially deposed. If the Roman Clergy take upon them to condemn him before he is heard, his Condition is worse than that of other men. If they presume to call a Council before he is condemned, they usurp his Authority, and act independently to the prejudice of the Chair, in such sort as was never heard of; there being no President or Copy but this, of such a Proceeding. Though the Pope were a Criminal, yet every one must not judg him. *I* suppose they will Confess there have been many wicked Popes, yet while the Pope is a Pope, no man without his Authority may call a Council. The thing is impossible therefore in it self. For he must First be condemned, before a Council could be called to condemn him; and before he could be condemned, the Council must be called. Which would seem among Protestants a Contradiction.

The Absurditie of the Plot, is another reason why we reject it. Three hundred Bishops in a persecution adventure their Lives to meet together, upon an unwarrantable Call before the Pope was convicted as a Criminal, and without knowing whether he would come to Judgment; though certainly knowing that none could compel him, convene him before them. They produce one Day 14. Witnesses, another Day 44. And care is taken, according to the Decree of the *Epilogus Brevis*: to compleat the number of 72. Witnesses: And when all is done, they confess they have no Power to condemn him. The Absurdities are not easily fathomed. How gross was it for the Roman Clergy to call a Council for the Deposing of a Pope, whom they before knew nothing could condemn but his own Sentence? How absurd, for them to judg the Pope, whom they continually teach no man can judg? How much more absurd for the Council to meet to depose him, who if he were pleased to declare their Sentence null, all was in vain? It is just as if a *Rebellious* Parliament should meet on their own Heads, to call their King to account, upon pretence of his Crimes. If this be admitted, all must be Disorder and Confusion in Kingdom.

If his Ingenuity had led *him* to depose himself, without giving all these Bishops the trouble, he might have done it at home. That he wanted Ingenuity, his denial of the Fact (before the Council) testifieth. Whereupon I wonder what brought him thither, or what Miracle made him stand before the Bar, at his Tryal? But had he not denied the Fact, the Ceremony had been lost of *producing seventy and two Witnesses*. Which relation to the putid Forgery of the *Epilogus Brevis*, as yet unmade, utterly mars the business.

The Council it self is the greatest evidence against it self in the World. If you please to give your self the trouble of reading it, either in *Peter Crab*, or *Surius*, or *Nicolinus*, or *Binius*, and compare it with the Letters of Pope *Sylvester* and the *Nicene Council*, recorded afterwards, you will find reason to believe the very same *Dunce* made them all. Those three being the absurdest pieces, that ever were seen with learned eyes.

For a Taste of this, take but the beginning of the two old pretended Originals, A. and C. to let go the third, which being made by latter men, is nothing to the purpose.

A.	C.
Dioclesiano & Maximiano Augustis. Cum multi in vitâ suâ asper si mentis suæ vacillitate mentiebantur, origine dicentes, quod Deorum Superstitio vanitas super se sentirent, & ad Sacrificandum eo tempore multi inducerentur per pecuniam, ut Sacrificarent Diis. Marcellinus itaque, &c.	Cum multi in vitâ suâ aspersu mentis suæ vacillitate mentiebantur, origine, dicentes, quod Deorum Superstitionem vanis super sentirent, & ad Sacrificandum eodem tempore multi inducerentur per pecuniam utthurificarent Diis. Marcellinus itaque, & c.

Take which you will, and try to construe it; you will find it impossible: yet in this Dialect he holdeth from end to end. Many things more we might speak, but we study brevity.

CAP. XX.

Divers things premised in order, first to the Establishment, and then to the Refutation of Constantine's *Donation; the first by* Binius, *and the latter by the Author. The Forgeries of* Marcellus, *Pope* Eusebius, *and* Binius *opened.*

Marcellus *a Roman sate five years,*[1] *six moneths, and twenty one days,* saith the Pontifical. He succeeded *Marcellinus*. There are two Decretal Epistles ascribed to him, and both counterfeit: The one is *concerning the Primacy and Authority of the Roman Church*: the other is written to *Maxentius the Heathen Emperour*, and a Tyrant. Concerning which last, *Binius* (in his Notes upon it) saith, *Hanc Epistolam, Anno 308. Scriptam, Additamentum aliquod accepisse, Res Scriptæ hic parùm sibi cohærentes indicant.* He holdeth it for a good Record; but there are so many things inconsistent in it, that he fears it has *taken a Dose,* and confesseth that some things were put in, by way of Forgery.

This is an easy way of defending. There was never any Deed forged, wherein the larger half, being *directed purely according to form of Law*, was not Good. But if for that cause, when it comes to be Scanned, the forger at every Detection should say, *This was forged indeed, but the rest is good*; the Court would laugh at him: And this is *Binius* his present Case.

In the time of *Marcellus* there was a Council called at *Eliberis, An.* 305. where they forgot *Binius* his *Council of Apostles at Antioch*; and among other Canons decreed this for one, *Placuit Picturas in Ecclesiâ esse non debere. Ne quod colitur & adoratur, in Parietibus depingatur.* They think it unlawful to put any Picture of what is adored, in the Church on the Walls. He takes much pains to pick this Thorn out of the Popes foot: but we leave him at his work, and proceed to

THE LIFE, EPISTLES, AND DE–
CREES OF *EUSEBIUS* POPE,
Out of the Pontifical of Pope
Damasus.

---

[1] Marginal gloss: *An.* 304.

Eusebius a Grecian sate nine years,[1] *four moneths, and three days.* *Binius* proveth, he could sit but *two years,* some *moneths, &c.* And whereas *Eusebius* saith, *the Cross was found in his days,* and Fathers the Invention of it upon one *Judas,* converted thereupon, and called (at his Baptism) *Quiriacus*; though he names the day of the moneth exactly, *the fifth of the Nones of May,* and instituteth an Holy-day thereupon; yet is all this rejected by *Binius* for a Fable. *For by the consent of all Ancient Writers,* saith he, *the Cross was found after the Nicene Council, by* Helena *the Mother of* Constantine *the Great.* Howbeit, there is a very formal *Epistle to the Bishops of* Tuscia *and* Campania, in the name of *Eusebius,* devoutly abusing H. Scripture, exalting Piety, and the Popes Chair; till at last it decrees an *Holy-day* for this happy Invention, solemnly enjoyn'd by the Authority of this Roman Catholick and Apostolical Bishop, though all this be as very a Cheat as any of the former. *Binius* has a cure for this too, but a very course one: *This part of the Epistle we confess to be counterfeit.* Vid. Bin. in loc.

Melchiades *an African sate three years,*[2] *eleven moneths, and eight days.* Binius saith, *two years,* &c. And reprehends the Pontificals Confusion, which I shall not stand to mention, having greater matters to declare.

In his time *Constantine the first Christian Emperour* arose: Concerning whom the Pontifical is silent in the time of *Melchiades,* having need of him in that of *Sylvester*: but *Binius* gives us this little Abstract of his History here.

After an Interval of seven days, Octob. 3. An. Christ. 311. *in the third year of the Emperour* Constantine, Melchiades *began to sit. In his time, six moneths from the return of Peace to the Church being scarcely past,* Maximinus *in the* East, *being Emperour with* Licinius, *stirred up a most grievous Persecution against the Christians, whom he called the Firebrands, and the Authors of all the Evils in the World.* Euseb. *l.* 9. *c.* 6. Maxentius *in the West oppressed the Empire with a grievous Tyranny: But* Constantine *his Fellow=Emperour that Reigned with him in the* West, *as* Licinius *Reigned with* Maximinus *in the* East, *being stirred up partly by injuries, and partly by the prayers of the* Romans, *resolved to suppress the Tyrant. When therefore he designed the War, he despised the Aids of the Heathen Gods, and determined in himself to implore only the Creator of Heaven and Earth, whom his Father* Constantius *adored. It happened therefore that while he was praying for Prosperity, he saw*

---

[1] Marginal gloss: *An.* 309.
[2] Marginal gloss: *An.* 311.

at Mid-day the Sign of the Cross, made with Beams of Light, appearing in the Heavens; in which these words were manifestly contained, IN HOC VINCE. *The Explication whereof when he had learned from our Lord Jesus Christ appearing to him in his sleep, and from his Priests; he undertakes the War against* Maxentius, *and happily conquers him. Which Victory being gloriously gotten, in acknowledgment that it came from that One Invisible and Immortal God, he erected a Trophy of the Cross in the midst of the City, with this Famous Motto*: HOC SALUTARI SIGNO, VERO FORTITUDINIS INDICIO CIVITATEM VESTRAM TYRANNIDIS JUGO LIBERAVI. Under this Saving Sign, the true Mark of Fortitude, I freed your City from the Yoke of Tyranny. *And as a manifest Token of his Liberality and Piety, he gave to* Melchiades *the Publick House in the* Lateran, *which heretofore was the Palace of* Fausta *the Empress.* Opt. Mil. *He restored the Goods of the Church, gave great Priviledges and Immunities to the Clergy, and made a Decree, that they should be maintained at the Publick Charge.*

In the latter end of this first *Tome*, *Binius* has a long Record of *Gelasius Cyzicenus*, in fair Greek and Latine, who being a very Ancient Author, confirms all these things, shewing the madness of *Maximinus*, and his destruction, the building of Churches, the evil manners of *Licinius*, the Victory which the *Religious* Emperour obtained against that *wicked* man, the *Peace* of the Churches after *Licinius* his Death, and the several ways whereby the good Emperour promoted the Christian Affairs.

Yet as if all this were a Dream, the Scene is immediately overthrown; *Constantine* is a Tyrant, a Murderer, an Oppressor, a Persecuter of the Church, and smitten with Leprosie from Heaven! namely for his great abominations: *Licinius* is innocent, and unjustly slain; but *Constantine* is made the Destroyer of peace. For in the Life of *Sylvester* the next Bishop after *Melchiades,* the Pontifical saith, *he was banished into the Mountain* Soracte. Upon which words, *Binius* further saith, that *Sylvester, fearing the cruelty of the Emperour, fled from the City, as his own Acts, and* Zozimus, *and* Sozomen *do probably shew.*

As for *Sylvesters Acts* so simply and freely cited here, meerly to cheat the Reader, he afterwards *[1] confesseth them to be a Forgerie. And as for *Zozimus* and *Sozomen*: those Words, [*Do probably shew.*] shew *Binius* to be a *Sophister*. He would fain have father'd the Story upon *Zozimus* and *Sozomen*: but his Courage failed him: for they speak not expresly, but *Probably shew*; that is, in his conceit, they give him colour

---

[1] The asterisk refers to the marginal gloss: **Bin. Not. In Constant. Edict.*

enough to side with a Cheat, a Forger, a Lyar, a notorious Counterfeit, *Damasus*, against all the true Antiquities and Histories in the World. The positive Relation of *Eusebius Pamphilus* an holy Father in the *Nicene Council*, that lived in those times, the Records of *Gelasius Cyzicenus* that ancient Author, and *Nicolinus*, the late Compiler of the Councils, that commend *Eusebius* as *the most faithful witness among Ecclesiastical Writers*, being palpably contradicted, while *Zozimus the Heathen* is favoured in some dark expression, wherein his Envy tempted him to carp at the Emperour; because he was next under God, the Author of so much Peace and Felicity amongst the Christians. As for *Sozomen* he was a Christian indeed, but too late an Author to contend with *Eusebius* and *Gelasius Cyzincenus*. Neither does *Binius* say he positively avers any such thing, but *probably shews* either a *Fox* or a *Fernbush*; Some frailty perhaps which proves *Constantine* a Man: but *Binius* should have produced clear Testimonies, as sound and authentick as the former, if he meant to swim against all Antiquity, in disgracing so glorious an Emperour, positively affirming him to be guilty of Murder, and Paricide, Apostacy, and Idolatry, Persecution, *&c.*

Binius acteth his part too far: for, if (as he saith) *Constantine counterfeited* himself to be an *Heathen* only to satisfie the People; *his great munificence, and kindness to the Christians having imbitttered the Multitude, so far, that it almost brake out into a Rebellion: for the appeasing of the Sedition therefore, he dissembled his Religion, upon Temporal Considerations, for which God was provoked*, Certainly he could never hope to be cured of his Leprosie, by going in earnest to the Heathen Priests and their Idols, as *Binius* pretendeth, when he was so deeply humbled, and in danger of Destruction.

But this whole pretence is overthrown, and the *Genius* of the Man more clearly displayed in the passage following.

In the Life of *Marcellus* with which we began the Chapter, and which was some years before this pretended necessity, he telleth us that *Maxentius, who studied to possess himself of the Tyranny of* Rome, *at his first entrance into the* Roman *Empire, feigned himself craftily to embrace our Faith; thereby to please the* Roman *people, and to take them with his Flatteries, for which cause he remitted the Persecution against the Christians: and put on such a shew of Piety, that for a time he seemed full of Courtesie, Love, and Humanity.* This he proveth out of *Euseb. l.* 8. *c.* 26. But for a purpose of which *Eusebius* was not aware: his design being hereby to justifie the Counterfeit *Epistle of Marcellus*, and to palliate the absurdities therein contained, the Popes ranting so foolishly out of the Bible, and threatning *Maxentius the Heathen Emperour*, with the Authority of his Predecessor *Clement*; while he was a Pagan Infidel. Now if *Maxentius* found it necessary to counterfeit himself a *Christian*, to please the People; *Constantine*, who found the minds of men far more inclinable to Religion then *Maxentius* did, was by consequent, more engaged to appear a Christian, than *Maxentius* was; that so he might also please the People. But voluble Wits in *partial* Heads are bended easily to any Cause, they fancy for their advantage: Otherwise the Cross in the Heavens, the Trophies upon Earth, the prevailing glory of *Christianity*, the victories of *Constantine*, the joy and exultation of the people, and the general applause with which he was received throughout the whole World, would have taught *Binius* another Lesson, than *Constantines* necessity to counterfeit himself an *Heathen*, which is the meer *Chymera* of a lying Brain: for which he is not able to produce any one Author in the World, worth the naming.

He produces the Testimony of *Eusebius* concerning the necessity of *Maxentius* his counterfeiting himself to be a *Christian*, but *Eusebius* speaketh not one word of any necessity lying upon *Constantine* to counterfeit himself an *Heathen*: but the contrary, so far, that *Binius*, who had quoted *Eusebius* so gravely before, brandeth him with the Reproach of an *Arrian*, because he crosseth his design now about *Constantines Donation*.

For the Donation is founded on *Constantines* Cure, his Cure on his Leprosie, his Leprosie on his Apostacy, his Apostacy upon a Necessity to comply with the perverseness of the *Heathen* people, whose Power was of too great a sway for his Design in the Empire: All which is contradicted by the continual decaying of *Heathenism* that then was day by day, and the growth of *Christianity*, which had taken such root and possession in the People, that there needed nothing but the change of the Emperour, to turn the *Empire* into *Christendom*. But this Necessity must be invented: for else it would seem impossible that he should turn Pagan, after our Saviour had appeared to him in his sleep, after he had seen the Cross in the Air, after he had set it up in his Standard, after all his Victories gotten under that glorious Banner, after he had erected its Trophy in the City, and made the World Glorious by his Munificence to the Churches.

For this Cause, a far off, and so long befoe the end could be discovered, to which it should be applied, does *Binius* take his Rise from the Fable in the *Donation*, and shape his Discourse to the Exaltation of the *See*, by rooting the *Donation* deeply in the Minds of men. For all his drift is to no other purpose, than to confirm the *Donation* of the Emperour, thereby to settle the Empire in the Chair: for the sake of which, he tramples upon the Emperour, wryeth Antiquity, wresteth Authority, citeth Forgeries and Heathen Authors, defaceth the History of the Church, and rewards the greatest of all Benefactors, with the basest ingratitude.

All these Wars are commenced *afar off*: for the strength of *Rome* is alwaies at a distance: near at hand she is weak and feeble; when he comes up close to the matter, though he makes a great semblance of its evident centainty, writing over head in Capital Letters, EDICTUM CONSTANTINI: And putting down the *Donation* under it at large, commenting on it also very formally, nay and writing in the Margin of his Notes, *Constantini Donatio defenditur*, and near the close of them, *Constantini Donatio confirmatur*: yet after all this, he confesses the Donation to be *Spurious*. His Design being no more, than to make a *Shew*, and cover that *Confession*; which meer necessity, at greatest pinch, wrested from him. His Confession lies in little roome, and his Notes are made for the assistance of *Confederates*; Such mighty Tomes for the Help of a sworn Party. As for the rest of men that are allured perhaps by the Magnificence of the Books to admire them, and to grace their Studies with them, such as *Lords* and *Princes*, he very well knows, they may feed their Eyes with Great Titles, and Glorious Shews afar off; but they will never penetrate such *Stupendious Volumes*, by reason of other Diversions, Labors, Cares, and Pleasures, which call them away to other secular Objects. So that they may easily be deceived with the outward Appearance and splendor of such great and learned Collections, which secret Design is the Mystery of the *Popish Councils*.

For in the Body of those Notes, *Binius* himself by many well studied Arguments sets himself strenuously to overthrow the *Donation*; and Fathers it on the Knavery of *Balsamon* a Greek, who produced it (as he pretends) with an intent to disgrace the *Roman Chair*; by making the World believe, that the Popes Supremacy came not by Divine Institution, but the Grant of the Emperour: Which he abhors as fickle, weak, and humane, chusing rather that the Popes Right should rest on the Scriptures.

Labbe, *Cossartius*, and the COLLECTIO REGIA follow *Binius* exactly, even to those Cheats *in the Margin*. But now it is high time to see the Contents of this wonderful *Donation*.

CAP. XXI.

The EDICT *of our Lord* CONSTANTINE *the Emperour.*

*I*n *the Name of the Holy and Individual Trinity,*[1] *the Father, and the Son, and the H. Ghos*t; Flavius Constantinus, Cæsar, *and Emperour, in Jesus Christ, one of the same H. Trinity, &c. To the most Holy and Blessed Father of Fathers* Sylvester, *Bishop and Pope of the City of* Rome, *and to all his Successors about to sit in the Seat of blessed* Peter, *to the end of the World: And to all our most Reverend and Catholick Bishops, amiable in God, made Subject throughout the World to the H. Church of* Rome, *by this our Imperial Constitution, &c.* It is too long to put it down formally, and at large: We shall therefore take only the chief Contents, as they lie in the Donation. It first contains a large account of the Articles of his Faith; Secondly, the story of his Leprosie, Cure, and Baptism: wherein the font is remarkably called *Piscina,* (the Popes *Fishpond* as it were) then he cometh to the Gift it self.

While I learned these things by the Preaching of the blessed Sylvester, *and by the benefit of the blessed* Peter, *found my self perfectly restored to my health, we judged it profitable, together with* * *all our Nobles,*[2] *and the whole Senate, my Princes also, and the whole People Subject to the Empire of the Roman Glory; that as S.* Peter *upon Earth seemeth to be made the Vicar of the Son of God, the Bishops also that are the Successors of him, the Prince of the Apostles, may obtain the Power of Principality given from us and our Empire, more than the Earthly Clemency of our Imperial Majesty is seen to have had; chusing the Prince of the Apostles, and his Successors, for our stedfast Patrons with God. And we have decreed that this H. Roman Church shall be honoured with Veneration, even as our Terrene Imperial Power is: And that the most Holy Seat of B.* Peter *be more gloriously exalted than our Earthly Throne; giving it Power, and Dignity of Glory, and Vigour, and Honour Imperial. And we decree and ordain, that he shall hold the Principality, as well over the four Principal Sees of* Antioch, Alexandria, Jerusalem, *and* *Constantiople,[3] *as over*

---

[1] Marginal gloss: A Forgery beginning in the Name of the Father, Son, and H. Ghost.
[2] The asterisk refers to the marginal gloss: *All the Nobles, and the Senate, converted in a moment.mmn
[3] The asterisk refers to the marginal gloss: *Not yet built.

all the Churches of God in the whole World. And by his Judgment let all things whatsoever, pertaining to the Worship of God, and the Establishment of the Christian Faith be ordained.

When *Binius* pleases to give Efficacy to a Miracle, all the World shall be converted in a moment. Notwithstanding all the Miracles and Victories before, *Constantine* was fain to counterfeit himself an Heathen for fear of the people: Now all his Nobles, and the Senate, are changed in an instant; and his Leprosie upon Earth has done more than his Cross in the Heavens. So easie it is to blow mens minds with a Breath, when they are dead and gone. *His Princes also, and the whole people subject to the Empire of the Roman Glory, judged it profitable, together with him, and his Nobles*, to do that which they abhorred before, to give to Banished *Sylvester*, and his Heirs, the Glory of the *Roman* Empire: As if that one Miracle had in a trice for Virtue outgone all our *Saviours*.

The last Clause contains something more than the Emperour had power to bestow. That a Lay-man should by Deed of Gift devise, and give away the power of determining all Controversies in Religion, to whom he fancieth; may be put among the Popes Extravagants (as some of their Decrees are called:) yet with *Constantinople*, (a City yet unmade) this also is given to the Pope in the present *Donation*. But upon good reason: *For it is just that the Holy Law should retain the Head of Principality there, where our Saviour, the Instituter of Holy Laws, commanded the B. Peter to undertake the Chair of his Apostleship.*

A merrier accident follows, *he bequeaths his Goods to the Dead*! It is true indeed he was allied to them, for he was dead when the Deed was made, as well as they. S. *Peter*'s Trustees having the management of his Pen, knew very well, that whatever he *gave to his most blessed Lords*, Peter *and* Paul, (since dead men never want Heirs) would fall to their share: and like our late Long Parliament, conspired to give large Boons to themselves, in form following.

'WE Exhort and admonish all, that with us they would pay abundant thanks to our God and Saviour Jesus Christ,[1] because being God in Heaven above, and in Earth beneath, he hath visited us by his H. Apostles, and made us worthy ro receive the H. Sacrament of Baptisme, and the health of our Body. FOR WHICH we grant to the H. Apostles themselves, my most Blessed Lords, *Peter* and *Paul*,[2] and by them also to B. *Sylvester* our Father, the chief Bishop and Pope of our

---

[1] Marginal gloss: *Ibid*.
[2] Marginal gloss: Constantine the Great gives his Cloaths to S *Peter* and S. *Paul* in heaven.

Universal City of *Rome*, and to all Bishops his Successors that shall ever sit in the Chair of B. *Peter*, to the end of the world, *Our Diadem*, to wit, the Crown of our Head, together with our Mitre, as also the Cloak on our Shoulders; *viz.* our Breast-plate which is wont to compass our Imperial Neck, as also our Purple *Clamys*, and Violet Cloak, and all the Imperial Attires. The Dignity moreover of our Imperial *Horsemen*:[1] Giving him also the Imperial Scepters, with all other Signs, Badges, Banners, and other Imperial Ornaments, with the whole manner of the Procession of our Imperial Highness, and the Glory of our Power.

'WE Decree also and Ordain to the most Reverend Clergy-men serving that H. Roman Church, in their divers Orders, the Height in Singularity, Power and Excellency, with the Glory whereof our most ample Senate seemeth to be adored; that is, that they shall be made *Patricii*, and *Consuls*.[2] As also we promulgate it for a Law, that they be beautified with the other Imperial Dignities. AND as the Imperial Army is adorned,[3] so do we Decree the Clergy of the Roman Church to be adorned: And as the Imperial Power is adorned with divers Offices, as that of Chamberlains, Porters, and all Guards; so we will have the Roman Church to be adorned.

'AND that the Pontifical Glory may shine most amply,[4] we Decree this also; That the Horses of the Clergy of the said Roman Church, be beautified with Caparisons, and Linnen Vestures of the whitest colour, and so to ride. And as our Senate useth Shoes, *cum Udonibus*, made bright and illustrious with fine white Linnen, so let the Clergy also do: And let the Heavenly, as the Earthly things are, be made comely to the praise of God.

'BUT above all, we give License to our most H. Father *Sylveser*, Bishop and Pope of the City of *Rome* himself, and to all that shall succeed him for ever, for the Honour and Glory of Christ our God, in the same Great, Catholick, and Apostolick Church of God, by our Edict, *Ut quem placatus proprio Consilio clericali voluerit, & in numoro religiosorum Clericorum connumerare, nullum ex omnibus præsumentum superbè agere.*'[5]

Binius for *Clericali* will have it *Clericare*, which he puts over against it in the Margin. Here are more Barbarismes than one: but I think

---

[1] Marginal gloss: The Popes Guard.
[2] Marginal gloss: Secular Power.
[3] Marginal gloss: The Popes Army.
[4] Marginal gloss: The Popes Horses.
[5] Marginal gloss: False Latine and Nonsense.

the drift is, *that no man but he whom the Bishop of* Rome *pleaseth, shall be made a Priest: and that no man so made, shall behave himself proudly against the Bishop of* Rome.

We have Decreed this also,[1] *That the same Venerable* Sylvester *our Father, the High-Priest, and all his Successors, ought to use the Diadem, to wit, the Crown which we gave him from off our Head, of pure Gold and Precious Stones, and to wear it on his Head, to the praise of God, and honour of S.* Peter. * *BUT because the most Holy Pope himself will not endure a Crown*[2] *altogether of Gold on the Crown of his Priesthood, which he bears to the Glory of the B.* Peter, *we have with our own hands put the Mitre of Resplendent White, signifying the most Glorious Resurrection of our Lord, on his Head:* * *And holding the Bridle of his Horse,*[3] *for the Reverence we owe to S.* Peter, *we served him in the Office of a Stirrup-holder: Ordaining, that all his Successors shall in single and peculiar manner use the same Mitre in their Processions, in imitation of our Empire.*

The Popes Modesty comes off purely: Because he would not have his Shaven Crown profaned with a Crown of Gold; therefore the Emperour must give him the Mitre too: because it was unlawful for him to wear the one without the other; that is, his Conscience made a scruple at the one, unless he might have both: being so made exactly like the Heathen Monarchs at *Rome, Pontifex Maximus,* and *Emperour* together.

The Regalities were affected, not for themselves; Alas, Ornaments are but shadows, the Body and Substance is the thing desired.

WHEREFORE that the Pontifical Crown[4] *may never wax vile, but be more exalted also than the Dignity of the Terrene Empire, and the Glory of Power: Behold, we give and leave as well our Palace,*[5] *as was before said, as the City of* Rome, *all* Italy, *and all the Provinces, places, and Cities of the Western Empire, to our foresaid most B. High Priest, and Universal Pope, and to the Power and Tenure of the Popes his Successors, by firm Imperial Censure,* Per hanc Divalem & Pragmaticum Constitutum;[6] *By this our Divine and Pragmatical Constitution, we Decree them to be disposed, and grant them to remain under the Right and Tenure of the H. Roman Church.*

Poor Priests are fain to cheat the people by witty Miracles, and small Devices, at *Shrines* and *Images,* for a little Silver and Gold. The

---

[1] Marginal gloss: *Ibid.*
[2] The asterisk refers to the marginal gloss: the Popes Modesty.
[3] The asterisk refers to the marginal gloss: *Constantine* the Great the Popes Groom or Stirrup-holder.
[4] Marginal gloss: *Ibid.*
[5] Marginal gloss: The Popes Dominions.
[6] Marginal gloss: The Popes Latine.

best of them can attain no more than Lordships, and the Territories of *Subjects*: As the Manours evidence, which are given to *our Lady of Loretto*, and those Lands which *Jesuites* squeeze out of dying men with the fear of *Purgatory*. But the Pope and his Cardinals find it not suitable to their State and Dignity, to juggle for less than Empires and Kingdoms; and therefore soar high, you see, in the present *Donation*.

'Wherefore, *saith the Emperour*,[1] we have thought it convenient to change and remove our Empire, and the power of our Kingdom into the Eastern Countries, and in the best place of the Province *Byzantium*, to build a City after our Name, and there to found our Empire. Because where the * Head of the Principality of Priests, and of the Christian * Religion is ordained to be by the Cœlestial Emperour,[2] it is not just that the Earthly emperour should there have any Power.'

Here is a high Career of notorious Heresie and Blasphemy together. S. *Peter* was called the Prince of Apostles, but the Pope is the *Head of the Principality*; nor Head of the Priests only, but *of the Christian Religion*: which I think none but our Saviour can possibly be. It smells rank of Blasphemy; but that the Priestly and Imperial Power should be incompatible, is Rebellion and Heresie. It shews how imcompatible *Popish* and *Imperial* Power is: Yet all these things are ratified by other *Dival Sanctions*, made by the Emperor, though recorded no where; as you may see in the words following.

BUT all these things we also have decreed,[3] *and ratified by other Dival Sanctions, and we decree them to stand unblemished, and unshaken, to the end of the World. WHEREFORE we protest before the Living God who commanded us to Reign, and before his Terrible Judgment by this our Imperial Constitution, that it shall not be lawful for any the Emperours our Successors, nor for any of our Nobles and Peers, or for the most Ample Senate, or for all the people of the whole World, now, or hereafter, from hence in all Ages, lying under our Empire, by any means to contradict, or break, or in the least to diminish these things; which by this our Imperial Sanction are granted to the Holy Roman Church, or to all the Bishops of the same. But if any Breaker or Contemner of these shall arise (which we do not believe) let him be knotted and ensnared in eternal Damnation, and find the Saints of God, and the Princes of the Apostles* Peter *and* Paul, *Enemies unto him, both in the Life present, and in that which is to come: and being burnt in the lower Hell, let him perish with the Devil and all the wicked.*

---

[1] Marginal gloss: *Ibid*.
[2] The asterisks refer to marginal gloss: The Pope the Head of Religion.
[3] Marginal gloss: The Sanction of the Decree.

The great Council of *Chalcedon*[1] consisting of 630 Fathers, lies under this Sentence; because they made the Patriarch of *Constantinople* equal with the Bishop of *Rome*: If *Constantine* the Great did make it, *with the consent of all his Nobles and the whole Senate, before all the Princes and People of* Rome, as is pretended in the Donation. It was too publick a thing not to be heard of, and too remarkable to be let pass in silence. Since therefore it is incredible, that so many Fathers should wilfully fall under the Curse, it is certain the whole Donation is a Counterfeit. Howbeit as the Substance of the Act, so the Ceremony is worth the observation.

But ratifying the Page of this our Imperial Decree, we laid it with our own hands on the venerable Body of the Blessed Peter *Prince of the Apostles, and there promising to that Apostle of God, that we would inviolably keep all these things, and leave them in charge to be kept by the Emperours our Successors, we delivered them to our blessed Father* Sylvester, *High-Priest, and* * *Universal Pope*,[2] *and to all the Popes his Successors, the Lord God, and our Saviour Jesus Christ allowing it, for ever, and happily to be enjoyed. And the Imperial subscription. The Divinity keep you many years, most holy and blessed Fathers. Dated in* Rome, *on the third day of the Kalends of* April. *Our Lord* Flavius Constantinus Augustus *the fourth time,* and Gallicanus *being Consuls.*

A NOTE.

No Emperour being ever accustomed, to stile himself *Our Lord*, &c. Those words *Our Lord* Flavius Constantinus, coming out of *Constantine's* own Mouth bewray the Donation, as made by some other, unless he were at the same time both his own Subject, and his own Emperour.

---

[1] Marginal gloss: *Council. Chalced. Can.* 28.
[2] Asterisk refers to marginal gloss: * *Gregory* the Great's Blasphemous Title.

CAP. XXII.

The Donation of Constantine *proved to be a Forgery by* Binius *himself. He confesseth the Acts of* Sylvester, *which he before had cited as good Records, to be Counterfeit.*

THose things (saith *Binius* in his Notes) *which are told concerning the Dominion and Temporal Kingdom, given to the See of* Rome, *are manifestly enough proved to be likely, by what we said in our Notes upon the former Epistle; as well as by the Munificence of the Emperour himself, never enough to be praised.*

Observe here the modesty of the man! He ought to prove the Instrument itself; but that he throws by, and talks of the *Dominion*, and *Temporal Kingdom*.

2. Neither will he undertake to prove it *certain*, but *likely*, that the Dominion and Temporal Kingdom was given to the See of *Rome*.

3. He cites his Notes on a counterfeit Epistle, to make it *likely*: For the Epistle going before was the *Epistle of Melchiades*, which he confesseth to be a Forgery.

4. *The Munificence of the Emperour makes it probable, that he gave away the Empire to the See of* Rome. If you will not believe this, you are an hard-hearted man; for *Binius* says it.

His Notes upon the *former Epistle*, to which he refers you, are these: 'That the things which are written in this Epistle concerning the Donation of *Constantine* to *Melchiades* and *Sylvester*, are true, is proved not only from hence, but most firmly also by the Authority of *Optatus Milevitanus*, a most approved Writer. For he writeth, *lib.* 1. *cont. Parm.* that *Constantine* and *Licinius* being the third time Consuls, to wit, in the year of Christ 313. a Council of 19 Bishops was held at *Rome*, in the Cause of *Cæcilianus* and the *Donatists*, in the *Lateran*, in the House of *Fausta*, which was the Seat of the Roman Bishop. Truly he doth not expresly write, that the House was given to *Melchiades* by the Emperour: but since no reason doth appear for which it is necessary, that the Convention of 19 Bishops should require larger Rooms out of the House of *Melchiades*, that wherein the foresaid Synod was assembled, to wit, the *Lateran*, or House of *Fausta*, can by no prudent person any more be doubted, to be given by the Emperour to *Melchiades* the Bishop of *Rome*.'

The *Lateran* is not so much as named in the Epistle of *Melchiades*; but that *he left the Imperial Seat, which the Roman Princes had possest, and granted it to the profit of the blessed* Peter, *and his Bishops.* Which considering what follows, is far more fit to be understood of the Emperours *leaving Rome,* and granting it to the Bishop: whence they pretend, he did go on purpose. So that the agreement between *Optatus Milevitanus,* and the Epistle of *Melchiades,* is very small, or none at all.

But admit that *Melchiades* and *Optatus Milevitanus* had said, both of them, that the *Lateran* was given to *Melchiades*; what is that to the *Dominion and Temporal Kingdom?* A single House, instead of an Empire! Though, that the House was given, *Opatus Milevitanus* doth not affirm, even by *Binius* his own confession.

How *the things in this Epistle* should be *concerning the Donation of* Constantine *to* Melchiades *and* Sylvester, is difficult to conceive; because *Melchiades* was dead before the Donation was made to *Sylvester*. It is very unlikely therefore that *Melchiades* should make mention of that *Donation.*

His Epistle talking of *Constantine his being President in the H. Synod that was called at* Nice, is a manifest Imposture, *Melchiades* being dead before the *Nicene* Council; as is before observed: Yet hence it is proved, that *Constantine* made a *Donation* to *Melchiades* and *Sylvester.*

Binius holdeth fast the *Donation*, though he lets go the *Epistle*. Like a Logician, who lets go the premises, but keeps the conclusion.

For it is most firmly proved by *Optatus Milevitanus.* What is proved by him? *That* Constantine *the Great gave the Lateran to* Melchiades. How is it proved? Why *he testifieth, that a Council of* 19 *Bishops met in* Fausta's *house in the* Lateran. *Truly he doth not expresly write, that the house was given to* Melchiades. But it seemeth probable to *Binius* his imagination: And so it is *most firmly proved by* Optatus Milevitanus, *a most approved Writer.* Thus *those things that are told concerning the Dominion and Temporal Kingdom given to the See of* Rome, *are manifestly enough proved to be likely by what we said in our Notes upon the former Epistle.* But it is better proved, *by the continual possession of those houses, by the space of thirteen Ages, until now;* as he afterwards observeth. Though the length of an unjust Tenure increaseth the Transgression.

Having first proved the *Donation,* he proceedeth thus. *Hoc Edictum à Græcis perfidâ Donatione (quâ, justa illud.* Virg. 2. Æneid. *Timeo Danaos & Dona ferentes; donare solent acceptum) mutilum esse, ac dolosè depravatum, hæ rationes evidenter demonstrant. These following reasons evidently shew this Edict of* Constantine, by the perfidious *Donation* of the Greeks, to be maimed, and *treacherously depraved.*

He enters upon the business gently, pretending at first (as if the Donation were true) that it was *depraved* by the Greeks. But afterwards, when he is a little warm in the Argument, and somewhat further off from his Sophistical Defences, he falls foul upon it as a *Counterfeit*, and rejects it altogether; as in the close will appear to the considerate Reader. But here let us see what Arguments he produceth, to prove it *maimed, and treacherously depraved.*

'1. Because it pretendeth the Primacy[1] of the Church to be granted 'by a Layman, which was immediately given to *Peter*, by God 'himself, and by our Lord Jesus Christ; as is manifest by those words, *'Thou art* Peter, *and upon this Rock will I build my Church.*

'2. The Emperour, by this Edict, is made to give a Patriarchal 'Dignity to the Church of *Constantinople*: Which if it be true, how 'then could *Anatolius*, the Bishop of *Constantinople*, be said to take the 'Patriarchal Dignity to himself long after; even after the Council of '*Chalcedon* was ended, *Leo, Gelasius,* and other Roman Bishops 'resisting him?

'How could the Church of *Constantinople* be a Patriarchal See at 'this time, wherein even the name of *Constantinople* was not yet given 'to *Byzantium.*

'3. This Edict was first published by *Theodorus Balsamon*, out of 'the Acts of *Sylvester* the Pope, falsly written in Greek under the name of *Eusebius*, Bishop of *Cæsarea:*[2] not that he might do any service to the Church of *Rome*, but that he might shew the Patriarchate of *Constantinople* to be the eldest. Which Acts of *Sylvester* were not known till a[3] thousand years after Christ, coming then forth in *Eusebius* his name, out of a certain Book of Martyrs; but were now increased by the Addition of this Edict of *Constantine*.

His design is, if it be possible, to clear the Church of *Rome* of this too palpable and notorious Counterfeit: And for that end he would fain cast it on the *Treacherous Greeks*, that he might thereby acquit the more Treacherous *Romans:* Which he further pursues in the clause following.

The new found Hereticks that oppose this Edict of Constantine, *translated out of* Greek *into* Latine, *with such great endeavour, and impertinent study; let them know, that in this they rather further our Cause,*

---

[1] Marginal gloss: Bin. *Not. in* Constan- [line break] tin. *Edict.*
[2] Marginal gloss: Forgeries in the Name of *Eusebius.*
[3] Marginal gloss: The Acts of *Sylvester* forged.

than fight against us: *Who do our selves, with* Irenæus, Cyprian, *and other Holy Fathers, as well* Greek *as* Latine, *profess the Priviledges of the Church of Rome, not to be conferred and given of men, but from* Christ *to* Peter, *and from Peter to his Successors.*

Where the faults are so great, we need not make a Remark on the common Cheat, *his vain Brag of the Fathers.* But this we may observe, that whereas the Popes Claim is somewhat blind to the Prerogative, which is pretended to be given to S. *Peter, Binius* hints at a proper Expedient to make it clear. For suppose our Saviour made S. *Peter* the Rock on which he built his Church: How comes the Pope to be that Rock? Since S. *Peter* being an Apostle immediately inspired, and able to pen *Canonical Scripture,* some of his Prerogatives were *Personal,* and died with him? He tells you, that the Priviledge was granted *from Christ to* Peter, *and from* Peter *to his Successors.* So that it was not *Christ,* but *Peter* that gave it to the Bishops of *Rome.* Now it would extremely puzzle him to shew, where *Peter* gave that power to the Bishops of *Rome;* in what place, at what time, by what Act, before what Witnesses. All he can produce, is S. *Clement's* counterfeit Letter, and that miscarries.

But *in opposing the Edict of* Constantine, *the Protestants further their Cause, rather than fight against them.* Is not this a bold Assertion? Their Popes have laid Claim to the whole Empire of the Western World, even by this very *Edict,* or *Donation of Constantine*: And yet the Protestants did nothing, when they proved it to be a Forgery. This *Donation* is an old Evidence, proving the Divine Right of *Peter's Primacy,* and the *Popes Supremacy*: Did they promote their Cause, that proved it to be a Cheat? Certainly they that have Fingers so long as to grasp at an Empire, and Foreheads so hard as to claim it by *Frauds,* will stick at nothing they can conceive for their advantage. Is it impertinent to discover Knavery in the Holy Roman Catholick Church; or Imposture in the Infallible Chair? And together with the Credit of *Rome,* to take away an Empire? Besides the *Spiritual Right* of being the *Rock,* there are ample *Territories* and *Cities* claimed, with a Temporal Kingdom.

Let him therefore pretend what he will, the Authority of such Instruments is very convenient: And because he knows it well enough, he produces the *Diplomata,* or the *Patents of other Kings and Emperours,* to confirm the Churches Secular Right, *extant,* as he saith, *in the Original, with their Imperial Seals; as particularly those of the Most Christian Princes of* France, *restoring those things which the* Longobards *took away.* But he does not tell you, by what Arts they got possession of those Territories at first, nor by what Ancient Evidences, Seals, or Patents, they held them before the *Longobards* touched them.

And because a Kingdom is of much Moment in the Church of *Rome*, he further saith, *As for the Dominion of things temporal given to the Church, herself proves them by the Broad Seals of the very Emperours giving them, yet extant in the Originals, and she quietly enjoyeth them.* How quiet her injoyment is, you may see by that stir and opposition she meeteth, and by all the clamour throughout the Christian World, that followeth her Usurpations. Which she defendeth here by the *Seals of Emperours* in general Terms, but what Seals they are, she scorneth as it were, to mention in particular. Which argueth her cause to be as *Bad*, as her pretence is *Bold*.

But as for the Rights granted to the same Roman Church, S. Leo, Fælix, Romanus, Gelasius, Hormisda, Gregorius, *and other their Successors, that flourished famously from the times of* Constantine, *have defended them,* saith he, *not by the Authority of this Constantinian Edict, but rather by Divine and Evangelical Authority, against all the Impugners of them.* The man is warily to be understood; for some of these, whom he pronounceth as Defenders, violently oppose their claim, as *Gregory* in particular: who for himself and all his Predecessors, renounceth that *Blasphemous Title*,[1] which *John of Constantinople* first arrogated, but the Bishops of *Rome* acquired afterwards, by the Gift of *Phocas*, the bloody Emperour. So that all these are *Mummers*, brought in, as it were in a Masque, to shew their vizars and say nothing. For of all these Roman Bishops mentioned by *Binius*, *Gregory* was the last: who testifieth,[2] that *none of his Predecessors ever claimed such a Title.*

We may further note, that he speaks here with much Confusion, because he speaks *of the Rights granted to the Roman Church*; but does not distinguish between the *Divine* and *Humane* Rights of which he is treating. For the Business he is now upon, is the *Temporal Kingdom*; in defending of which these Popes down to *Gregory* did forbear to use the Authority of this *Constantinian Edict*, as he calleth it (by way of scorn) not because they had it not, but rather (as he pretends) because they had no need of it, having enough to shew by *Divine and Evangelical Authority* for the same. Which is another pretence as bold and impudent as the former. For, I think, none of his own Party will aver, that the Bishop of *Rome* can claim *a Temporal Kingdom* by the Holy Scripture.

---

[1] Marginal gloss: *Greg. lib.* 6. *Ep.* 30.
[2] Marginal gloss: *Greg. lib.* 4. *Epist.* 30.

As for any other Claim by this *Constantinian Edict*, or any *Donation* else of *Emperours*, before the *Longobards*, he slighteth all: especially the Authority of this *Constantinian Edict*, concerning which, he saith, 'None of all those, who sate over the Church before the year 1000. many of which saw the genuine Acts of *Sylvester* recited, concerning which we spake above, is read to have made any mention of this Edict. For as much as the *Counterfeit Edict* was not yet added to the Acts by the Greek Impostors.'

He does not tell us how he came to know, that many of the *Roman* Bishops saw *the genuine Acts of* Sylvester, before the year 1000. that being an Artifice or Color only, as if there were two divers Books of *Sylvesters Acts*, and the one a true one. He tells us not a word of the Contents that were in them: but he before told us plainly, that *the Acts of* Sylvester *the Pope, were falsly written in Greek under the name of* Eusebius *Bishop of* Cæsarea, *that they were not known till* 1000. *years after Christ, coming then forth in* Eusebius *his Name.* And now he telleth us as plainly, that *the Counterfeit Edict was not yet added to the Acts by the Greek Impostors.*

The poor *Greeks* on whom he layes all the Load of Imposture, never injoyed the benefit of these Acts, nor ever pleaded the Imposture as the *Latines* did. And in all likelyhood they made it, that laid Claim and Title to the Supremacy by it. Since therefore the Question is come to this, *Who were the Impostors?* we must define against him, that *the Counterfeit Edict was added to the forged Acts, not by* the *Greek,* but *Latine Impostors.*

For how Counterfeit so ever he will have it, *Pope* Adrian *in his Epistle to* Constantine *and* Irene, *which remains inserted in the* Nicene *Council, recites this whole History almost in the same manner, and so confirmes it by the Truth of this Edict.* As *Binius* himself telleth us on the words *Ipse enim.*] So that the *Edict* was pleaded long before the *Greeks* added it to the Acts of *Sylvester.* For Pope *Adrian* died in the year 795, and the Acts of *Sylvester* were unknown till the year 1000. Yet this *Adrian* founded his Epistle to the Emperour and Empress, in the second *Nicene Council, upon the truth of this Edict.* And in very truth, the Story he telleth is the same of *Constantine's Leprosie,* &c. contained in the *Donation.* Which if *Binius* had been pleased to remember, was published by the *Latines* in *Isidore Mercator's Collection of the Councils,* about the year 800. Where the *Greeks* in all probability first found it, and were cheated, (as many Wiser men have since been) with the appearance of it there. So that searching it up to the Fountain Head, it rests still among the *Romans*.

By the way, to shew you that *Binius* is his Crafts-Master, over against these words concerning *Adrian* before mentioned, he putteth down that Famous Marginal Note; *Donatio* Constantini *confirmatur, The Donation of* Constantine *is confirmed*; not by *Binius*, as the simple Reader would suppose, but by *Adrian*'s *Epistle*, recorded in the 2 *Nicene Council*, and expresly containing the whole Fable of *Constantine*'s Leprosie, Vision, and Baptism. So that the first that ever knew it in the World, for ought I can yet perceive, was this *Adrian*, of whom we have spoken somewhat before.

Now he comes to shew, how greedily the Popes received this Cheat of the Greeks. *Among*[1] *those who received the Acts of* Sylvester *in good sooth, corrupted thus with the addition of this counterfeit Edict, by an evil Art, and by the sorry faith of the Grecians carried out of the East into the West, and that earnestly defended them as Legitimate and Genuine, and pure from all fraud and Imposture, the first is found*, saith he, *to be Pope* * Leo *the Nineth:*[2] *Who in an Epistle to* Michael *of* Constantinople, *and* Leo *of* Acridanum, *Bishops, in the year of our Redemption*, 1054. *makes mention of the Donation of this* Constantinian *Edict, made to* Sylvester. *From whence, I believe, it was, that much Faith and Authority being hereby added unto it, very many of the* * Gravest *and most Learned Doctors*,[3] *without any suspition of Fraud or Imposture, with good Faith did read and receive it.*

He makes a large Confession here; wherein three things are fit to be noted. *The first that ever used this Edict was a Pope*: Pope *Leo* 9. 2. *He used it immediately after it came forth*: For *Sylvesters* Acts came forth about the year 1000. *being afterwards increased with the Addition of this Edict of* Constantine; *and some* 54 *years after, the Pope made use of the Donation in it*. Wherein *he is followed by many, very many of the Gravest and most Learned Popish Doctors*; which is the third thing to be noted. This fault of the Popish Doctors, who did *read and receive* this Donation of *Constantine, without any suspition of Fraud and Imposture*, being by *Binius* charged upon the Pope. The Shepherd went out of the way, and the Sheep followed him. The Captain, and the Herd, did all stray and miscarry: *Leo* 9. being somewhat like the Dragon in the *Revelation*, that threw down the third part of the Stars with his Tail.

---

[1] Marginal gloss: *Bin. Not. Edict. Constan.* or Bin. Not. Edict. *Constantin.*
[2] The asterisk refers to the marginal gloss: Pope *Leo* 9. citeth the Donation.
[3] The asterisk refers to the marginal gloss: The Gravest and most Learned Doctors among the Papists use it without any suspicion.

Binius his Cure is but the shift of a *Mountebank*, to save his Credit. There are Errours and Heresies in the *Donation of Constantine*, which whosoever receiveth the *Donation*, he receiveth them in like manner: And to say, that the Head and its Members in the Church of *Rome* were deceived *by the Evil Art and sorry Faith of the Grecians*, while they licked up this Vomit of *Balsamon*, for the Popes advantage; is but a sorry shift, a Corrosive that eats like a Canker. For it shews how the Holy Catholick Roman Church may be *deceived*; Head and Members, Pope and Doctors, Priests and People. They were imposed on by an *Evil Art* it seems, and swallowed down *Heresie* in *Constantine*'s *Donation*.

But that *Binius* lyes in his prevarication about the *Greeks*, and that the *Greeks* were not the Authors of the Donation, and that it did not intend to hurt the Popes Chair, is evident by this. The Donation was made not to overthrow, but confirm the *Divine Right* of the Popes Supremacy, point blank against what *Binius* pretends. He that made it had an eye both to the *Temporal* and *Spiritual* Priviledges of the *Roman* Chair. For the *Donation* applieth those Scriptures, on which the Popes build their Right, to S. *Peter*'s Successors, and makes the Emperour to note, that the Will of our Saviour was the Root of all his Kindness to the Chair: nay it expresly throws all on our Saviours Institution. *For it is just, that the Holy Law should retain*[1] *the Head of the Principality there, where our Saviour, the Instituter of H. Laws, commanded the blessed* Peter *to undertake the Chair of the Apostleship.* Where you may note another fetch of the Papists: Lest what our Saviour did to S. *Peter* should seem too remote to concern *Rome*; that they might make the Channel of Conveyance clear, these old Counterfeits record, that S. *Peter* did not come to *Rome* by chance, but being invested in so great an Hereditary Power, our Saviour chose the place where it should rest: and that *Peter* came to *Rome*, and there undertook the Chair of his Apostleship, *by our Saviours Commandment*. Which if they could make the World believe, their work would be half done. So that it utterly destroys the Interest of the *Greeks*, and the Donation is Root and Branch altogether *Roman*. Neither did the *Greeks* ever use it to disgrace the Roman Church, for ought I can find, though the Romans used it, to magnifie their Church above all other Churches.

---

[1] Marginal gloss: *Constantin. Donat.*

CAP. XXIII.

Melchiades *counterfeited*. Isidore Mercator *confessed to be a Forgery. The Council of* Laodicea *corrupted, both by a Fraud in the Text, and by the False Glosses of the Papists.*

The Forgery put out at first in the name of Melchiades, *concerning the Primitive Church, and the Munificence of the Emperour* Constantine, hath now gotten a clause added to the Title, viz. *Falsly ascribed to* Melchiades: In *Binius, Labbé*, and the *Collectio Regia*. Upon those words, *Falsly ascribed to Melchiades, Binius* speaketh thus. 'That this Epistle was ascribed to *Melchiades*, appeareth *Can. Futuram* '12. *q.* 1. *& Can. Decrevit. Dist.* 88. which bearing the name of *Melchiades*, contain for the most part the things which are written here. It appeareth from hence also, that hitherto it was commonly put in the former Edition of the Councils, just after the Decrees of *Melchiades* the Pope.' Thus was this counterfeit Epistle placed among their Laws and Councils. 'But that it was noted with the false[1] Title and name of *Melchiades*, appeareth from hence; (saith he) because it maketh mention of the *Nicene* Council: which by the consent of all men happened after the death of *Melchiades*, and after the Baptism of the Emperour: not under *Melchiades*, but under *Sylvester*, in the year of Christ 325. being the 20 year of *Constantine*, as almost all Historians unanimously do testifie. Perhaps therefore it is more true, that *Isidore* himself, being a Compiler, rather than a Collector, was the Author of this Epistle:[2] Which it is certain was made out of the third Canon of the Council of *Chalcedon*, and a certain fragment of the 24 Epistle in the 1. Book of Pope *Gregory*, and the History of the *Nicene* Council.' *Baron. An.* 312. *Nu.* 80.[3]

Here we come to know the manner how Decretal Epistles were made: Good passages stoln out of the *Fathers*, are clapt Artificially together, and a Grain or two of *Interest*, thrust neatly in, makes up an *Epistle*. This of *Binius* is plain dealing. *Isidore* is confessed to be a *Compiler*, that is, a Forger, rather than a *Collector*, or Recorder of the Councils.

*Note this well: because *Isidore* is the Fountain (a muddy dirty one) out of which they drink their waters.

---

[1] Marginal gloss: *Ibid*.
[2] Marginal gloss: *Isidore* a Forger.
[3] Intended marginal gloss: *Baron. An.* 312. *Nu.* 80.

This acknowledgment is the more considerable, because *Baronius*, *Labbè*, and *Cossartius*, and the *Collectio Regia*, herein do keep *Binius* Company.

Confessing it to be stoln out of S. *Gregory*, he acknowledgeth it to be made almost 300 years after it was pretended: Which draws near to the time of *Hadrian* the *First*, and sheds another Ray of Light on the Original of these Impostures.

In the time of *Sylvester* there happened many Councils. One Feather is finely thrust in, into that at *Arles*, to adorn the Papacy: The Pope is set before the Emperour. In that of *Ancyra*, the *Marriage of Deacons is permitted*. Can. 1. *Priests also were not compelled to leave their Wives, unless they were taken in Adultery.* Can. 8. *The Cup and the Bread were both given to the People.* Can. 13. In the Council of *Laodicea* it is determined, that *the Scriptures should be read on the Sabbath days.* Can. 16. And *that we ought not to leave the Church of God, and go and call upon Angels, and make Congregations which are known to be forbidden. If any one therefore be found observing this hidden Idolatry, let him be accursed; because he leaves our Lord Jesus Christ the Son of God, and gives himself over to Idolatry.* Can. 35.

The Invocation of Angels, though they were known to be Angels, is by the Council of *Laodicea* called *Idolatry*: Which vindicates Dr. *Stillingfleet*, in his acceptation of the word *Idolatry*, from the cavils of his Adversary. The Council esteemeth the very *calling upon Angels a forsaking of Christ, and an hidden Idolatry.*

Many attempts have been made to overthrow the *Canon*: I should be tedious, should I give you all their several ways to evade it. That which lies under my Cognizance, is their corrupting of the place.

Angelus and *Angulus*, being two words in the Latine, near of Kin, though in the sense they differ much, the one signifying an *Angel*, the other a *Corner*; some have been so bold, as to turn *Angelos* into *Angulos*, Angels into Corners: making the Canon to run thus; *We ought not to leave the Church of God, and to go and call upon Corners.* Though neither the sense of the place, nor the word in the Greek Tongue, nor the occasion of the Canon will bear it.

Binius indeed is not so bold as to put it into the *Text*, but as a *various Reading* he puts it over against the Text in the Margin; to stumble the Reader, or make him obdurate.

Theodoret, an Ancient Father, living near the times of this Council,[1] observes that by this Canon *those Hereticks were condemned, who taught*

---

[1] Marginal gloss: *Theod. in Colos.* 2.

that Angels were to be worshipped: As *Binius* himself upon the place confesseth.

Epiphanius, among other Hereticks,[1] mentions the *Angelici*; against whom, in all probability, this Canon was made.

Bellarmine defends *Theodoret*, and approves of his Exposition.[2] *For there is no doubt* (saith he) *but* Theodoret *was sound and Orthodox in his Opinion, concerning the Worship of Angels*. But then he has a fetch to clear the Church of Rome: *Not every pious Veneration of Angels is forbidden, but that only which is due to God*. Doubtless *Theodoret* was willing to give a *pious Veneration to Angels*; but neither he, nor the Council of *Laodicea*, knew of any *pious Invocation of them*.

But we leave these to come unto *Binius*. In his Notes upon *Pius his Epistle* before mentioned, he saith, 'The words of S. *Paul*, Colos. 2. are written, not as *Hierom* supposeth against the *Jews*, who believed the Stars of Heaven to be Angels; nor against the *Simonaici*, as *Bellarmine* supposed; but rather against the pernicious Doctrine of *Cerinthus*: who holding Christ to be a naked man, extolled all the Angels, as the Makers of the World, above him.' Yet a little after he saith the clean contrary: 'That *Cerinthus* did not only not teach, that Angels were as Makers of the World to be adored; but rather they were to be had in hatred, as the Authors of evil.' For the one he citeth *Irenæus*, *Epiphanius*, and *Tertullian*: *Baronius* for the other: And (which is very strange) himself sideth with all. Which you must conceive to be a *neat* effect of *clean conveyance*: For by how much the more impossible the Operation is, the *Juglers* slight is the more to be admired. In very truth, his behaviour is such, that it makes me too justly to fear, they say any thing in every place, that will serve their turn, make Cyphers of the Fathers, and care not a farthing how much they contradict themselves, so they be not discerned in doing it: Nay, his contradictions are so palpable, as if long custom had made him careless of being seen too, and deprived him of his feeling: For Lyars, speaking truth and falshood indifferently, for a long time, at last note not themselves, nor well apprehend which of the two they are speaking. And they that make a *Trade* of contradictions, inure themselves, by long habit, till they become insensible: Which (if need be) we shall more fully and clearly shew, out of *Binius* himself, upon this occasion.

---

[1] Marginal gloss: *Epiphan. Hæres.* 60.
[2] Marginal gloss: *Lib.* 1. *de SS. Beat.* cap. 20.

CAP. XXIV.

Learning of Alphonsus Pisanus. *The counterfeit Epistles of* Sylvester, *and that Council. A* Roman Council *wholly counter-feited. Letters counterfeited in the Name of Pope* Mark, *and* Athanasius, *and the Bishops of* Egypt, *to defend the Forgeries that were lately added to the* Nicene *Council.*

Binius hath the Code of the *Nicene* Council, fairly written in Greek, and at the end of it ΤΕΛΟΣ: or in Latine, FINIS.

After this, in another place, (by it self) under the name of *Alphonsus Pisanus*, with the Patronage of *Francis Turrian*, he bringeth in a whole Legend of Canons, to the number of fourscore, Fathered all upon the *Nicene* Council.

In the *Code* it self there are the Epistles of *Alexander Alexandrinus, Constantine the Emperour*, and the whole *Synod*, the *Emperours Oration*, the *Recantation of* Theognis *and* Eusebius *Bishop of* Nicomedia, the *Nicene Creed*, and the 20 *Canons of the Nicene Council*. All curiously written in fair Greek.

Out of the *Code*, after Τέλος, there is a counterfeit List of the Bishops *Subscriptions* (but miserably depraved) to put the better face on the rest of the Forgeries: and like many other of the *Frauds*, written only in Latine. Then there is an humble Letter, whereby the Council submitteth it self to the Popes Censure; but in the Column on the other side (for there are 2 Columns in the Leaf) it is defaced with an empty Blank, for want of a Greek Copy.

For fear this Letter should not be seen often enough, he hath it again, with the Answer of Pope *Sylvester* thereunto; both recorded in another place, near to the *Arabick* Canons; detected by these marks: They are without any Greek Copy, are not among the Acts of the Council, are full of mistakes and Barbarismes, and clearly refelled by the Genuine Acts of the Council it self.

The Epistles are these.

SYNODI NICÆNÆ
Epistola
AD *SYLVESTRUM* PAPAM.

'Beatissimo Papæ Urbis *Romæ*, cum omni Reverentiâ colendo, *Sylvestro*; Hosius Episcopus Provinciæ *Hispaniæ*, Civitatis *Cordubæ*;

Macarius Episcopus Ecclesiæ Hierosolymitanæ, *Victor* & *Vincentius* ex Urbe *Romæ,* Ordinati ex directione tuâ.

'QUONIAM omnia corroborata de Divinis Mysteriis Ecclesiasticæ utilitatis, quæ ad robur pertinent Sanctæ Ecclesiæ Catholicæ & Apostolicæ, ad sedem tuam Romanam explanata, & de Græco redacta sunt, scribere consitemur, nunc itaque ad vestræ Sedis argumentum accurrimus roborari. Itaque censeat vestra Apostolica Doctrina, Episcopos totius vestræ Apostolicæ Urbis in unum convenire, vestrumque habere Concilium, sicut docet mystica Veritas, ut firmetur nostra Sanctimonia, gradusque sixos, vel textus Ordinationis tuæ Sanctimoniæ nostra possit habere Regula. Quoniàm decet numerum dictorum tuorum Coepiscoporum à te discere gradus vel ordinis constituere Urbis. Quicquid autem constituimus in Concilio Nicæno, precamur vestri oris consortio confirmetur. Oret Beatitudo tua pro universo Concilio. Data 8. Kalend. *Julias.* Accepta 13. Kalendas *Novembris, Paulino* & *Juliano* summis Conf. libus.'

There are a great many faults in it, which *Binius* mendeth; but he did not consider how accurate they were in Dating *the time wherein the Letter was received*: nor how much the Council condescended to the *Bishop of Rome,* while they wrote in Greek to the *common people* of *Alexandria*; but translated their Acts into *Latine,* for the *Popes* understanding. *Ad sedem tuam Romanam explanata, & de Græco redacta.* As if the Pope and his Clergy were unacquainted with the Greek Tongue.

RESCRIPTUM SYLVESTRI
ad Synodum Nicænam.

SYLVESTER Episcopus Sedis Apostolicæ & Sanctæ Catholicæ Ecclesiæ Reverendæ Religionis Urbis Romæ, *fratribus & Coepiscopis, qui in* Nicænum *Concilium convenerunt in Domino Salutem.*

GAUDEO *promptam vos Benignitatem servare. Nam & confirmo figoque ad vestræ Doctrinæ reclamantes de Mysterio vel unitate Trinitatis Chrysmatis vos secundùm Dicta & Doctrinam Evangelicam Sanctam accepisse Gratiam. De quo Examinationis probo vera fuisse & esse mansura, quæ in vestrum nostrumque manævere Mysterium. Meum Chirographum & Discipulorum meorum offero in vestro Sancto Concilio, quicquid constituistis unà parem dare consensum. Atque in gremio vestræ Synodi parva propter Disciplinam Ecclesiæ alligabo præcepta, propter* Victorinum *qui arbitrio suo quicquid vellet affirmabat, & Cyclos Paschæ pronunciabat fallaces, & cum Episcopis totius Urbis* Italiæ *examinatam universitatis vestri Sancti Concilii dignetur accipere veritatem. Et aliâ* manu, *Oret pro nobis Beatitudo vestri Sancti Concilii Trecentorum Decem & Octo: ut Charitatis quæ vobis data est Domini nostri Jesu Christi servetur Augmentum. Data* 5. *Kalendas* Novembr. *Accepta* 4. *Idûs* Februarii, Constantino *Septiès &* Constantio Cæsare *Quarto Consulibus.*

Though the Nonsense be the most horrible that ever was seen, the exactness is great: For in token of the Spirit of Prophecy, the Bishop of *Rome* telleth them at *Nice*, that they were *three hundred and eighteen*, and dateth the day on which his Letter was received: which I think was extraordinary.

But there is a contradiction in these Dull Letters, that mars all. They at *Nice* inform the Pope, that *all the Bishops of the Apostolical City were assembled in one, and held his Council* for him there: The Pope on the other side tells them of a Council at *Rome* of the Bishops *of all the City of* Italy *(assembled) whence* he sent *the Truth examined by his Disciples there* (as he calls them) for them at *Nice*, to receive: which he prayes them to accept, &c. I confess the nonsense so terrible, that it is difficult to construe it to any sense at all: but divers circumstances interpret the words so, that *Præcepta* signifie *Canons*, and *Episcopi totius urbis* Italiæ, the Roman Synod under *Sylvester*: As those other words, *Meum Chirographum & Discipulorum meorum offero*; his own Subscription, and the Subscription of the Bishops under him, whereby he confirmed the *Nicene* Council.

For the Legend goes, that while the Council was sitting at *Nice* of 318 Bishops, *Sylvester* called a Council at *Rome* of 267 Bishops; where they made Canons as they did at *Nice*, and as good luck was, confirmed the Council there: Else all at *Nice* had not been worth a Rush. And to this *Roman* Council *Sylvester* relateth, when he saith, *I send you mine, and my Disciples hands to give our joynt consent to all that you have orained.* This is that Council which made the *Epilogus Brevis*, the commending of which to the *Nicene* Council, (were there nothing in the Letter beside) would disgrace it for Cosin-German to that putid Forgery, so often touched in the *Epilogus Brevis*.

This Council is set by *Binius* (I known not why) before the *Nicene* Council; though it professeth it self to be held *at the same time.* Perhaps the reason is, that they could not be set down both together, and Priority was to be given to the Synod at *Rome*.

The Title of this Council is,
CONCILIUM ROMANUM
Aliud, sub Sylvestro *Papa Primo.*

It immediately follows *Constantines Donation*, and dependeth on the truth of the same.

The Popes *See* is magnified therein above the Skies; and for that reason it shineth among the Councils, as a Direful Comet among the Stars of Heaven.

The Proem set before it bears the name of the *Epilogue*, Epilogus brevis, &c. *A short Epilogue of the following Roman Council.* A Trip in the Threshold bewraying the Author. A Learned Council it was, no doubt, that began with the conclusion: For the *Epilogue* is the close of any discourse, the *Prologue* is the beginning.

But this First is a small Indecency, we proceed to the matter. The *Nicene Council* has the good fortune of being full of smoothness, clarity and Majesty: But *Binius* finds this so rude and rough, that he is fain to clear the way by a *Premonition to the Reader*.

The following Canons were written verbatim,[1] saith he, *out of two Ancient Copies, which in many places, by reason of the depravation of the Exemplars, can scarcely, or indeed not at all, be understood. Let the Reader censure favourably, and communicate, if he hath, something more certain.*

You must touch it gingerly you see, or it will fall to pieces. *Solecismes* and *Nonsense* are like Rust and Cobwebs, signs of *Antiquity* in the *Roman Church*: Else certainly they would never have dared to present such *Mouldy* Instruments to the Face of the World. * But such Councils[2] are fit to support the *Mystery of Iniquity*, which is made a *Mystery*, by making and supporting such Councils.

Since the *Canons* are so rude, we will let them go, and come to the *Epilogus*, which beareth the force of the most Authentick Canon.

Therein it is recorded, that *in the time of* Sylvester *and* Constantine *the most holy Emperour, while* 318 *Bishops sat in Council at* Nice, *by the Command of* Sylvester; *on the thirteenth of the Kalends of* July, *there was a Council of* 267 *Bishops convened at* Rome, *by the Canonical Call of the Pope: That again condemned* Callistus, Arrius, Photius, *and* Sabellius, *before condemned in the* Nicene *Council, and ordained, that no* Arrian *Bishop returning, should be received by any but the Bishop of the place. In which also, by the consent and Subscription of all, it was ordained, That no Lay-man should accuse a Clergy-man, and that no Priest should accuse a Bishop, no Deacon a Priest, no Sub-Deacon a Deacon, no Acolythite a Sub-Deacon, no Exorcist an Acolythite, no Reader an Exorcist, no Door-keeper a Reader. It was further ordained, that no Bishop should be*

---

[1] Marginal gloss: Bin. *in Concil.* Rom. *sub* Sylvester.
[2] There is a manicule (☞) printed in the outer margin.

condemned but by the Testimony of at least threescore and twelve Witnesses, nor shall the Highest Priest be judged by any, &c.

This Decree is put among the Popes Laws by *Ivo Cartonensis,* &c. Doubtless to the very great case and satisfaction of the *Roman Clergy:* For it reaches down, you know, to the lowest Orders of *Readers* and *Door-keepers.* So that they may write as many Forgeries as they will: If it be a Pope, no man can condemn him: If it be a Bishop, no less than three score and twelve Bishops, must on their Corporal Oath prove the Fact against him: forty four *Equals,* against a Cardinal-Priest, twenty six must depose against a Cardinal-Deacon of the City of *Rome,* and seven against a Door-keeper; all which must be at least his Equals. A Marvellous Priviledge for *the City of Rome*! Which word *Rome,* though annexed only to *Cardinal-Deacons,* yet, for ought I know, the Judge will interpret its Extent, to all the other Orders; or use it *Equivocally,* as himself listeth, or as his Superiour pleaseth. So that in Causes pertaining to the Interest of the *Roman Church,* other Priests perhaps, beside them in the City of *Rome,* shall enjoy the benefit of this Law; but in Causes displeasing the Pope, and his Accomplices, none shall enjoy it, but the Priests of *Rome.* Many such *Trap-doors* are prepared in Laws, where Rulers are perverse and Tyrannical; and whether this be not one of those, I leave to the Readers further Examination.

Mark succeeded *Sylvester* in the See of *Rome*: Between whom, and *Athanasius,* there were certain Letters framed, that stand upon Record to this day, to prove the Canons of the *Nicene* Council to be *Threescore and ten.* Heretofore they were good *old* Records magnificently cited: but now they are worn out: for *Baronius* and *Bellarmine* have lately rejected them; who are followed by *Binius,* as he is by *Labbe* and *Cossartius* and the *Collectio Regia,* all concluding the Letters to be Forged. The three last have this Note upon that of *Athanasius. Hanc surreptitiam & ab aliquo confict am fuisse quinque rationibus ostenditur, &c.*

'That this Epistle is a Counterfeit devised by some body,[1] appeareth evidently by five reasons. Whereof the first is this, In the Controversie between the African Churches, and the Roman Bishops, (*Zozimus* and *Boniface)* concerning the number of the *Nicene* Canons, this Epistle was unknown. 2. *Athanasius,* as is manifest by what went before was at this time fled into *France,* and so it could not be written from *Alexandria* and from the Bishops in *Egypt.* 3. That Divastation fell upon the Church of *Alexandria* many years after these times in the Reign of *Constantius,* &c. As *Athanasius* himself witnesseth in his

---

[1] Marginal gloss: *Bin. in Ep. Athan. ad Marc.*

Epistle *ad omnes Orthodoxos*. 4. *Mark* died in the Nones of *October* this present year: *Constantine* himself being yet alive. 5. If Pope *Mark* had sent a Copy of the *Nicene* Council out of the Roman Archives, to them at *Alexandria*, surely the Roman Copy and that of *Alexandria* would have agreed thenceforth as the same: How then were those three Canons wanting in the Copy, which S. *Cyril* sent from *Alexandria* to the Africans, which were found in the Roman Copy?'

He pointeth to the *Commonitorium* sent from *Rome* to the Sixth Council of *Carthage*; and verifies all the Story we have related; by rejecting these Letters of *Mark* and *Athanasius*, made on purpose to defend the Forgeries there detected. For which he cites *Baron. An.* 336. *nu.* 59, 60. and *Bellarm. de Rom. Pont. lib.* 2. *cap.* 25.

This Epistle was alledged by *Harding* against *Jewel*, and by *Hart* against *Rainolds* for a good Record. How formally it was laid down by the Elder Collectors you may see with your eyes: and may find it frequently cited by the most learned Papists. Such as these being their best and only Evidences.

After *Mark Julius* succeeded. *The Epistle sent by the Bishops of the East to Pope* Julius I. *is now confessed to be a Forgery.*[1] *Veram & germanam non extare præter authoritatem* Baronii *illud asserentis, ea quæ supra in principio Epistolarum* Julii *annotavi confirmant*: Saith *Binius*. Again he saith, 'This Epistle which is put in the second place, bearing the names of the Bishops of the East, seems to be compiled by some uncertain Author, both by the concurrent Testimony of *Sozomen*, and *Socrates*, and because thou mayest observe many things to be wanting, and some in the words and things expressed to be changed',

Rescriptum Julii] The Epistle which *Julius* returned in answer hath the like Note upon it. *Hanc mendosam, corruptam, & a quodam ex diversis compilatam*, &c. That this Epistle is counterfeit, corrupt, and compiled by some body out of divers Authors, the Counsulships of *Felicianus* and *Maximianus* evidently shew, &c.'

The matter in these Epistles is *the Popes Supremacy; the unlawfulness of calling Councils, but by his Authority; his Right of receiving Appeals*; with other Themes, which Ambition and self Interest suggest, and of which genuine Antiquity is totally silent.

Having so fortunately glanced upon the Sixth Council, I shall not trouble the Reader with any more: but bewailing what I observe, beseech him earnestly to weigh this *Business walking in the Dark*, and take heed of a *Pope* and a *Church*, that hath exceeded all the World

---

[1] Marginal gloss: *Bin. in Epist. Julii.*

in Forgerie. For let the Earth be searched from East to West, from Pole to Pole, Jews, Turks, Barbarians, Hereticks, none of them have soared so high, or so often made the Father of Lies their Patron, in things of so great Nature and Importance. Since therefore the Mother of Lyes hath espoused the Father of Lies for her assistance, and the accursed production of this adulterate brood is so numerous; I leave it to the Judgement of every Christian, what *Antiquity* or *Tradition* she can have, that is guilty of such a Crime, and defiled with so great an Off-spring of notorious *Impostures*.

AN
APPENDIX.

Cardinal Baronius his Grave Censure and Reproof of the Forgeries: His fear that they will prove destructive and pernicious to the See of Rome.

A *piarius*, a Priest of the Church of *Africa*, being Excommunicated by his *Ordinary*, for several notorious crimes, flies to *Rome* for Sanctuary; *Zozimus* the Bishop receives him kindly, gives him the Communion, and sends Orders to see him restored. Hereupon the *African* Churches convene a Council, namely, the *sixth Council of Carthage*, whence they send a modest Letter, but as Sincere as Powerful, shewing how after all shifts and Evasions, *Apiarius* had confessed his Enormities; and that both the *Nicene Council*, and clear *Reason*, was against the disorder of such *Appeals*: All Causes being to be determined in the Province where they arose, by a Bishop, Patriarch, or Council, upon the place. *Otherwise, say they, how can this Beyond-Sea Judgment be firm,*[1] *where the necessary appearance of Witnesses cannot be made, either by reason of weakness of Nature, or Old Age, or many other Impediments?* They decry the Innovation of the Bishop of *Rome* in arrogating that Authority, *lest the smoakie Puff of the pride of this World should be brought into the Church of Christ.*[2] This Epistle is on all sides owned and confessed to be a good Record. It was sent to *Celestine* the Successor of *Zozimus* and *Boniface*.

About 100 years after, *Eulabius* sate in the Chair at *Alexandria*, (some call him *Eulalius*:) Between him and *Boniface* 2. there are two Epistles extant, out of which it is gathered, that after the sixth Council of *Carthage*, the African Churches were Excommunicated by the Roman for 100 years, and reconciled at last upon the Submission of *Eulalius*, Archbishop of *Carthage*, accursing S. *Augustine*, and his own Predecessors.

Concerning these two Epistles, Cardinal *Bellarmine* giveth his Opinion thus: *Valdè mihi eas Epistolas esse suspectas, &c.* 'I have a mighty suspition of these Epistles:[3] For first they seem to be

---

[1] Marginal gloss: *Epist. Council. Carth. 6. ad Cælestin.*
[2] Marginal gloss: *Ibid.*
[3] Marginal gloss: Bel. *de Sum. Pont. lib.* 2. *cap.* 25.

repugnant to those things which we have spoken concerning the Union of S. *Augustine, Eugenius, Flugentius,* and other Africans with the Roman Church: And again, either there was no *Eulabius* of *Alexandria*, to whom *Boniface* seemeth to write; or at least there was none at that time: as is evident out of the Chronology of *Nicephorus* of *Constantinople*. Besides, *Boniface* intimates in his Epistle, that he wrote at the Commandment of *Justinus* the Emperour. But *Justinus* was dead before *Boniface* began to sit; as is manifest out of all Histories. Moreover, the Epistle which is ascribed to *Boniface*, consists all of it almost of two fragments, of which the one is taken out of the Epistle of Pope *Hormisda* to *John*, the other out of the Epistle of S. *Gregory* to the Bishops of *France*: even the 52 Epistles of his fourth Book. Now S. *Gregory* was not born at that time: nor is it credible that *Gregory* took those words out of *Boniface*, since the Stile is altogether *Gregorian*.

'In the Epistle also which is Fathered upon *Eulabius* the *Carthaginian*, there is a Sentence of S. *Gregories* inserted, out of the 36 Epistle of his fourth Book: and the rest of that Epistle is nothing but a fragment of an Epistle of *John*, the Bishop of *Constantinople*, to Pope *Hormisda*.'

Notwithstanding all these reasons, *Bellarmine* is afraid to *damn* the Epistles: but Cardinal *Baronius* is a little more bold. He judges it inconvenient for the Church of *Rome*, that any such Forgeries were ever made: And upon the occasion of these *two Epistles*, utterly disgraces *Isidore Mercator* for a meer *Impostor*.

Whether in so doing he salves the Sores of the *Roman* Church, that hath been guilty of *vending* them, the experience of Ages yet to come, will hereafter evidence. In the mean time let us see what he saith.

In Not. Martyrol. ad 16. *Octobr.* he layeth down these words: *Scias falsam & adulterinam Epistolam illam, quæ fertur nomine* Bonifacii 2. *&c. Know, that the Epistle which is carried abroad in the name of* Boniface 2. *to* Eulalius *Bishop of* Alexandria, *which is extant, and published in the second Tome of the Councils of the latter Edition, is false and adulterate.*

And speaking concerning the Schism, Excommunication, and Re-union of the African Churches, he saith, *Si hæc verá sunt, &c. If these things are true, certainly then all the Martyrs and Confessors, which were at that very time crowned with Martyrdom in the* African *Church, or otherwise waxed famous by the Merits of their Eminent Sanctity, must be blotted out of the List of Saints, which* THE HOLY ROMAN CHURCH *it self hath, in its Martyrology, numbred among the Martyrs, or reckoned among the Confessors. Since it is most manifest by a thousand Sentences of*

Cyprian, Augustine, *and all the Fathers, that out of the Church there can be no Martyrdom, nor any kind of Sanctity.*

If Lyes were always consistent, *Truth* would be amazed. God doth infatuate the Counsels of his Enemies, and turn their Wisdom into Foolishness. They run into inconveniences, sometimes so great, that they cannot be remedied. Could a Lye shun all inconvenience, and see to its Interest on every side, it would be as wise and perfect as Truth it self.

Quin ampliùs ex Collegis Aurelii, *&c.*[1] 'But yet further, among other Companions of *Aurelius*, the most holy Father S. *Augustine*, the most glorious Beam of the Catholick Church, was accused in that Epistle. Who being clouded with the same Myst of Schism, must (if those Epistles be true) be blotted out of the Class of the Doctors of Holy Church, out of the number of Saints, nay out of the Martyrology; nor only so, but out of the Kalender of the HOLY ROMAN CHURCH. For it is most certain, that after the aforesaid *Aurelius*, he departed this life, within the space of the time before-mentioned. What should I reckon the *Fulgentiuses*, the *Eugeniuses*, and others, almost innumerable men, most Famous for Holiness and Learning, to be accounted in the same condition?'

It is a common Artifice in the *Church of Rome*, to propagate these Forgeries as far as they are able, by them to possess the minds of men with great apprehensions of the Popes high and Infallible Power; and if at any time they are detected, to cast the blame on *private* persons: while the Church is free (they pretend) from such Abominations. I desire you to note therefore, that the HOLY ROMAN CHURCH it self is the Author of Her *Martyrologies* and *Kalendars*, and that the HOLY ROMAN CHURCH *her self* hath Canonized her *Saints*, and made *Holy-days*, and put them into her *Breviaries*: And it was this very HOLY ROMAN CHURCH, that put the *counterfeit Council of Sinuessa* into her *Martyrologies*, the Lying Legend of *Sylvester* into the *Roman Breviary*, Authorized by three Popes, and the Council of *Trent*; and her counterfeit *Decretals* among her Laws, in all her *Consistories*, and Ecclesiastical Courts of *Highest Judicature*. So that if *Baronius* do not err, the ROMAN CHURCH is liable to the Charge of these Bastard-Antiquities: For which cause he might well break out into that angry Extasie, *Ecce in quod Discrimen Unus* Isidorus Mercator,[2] *illarum Epistolarum Collector, res nostras adduxit! ut ex eâ parte*

---

[1] Marginal gloss: *Ibid.*
[2] Marginal gloss: *Ibid.*

periclitari videatur Ecclesia, &c. 'Behold into what peril, one *Isidore Mercator*, the Collector of those Epistles, hath brought our Affairs! So that the CHURCH seemeth on that side to be endangered, if we shall say, those things which he hath collected, or rather feigned, be firm and certain.' If the Roman Church be found guilty of Forgery, in *Baronius* his judgment, she is utterly ruined.

It is of no small Importance, did he only confess the things to be feigned (rather than collected) which their great Matters of the Councils find in *Isidore*, their first Author. But his acknowledgment of the hazard which the *Roman Church* runneth, is more. For they have so many Subterfuges about the *Roman Church*, that it is more difficult to find it, than to vanquish it. It was not the Pope in a *formal Council*, that Excommunicated the Church of *Africa*, or that put her Saints first into the Roman Martyrologies, yet it was the *Holy Roman Church*. And indeed, if the *Holy Roman Church*, and her Authority, be not to be found in her *Mass-books* and *Breviaries*, her *Courts* and *Consistories*, her *Laws* and *Decrees*, her *Martyrologies* and *Kalenders*, her *Popes* and *Doctors*, I know not where to meet with Her: And if nothing else be the *Roman Church* but a Pope and Council United, the *Roman Church* is but a blinking business. There is no *Roman Church* (upon this account) sometimes for two or three Ages together: for she always vanishes upon the dissolution of the Council.

The *Roman Church* is in a great strait; but she may thank her self. She threw her self into this *Peril*, by making her self a Schismatick, an Usurper, a Forger. She first breaks the *Rule*; and if the Pope and his Doctors about him be the *Roman Church*, as they certainly must needs be; (for all that depart from them, shall be Schismaticks:) if the Head of the Church, and all the Members that cleave unto it, be the *Roman Church*, she first brake the *Rule*, and then forged *Ancient Canons* in the Name of the *Nicene Council*, to defend her Exorbitancy: she cut her self off from the true Church in the sixth Council of *Carthage*, by a perverse inveterate obstinacy; and to acquit her self afterwards, laid the Curse and Scandal upon others. She pretends, at least, that the most Holy Churches were Excommunicated; that 217 Bishops in a Sacred Council, *Alypius. S. Augustine, Aurelius,* and all his Collegues, were *puffed up with pride by the Instigation of the Devil*, and accursed by a *Dreadful Excommunication*: for so it is in the *Epistle of Boniface* 2. to *Eulalius*. And now she hath nothing left to support her Enormity, but that *Greatness* alone, which by these Forgeries she hath acquired and maintained. These *Thorns* are never to be pulled out, but the *Veins* and

Sinews will follow after: For in rejecting these (Thorns in her sides) all her *Authority, Infallibility, Antiquity, Tradition, Unity, Succession, Credit* and *Veracity* is gone.

As for *Baronius*, and the way he takes, a man may safely throw away the Sword, when he has killed the Enemy: but the Church of *Rome* is not arrived to such an happiness. Politicians pull down the *Ladder* by which they have gotten up to the *Top* of their desires. But the case is altered here: They are undone, if the *Ladder* be removed. To acknowledge these *Helps* to be Forgeries, is their apparent *Ruine*.

Some Papists use these Counterfeits, by vertue of which their Predecessors acquired, and established their Empire, as *Usurpers* do *Traytors*, by whose villanous help they are seated in the Throne. But they can never wash off the Guilt they have contracted; nor make the Act, or the Crime (committed once) to be again *undone*. After 700 years enjoyment of the Benefit, they begin to slight the means of acquiring it: But it is, because they cannot help it. The Cheat is detected, and they would fain perswade the World they are Innocent of it. All of them either hold these things to be no *Forgeries*, or (if *Forgeries*) to be *none of theirs*. The Confession is not Genuine, like that of S. *Peter*; rather it is awkward and untoward, like that of *Apiarius*; whose Confession the sixth Council of *Carthage* observes to be *forced*. For after he had obstinately persisted, as long as possible, in an impudent denial, reviled his Judges, abused the *Roman* Chair, disordered the Church, and inflamed the World, when God had brought him into so vast a strait, that he could do no otherwise: then the *Fraudulent Dissembler*, as they call him, fled to Confession; but the Root of his Malevolence he retained in him.

Some Papists confess these Forgeries, but deny them to be theirs: They confess the things, but justifie themselves. The things they say are *Forgeries*, but themselves no *Forgers*: And whether of the two be the greater Impudence, is hard to define: They confess the *Fraud*, but make no *Restitution*. All their Drift is to save their *Skin*: when one pretence is broken, they fly to another: nay, they go on to quote these things, even now they confess them: where they are not detected they still do quote them; and wish still, they were as able to conceal and defend them, as ever: For for one that knows them, they meet with a thousand that are ignorant of those devices. There they dissemble their Conviction, and hide their Confession with the Ignorant, and before such make shew of these Frauds, as of great and glorious Antiquities; though, like *Proteus*, they transform themselves into other shapes before the more Learned. They find it meet and necessary to sail with every Wind, and to adapt themselves fitly in their discourses both to them that know them, and to them that know them not; with them that know them they seem to decry the Impostures.

These things I speak, not to the poor simple *seduced* Papists, who did they believe and know these things, would abhor them to the Death; but to the *Seducers* themselves, who so delude the Ignorant, and are by all *Methods* ever busie in carrying on the Cause of the *Temporal Kingdom of the Church of* Rome: as by their obstinate practises is most apparent.

Baronius himself bewrayeth his Confession to be without any purpose of amendment; even by the Defence he maketh, for his good Old Friend, the Bastard *Isidore*.

A *Jerom of Prague*, or a *John Huss*, a *Latimer*, or a *Ridley*, though never so holy and pure in other things, were to be cursed with *Bell, Book and Candle*, if the least Errour appeared in them, that reflected on the Popes *Security*: Though never so Innocent, they were with all violent fury pursued to the Fire. But if a man have this one Vertue, of maintaining the Popes *Interest*, he may lye, and cog, and cheat, and forge; abuse Apostles, Councils, Fathers, and be followed by an Army of Popes and Doctors: becoming a *Zealous* and Venerable Saint notwithstanding. *Hincmarus* of *Rhemes* could hardly escape, for offering to mutter against *Isidore*. But *Isidore* himself, because he did the Pope Service, though he be a *Sacrilegious* person, and deserves all that can be called *Bad*, for the incomparable height and depth of his *Villany*; yet he is received to fair Quarters, and well esteeemed of by Cardinal *Baronius: Testimonium illi perhibeo (utar verbis Apostoli)* (saith he) *quòd Zelum habuit, sed non secundùm Scientiam,* &c.

I will give him this Testimony, (and here I will use the words of the Apostle) He had a Zeal, but not according to knowledge. For because the contention of Aurelius, *Bishop of* Carthage, Augustine, *and other African Bishops, seemed to him a little more hot than it should be, with* Boniface *and* Celestine *the Roman Popes, in the Cause of* Apiarius *the Priest: he supposed it expedient, in that Epistle which he feigned in the name of* Boniface, *to patch up what was cut away. But away with these things! The Church of God is not founded, nor does it lean upon Chaff, it self being the Pillar and Ground of Truth.* Baron. Martyrol. Octob. 16.[1]

I will not note, how he abuseth the *Scriptures*, nor how he wresteth the Words of the H. Apostle, to cover a filthy piece of Knavery: nor yet in what sense he maketh the last words, which he uttereth, to sound;

---

[1] Baron. Martyrol. Octob. 16., perhaps intended as a marginal gloss.

concerning the *Roman* Churches being *her self the Pillar and Ground of Truth*. Though matters are so carried, as if she were great enough to be her own *Support*, and without being founded on any other, were her own *Foundation*. All I shall observe, is, that *Hadrian* 1. and *Leo* 9. have been very zealous and tender of these Records: that *Benedictus Levita* got them confirmed by the *Roman Chair*: that several Popes, since *Leo* 9. have imbraced, countenanced, and furthered them, as Pope *Paul* V. and *Sixtus* V. in particular: that *Isidore Mercator*, whom *Baronius* confesseth to be a Cheat, is the common Father of the *Popish Compilers*: That the *Codes*, or *Tomes* of the *Councils*, at this day received in the *Roman Church*, for good and Sacred *Records*, are by these *Collectors, James Merlin, Peter Crab, Laurentius Surius, Carranza, Nicolinus, Severinus Binius, Labbe,* the *Collectio Regia*, old *Ivo, Gratian*, &c. have digested these Impostures, and recorded them as the *Sacred Authenticks* of the *H. Catholick Church*: that whole Armies of *Cardinals, Archbishops, Bishops, Doctors, Schoolmen, Jesuites, Monks, Fryars, Canonists*, &c. have cited them for many Ages as true Records: that *Turrian* in particular (with divers others) have set themselves strenuously to defend them: that they have imposed the Cheat upon *Kings* and *Emperours*: that the Forgeries are backed with the Authorities of *Popes, Emperours, Kings,* &c. All, no doubt, *having a zeal, but not according to knowledge*; that is, being exceeding regardful of the Interest of the Chair, and studiously maintaining the *Temporal Kingdom of the Church*, as they call it; but erring in the *manner*. While they thought this the way to advance her, which is now become her apparent shame, and a probable means (without sudden amendment) to bring her to Confusion.

That Princes may a little more clearly see into the Mystery of these counterfeit *Decretals*, it is meet, in the close of all, to expose to the view of the World one *Passage*, out of many other, which we have passed over in silence. The Design of it touches Kings and Emperours to the *Quick*, though (for greater security to the Chair) it be covertly expressed. It is in the Oration of S. *Peter* to the people of *Rome*, in S. *Clements* Letter to S. *James*; and it is commended to the consideration of the World by all the *Popish Compilers* of the Decrees and Councils, from *Isidore* downwards.

It is revived in the first Epistle of *Anacletus*, as *Binius* * oberves:[1] And *expresly* repeated (because they will make much of it) in the[2]

---

[1] The asterisk refers to the marginal gloss: *Bin. Marg in Clement. Epist.* 1.
[2] The asterisk refers to the marginal gloss: *Fab. Epist.* 1.

counterfeit Letter of * *Fabianus*, a Roman Bishop and Martyr, that lived about 1400 * years ago,¹ to this purpose.

*When he had said these things,*² *and many more like unto these, looking upon the people, again, he said, And you my dearest Brethren, and Fellow-Servants, obey this * Man*³ *that presideth over you to teach you the Truth,* IN ALL THINGS: *Knowing, that if any one grieveth him, he receiveth not* Christ, *who intrusted to him the* Chair of Teaching: *and he that receiveth not* Christ, *shall be judged not to have received* God *the* Father: *and therefore neither shall himself be received into the Kingdom of Heaven,* &c. *But ever coming together to* Clement, Date omnes operam pro ipso sentire, (it is an Emphatical expression) *make it your business to be of his Opinion; and with your utmost study to shew your favour towards him: Knowing, that for every one of your sakes, the Enemy is more inraged against him alone, and stirs up greater Wars against him. Ye ought therefore to endeavour with your utmost study, that being all knit together in the Bond of love towards him, ye may cleave unto him with a most perfect affection. But you also be sure to continue unanimous in all Concord, that you may so much the more easily obey him with one Consent and Unanimity. For which, both you may attain Salvation, and be, while ye obey him, may more readily bear the weight of the Burden laid upon him.* They must with their *utmost study* favour him, and bend all their Charity to each other, [for this very end] that they may cleave the faster unto him; for doing which, they shall attain *Salvation*. This environs the Popes Chair with Armies of *Well-wishers* and *Servants*. But the *Dangerous Passage* follows, which shakes all the Thrones and Kingdomes in the World! Lest they should be an Army of silly *Sheep*, and simple *Doves*, wanting the *Serpents* Fraud and *Sting*. He admonisheth them further, that they all must be Enemies to their Popes Enemies, and hate all that he hateth. I leave Kings and Princes to judge of the words.

Quædam etiam ex vobis ipsis intelligere debetis, &c. *Some things also ye ought to understand of your selves; If there be any thing which he dares not evidently and manifestly speak out, for fear of the Treacheries of evil men. As for Instance: If he be an Enemy to any one for his Deeds, do not ye expect that he should tell you, Be ye not Friends with such an one: but ye ought prudently to observe, and to do his Will without any Admonition, and to turn form him, against whom ye perceive he is an Enemy; nor so much as to speak to him, with whom he speaketh not,* &c. *That every one in*

---

¹ The asterisk refers to the marginal gloss: *An. Christ* 238.
² Marginal gloss: *S. Peters* Forged Oration.
³ The asterisk refers to the marginal gloss: The Roman Bishop.

fault, while he covets to regain all your Friendships, may the sooner make haste to be reconciled to him who is over all; and by this return to Salvation, while he begins to obey the Admonitions of his Superiour. But if any one shall be a Friend to those to whom he is not a Friend, or speak to those to whom he speaketh not, he is one of them, &c.

This dangerous Intimation is a sufficient hint for *Jesuitical* Souls: He declares his Principle, that he is an *Enemy* to some, contrary to our Saviours Order: and gives order to his Disciples to guess at his meaning, and without any publick notice to execute the same. *Hatred* removes its Object; he hates, *and they must do his Will without Admonition.* If they mistake his meaning, provided they do it out of Zeal, he can easily connive at it: which suits with their Practises, of Poysoning Emperours, Murdering Kings, attempting on Queens, their Massacre at *Paris*, the Gunpowder-Treason, *&c.* The *Instruments* of which Acts, are by such Records rather favoured than discouraged; and some of them Canonized, rather than punished in the See of *Rome.*

FINIS.

Textual Emendations and Notes

Emendations are recorded by page and line number. References to various volumes are to *The Works of Thomas Traherne*, ed. Jan Ross (Cambridge: D.S. Brewer 2005–).

Dedication

323. penultimate line: 'The VSE', V and U were interchangeable in the seventeenth century.

To the Reader

331. 27 *Guile of Deception* in the *Evening*, marginal gloss: *Ibid.* in CUL (7.41.24 / Peterborough C.4.18).
332. 12 attempted, printed with a backward 'p' in CUL (7.41.24/Peterborough C.4.18), LC, WF, LPL, BCL, OB, WCO, and WTN.
332. 32 very Poinant and Emphatical, marginal gloss, *Ibid.* Marginal gloss not in NU, but in CUL (7.41.24 / Peterborough C.4.18).
333. 15 enough, printed as 'e=nough' in NU, CUL (7.41.24 / Peterborough C.4.18), WF, LPL, BCL, OB, WCO, and WTN.
333. 16 those of the people., no full stop or any kind of punctuation in NU, LC, CUL (7.41.24 / Peterborough C.4.18), WF, LPL, BCL, OB, WCO, and WTN copies.
333. 17 *Indices Expurgatorii*, see *CH*, Vol. III, 'Antichrist', pp. 96–113, especially p. 109, line 541, for a direct reference to 'Index Expurgatorius' as well as to *RF*, p. 110, lines 561–3.
334. 8 and to expatiate downwards, would over-swell the Book, Traherne clearly limits the scope of his book and lets the readers know exactly what years he is covering. In contrast, Thomas Comber's work on Roman Forgeries extends to five books, perhaps more.

Chapter II

347. 24
–348. 4 'CCVI. Altogether following the Decrees ... to be extolled and magnified, being the second after it, *&c.*', there are single quotation marks to the left of this entire quotation in NU, CUL (7.41.24 / Peterborough C.4.18), LPL, HCL, HL, BCL, OB, WCO and WTN.
347. 32 [called], brackets in CUL (7.41.24 / Peterborough C.4.18), WF, LPL, BCL, OB, WCO, and WTN.
348. 10 against him ... *was the runner of the Antichrist*, marginal gloss: *Greg. Lib.* 6. *Epist.* 30. *Lib.* 4. *Epist.* 32. *Lib.* 6. *Epist.* 30. In NU and both CUL (7.41.24 / Peterborough C.4.18) copies.

494 *The Works of Thomas Traherne*

348. 14 And to this purpose, marginal gloss: *Greg. Lib.* 4. *Epist.* 34, in NU and both Cul copies (7.41.24 / Peterborough C.4.18).

349. 1 Council was called at Rome, marginal gloss: Helvic, *Chronol.* In NU and both CUL (7.41.24 / Peterborough C.4.18) copies.

349. 14 *Boniface III ... contention*, marginal gloss: Platin. *In vit.* Bonif. 3. In NU and both CUL (7.41.24 / Peterborough C.4.18) copies.

349. 34 [*the Roman Bishop*], brackets in NU, CUL (7.41.24 / Peterborough C.4.18), LPL, HL, HCL. BCL, OB, WCO, and WTN.

350. 1 [*Legate or*], brackets in NU, CUL (7.41.24 / Peterborough C.4.18), LPL, HL, HCL, BCL, OB, WCO and WTN.

351. 5 [Bishops], brackets in NU, CUL (7.41.24 / Peterborough C.4.18), LPL, HL, HCL, LC, WF, BCL. OB, WCO and WTN.

Chapter III

352. 7 suffered by the ... Zozimus), marginal gloss: Platin. *in vit*, Zozim 1.

352. 22 2. *Nicene* Council ... images, marginal gloss: *Councul. Nicene.* 2. *An.* In NU and both CUL (7.41.24 / Peterborough C.4.18). HL, HCL, LC, WF, BCL. OB, WCO and WTN copies.

353. 2–4 which when *Hincmarus* ... to write against, marginal gloss: Baron. *An* 865. *nu.* 6. In NU and both CUL (7.41.24 / Peterborough C.4.18), HL, HCL, LC, WF, BCL. OB, WCO and WTN copies.

353. 7 every Creature being naturally affectionate to its own *Brood*, and prone to study its preservation., see *C* 1, 94: 'I desire to learn of Thee, to becom in Spirit like unto Thee, I desire not to learn of my Relations, Acquaintance, Tradesmen Merchants or Earthly Princes to be like unto them; but like unto Thee the King of Glory...'. The RC church is too narrow in its affections. A golden rule to Traherne: affections must radiate outward toward all, be inclusive and exclusive.

353. 9 The Church of Rome ... Edition, marginal gloss: Baron. ibid. In NU, HL, HCL, LC, WF, BCL. OB, WCO and WTN and both CUL (7.41.24 / Peterborough C.4.18) copies.

353. 12 It is recorded by *Justellus*, that the forementioned *Hadrian* was careful to give *Charles the Great* a Copy of the Councils, marginal gloss: F. Tom. 2. Council [?] Jus [?], in NU, CUL (7.41.24 / Peterborough C.4.18), LPL, HCL, LC, WF, BCL, OB, WCO and WTN. Perhaps a reference to Henri Justel, a French Huguenot, son of Christophe Justel. Henri edited and published his father's 'Bibliotheca Juris Cononici veteris, in duos tomos distributa' (Paris, 1661).

354. 13 books by S. *Clement*, S. *Peter*'s Successor, marginal gloss: *Apost. Ca* 1.64, in NU and CUL (7.41.24 / Peterborough C.4.18,)NU, LPL, HCL, LC, WF, BCL, OB, WCO and WTN.

354.25–8 In token (doubtless) ... among those of the *Apostles*, marginal gloss: *Ibid.*, in NU and CUL (7.41.24 / Peterborough C.4.18), NU, LPL, HCL, LC, WF, BCL, OB, WCO and WTN.

354. 35 *Cui Bono?*, 'to what purpose' or 'for whose benefit?'

355.8–10 As may perhaps in another Volume be more fully discovered, when we descend from these *first*, to succeeding Ages; was Traherne planning to write two volumes about the Church of Rome? This certainly implies that he was. Or, was he referring to *CH*, 'Antichrist', 'Antiquitie', 'Apostasie'. Traherne planned a topic under 'Idotatrie'. See Vols. II, p. 524 and III, pp. 96–127. See also *CH*, Vol. III, p. 110 under 'Antichrist' where Traherne alludes to *RF*, 'we have prepared a whole Tract upon that theme, (an intire volume) fit to be published.'

355. 12 Tares among Wheat, see Matthew 13.

355. 16 perhaps by some doctors and bishops, followed by 'now' to read 'perhaps by some doctors and bishops now'. Errata reads 'p. 35 line 15 dele *now* (see p. 328 in present text). In NU, WF, HCL, BCL and OB 'now' has been deleted, but is missing in BL, LPL, CUL (7.41.24 / Peterborough C.4.18), and WTN.

356. 11 Oyster shell, printed as 'Oyster=shell in NU, CUL (7.41.24/ Peterborough C.4.18), BL, LPL, LC, BCL and WTN.

356. 16 new Orders of *Jesuites*, Jesuites were a late order (1540). See Gale's treatise, *The True Idea of Janseisme, both Historick and Dogmatick*. (London: Printed for Th. Gilbert in Oxon., 1669) on 'Jansenisme', especially his arguments with Jesuites who introduced Pelagianism (man can gain his own salvation without the assistance of grace) relates to Bradwardine. See J. Owen's preface sig. A4v. See Gale pp. 3, 4 and esp. 5, 'this Jesuistick design, for the reviving of Pelagianisme, being discovered by some sober Reforming Papist, they put forth their most vigorous endeavors, for the timely preventing thereof, and confirming the Doctrine of *Free Grace*, asserted by Austin, &c. p. 3: for Pelagius and his Adherents having made it their Business to advance *corrupt Nature*, and place it on the *Royal Throne of Soveraign Grace*, the Lord raised by Austin and other worthy Instruments to give check to these Antichristian Infusion.'

356. 22 like *Sappho*'s Birds, probably a reference to Sappho's 'Hymn to Aphrodite', stanzas 2 and 3: 'On that day, / you heard my distant voice, nodding, / you left your father's golden chambers and yoked your / two swift companion birds to your glittering chariot. / They fluttered through the spreading sky and / brought you hurriedly down here, / next to me, / here, upon the black soi.' Sappho was a Greek poet (c. 630–c. 570) from the island of Lesbos, known for her lyric poetry.

356. 39 *James Merlin*, James Merlin, or, Jacques Merlin (d. 1541), a French theologian, born in latter part of the fifteenth century, held a doctor of theology at Navarre (1499), was lecturer on divinity to the chapter of Saint-Etienne de Limoges, curate at Montmartre, and chief penitentiary of the Cathedral of Notre-Dame, where he had been resident canon. In 1527 King Francis I had him arrested and incarcerated in the Louvre for preaching against courtiers suspected of sympathizing with the reform movement. For two years after his incarceration he was confined to his residence at Nantes. In 1530 he was installed as grand-vicar to the bishop of Paris as well as curate and archpriest of La Madeleine. His collection of the four general councils of which Traherne writes was first published in Paris, 1524 in folio, with reprints in 8vo, Cologne, 1530, and Paris, 1535.

358. 15   *Hamor* and *Shechem*, marginal gloss: Gen 34. Schechem raped Jacob's daughter Dinah, and Hamor, Schechem's father, wanted the marriage, so that he could take over the clan of Jacob eventually. The tribe of Levi, however, slaughtered Schechem, Hamor and the whole town.

358. 37   love of the world that, substituted in ink for 'obstinate perverseness'; see Errata, p. 328, which directs: 'p. 43 l. 21 r *love of the world that*'; there is however no instruction to delete 'obstinate perverseness'. The sentence originally read 'these are a sufficient instance of the *incredible* obdurateness of mans heart, and his obstinate perverseness allures his hopes'. In both CUL (7.41.24 / Peterborough C.4.18) copies 'Lov of the World' is inserted in ink above 'obstinate perverseness', which has been deleted, with 'that' inserted after 'perverseness', so that the sentence reads 'and his Lov of the World that allures his hopes, as the immediate Crown of his Labours'. The WTN copy reads 'Love of the World that'; the Union copy however inserts '& lov of ye World y^t' above 'perverseness' with a caret under 'y^t'; there is however no deletion, so that the sentence reads 'and his obstinate perverseness & lov of the World y^t' allures his hopes, as the immediate Crown of his Labours'; in the BCL copy 'obstinate perverseness' has been crossed through and replaced by 'Love of ye world, y^t'; the HCL copy reads '& lov to ye World y^t', with 'obstinate perverseness' deleted. In both the WF and BL (1019.c.19) copies '& lov to ye World y^t' is written above 'obstinate perverseness', which is not deleted; however in the BL copy (861.D.10) 'Lov of ye World y^t' is written above 'obstinate perverseness', which is deleted'. [NB: 'to' in the WF, HCL, and BL (1019.c.19).] LPL read 'obstinate perverseness' with no substitution; LPL Main Collection H1763.T7, '& lov to ye World that' is written above 'obstinate perverseness', which is not deleted; in the BCL copy 'obstinate perverseness' has been crossed through and replaced by 'Love of ye world, y^t'; in the OB copy 'Lov of ye World y^t' has been inserted and 'obstinate perverseness' deleted; in the WCO copy 'lov of ye World y^t' has been inserted with 'obstinate perverseness' deleted. There is no instruction in the Errata to insert '&' or 'and' before 'love'. 'Love of the World that' was probably intended to substitute for 'obstinate perverseness', because of '*the incredible* obdurateness of mans heart' in the line above and because of the absence of '&' in the Errata. Both 'obdurateness' and 'obstinate perverseness' suggest a stubborn hard-heartedness and inflexibility, or a stubborn adherence to one's own beliefs or opinions. I have chosen 'Love of the Word that' as in the Errata and deleted 'obstinate perverseness' because of repetition of meaning. The instructions in the Errata are unclear and the exact reading uncertain.

358.36–7   these are a sufficient instance of *incredible* Obdurateness of mans heart, and his Lov of the world allures his hopes, as the immediate crown of his Labours, note in Introduction about Traherne's editing of the printed work.

359. 4   See Also *C* IV, 9–10, etc. Putting off happiness.

359. 6   Dr. *Stillingfleet*, in his Book of *Popist Counterfeit Miracles*: Traherne may be referring to either *A Rational Account of the Grounds of the Protestant Religion* (1665) or *A Discourse concerning the idolatry practised in the Church of Rome* (1671). The work may also be in manuscript form.

Chapter IV

360. 1–4 *James Merlin's ... Isidore*, with some Collections and Additions of his own. He positively affirmeth him to be that Famous *Isidore* of *Hispalis*, a Saint, a Bishop, and a Father of the Church: though *Blondel* and Dr. *Reynolds* accurately observe, S. *Isidore* of *Hispalis* was dead 40, 50, 60 years, before some things came to pass that are mentioned in that Book of the Councils.

360. 3 *Isidore of Hispalis*, a Saint, a Bishop and a Father of the Church, St. Isidore (c. 560–636). The most important of his works is the 'Etymologiae', an encyclopaedia of the knowledge of his time, containing information on subjects such as grammar, rhetoric, mathematics, medicine, and history, as well as on the books and offices of the Church and other theological matters. The work received its name from the (frequently quite fanciful) etymological explanations of the words signifying the different subjects.

360. 7 David Blondel (1591–1655), a French Protestant church historian and clergyman, born at Châlons-sur-Marne in 1591, and died on April 6, 1655. He was educated at Sedan and the Genevan Academy. For most of his life he was a country pastor at Roucy, refusing a chair of theology at Saumur in 1631, although in 1645 he was created an honary professor there. In 1650 he succeeded G. J. Vossius in the professorship of history at Amsterdam. His most important work was *Pseudo-Isidoru et Turrianus Vapulans*, finally discrediting the historicity of the False decretals. All of his works are listed in the Roman Catholic Index of Forbidden Books.

360. 7 *Turrianus Vapulans*, i.e., Francisco Torres, also known as 'Turrianus' (c. 1504–1584), Jesuit patristic scholar and well-known Roman Catholic controversialist. He served as Papal theologian at the Council of Trent. He attributed the 'Apostolic Constitutions' to St. Clement of Rome, and defended the authenticity of the 'Apostolic Canons', the 'False Decretals', and the 80 Nicene Canons, all of them spurious, as well as that of the genuine Acts of the Sixth and Seventh General Councils.

360. 9 *Vasaeus*, Johnnes Vasaeus (b. 1511), Jan Was or Waes, born in Bruges, studied in the Collegium Trilingue in Leuven, where he met Ferdinand Columbus, second son of Christopher Columbus, who persuaded him to go to Spain with him, where he became the first librarian of Ferdinand's personal library, a collection dedicated to the discoveries and voyages of Christopher Columbus. After Ferdinand died in 1539, his library (approximately 10,000 volumes) was given to Seville Cathedral, and Vasaeus's contract was terminated. He then became the head of a school in Braga, and in 1541 taught in the Universidade de Evora, both in Portugal.

360. 24 *Honoratus*, St. Honoratus (c. 350–429), Archbishop of Arles, of a consular family, converted to Christianity and went with his brother on a pilgrimage to the holy places in Syria and Egypt. Upon his brother's death, he returned through Rome, settling on the island of Lérins, where he founded (c. 410) a monastary. He became Archbishop of Arles in 426, where he was active in establishing Christianity and continued to direct his monastary. His successor was St. Hilary of Arles. His writings have been lost.

361. 1 *Possevin*, Antonio Possevino (1533–1611), a Jesuit controversialist and bibliographer, active politically in the Counter-Reformation, especially

against the spread of Calvinism; he was also connected with the Aristotelian revival associated with Francis Robortello and Vincenzo Maggi (1498–1564). As a papal legate, he was the first Jesuit to visit Moscow, vicar general of Sweden, Denmark and northern islands, Muscovy, Livonia, Russia, Hungary, Pomerania and Saxony between 1578 and 1586.

361. 1 *Hart* in his Conference with *Reynolds*, see *CH*, Vol. I, Introduction p. xxiii, and Vol. III, Introduction, and 'Antichrist' (pp. 97–113) and 'Antiquitie', pp. 118–23. Traherne relied ... on John Jewel's *A Replie unto M. Hardinges Answeare* (London, 1565), *A Defence of the Aplogie of the chruche of Englande* (London, 1567) and *An Exposition upon the two Epistles of the Apostle Sainct Paule to the Thessalonians* (London, 1583) as well as John Rainolde's *The Summe of the Conference betwene John Rainoldes and John Hart: Touching the Head and the Faith of the Church* (London, 1584), all sources directly linked to *Roman Forgeries* (London, 1673)'.

See *CH*, 'Antichrist', Vol. III, p. 109, where Traherne refers to the Index Expuratorius, and under "Antiquitie', p. 118, where he refers to Hart and Genebrand.

Génébrard (1537–1597), French Roman Catholic exegete and Hebraist, moral and dogmatic theologian, appointed Archbishop of Aix-en-Provence in 1593: 'Concerning the Lies and Forgeries. Dreams and Lying Wonders, fals and feigned miracles, spurious Books and Counterfeit Records which Satan and antichrist have vented abroad the World', see Bishop Jewel, Dr Reinolds and Mr Perkins. 'Even volumes themselvs will not contain all the Villanies they have done of that Kind. There is a whole Book which they have contrived Directing Printers how to Corrupt the Fathers. Tis called Index Expuratorius.'

361. 2 Reynolds, John (1549–1607), Anglican divine (spelled variously John Rainolds, Reinolds). A native of Pinhoe, Devon, educated at Corpus Christi College, Oxford, where he was elected a Fellow in 1568. As reader in Greek in his college (1577–8), he became well known through his successful lectures on Aristotle's *Rhetoric*. Resigning his Fellowship in 1586, probably through difficulties with William Coke, the president, he taught for a time at Queen's College. In 1593 he became Dean of Lincoln and in 1598, by an arrangement welcomed to Corpus, where Coke's rule was much disliked, exchanged this office with the president. By this time Rainolds had won a reputation as a skilled champion of Calvinism, and at the Hampton Court Conference (1604) he was the chief representative of the Puritan Cause. Among the things of the Book of Common Prayer to which he objected were the sign of the Cross in baptism, the ring in marriage, the use of the Apocrypha, and the churching of women. Though the Puritan objections were overruled at the conference, Rainolds did not fall from favour. He was given a prominent part in preparing the Authorized Version of he Bible, sitting in the company that translated the Prophets. His high character and wide learning won him respect even from his theological adversaries.

361. 7 *Siricius* (334–399), Pope 384–399, successor of Pope Damasus I and succeeded by Pope Anastasius I, was the first pope to issue decretals, two against decrees concerning clerical celibacy. He also took severe measures

Textual Emendations and Notes

against the Manichæans at Rome.

361. 23 *that the causes of Bishops ... with the residue*, marginal gloss: Baron. *An. Christ.* 862. *nu.* 4, in NU and CUL (7.41.24 /Peterborough C.4.18) copies.

361. 29 *It is certain ... a business as this*, marginal gloss: *Ibid. nu.* 5, in NU, CUL (7.41.24 / Peterborough C.4.18) copies.

362. 35 *That the same* Riculphus ... *in all things*, marginal gloss: Baron. *An.* 365. *nu.* 6, in NU and CUL (7.41.24 / Peterborough C.4.18) copies.

363. 25 which putteth me in mind of *Cacus* his device, who being a strong Thief ... they might not be tracked, but seem to be gone another way': in Roman mythology Cacus was a fire-breathing giant and son of Vulcan, who lived in a cave in Italy, the future site of Rome. He was also a cannibal, who nailed the heads of his victims to the entrance of his cave. According to Evander, Hercules stopped to pasture his own recently stolen cattle from Geryon near Cacus's lair; while he slept, however, Cacus stole eight of the cattle – four bulls and four heifers – dragging them into his cave backwards by their tails, so as to leave a trail in wrong direction. See Virgil, *Aneid*, Book VIII, lines 200–15.

364. 11 *An* 865, *nu.* 7, in NU and CUL (7.41.24 / Peterborough C.4.18) copies.

364. 33 Statesmen, originally 'Privy Councils'; in NU, BCL, OB and HCL copies substitute 'Statesmen' for 'Privy Councils', which has been deleted; in the WF copy, 'Councils' has been crossed through and 'statesmen' written in the margin. However, the CUL (7.41.24 / Peterborough C.4.18), BL (1019.c.19 / 861.D.10), LPL, LC and WTN copies have no correction and read 'Privy Councils'. The instruction in the Errata is unclear, 'p. 55 for *Council* r. Statesmen'. The reading is doubtful; 'Privy Statesmen' seems unlikely. I have substituted 'Statesmen' for the phrase 'Privy Council'.

365. 13 *But he who first published ... in themselves*, marginal gloss: *Ibid. nu.* 7, in NU and CUL (7.41.24/Peterborough C.4.18) copies.

365. 16 *Epistle*, printed as 'Fpistle' in CUL (7.41.24 / Peterborough C.4.18) copies.

365. 38 Hispalis, printed as 'Hi–lpalis' in NU, CUL (7.41.24 / Peterborough C.4.18), LPL, HC, HCL and WF.

365. 39 Ildephonsus, c. 607–667, appointed Archbishop of Toledo in 657; attended Councils of Toledo in 653 and 655.

367.4–5 Cardinal *Bellarmine* ... from the Popes themselves, marginal gloss: Bellarm. *de Rom. Pont. lib.* 1. *cap.* 14; in NU and CUL (7.41.24 / Peterborough C.4.18).

367. 14 Marcellus, d. c. 374, Bishop of Ancyra and strong supporter of Homousion at the Council of Nicaea.

367. 37 Dr. *Reynolds ...* with *Hart*, marginal gloss: *Confer. Cap* 8. Divis. 3; in NU and CUL (7.41.24 / Peterborough C.4.18).

368. 5 *or thereabout*, full stop missing in NU.

368. 18 *Harding*, in his book against Bishop *Jewel*, refers to the so-called Harding–Jewel debate. Thomas Harding (1516–1572), theologian, controversialist and professor of Hebrew at New College, Oxford, who returned to the Roman Church, after professing reformed ideas, and John Jewel (1522–1571), bishop of Salisbury, controversialist and apologist. See John Jewel, *Apologie of the Churche of England* (1562 and 1564), *A Replie unto M. Hardinges Answeare* (London, 1565); *A Defence of the Apologie of the Churche of Englande*

(London, 1567); and John Rainolde, *The Summe of the Conference betwene John Rainoldes and John Hart: Touching the Head and the Faith of the Church* (London, 1584); and Thomas Harding, *Confutation of a book called Apology of the Church of England* (1565). *Answer to M. Jewel's Challenge* (1564). See also *Commentaries of Heaven* in *The Works of Thomas Traherne*, ed. Jan Ross (Cambridge: D.S. Brewer, 2005–), Vol. II, Introduction, p. xviii, and Vol. III, 'Antiquitie', p. 114 and 'Assumption', p. 291.

Chapter V

369. 10   That all the Primacies ... the *Mother of us all*, in NU and CUL (7.41.24 / Peterborough C.4.18), there are single quotation marks to the left of each line in this quotation.

370. 6   *Magdenburge*, final 'e' not in Errata. *Magdenburge*, and: see Errata (p. 328), 'p. 66 l. 16 aft. Magdenburg r. *and*'. Inserted in ink NU, OB and CUL (7.41.24) copies; in the WF, BCL, OB and HCL copies an ampersand (&) has been inserted after 'Magdenburge'; no correction has been made in WTN, BL (1019.c.19 / 861.D.10), CUL (7.41.24 / Peterborough C.4.18) or LPL.

370. 15   *Gratian* sheweth ... among the Learned, marginal gloss: D*ist* 19. De *Epistolis;* in LPL, LC and CUL (7.41.24 / Peterborough C. 4.18).

370. 25   open and known Lies. *Anacletus*, that, marginal gloss: Dist. 9. Juxta Sanctorum; in NU, CUL (7.41.24 / Peterborough C.4.18) and LPL

370. 25   *Anacletus ... Peter*, marginal gloss: Dist. 97 Juxta Sanctorum; in NU, LPL, LC and CUL (7.41.24 / Peterborough C.4.18).

371. 5   themselves, written as them= [page break] selves.

371. 35   Cardinals in *Rome* in the time of *Constantine*, marginal gloss: *An.* 320; in NU and CUL (7.41.24 / Peterborough C.4.18).

372. 1   'You 80 Bishops, ... of that Synod', there are single quotation marks to the left of each line of this quotation; in NU, CUL (7.41.24 / Peterborough C.4.18), LPL (Main Collection A69.3 / T67 and H1763.t7) and BL (1019.c.19 / 861.D.10).

372. 13   *Mark* was dead 9 years before the Burning happened, marginal gloss: Bin. *Tom.* 1. *in vita* Marc; in NU, CUL (7.41.21.4 / Peterborough C.4.18), LPL (A69.3 / T67 and H1763.t7) and BL (1018 c.19 / 861. D.10).

373. 13   Marginal gloss: Bell. *de Rom. Pont. lib. 4. cap. 9.* Baron. *An. Christ.* 357. Liberii 6, *nu.* 32, 33; in NU, CUL (7.41.24 / Peterborough C.4.18), LPL (A69.3 / T67 and H1763.t7) and BL (1019.c.19 / 861.D.10).

373. 17   Marginal gloss: Bin. *in vit.* Liberii; in NU, CUL (7.41.24 / Peterborough C.4.18), LPL (A69.3 / T67 and H1763.t7) and BL (1019.c.19 / 861.D.10).

373. 26   Bellarmine and Platina consent to this, marginal gloss: Bellarm. *ut supra*; in NU, CUL (7.41.24 / Peterborough C.4.18), LPL (A69.3 / T67 and H1763.t7) and BL (1019.c.19 / 861.D.10).

373. 34   Next the Epistle of *Damasus* to *Hierom*, and *Hierom*'s Answer, marginal gloss: Bin. *Not. In Epist. 3.* Damasi. *&c in Epist.* Hieron. *ad* Damas.; in NU, CUL (7.41.24 / Peterborough C.4.18), LPL (A69.3 / T67 and H1763.t7), and BL (1019.c.19 / 861.D.10).

374. 23   *Hilarius, Simplicius*, commas inserted by editor.

Textual Emendations and Notes 501

374. 24 the most of which do much exceed our compass of the first 400 years, and are too late for our cognizance. Traherne reminds his audience of the boundaries of discussion of the False Decretals.

375. 23 *Deleatur*, a written mark on a proof-sheet indicating a section to be deleted. mist; in NU, WF, LPL (Main Collection SR3, H1763.t7 / Sion Aarc Octavo A69.3/ T67), CUL (7.41.24 / Peterborough C.4.18), HL, HCL, BL (861.D.10 / 1019.c.19) WTN, BCL, OB, WCO and LC all read 'mist'; a seventeenth-century variant spelling for 'missed'.

375. 34 Binius, and all the Popish compilers ... honour has made us satisfaction, Traherne's attempt at humor?

376. 6 poyseth, Traherne is perhaps making a word play here with 'poysen' above, 'poyseth' meaning 'adding weight' (here by foul means; 'size and number' suggest this meaning); a seventeeneth-century variant for 'poise', to add weight to'; 'poyseth' is in NU, CUL (7.41.24 / Peterborough C.4.18), LPL (A69.3 / T67 and H1763.t7) and BL (1019.c.19 / 861.D.10); or may be a printing errour for 'poyseneth'.

376. 12 *Philtres*, a potion or drug to enchant or produce a magic effect.

377. 10 p. 82, printed upside down as '28' in the CUL (7.41.24) copy; printed as 82 in CUL (Peterborough C.4.18), NU, HL, HCL, BCL, OB, WTN and LPL (SR3, H1763.T7, and Sion Aarc Octavo A69.3 / T67).

Chapter VI

378. 24 1535, corrected in ink from 1635 in NU, HCL, BCL, OB, BL (1019.c.10), WF and LC copies, but not in the CUL (7.41.24 / Peterborough C.4.18), WTN, BL (861.D.10) and LPL (Sion Aarc A69.3 / T67 or H1763.T7) copies. Merlin's *COLLECTION* was first published in 1524; see above. Title in Latin reads: *Conciliorum Quatvor Generalium. Niceni, Constantinopolitani. Ephesini, et Calcedonensis. Que diuus Gregorius magnus tang[uam] quatuor Euangelia colit ac veneratur.: Tomvs Primvs. Quadraginta quoq[ue] septem conciliorum prouincialium authenticorum. Decretorum etiam sexagina nouem pontificum ab apostolis & eorundem canonibus usq[ue] ad Zachariam primum, Isidoro authore. Item bulla Aurea Caroli IIII. Imperatoris, de electione Regis Romanorum. Tomus secundus. Aliorum aliquot conciliorum generalium. Practica Quintae Synodi Constantinopolitanae. Sexta Synodus Constantinopolitana. Acta concilij Constantiensis. Decrta concilij Basiliensis. Approbatio actorum Concilij Basiliensis per N. P. Confimatio constittionum Friderici & Carolinae,* by Jacques Merlin.

380. 12 *Medusa's Head of Snakes*, in Greek mythology Medusa was a monster, a Gorgon, a winged human female, with a hideous face and living venomous snakes in place of hair. Anyone who look upon her was turned to stone. See Ovid, *Metamorphoses*, Books IV, V, VI.

380. 13 *Pontificians*, adj., noun, obs. for 'pontificial', a bishop, specifically the pope, 'pontiff'; and adherent of pontifical rule.

380. 15 *to depress the proud, to weary the voluptuous, to bring down the ambitious, to take the little Foxes that spoil the Vineyard of the Church,* see Song of Solomon, 2.15 and 1 Corinthians 7.1.

381.	5	*Stones of* David that kill Goliah, see 1 Samuel 17. CUL (both copies) and NU spell it 'Goliah'.
381.	9	Pearl of Price, see Matthew 13.46.
381.	20	so hard a Father, that he soweth Tares instead of Wheat, see Matthew 13 for the parable of the tares, especially verses 24–29.
381.	21	and giveth Stones instead of Bread, see Matthew 7.9.
381.	22	for Eggs feedeth us with Scorpions, see Luke 11.12.
382.	19	hated the Light, because their Deeds were evil, see John 3.19.
382.	30	For *Sinon* was let loose, with as little Artifice as this, to the Destruction of *Troy*, Sinon was a Greek, posing as a deserter, who persuaded the Trojans to take the Trojan Horse into their city. Hidden within the belly of the horse were the best of the Greek soldiers, fully armed. When night fell, Sinon opened the horses's belly and released the Greeks, who killed the Trojan guards and opened the gates of the city to the rest of their forces, who destroyed the city. See Virgil, *The Aeneid*, Book II, especially lines 77–267. Sinon became a symbol of a liar and deceiver.
382.	39	An Ass may be expected to meddle with a Harp, as soon as a Merchant with the Mysterious Records of the Church, Traherne's sarcastic humour.

Chapter VII

387.	6	First he observeth, marginal gloss: Turrian *in* Clement *Epist.* 1. In CUL (7.41.24) and BL, but not in NU, LPL, WTN, HCL, HL.
388.	19	Solomon *saith, Look diligently to the face of thy Cattel and consider thy Herds*, &c., see Proverbs 27.23.
388.	22	Having noted how S. *Paul* transferred a certain business on himself and *Apollos*, perhaps a reference to either 1 Corinthians 1.12–17 or 1 Corinthians 3.5–15.
388.	33	fifth, written as 'fit' corrected in the text in ink to 'fifth' in NU, HCL and OB copies; in the WF copy 'fifth' has been written in the margin. In the BCL copy 'th' has been written at the end of the word. There is no correction in the CUL (7.41.24 / Peterborough C.4.18), LPL (Main Collection SR3, H1763.T7 and Sion Aarc Octavo A69.3 / T67), BL (1019.c.19 and 861.D.10) or WTN copies, which reads 'fit'. See Errata (p. 328 in present text), 'p. 104 line 16 for fit r fift.'

Chapter VIII

390.	18	1608, corrected in ink from '1618' to '1608' in NU, HCL, HL, BCL, OB, BL (1019.c.19) and WF, but not in CUL (7.41.24 / Peterborough c.4.18), BL (861.D.10), LPL (Main Collection SR3, H1763.T7 and Sion Aarc Octavo A69.3 / T67), WTN, BCL or WCO.
391.	38	Honest *Turrian* zealously, and magnified by *Nicolinus* as the *Coronis* of the Apostles Canons, marginal gloss: *Vid. Cap. 11*. Poorly printed with '11' missing in the CUL (7.41.24) copy but inserted by hand in ink in NU, BL (1019.c.19), BCL, WF and HCL; no correction is made in the OB, BL (810.D.10), CUL Peterborough (c.4.18), LPL (Main Collection SR3, H1763.T67 / H1763.t7) or WTN.
392.	3	with, printed as 'wtih'; in NU and CUL (7.41.24 / Peterborough C.4.18),

Textual Emendations and Notes

LPL (SR3, H1763.t7 and Sion Aarc Octavo A69.3 / T67) BL, BCL, OB, WCO.

392. 15 *Out of thine own mouth thou shalt be justified, and out of thine own mouth thou shalt be condemned*, a conflation of several verses: see Matthew 12.37, Luke 19. 22 and Job 15.6.

Chapter X

397. 14 *Did I follow them throughout all Ages. ... This I speak especially upon the last*, from *Binius* downward, Traherne reminds reader of the limits of his subject.

Chapter XI

398. *NIcolinus his Tomes ... with Council of* Carthage. 'An Abridgment of the Chapters' reads '*of* Nicolinus his tomes, and their Contexts for the first 420 years. How full of Forgeries. His Testimony concerning the sixth Council of Carthage; with his was of defending the Popes Forgery therein.

401. 13 *Laws are like Spiders ... through them*, recorded in Tilley, L116, p. 371 as 'Laws catch flies (little flies) but let hornets (great flies) go free', pp. [446–7]. Recorded also in *The Oxford Dictionary of English Proverbs*, compiled by William George Smith, third edition, edited by F. P. Wilson (Oxford: At the Clarendon Press, 1970), p. 446, as 'Laws catch flies but let hornets go free.'

403. 5 *Jacobus Leschasserius*, see *De Volabulis ad geographiam juri Romani pertinentibl obervatio*. 8 Vo. France. 1617.

405. 4 *Treatise of the Right use of the Fathers*; it originally read '*Daille* in his *Treatise of the Right of the Fathers*, Cap. 4. pag. 45, 46, 47'; in NU, BCL, OB, WF, BL, WTN, BL (1019.c.19), LPL (Sion Aarc Octavo A69.3 / T67 or H1763.T7) and HCL copies the word 'use' has been inserted by hand from Errata (p. 296), 'p. 137 l. 71 r Right use of the Fathers'; there is no correction in HL, CUL (7.41.24 and Peterborough C.4.18), WCO, BL (861.D.10), LC, WTN.

Chapter XII

406. 9
–407. 26 *It fell out conveniently for me ... Venice* VI. Kal. *Octob.* M.D. LXXXV, there are quotation marks in the left margin at every line of the quotation from Nicolinus.

406. 14 Majesty, misprinted as 'Ma- / sty' in BL (861.D.10 and 1019.c.19) LPL (Main Collection SR3, H1763.T7), HL, HCL, NU, CUL 7.41.24 / Peterborough C.4.18).

406. 16 Veneration, full stop missing in BL (861.D.10 and 1019.c.19) LPL (Sion Arc SR3, Main Collection H1763.T7), HL, HCL, NU, CUL 7.41.24 / Peterborough C.4.18).

Chapter XIII

412. 22 *Devil is wont to deceive many, and so doth very oftentimes delude the imprudence of some by a similitude of Piety*; in WF, LC, CUL (7.41.24),

504   *The Works of Thomas Traherne*

		BCL, OB, WTN, BL (1019.c.19 and 861.D.10), LPL (Sion Aarc Octavo A69.3 / T67 and Main Collection H1763.T7), HCL, HL, NU there is a printed manicule (☞) pointing to this section.
413.	17	Proverb, *Woe be to the Sheep, while the Fox Preacheth*, The Oxford Dictionary of English Proverbs, third edition (Oxford, 1970, p. 285), records, 'When the Fox preaches, then beware your geese'. See also Morris Palmer Tilley, *A Dictionary of Proverbs in England in the Sixteenth and Seventeenth Centuries* (Ann Arbor, MI, 1950), p. 241, F656, 'Woe to the Geese that have the Fox for their priest'; and F656, 'When the Fox preaches beware your geese'. See also Matthew 17.15, 'Beware of false prophets, which come to you in sheep's clothing, but inwardly they are ravening wolves'.
413.	20	*In the Pit which he made for others, is himself fallen*, see Psalm 7.15.
413.	21	the unpardonable sin, himself *blasphemes the Holy Ghost*, see Matthew 12.31–32 and Mark 3.28–29.
413.	23	*Father of Lies*, see John 8.44.
414.	1	*the wickedness of the Devil, who deludes men with a shew of Piety*; probably a reference to 2 Cor. 11.14, where he may appear as an angel of light.

Chapter XIV

415.	29	[Transeunt], in NU 'Transcant' is corrected by hand in the text to 'Transient', changing the 'c' to 'i', deleting the 'a'; in WF 'Transceant' is corrected to 'Transeant' by hand in the text, crossing through the 'c'. HL, PB, BCL correct from 'Transceant' to 'Transeunt'; in HCL 'e' and 'u' have been printed over the word; BCL and OB read Transent, with 'with "u" inserted to read 'Transeunt'; there is no correction in CUL (7.41.24, Peterborough C.4.18), BL (1019.c.19 and 861.D.10), LPL (Sion Aarc Octavo A69.3/T67 or Main Collection H1763.T7), WCO or WTN. I have followed the Errata (p. 328) where the instructions are as follows: p. 157 l. ult. r. 'Transeunt'. Traherne probably means here an Eye (or person) that gives only a fleeting or transitory glance, with no lasting impression.
417.	21	Tradition., no full stop after 'Tradition' in LPL (Main Collection SR3, H1763.T7 and Sion Aarc Octavo (A69.3/T67) BL (1019.c.19 / 861.D.10); full stop lightly printed in NU, HCL, HL, BCL, WF, LC, OB.
418.	17	as Fire hardens Clay, and softens Wax, see Morris Palmer Tilley, *A Dictionary of the Proverbs in England in the Sixteenth and Seventeenth Centuries* (Ann Arbor, MI, 1950), p. 641, S 980: 'The same sunne works several effects upon Waxe and Clay: for it softens the one, and hardneth the other'.
420.	1	*Cuttle, in his own Ink, that he might vomit up the Hook in the dark, and scape away*, 'Cuttle' refers to the common cuttlefish, also called 'ink-fish' from its power to eject a black fluid from a sac, so as to darken the water and hide itself from enemies in pursuit.
421.	15	conjecture, comma is missing in NU copy; there is a comma in LPL (Main Collection SR3, H1763.T7 / Sion Aarc Octavo A69.3/67), CUL 7.41.24 / Peterborough C.4.18.
421.	22	*To the Jews*, saith S. Paul, *I became as a Jew that I might gain the Jews*, see 1 Corinthians 9.20.

Textual Emendations and Notes 505

Chapter XV

423. *Falsely*, CUL (7.41.24) reads 'Falsity'; WF and OB corrected to 'Falsely'; NU reads 'Falsely', with 'el' written over 'it'; BCL reads 'Falsely, with 'y' added in ink; HCL reads 'Falsely', with 'ely' written over 'ity'. 'An Abridgment of the Chapters' reads 'falsly' (sigs. B8^V–C2^V in text; p. 337, Cap. 15, in present text). No correction was made in HL, LPL (Sion Aarc Octavo A69.3/T67 and Main Collection H1763.T7), OB, BL (1019.c.19 and 861.D.10) or WTN copies.

424. 24 When Ioe the Witch of *Endor* raises up *Samuel*, see 1 Samuel 28.3–20.

424. 32 For as Light answered Light in *Solomons Buildings*, perhaps a reference to the Kabbalah, which portrays Solomon as having sailed through the air on a throne of light placed on an eagle, which brought him near the heavenly gates as well as to the dark mountains behind which the fallen angels Uzza and Azzazel were chained; the eagle would rest on the chains, and Solomon, using the magic ring, would compel the two angels to reveal every mystery he desired to know.

425. 25 Marginal gloss: *An*. 15. Incompletely printed in CUL Peterborough C.4.18, but completely printed in 7.41.24.

425. 29 twenty four years, comma missing in NU copy.

425. 38 S. *Peters's Name*, full stop missing in CUL and NU.

426. 3 *Gibeonites old Bottles, clouted Shooes, and mouldy Bread*, see Joshua 9.3–6.

Chapter XVI

430. 8 heedlesly, CUL (7.41.24), WF, NU, BL (1019.c.19 / 861.D.10), HL, HCL, LPL (Main collection SR3 H1763.T7 and Sion Aarc Octavo A69.3 / T67), BCL, OB and WTN read 'heedlesly'.

430. 16 him:, printed as 'him:' in CUL (7.41.24), LPL (Main Collection SR3 H1763.T7), HL, HCL, BCL, OB, WTN, BL (861.D.10 and 1019.c.19), NU; but not in CUL Peterborough C.4.18.

430. 23 Peter., no full stop in NU.

431. 10 *Binius*, printed in NU as 'B*inius*', as in line 33; corrected for consistency.

431. 23 S. *Clement* sendeth, full stop missing in CUL (7.41.24 / Peterborough C.4.18); full stop in WF, LPL (Main Collection SR3, H1763 T7 and Sion Aarc Octavo A69.3 / T67), BL (1019.c.19 and 861.D.10), OB, BCL, WTN, HL, HCL.

432. 2 *unskilful*, NU reads '*unskilfuI*'.

433. 2 S. *James*, full stop after 'S' missing in CUL (7.41.24 / Peterborough C.4.18), WF, LPL (Main Collection SR3, H1763.T7 and Sion Aarc Octavo A69.3 / T67), LC, BL (861.D.10 and 1019.c.19), HL, HCL, BCL, OB, WTN, NU.

433. 13 S. *James, De Sacratis vestibus, vel vasis*. Title of letter.

433. 18 *Pall*, reference is unclear; probably refers to the stiffened linen cloth used to cover the chalice; it may also refer to the hanging for the front of the altar, or to a richly woven altar cover (although mentioned below).

433. 25 *Fryers Coul*, seventeenth-century variant of 'cowl', a hooded robe of a monk.

Chapter XVII

434. 1 Pope Hyginus, Bishop of Rome c. 138–42. Born in Athens, he served as Pope during the heretical teachings of the Gnostics, who taught that the God of the Old Testament and Christ of the New Testament were two different Gods. He died a martyr and was made a Saint by the Roman Catholic Church. His feast day is January 11.

434. 8 Binius, printed as 'Binius' in CUL (7.41.24), NU, WF, BCL, OB, WTN, LPL (Main Collection SR3 H1763.T7 and Sion Arc Octavo A69.3 / T67), HCL, BL (861.D.10 and 1019.c.19), LC.

434. 24 *that* Easter *should be observed on the Lords Day*, see *CYB*, 'Of the Coming of the H. Ghost' in Ross, Vol. IV, pp. 114–49, especially

434. 26 *baptized*, &c., followed by a comma not a full stop in CUL (7.41.24 / Peterborough C.4.18), NU, WF, BCL, OB, WTN, LPL (Main Collection SR3, H1763.T7 and Sion Aarc Octavo A69.3 / T67), HL, HC, LC, BL (861.D.10 and 1019.c.19).

434. 29 *Salute Asyncritus, Phlegon, Hermas, Patrobus, Hermes*, see Romans 16.14.

435. 13 *Popes Brother*, printed as '*Popes Brother*' in CUL (7.41.24), NU, WF, BCL, OB, WTN, LPL (Sion Aarc Octavo A69.3 / T7), HL, HCL, BL (861.D.10 and 1019.c.19); correctly printed in LPL (Main Collection SR3, H1763.T67), LC.

435. 21 *Binius ... Pius*, CUL (7.41.24) and NU print 'Binus ... Pius'.

436. 2 *Binius*, printed as 'Binus' in CUL (7.41.24), NU, WF, BCL, OB, WTN, LPL (Main Collection SR3, H1763.T7 and Sion Aarc Octavo A69.3/T67), HL, HCL, LC, BL (861.D.10 and 1019.c.19).

436. 29 *Dicendum*s, a reply, answer or defence.

436. 32 of these Hermes one, 'one' is inserted in ink from above the line in CUL (7.41.24 / Peterborough C.4.18), NU, HCL, WF, OB, BCL, LPL (Main Collection SR3, H1763.T7 and Sion Aarc Octavo A69.3/T67), but not in WTN, BL (1019 c.19 and 861.D.10), LC.

437. 3 *Tertullian's Poetrie*, as in CUL (7.41.24), NU, WF, BCL, OB, WTN, LPL (Main Collection SR3, H1763.T7 and Sion Aarc Octavo A69.3/T67), HL, HCL, BL (861.D.10 and 1019.c.19), LC.

437. 16 *shape of a Shepheard*, as in CUL (7.41.24 / Peterborough C.4.18), NU, WF, BCL, OB, WTN, LPL (Main Collection SR3, H1763.T7 and Sion Aarc Octavo A69.3 / T67), HL, HCL, BL (861.D.10 and 1019.c.19).

438. 2 *for in him dwelleth all the fulness of the Godhead bodily: that ye may be repleat in him, who is the Head of all Principality and Power*, see Colossians 2.9–10.

438. 6 *thou are* Peter, *and upon this Rock will I build my Church*, see Matthew 16.18.

438. 9 *hold the Head, from which all the Body by Joynts and Bands having nourishment ministered, and knit together, increaseth with the increase of God*, see Colossians 2.19.

438. 17 *in whom all the fulness of the Godhead dwelleth Bodily*, see Colossians 2.9.

438. 22 *Kingdom of Heaven to whom he will*, no full stop in CUL (7.41.24 / Peterborough C.4.18), NU, WF, BCL, OB, WTN, LPL (SR3, H1763.T7 and Sion Aarc Octavo A69.3 / T67), HL, HCL, BL (861.D.10 and 1019.c.19), LC.

Textual Emendations and Notes 507

438. 24   though it, printed as 'though it it' in CUL (7.41.24 / Peterborough C.4.18).

438. 28   but the Popes: nor be obeyed for himself, printed as 'but the Popes:nor be obeyed for himself', with no space between 'Popes:' and 'nor'. in CUL (7.41.24); there is a space in CUL Peterborough C.4.18. WF, BCL, OB, WTN, LPL (Main Collection SR3, H1763.T7 and Sion Aarc Octavo A69.3 / T67), HL, HCL, BL (861.D.10 and 1019.c.19) copies.), NU, WF, BCL, OB, WTN, OB, WTN.

438. 36   *Ovid* makes use of the *Cock*, and his *Crowing* in the Morning, the exact reference being obscure; see Ovid, *Metamorphoses*, Book XI, lines 162–3, 'There is no wakeful, crested cock with his loud crowing summons the dawn'.

438. 36   Only as *Ovid* makes use of the *Cock*, and his *Crowing* in the Morning, to introduce the fable of *Alector*, the reference to *Alector* is obscure; it may refer to Alector, a son of Anaxagoras and father of Iphis, king of Argos. He was consulted by Polyneices as to the manner in which Amphiaraus might be compelled to take part in the expedition against Thebes. See Homer, *Odyssey*, 4.10. See also *The Iliad*, 17.602.

439. 3   *Damasus.*, no full stop in CUL (7.41.24), NU, WF, BCL, OB, WTN, LPL (Main Collection SR3, H1763.T7 and Sion Aarc Octavo A69.3 / T67), HL, HCL, BL (861.D.10 and 1019.c.19), LC.

Chapter XVIII

440. 9
–441. 16   In NU copy, p. 207 ('THE FIRST EPISTLE … neither failes of Greatness, [nec a fructibus inanescit]') and p. 208 ('nor waxes vain … of the Calend, or *July*: praying God') are followed by 222 and 223. The pages are reprinted in their proper order at pp. 222 (*'exceeding many most Learned men … or is it by the'*) and 223 (*'common Assent of all believed … against an apparent false'*).

440. 13   Cornelius, there are single quotations at the beginning of every line, starting at 'Cornelius' and ending with 'the Name of the Lord'. Because of the dropped capital letter 'C' however I could not insert the quotation mark at this point.

440. 14   Serve, printed as '*S*erve' in NU, CUL (7.41.24 / Peterborough C 4.18), WF, BCL, OB, WTN, LPL (Main Collection SR3, H1763.T7 and Sion Aarc Octavo A69.3 / T67), HL, HCL, BL (861.D.10 and 1019.c.19).

440. 16
–441.20   Considering the Benevolence of your Charity … Name of the Lord, there are single quotation marks to the left of each line of this section in NU, WF, LC, BCL, OB, WTN, LPL (Main Collection SR3, H1763.T7 and Sion Aarc Octavo A69.3 / T67), HCL, BL (861.D.10 and 1019.c.19).

440. 19   Known, printed as '*K*nown' in CUL (7.41.24 / Peterborough C 4.18), NU, WF, BCL, OB, WTN, LPL (Main Collection SR3, H1763.T7 and Sion Aarc Octavo A69.3/T67), HL, HCL, BL (861.D.10 and 1019.c.19).

440. 20   us in the Church of *Rome*, printed as 'us in theChurch of *Rome*' in NU, CUL (7.41.24 / Peterborough C 4.18), WF, BCL, OB, WTN, LPL (Main Collection SR3, H1763.T7 and Sion Aarc Octavo A69.3 / T67), HL, HCL, BL (861.D.10 and 1019.c.19).

440. 24   Increases, reads *I*ncreases in CUL (7.41.24 / Peterborough C 4.18), NU, WF, BCL, OB, WTN, LPL (Main Collection SR3, H1763.T7 and Sion Aarc Octavo A69.3 / T67), HL, HCL, BL (861.D.10 and 1019.c.19).

441. 7   Ostiensian Way (Via Ostiensis), an important road in ancient Rome, running approximately nineteen miles west from the City to the Port of Ostia Antica, from which it took its name. According to tradition, St Paul was beheaded at Rome during Nero's persecution of the Christians in AD 67, and led out to a place known as *Aquae Salviae*, near the third mile-stone on the Ostian Way. He was buried by a Christian matron, Lucina, on her own property. It was not a subterranean cemetery but one on the surface, hemmed in between the Ostian Road and another road, Via Valentiniana, which has now disappeared. In the fifth century a memorial chapel was erected, the remains of which were discovered in 1867 under the present church of S. Paolo alle Tre Fontane; in 1875 during excavations behind this church a number of coins of Nero were discovered. Although there is no extant written account, St Peter was crucified at Rome during Nero's reign (AD 54–68) in the Mamertine prison, where the church of San Pietro in Carcere now stands. He was, according to Tertullian (d. c. 225), crucified with his head downwards, having requested this form of death (see Eusebius ii. i). The body of St Peter was buried in a small cemetery on the Vatican hill close to the place where he was crucified, with, according to Tertullian, with his head downwards, having requested this form of death (see Eusebius, *Church History* ii. i).

441. 18   What shall I return unto the Lord, for all he hath returned to me? I will take up the Cup of Salvation, and call upon the Name of the Lord, see Psalm 116.12–13.

442. 12   *Lucina*, a devout Christian matron of wealth and property, who lived near Rome during the time of St Peter and St Paul.

442. 19   *Palace*, printed as '*Palace*' in CUL (7.41.24), NU, WF, BCL, OB, WTN, LPL (Main Collection SR3, H1763.T7 and Sion Aarc Octavo A69.3 / T67), HCL, BL (861.D.10 and 1019.c.19).

442. 33   *What shall I give unto the Lord for all his Benefits towards me? I will take up the Cup of Salvation, and call upon the Name of the Lord*, see Psalm 116.12–13.

443. 20   *As by the testimony of S. Gregory the Pope we demonstrated above*, see above pages 000–00 [436–8].

443. 23   The pride of *Rome* is founded like that of the great Whore, see Revelation 17.1.

Chapter XIX

444. 2   *Dioclesian.*, no full stop in NU.

444. 16   *His on Sentence ... After those of* Magdenburg, these two sentences are separated by a wide space, and a large pilcrow

444. 17   ¶ has been inserted in ink in CUL (7.41.24), NU, WF, BCL, OB, WTN, LPL (SR3, H1763.T7 and Sion Aarc Octavo A69.3 / T67), HL, HCL, BL (861.d.10 and 1019.c.19). A new paragraph makes sense within the context.

445. 2   is, notwithstanding, printed as 'is, notwithstanding' in NU, CUL (7.41.24),

Textual Emendations and Notes   509

		WF, BC, OB, WTN, LPL (Main Collection SR3 H1763.T7 and Sion Aarc Octavo A69.3 / T67), HL, HCL, BL (861.D.10 and 1019.c.19).
445.	18	Mercellinus, spelled as both 'Mercellinus' and 'Marcellinus'.
445.	29	*out of thine own mouth thou shalt be justified, and out of thine own mouth thou shalt be condemned*, see Matthew 12.36–37 and Luke 19.22.
445.	34	*weight, [219]*, page number missing in NU copy.
445.	36	Marcellinus, spelled both as 'Marcellinus' and 'Mercellinus'.
446.	12	clears [220], page number missing in NU copy.
446.	17	*the Receiver is as bad as the Thief*, see Morris Palmer Tilley, *A Dictionary of Proverbs in England in the Sixteenth and Seventeenth Centuries* (Ann Arbor, MI, 1950), p. 567, R52; and *The Oxford Dictionary of English Proverbs*, third edition (Oxford, 1970), p. 667. See also Proverbs 29.24.
446.	35	Strong ones too, printed as 'Strong ones to' in CUL (7.41.24 / Peterborough C.4.18), NU, WF, BCL, OB, WTN, LPL (SR3, H1763.T7 and Sion Aarc Octavo A69.3 / T67), HL, HCL, BL (861.D.10 and 1019.c.19).
447.	6	P. 222, in CUL (7.41.24) text misnumbered and page number reads '202'.
447.	16	*Breviaries*, printed as '*B*reviaries' in 1673 CUL (7.41.24 / Peterborough C.4.18), NU, WF, BCL, OB, WTN, LPL (Main Collection SR3, H1763.T7 and Sion Aarc Octavo A69.3 / T67), HL, HCL, BL (861.D.10 and 1019.c.19).
447.	24	Pages 222 and 223 are printed as 202 and 203 in CUL (7.41.24); in Union copy page 222 is printed as 202; 225 as 205; pp. 223 and 224 are missing.
447.	38	Love, printed as '*L*ove' in (7.41.24 and Peterborough C.4.18), NU, WF, BCL, OB, WTN, LPL (Main Collection SR3, H1763.T7 and Sion Aarc Octavo A69.3 / T67), HL, HCL, BL (861.D.10 and 1019.c.19).
448.10-15		'These Words be false … Army against the Persians', there are single quotation marks to the left at every line in this section in NU, BL (861.D.10 and 1019.c.9), Peterborough (C.4.18), WF, BCL, OB, LPL (SR3, H1763.T7).
448.	18	Notes on the word *Sinuessa*; in BL (861.D.10 and 1019.c.9), Peterborough (C.4.18), WF, BCL, OB, LPL (SR3, H1763.T7) copies '*Sinuessa*' is followed by 'num.]'; missing in CUL (7.41.24), BL (861.D.10 and 1019.c.19), HCL, CUL (7.41.24), NU, HCL.
448.	22	admired at all, 'at al' in CUL (7.41.24) and LPL (Main Collection SR3, H1763.T7), BL (861.D.10 and 1019.c.19).
448.	27	made, full stop missing in CUL (7.41.24), WF, LPL (Main Collection SR3, H1763.T7 and Sion Aarc Octavo A69.3 / T67), BL (861.D.10 and 1019.c.19) BCL, OB, WTN.
448.18–27		'So called from the City *Sinuessa* … Cities hath bin also made'.
448.	30	That other Place[s] have been lost we know, printed as 'That other Place have been lost we know' in CUL (7.41.24 / Peterborough C.4.18), NU, WF, BCL, OB, WTN, LPL (Main Collection SR3, H1763.T7 and Sion Aarc Octavo A69.3 / T67), HL, HCL, BL (861.D.10 and 1019.c.19); the letter 's' inserted for clarity.
448.	33	Trumpet of the famous, CUL (7.41.24) reads 'Trumpet of fame'; NU, WF, BCL, OB, WTN, LPL (Main Collection SR3, H1763.T7 and Sion Aarc Octavo A69.3 / T67), BL (1019.c.19 / 861.D.10), Peterborough (C.4.18) read 'Trumpet of the Famous'.

448. 37 In CUL (7.41.24) and NU to the left of this paragraph is drawn a manicule pointing upward (☝): this does not appear in LPL, Peterborough (C.4.18) or BL (1019.c.19 / 861.D.10). Does this refer to the note below?

448. 40 Does this refer to pp. 114–15 (in this text p. 379): He [Binius] has a *Pseudo-Catholick* Council at *Rome* under Pope *Sylvester*, with the same Premonition *to the Reader*, word for word, which he set before the *Sinnessa* Council, *Propter Exemplariorum intolerabilem niminamque & Differentiam, & Depravationem*, &c.

449. 5 but Spurious Copy, printed as 'butSpuriousCopy' in CUL (7.41.24 / Peterborough C.4.18), NU, WF, BCL, OB, WTN, LPL (Main Collection SR3, H1763.3T7 and Sion Aarc Octavo A69.3/T67), HL, HCL, BL (861.D.10 and 1019.c.19).

449. 14 pull off, in NU 'pull of'.

449. 17 *intolerable*, printed as *'in tolerable'* in CUL (7.41.24 / Peterborough C.4.18), WF, BCL, OB, WTN, LPL, BL, NU.

449. 22 to remember how Peter's *Denial*, CUL (7.41.24 / Peterborough C.4.18), NU, WF, BCL, OB, WTN, BL, HL, HCL, LPL copies read *'to remember how Peter Denial'*; apostrophe 's' inserted for clarity.

449. 22 Peter's *Denial*, see Matthew 26.69–75; Mark 14.66–72; John 18.25–27.

449. 23 *there is joy among the Angels over one Sinner that repenteth*, see Luke 15.7.10.

449. 25 *and according to the Proverb, fought manfully after he ran away*; reference uncertain.

450. 25 to be uttered., no full stop in NU copy; full stop in CUL (7.41.24 / Peterborough C.4.18), LPL (SR3, H1763.T7 / A69.3 / T67), BL (861.d.10 / 1019 c.19),

450. 29 *Out of thine own Mouth thou shalt be justified, &c.*, see Matthew 12.36–37.

450. 39 or any, printed as 'orany' in CUL (7.41.24 / Peterborough C.4.18), NU, LPL, BL, HCL, BCL, WCO, OB, WTN.

451. 4 presume to call, printed as 'presume to (backward comma) 'call', in CUL (7.41.24 / Peterborough C.4.18), NU, WF, LPL, BL, BCL, WCO, OB, WTN, HCL.

451. 29 It is just as if a *Rebellious* Parliament should meet on their own Heads, to call their King to account, upon pretence of his Crimes., a reference to Charles I?

451. 32 Disorder, printed as '*Disorder*' in NU, BL, LPL, CUL (7.41.24 / Peterborough C.4.18), HL, HCL.

Chapter XX

453. 13 it, printed as 'ir' in CUL (7.41.24 / Peterborough C.4.18), NU, BL LPL.

453. 14 Detection should say, printed as 'Detection- [line break] should say' in CUL (7.41.24 / Peterborough C.4.18) and NU.

453. 21 He takes much pains to pick this Thorn out of the Popes foot, perhaps a reference to the common medieval folktale of Androcles and the Lion, ascribed to to Aesop's *Fables*.

454. 6 *Nones*, in the ancient Roman calendar, the ninth day before the ides of a month; the seventh of March, May, July, and October, and the fifth day of the other months.

Textual Emendations and Notes 511

455. 26 *Constantine* is a, printed as '*Con* [line break] *antine* ia Tyrant' in CUL (7.41.24 / Peterborough C.4.18), NU, WF, LPL, BL, HL, HCL.
455. 36 [*Do probably shew.*], brackets in NU.
456. 11 too late an Author, misprint as 'Authot' in CUL (7.41.24 / Peterborough C.4.18), NU, LPL.
456. 16 former, the comma after 'former' is printed as an upsidedown backward semicolon below the line in NU, CUL (7.41.24 / Peterborough C.4.18), WF, LPL, BL, BCL, WCO, OB, WTN, HL, HCL.

Chapter XXI

460. 14 trice, obs., a 'trice' is a pulley; 'in a trice', at a single pluck or pull and, hence, in a short period of time; a moment, or instant.
460. 29 and like our late Long Parliament, which sat from 1640 until 1648, when it was purged by the New Model Army. See Commentary, Volume IX.
460. 31 We Exhort and admonish all ... *superbè agere*, there are single quotation marks at the beginning of each line for this section in CUL (7.41.24 / Peterborough C.4.18), NU, WF, LPL, BL, BCL, OB, WTN, HL, HCL.
461. 5 *Clamys*, i.e., 'Chlamys', a fine woolen mantle fastened at the shoulder, worn by men in ancient Greece. During the middle Byzantine period, the Chlyamys was the ceremonial wear of emperors and high officials on formal occasions. It was highly decorative with bright patterned silk, embroidered borders and encrusted by gems. Usually only the emperor alone could wear the purple chlamys.
461. 12 Caparisons, an ornamental cover placed over a horse's saddle or harness.
461. 13 *Udonibus*, a sock of felt or fur.
463.7–13 'Wherefore, *saith the Emperour* ... should there have any Power,' there are single quotation marks to the left of each line in this paragraph in CUL (7.41.24 / Peterborough C.4.18), NU, WF, LPL, BL, BCL, PB, WTN, HL, HCL.

Chapter XXII

465.7–32 That the things which are written ... *Melchiades* the Bishop of *Rome*, there are single quotation marks to the left of each line in this paragraph in NU, WF, CUL (7.41.24 / Peterborough C.4.18), LPL, BL, BCL, OB, WTN, HL, HCL.
465. 18 these: printed as 'these:' in CUL (7.41.24 / Peterborough C.4.18), NU, WF, LPL, BL, BCL, OB, WTN, HL, HCL.
466. 20 before the *Nicene* Council, '*Nicene*' is printed as '*N*icene' in CUL (7.41.24 / Peterborough C.4.18), NU, WF, LPL, BL, BCL, OB, WTN, HL, HCL.
466. 23 the premises, but, 'but' is printed with final 't' in subscript as 'bu$_t$'; 'but' in NU, CUL (7.41.24 / Peterborough C.4.18), WF, LPL, BL, BCL, OB, WTN, HL, HCL.
466. 26 *Council of 9 Bishops*, NU prints '*Council of 19 Bishops*'; CUL prints '9'; there is however a wide space between 'of' and '9', so that the '1' was not set properly by the compositor; '19' in CUL (7.41.24 / Peterborough C.4.18), WF, LPL, LC, BL, BCL, HL, HCL, OB, WCO.
466. 28 *given to* Melchiades., in Union copy 'But' is printed as 'Bu$_t$', with final 't' in subscript; printed as 'But' in CUL (7.41.24 / Peterborough C.4.18), Folger,

LPL, LC, BL, BCL, HL, HCL, OB, WCO.

466. 38 *Timeo Danaos & Dona ferentes*, Virgil, *The Aeneid*, Book ii, line 49, 'as with the edict (manifestation) of the Greeks treacherous gift … they are maimed, crafty and depraved, as these reasons evidently demonstrate'.

467.10–29 1. Because if pretendeth … of this Edict of *Constantine*, there are single quotations marks to the left of each line in this quotation in NU, CUL (7.41.24 / Peterborough C.4.18), WF, LPL, LC, BL, BCL, HL, HCL, OB, WCO.

467. 12 *Thou art* Peter, *and upon this Rock will I build my Church*, see Matthew 16.18.

467. 23 falsly, as in NU, CUL (7.41.24 / Peterborough C.4.18), WF, LPL, LC, BL, BCL, HL, HCL,OB, WCO.

467. 31 notorious Counterfeit:, printed as notorious 'Counterfeit:' in NU, CUL (7.41.24 / Peterborough C.4.18), WF, LPL, LC, BL, BCL, HL, HCL, OB, and WCO copies.

468. 1 Irenaeus, printed with the ligature in subscript in CUL (7.41.24 / Peterborough C.4.18), NU, WF, LPL, LC, BL, BCL, HL, HCL, OB, WCO.

468. 5 Where the faults, NU copy reads 'fau ts' with 'l' missing. The 'l' in 'faults' is very lightly printed in CUL (7.41.24 / Peterborough C.4.18), WF, LPL, LC, BL, BCL, HL, HCL. OB and WCO copies read 'faults'.

468. 39 Longobards, i.e., Lombards, 'Long Beards'.

469. 23 *Mummers*, or, 'guisers' or 'disquisers', are actors in a dumb show, who usually wear masks; the word is often applied contemptuously to religious ceremony considered to be silly or hypocritical.

469. 24 Masque, a form of festive courtly entertainment, popular in the sixteenth and seventeenth centuries; it consisted of music, singing, dancing and acting in dumb show, the actors being masked and habited in character.

469. 30 *Kingdom*, misprinted in NU text as 'Klngdom'.

470.4–17 None of all those … Greek Impostors, there are single quotation marks at every line of this quotation in CUL (7.41.24 / Peterborough C.4.18), NU, WF, LPL, LC, BL, BCL, HL, HCL, OB, WCO.

470. 17 *to the Acts by the Greek Impostors*, 'Impostors' may read 'Imposters' in NU copy.

470. 35 Which if *Binius*, printed as '*Binus*' in NU text.

471. 1 to shew you that *Binius*, printed as '*Binus*' in CUL (7.41.24 / Peterborough C.4.18), NU, WF, BL, BCL, HL, HCL. OB and WCO copies, text.

471. 30 This fault of the [275], p. 275 missing in NU copy.

471. 34 Dragon in the *Revelation*, that threw down the third part of the Stars with his Tail, see Revelation 12.4.

472. 5 while they licked up this Vomit of, see 2 Peter 2.22.

472. 32 destroys, text as printed as 'destroy^s', with superscript 's' in CUL (7.41.24 / Peterborough C.4.18), NU, WF, BL, LPL, BCL, OB, WCO.

Chapter XXIII

473.5–10 That this Epistle was ascribed to … Decrees of *Melchiades* the Pope, there are single quotation marks to the right of each line of this quotation in NU, CUL (7.41.24 / Peterborough C.4.18), BL, BCL, HCL, LPL, LC.

Textual Emendations and Notes 513

473. 10   Thus was the counterfeit ... Laws and Councils, marginal gloss: *Ibid.*, missing in NU, included in CUL (7.41.24 / Peterborough C.4.18), BL, BCL, HCL, LPL, LC.

473. 12   But that it was noted with the false Title and name of *Melchiades* ... History of the *Nicene* Council. Baron. *An.* 31. *Nu.* 80, there are single quotation marks to the right of each line of this quotation in NU.

473. 18   *Isidore himself,* marginal gloss: *Isidore* a Forger, not in NU, but in CUL (7.41.24) copy.

473. 19   of this Epistle:, there is a full stop after 'Epistle' in CUL (7.41.24 / Peterborough C.4.18), NU, BL, BCL, HCL, LPL, LC copies; comma and a colon in NU. It was not uncommon for Traherne to use a full stop as a comma.

473. 22   Baron. *An.* 312. *Nu.* 80., perhaps intended as a marginal gloss.

474. 22   which vindicates Dr. *Stillingfleet*.

475. 13   of S. *Paul*, Colos. 2., see Colossians 2.18, 'Let no man beguile you of your reward in a voluntary humility and worshipping of angels, intruding into those things which he hath not seen, vainly puffed up by his fleshly mind.' The whole of Colossians 2 is a defense of Christ as the Godhead incarnate, maker of all things, both visible and invisible, as well as a warning of false teaching and mysticism.

475.13–21   The words of S. *Paul*, Colos. 2. are written ... as the Authors of evil, there are single quotation marks to the right of each line of this quotation in NU.

475. 14   not as *Hierom* supposeth; *Hierom* is Jerome.

Chapter XXIV

476. 2   ΤΕΛΟΣ, Telos, Greek for 'the end, goal or purpose'.

476. 21   NU text reads 'marks'; Traherne however may have intended 'remarks'.

477.3–16   QUONIAM omnia corroborata ... *Paulino* & *Julino* summis Conf.libus., there are single quotation marks to the left of each line in this quotation in NU.

477. 17   page 287 is missing in NU copy.

477. 19   Council, correction in ink NU copy to 'C' from ')'.

478. 4   Cæsare, in NU, BL, WF and CUL (7.41.24) copies printed as 'Ca sare' not however in Peterborough (C.4.18.).

478. 28   *joynt consent to all*, full stop after 'all' in NU.

478. 31   in the Letter beside, page 290 missing in NU.

478. 31   Cosin-German, a person's first cousin; used figuratively as something or someone closely related or allied to another; a near relative.

479. 22   Face of the World. * But such Councils, there is a manicule (☞) printed in the right margin of p. 291 in NU, BCL, OB, WTN, HCL, HL, BL (1019.c.19 and 861.D.10), LPL (Sion Aarc Octavo, A69.3 / T67 and H1763.t7), CUL (7.41.24 / Peterborough C.4.18), LC.

479. 27   *in the time of* [292] Sylvester, page numbers 292–3 missing in NU.

480. 31
–481. 7   That this Epistle is a Counterfeit ... found in the Roman Copy, there are single quotation marks to the left of each line in this quotation in NU.

481.13–31   'This Epistle which is put ... *Maximus* evidently shew, &c.', has single

481. 26 quotation marks in the left margin at each line in this quotation in NU.
481. 26 'to be changed', NU text has a comma following 'changed'; the printer perhaps erroneously inserted a line break after 'changed', for '*Rescriptum Julii*]' which may be the source of the quotation and was probably intended as a marginal gloss. The beginning of the next paragraph would have started with 'The Epistle which *Julius* returned'. I have followed the text as in CUL (7.41.24 / Peterborough C.4.18) NU.

Appendix

483. 27
–484. 19 I have a mighty suspicion ... to Pope *Hormisda*, there are single quotation marks to the left of each line in this quotation in NU text.

484. 12 Epistles, printed as '52 Epistle', in CUL (7.41.24 /Peterborough C.4.18) and NU.

484. 38 HOLY, printed as 'HOYL' in CUL (7.41.24 /Peterborough C.4.18).

485. 4 infatuate, reduce to foolishness and folly; frustrate and bring to nothing.

485.9–20 But yet further ... in the same condition, there are single quotation marks to the left of each line in this quotation in NU.

485. 13 Doctors of Holy Church, CUL and NU texts print 'Doctors of Holy Church'; there may be a missing 'the' before 'Holy Church'; I have left as printed because this section is a quotation.

485. 24 and if at any time, 'and if at at any time' in NU.

485. 30 this very HOLY ROMAN CHURCH, there is an 'R' missing in CHURCH in CUL (7.41.24 /Peterborough C.4.18).

486. 1–5 Behold into what peril, one *Isidore* ... be firm and certain, there are single quotation marks to the left of each line in this quotation in both the CUL (7.41.24 /Peterborough C.4.18) and NU copies.

486. 20 is but a blinking business, Traherne may mean by 'blinking' evasive and self deceptive.

488. 36 Baron. Martyrol. Octob. 16., this may have been intended as a marginal gloss.

489. 21 *having a zeal, but not according to knowledge*, see Romans 10.2.

490. 7 *and he that receiveth not* Christ, *shall be judged not to have received* God *the Father: and therefore neither shall himself be received into the Kingdom of Heaven*, a conflation of several biblical verses; see Matthew 10.44; Mark 9.37; Luke 9.48; Luke 18.17; and John 3.18.

490. 25 *Passage* follows, the final 's' on 'follows' is in subscript 'follow$_s$'.

APPENDIX

THE WILL OF THOMAS TRAHERNE, AS REGISTERED IN THE PREROGATIVE COURT OF CANTERBURY

MEMORANDUM that Thomas Traherne late of Teddington of the County of Midd Clerk deceased in the time of the sickness whereof he dyed and vpon or about the Seaven and Twentyeth of September 1674 having sent for John Bredo Gent to come to him the said Thomas Traherne then lying sick at the Lady Bridgmans house in Teddington and the said Mr Berdo being come vnto him he the said Thomas Traherne being then of pefect mind and memory vsed these or the like words to the said Mr. Berdo vizt. I haue sent for you to make my Will for mee or to that effect Whereupon the said Mr Berdo asked of him the said Mr Thomas Traherne whether he would haue it made in Writing To which the said Thomas Traherne answeared in these or the like works vizt Noe I haue not so much but that I can dispose of it by Word of Mouth or to that effect And the said Thomas Traherne being then of perfect mind and memory by Word of Mouth with an intent to make his Will and to settle and dispose of his Goods and Estate did vtter and speake these or the like words vizt. Whereupon the said Mr Merdo asked of him the said Mr Thomas Traherne whether he would haue it made in Writing To which the said Thomas Traherne answeared in these or the like words vizt Noe I haue not so much but that I can dispose of it by Word of Mouth or to that effect And the said Thomas Traherne being then of perfect mind and memory by Word of Mouth with an intent to make his Will to settle and dispose of his Goods and Estate did vtter and speake these or the like words vizt I desire my Lady Bridgman and her daughter the Lady Charlott should haue each of them a Ring And to you (speaking to the said Mr. Berdo) I give Tenn Pounds and to Mrs Cockson Tenn shillings and to Phillip Landman ffyve shillings and to John Rowland the Gardiner ffyve shillings and to Mary the Laundry maid ffyve shillings and to all the rest of the servants half a crowne apeece. My best Hatt I give it to my brother Phillipp And sister (speaking to Mrs Susan Traherne the wife of his brother Phillipp which Susan was then present) I desire you would keepe it for him And all the rest of my Clothes that is worth your acceptance

I give to you And for those that are not worth your accepting I would have you to giue them to Phillipp Landman or to whome you please with my old Hatt All my Books I give to my brother Phillipp And (still speaking to the said Mrs Susan then present) I make you and my brother Phillipp my whole Executors which words or the like in effect The said Thomas Traherne being then of perfect mind and memory did then utter Animo testandi and with an intent that the same should stand and be as and for his last Will and Testament in the prescence and hearing of John Berdo Alice Cockson and Mary Linum.
John Berdo Alice Cockson The Mark of Mary Linum.

Proved at London 22 Oct 1674 by Susan Traherne, one of he Executors, to whom administration was granted, power being reserved of making the like grant to Philip Traherne, the other executor, should he ask for the same.[1]

---

[1] See Bertram Dobell, ed., *The Poetical Works of Thomas Traherne, B.D., 1636?–1674* (London, 1903), pp. 167–8.

Brooke's account of the discovery of Thomas Traherne's manuscripts

The Story of the Traherne MSS. by their finder.[1]

The announcement in the columns of our contemporary the 'Athenæum' of the approaching publication of a fresh manuscript of the lately discovered poet, Thomas Traherne, recalls the curious story which so respectable an authority as the 'Quarterly Review' regarded as 'one of the most romantic in the annals of English bibliography'.

As the writer of this article was the original discoverer, and many of the details have not yet appeared in print, the following may be of more than passing interest.

It has been my fortune during half a century's study of English poetry, sacred and secular, to make many curious finds. Such was the unique copy of Pope's 'Ethic Epistles', 1743, suppressed by Lord Bolingbroke on Pope's death and now, as Dr. Garnett told the writer, justly regarded as the prize of their Pope documents, it having been secured for the British Museum after I had sold it to the late Colonel Grant. Such, also the unique holograph manuscript of Richard Krashaw, containing poems no where else found, and also in the British Museum. Such the unknown first hymnbook of John Wesley issued during his visit to America in 1737, which, bought for half a guinea, has fetched first £20.10p(?) and then in 1905, £106 and which went to America, (though not before a facsimile reprint had been published by the Wesleyans here).

There are minor discoveries, like those of Bishop Ken's unique tracts, but all yield the [poem?] interest and importance to that of the subject of our paper.

Occupied as I have always been in business life, in London, for many years the Saturday half holiday has been spent in the quarters

---

[1] Bodleian MS Dobell c.56, fols. 54^r–59^r. This was probably written in early October 1910. The allusion to the announcement of a New Traherne manuscript is to H. I. Bell's edition of Philip Traherne's manuscript copy of Thomas's poems, *Poems of Felicity* (Oxford: at the Clarendon Press, 1910). See 'A New MS of Thomas Traherne', *The Athenæum*, No. 4327 (October 1, 1910): 389–90.

frequented by book lovers and as the volumes purchased from the penny or two penny stall were generally numerous, it follows that they were frequently laid aside for investigation at a more convenient season, and that that season occasionally, was long in coming.

Thus it was, that I had manuscripts which as I was, with scanty leisure, engaged [in?] quite other literary work that two of the Traherne MSS fell quite unknowingly into my hands. One was purchased in Whitechapel, the other in the Farringdon Road. The two, certainly, did not cost their owner a shilling but they were purchased at different times, and were as said above, laid aside. A letter from the Rev Dr Grosart, a literary correspondent of some thirty years standing brought the purchase to memory and I examined the folio MS. The poems caught at once my heart and fancy. So strong was the resemblance between the new poems, and some of Henry Vaughan's specially 'The Retreat', that I thought they must be his or failing him his twin brother, Thomas Vaughan's. 'If not' I wrote to Dr Grosart, 'we are in the presence of a Third and hitherto unknown poet greater than either'. The prophecy has been fulfilled! They are not Henry or Thomas Vaughan's but they are Thomas Traherne's. Dr Grosart offered £5, for the folio manuscript, and in the same letter, asked if I had any other seventeenth century manuscripts for sale. I had, but none of any great interest, till on opening one the 'Four Centuries of Meditations' I found to my intense surprise one of the poems identical with one in the folio and headed 'Upon these pure and virginal thoughts which I had in my childhood I made this poem' proving conclusively that however long the manuscripts had been separated, they were both in the same hand, and (though we did not then know it), that hand, Thomas Traherne's.[1] I wrote at once to [him] pointing out this almost incredible coincidence, and he at once secured the second manuscript at the same price. In fact, the manuscript reached him on Sunday morning, when he was on holiday in Wales, and so eager was he to make it his own, that to my mingled astonishment and amusement I found on the Monday morning a letter containing the sum in gold and silver, the Welsh apparently having more respect for the sabbath than the old Scottish Presbyterian divine. Dr Grosart lived and died in this belief he had prepared a prospectus of a new edition of Henry Vaughan in which these were to be included. I saw him both at the British Museum and his Temperance hotel, on his last visit to

---

[1] Traherne's, followed by 'Still thinking they were Henry Vaughan's Dr Grosart came over from Dublin' deleted.

London and when we parted, it was with his words of blessing and farewell and the knowledge that the new edition might never appear.

Six months later, he was at rest, and in due course I was called on to give my idea as to the value of a portion of his library. In the list of these, I recognized my two Vaughan volumes, so I called the attention of my employer to these. Ultimately Mr Charles Higham became their possessor after some negotiations, and then it was that Mr Bertram Dobell, their editor and annotator came on the scene. I had mentioned to him that Mr Higham had them, and he bought them at once. But unlike Dr Grosart and myself, his critical taste did not recognise them as Vaughan's. Curiously enough some years before, when preparing my edition of Giles Fletcher's 'Christ's Victory and Triumph' for Messrs Griffith Farran and Co's Ancient and Modern Library, I had included in it a short poem the "Ways of Wisdom" from a little anonymous book of 1699. This was so much in the style of the new poems that it seemed probable they were by the same author. But Mr Dobell at once perceived that if, as the preface to the 1699 book asserted the author had been Chaplain to Lord Keeper Bridgeman he could not possibly have been Henry Vaughan, who was a doctor, not a divine, nor Thomas Vaughan, who had long been dead.

I was then instructed by Mr Dobell to see if I could trace any one whom Sir Orlando Bridgman had employed as chaplain, and a little research showed me that Thomas Trahern had been appointed by him, and resided with him moreover, that Traherne died in the Lord Keeper's house four months after Bridgman's own death in the same building.

At last then we had found the right name but when we found two books of Traherne's had been issued, one Romish Forgeries, 1674 [sic] of no literary value and the other Christian Ethics [sic] 1675 which Traherne did not live to see through the press, doubt was no longer possible.

And to make assurance doubly sure, some of the verse given in the 'Christian Ethics [sic]', reappears in one of Mr Dobell's MSS.

The reception given by the press and the public to Mr Dobell's admirable editions, first of the poems, and then of the Divine Meditations, has been gratifying.

But as if to this strange chapter of accidents no element should be wanting, it now turns out that Philip Trahern or Traheron had actually prepared an edition of his brother's poems for the press, of which Vol 1 is in the British Museum. The new find contains some thirty nine fresh poems as well as fresh texts of some published by Mr Dobell. Some of the new, at least equal if they do not excel those previously issued.

Moreover, Philip Trahern himself contributes two poems, and it has [*sic*] now known that he died at Wimborne Minster in 1723 where he had long been minister.

This, at once, opens a fresh field of investigation. The Dobell MSS (we should have stated Mr Dobell has a third M.S. which Dr Grosart had had and never recognized) are believed to have come from Hereford from the library of an antiquary named Skip. But the new British Museum MS is a transcript, not an original. This suggests two families of MSS, Thomas Trahern's own, and his brother Philip's carefully prepared transcripts. So that we now have,

A. Thomas Traherne's printed volumes, 1674 [*sic*], 1675 and the posthumous little book, 1699.

B. The three MSS one folio, and two octavo now in the possession of their Editor and Publisher Mr. Bertram Dobell.

C. The new MS. now in the British Museum.

Even this however by no means exhausts the possibilities for Mr Dobell's MSS give references to others at present unkown, while the words Vol 1, on Philip Trahern's MS. and the fact that some poems of Mr Dobell's edition do not occur in the new volume would seem to show he may have prepared Vol 11 in a similar manner. And moreover, where are Thomas Traherne's sermons not to mention Philip's?

It is quite possible, that the final chapter of this bibliographical Romance is as yet unwritten.

And research in other directions may be fruitful, For example two boys, Philip and Thomas Trahern were entered at Eton in 1695, and these are most probably Philip's sons. And again the connection between Bartholomew Traheron or Trahern has not been traced. He is well known as an Elizabethan reformer, and was probably the grandfather of Thomas and Philip Trahern. More light on these points is needed, And after the recent discoveries and identifications may reasonably be looked for. If people would only examine the treasures which lie about in odd corners, and would take no thing for granted, other seventeenth century authors, besides Thomas Traherne would receive tardy but well merited recognition.

Will. T. Brooke

Glossary

Affray	to disturb or frighten
Apocryphal	from a Greek word for hidden, concealed; 'Apocrypha' was used by the Church for early books that were not part of the collection of books that had canonical authority. The Church of Rome accepted several of them as a sort of second canon, explaining the word to mean the source was hidden. Protestants rejected them as lacking authority and not part of the canon. The term 'apocryphal' came to mean lacking credibilty, or spurious
Arcanum	from Latin for 'secret'; the word is related to an ark or chest, and refers to mysterious knowledge or information only accessible to the initiate
Arrogate	to presumptuously appropriate or claim something for oneself without right
Behoof	profit, advantage
Beulah	Hebrew meaning 'married'; used in Isaiah 62.4 symbolically to describe the renewed covenant relationship between the restored Jews and God
Bewraid	obsolete form of bewray
Bewraying	to disclose or betray, to accuse, to expose or reveal unintentionally
Bile	bile is stored in the liver to assist digestion
Boggle	to start with fright or amazement, overwhelmed with wonder or bewilderment or alarm, be startled
Commentious	contrived
Complacent	the state of being pleased or satisfied, or of being pleasing or agreeable to others; a feeling of contentment
Consarcinatus	from 'consarcino', to sew, stitch, or patch together

Conversation	the manner of conducting oneself in the world of society; social intercourse
Dehort	to persuade or exhort a person against a certain course, purpose or action
Devolving	to pass to by inheritance or legal succession
Dival Sanctions	imperial sanctions
Ductures	a tubular passage through which a substance is conveyed; a bodily passage, especially one for secretion; in general, a movement in some direction, guidance or leading
Effeminate	marked by unbecoming delicacy or over refinement, not manly
Fardel	bundle
Fautors	someone who actively encourges or assists someone in carrying out an action, usually a crime
Fetch	stratagem or contrivance
Gall	something bitter to endure, a poison; or a plant and its bitter fruit, like wormwood; metaphorically for travail and a bitter experience
Gueld	seventeenth-century variant of 'geld', to castrate or emasculate; more commonly to impair the strength or force of something; to weaken or enfeeble, now obsolete
Humor	given to making objections, cavilling, peevish, captious
Ingenuity	being free born, or having qualities associated with being free born, distinquished, intellectual, nobility of character
Irrepsisse	perfect active infinitive of *irrepo*, to creep in or upon
Janizaries	soldiers in an elite guard of Turkish troops organized in the fourteenth century and abolished in 1826
Jars	a jolt or shock caused by discord or inharmonious sounds
Leasing	lying, falsehood

Liber	'lib', from Latin, the inner bark of a tree; in the ancient world dried bark was used to write on; a book, work, treatise; a division of a work or book: 'tres libri de Natura Deorm'; a list, catalogue, register; a letter, epistle
Malepert	seventeenth-century variant spelling of 'malapert'; presumptuous, impudent, bold
Material Cause	the cause that gives matter to a thing, or the principle from which a thing comes into being
Momentany	obs. for momentary, lasting for a moment
Obnoxious	liable to punishment; exposed to harm, subject to injury, liable to punishment or censure, guilty
Ordinary	in Ecclesiastical sense, one who has by his own right and not by special deputation immediate jurisdiction in a ecclesastical case, such as an Archbishop over a province
Polycarp	S. Polycarp, S. John's disciple
Praeludium a	prelude or introduction
Prelation	preferment and ultimately exaltation, as with a 'prelate'
President	i.e., precedents; preceding in time and order; leading position, superior, foremost
Proficuous	profitabale, advantageous, beneficial and useful (from late Latin *proficu-us*, beneficial)
Prolatory	from 'prolate', obs. to lengthen out in utterance or bringing forth of words; there is no adjectival form in the *OED*
Putid	(rare) stinking, rotten, foul, putrid; intellectually or morally rotten or worthless and therefore offensive
Quadragesima	the forty days of Lent; now refers to the first Sunday of Lent after Ash Wednesday. Traherne probably means the forty days of Lent
Quadrat	i.e., quadrate; corresponding, agree
Rash	a rapid, hasty, brisk or unthoughtful movement
Ravine	prey, as in an eagle that fills her nest with ravine
Refel	to prove an argument or opinion false or untenable
Resentment	a natural or spontaneous feeling, to feel something deeply and sharply

Rife	widespread, numerous
Shufling	a shifting of something from one place to another; shifty or evasive action or behaviour
Simony	lying, sacriledge
Simple	a medical term for a treatment not mixed or compounded with other ingredients
Sleight, v.	variant spelling of slight, to treat with indifference or disrespect, to disregard, disdain, ignore; or to deal deceifully
Sleight, n.	deceitful craftiness or strategem, cunning or deceit
Splenetick	given to melanchoily, marked by bad temper, given to fits of angry disposition, impatience or irritability
Substraction	obsolete form of 'subtraction'
Thrasonical	given to bragging and boasting, vain glorious
Timerous	full of apprehension, fear, timid
Tittle	an ornamental curl or horn written at the top of a Hebrew letter that distinguishes it from another letter; used to refer to the smallest part of the Law in Matthew 5.18 and Luke 16.17
Transeunt	temporary or not permanent; extrinsic or not inherent; in philosophy, productive of effects outside the mind
Travail	seventeenth-century rendering of 'travel'
Unisone	perfect agreement, harmony
Violence	that which moves against its inherent motion; intense, vehement, or extreme
Wen	an abnormal growth, like a wart or lump, a protuberance of the body
Wormwood	an herb often used to help digestion. When 'bile' and 'wormwood' are used together, it means a source of bitter mortification